Soviet and Russian Ekranoplans

Sergey Komissarov and Yefim Gordon

Crécy
www.crecy.co.uk

Crécy
www.crecy.co.uk

Contents

SOVIET AND RUSSIAN EKRANOPLANS
Sergey Komissarov and Yefim Gordon

Second edition
Published by Crécy Publishing Ltd 2020

First edition published 2010

A CIP record for this book is available from the British Library

ISBN 978 1 910809 36 5

Printed in India by Replika Press Pvt. Ltd.

Crécy Publishing Limited
1a Ringway Trading Estate, Shadowmoss Road, Manchester M22 5LH

www.crecy.co.uk

Design concept and layout by Polygon Press Ltd. (Moscow, Russia)

Line drawings by Gennadiy Petrov, Central Hydrofoil Design Bureau, Beriyev TANTK, Arctic Trade and Transport Company (ATTK).
Colour artwork by Viktor Mil'yachenko.

This book is illustrated with photos by Yefim Gordon, Sergey Komissarov, Helmut F. Walther, as well as from Yefim Gordon archive, Sergey and Dmitriy Komissarov archive, Gennadiy Petrov archive, Sergey M. Ganin archive, Pavel G. Tkachenko archive, Helmut Walther archive, Central Hydrofoil Design Bureau, Beriyev TANTK, Amphibious transport Technologies JSC, Arctic Trade and Transport Company (ATTK), Wingship Company (Russia), The Russian Aviation Research Trust, Books by Pavel I. Kachur, Aleksandr I. Maskalik, V. F. Plotnikov, Military Parade magazine, AON (General Aviation) magazine and from the following web sources: www.aero.kiev.ua, http://airboat.fatal.ru, www.aircraft.clan.su, www.airfoil-development.com, www.an2plane.ru, www.attk.ru, www.australianhovercraft.com, www.aviajournal.com, www.aviaport.ru, www.aviationexplorer.com, www.avicopress.ru, www.discaircraft.greyfalcon.us, http://ekranoflot.com, http://ekranoplan.ru.narod.ru, www.ekranoplane.ru, www.ekranoplan-hit.ru, www.entropyworld.narod.ru, http://en.wikipedia.org, http://flot.com/forum, http://forum.flot.su, www.ghdstudios.com, www.hovercraft.su, www.hs-ships.ru, http://ipfg.ru, www.isobrel.ru, www.kai.ru, http://katermarket.ru, www.news.cnet.com, www.oborona.ru, www.reaa.ru, www.se-technology.com, http://sivnia.ru, www.snowjeep.com, www.techavia.ru, http://wapedia.mobi, http://vtol.boom.ru, www.zpkb.com, www.trekvolga.com, http://rufut.ru, https://nauka-tehnika.com.ua, www.ato.ru, https://www.korabel.ru, www.rdc-aqualines.ru, www.ekranoplani.ru, https://gmichailov.livejournal.com, www.palio.ru, www.indbooks.in/mirror5.ru, www.nevskii-bastion.ru, http://vpk.name, http://www.aerohod.ru.

INTRODUCTION

This book is a revised and expanded edition of two similar publications which made their appearance in 2002 and 2010. They showed Russia's role and achievements in the development of ekranoplans, or wing-in-ground effect (WIG) craft – a new and fairly exotic means of transport. These achievements attract much interest in many countries. After all, it was in Russia (to be precise, the then Soviet Union) that pioneering work in this field of technology brought about results that have yet to be surpassed. The 2010 edition has proved to be very popular with the readers and has been sold out. This justifies the publication of the present edition. In this introduction the reader will find a general review of the work accomplished by Russian design bureaux and production plants in this field of technology, while a description of specific designs will be covered in subsequent chapters. The authors have chosen to devote a special chapter to the description of new events and designs of the last decade, as well as to some remarks updating the previously published information.

To begin with, a few words about the subject of this book. Wing-in-ground-effect craft making use of a dynamic air cushion are vehicles operating in close proximity to a supporting surface. This is usually water, but basically it makes no difference whether a WIG craft is operating over water or over land – provided that the ground surface is sufficiently even and flat.

A feature common to an aircraft and a WIG craft is wings generating lift due to aerodynamic forces. However, in the case of the WIG craft this lift is augmented owing to the ground effect created by compression of the ram air stream between the wings and the supporting surface. A higher lift/drag ratio enables a WIG craft to obtain the same lift at lower speeds and lower engine power compared to aircraft. As a result, the WIG craft are, in principle, more fuel-efficient compared to aircraft.

Since large flat areas on land are not a common occurrence, WIG craft are in most cases intended for use over water. Operation from the surface of lakes, rivers or seas of necessity introduces some features of water-borne vessels into the design of WIG vehicles. Historically, a number of WIGs emerged as a kind of attempt to lift water-borne craft out of the water for the purpose of achieving higher speeds, and in many cases WIG craft were built at shipyards. Small wonder that the question is posed sometimes whether one must regard these new craft as very low-flying aircraft or as ships that have lifted themselves out of the water.

It would appear that both definitions might be appropriate, since the concept of WIG vehicles embraces a wide variety of craft featuring quite substantial differences. They may tend to be closer to one or the other of the two extremes, but, generally speaking, they are always something of a hybrid. On the one hand, a WIG vehicle in cruise flight is subjected to aerodynamic forces, much in common with conventional aircraft, while the hydrodynamic forces act on it only during take-off and landing – or rather alighting. On the other hand, WIG craft operating in close proximity of the water surface in a marine environment have to be subjected to the same rules and requirements as usual marine vessels in terms of traffic safety.

The latter consideration has played an important role when it came to establishing a formal classification of WIG vehicles with a view to adopting rules concerning their certification and safety regulations. Three basic categories have been formally adopted for this purpose.

The first of them (Type A) encompasses vehicles that can be operated only within the height of the surface effect. They usually feature wings of low aspect ratio (up to 1) and are fitted only with a rudder, there being no elevator; the 'driver' (or should we say helmsman?) does not have to possess piloting skills and steers the vehicle in much the same way as an ordinary speedboat. In Russian parlance, such vehicles are termed Dynamic Air Cushion Vessels, or WIG vessels (ekranoplan boats). Among Russian designs, such examples as the Volga-2, Amphistar and Raketa-2 (described in subsequent chapters) may be cited.

The second category (Type B) includes vehicles which are capable of leaving the surface effect zone for a short while and making brief 'hops'. The altitude of such a 'hop' must not exceed the minimum safe altitude of flight for aircraft, as prescribed by International Civil Aviation Organisation (ICAO) regulations (150 m/500 ft). In Russian parlance such vehicles are regarded as WIG craft (*ekranoplans*) proper; they feature wings with an aspect ratio of up to 3 and are provided with elevators. They are controlled by pilots. Among Russian designs this category is represented by the Orlyonok, KM, Strizh, ESKA-1 and others.

The third category (Type C) covers WIG vehicles capable of flying outside the surface effect zone for a considerable time and of climbing to altitudes in excess of the minimum safe flight altitude for aircraft, as prescribed by ICAO regulations.

This classification subdividing the WIG vehicles into types A, B and C was formulated by Russian organisations and submitted by Russia to the International Maritime Organisation (IMO) and ICAO for their consideration. Thanks in no small degree to determined efforts of the Russian side it has proved possible to reach within the framework of IMO an agreement on a number of basic issues pertaining to legal, technical and operational aspects of WIG craft.

At its 76th session held on 2nd-13th December 2002 the IMO Maritime Safety Committee endorsed a provisional code of WIG craft safety. It contains the classification presented above, along with detailed stipulations concerning technical features of ekranoplans, their modes of operation, maintenance, passenger safety etc.

For the first time international documents were evolved that provide rules for commercial operation of WIG craft and for their safety. These documents represent an important milestone. They have given an expression at a high level for an international recognition of WIG craft as a new and promising means of maritime transport and provided a legal basis for its further development and commercial operation on international sea routes.

Against this background, let us take a look at the story of WIG craft design and production in the Soviet Union and modern Russia.

Early research on ground effect and of efforts aimed at creating practicable WIG vehicles dates back to the 1920s and 1930s when work in this field was started in several countries. As is well known, the first-ever self-propelled WIG vehicle was built by Toivo Kaario, a Finnish engineer, in 1935. His experiments were followed up by research and practical design work in the USA, Germany, Sweden, China, Australia and other countries (a brief review of the work on *ekranoplans* outside Russia can be found in Chapter 7).

The Soviet Union also joined the 'club' of countries working on the WIG craft. Theoretical and experimental work in this direction was started in the USSR in the 1920s (experimental work by Boris N. Yur'yev, 1923). Further work followed in the 1930s, when a whole set of theoretical studies and experiments in the field of ground effect research was performed by Yakov M. Serebriyskiy and Sh. A. Biyachuyev. The results of this work were published in specialised literature.

In the early 1930s the first steps in practical design of WIG craft in the USSR were made by Pavel Ignat'yevich Grokhovsky, an aviation engineer and inventor renowned for his energy and innovative ideas. In 1932 Grokhovskiy, aided by a group of his associates, designed a full-scale mock-up of a sea-going flying vehicle featuring a twin-hull layout. The two hulls served as a sort of endplates for a wide-chord wing centre section; the forward section of each of the hulls housed an M-25 radial (a copy of the Wright R-1820-F3 Cyclone) delivering some 700 hp and driving a tractor propeller. The wing was provided with a flap which was intended to increase the lift on take-off and landing. The flying prototype was never built, but this layout was used in many designs of WIG craft in later decades.

An artist's impression of Pavel I. Grokhovskiy's *ekranoplan* project of 1932.

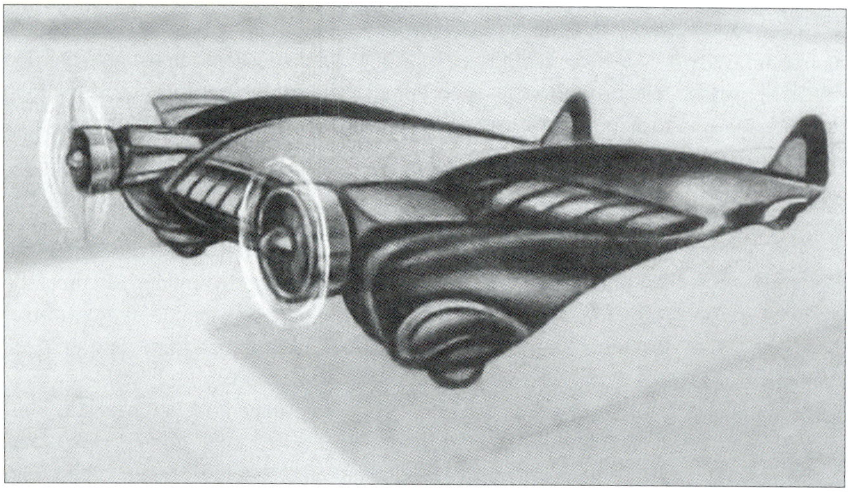

However, it is Rostislav Yevgen'yevich Alekseyev (1916-1980), an outstanding scientist and designer, who must be credited with having played a paramount, decisive role in shaping the course of research, design and construction of WIG vehicles in Russia. His was the conceptual approach and design philosophy; he may truly be regarded as the founder of the Russian wingship construction. Alekseyev started his activities as a builder of hydrofoil ships in his capacity of the chief of the TsKB-19 shipbuilding design bureau based at Gor'kiy (at present Nizhniy Novgorod). In 1958 it was reorganised into the Central Hydrofoil Design Bureau (CHDB, or TsKB po SPK – *Tsen**trahl'**noye kon**strook**torskoye byu**ro** po soo**dahm** na pod**vod**nykh **kryl'**yakh*). An impressive range of highly successful hydrofoil vessels designed under Alekseyev's guidance was developed and put into operational service. As recognition of R. Alekseyev's outstanding contribution to the creation of hydrofoil ships, he was awarded the degree of Dr. Sc. in technical sciences *honoris causa* in April 1962. Yet, it was his work on WIG craft – work veiled in utmost secrecy for many years – that was destined to become the most prominent and significant part of his creative activities.

The Central Hydrofoil Design Bureau became actively engaged in WIG craft design in the early 1960s. But as early as 1957 Rostislav Alekseyev had demonstrated a small model of a vehicle making use of ground effect. In 1958, at his initiative, work began on the construction of a research and experimenting facility near the town of Chkalovsk on the Gor'kiy Reservoir (later it was known as IS-2 – *ispy**tah**tel'naya **stahn**tsiya*). It incorporated an experimental production facility and unique installations, many of which were created with the express purpose of studying the surface effect. The IS-2 became one of the main subdivisions of the CHDB, supplying it with the scientific information required for the practical design of WIG craft.

This design work was based on the concept of autostabilisation of the wings of a WIG vehicle relative to the interface between the supporting water surface and the air. This concept proved basically sound and was subsequently incorporated in all

Rostislav Ye. Alekseyev, Chief Designer of the Central Hydrofoil Design Bureau.

WIG projects issued by the design bureau. On its basis a search was initiated for suitable aero-hydrodynamic layouts; initially, one of these featured two sets of wings arranged in tandem. The first 3-ton (6,600-lb) SM-1 *ekranoplan* built in 1961 at IS-2 was fitted with two sets of wings. Research revealed that the tandem-wing layout is practicable only in very close proximity to the surface and is unable to ensure the necessary margin of stability and safety, once the craft leaves this close proximity. Experiments with this tandem-wing machine ended in a crash. Alekseyev arrived at the decision to make use of a classic aircraft layout (one set of wings and a tail unit) which was to be subjected to modifications designed to ensure stability and controllability during cruise flight in ground effect. In particular, low-set or mid-set wings of much lower aspect ratio (around 3) were adopted. An important feature was the use of an outsize horizontal tail; it was to be placed sufficiently far aft and high up relative to the main wings so as to minimise the influence of the downwash induced by the wings depending on the flight altitude and pitch angle.

Ten experimental WIG vehicles featuring this layout were built in the Central Hydrofoil Design Bureau, their weight and dimensions growing with every successive machine. These were the machines in the SM series (SM stands for *samo**khod**naya mo**del'*** – self-propelled model), with an all-up weight of up to 5 tonnes (11,000 lb); a detailed description is given in Chapter 1.

Design experience gained by Rostislav Ye. Alekseyev in developing these machines enabled him to take a bold decision to initiate the design of gigantic WIG vehicles with an all-up weight of more than 400 t (880,000 lb). In 1962 the Central Design Bureau was engaged in project work on a combat WIG craft intended for anti-submarine warfare (ASW) weighing 450 t (990,000 lb); two years later the design team in Nizhniy Novgorod started designing the T-1 troop transport/assault WIG craft.

It should be noted that the very considerable scope attained by the activities of the Central Design Bureau of Hydrofoils was due to the fact that the new means of transport had attracted much interest on the part of the military. The Soviet Navy took much interest in the military potential of *ekranoplans*; it became the main customer for Alekseyev's CHDB. As a consequence, for many years this work was highly classified. Thus, construction of WIG vehicles in the Soviet Union received a boost from military programmes. In the opinion of military specialists both in the Soviet Union (and nowadays in Russia) and in the West, large WIG vehicles can be employed for a wide range of missions in the armed forces, notably in the Navy. These include troop transportation, ASW, anti-shipping strikes with guided missiles, patrol missions etc. The most ambitious projects envisaged the use of WIG craft as flying aircraft carriers! An inherent advantage of WIG vehicles when used in warfare is their ability to remain undetected by enemy radar thanks to the low altitude of their flight; the lack of contact with the sea surface makes them undetectable by acoustic means (sonar devices). WIG vehicles are capable of operating not only over water expanses but also over snow-covered stretches of land and over ice fields. This makes them eminently suitable for use

One of Alekseyev's sketches from 1947 showing an early concept of WIG vehicles using the tail-first layout. The upper one is particularly unusual, since each wingtip rests on a small auxiliary wing flanked by floats. Note that the foreplanes are attached to the fuselage by a pylon and feature three floats.

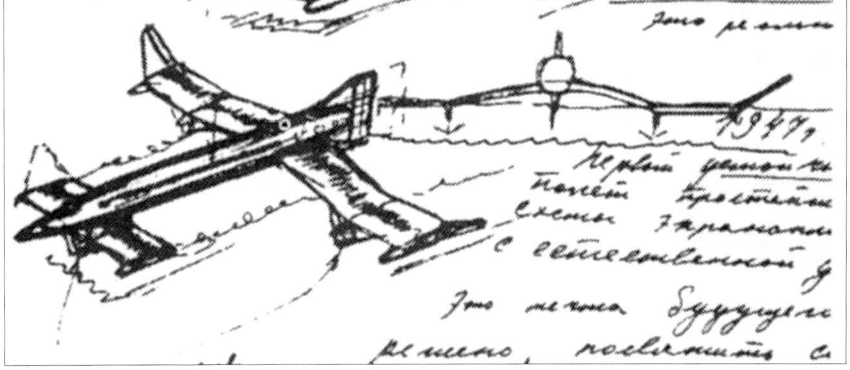

A working meeting at the Central Hydrofoil Design Bureau; Rostislav Alekseyev (standing) heads the meeting. A model of a hydrofoil vessel can be seen on the desk.

in Polar areas. Their high speed ensures their quick response to the changing battlefield situation, and their high load-carrying capacity enhances their capability for accomplishing various missions and carrying a wide range of weapons.

It must be noted that Admiral Sergey G. Gorshkov, the Navy's Commander-in-Chief, was at first somewhat sceptical of WIG craft. Once he asked the CHDB designers: what was a WIG craft – a flying ship or a floating aircraft? If it was an aircraft, the Navy would task Tupolev with preparing a project, if it was a ship, the task would go to CHDB. Naturally, the designers answered in unison that it was *'a ship, but with many distinctive features of a flying vehicle'*!

In assessing the suitability of the WIG craft for ASW, one should bear in mind that, owing to their low flight altitude, WIG vehicles cannot be equipped with sonobuoys. However, they possess a wider range of capabilities for making use of a dunking sonar when afloat. Moreover, thanks to their large dimensions they can, in principle, be fitted with ASW weapons normally carried by surface ships, to be used without becoming airborne.

Large-scale models of WIG craft built by the CHDB were tested in free flight on open water, using a hydrofoil boat as a tug, as shown here.

WIG vehicles are superior to amphibious aircraft in sea-going capabilities and endurance; they can be armed with more potent missiles possessing longer range. However, they have their limitations associated with the need for target designation from an external source (amphibious seaplanes can provide target designation for their weapons when flying at high altitude).

The projects of an ASW WIG vehicle and the T-1 troop-carrying WIG vehicle developed at CHDB never left the drawing board. On the other hand, in 1966 the Design Bureau built, in response to an order from the Navy, a WIG craft designated KM (*ko**rah**bl'-ma**ket*** – a 'mock-up', i.e., prototype ship). With its fuselage length of 97 m (320 ft), wing span of 37 m (123 ft) and all-up weight of 430 t (948,000 lb), this gigantic machine was a unique piece of engineering. In a record-setting flight its weight reached 540 t (1,190,000 lb), which was an unofficial world record for flying machines at that time. Rostislav Alekseyev argued that the construction and testing of such a WIG craft would provide invaluable experience for the designing of military ekranoplans and civil transport ekranoplans with an AUW of about 2,000 tonnes (4,410,000 lb). He was convinced that large WIG vehicles offered important aerodynamic advantages and represented a promising line of development. Of course, a decision to proceed from small experimental vehicles directly to a giant machine was a technical risk, but it acquitted itself in the end. In 1964, when the activities of CHDB became a subject of critical scrutiny, the design work on the KM was endorsed, among others, by TsAGI, although this authoritative scientific institute had its own ideas, differing from those of Alekseyev, on the optimum layout for ekranoplans.

Creation of large sea-going *ekranoplans* required a new test facility located on a sea shore. Such a test facility was set up on the Caspian Sea, near the town of Kaspiysk in Daghestan. This facility served as base for the testing of the KM and a further two types of large *ekranoplans*.

The abovementioned KM, dubbed 'Caspian Sea Monster' in the West, underwent comprehensive testing in the course of 15 years of operation. It marked the completion of a whole range of research and practical design tasks associated with approbation of the WIG concept as a whole and evolving the scientific basis for their design, construction and testing. The results of this work made it possible to create a theoretical and methodological basis for designing and building practicable examples of WIG vehicles of different classes.

One of these was the *Or**lyo**nok* (Eaglet) troop transport/assault ekranoplan with a take-off weight of 140 t (309,000lb). It was capable of transporting

As these pictures show, Rostislav Alekseyev was a pilot and personally tested many of his *ekranoplans*.

a 20-tonne (44,000-lb) cargo at a speed of 400 km/h (248 mph) to a distance of up to 1,500 km (930 miles). Construction of the Orlyonok was conducted at the Volga Shipyard which was set up on the basis of CHDB's experimental production workshops in 1970. Three examples of the Orlyonok (Project 904) were delivered to the Navy for evaluation. Their service career proved to be far from an unqualified success. Normal operation was hampered, above all, by circumstances of bureaucratic nature. The WIG machines were operated by the Navy, yet their crews had to include pilots because in certain operational modes they had to be piloted like aircraft. However, neither the Air Force nor the Naval Aviation showed any enthusiasm for these machines and sought to 'prove' in every possible way that they could not be regarded as flying machines – unabashed by the fact that provision was made for operating them also out of surface effect and there were plans for long-range ferrying flights at high altitude. Yielding to this pressure, the Navy top brass then decided that WIG craft should be classed as 'ships with aircraft-like properties'.

In turn, the Central Hydrofoil Design Bureau clearly underestimated the 'aviation' aspect of the matter and had failed to consult the Air Force on the methods of testing, which gave rise to justifiable complaints. Arrangements required to facilitate operational use of the machines delivered to the Navy suffered setbacks and delays. Series production of WIG craft for the Navy was expected to amount to several dozens of examples, but these plans failed to materialise. Introduction of new types of weaponry in the USSR, following a pattern common to many countries, depended heavily on lobbying on the part of this or that person in the top echelon. The Soviet Union's Minister of Defence,

The missile-armed Loon' demonstrated the practicality of using WIG vehicles for combat applications.

The prototype of the Orlyonok in cruise flight.

Marshal of the Soviet Union Dmitriy F. Ustinov supported the idea of WIG vehicle construction, but he died in 1985. Marshal Sergey L. Sokolov, the new Minister of Defence, influenced by the newly appointed Commander-in-Chief of the Navy Fleet Admiral Vladimir N. Chernavin, ordered that all the funds available to the Navy be used for the construction of submarines. A crash suffered in 1992 by one of the Orlyonok machines was hardly conducive to improving the atmosphere around their integration into the armed forces. This was further aggravated by the transfer of the WIG machines from ordinary naval units to the Naval Aviation – airmen were not overly enthusiastic about the new hardware. Deprived of the necessary attention and supplies, the base where the WIG craft were stationed began to fall into decay. Eventually the three surviving machines (two Orlyonoks and one Loon') were struck off charge on the pretext of difficulties associated with maintenance and repairs, That marked, for the time being, the end of operational use of transport and combat WIG vehicles in the Russian Navy.

There is an episode in the story of the Orlyonok which eloquently bears witness to the character of both the machine and its creator, Rostislav Alekseyev. In 1975, during one of the test flights, Alekseyev was on board. The pilot, who had little experience with this type of vehicle, impacted the machine heavily right on the crest of a wave. The crew did not grasp the situation. Only Alekseyev, who had taken a look from the upper hatch, knew what had happened. Without a word, he took over the controls, gave full throttle to the nose-mounted booster engines and delivered the machine to its base which was 40 km (25 miles) away. Only then could the crew take a look at the machine. They were stunned by the sight: the vehicle had lost its tail! The rear fuselage, complete with the tail unit and cruise engine, had simply broken off on impact and sunk! The fact that the Orlyonok still made it safely back to base bore witness both to the designer's presence of mind and piloting skill and to the machine's qualities. However, this episode gave a welcome tool into the hands of Alekseyev's detractors and those who were intent on closing down the work on WIG vehicles. The episode was followed by 'administrative measures' (i.e., repercussions) which boiled down to victimising the designer. In September 1975 Alekseyev was dismissed from the post of Chief Designer of the Orlyonok project (he was replaced by V. V. Sokolov in this capacity). Alekseyev was demoted to a modest post of a section leader and was compelled to with-

A fine view of the cruising Orlyonok, showing the wake of spray the machine leaves.

draw from practical design, being tasked solely with research work. Thus, he was deprived of the possibility to make full use of his creative potential. Nevertheless, he did not give up. During the last years of his work Rostislav Alekseyev devoted his attention to evolving technical proposals to meet the Navy's requirements for WIG vehicles intended for various duties, such as transport and troop landing vehicles, ASW craft, missile-carrying machines etc. A significant volume of theoretic and experimental work was conducted under his guidance with a view to creating a scientific and techni-

Chief Designer Rostislav Ye. Alekseyev in the late 1970s.

cal basis for the projecting of large ekranoplans. In 1978, in his report at a technical conference in the Central Shipbuilding Institute named after Academician Aleksey N. Krylov (TsNII – *Tsen**trahl'**nyy naa**ooch**no-is**sle**dovatel'skiy insti**toot***; oddly, the institute's shipbuilding specialisation is not reflected in the official Russian name), Alekseyev submitted results of studies concerning the aerohydrodynamic layout of an aircraft-carrier ekranoplan. He visualised this vehicle as a machine of integral layout (flying wing) without a separate fuselage and traditional tail unit, wingtip endplates playing the role of vertical tails.

It was at that time (1976) that the Chkalovsk-based branch of CHDB (IS-2) was reorganised into a branch of the Krylov Central Shipbuilding Institute (TsNII) in Leningrad (now St. Petersburg).

A few words must be said about Rostislav Alekseyev's relations with the nation's leaders and top figures in the industrial and military circles. Alekseyev enjoyed full support from Nikita S. Khrushchov until the latter was ousted from leadership in 1964. That marked a worsening of the 'climate' around Alekseyev's work. A valuable asset for Alekseyev was the support from Marshal Ustinov, the Minister of Defence and an important figure in the Communist Party leadership with defence as his special concern. On the other hand, Alekseyev's work met with overt and covert opposition from the Minister of Shipbuilding Industry Boris Ye. Butoma who, while being an unquestionably efficient manager in his branch, was sceptical about WIG craft and, moreover, had personal ill feelings towards Alekseyev – mainly because of the latter's independent behaviour.

Rostislav Alekseyev died in 1980. It fell to the lot of his associates and successors to undertake the work which marked an important stage in the activities of the Central Hydrofoil Design Bureau. This was the creation of the Loon' (Hen Harrier) – a 400-tonne missile carrier armed with *Mos**kit*** (Mosquito) anti-shipping missiles. It was launched in 1987 and tested in 1989. Construction of a second example of this machine was envisaged, but collapse of the Soviet Union drastically affected the programme (see Chapter 1 for details of the 'operational career' of the Loon' and Orlyonok WIG vehicles). The second example, already under construction, was to be completed as a search-and-rescue machine. Accordingly, conversion work was started, but this project, too, stranded due to various political and economic reasons.

Long before Rostislav Alekseyev's demise the top management of CHDB was taken over by other persons. In 1968 V. V. Ikonnikov was appointed the head and Chief Designer of the Central Hydrofoil Design Bureau; he occupied these post well into the 1970s (in 1968 Alekseyev was placed in charge of a separate *ekranoplan* section of the CHDB as Chief Designer). Ikonnikov's successor was B. V. Choobikov. For a while this organisation was headed by General Director I. M. Vasilevskiy and, finally, by S. V. Platonov. In the early 1990s, after the demise of the Soviet Union and the onset of radical economic and political transformations, the Central Hydrofoil Design Bureau, now named after Rostislav Ye. Alekseyev, was transformed into a joint-stock company. The scope of its activities in the field of the WIG craft design was drastically reduced due to the lack of funding and state orders, and the emphasis shifted to small machines intended for commercial uses. Some of the projects were developed with a view to foreign markets and partnership schemes with investors from abroad but such plans did not bear fruit. (The situation around the CHDB is described in greater detail in Chapters 1 and 6.)

While the Central Hydrofoil Design Bureau in Nizhniy Novgorod enjoyed for many years the position as Russia's leading developer of heavy seagoing WIG craft, it was not a monopolist in its field.

In the course of the last five decades questions of WIG research and practical design have been dealt with by quite a number of organisations, big and small, including design bureaus, scientific institutions, commercial firms, student design teams and individual enthusiasts. Here are some of these organisations:

WIG vehicles have occupied an important place in the activities of Robert Lyudvigovich Bartini, a

Like most of Alekseyev's WIG vehicles, the Orlyonok utilised an aircraft-type layout.

well-known Soviet aircraft designer who made a significant contribution to evolving the theory of dynamic air cushion vehicles and prepared a number of designs which failed to reach the hardware stage, with the exception of the 14M1P (they are described in detail in Chapter 2).

At a certain stage in his career Bartini continued his activities within the framework of Gheorgiy Mikhaïlovich Beriyev's design bureau (now the Taganrog Aviation Scientific and Technical Complex named after G. M. Beriyev). This is where his 14M1P was built. Also other Beriyev engineers and

A typical feature of Alekseyev's WIGs was the use of engine exhaust for creating an air cushion under the wings on take-off.

Opposite page: Robert Bartini's VVA-14 amphibian utilising WIG technology.

design teams were engaged in WIG vehicle design; in 1965 they designed and built the Be-1 experimental WIG vehicle. Several WIG craft projects were developed by Beriyev. During the last decades engineers of the Taganrog firm have been working with designs of large (even gigantic) aircraft of this type combining the features of a WIG vehicle and a traditional amphibious flying boat. (see Chapter 3).

The Sukhoi Design Bureau established co-operation with the Central Hydrofoil Design Bureau; in the course of 10 to 15 years (before 2002) it developed several WIG projects such as the S-90, S-90-8 and S-90-200. They are described in Chapter 4.

Nizhniy Novgorod remains an important centre of activities associated with *ekranoplan* design and production. In the 1990s it saw the emergence of a number of small firms established in the early 1990s. The most important among them is the Technology and Transport Joint-Stock Co. (later renamed Amphibious Transport Technologies, now a subsidiary of the ATTK) which has developed the Amphistar passenger WIG speedboat. Among other companies mention must be made of the now defunct Amphicon (a Russian acronym meaning *amfi**beey**nyye kon**strook**tsii* – amphibious designs), Transal (an acronym for ***Trahns**port Alek**sey**eva* – Alexeyev's Transport), Plast and other companies, some of which, however, switched over to ACVs rather than WIG craft. In Moscow the Roks-Aero company was working with WIG designs in the early 1990s; the KOMETEL company and its successor, the IFPG, is active there at present. Some activity in the field of the ekranoplan design took place for some time in the Almaz Central Design Bureau in Leningrad (now St. Petersburg) and in the Zelenodol'sk Design Bureau. Some design activities have taken place in Siberian cities (Ulan-Ude, Abakan) as a sequel to Amphicon's work.

In the course of the last 50 years (from the 1960s onwards) a whole series of light WIG vehicles was designed and built by young designers working within enthusiast designer groups or so-called student design bureaus that had been established at a number of aviation institutes (colleges). Here mention must be made of such teams within TsLST (*Tsen**trahl'**naya labora**tor**iya spa**sah**tel'noy **tekh**niki* – Central Laboratory for SAR Technology), MVTU (*Mos**kov**skoye **vys**sheye tekh**nich**eskoye oo**chil**ischche* – Moscow Higher Technical College named after Nikolay E. Bauman), MIIGA (*Mos**kov**skiy insti**toot** inzhe**neh**rov grazh**dahn**skoy avi**ah**tsii* – Moscow Institute of Civil Aviation Engineers), MAI (*Mos**kov**skiy aviatsi**on**nyy insti**toot*** – Moscow Aviation Institute), RKIIGA (***Rizh**skiy krasnozna**myon**nyy insti**toot** inzhe**neh**rov grazh**dahn**skoy avi**ah**tsii* – Riga Red Banner Institute of Civil Aviation Engineers), KnAPI (*Komso**mol'**skiy-na-A**moo**re politekh**nich**eskiy insti**toot*** – Komsomolsk-on-Amur Polytechnic Institute), IPI (*Ir**koot**skiy politekh**nich**eskiy insti**toot*** – Irkutsk Polytechnic Institute) and KAI (*Ka**zahn**skiy aviatsi**on**nyy insti**toot*** – Kazan' Aviation Institute).

Problems pertaining to WIG vehicles are studied by such scientific institutions as the A. N. Krylov Central Shipbuilding Research Institute (TsNII) in St. Petersburg, TsAGI (*Tsen**trahl'**nyy **aero****ghid**rodina**mich**eskiy institoot* – Central Aero- and Hydrodynamical Institute) in Moscow and Zhukovskiy, SibNIIA (*Si**beer**skiy na**ooch**no-is**sle**dovatel'skiy insti**toot** avi**ah**tsii* – Siberian Aviation Research Institute) in Novosibirsk, the Irkutsk State University in co-operation with the Russian Academy of Sciences. In the Ukraine, then part of the USSR, theoretical studies and practical design work on ekranoplans were conducted in Kiev-based Hydrodynamics Institute, in KhAI (***Khar'**kovskiy aviatsi**on**nyy insti**toot*** – Khar'kov Aviation Institute) and a voluntary design bureau at Khar'kov aircraft plant) and in the Nikolayev Shipbuilding Institute.

What are the general trends and prospects in the activity of Russian organisations in the field of WIG design and production at present?

As to military applications, during the 1990s it appeared that the need for WIG vehicles in the Armed Forces of Russia had fallen drastically. One of the reasons for this was presumably the radical change in the world situation as compared to the Soviet period. The confrontation between social systems and military alliances had given way to normal relations between Russia and the West, entailing a revision of the scope and character of Russian military programmes. To a certain extent this reflected the euphoria based on the hopes of a cloudless relationship with the former Cold War adversaries. As a consequence, defence needs did not receive due attention. Another factor was the marked worsening of the economic situation in Russia in the 1990s. Budgetary restrictions drastically reduced the resources that could be used by the Armed Forces for funding the development and acquisition of new military hardware. These limitations harshly affected the traditional armaments, entailing, for example, a severe curtailment of the construction of new ships for the Navy. It was unrealistic to expect that priority would be given to an exotic type of military materiel.

In these circumstances the design bureaux engaged in WIG vehicle design were compelled to stake on designing machines intended for commercial application. The prospects of commercial use of WIG craft, however, remain unclear to this day. To win a secure place in the world transport system, the new means of transportation has to overcome

СССР-19172

many obstacles. The competition between WIG craft and traditional means of transport (aircraft, ships) can, i.a., take the form of covert opposition from certain quarters to introduction of WIG vehicles on lucrative sea routes. However, the main thing is the objective factor – namely, the ability of WIG vehicles to demonstrate economic advantages over traditional air and sea transport. Here WIG vehicles have on the credit side their far superior speeds as compared to displacement vessels and greater load-carrying capacity per unit of engine power or thrust as compared to aircraft. Research on transport economics undertaken by a number of organisations in Russia and in the West revealed a niche which could be filled by WIG vehicles. It is passenger and cargo transportation on transoceanic trunk routes, as well as transport communications between islands in an archipelago and between islands and the mainland. WIG craft are presumed to have no need for a pier (as distinct from ships) or an airfield (as distinct from aircraft). This is important, since it is uneconomical to build a seaport or an airport in areas with low traffic intensity.

In practice, the economic efficiency of WIG craft has not yet established itself as something indisputable. One of the factors affecting it is the relatively low payload to all-up weight ratio of the WIG vehicles built to date (due to the use of shipbuilding, rather than aircraft technologies in construction and to the necessity to carry as dead weight the booster engines which are required only at take-off).

Be it as it may, at the end of 1980 and the beginning of 1990s the Russian design bureaux specialising in the designing of WIG vehicles set about designing machines intended for commercial application both at home and abroad. In 1993 designer V. V. Sokolov, a disciple of Rostislav Ye. Alekseyev, voiced an optimistic opinion: *'Research done by specialised institutes shows that the expected high productivity of* ekranoplans *leading to their profitability fully meets the demands of potential buyers and the trends in the development of transport systems; therefore, commercial* ekranoplans *can become a reality already in the nearest future'.*

There was no prospect of obtaining the necessary funding from the State budget, so the design bureaux and companies in question pinned their hopes on establishing co-operation with foreign partners who were expected to make the necessary investments. International co-operation was expected to provide the basis not only for the introduction of WIG craft into cargo and passenger transportation, but also for the employment of this new means of transport in systems for aerial launch of space shuttles, in international maritime SAR systems etc.

These plans and intentions had, generally speaking, a certain realistic foundation. Russia is universally recognised to have far outstripped other countries in design and construction of WIG vehicles, especially large sea-going craft. A noteworthy comment on this score was made by Vladimir N. Kirillovykh, Chief Designer of the Central Hydrofoils Design Bureau. In December 2001 he said in an interview to a Russian magazine that Russia was some twenty years ahead of other countries as far as the technology of WIG vehicle construction was concerned. *'There are many amphibious craft in the world today, but all of them are unsuitable for use at sea,* – said he. – *Nowadays only Russia is in possession of technology required for the construction of precisely the sea-going* ekranoplans'.

Several countries displayed interest for getting access to the advanced Russian know-how in WIG design. In 1992 an authoritative group of US specialists visited the *ekranoplan* base in Kaspiysk to gain first-hand impressions of the Russian achievements and assess the prospects of co-operation. In the USA interest was shown for making use of the Russian experience in connection with some plans for gearing WIG vehicles to military tasks. However, this did not lead to any joint ventures with practical results.

In 1990s the Sukhoi Design Bureau concluded an agreement with a Singapore company on joint development of a WIG vehicle for cargo and passenger transportation in South-East Asia. Unfortunately the agreement stranded for financial reasons. This and other similar efforts brought no results – not a single joint project has been brought to fruition. The main reason is the lack of the necessary funding on the part of Russian partners.

At present the following trends can be observed as regards the practical use of WIG vehicles in Russia. Firstly, it is the relatively cheap smaller-size craft carrying 8 to 12 passengers that are used as a first step in the introduction of the new means of cargo and passenger transportation. This is due both to a cautious approach of carriers to the new technology and to a lack of financial means for developing and buying bigger and costlier machines. Nevertheless, several private companies (IFPG, ATTK, Alien-Chkalovsk) have developed programmes envisaging the design, manufacture and operational service of larger craft intended to transport 50-100 and more passengers or a corresponding cargo. Secondly, many projects developed earlier by Russian design bureaux or under development at present represent Type B and C WIG vehicles, yet the emphasis is placed on the introduction of Type A machines (DAC vessels) intended for operation only within ground effect. In Russia the introduction of WIG craft is associated first and foremost with the development of river transport in shipping agencies of inland waterways, such as the rivers of Volga, Oka, Kama, Ob', Irtysh, Yenisey, Amur, Lena etc. The reason is simple. Type A WIG vehicle are certified according to requirements for river-going and sea-going ships, while certification of vehicles capable of operation out of ground effect is effected according to requirements for aircraft. This makes the certification procedure in the latter case far more complicated and costly – an important consideration for operators with limited resources. Therefore introduction of Type B and C WIG vehicles into commercial operations in Russia can be expected only when some experience in the operation of Type A machines has been accumulated and potential operators have considerably improved their financial situation.

There appears to be a revival of interest in *ekranoplans* on the part of the Russian military, although there is no evidence yet of any specific plans for their introduction into the arsenals of the armed forces, nor is there any well thought-out general concept of the role of *ekranoplans* in the nation's defence. The first tangible sign of a possible comeback of military application of the WIG technology was the decision of Russia's Border Guard Agency to order 12-seat EK-12 machines; in 2007 an example of this vehicle owned by the Border Guards was displayed at the MAKS-2007 air show. Operational testing of the machine attracted much interest on the part of the Russian Navy, whose specialists came to the conclusion that much larger WIG vehicles were required for sea operations. A prospective *ekranoplan* for the Navy must be in the 50-tonne (110,000 lb) class. Projects in this category already have been developed for civil applications, but eventual machines tailored for the Navy will presumably be designed from scratch to meet fully the special requirements. In the course of public discussions on the subject of WIG technology representatives of the Navy voiced the opinion that the proper course of action would be to explore the possible regions suitable for *ekranoplan* operations, to determine the tasks that could be tackled by *ekranoplans* and to define the requirements that these machines have to meet. Then the technical specifications must be drawn up which, in addition to technical parameters, must define the tactical pattern of their operational use. The next stage will be to determine the organisation which will undertake the design and manufacture of the ekranoplans in question. But prior to that sufficient operational experience must be obtained with the EK-12 *ekranoplan*, which is being introduced into service now.

During the last four or five years the need for reviving WIG vehicle development and construction, particularly with defence tasks in mind, has been repeatedly raised in the mass media by politicians and military specialists. This appears to have had some influence on the attitude to this question in the official quarters. On several occasions the First Deputy Prime Minister Sergey B. Ivanov expressed his belief that concerted efforts should be made to revive the WIG vehicle manufacture in the country. Some interest for WIG vehicles has been displayed by the Russian Ministry for Emergency Situations (EMERCOM). It remains to be seen to what extent these declarations will be put into practice.

At present the Russian industry is capable of building *ekranoplans* comparable in size to large airliners, provided this is backed up by a national programme and the necessary funding. As for the construction and operational use of WIG vehicles in the super-heavy class (1,000 t/2,200,000 lb and more), implementation of such projects by the Russian industry alone seems quite Utopian in the nearest future, bearing in mind the huge expenses involved in designing, testing, development and construction of such monsters.

Further work of the Russian design bureaux engaged in the projecting of WIG vehicles will presumably proceed under the conditions of tough competition from Western countries having greater financial resources at their disposal. Furthermore, some Asian countries – China, South Korea and Japan – are emerging as serious competitors in this field, too. Enthusiasts of *ekranoplan* construction in Russia try to impress upon the Russian Government the need for a determined effort designed to preserve and enhance Russia's lead in the theoretical research and practical implementation of this new means of transport. A few years ago Dr. Sc. Aleksandr I. Maskalik, one of the designers of the Amphistar WIG vehicle, said: *'Yes, we are still retaining advanced positions in the construction of* ekranoplans*, but Western contenders are now making their presence more and more acutely felt. If no urgent measures are taken, we can lose this advantage completely'*. These words sound still more topical today.

In the following chapters the reader will find a description of the most significant designs of WIG vehicles created in Russia (when dealing with the Soviet period, mention is made of designs evolved in other republics of the USSR, notably in the Ukraine and the Baltic republics). Four separate chapters are devoted to historically the most prominent Soviet design bureaux in this field, while the following two chapters deal with designs emanating from enthusiasts, scientific institutions and the present-day Russian design bureaux and commercial companies. However, the range of types covered here is by no means exhaustive. Finally, a special chapter is devoted to a brief review of the trends and achievements in WIG design in countries outside Russia, to give the reader a background against which the Russian activities should be judged.

The authors feel that a few words are called for concerning the terminology used in this book. The terminology pertaining to the subject under consideration, both in English and in Russian, shows a number of variations of some basic terms. In some cases, Russian terms have no direct equivalent in English. Therefore the authors deem it necessary to mention here their personal preferences in translating some basic definitions and notions.

The subject of this book is a new means of transport associated with ground effect, or surface effect. Accordingly, the generally accepted English term for the machines in question is 'wing-in-ground-effect vehicle', with such variations as ground effect vehicle (GEV), 'wing-in-surface-effect vehicle', 'wing-in ground (surface) effect craft, wing in surface effect ship (WISES). These terms are often abbreviated to WIG vehicle (craft), less frequently WIGE vehicle. However, we also have the American term 'wingship', and one can encounter such variations as 'WIG aircraft', reflecting the uncertainty as to whether one should regard the new transport means as fish or fowl. In addition, the Russian term 'ekranoplan' (pronounced *ekrano***plahn**), sometimes spelled 'ekranoplane', has received a measure of currency in some English-language publications. Its use in Russian publications reveals some variations in the understanding of the word by different authors. Generally it is understood to cover all types of WIG vehicles, but sometimes it is used restrictively with reference to vehicles operating in ground effect only, as distinct from the Russian term '*ekrano***lyot**' which refers to WIG vehicles capable of operating also out of ground effect and especially to those capable of high-altitude flying.

The authors have chosen to make use basically of the term 'wing-in-ground-effect vehicle', or 'WIG vehicle', with variations as appropriate, but occasionally the reader will encounter the Russian words '*ekranoplan*' and '*ekranolyot*' reflecting the style and usage of Russian official documents. Some difficulty arises in translating the term '*ekranolyot*'. Translating it as 'WIG aircraft', while technically correct, can be ambiguous, since this term sometimes covers the general notion of WIG vehicles. Therefore it was considered wise to adapt translation to the context and to make use, where appropriate, of the modern (IMO) classification of Type A, B and C vehicles.

Much emphasis has been placed in recent years on putting the simplest WIG vehicles operating exclusively in ground effect (Type A vehicles) on the same footing with ships in terms of certification. This has given rise to in Russian terminology such as ***kah****ter-ekrano***plahn** (WIG boat) or ***sood****no na dina***mich***eskoy voz***doosh***noy po***doosh***ke* (dynamic air cushion vessel), as distinct from a 'real *ekranoplan*' which is supposed to possess at least a measure of ability to fly out of ground effect.

In describing the powerplants of WIG vehicles, the Russian terminology makes wide use of the word *pod***doov** which means 'blowing' and is usually rendered descriptively as directing (deflecting) streams of air or jet efflux beneath the wings for the purpose of forming a static air cushion under them for take-off. In Western parlance, this is often rendered by such terms as power-augmented ram air cushion (PAR) etc. Engines installed in a WIG vehicle specially for this purpose are termed variously as assisted take-off engines, lift engines or booster engines (the latter term is used in the book). These are only examples of the variations that can be encountered.

The reader will often encounter in this book the term 'composite layout wings', corresponding to the Russian term *sostav***noy***e kry***lo** – a wing design that combines a low-aspect-ratio centre section with high-aspect-ratio outer wing panels.

With all the aforesaid in mind, we hope, the reader will forgive minor inconsistencies in terminology that may eventually be found in this book.

Acknowledgements

This book is based on published materials and on information supplied by some of the organisations engaged in WIG craft design and construction. Books and magazine articles by E. A. Aframeyev, V. B. Diomidov, Yevgeniy P. Groonin, Pavel I. Kachur, Ye. A. Kramaryov, Yu. V. Makarov, Aleksandr I. Maskalik, A. V. Nebylov, Gennadiy S. Panatov, V. F. Plotnikov, D. N. Sinitsyn, V. V. Sokolov, I. M. Vasilevskiy, P. P. Yablonskiy, V. Bukovskiy, Yu. Varakosov and others have proved particularly valuable.

The authors would like to thank Keith Dexter, Sergey M. Ganin, Andrey Sal'nikov, Konstantin Udalov and Avico Press Ltd., the EKIP Concern, the ATT and ATTK Joint Stock Companies and the Wingship Company for the materials used in the making of this book, and Gennadiy F. Petrov and Pavel G. Tkachenko for the photos they kindly supplied.

Special thanks go to Gennady Petrov for his line drawings (pp. 16, 20, 21, 22, 24, 29, 35, 37, 75, 189, 246) and to Helmut Walther for his valuable photos from Nizhniy Novgorod.

Finally, the authors thank Dmitriy Komissarov for his assistance in the preparation of this book.

CHAPTER ONE

ALEKSEYEV, THE PIONEER

STANDARD-SETTING DESIGNS

The history of the establishment and development of the Central Hydrofoil Design Bureau has been presented in the introductory chapter. Here follows a description of its designs.

Vehicles in the SM series

At the initial stage of the work on WIG vehicles in the Central Hydrofoil Design Bureau several light machines were built under the common designation SM (*samo**khod**naya mo**del**'*, self-propelled model), individual designs bearing a succession of numbers from 1 to 8. They were proof-of-concept vehicles used to check the surface effect and evolve technical features which came into use later when development of WIG vehicles intended for practical operation was started. Their testing was conducted at a special test facility built on the bank of the Gor'kiy Reservoir (the IS-2 base) which was well equipped with various test facilities.

SM-1

This machine was designed in 1960 and built in 1961at the Chkalovsk test facility, making its first flight on 22nd July with the designer Rostislav Ye. Alekseyev at the controls. It had two sets of wings arranged in tandem and fitted with endplates. The front wings of rectangular shape with an aspect ratio of 1.26 had ailerons/flaps, the aft wings with an aspect ratio of 1.35 were of trapezoidal planform and were mounted at virtually the same height as the front wings. The aft wings were fitted with

Rostislav Yevgen'yevich Alekseyev, head of the Central Hydrofoil Design Bureau.

The SM-1 during trials. Note the three open cockpits, the uncowled engine and the auxiliary fin immediately ahead of it.

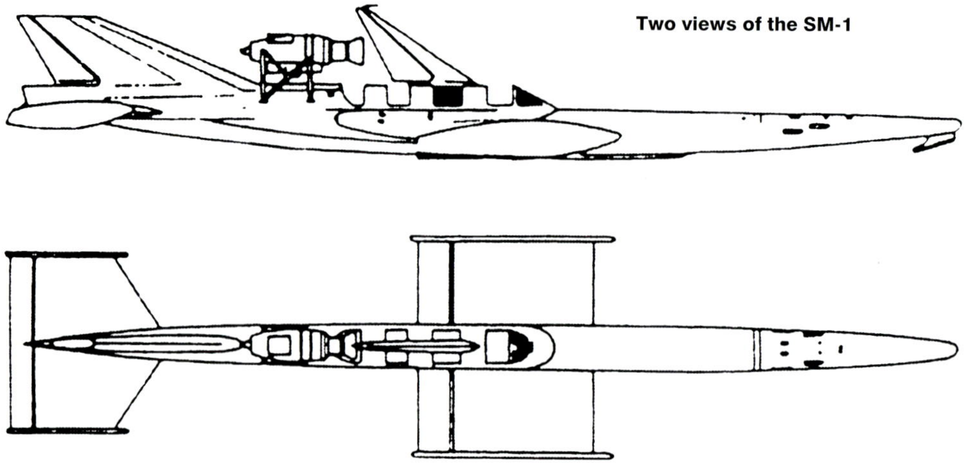

Two views of the SM-1

elevators on their trailing edges. A turbojet engine with no cowling but with a funnel-shaped air intake was mounted on top of the fuselage behind a three-seat open cockpit. The three seats were located in tandem on the vehicle's axis; provision was made for a fourth crew member. An interesting feature of the design was the provision of an extra vertical control surface: in addition to the conventional aft-mounted fin-and-rudder assembly, there was a smaller fin-and-rudder placed atop the fuselage behind the first cockpit.

The tests revealed satisfactory stability and controllability in the ground effect flight mode. As the tests progressed, Alekseyev grew more and more confident of his machine – to such an extent that in the late autumn of 1961 he invited high-ranking guests to take a look at it. Those invited were Marshal Dmitriy F. Ustinov, secretary of the Communist Party's central committee; Boris Ye. Butoma, the Minister of Shipbuilding Industry; and Admiral Sergey G. Gorshkov, Commander-in-Chief of the Navy. The guests were so impressed by what they saw that they accepted the invitation to take a ride in the experimental vehicle. Dmitriy Ustinov was very pleased with the ride and instructed Boris Butoma to give all the necessary assistance to Alekseyev.

Specifications of the SM-1

Wing span	5.0 m (16 ft 4¾ in)
Length	20.0 m (65 ft 7 13/32 in)
Height	1.53 m (5 ft 0 in)
All-up weight, kg (lb)	2,830 (6,240)
Cruising speed, km/h (mph)	170 (106)
Maximum speed, km/h (mph)	270 (168)
Powerplant	One turbojet of unspecified type
Engine thrust , kgp (lbst)	n.a.

The SM-2 skims along the water surface before becoming airborne. Note the pitot intake of the forward engine. The vertical tail appears disproportionately large in this view.

The SM-2 in wing-borne flight, showing the air intake and nozzle of the rear-mounted cruise engine. The curved strakes on the aft fuselage underside were probably meant to improve the hydrodynamic properties.

Successful tests of the SM-1 corroborated the basic concept of flight in close proximity of a supporting surface. A speed of 200 km/h (124 mph) was reached; the vehicle's stability and handling characteristics during flight close to the supporting surface (water, snow-covered stretches of land) proved to be satisfactory. Yet the tests revealed insufficient seaworthiness and excessively high take-off and landing speeds. The latter may be regarded as one of the main drawbacks of the tandem layout, another being the vehicle's excessive sensitivity to unevenness of the supporting surface. Furthermore, the SM-1's range of stable flight modes proved to be very limited, as regards the height above the supporting surface and the pitch angle.

In January 1962, during one of the test flights, the SM-1 soared into the air of its own accord, leaving the ground effect zone, and then 'fell through', impacting the ice, when the pilot shut down the engine. The machine was damaged and the crew sustained minor injuries. That brought the SM-1's testing to an end – the machine was not repaired.

Two stills from a cine film showing the SM-2 in action (in cruise mode).

Starboard side view of the SM-2 in cruise mode. The black spots on the sides of the nose are the forward engine's nozzles.

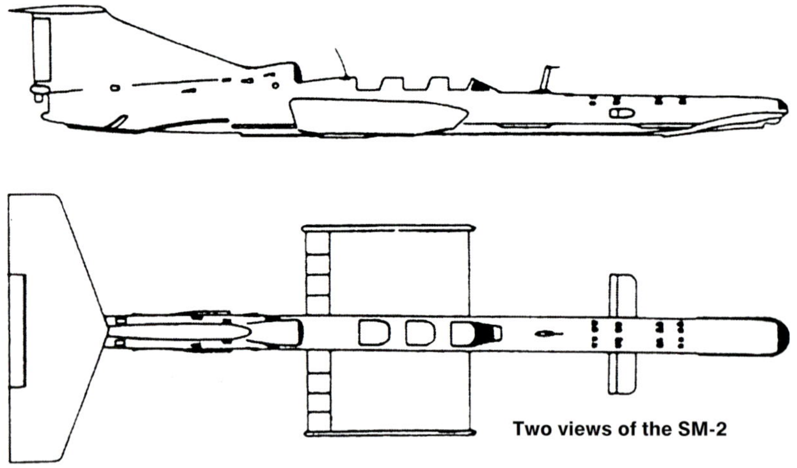

Two views of the SM-2

Specifications of the SM-2	
Wing span	5.0 m (16 ft 4 55/64 in)
Length	20.0 m (65 ft 7½ in)
Height	1.5 m (4 ft 11 in)
All-up weight, kg (lb)	3,200 (7,056)
Cruising speed, km/h (mph)	160 (99)
Maximum speed, km/h (mph)	270 (168)
Powerplant	2 x RU-19-300 modified
Engine thrust , kgp (lbst)	2 x 900 (1,984)
Crew	3

SM-2

This machine built in 1962 was initially fitted with two wing sets arranged in tandem. It was damaged by a hangar fire before the trials could begin and reworked in the process of restoration to feature an aircraft layout. This aero-hydrodynamic layout with one set of wings, T-tail and a device for power-augmented take-off was adopted for all subsequent vehicles designed in the Central Hydrofoil Design Bureau. The SM-2 served for studying the influence of take-off booster blowing devices on the take-off performance of WIG vehicles (that was the first time Alekseyev used such a device). The booster engine located in the front fuselage was fitted with bifurcated flattened nozzle extensions placed wide apart on both sides of the fuselage; they directed the jet efflux under the wings. Initially it also served as a cruise engine, but the thrust of the bifurcated nozzles proved insufficient, and a separate cruise engine was installed in the aft fuselage under the fin. Both engines were 900-kgp (1,984-lb st) Tumanskiy RU19-300 turbojets in a 'marine' version featuring enhanced corrosion protection.

On completion of the testing the vehicle was upgraded: the swept-back wing leading edges were replaced by straight leading edges to improve the effect from blowing, resulting in a rectangular wing planform. In this version the vehicle was redesignated SM-2P (P presumably stands for *pri-amo'u**gol'**noye* [*kry**lo***] – rectangular wings).

Thanks to the lift augmentation (blowing) the take-off performance of the SM-2 was considerably improved as compared to the SM-1. The tests corroborated the soundness of the basic design layout and enabled the designers to use it in their further work.

In early May 1962 the SM-2 was shown to the country's government and personally to Nikita S. Khrushchov (this was done at the initiative of Dmitriy Ustinov). The vehicle was urgently transported to Moscow on a sling by a Mi-10 helicopter. This was

The SM-3 moves across a snow-covered field. Like most of the vehicles in the SM series, it looked pretty hair-raising! This view illustrates well the extremely wide chord of the wings.

Here the SM-3 is seen in wing-borne flight, travelling higher above the ground.

A still from a cine film showing the SM-3 during trials.

done at short notice, and the test team had no time to fit the rear engine – the vehicle had to be sent for demonstration with the front engine only. Being underpowered, it could not show to advantage all its capabilities, yet the general impression was favourable. Later, with both engines in place, the vehicle displayed good performance and could even fly above sand-bars.

SM-3

This single-seat experimental machine built in 1962 was used for studying the aerodynamic layout with low aspect ratio wings. The wings of this WIG vehicle had a chord twice as big as on the previous machines, the aspect ratio being a mere 0.48. The vehicle had a T-tail. An unorthodox device for blowing under the wing was used: the air bled from the compressor of the RU19-300 engine placed in the front fuselage was ejected through nozzles located along the wing leading edge on its lower surface. Thereby an efflux curtain was created along the entire leading edge. The tests revealed that the use of the wing with a very low aspect ration had resulted in an oscillatory lateral instability during flights at a height of more than 1.5 m (16 ft) above the supporting surface.

Specifications of the SM-3	
Wing span	8.9 m (29 ft 2½ in)
Length	14.5 m (47 ft 7 in)
Height	1.3 m (4 ft 3¼ in)
All-up weight, kg (lb)	3,400 (7,500)
Cruising speed, km/h (mph)	140 (87)
Maximum speed, km/h (mph)	180 (112)
Powerplant	1 x RU19-300
Engine thrust , kgp (lbst)	900 (1,984)

SM-4

This three-seat machine built in 1963 as a derivative of the SM-3, was conceived by Alekseyev as quarter-scale prototype of a fully fledged WIG craft. It differed in having two engines – a booster engine and a cruise engine. The 2,180-kgp (4,800-lbst) Tumanskiy KR7-300 booster turbojet located in the forward

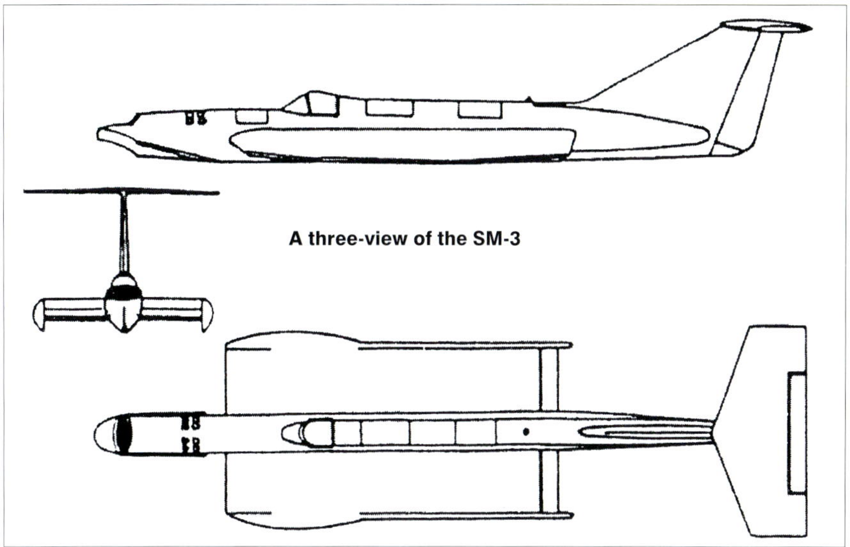

A three-view of the SM-3

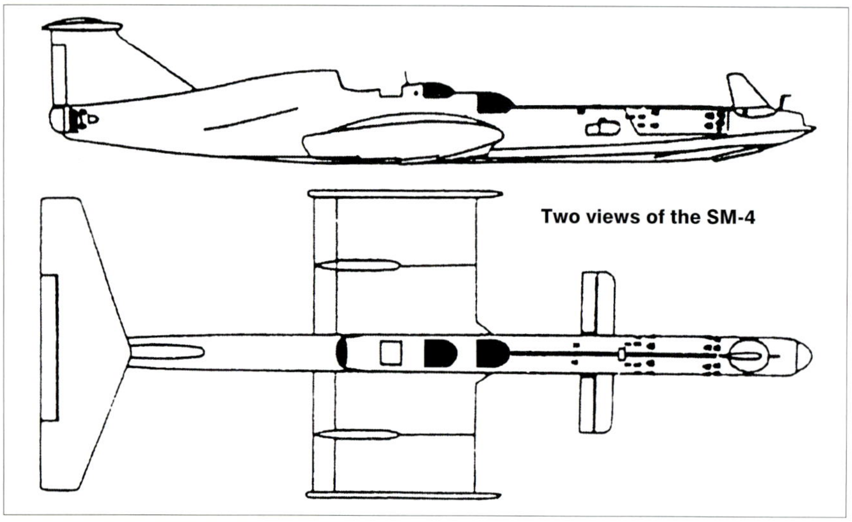

Two views of the SM-4

Specifications of the SM-4	
Wing span	7.6 m (24 ft 11¼ in)
Length	20.0 m (65 ft 7½ in)
Height	1.96 m (6 ft 5 in)
All-up weight, kg (lb)	4,800 (19,580)
Cruising speed, km/h (mph)	140 (87)
Maximum speed, km/h (mph)	230 (143)
Engines, type and thrust, kgp (lbst)	1 x KR-7-300, 2,000 (4,410) 1 x RU19-300, 900 (1,984)

The SM-4 in flight over the shallows. Note the front engine nozzles flanking the fuselage sides.

Two views of the SM-4 coming out onto a gently sloping river bank.

fuselage was fitted with steerable nozzles for directing the jet efflux under the wings. The flattened nozzles stood proud of the fuselage sides. The RU19-300 cruise turbojet was located in the aft fuselage; placed in its efflux was a gas rudder for directional control at low speeds. The tail unit featured a fin of reduced area with a small rudder. An additional all-movable vertical control surface was mounted on the extreme nose, looking like a rhino horn.

The wings fitted with endplates were attached to the boat hull-type fuselage in its centre portion; they were rectangular in planform and had an aspect ratio of 2. The wing flaps were divided into two sections and were spring-loaded to reduce the loads during contact with the water. Two pilots sat in two separate enclosed cockpits staggered vertically; a third open cockpit at the rear was intended for a test engineer. The two front cockpits were each equipped with a full set of controls, which permitted the vehicle to be used for pilot training (the instructor sat in the upper cockpit). The SM-4 was written off in the summer of 1966.

SM-5

Built in 1963, this machine was a quarter-scale analogue of the giant KM WIG vehicle, then under development. The SM-5 had wings of rectangular planform with endplates and spring-loaded flaps divided into several sections. The boat-type fuselage had planing steps on its lower surface and was hydrodynamically shaped to ensure good seaworthiness. The enclosed cockpit was located in the forward fuselage; placed behind it was a booster engine with pivoting nozzles on both sides of the hull which directed the jet efflux under the wings.

The cruise engine was placed ahead of the fin, its air intake occupying a position above the wing centre section. The intake was protected from water spray ingestion by a special U-shaped guard. The engine's bifurcated nozzle flanked the sharply swept fin. The craft had a T-tail with a full-length rudder whose lower portion was located below the waterline, serving as a water rudder.

The SM-5 was used, among other things, for the development of an autopilot system specially tai-

Specifications of the SM-5	
Wing span	19.4 m (63ft 7¾ in)
Length, m	18.0 m (59 ft 0¾ in)
Height	1.52 m (5 ft 0 in)
All-up weight, kg (lb)	7,300 (16,100)
Cruising speed, km/h (mph)	140 (87)
Maximum speed, km/h (mph)	230 (143)
Powerplant	One boost engine and one cruise engine (turbojets)

The SM-5 in cruise flight, showing the booster engine nozzles, main engine spray guard and bifurcated nozzle.

A three-view of the SM-5, with an added side view (top) of the original configuration without the cruise engine spray guard.

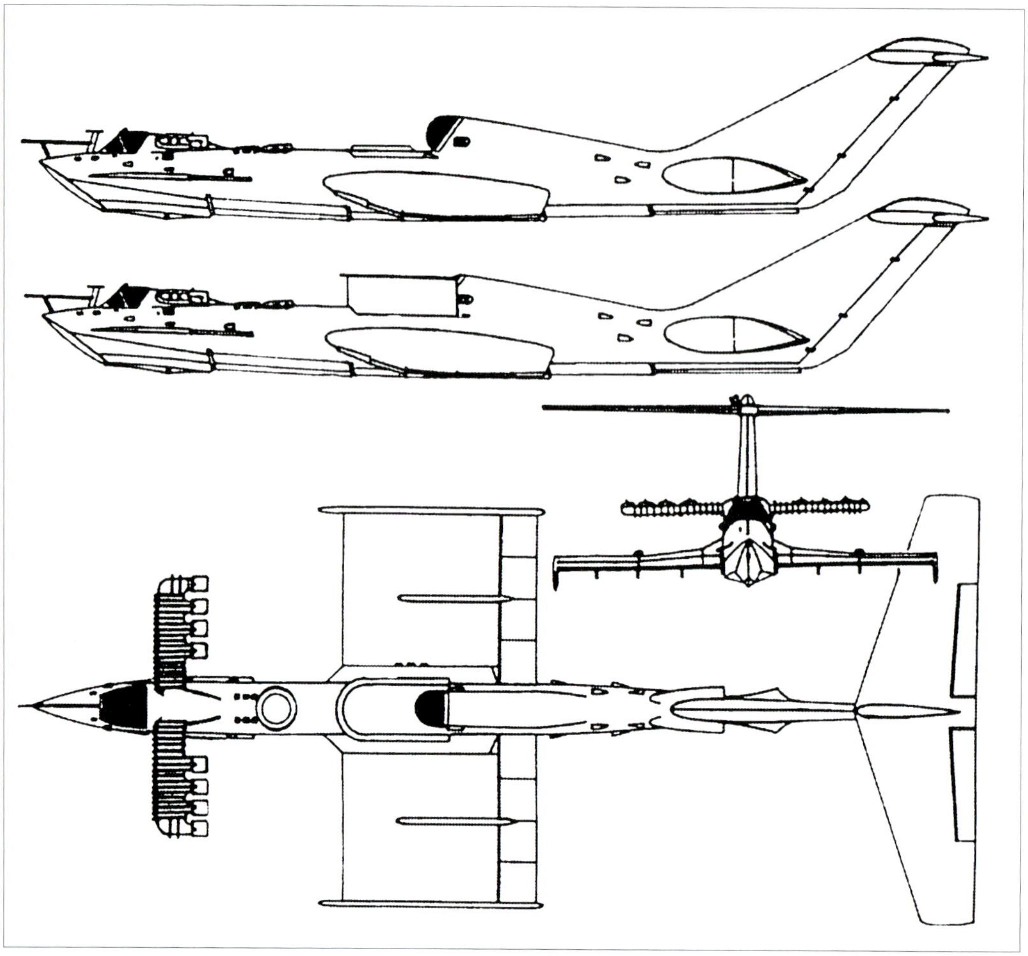

CHDB designers and test engineers gather round the SM-6 on the shore of the Gor'kiy Reservoir.

lored to the needs of WIG vehicles. Flights with this system installed were performed under the direction of Vladislav Diomidov, an autopilot specialist from the Elektropribor Central Research Institute in Leningrad. On several occasions Rostislav Alekseyev personally took part in these flights which were considered risky at that time. The flights with the autopilot system in action were performed at the Gor'kiy water reservoir (the IS-2 test facility), starting in the late spring of 1964. The vehicle performed 43 tacks of 6 to 8 minutes' duration at a speed of 120-140 km/h (74.5-87 mph) and a height of 0.2-0.5 m (0 ft 7$\frac{7}{8}$ in to 1 ft 6$\frac{21}{32}$ in). The tests corroborated the possibility of effective damping and stabilisation of the flight of a winged vehicle at extremely low altitudes.

On 24th August 1964 the SM-5 crashed during a test flight on a windy day. Immediately after lift-off, when the stabilisation system had not yet been switched on, the vehicle was caught in a powerful head-on gust of wind and began oscillating violently in pitch, bank and height. It banked abruptly and pitched up. Instead of throttling back the engines, the pilots gave them full throttle for climb, but the machine, leaving the ground effect zone, lost stability, banked and entered a dive, impacting the water surface. The crew was killed. This was the first fatal crash of a WIG vehicle in the SM family.

After this crash the work on the KM was suspended and the programme ran the risk of being cancelled completely, but eventually the supervising authorities permitted the resumption of work and limited their sanctions to reprimanding the Chief Designer. He was tasked with establishing a fully fledged flight test service staffed with highly skilled pilots. Appropriate measures were promptly taken by Alekseyev.

SM-6

Despite its sequence number, this experimental machine was completed after the SM-2P7 and SM-8 machines, making its appearance in 1970. But its origins date back to April 1964 when the basic layout of this machine was finalised by its chief designer. The vehicle was envisaged as a two-seat analogue of the projected T-1 troop transport *ekranoplan*; it featured similar low-set wings and separate booster and cruise engines, with the splayed installation of two booster engines in the forward fuselage. Construction of the two-seat machine began in October 1966, but the demise of the T-1 project led to delays. Not before September 1969 did the Navy resume the funding of the SM-6's construction. The SM-6 was completed at the Volga shipyard by 30th December 1970. A static test airframe was also built; it received the designation SM-6A.

The SM-6 in cruise mode, seen from a chase aircraft.

The SM-6 was intended for studying aero- and hydrodynamics and structural strength issues, as well as for evolving technical features for the Orlyonok heavy troop-carrier/assault WIG vehicle which was later evolved from the SM-6. The experimental craft could also be used for training purposes. Its powerplant comprised three engines: an Ivchenko AI-20K turboprop engine driving an AV-68 four-bladed propeller for cruise, mounted atop the fin, and two Mikulin RD-9B booster/cruise turbojet engines in the nose. Their location anticipated precisely the powerplant layout of the future Orlyonok. Like its bigger stablemate, the SM-6 featured a normal aerodynamic layout of a boat-hulled low-wing aircraft with a T-tail. As distinct from other machines in the SM series, it had more harmonious aircraft-like contours. The airframe was made of steel and AMG-61 aluminium/magnesium alloy and was protected from corrosion by a special coating and by electrochemical devices. The fuselage was of beam-and-stringer construction. The hull bottom in

Specifications of the SM-6

Wing span	14.8 m (48 ft 6$\frac{3}{4}$ in)
Length	31.0 m (101 ft 8$\frac{1}{2}$ in)
Height	7.85 m (25 ft 9 in)
Wing area, m^2 (sq ft)	73.8 (794.5)
All-up weight, kg (lb)	26,500 (58,432)
Booster engines, type and thrust, kgp (lbst)	2 x RD-9B, 2,100 (4,630)
Cruise engine, type and power output, hp	AI-20K, 3,750
Cruising speed, km/h (mph)	350 (218)
Range, km (miles)	700 (642)

The logo of the Volga Shipyard

Above: The SM-6 was, in effect, a subscale prototype for the future Orlyonok. It is probably seen just before touchdown; the hydroskis (equipped with wheels for taxying on the ground) are visible under the forward fuselage and wing centre section.

Below: Despite the fact that the SM-6 sports a different side number (6M79) in this view, it is still the same craft; the number was changed to 6M80 to confuse would-be spies. The last two digits do NOT denote the year, the sole SM-6 having been first flown in 1972!

Above: The SM-6 in cruise flight. Note how the pressure of the dynamic air cushion 'irons out' the waves while the vortices from the wingtips generate characteristic trails on the water.

Below: The SM-6 in relatively high-altitude flight for a WIG vehicle of this class; the tell-tale wake on the water is almost gone. Note that the booster engines are equipped with six-lobe nozzles – probably serving the same purpose as the 'hushkits' on the BAC One-Eleven.

The SM-6 comes ashore under its own power, waves washing over the top of the wings. An ATs-40(375)-Ts-1 fire engine stands by, just in case.

its final configuration was shaped by steps and by two hydro-skis to which the main and nose undercarriage units were attached.

In July 1971 the SM-6 was transferred to the IS-2 test facility at Chkalovsk where the engines were ignited for the first time in August, followed by test runs on water and then flight tests. An important event was a show arranged some time later at the Chkalovsk test facility for Air Marshal Ivan I. Borzov, Commander of the Naval Aviation. Test pilots

Here the SM-6 is seen entering the water from the sandy shore of the Gor'kiy Reservoir. Note the elevator mass balances.

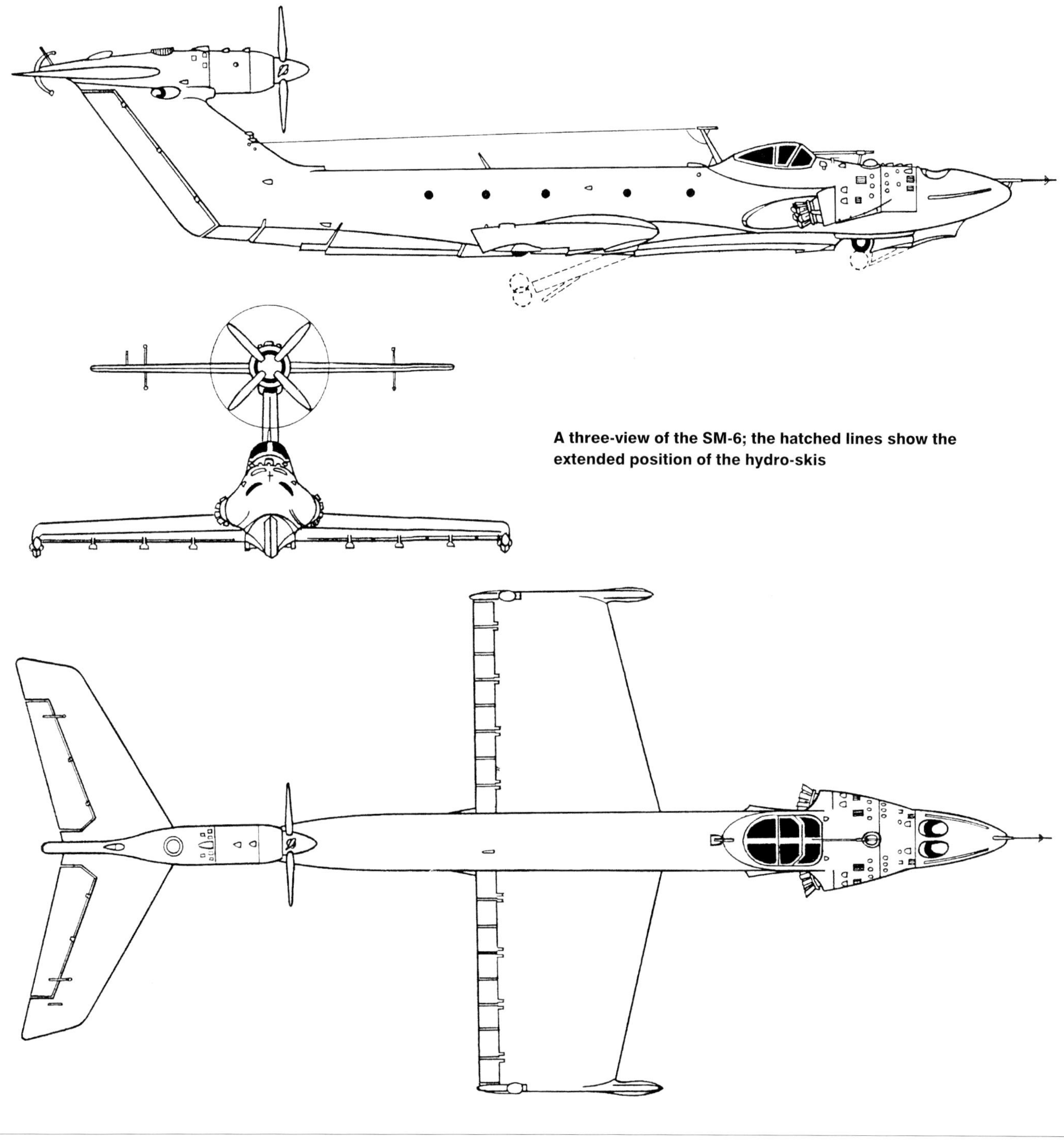

A three-view of the SM-6; the hatched lines show the extended position of the hydro-skis

demonstrated the SM-6 in the aquaplaning and ground effect flight mode, followed by a flight of the UT-1 (described later in this chapter) in an out-of-ground-effect mode. Borzov was duly impressed; he assessed what he had seen as 'flight at extremely low altitudes' and noted that such flights should be performed by experienced pilots.

In February-March 1972 the SM-6 was tested in flights above ice- and snow-covered stretches with the hydroski fitted. Somewhat later the SM-6 was modified – a tail skid was fitted; the vehicle was provided with the main and nose hydroskis featuring main and auxiliary shock-absorbing cylinders. A similar device was later used on the Orlyonok troop-carrier *ekranoplan*. The next stage was the fitting of a wheeled undercarriage, whereupon the SM-6 passed tests for seaworthiness and amphibious properties.

The vehicle was used for various tests, including the use of braking parachutes (in 1974). In late 1974 the SM-6 was transferred to the test base at Kaspiysk on the Caspian Sea.

Of all the vehicles in the SM series the SM-6 had the most aesthetically pleasing, aircraft-like forms. This view shows well the powerplant arrangement with the dorsal 'nostrils' of the RD-9B booster engine air intakes, with spray dams below them, and the dorsal exhaust of the AI-20K cruise engine. Note how the turbojets are angled outwards.

From early 1976 the SM-6 was modified again to bring its hydroskis to the standard used on the Orlyonok (which had been built in the meantime). The subsequent flight testing of the SM-6 at Kaspiysk confirmed the soundness of the *ekranoplan*'s aerohydrodynamic layout and the efficiency of the hydroskis. Test flights of the SM-6 went on until the end of the 1980s. Almost every year the vehicle underwent some sort of modification. In addition to basic research, the flights were used to solve questions arising in the course of operation of the Orlyonok *ekranoplans*.

SM-2P7

This single-seat vehicle was built in 1964 for studying take-off and landing performance, problems of stability of flight over a supporting surface and the possibilities of optimising the aerodynamic layout of a single-engined WIG vehicle. The SM-2P7 was a development (a conversion) of the earlier SM-2P in which the nose-mounted RU19-300 engine was replaced by a Tumanskiy KR7-300 turbojet. This short-life engine rated at 2,180 kgp (4,800 lbst) was intended primarily for supersonic UAVs. For the SM-2P7 it was derated to a maximum thrust of 2,000 kgp (4,410 lbst), serving both as a booster and a cruise engine. The exhaust gases passed through a row of nozzles placed parallel to the wing leading edge within approximately half of the span. Nozzle deflectors were used for directing the jet efflux under the wings in the blowing mode during take-off. The enclosed cockpit was placed amidships.

The rectangular wings of the SM-2P7 had an aspect ratio of more than 2.4; they were fitted with spring-loaded multi-section flaps and endplates. The vehicle became airborne at a speed of 150 km/h (93 mph) after a take-off run of 600-800 m (1,970-2,625 ft) which took 35-40 seconds.

The SM-2P7 pictured during the take-off run. Note the nose air intake and the outriggers carrying the engine nozzles.

Specifications of the SM-2P7	
Wing span	9.5 m (31 ft 8⅜ in)
Length	19.4 m (63 ft 7¾ in)
Height	1.54 m (5 ft 0½ in)
All-up weight, kg (lb)	6,300 (13,890)
Lift-off speed , km/h (mph)	150 (93)
Cruising speed, km/h (mph)	130 (81)
Maximum speed, km/h (mph)	270 (168)
Landing speed, km/h (mph)	140 (67)
Powerplant	1 x KR7-300
Engine thrust , kgp (lbst)	2,000 (4,410)

SM-8

The SM-8 WIG vehicle built in 1967 became the second quarter-scale analogue of the KM *ekranoplan*; it reflected the changes introduced into the layout of the KM in the course of its design. The SM-8 became the last in the family of SM experimental flying vehicles whose testing furnished results essential for the creation of *ekranoplan* theory and for evolving the methods of designing and developing new models of heavy WIG vehicles for military and civil applications. The testing of the SM-8 proceeded in parallel with the testing of the KM; the analogue served for checking the methods of testing its bigger stablemate.

Here the SM-2P7 is seen on the point of transitioning to wing-borne flight.

Above and below: The SM-8 was a subscale analogue of the KM vehicle. Except for the dorsal excrescences, from a distance it looked extremely similar to its 'big brother'. The 'smokestack' above the wing leading edge is the protected intake of the forward engine. The full-length rudder acted as a water rudder when afloat.

The SM-8 was propelled by a turbojet located in the upper part of the fuselage ahead of the fin. Its air intake was protected from spray by a U-shaped guard and the nozzle was bifurcated, as on the SM-5. To emulate the blowing (booster) engines of the KM, the SM-8 was provided with a special nozzle device in the front fuselage intended to direct part of the gases bled from the engine under the wings. According to some reports, the vehicle was powered by *two* KR7-300 engines, one of them serving as the cruise engine and the other as a booster engine located in the nose. This would explain the purpose of the funnel-shaped structure above the fuselage which must have been the air intake of the booster engine located immediately aft of the cockpit.

Both the SM-8 and the KM were test flown by V. F. Loginov, commander of the flight test detach-

ment of the CHDB, and by leading test pilots D. T. Garbuzov, V. T. Troshin, M. A. Semyonov and V. S. Kudrin, In 1968 the SM-8 was tested in still water conditions and in different sea states with the primary purpose of assessing the craft's seaworthiness, controllability and manoeuvrability, take-off and alighting performance and the machines behaviour during flight at different angles to the waves' movement. Particular attention was paid to mastering the techniques of handling the craft above the water for the purpose of evolving recommendations for piloting the KM *ekranoplan*.

Further seaworthiness tests of the SM-8 were conducted in May-June 1969. Its amphibious qualities were checked on 10th June 1969 when the machine made passes above an unprepared grass-covered bank, stretches of marshland, sand-bars and the like. The SM-8 served as a testbed for a

Above and below: The SM-8 in cruise flight. These photos show the massive intake spray guard and bifurcated nozzle of the main engine, the 'garden rake' immediately aft of the cockpit with nozzles emulating the KM's booster engines, the flap actuator fairings and the strong dihedral of the tailplane.

Another view of the SM-8 over the Caspian Sea.

Like the SM-5, the SM-8 had a strut-mounted pitot ahead of the windscreen. The wing and tailplane trailing-edge portions were striped.

damping and stabilisation system known as *izdeliye* (article) 127, developed by the Leningrad-based Elektropribor research institute. In 1969 it was fitted with special devices for spreading evenly in the horizontal plane the efflux from the nozzles of the nose-mounted engine.

In addition to research flights, the SM-8 was used for pilot training.

The construction and testing of the SM series (SM-1 through SM-8) were directly connected with the creation of designs that marked the apex of achievements of the Central Hydrofoil Design Bureau – the vehicles known as KM, Loon' and Orlyonok. Therefore it is logical to give the description of these designs here. Description of later machines in the SM series will be given separately.

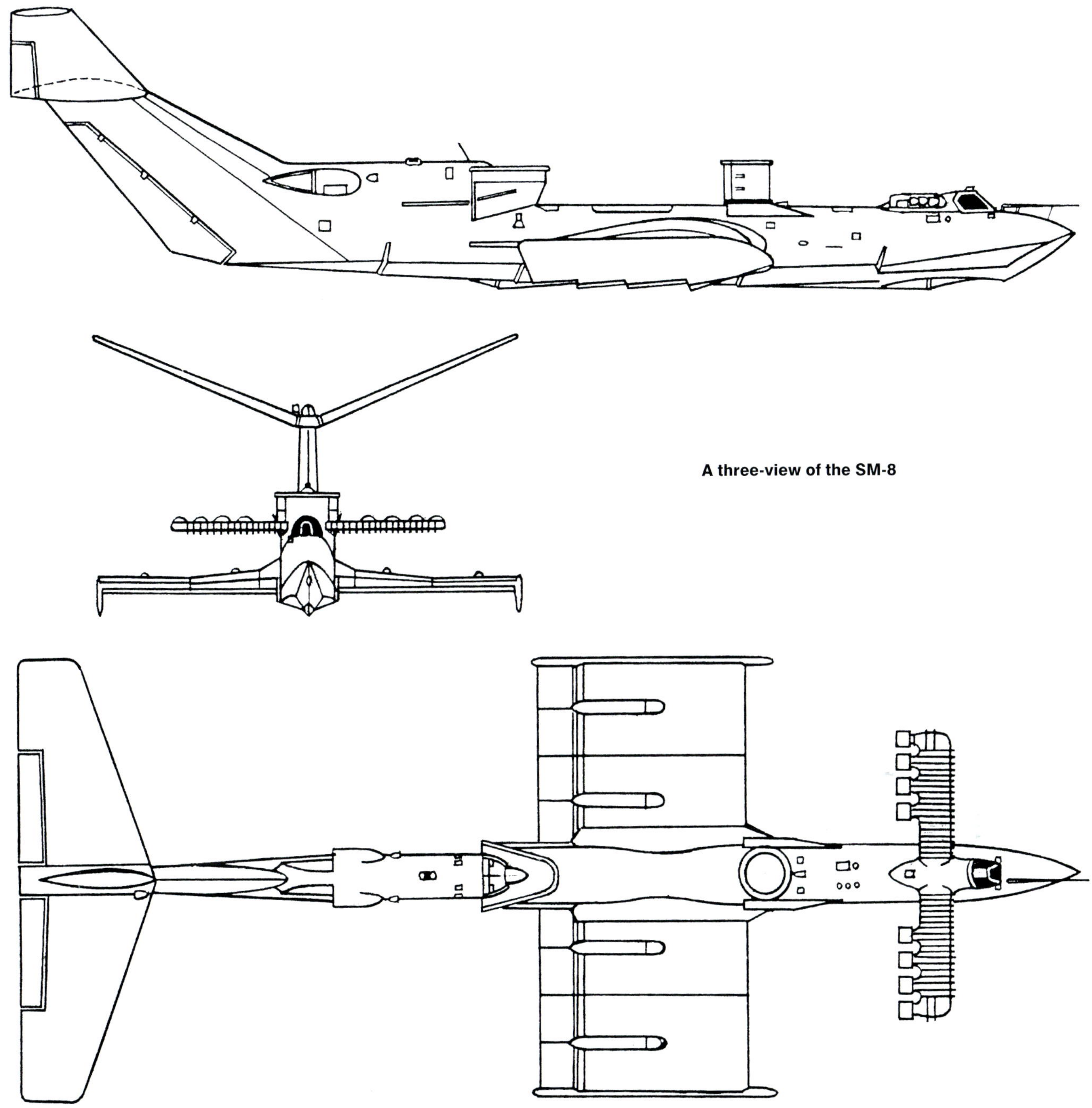

A three-view of the SM-8

Specifications of the SM-8	
Wing span	19.4 m (63 ft 7¾ in)
Length	18.5m (60 ft 8½ in)
Height	1.52 m (5 ft 0 in)
All-up weight, kg (lb)	8,100 (17,860)
Cruising speed, km/h (mph)	220 (137)
Practical range, km (miles)	120 (75)
Flight altitude in WIG mode, m (ft)	1.2 (4)
Seaworthiness	Sea state 3

KM

In 1963, in response to an order placed by the Navy, construction was started at the 'Volga' shipyard near Gor'kiy (now Nizhny Novgorod) of a gigantic WIG vehicle which was designated KM (*ko**rah**bl'-ma**ket*** – 'dummy ship', or rather prototype ship). It was a machine of staggering dimensions, the length of the hull being 97.4 m (319 ft 6¾ in with a wing span of 37.6 m (123 ft 4⅜ in) and a height of 22.0 m (72 ft 2⅛ in). It was launched at the Volga Shipyard on 22nd June 1966 and transferred

The fuselage (hull) of the KM in the assembly jig at the Volga Shipyard in Gor'kiy.

Above: The flight deck section of the KM, with the glazing framework yet to be fitted.

for testing to Kaspiysk (a naval base on the Caspian Sea). The transfer operation was performed under the conditions of utmost secrecy, the vehicle being towed along the Volga River strictly at night.

Upon arrival at Kaspiysk, preparations started for the first flight, the KM being placed in a floating dock. A curious episode happened shortly afterwards. Zealous officials supervising the programme came to Kaspiysk and adamantly demanded that tangible results of the work be presented at once. Unabashed, Alekseyev decreed that the machine be 'flight tested in the dock'. The KM was securely tethered and all its ten engines were started, reaching 40% of the rated thrust. The dock with the giant machine began to move, the strained anchor chains being on the point of breaking. Having impressed the officials, Alekseyev gave the order to shut down the engines.

Eventually, the KM was cleared for testing on water and in the air. On 18th October 1966 the KM performed its first sea-going trials with pilot Loginov as captain. In actual fact, Alekseyev himself was at the controls (despite an official ban for the Chief Designer to act as a test pilot). After reaching a speed of 200 km/h (124 mph) on the water, the KM continued the run in the aquaplaning mode, accompanied by a Yak-12 chase aircraft. Alekseyev was tempted to make a hop, but Loginov found this premature. During the first runs one of the flap sections on the port wing had suffered damage, but this did not prevent the craft from being put to sea-going tests again on 19th October. This time, too, speeds of 200-250 km/h (124-155 mph) were attained in the aquaplaning mode.

Two views of the KM afloat on the Caspian Sea, with attending tug and tanker.

The KM in cruise mode, seen from a Yak-12 chase aircraft and from a ship.

The KM at rest a short way from the Caspian Sea shore. The camel in the foreground appears to be saying *humph*. You can take your pick, boy.

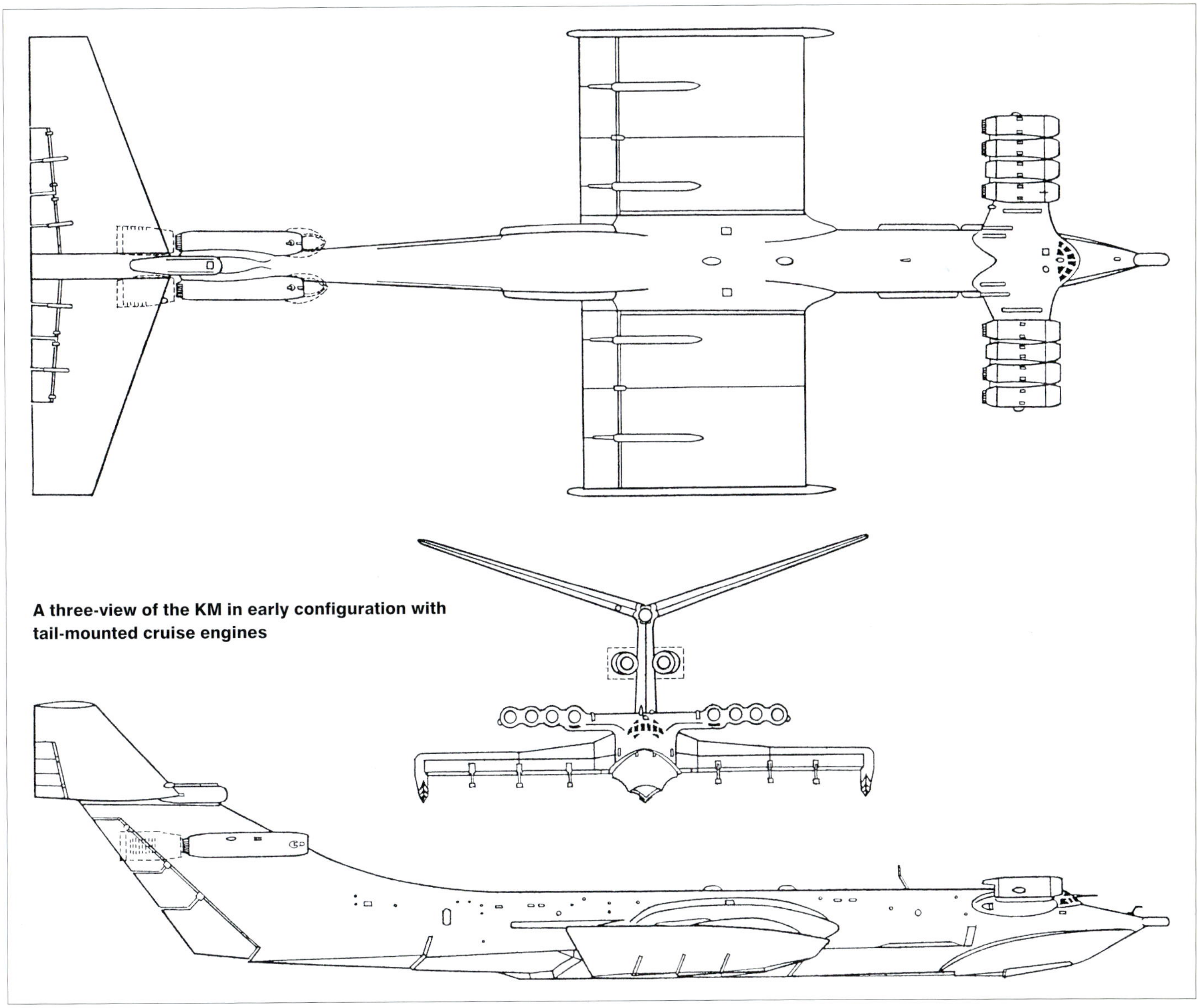

A three-view of the KM in early configuration with tail-mounted cruise engines

Originally the KM had tail-mounted cruise engines with air intake spray guards.

Head-on view of the KM afloat as the tech staff performs routine checks.

The first phase of the aquaplaning trials was completed on 25th October 1966, when the KM was towed back to the Kaspiysk base from the test area. Everything had gone well, except for one thing. The flights revealed insufficient stiffness of the hull which, at one point, began to snake. The problem was cured by reinforcing the hull with 10- and 20-mm (0$\frac{25}{64}$ in and 0$\frac{25}{32}$ in) metal sheets. One more problem to be tackled was the contamination of the Dobrynin VD-7 turbojets by ingested sea water which led to damage and reduced the life of the engines. It became apparent that turbojet and turboprop engines intended for ekranoplans had to be specially adapted for operation in a maritime environment.

The winter period of 1966-67 and the spring of 1967 were used for effecting various improvements to the airframe and equipment of the KM, while the crew practised piloting on the SM-2P7 experimental vehicle. Preparations for the resumption of sea-going and flight test of the KM started in the summer of 1967.

Some sources regard 18th October 1966 as the date of the first flight of the KM, but this is apparently a misunderstanding. In fact, the giant ekranoplan became airborne for the first time considerably later – on 14th August 1967. The first flight lasted 50 minutes, with Alekseyev himself at the controls. The huge vehicle flew at a height of

The KM had several identities, originally wearing the tail number '01 White'.

This view shows the anchor chain and the ladders allowing access to the eight booster engines.

04

04

04

A view of the KM from the height of its dihedral T-tail. The two-section flaps are visible. Note that the deflector vanes of the Nos. 1-4 engines are lowered into take-off position while those of the Nos. 5-8 engines are in raised (cruise) position.

Opposite page: Three views of the KM at a later point in its career with the new tail number '04 White'. Here the vehicle leaves a moderate amount of spray in its wake.

The KM had a forward-facing crew cockpit, the flight engineer sitting centrally behind the pilots. Note that some of the co-pilot's instruments are missing.

Each pilot had his own bank of ten throttle levers, the centre pair being longer. Here the flight engineer works the co-pilot's throttles.

The KM seen at a still later date, sporting the tail number '07 White'. The stripes on the hull were blue (upper) and red edged in white. Here the machine kicks up a lot more spray.

Two more views of the KM in late guise as '07 White'. The hinged flaps on the booster engine nozzles are in cruise position. Note the heat-resistant panels on the top section of the three-section rudder protecting the skin from the efflux of the cruise engines. The bottom section doubles as a water rudder.

some 4 m (13 ft) and a speed of 400-450 km/h (249-280 mph). In his report to the commission that witnessed the testing Alekseyev described the first flight as fully successful. All subsequent test runs of the KM in 1967 were performed in the WIG flight mode. The flights took place mainly over water, but on one occasion the pilots made a mistake and flew over a 2-km (1.2-mile) stretch of land (a small island) without any undue consequences, thus demonstrating the *ekranoplan*'s ability to fly above dry land.

In the course of testing the optimum flight altitude in ground effect proved to be 4 to 14 m (13 to 46 ft). At that time the KM was the largest flying vehicle in the world – its weight in one of the flights reached 544 tonnes (1,299,300 lb)! Nominally, the vehicle had a maximum displacement of 500 tonnes (1,102,500 lb) and could carry a useful load

of 150 tonnes (330,750 lb). Small wonder that it was nicknamed 'Caspian Sea Monster' in the West (later some Russian journalists, too, deciphered KM as *Kaspeeyskiy monstr*). This huge machine was powered by ten Dobrynin VD-7 turbojets; of these, two engines located at the fin leading edge served as cruise engines, while the remaining eight engines were mounted in two packages of four on the forward fuselage sides, performing the role of booster engines for power-augmented take-off. The eight nose-mounted VD-7 *sans suffixe* engines had a thrust of 9,500 kgp/20,950 lbst apiece and the two VD-7M cruise engines delivered a thrust of 10,500 kgp/23,150 lb st each). The machine reached a

Above right: The KM (coded '07 White') cruises at full speed, trailing almighty plumes of spray. The elevators terminate at about half-span of the horizontal tail.

Right: Close-up of the KM's forward fuselage as the craft cruises. The anchor can be seen stowed under the bows.

Below: WIGs of a feather flock together? The SM-6 and the KM off the Caspian Sea coast, with the latter craft's forward engine cowlings open for maintenance. The people swarming over both machines like ants illustrate the sheer bulk of the KM; note that the tail number has been changed AGAIN (to '08 White').

A harbour tug tows the KM in its ultimate configuration to the pier. The cruise engines have been relocated to a pylon above the flight deck, which also carries a saucer radome. Note that the booster engines, too, have been retrofitted with spray guards. Also, the machine appears to carry no tail number now.

maximum speed of 500 km/h (310 mph), the cruising speed being 430 km/h (267 mph).

In the course of its testing the KM underwent a number of modifications some of which were rather substantial. For example, in 1979 the cruise engines placed on the fin were transferred to a pylon mounted over the forward fuselage so as to lessen spray ingestion. The cruise engines (and later the booster engines as well) were provided with spray deflectors on the intakes.

In the course of testing Alekseyev conceived the idea of using braking parachutes for the purpose of reducing the landing (alighting) speed of the KM, but the work on the development of such a parachute specially for *ekranoplans* did not result in a practical solution.

The KM had good manoeuvrability, stability and handling; it could perform tight turns with large bank angles, the wingtip float touching the sea surface. This machine flew for 15 years and earned a reputation for being a very reliable transport means. Comprehensive tests and experiments conducted on the KM proved extremely valuable in evolving the scientific basis for the design, construction and testing of ekranoplans. Unfortunately, in December 1980 the KM crashed due to pilot error. The pilot, who had not been at the controls of the big machine for a long time, overdid the pitching up on take-off. The machine began to rise steeply. Losing his head, the pilot abruptly throttled back the engines and applied the elevator in a fashion contrary to flight manual instructions. The winged ship rolled to port, impacted the water surface and sank; the crew escaped unhurt.

There was only one flyable example of the KM. During different stages of its test programme and service it wore different two-digit tactical numbers. Available photos show the wingship carrying the numbers '01 White', '04 White', '07 White' and '08 White'. One can come across reports erroneously mentioning the existence of a second flight test example.

Some Russian and foreign publications use the designation KM-1, but its veracity is unconfirmed.

Orlyonok (Project 904)

This troop-carrier/assault WIG vehicle designed in response to an order from the Navy made its first flight from one of the channels of the Volga River in 1972. After this, disguised as a Tupolev Tu-134 airliner, the prototype was transported on a barge to Kaspiysk to be tested in sea conditions. It was the first WIG vehicle intended for speedy transportation of troops and materiel. Its cargo hold measuring

21 m (68 ft 11 in) in length, 3.2 m (10ft 6 in) in height and 3.0 m (9 ft 10 in) in width made it possible to transport self-propelled vehicles that were on the strength of the Soviet Marines.

The Orlyonok featured an aircraft layout. It was an all-metal cantilever monoplane with a fuselage provided with hydrodynamic elements in its lower portion (planing steps, hydroskis etc.); it had low-set wings and a T-tail with a horizontal tail of considerable dimensions. Its powerplant comprised two Kuznetsov NK-8-4K booster turbofans rated at 10,500 kgp (23,148 lbst) for take-off (provision was made for their eventual replacement with 13,000-kgp/28,660-lbst NK-87 turbofans) and one 15,000-ehp NK-12MK cruise turboprop (a version of the NK-12M used on the Tu-95 bomber) driving AV-90 eight-blade contra-rotating propellers. All the engines were maritime versions of the respective aircraft engines. The booster engines were fitted with special pivoting nozzles and used not only for creating an air cushion on take-off by directing their efflux under the wings (blowing mode) but also for acceleration to cruising speed. The dorsal air intakes of the turbofan engines were blended into the contours of the forward fuselage, which reduced drag and helped protect the engines from corrosive sea spray. The cruise engine was located at the junction of the fin and horizontal tail; being placed so high, it was less vulnerable to spray ingestion at take-off and landing and to salt contamination from aerosols whose density depends on the height over the sea surface.

The fuselage of the Orlyonok was of beam-and-stringer construction; it was divided into three sections – forward, centre and aft. The centre fuselage accommodated the cargo hold accessed by swing-

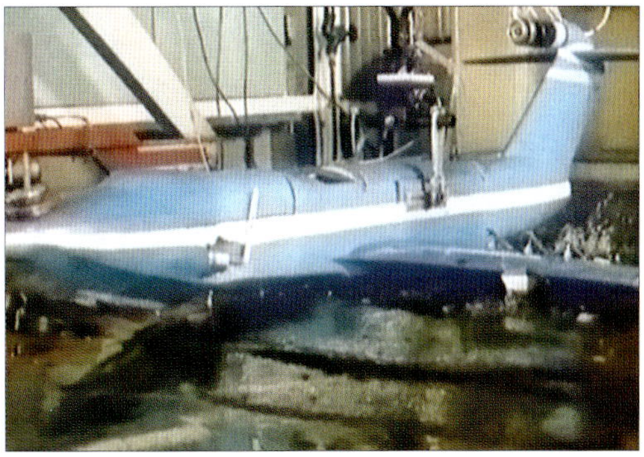

A model of the Orlyonok assault/transport WIG vehicle undergoes testing in the towing basin.

The Orlyonok puts to sea in a flurry of spray. Only the prototype wore this civil-style colour scheme. Note the elevator actuator fairings and the four-section elevators.

Above: A full frontal of the Orlyonok prototype on its hardstand at Kaspiysk. From this angle the vehicle has a squat and rather ungainly look. The photo shows well the eight-bladed AV-90 contraprop of the cruise engine and the wing leading edge camber.

This is how the Orlyonok's forward fuselage swung open through 92° for loading and unloading. Note the snap-action vehicle loading ramps, the twin-gun dorsal turret immediately forward of the fuselage break point, the collision avoidance radar in a thimble radome and the pylon-mounted 'saucer' of the navigation radar.

Above: A Soviet BTR-60PB eight-wheel armoured personnel carrier is about to roll off the Orlyonok. This view shows the design of the double-hinged loading ramps, the overhead actuating cylinder of the forward fuselage, the bulkhead with a flight deck access doorway and the numerous securing clamps around the hatch perimeter. The latter is understandable, considering the high stresses in the area.

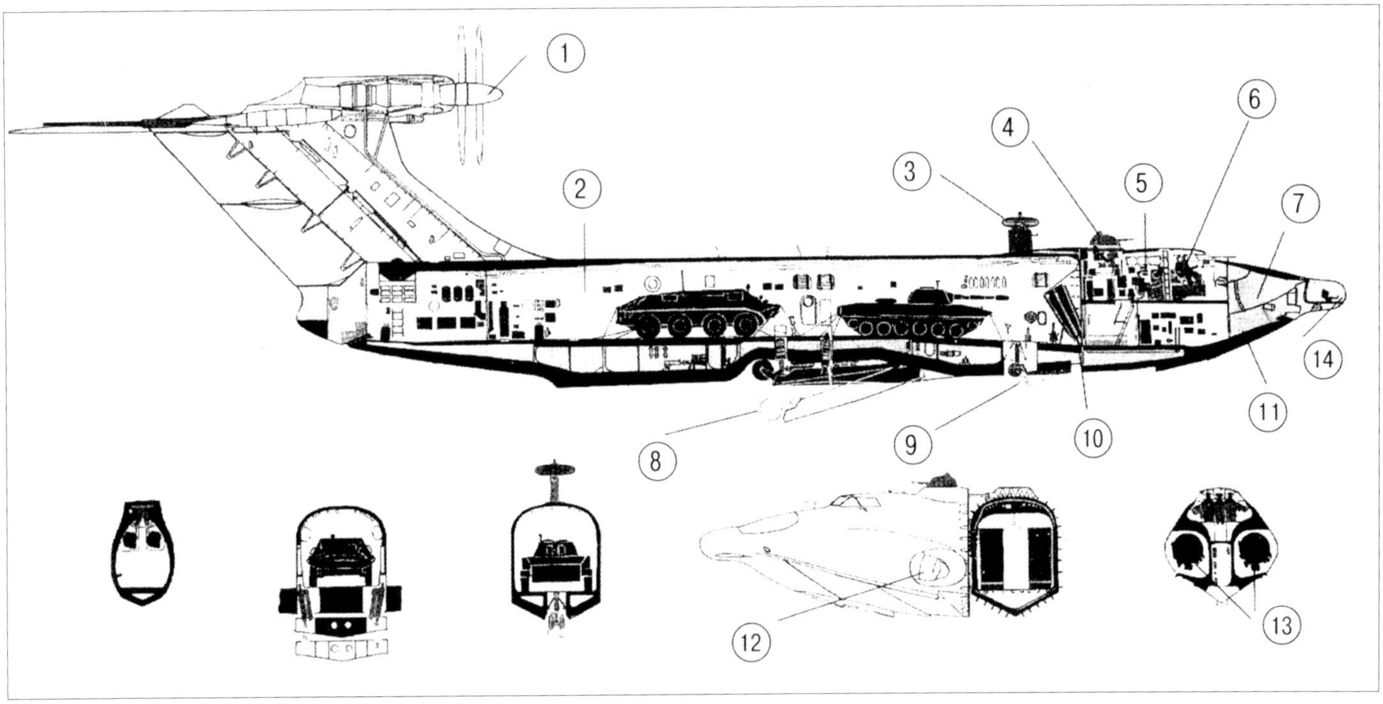

A cutaway drawing of the Orlyonok, with a PT-76 amphibious tank and a turret-less BTR-60P in the cabin.
1. NK-12MK cruise engine. 2. Cargo cabin. 3. Ekran 360° navigation radar. 4. Powered turret with twin 12.7-mm NSV machine-guns. 5. Navigator's workstation. 6. Captain's, co-pilot's and flight engineer's seats. 7. Booster engine inlet ducts. 8. Rear hydroski with shock absorbers and four-wheel main gear unit. 9. Forward hydroski with twin-wheel nose gear unit. 10. Vehicle loading ramps. 11. Forward fuselage section hinged to starboard. 12. Movable booster engine nozzle. 13. NK-8-4K booster engine. 14. Collision avoidance radar.

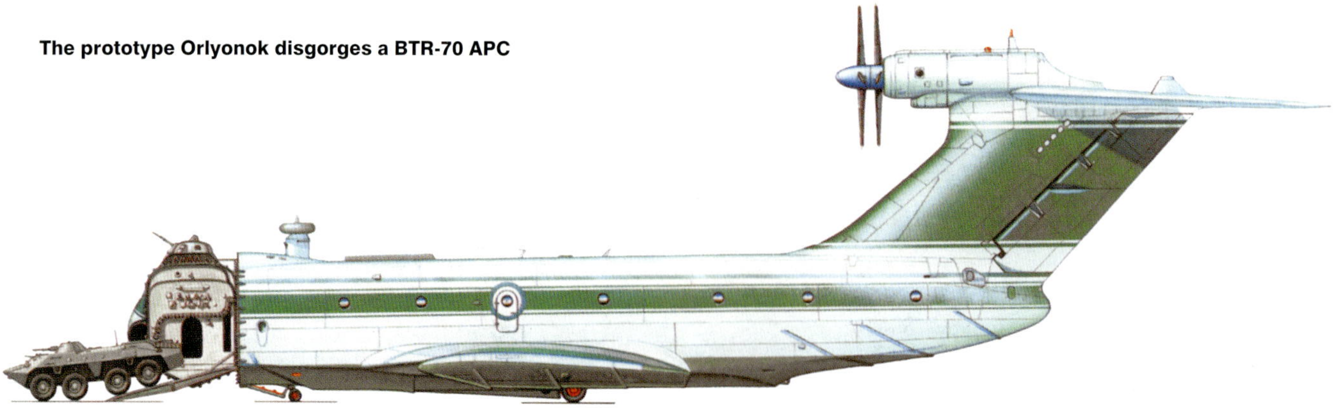

The prototype Orlyonok disgorges a BTR-70 APC

ing the hinged forward fuselage 92° to starboard. The hinged part of the fuselage housed the flight deck, the booster engines and a radar in a thimble radome. The aft fuselage housed a compartment for auxiliary power units and accessories required for starting the main engines and operating the vehicle's electrical and hydraulic systems. Placed dorsally on the hull were a turret with twin 12.7-mm (.50 calibre) Nikitin/Sokolov/Volkov NSV-12.7 Utyos heavy machine-guns, the antenna of a 360° navigation radar, direction finder aerials, communication and navigation equipment aerials. To reduce the

Stills from a cine film showing a BTR-60PB (with the turret and KPVT machine-gun under canvas covers) being unloaded from the Orlyonok prototype.

The Orlyonok's cabin was only just wide enough for the BTR-60 – there were only a few inches to spare.

A production Orlyonok coded '26 White' (the S-26) in Russian Navy markings

The captain of an Orlyonok in the left-hand seat. Interestingly, here he is wearing a simple headset but no helmet.

As this view shows, the captain's instrument panel of the Orlyonok was rather sparsely 'populated' but featured some sort of rectangular display.

Left row: Three interesting aspects of a production Orlyonok, showing the protective grilles on the air intakes (meant to prevent bird ingestion) and open engine cowlings.

The co-pilot of an Orlyonok – in this case wearing a ZSh-7 'bone dome' helmet.

shock loads in the take-off and landing mode the designers introduced hydroskis shaped as simple deflectable panels. The main hydroski was placed under the centre fuselage. A smaller hydroski was installed in the forward part of the hull. The craft was equipped with a wheeled undercarriage intended for beaching the machine and moving along paved taxiways on the shore. The wheel undercarriage comprised a steerable twin-wheel nose unit and a ten-wheel main unit which is combined with the main hydroski.

The navigator of the Orlyonok at his workstation. Note the flight deck escape hatch.

Above: The Orlyonok prototype before touchdown with the rear hydroski fully deployed. Interestingly, the entry doors amidships are not yet marked externally.

Below: The prototype caught by the camera in a banking turn. Note that the Soviet Navy flag has been added on the tail, revealing the craft's true owner.

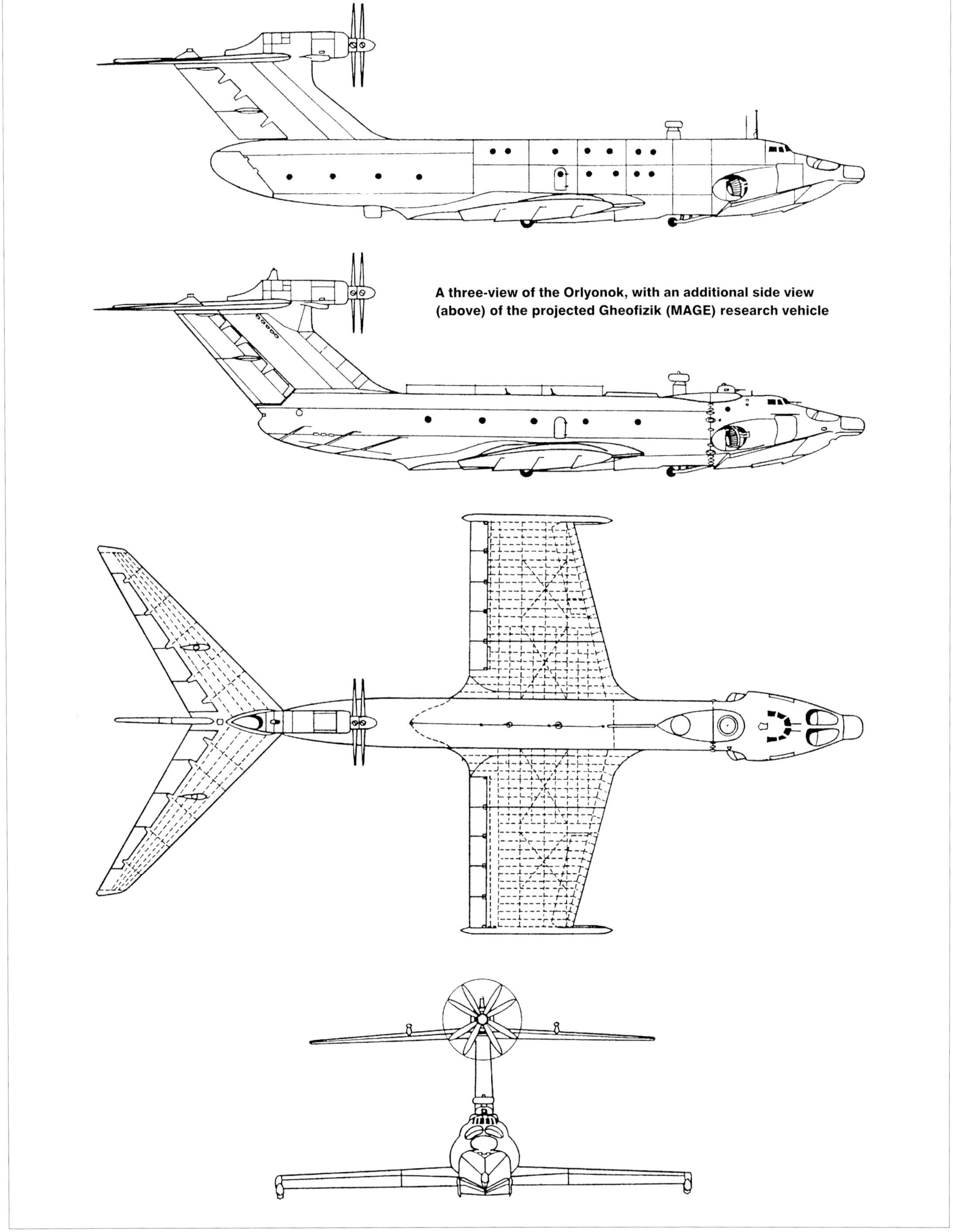

A three-view of the Orlyonok, with an additional side view (above) of the projected Gheofizik (MAGE) research vehicle

Seen from an An-26 transport, the Orlyonok prototype makes a gentle turn to port, trailing plumes of spray. The keel and wing endplates leave a characteristic triple wake. The booster engine intakes are well visible, as is the large span of the horizontal tail.

Opposite page:

The booster engines of the Orlyonok create a tremendous amount of spray as the vehicle enters the water.

Another air-to-air study of the Orlyonok. Note the APU exhaust at the base of the rudder to starboard, the HF aerial spike pointing aft from the fin top and the phoney circular markings around the entry doors (which in reality are rectangular).

The Orlyonok prototype comes out onto a sandy beach.

One more fine study of the Orlyonok prototype in its element.

The Orlyonok taxies on the water at low speed, the waves washing across the top of the wings.

Above: The Orlyonok prototype sweeps past the Soviet Navy/Caspian Flotilla rescue vessel GKS-13 standing at anchor. The hull number reveals this was formerly a Type 513 hydroacoustic monitoring vessel (GKS = ghidroakusticheskoye kontrol'noye soodno).

The low-set wings of trapezoidal planform, comprising an integral centre section and outer wing panels of torsion box construction, were fitted with flaperons. The wing undersurface incorporated special leading-edge flaps close to the tips, deflected 70° during take-off. The wingtips carried floats doubling as endplates. The floats, as well as the hull, featured planing steps to help attain the aquaplaning mode during take-off. The wing high-lift devices were used for creating an air cushion which lifted the vehicle out of the water. During take-off the efflux of the jet engines was directed under the wings; the pilot lowered the flaperons and leading-edge flaps, thus barring the way for the gases tending to escape fore and aft. The increased pressure under the wings lifted the machine out of the water. The main part of the wings, with the exception of the leading-edge flaps and flaperons, was watertight. The wings were divided into 14 watertight bays, two of which were used for fuel.

The sharply swept T-tail comprised a fin with a two-section rudder and large-span stabilisers with four-section elevators. The fin had a leading-edge sweepback of 40° and was built integrally with the hull. The horizontal tail had a leading-edge sweep of 45°.

The Orlyonok was equipped with the *Ekran* (Screen) navigation suite which included a surveillance radar mounted in a saucer-shaped fairing on a pylon above the fuselage. A thimble radome in the nose housed the Ekran-4 high-definition navigation radar intended to ensure collision avoidance.

To relieve the crew workload in flight, provision was made for automatic stabilisation of the altitude (by deflecting the flaps), the pitch angle (by deflecting the elevators), the heading (by deflecting the rudder) and the bank angle (by deflecting the flaperons). The machine could also be flown in manual control mode.

The introduction of autopilots on the Orlyonok WIG craft merits a few details. Analysis proved that on ground effect vehicles, proper movement was unstable in some flight modes, which necessitated the use of an autopilot. When Rostislav Alekseyev sought the assistance of aviation engineers dealing with aircraft autopilot systems he was flatly rebuffed with the following succinct answer: *'Aviation rules forbid engaging an autopilot during flights at altitudes below 500 m [1,640 ft]; consequently, the development of autopilots for WIG craft flying at low altitudes is pointless'*. Alekseyev had no choice but to look for autopilot specialists within the shipbuilding industry and thus established contacts with the Elektropribor (= electric device) Central Research Institute in Leningrad, now St. Petersburg. The work of this institute resulted in the development of the

Opposite page: Two colour shots of the Orlyonok prototype with the doors marked but the Navy flag not yet applied. The basic colour of the wings is light grey.

Here the craft commences a port turn, with rudder deflection and left bank clearly visible.

One more view of the first Orlyonok in cruise flight. The transverse strakes in the nose air intakes are airflow guides.

Smena-3 (Crew shift) and Smena-4 autopilot systems which were flight tested on the Orlyonok and Loon' ekranoplans at the Caspian Sea between 1978 and 1989. These systems duly took into account the specific aspects of the ground effect flight mode, as distinct from high altitude flight. They ensured top quality damping, stabilisation and manoeuvring in both horizontal and vertical planes. In particular, vigorous and safe banked, slip-angled, altitude-hop and thrust-variation turns were ensured. The tests proved that the problem of the autopilot failure safety had been resolved correctly. The quality and reliability of the automatic control system and the failure safety of the equipment were rated very highly by state acceptance commissions, flying crews and personally by Rostislav Alekseyev.

Coming back to the Orlyonok's description, it may be noted that the craft is provided with devices normally fitted to ships. These include the sea navigation lights, anchoring and towing equipment.

Here are some basic characteristics and performance figures. The machine measures 58.1 m (190 ft 7 in) in length and 31.5 m (103 ft 4 in) in wing span, the width and height of the hull being 3.8 m (12 ft 6 in) and 5.2 m (17 ft) respectively; it has an all-up weight of 125,000 kg (275,600 lb) and an empty weight of 100,000 kg (220,500 lb). The Orlyonok's maximum speed is 400 km/h (249 mph), the cruising speed being 360 km/h (224 mph). The height of flight over the supporting surface can vary from 0.5 m to 5 m (1 ft 8 in to 16 ft), the optimum height being 2 m (6 ft).

In addition to the prototype, which crashed in 1975 (see below), an initial batch of three Orlyonoks was manufactured; they were adopted for squadron service by the Navy and underwent evaluation from 1979 onwards. Each of the three examples had its own factory designation; these Project 904 machines were designated S-21, S-25 and S-26. Originally the machines wore ship-type three-digit 'hull numbers' 610 (S-21), 630 (S-25) and 650 (S-26) and no star insignia, but were aptly reserialled '21 White', '25 White' and '26 White' respectively for the greater part of their service career. In the Navy they were known as the MDE-150, MDE-155 and MDE-160 respectively (MDE presumably means *mor**skoy** de**sahnt**nyy ekrano**plahn*** – sea-going transport and assault WIG vehicle). The three machines were taken on charge by the Navy on 3rd November 1979, 27th October 1981 and 30th December 1981 respectively. The Naval Com-

Opposite: 'Eagle eyrie' at Kaspiysk, with two of the three production Orlyonoks undergoing routine maintenance (the one nearest to the camera wears its original serial '610 White'). Note the open overwing entry doors; these probably served for troop disembarkation during assault operations.

Above: The same base at a later date, with all three production Orlyonoks on the hardstand; left to right, the S-26 ('26 White'), S-25 ('25 White') and the ill-starred S-21 ('21 White'). Interestingly, the S-25 and S-26 are painted a lighter shade of grey than the first production machine.

Left: A rare view of two production Orlyonoks flying in line abreast formation.

The nose of a production Orlyonok adorned with appropriate eagle nose art and red stars added to the wings. Note the booster engine nozzle travel limits.

26

26

mand presumed that the WIG vehicles would demonstrate high effectiveness (considerable speed and ensuing capability for surprise actions, capability for overcoming anti-assault obstacles and minefields) and would ensure the seizure of bridgeheads at a coastline defended by the enemy. There were plans in hand for manufacturing 11 Orlyonok (Project 904) machines during the 12th and 13th five-year economic development plan periods (1981-1990), to be followed by the construction of transport and assault WIG craft of a new type (with a new project number) possessing greater cargo carrying capacity. Preparations were made for establishing a WIG vehicle unit in the Red Banner Baltic Fleet. However, for several reasons these plans did not come to fruition. The Orlyonok WIG craft were doomed never to leave the Caspian Sea.

Initially they were operated by the specially established 236th Squadron of WIG vehicles within the brigade of transport and assault ships of the Red Banner Caspian Flotilla. Later an idea cropped up of transferring the WIG vehicles under the authority of headquarters of the Naval Aviation, but these plans met with much opposition on the part of the latter. An end to these disputes was formally put by Order No. 0256 issued by the Minister of Defence on 12th November 1986 under the terms of which ekranoplans became part of the aviation element of the Navy's Fleets. The document prescribed that WIG vehicles, as well as aircraft and helicopters, must be regarded as a class of the Naval Aviation's weaponry. In accordance with directive No. DF-035 dated 21st April 1987 the WIG craft unit, renamed 11th Air Group, was formally placed under the command of the Black Sea Fleet, albeit it retained its former base on the Caspian Sea – the town of Kaspiysk.

The incorporation of the WIG vehicles into the normal activities of the armed forces was not trouble-free and was not pursued all too vigorously. Much time was spent on repairs and modernisation (albeit the machines were almost brand-new!). There were difficulties with crew training. By 1983 four crew captains had received sufficient training; all of them had previously flown the Beriyev Be-12 Chaika (*Mail*) ASW amphibian. Up to 1984 crew training was undertaken in accordance with the 'Provisional course for training the crews of *ekranoplan* ships' prepared by the Combat Training Department of the Navy. Later the manual was reworked with participation of the Combat Training Section of the Naval Aviation.

In 1983 GNII-8 VVS (State Research Institute No. 8 of the Air Force) joined in the testing of one of the Orlyonoks. This was done in response to a request from the Naval Aviation's headquarters, albeit without much enthusiasm. The institute justifiably reproached the developers of the WIG vehicle for having prepared an operation manual for the crew without the participation of test pilots. Its form and contents were quite out of keeping with the standards to which operation manuals for crews of aircraft and helicopters were prepared. There were also other complaints and remarks.

Some interesting details concerning the operational service of the Orlyonoks were disclosed in an internet forum discussion by a person who had served with the *ekranoplan* unit based on the Caspian Sea. Major (in the reserve) Ravil' Dolotkazin served with the 236th *Ekranoplan* Squadron at the Kaspiysk base in 1980-1991. He noted, for example, that the *ekranoplans* were flown, according to instructions, at a height of 1 to 10 m (3 to 30 ft) and at speeds not exceeding 385 km/h (239 mph). Rising to higher altitudes was problematic – not only because of the aerodynamic qualities inherent in the design but also because the necessary equipment for flights in the aircraft mode was lacking. There were no aneroid altimeters, no parachutes and no emergency escape systems.

Yet, the crew of the S-21 craft undertook, at its own initiative and in utmost secrecy, several flights out of ground effect. The crew captain informally obtained personal consent of every member of the crew to such a dangerous experiment – everybody had the right to refuse; yet, nobody backed out. Such flights, performed in excellent weather conditions, lasted 20-30 minutes. The altitude attained was in excess of 100 m (330 ft), maybe even up to 300 m (about 1,000 ft). The captain, a very experienced pilot, later told his colleagues that piloting the *ekranoplan* at such altitudes was difficult. The control surfaces, especially the ailerons, lost their effectiveness. The flight became unstable, involving the risk of stalling and entering a spin, and placed a heavy strain on the pilot who constantly had to parry deviations from the flight path. On the other hand, the Orlyonok was very stable when flying in ground effect.

A different source describing the same situation states that Rostislav Alekseyev was on board the Orlyonok during such flights; they were performed at an altitude of 80-100 m (260-330 ft) and out of sight of the base for concealment. The pilots considered the vehicle to be quite controllable, albeit somewhat sluggish in a bank.

Routinely, the Orlyonoks were flown with a reduced fuel load of 22 tonnes (48,510 lb), the full fuel load being 28 tonnes. A typical mission with the reduced fuel load was a flight on the route from Kaspiysk to Astrakhan' (350 km/217 miles), then from Astrakhan' to Baku (800 km/497 miles) and finally from Baku to Kaspiysk (450 km/280 miles), which adds up to 1,600 km (994 miles).

The Russian Navy flag (known as the St. Andrew's Flag) as applied to the *ekranoplans*

Two views of the Orlyonok designated S-26 ('26 White') in post-Soviet guise with the Russian Navy flag on the fin replacing the Soviet flag. Note that the planing bottom, wing leading edges and wingtip floats are repainted black.

Unfortunately, mastering the new hardware was not free from incidents and crashes. In 1975 the Orlyonok prototype undergoing tests beached on a rocky sand-bar. Blowing from the booster engines made it possible to lift it off the rocks and safely return to base, but the episode had its consequences. The hull of the prototype machine was made of K282T1 alloy which, while possessing sufficient strength, was on the fragile side. Obviously the contact with the rocks left its traces – cracks in the aft fuselage which went unnoticed at that time. In one of the subsequent test flights, when the craft made a touch-down in rough seas, the aft fuselage/tail unit broke off and sank. Chief Designer Rostislav Ye. Alekseyev, who was on board, reacted instantly by taking over the controls. He ordered the mechanics to reset the thrust deflectors from blowing (vectored thrust) mode into the cruise (horizontal thrust) position and give the engines full throttle. The machine changed its trim and adopted a negative pitch angle, raising the gaping hole in the aft fuselage above the water surface. In this way, exercising a superb mastery of the vehicle, Alekseyev managed to bring the crippled machine safely back to base in planing mode (the consequences of this episode for the Chief Designer are described in the introductory chapter).

The severely damaged machine was returned to Gor'kiy for restoration which, in fact amounted to building a new machine. As a consequence of the accident, Alekseyev reworked the design, utilising the AMG-61aluminium/magnesium alloy instead of the previously used K282T1 alloy. It was at this stage that the Orlyonok's design came to incorporate the shock-absorbing hydroski coupled with a set of wheels. Some time later the rebuilt machine was ready for flight testing again. This marked the beginning of a period when every year between June and December the factory testing and interdepartmental acceptance trials were conducted – they involved consecutively the three Orlyonok examples and later the Loon' WIG craft (described later in this chapter). By 1989 the three Orlyonok *ekranoplans* performed 438 take-offs and landings between them and performed 118 beachings.

On 12th September 1992 another crash occurred, this time accompanied by a loss of life. The first production Orlyonok with the factory designation S-21 left its base in Kaspiysk to take part in preparations for a demonstration of Russian WIG

Right and below: This model of a projected commercial passenger version of the Orlyonok was displayed at the MAKS-93 airshow, complete with water basin with artificial waves. Note the fat dorsal fairing ahead of the fin.

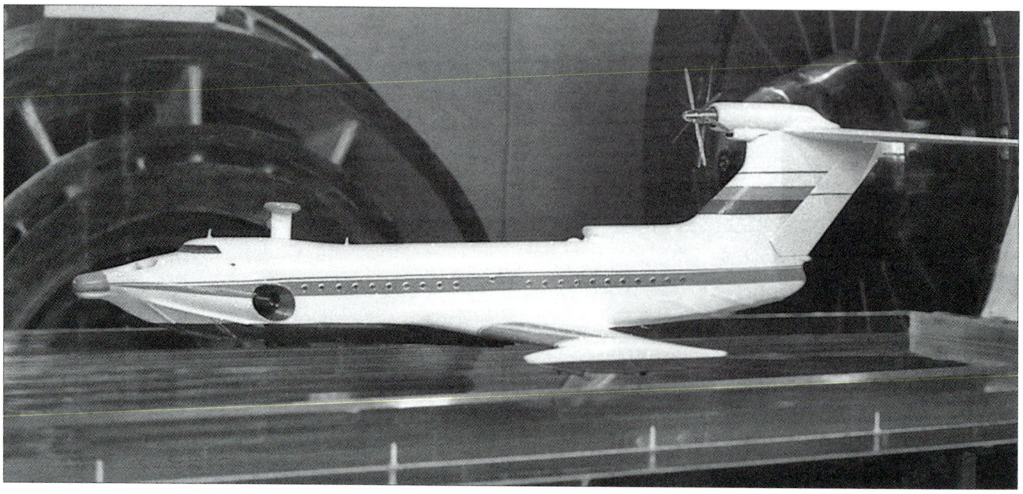

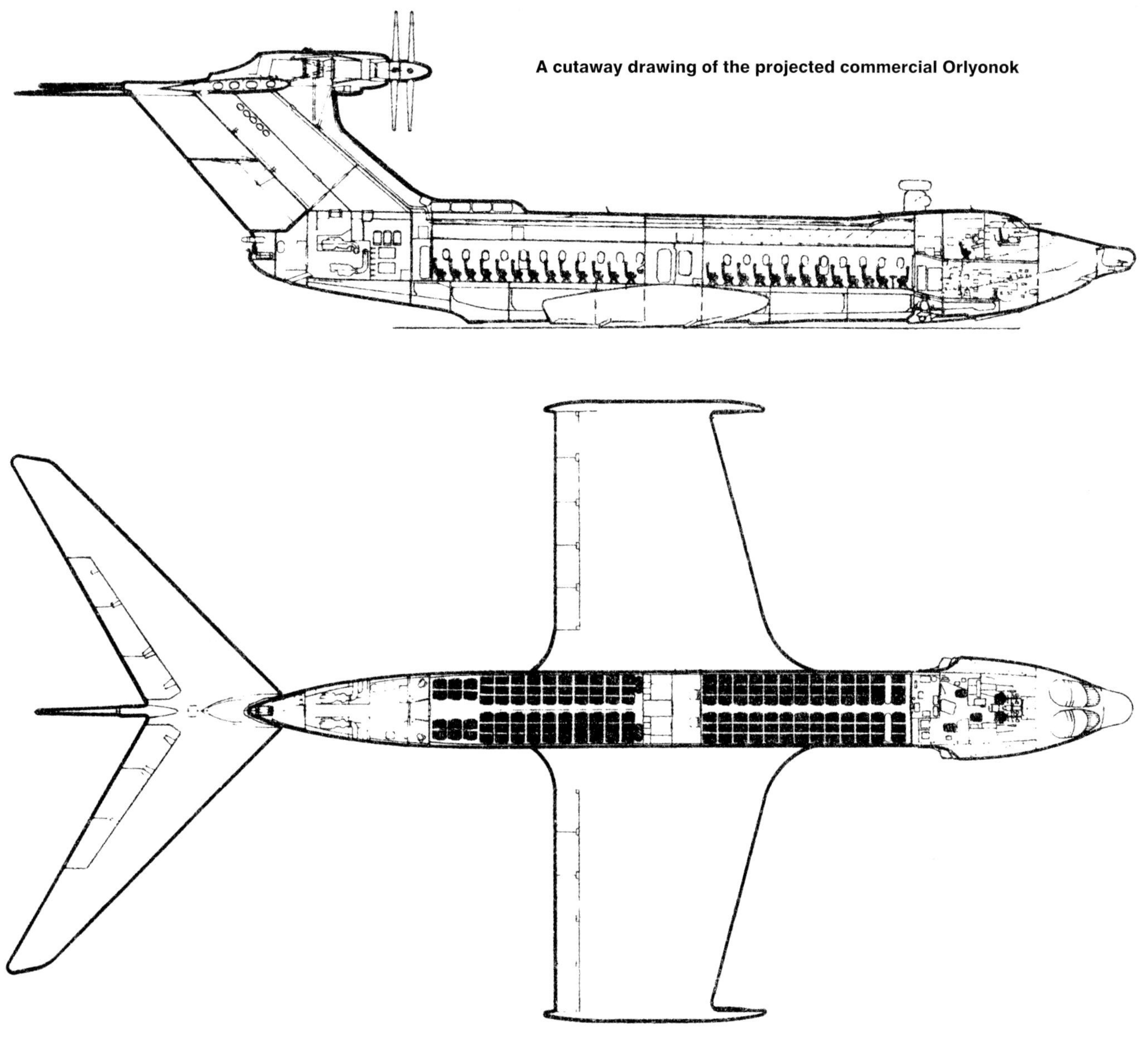

A cutaway drawing of the projected commercial Orlyonok

craft to foreign guests who were to include representatives from the US company Aerocon. While cruising at 350 km/h (217 mph), the Orlyonok suddenly began to pitch down. To parry this, the crew captain gave full throttle to the cruise engine and hauled back on the control column. As a result, the machine soared in a steep climb. Having reached a height of 40 m (130 ft), it stalled and crashed into the sea, bounced, pulled up a second time and impacted again, sustaining severe damage. Nine of the ten crew survived, albeit with injuries, and were eventually rescued. The tenth crew member – the flight engineer – was killed. The crippled Orlyonok drifted 110 km (60 nm) and was eventually blown up – the Russian Navy could not afford the price asked for its retrieval by salvage companies. It was presumed that the crash had been caused by a failure of the automatic stability system, albeit pilot error is also cited.

After this the remaining WIG complement of the Navy came to include two Project 904 machines (Orlyonok) and one Project 903 machine (Loon'). Quite clearly, for many they were a thorn in their flesh. Gradually, the *ekranoplans* began to sink into oblivion – there were many other things to think of. The vehicles gradually fell into disrepair to the point of no longer being airworthy. Finally, in 1998 the command of the Navy issued an order requiring the Orlyonok WIG vehicles to be written off on account of their alleged unsuitability for repairs and refurbishment.

Fortunately, at least one example of the Orlyonok has been saved for posterity. A few years ago Moscow's Mayor Yuriy M. Luzhkov conceived the idea of setting up a Naval Museum in Moscow. A

A model of another projected passenger version of the Orlyonok designated Orlyonok-P. It features compound-type wings with swept-back dihedral outer panels and an unswept horizontal tail. Again, there is a fat dorsal fairing ahead of the fin.

Two more views of the same model. showing the wing shape. The model bears Ekranoflot titles (a supposed *ekranoplan* operator named by analogy with Aeroflot Russian Airlines, the Russian flag carrier.

site for the museum was chosen at the Khimki Reservoir at the northern outskirts of Moscow. The idea found support from the Government of the Russian Federation. In 2006 the museum was inaugurated, a diesel-powered submarine becoming its first exhibit. But Luzhkov's dream was to obtain one of the Orlyonok *ekranoplans* for the museum, and he succeeded in making it come true. On 7th September 2006 the government adopted a resolution 'On the transfer to the state property of Moscow City of the Project 904 ekranoplan S-26 Orlyonok and the Project 1205 hovercraft D-357 Skat, decommissioned by the Navy and demilitarised, to be placed in Moscow as museum exhibits'.

In 2007 the *Skorosnoy flot* (High-speed Fleet) Joint-Stock Co., which by that time incorporated the Alekseyev Central Hydrofoil Ship Design Bureau, performed all the work associated with the demilitarisation and declassification of the S-26 and effected its transportation by river waterways from its base at Kaspiysk to Moscow. To pass through locks, the machine had one of its wings detached and propellers removed. Upon delivery the ekranoplan was reassembled and prepared for installation as a museum exhibit. The same was done with regard to the mentioned hovercraft. In 2008 the JSC 'Skorosnoy flot' refurbished the Orlyonok and the hovercraft, and they took up their places at Khimki, sharing the company of the Museum's first exhibit – a submarine. The Orlyonok was raised on a pedestal.

ASW version of the Orlyonok

The Project 904 WIG craft served as a basis for a project of an *ekranoplan* intended for ASW duties. The machine was to be equipped with a highly sensitive dipping sonar system which could be used with the machine afloat. No prototype was built. The project is represented by a model in the museum of the CHDB in Nizhniy Novgorod.

The Orlyonok served as a basis for several versions intended for civil applications. These include the following projects:

Sea-going passenger WIG vehicle

Several passenger versions of the Orlyonok were studied by the Design Bureau. In its initial form this variant fully retained the basic configuration of the baseline Orlyonok, differing only in being demilitarised and fitted out in accordance with the new tasks. Importantly, the original wing design of the Orlyonok was retained. Here are its basic characteristics: normal take-off weight, 125 t (275,000 lb); maximum TOW, 140 t (308,000 lb), payload, up to 20 t (44,100 lb) in cargo configuration, 150 passengers in passenger configuration or 30 passengers and 17 t (37,480 lb) of cargo in combi configuration; cruising speed, 350 km/h (217 mph); range, up to 1,500 km (930 miles); wave height during take-off and landing, 1.5 m (5 ft) at normal TOW or 0.5 m (1 ft 8 in) at maximum TOW.

A-90.150

This designation has been applied in Western sources to a somewhat revised projected passenger version of the Orlyonok. According to an advertising booklet from the Design Bureau (which does not mention the A-90.150 designation), it is intended to carry 100 to 150 passengers in a single-deck variant and 300 passengers in a double-deck variant. It was presumed that it could be used on regular passenger routes for transporting 150 passengers or be used as a passenger/cargo transport for speedy delivery of goods and shift crews to offshore oil rigs, fishing vessels and Polar research stations (the latter case involved landing on ice). With a powerplant identical to that of the baseline version, it had a take-off weight of 110-125 t (242,500-275,000 lb), a cruising speed of 400 km/h (249 mph) and a range of 2,000 km (1,240 miles). Further particulars included a crew of five, a de-luxe seating arrangement for 65-75 passengers, a single-deck seating arrangement for 100-150 passengers and a double-deck configuration seating up to 300 passengers. The single-deck passenger compartment had a length of 25 m (82 ft 0 in), a width of 3.3 m (10 ft 10 in) and a height of 3 m (9 ft 10 in).

Orlyonok-P

This passenger version of Orlyonok (P presumably stands for *passa***zheer***skiy* – passenger, used attributively) features new composite layout wings. A model of the craft shows swept dihedral outer wing panels of smaller chord and higher aspect ratio added to the main wings outboard of the end-plates/floats. This was expected to give the Orlyonok-P a lift/drag ratio that is one-third higher than that of the basic model; its fuel consumption would be on a level with that of advanced aircraft under development at that time. The horizontal tail was also new, having no sweepback.

The basic specifications and performance of the Orlyonok-P were initially advertised as follows: displacement (take-off weight), up to 140 t (308,640 lb); payload, 40 t (88,180 lb); range, 2,000 km (1,240 miles); speed, 375 km/h (233 mph), seaworthiness at take-off and landing, sea state 4; crew, 6. Later, revised figures were published (see table).

Orlyonok-Gr sea-going cargo WIG vehicle

This was a 'demilitarised' version of the baseline troop transport and assault Orlyonok, retaining its loading feature – the forward fuselage swinging to starboard. It is capable of transporting 30 t (66,000 lb) of cargo to a distance of 1,000 km (620 miles), the maximum range being 2,000 km (1,240 miles). Cruising speed- 400 km/h (249 mph). It is presumably this particular version that has been advertised as the Orlyonok-Gr (*groozo***voy** – cargo, used attributively). It was intended for speedy delivery of wheeled and tracked vehicles, including deliveries to sites on a sea shore without any unloading facilities. The dimensions of the cargo hold were as follows: length, 21 m (68 ft $10\frac{49}{64}$ in); width, 3.2 m (10 ft 6 in); height, 3 m (9 ft $10\frac{7}{64}$ in).

More recent official specifications for the Orlyonok-P and Orlyonok-Gr are given in the table below. Note that they differ somewhat from the figures quoted in the text, but this presumably reflects the changes introduced at various stages of the design work.

Provisional specifications of the Orlyonok's projected commercial versions

	Orlyonok-P	Orlyonok-Gr
Register class according to the IMO classification	B	B
Displacement, tonnes (lb)	125 (275,625)	Up to 140 (308,700)
Draught	1.5 m (4 ft 10 in)	1.6 m (5 ft 3 in)
Speed, km/h (mph)	350-400 (217-249)	375-425 (233-264)
Passenger capacity, persons	150	-
Cargo capacity, tonnes (lb)	-	up to 40 (88,200)
Powerplant:		
Cruise engines, number and output, kW	1 x 11,030	1 x 11,030
Booster engines, number and thrust, kgp (lbst)	2 x 10,500 (2 x 23,150)	2 x 10,500 (2 x 23,150)

MAGE

This sea-going Arctic prospecting WIG vehicle (MAGE = *mor***skoy** *ark***tich***eskiy ghe***o***logorazve***dochnyy** *ekrano***plahn**) is intended for prospecting on the shallow-water shelf of the Arctic seas and for transportation tasks related to this work.

It differs from the baseline Orlyonok not only in having the armament and troop-carrying equip-

Above: An artist's impression of a projected geological prospecting version of the Orlyonok known as Gheofizik (Geophysicist) or MAGE (the acronym means 'sea-going Arctic prospecting WIG vehicle').

Below: The Gheofizik in action, moving at low speed and towing what appears to be a submerged sensor array supported by buoys. Note the rear doors used for loading and deploying the sensors.

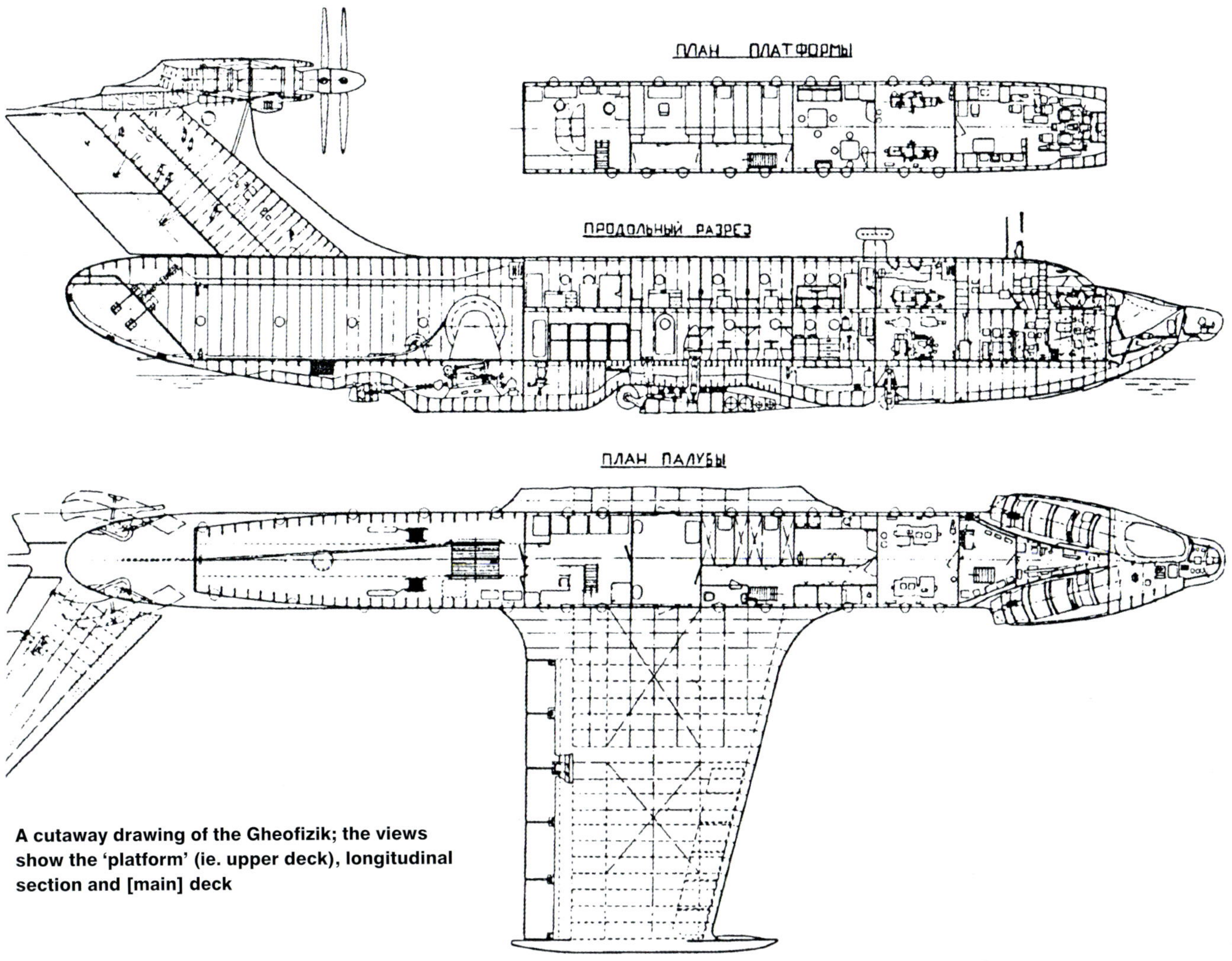

A cutaway drawing of the Gheofizik; the views show the 'platform' (ie. upper deck), longitudinal section and [main] deck

ment deleted, but also in some structural details. The height of the hull (fuselage) has been increased. The aft fuselage features clamshell doors and houses special equipment which permits the machine to take samples of ground from the sea bed and perform prospecting with the use of seismoacoustic, magnetometric and gravimetric methods. Scientific equipment carried by the craft included, in particular, the Progress seismic station, an echo sounder, an ***In**ey-P* (Hoar Frost) analogue recorder, MVS magnetic variation stations, a data storage device and other onboard devices. These are supplemented by a number of immersible devices, such as the ADSR seismic sensors, proton magnetometers, the GMT-D bottom gravimeter, the PSK-6 chains of seismic explosive charges. Sampling from the sea bed is performed with the help of the Okean-0,25 excavator and sampling pipes.

The aft fuselage houses a retractable water propulsor for low-speed motion when afloat – a propeller screw in an annular duct driven by a diesel engine. This propulsor is used in the course of the prospecting work which is performed at a speed of 5-10 km/h (3-6 mph). The MAGE with a normal AUW of 138 tonnes (304,230 lb) is capable of attaining a speed of 390 km/h (231 mph) in cruising flight and has a range of 2,000 km (1,240 miles)

The MAGE is also known as *Gheo**fiz**ik* (Geophysicist).

SAR WIG vehicle

This version was intended for search and rescue work for the benefit of the merchant fleet and the Navy, for delivering rescue teams to accident and natural disaster sites in the vicinity of off-shore drilling rigs, platforms and inhabited places at the coastline, as well as for rendering assistance to people affected by these disasters and evacuating them from those places. With a crew of 16, including pilots, rescue workers and medical attendants, the machine was to take on board 95 rescuees (up to 150 in an emergency). The machine was to have a normal AUW of 125 tonnes (275,570 lb), a maximum AUW of 140 tonnes (308,640 lb), a cruising

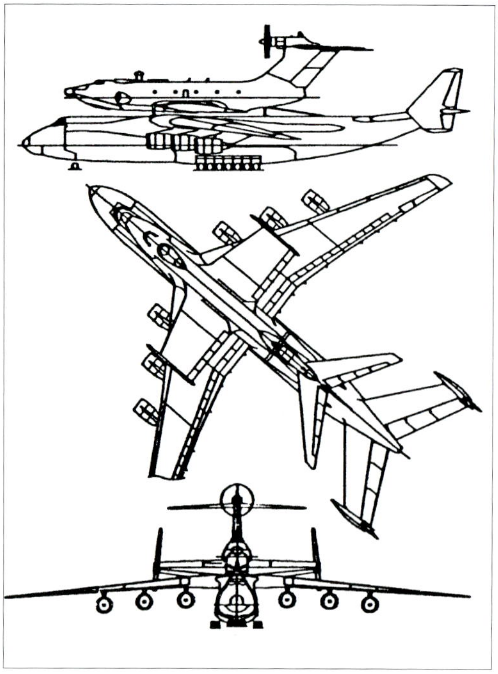

A three-view of a maritime rescue system consisting of an Orlyonok carried piggy-back by the An-225.

speed of 400 km/h (248 mph) and a range of up to 3,000 km (1,863 miles). The medical section of the fuselage included an intensive therapy ward. The rescue equipment included two inflatable boats with outboard motors, six life rafts and 120 individual life jackets.

Mriya/Orlyonok Aviation and Maritime Search-and-Rescue System

This SAR complex was evolved by the Alexeyev Central Hydrofoil Design Bureau together with the Antonov Design Bureau. Its task consists in detecting the accident site at the sea surface, performing rescue work and rendering the necessary assistance to people in distress. The complex comprises the An-225 Mriya (Dream/*Cossack*) carrier aircraft and the Orlyonok WIG vehicle carried on top of its fuselage. The overall weight of the system is 610 tonnes (1,345,000 lb). The An-225, the biggest transport aircraft in the world, had already demonstrated its ability to carry similar loads externally when it ferried the Buran space shuttle.

Once an accident has been reported, the An-225 with the Orlyonok attached to it 'piggy-back' takes off, heading for the disaster area. With an intermediate landing (if needed), the system can deliver a rescue team to any site in the World Ocean within 10 to 12 hours. In the vicinity of the accident site the Orlyonok starts its engines and detaches itself from the carrier aircraft, making a gliding

A computer-generated image of the Mriya/Orlyonok combination in flight.

descent to the water surface where it alights. According to the project plan, the Orlyonok was to be fitted out with special equipment enabling it to render urgent medical aid and accommodate up to 70 survivors.

In accordance with the designers' concept five to seven systems making part of a unified SAR system would be located in different areas of the World Ocean. This international system was expected to cover virtually all major maritime traffic routes, fishery areas and areas of off-shore oil and gas extraction. Since both components of the SAR system had already been created and had undergone operational trials, it was presumed that the development of such a system would be less costly than establishing other similar systems. According to some estimates based on maritime disaster statistics and shipping trends for the late 1990s, seven An-225/Orlyonok systems would have performed not less than 210 to 250 rescue operations in high seas per year. However, a prerequisite for putting such a plan into effect was the setting up of an international rescue service. Unfortunately, this project was not put into practice.

It remains to be added that all the civil versions of the Orlyonok listed above remained paper projects.

Loon' (Project 903) missile-carrying *ekranoplan*

In the late 1980s the work of the Central Hydrofoil Design Bureau on WIG vehicles intended for military application led to the creation of a unique machine – a missile strike *ekranoplan*. Bearing the manufacturer's designation 'Project 903', it was subsequently named Loon' (Hen Harrier). According to some sources, it was initially named ***Oot**ka* – 'duck', but this sounded totally unwarlike and could also be interpreted as 'canard', that is, something bogus. The machine's Chief Designer was Vladimir N. Kirillovykh. This machine with a hull length of 73.80 m (242 ft 1¾), a wing span of 44 m (144 ft 4$\frac{9}{32}$ in) and a wing area of 550 m^2 (5,920 sq ft) was launched on 16th July 1986. Its empty weight reached 243,000 kg (535,815 lb), the maximum AUW being 380,000 kg (837,900 lb). Its design was based on the layout which had already been verified on such vehicles as the KM and the Orlyonok, that is, the 'aircraft' layout – a monoplane with wings of trapezoidal planform and a swept T-tail.

The Loon', however, differed substantially from its predecessors. The entire powerplant comprising eight Kuznetsov NK-87 turbofans rated at 13,000 kgp (28,660 lbst) each was located on the forward fuselage in packs of four. Thus, the engines served both as booster (blower) engines and cruise engines. This was apparently associated with another special feature of the machine – the placement of its offensive armament. Mounted dorsally on the fuselage in tandem pairs were six angled launch tubes with 3M80 *Mos**kit*** (Mosquito) anti-shipping missiles (NATO code name SS-N-22 *Sunburn*) developed under the guidance of Aleksandr Ya. Berezniak. This is a potent ramjet-powered supersonic missile which has no counterparts in other navies of the world. During the launch of these missiles there was a risk of the combustion products being ingested by the cruise engines previously placed high on the tail, which could cause them to flame out. Installing all the engines on the forward fuselage eliminated this danger.

As distinct from the low-wing Orlyonok, the Loon' had mid-set wings; otherwise, they were similar to those of its predecessor and were of multi-spar metal construction which was made watertight. Placed on the bottom of the hull was a hydroski device intended to cushion the impact when alighting on water. As distinct from the Orlyonok, the Loon' was not fitted with a nose hydroski and had only one hydroski under the centre fuse-

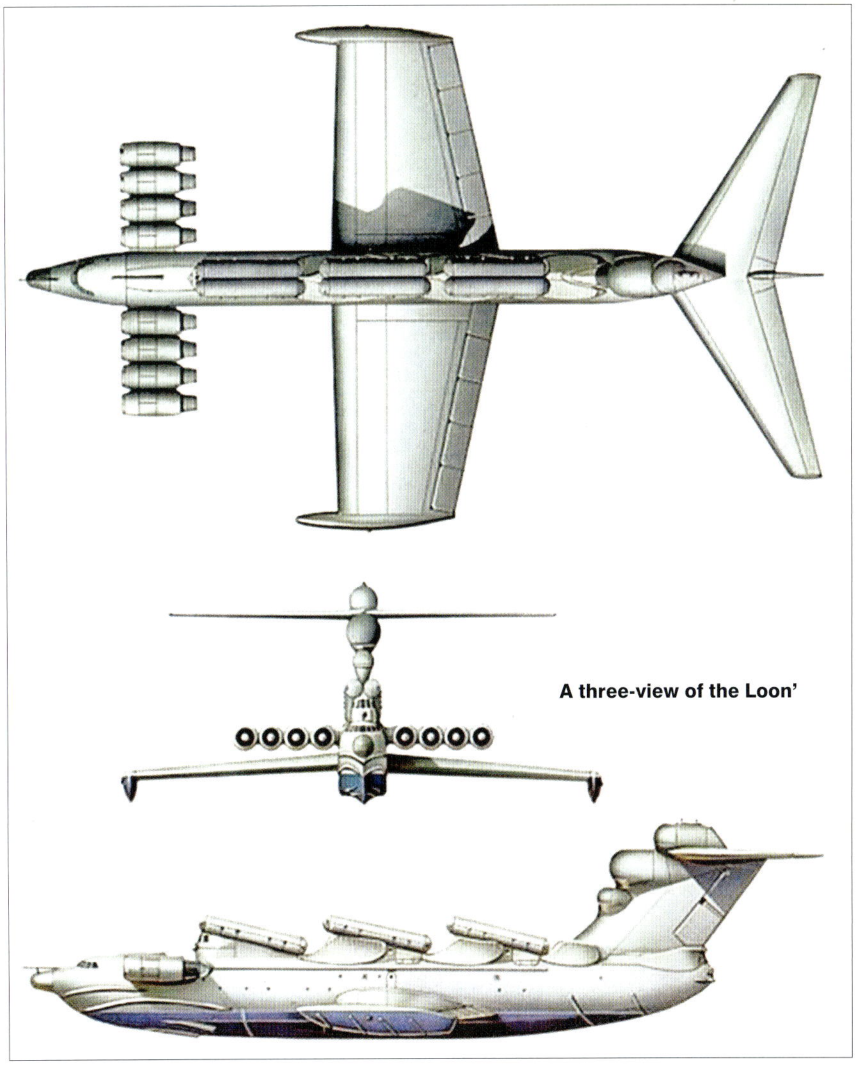

A three-view of the Loon'

lage; it had smaller dimensions and a pronounced deadrise (V-shaped bottom) which helped cushion the impact on touchdown. There was no wheeled undercarriage.

The Loon' was equipped with a radar for air and surface target detection and with a navigation radar, as well as with an ECM suite. They were housed in three huge dielectric fairings at the top of the fin – a feature that gave the craft a very distinctive appearance indeed. The Loon' was equipped with the *Pritok* (Tributary) navigation suite which was considerably improved in comparison with the Splav (Alloy) system used on the Orlyonok. In particular, an improved azimuth and heading gyro-

The photos on this page show a model of the Loon' in the towing basin where scaled-height waves are generated to represent high seas. Note the functional flaperons and the movable nozzles emulating the nozzle vanes of the boost/cruise engines. The missile launch tubes are omitted.

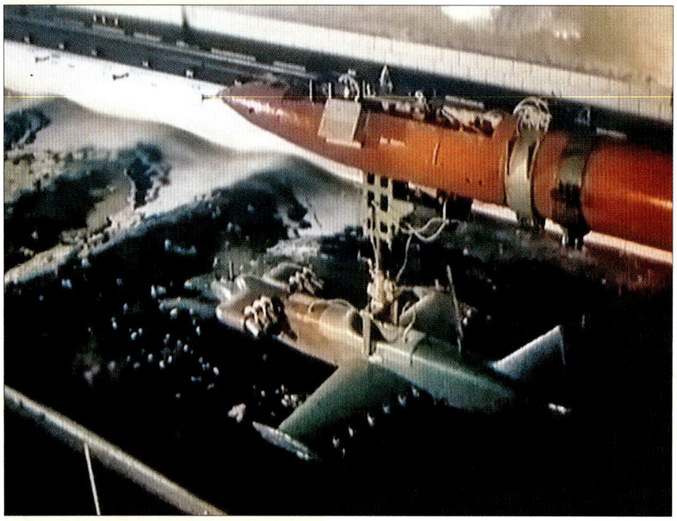

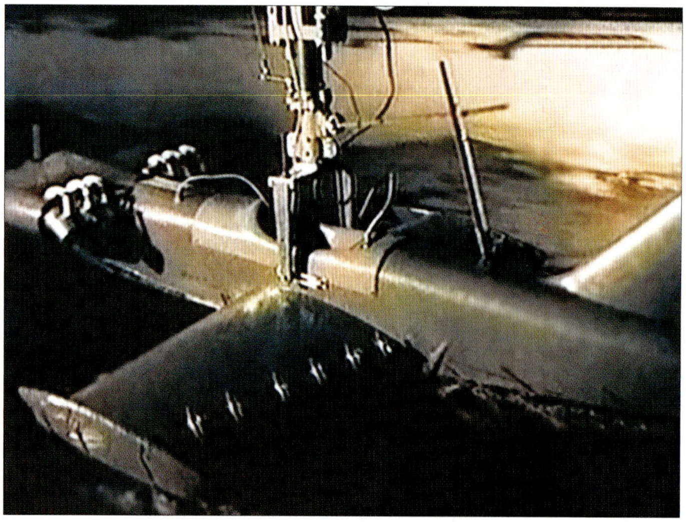

The Loon' fires a Moskit missile in cruise flight. The pall of smoke shows clearly why the designers chose to mount all eight engines on the forward fuselage.

scope ensured greater precision in laying the course. Furthermore, it showed the angles of bank and pitch (the latter was of importance for the missile launch system), the speed, the latitude and, with the help of calculations, the longitude. A satellite navigation system was also provided.

The defensive armament consisted of two gunner's stations borrowed directly from the Ilyushin IL-76M military transport, one facing forward and the other aft. Each had a UKU-9K-502 turret mounting two 23-mm (.90 calibre) Gryazev/Shipunov GSh-23 double-barrelled cannons.

The machine's performance included a maximum speed of 500 km/h (310 mph), a cruising altitude of 1-5 m (3-15 ft), and a range of 2,000 km (1,240 miles). It had an endurance of 5 days when afloat and could perform a take-off or alight at a sea state of 5-6. The vehicle carried a crew of 15.

Armed with Moskit anti-shipping missiles, the WIG vehicle flying at ultra-low level at a speed of 350-400 km/h (218-249 mph) could deal a devastating blow to the potential enemy's naval units and leave the scene unimpeded.

The testing of the Loon' (which was given the factory designation S-31) took place on the Caspian Sea. The test programme started on 30th October and was completed on 26th December 1989. In the course of these tests a total of 42 hours

The rear end of one of the paired launch tubes with the right cover closed and open, showing the nozzle of a Moskit ASM. Note the swinging arms and the lateral lock retaining the cover in the open position.

This reasonably accurate artist's impression of the Loon' appeared in the *Soviet Military Power* brochure published by the US Department of Defense.

and 15 minutes of operation was logged; of these 24 hours were logged with the craft airborne in the WIG cruise mode.

According to reports in the Russian press, *'the Project 903* ekranoplan *No. S-31 underwent operational testing in 1990-1991'*. In the course of this trial operation live missile launches were made from the dorsal launch tubes, as available photos testify. The machine met the design requirements, but it was ill-fated. Initially, in line with the provisions of directive No. 252-73 issued by the Communist Party Central Committee and the Soviet Council of Ministers of 26th March 1980, the warship construction programme envisaged the completion of four Project

A Mil' Mi-14PS SAR helicopter approaches the Loon' as the craft is towed to deep water (note the towing line). The forward gunner's station is visible below the Nos. 1 and 2 launch tubes.

The Loon' executes a tight turn to port on the water, leaving a foaming wake and a pall of water spray.

903 machines in the 12th and 13th five-year plan periods (1981-1990); later the planned figures were increased. Plans were in hand for the construction of six Project 903 WIG vehicles up to 1995 and another four machines of this type before 2000. However, in the late 1980s there came a change of heart towards the WIG vehicles in the command of the Navy. In 1989 it was decided to limit the construction of the attack WIG machines to just one example. A decision was taken to convert the second example of the Loon', then under construction, into a SAR vehicle (see below).

As for the sole example of the Loon' combat *ekranoplan*, it was withdrawn from service and is stored at Kaspiysk. According to one document, *'in order to preserve the missile-armed* ekranoplan, *the*

The Loon' in cruise flight, clearly showing the paired missile launch tubes with associated blast deflectors and the fin-mounted guidance/ECM antenna array. The defensive armament, complete with gunner's stations, was borrowed from the IL-76M transport.

A Moskit missile is seen just as it exits the No. 2 launch tube, belching flames.

More video imagery of the Loon' cruising over the Caspian Sea; the camera platform is an An-26.

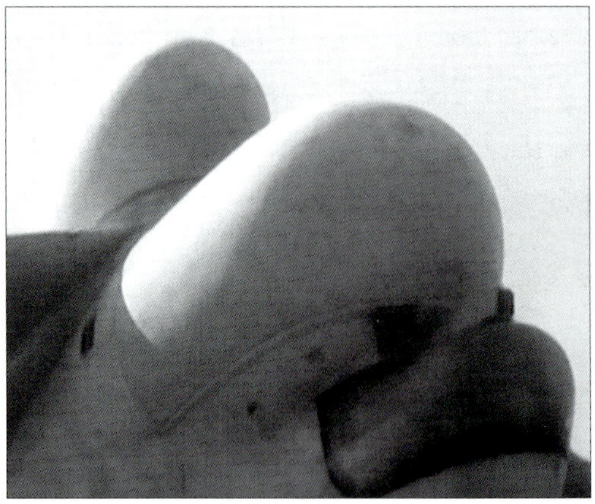

Here the Loon' skimming over the sea is seen from a surface ship.

Above right: Close-up of the three radomes mounted on the vertical tail.

The Loon' in its floating dock at Kaspiysk. The flaperons are fully deflected into take-off position.

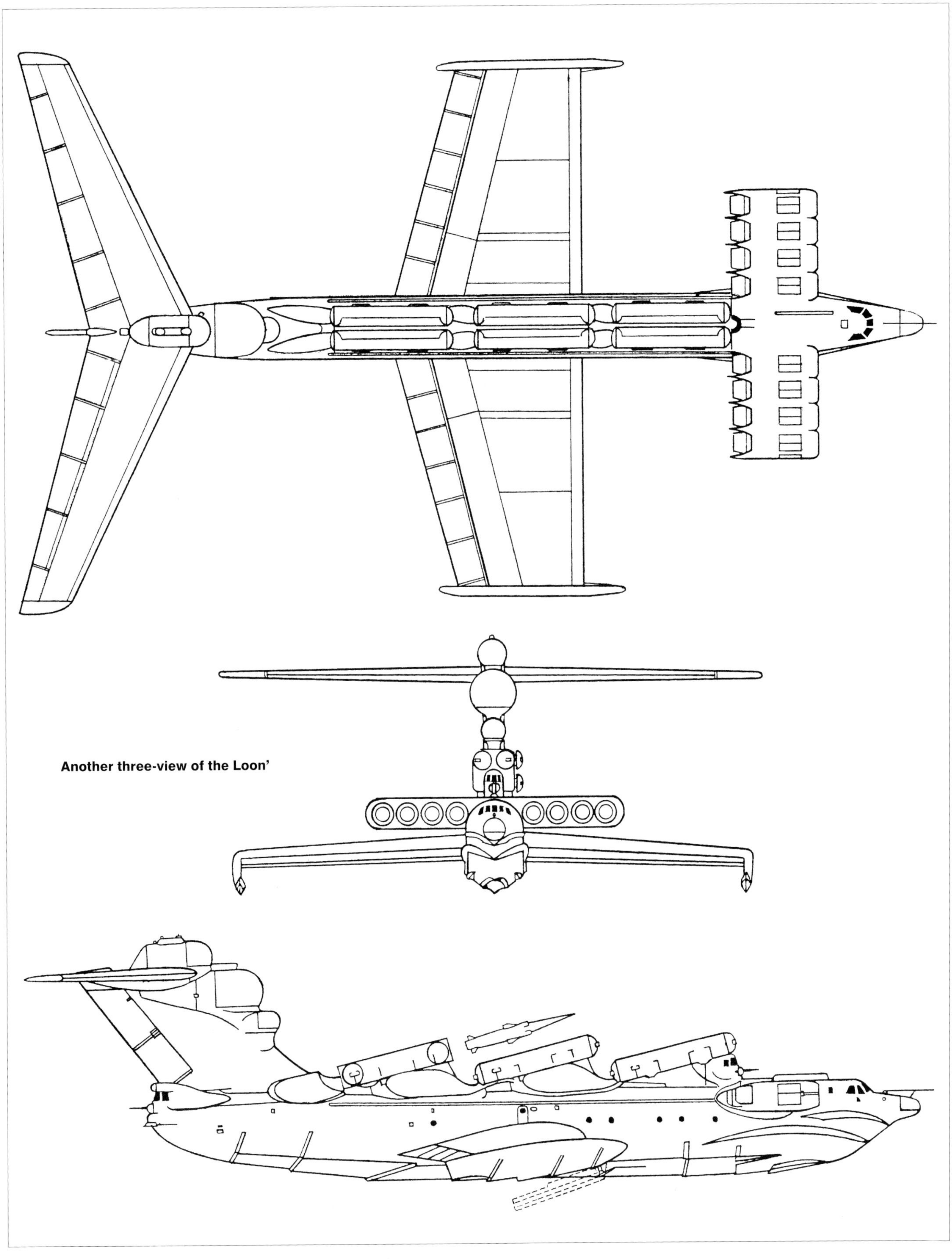

Another three-view of the Loon'

Right and far right: The three pairs of missile launch tubes and their blast deflectors.

Below right: The two quadruplets of NK-87 engines with intake centrebodies and inlet covers. Oddly, only the No. 3 engine is fitted with a foreign object damage (read: birdstrike) protection grille.

Below: A full frontal of the Loon' languishing in the floating dock at Kaspiysk.

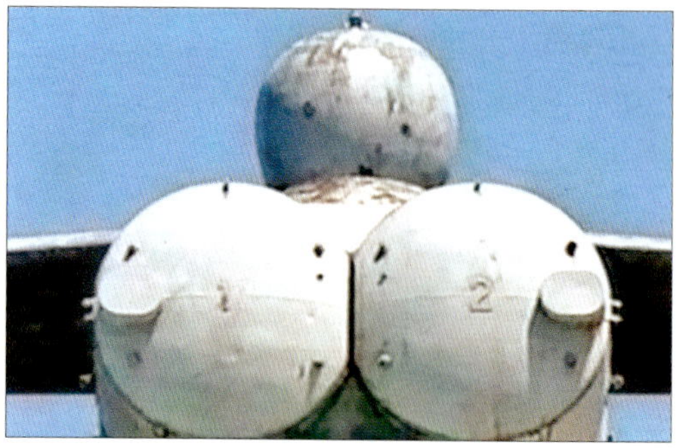

Top right: Another view of the missile launch tubes and the forward gunner's station. The cannons have been removed from the turret.

Above right: The properly marked front covers of the Nos. 1 and 2 launch tubes.

Another view of the Loon' at Kaspiysk. The inscription reading *Tikhiy khod!* (Low speed!) is an instruction to vessel captains.

Commander-in-Chief of the Navy took a decision providing for its preservation at the territory of the 11th Air Group and for transforming it into the air base (for storage of the ekranoplan*), with one crew complement to be retained at the base'.*

In 2002 the Russian Navy command came to the conclusion that the missile-carrying *ekranoplan* could well provide reinforcement to the depleted naval forces of the Russian Federation in the Caspian Sea. This was the result of the then President Vladimir V. Putin's visit to the Caspian Sea region where he, among other things, studied the situation in Russia's regional defences. The President tasked the Navy command with strengthening the Russian military presence on the Caspian Sea to a level commensurate with Russia's status as the strongest of the states sharing the coastline of that sea. As a result, Chief of the General Staff Anatoliy Kvashnin signed a directive calling for bringing the missile-carrying WIG craft back into service.

In May 2002 the Russian MoD daily newspaper ***Kras**naya Zvez**da*** (Red Star) reported that a special commission set up by the Chief of General Staff was busy with refurbishing the Loon' and getting it ready for renewed service. The newspaper asserted that the necessary funding had been provided and a new crew had been selected. However, all this fuss came to naught and the Loon' was doomed to remain in a pitiful state to this day.

The port engine package of the Loon' with the lower cowling panels open. Minor damage to the No. 1 engine intake is evident.

Spasatel' SAR vehicle (Project 9037)

The second example of the Loon' attack *ekranoplan* (factory designation S-33) ordered by the military was 80% complete when the work was halted and the machine was preserved with an imminent

The Loon' sits in storage at the Kaspiysk base, with maintenance platforms under the engine nacelles. Note the upper section of the rudder deflected differentially from the lower section. The tail in the foreground belongs to another *ekranoplan*.

Two towing basin models of the Loon' at the CHDB. The third model in the background represents a projected but unbuilt commercial WIG with twin vertical tails topped by an unswept stabiliser.

Two wind tunnel models of the Spasatel' suspended belly to belly in the wind tunnel.

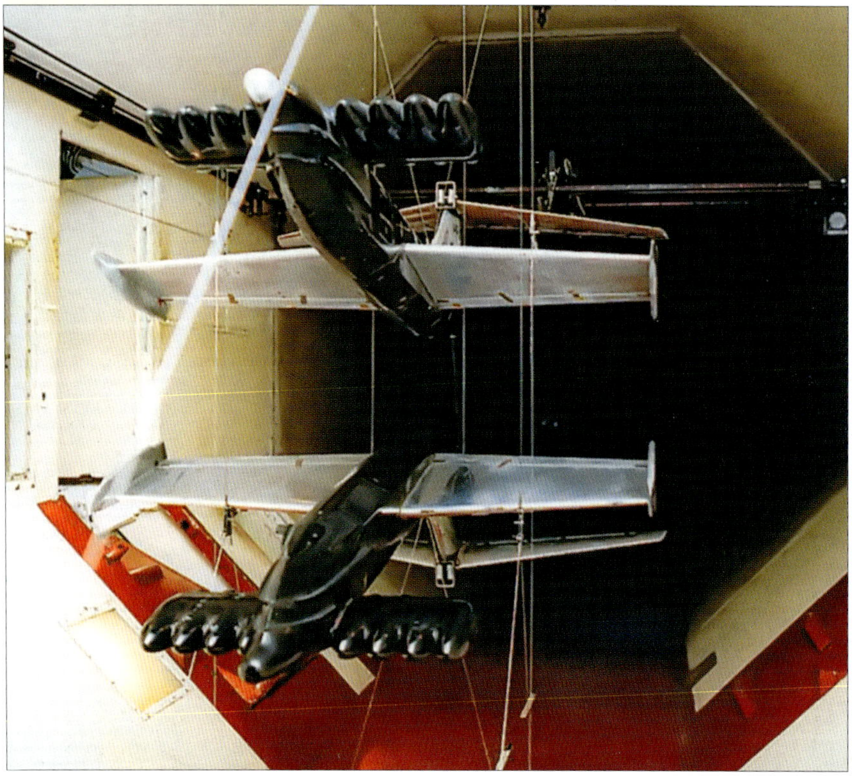

prospect of being scrapped. However, it was saved from that fate through a conversion for civil use. Research performed on the Loon' airframe in 1990-91 confirmed that this machine possessed a considerable potential for conducting search and rescue (SAR) work. In 1992 a plan cropped up in the Ministry of Defence, providing for the conversion of this machine into a SAR vehicle for the benefit of the Navy. A technical project was prepared under the direction of Chief Designer Vladimir N. Kirillovykh, and work was started at the Volga Shipyard in Nizhniy Novgorod with a view to converting the second example of the Loon', then under construction, into the *Spasatel'* (Rescue worker) WIG vehicle.

The equipment suite of this machine (Project 9037) enabled it to transport anything between 150 and 500 persons. In the floating hospital version it would provide accommodation for 80 patients on beds. The internal volume was such that the Spasatel' could take 700 to 800 persons on board and remain afloat in a stormy sea waiting for aid to come. This WIG vehicle can take off and alight in sea state 5 and perform cruise flight regardless of the sea state; the rescue means can be deployed directly on its wings. The project provides for an onboard hospital with a surgery room and an intensive therapy ward, as well as a separate place for special treatment needed by those affected by radiation during nuclear powerplant accidents, or by fire or chemical burns. The idea was that improved WIG craft of the Spasatel' type could become the basis of a worldwide SAR system that could be set up under the auspices of the United Nations.

Seven crew members (apart from the navigator and the medical personnel) were accommodated in a flight deck in the forward fuselage, while the navigator and a team of rescue workers sat in an aft compartment at the top of the fin affording excellent, nearly all-round view. The crew was to be provided with inflatable boats, ladders and other rescue means suited for actions under the conditions of a stormy sea.

In addition to aiding those afflicted by 'usual' disasters at sea (a sinking ship etc.), the Spasatel' was to be provided with the means of handling special situations, such as a fire on a ship or a burning oil slick and an emergency on a submerged submarine. For extinguishing fires, the Spasatel' would be equipped with a fire fighting system, including a special tank with 20 tonnes (44,100 lb) of foaming agent. In addition to traditional methods of extinguishing fires, the WIG craft can make use of the powerful jet efflux from its eight engines which, when operated in the boost (blowing) mode, raise a mighty cloud of spray.

In the case of a submarine in distress, the craft would carry piggy-back a deep-sea diving vehicle capable of accommodating 24 persons; this vehicle would be able to carry out rescue operations under the water. It would also carry a decompression chamber. To combat pollution from oil spillages at sea caused by tanker disasters, the Spasatel' could carry a container with floating barriers to an overall length of 3,000 m (9,840 ft). All these sets of equipment for different missions could be used on the same machine that would be properly equipped according to the situation. Furthermore, the Spasatel' was capable of delivering rescue parties and their equipment to offshore oil rigs and of evacuat-

Top left: The Spasatel' sits in the assembly hangar of the Volga Shipyard amidst a jumble of work platforms. The flight deck glazing is seen here.

Top: The flight deck roof (with dorsal escape hatch) and the engine pylon attachment area. The open maintenance access hatch is seen at the foot of the picture.

Above left: A look inside the cabin of the unfinished Spasatel'.

Above: The flight deck interior as it is now, showing the escape hatch and the glazing frame.

Two of the air intakes, with the foreign object damage prevention grilles already in place. These were fitted to all eight intakes.

The substantially complete Spasatel' in the assembly shop. Note the glazed observation cabin at the top of the fin.

ing the personnel of such rigs; it could be used for rendering assistance to the population in distress in the event of natural disasters in littoral areas. The Spasatel' was also capable of setting afloat ships that had run aground.

Performance figures for the Spasatel' include a speed of 400-550 km/h (249-342 mph) during cruise flight in WIG mode and 750 km/h (466 mph) during flight at an altitude out of ground effect. In the latter case the machine's service ceiling is 7,500 m

The outer wing panels of the Spasatel' are temporarily attached to the top of the fuselage and temporary floats mounted on the wing centre section stubs, allowing the craft to be towed through narrow channels.

Overall view of the Spasatel' SAR craft nearing completion.

(24,600 ft). In the search mode the Spasatel' is to fly at an altitude of 500 m (1,640 ft). A different source cites a range of 4,000 km (2,486 miles) and a 3,000-km (1,864-mile) tactical radius of action on condition of refuelling at sea from a ship that would arrive at the site within five days (the limit of self-contained operation for the Spasatel'). The cruise flight in the WIG mode is performed at a height of 1 to 4 m (3 to 13 ft), the search is best performed at an altitude between 100 and 300 m (330-980 ft), the ferry flight

The tail unit of the Spasatel' (minus the outer portions of the horizontal tail), showing the fin-top navigator's station/'crow's nest'. Note the upward-hinged tailcone allowing rescue rafts to be launched.

Top and above: Four more views of the Spasatel' at a later date, showing the nose radome and the prominent spray dams at the bows. Note the different grades of metal used for the hull.

Right: The engine nacelles with open upper cowlings.

Far right: The port temporary float and the outer wing panels mounted dorsally for the anticipated ferrying operation.

Two views of the Spasatel' from the work platforms at the observation cabin level.

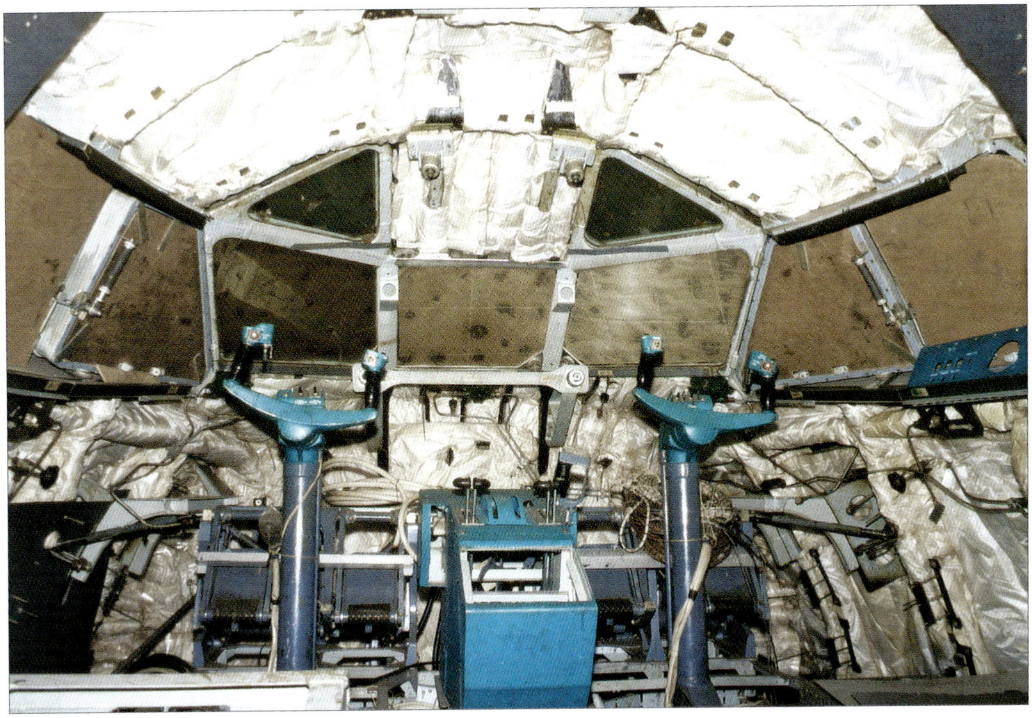

The flight deck of the unfinished Spasatel', showing the control columns, rudder pedals, central control pedestal and heat/sound-proofing blankets. All avionics and instrument panels have yet to be installed.

altitude is 3,000 m (9,840 ft). The vehicle has a length of 73.8 m (242 ft 1¾ in), a wing span of 44.0 m (144 ft 4¼ in), a height of 19.2 m (63 ft 0 in) and a draught of 2.5 m (8 ft 2½ in) when afloat.

Models of the Spasatel' exhibited at various air shows display some external differences, such as the presence or absence of a small saucer radome atop the fin, a spine atop the fuselage and the num-

Here the Spasatel' is seen with the outer wings in place. Note the temporary railings along the wing trailing edge.

An artist's impression of a rescue WIG base, with two Spasatel' vehicles moored in bays and a third example in a floating dock.

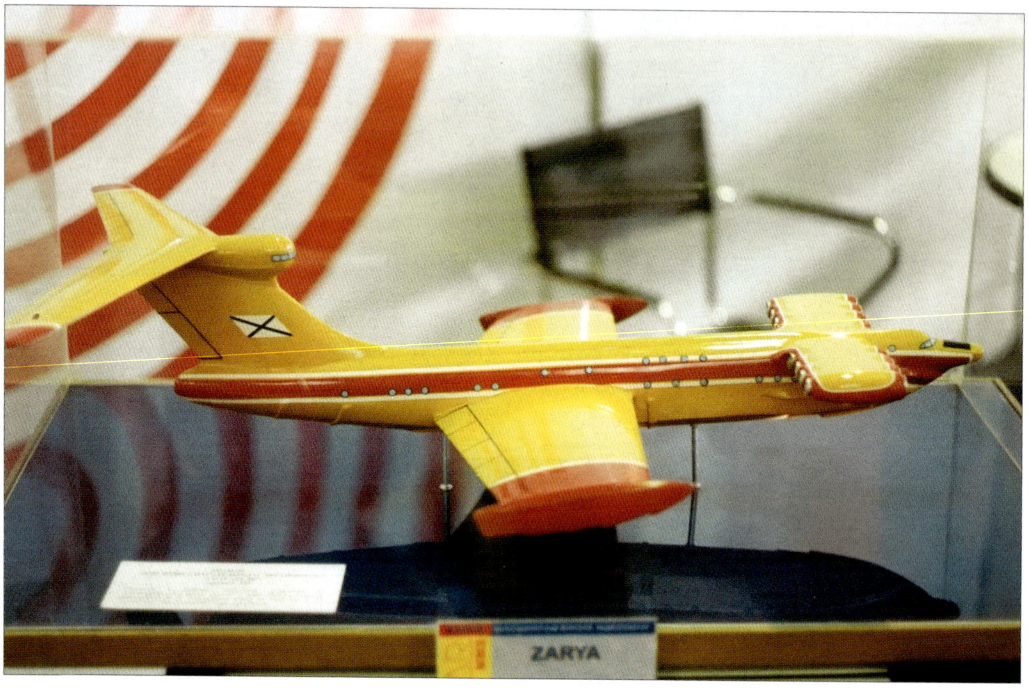

A model of the Spasatel' in Russian Navy colours at the display stand of avionics manufacturer Radar-MMS at one of the International Maritime Defence Shows in St. Petersburg. The name *Zarya* (Dawn) applies to a radar (developed by Radar-MMS) to be installed on the vehicle.

Another view of the same model. Note the window arrangement indicative of a double-deck layout, the fin root fillet, the fuselage spine and the tail-mounted saucer radome of the Zarya radar.

A cutaway model of the Spasatel' as actually built. It was displayed at one of the Hydro Aviation Shows in Ghelendzhik.

Another view of the same model, showing the straight fin leading edge. No tail-mounted radar is present here.

The model shown at Ghelendzhik was in civil colours and wore the CHDB logo, plus Red Cross markings.

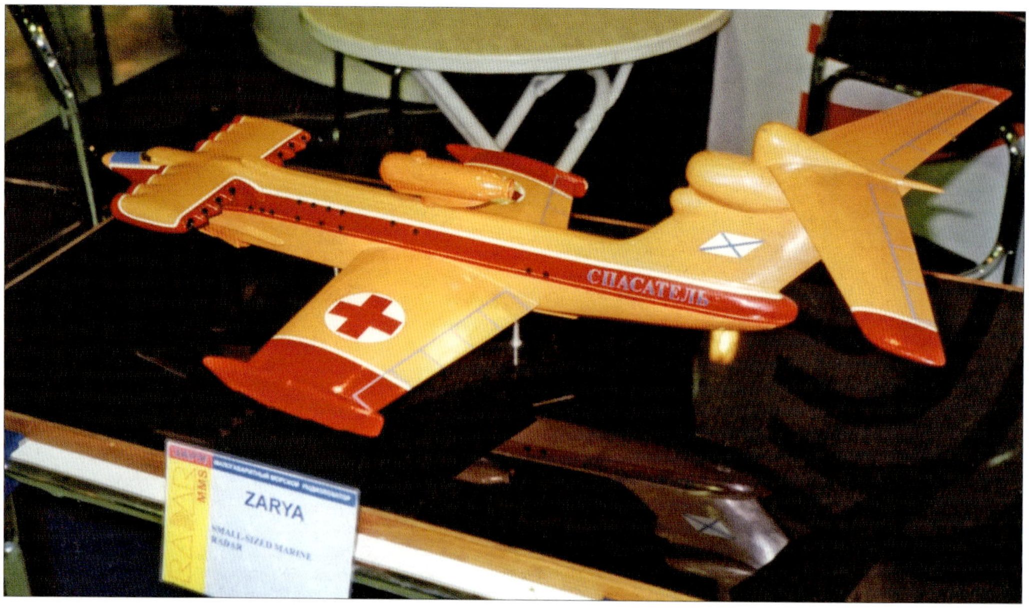

Two views of yet another display model of the Spasatel' in Navy colours. Strangely enough, it has a Loon'-style tail treatment with triple radomes and no observation cabin. A deep-sea diving vehicle is carried piggy-back. Again, the model is used to advertise the Radar-MMS Zarya radar.

This artist's impression shows the Spasatel' in fire-fighting configuration with a dorsally mounted foaming agent tank; the water is ejected from water cannons at the tips of the horizontal tail. Note the inflatable rescue rafts.

ber and shape of bulges on the fin leading edge. One of these models illustrated the use of the ***Zarya*** (Dawn) small-sized marine radar developed by the St. Petersburg-based company Radar-MMS.

WIG vehicles of the Spasatel' type were intended to form the basis of special SAR units within the Russian Navy's North and Pacific Fleets. Furthermore, the idea was that improved Spasatel' *ekranoplans* could become the basis of a world-wide SAR system that could be set up under the aegis of the United Nations. However, these plans were not destined to be implemented.

It was envisaged that the Spasatel' would leave the assembly shop in 1994 (a different source cites 1998), but the work tempo was slowed down owing to insufficient funding from the Ministry of Defence, and for some time the project was, in fact, 'put on ice'. In December 2001 a press report appeared stating that construction of the Spasatel' was

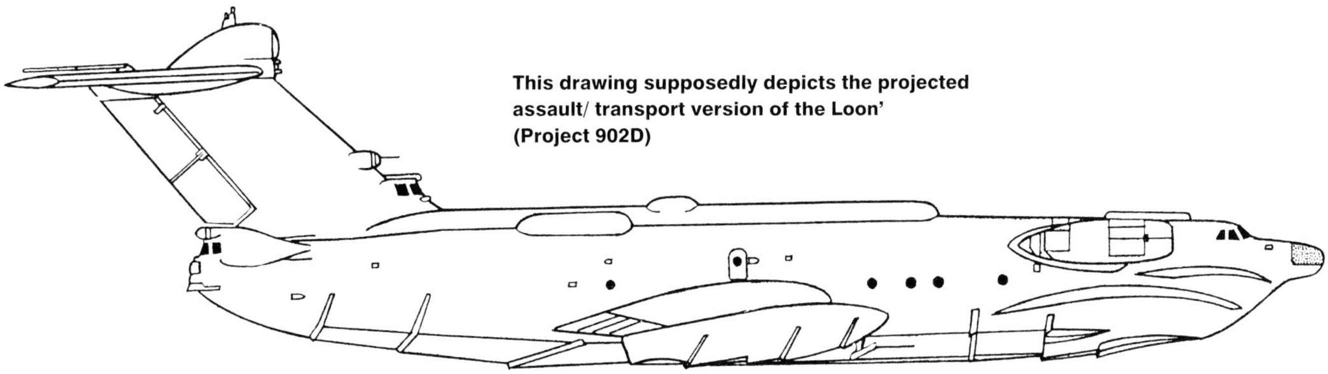

This drawing supposedly depicts the projected assault/ transport version of the Loon' (Project 902D)

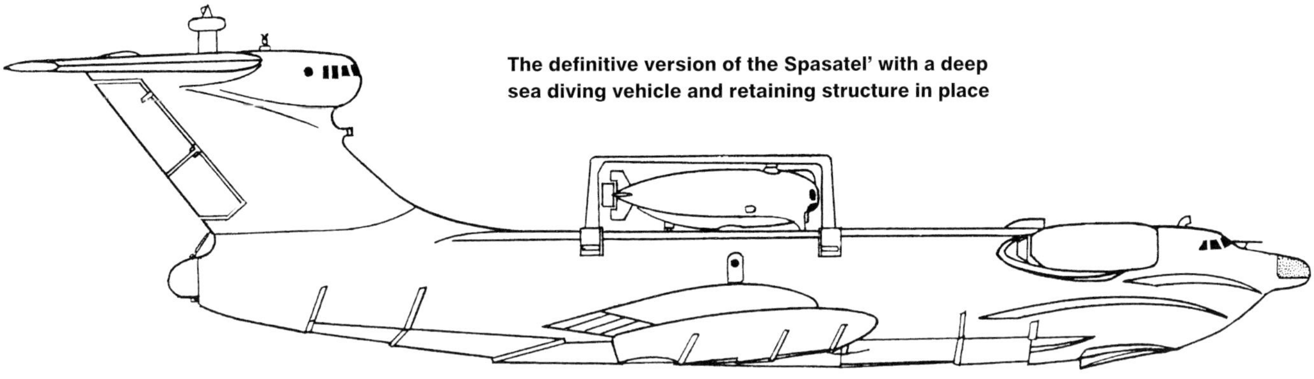

The definitive version of the Spasatel' with a deep sea diving vehicle and retaining structure in place

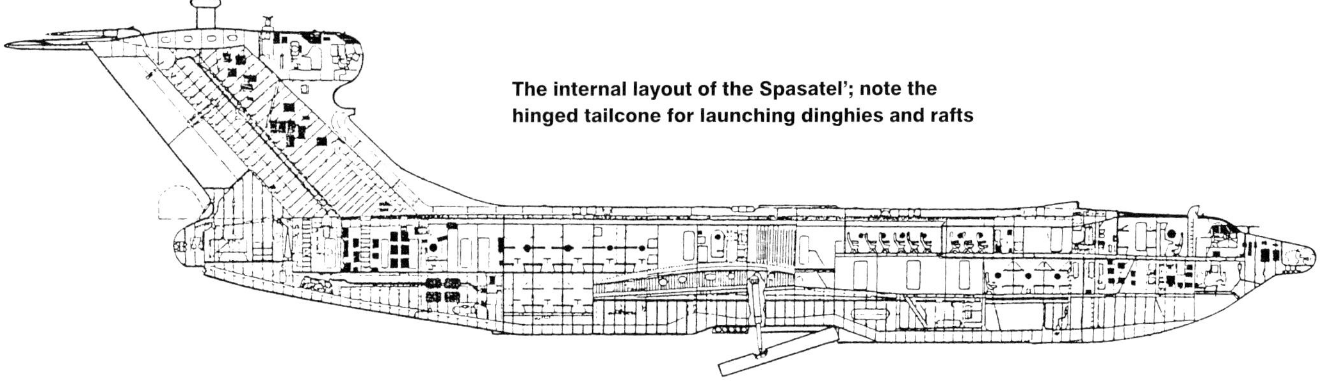

The internal layout of the Spasatel'; note the hinged tailcone for launching dinghies and rafts

approaching its completion – under the influence of a number of tragic accidents, such as the demise of the nuclear missile submarines SNS *Komsomolets* (K-178) and RNS *Kursk* (K-141) and of the car ferry M/V *Estonia* a decision was taken to speed up the construction of this vehicle capable of providing urgent relief in the event of a marine disaster. According to reports, the testing of the Spasatel' was expected to begin at Lake Ladoga as early as 2002, given a favourable course of events.

Unfortunately, these hopes proved ill-founded. To this day the Spasatel' has not been completed and its prospects are bleak.

Until recently, the Spasatel' programme had been 'kept afloat' by the holding company High-Speed Ships which had the Central Hydrofoil Design Bureau as one of its subsidiaries.

Project 902D troop-carrier ekranoplan

Some sources claim that the Project 903 Loon' missile-carrying WIG craft was preceded by a project of a troop-carrier *ekranoplan* designated Project 902 (902D). It is credited with a capacity for carrying 900 troops. This project, the existence of which remains unconfirmed, was allegedly reworked into the project of the missile-carrying Loon', initially designated Project 902R.

Further designs in the SM series

SM-9 Ootka

This was an experimental WIG vehicle featuring a canard (tail-first) layout with the horizontal tail mounted on the front part of the hull, hence the name ***Oot**ka* (Duck, or Canard). Other noteworthy features of the SM-9 were the nose-mounted tractor propeller and the so-called composite layout wings combining a low-aspect-ratio centre section with high-aspect-ratio outer wing panels. Rostislav Alekseyev undertook the design of this craft for the purpose of studying the peculiarities of behaviour of vehicles with this wing layout during flight in ground effect. Furthermore, the nose-mounted propeller served the purpose of studying a novel feature – the use of propellers as a means of blowing in the power-augmented take-off mode (instead of using jet efflux). Finally, this vehicle was intended for studying the use of an inflatable cushioning device in the landing mode.

This three-seat vehicle had a fuselage placed on top of the short-span, wide-chord wing flanked by pylons which rested upon three inflatable multi-section pontoons (two just inboard of the tips and one on the centreline). The fuselage nose housed a 130-hp piston engine which drove a tractor propeller mounted at the end of the elongated nose section. The forward fuselage also carried a steerable foreplane. Underneath the fuselage there was a pylon to which a circular-section inflatable balloon was attached. Attached to the main wing in its rear part were outer wing panels which had moderate dihedral, allowing them to remain within the ground effect zone.

The SM-9 was the first Soviet *ekranoplan* to use a propeller for the blowing-assisted take-off. The use of blowing in the cruise mode made it possible to reduce by half the speed of the craft above the supporting surface as compared with the high-speed *ekranoplans*. Instead of the 200-500-km/h

Above: Poachers beware! ...or what? The SM-9 experimental WIG vehicle bore *Rybnadzor* (Fisheries Control Agency) titles. Here it is shown in late configuration with gull wings and canted wingtips. Only the pilot's cockpit is visible here, the other two seats being closed by a fairing.

This view illustrates the gull wings, the vertical tails and auxiliary engine/propeller packs (used for enhancing directional control) at the wing crank, the engine cooling intake and the movable vanes aft of the main propeller shroud. The outer floats are located inboard of the wing centre section tips, and a third float is barely discernible on the centreline.

(124-311-mph) range of speeds the vehicle could be operated in the speed range between 100 and 250 km/h (62-155 mph). The landing speeds were proportionately reduced by half, too. This considerably reduced the loads and stresses affecting the vehicle. The use of the inflatable cushioning device also helped reduce the stresses and enhanced the vehicle's amphibious qualities.

Rostislav Alekseyev started the testing of the SM-9 in the winter of 1977-78. The first flight, with Alekseyev at the controls, took place on 9th December. The testing revealed that the propeller-effected blowing was much more efficient that the blowing with the use of turbojet efflux. The SM-9 was thoroughly tested both in winter and summer conditions. The tests showed that the layout used in this design made the flight in the WIG mode more secure and considerably reduced the stresses. However, it also became apparent that the vehicle had insufficient longitudinal stability and directional controllability. To remedy this, Alekseyev introduced some modifications. In 1978 the span of the main wing was increased, the outer wing panels were raised to a greater height over the supporting surface (this was done by using a gull-wing configuration). To increase directional controllability, special control devices were installed on the outer wing panels. These were 20-hp piston engines fitted with tractor propellers creating differential thrust.

An available photo of the SM-9 shows the vehicle in this modified configuration. It features an open pilot's cockpit (two more cockpits located further aft are hidden by a fairing) and a shrouded tractor propeller with airflow control vanes at the tip of the elongated fuselage nose. The foreplanes are not readily discernible, but must be there. The fuselage rests on a low aspect ratio wing of rectangular planform, flanked by floats, with a third float on the centreline. The main wing is supplemented by narrow-chord outer panels attached at the aft ends of the floats. The outer wing panels have a marked gull wing configuration and are provided with endplates resembling turned-down tips. Placed atop the outer wing panels at the kinks are two fins with rudders. Also discernible are the auxiliary engines with small propellers. The vehicle carries '*Rybnad**zor***' (Fisheries control) titles. According to the IMO classification, the SM-9 is a Type B vehicle capable of operating out of surface effect for brief periods for the purpose of avoiding obstacles.

The main specifications of the modified SM-9 are as follows: crew, 1-3; length, 11.14 m (36 ft 7 in); span, 9.85 m (32 ft 4 in); height, 2.57 m (8 ft 5 in); all-up weight, 1,750 kg (3,860 lb); cruising speed, 120 km/h (75 mph). In its initial version the SM-9 had a length of 11.69 m (38 ft 4¼ in) and a span of 12.61 m (41 ft 4½ in).

A WIG vehicle based on the SM-9 (project)

Numerous project 'variations on the SM-9 theme' were studied by Alekseyev. One of them, being essentially similar to the initial configuration of the SM-9, differed in having the open forward cockpit and rear fairing replaced by an common canopy enclosing the three seats located one after another. Incidentally, it was also intended for the fisheries control agency, as witnessed by the inscription on the hull in the artist's impression. This machine featured an unshrouded tractor propeller mounted in the similarly elongated fuselage nose. The nose boom carried fairly large-span foreplanes. The wing outer panels featured marked dihedral and sweepback, with no endplates. The fins were placed on top of the outer wing panels at mid-span.

This picture gives some idea of how many project configurations were explored at the CHDB. The models are obviously not to the same scale.

An artist's impression of a vehicle similar to the SM-9 and again wearing Rybnadzor titles.

SM-11

Little is known about this machine, designed and built in 1985. According to some sources this was a Type B WIG vehicle, in the IMO classification, capable of leaving the surface effect zone for brief periods. Some sources claim that in its layout this was a 'flying wing' with compound sweepback on the leading edges. However, a scientific publication (Proceedings of the First International Conference on *Ekranoplans*, St. Petersburg, 1993) carried an artist's impression of a vehicle captioned as *'an SK WIG craft with a small-size horizontal tail'* (SK may stand for *sostav**noy**e kry**lo*** – composite layout wing). This small single-seat vehicle had large-span wings comprising a wide-chord centre section and swept-back outer panels which were attached to the floats flanking the wing centre section. The outer wing panels had a gull-wing configuration and were fitted with endplates. The vehicle had a T-tail with a small-span horizontal tail. A cruise engine of unknown type, driving a tractor propeller, was mounted at the junction of the fin and the stabilisers. It was supplemented by two propellers located on the sides of the forward fuselage; these were apparently driven through extension shafts by a single engine housed in the fuselage. There are reasons to believe that this drawing depicted the SM-11. The wing layout of this machine was similar to that of the LK project (LK presumably means *le**ta**yushcheye kry**lo***, flying wing) which was also illustrated in the publication. In this project Alekseyev took the 'flying wing' layout with a wing with an aspect ratio that was rather high for a WIG vehicle (of the order of 5). By selecting an optimum airfoil section and making use of automatic oscillation damping and stabilisation systems he tried to solve the problems of stability of flight in ground effect for this new layout. However, a positive solution for 'flying-wing' WIG vehicles was not reached at that time.

The SM-11 was tested in late 1980s, shortly before the break-up of the Soviet Union. It was allegedly destroyed after the completion of testing because its creators *'did not wish it to fall into alien hands'*, whatever this may mean.

Here are some characteristics: crew, 1; length, 6.96 m (22 ft 10 in); span, 9.94 m (32 ft 7 in); all-up weight, 600 kg (1,320 lb); cruising speed, 110 km/h (68 mph).

WIG Vehicles for Military Purposes – Projects that Failed to Materialise

Project 1133 ASW WIG vehicle

Design work on this machine weighing 450 t (990,000 lb) started in 1962, but the design did not reach the hardware stage. No other information is available, apart from a drawing published in 2006 and presented here. The picture shows a machine described as 'a predecessor of the KM'; it is very similar in layout and dimensions to the KM and differs primarily in the arrangement of the cruise engines. Instead of two turbojets flanking the fin, it comprises four turboprops (presumably NK-12Ms) placed on the leading edge of the stabiliser. The project remained on the drawing board, but its basic elements were incorporated in the KM design.

T-1 troop transport WIG vehicle

In 1964 Alekseyev came to the conclusion that ekranoplans could be used by Airborne Troops as a means of delivery of troops and military hardware to sites where they were to be put into action. A WIG vehicle was capable of delivering a landing party to a strip on the coast or in the enemy's rear – something that could not be performed by transport aircraft. In co-operation with representatives of the Airborne Troops the Design Bureau evolved technical requirements for a military transport WIG vehicle which were agreed with the appropriate scientific institutions of the Ministry of Aircraft Industry and of the Air Force and finally approved by the Air Force on 31st July 1964. In October 1964 the Communist Party Central Committee and the Council of Ministers adopted a resolution calling for the development of a preliminary project of a military transport WIG vehicle, which was to be effected in 1965. The project received the designation T-1, with V. V. Sokolov as the project designer. On 28th December 1965 the advanced development project of the T-1 was sent for review to the customer (the Soviet Air Force), to the Ministry of Shipbuilding and to the research institutions of this ministry and of the Navy.

Rostislav Alekseyev officially presented this project in TsAGI on 12th February 1966. The project was praised by specialists, but there was also some criticism. Later in the same month the project passed a critical review at a high-level meeting in the Chkalovsk branch of the CHDB with the participation of the Minister of Defence, Commander of the Airborne Troops, Commander-in-Chief of the Navy, the Minister of Shipbuilding and other high-ranking officials. The machine presented to the in the shape of general arrangement drawings was a flying vehicle with low-set wings, measuring 70 m (229 ft 8 in) in length and 38 m (124 ft 8 in) in wing span. Its empty weight was 105 tonnes (231,525 lb), the normal payload was 20 tonnes (44,100 lb), the cargo-carrying capacity in overload configuration being 40 tonnes (88,160 lb). This enabled the T-1 to carry a medium tank and an infantry platoon with all its weapons and equipment or 150 troops over a distance of 4,000 km (2,486 miles) in the WIG

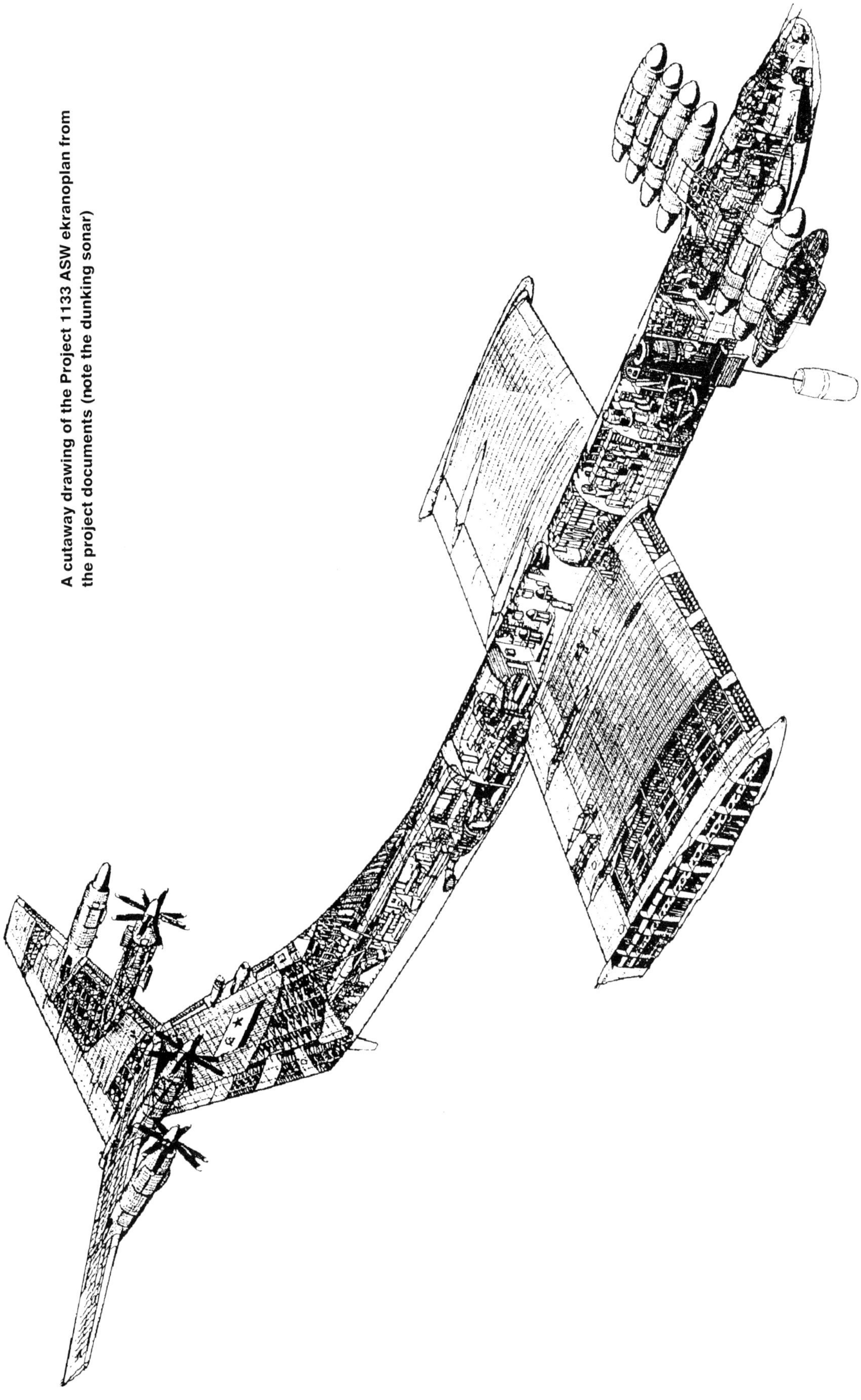

A cutaway drawing of the Project 1133 ASW ekranoplan from the project documents (note the dunking sonar)

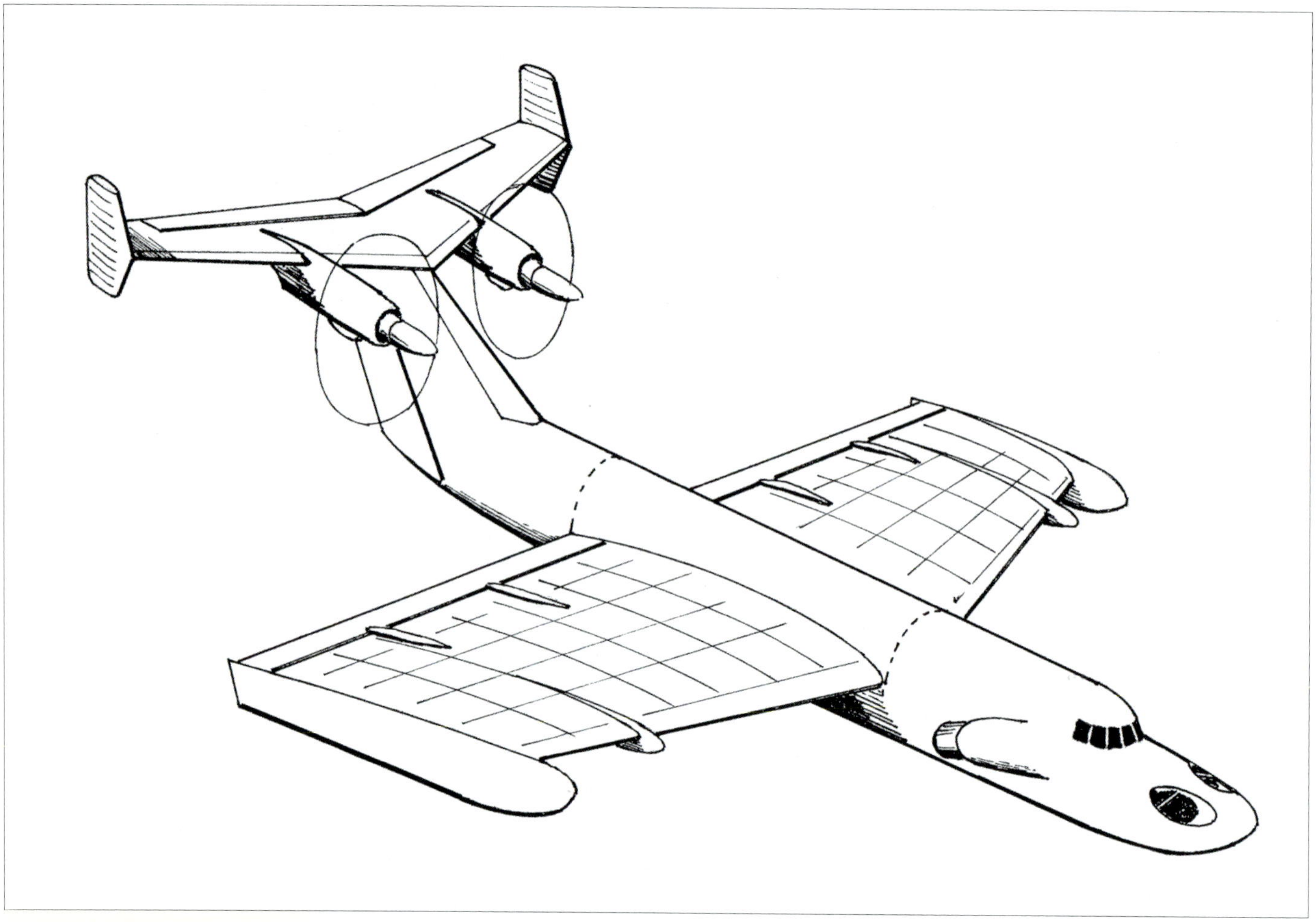

An artist' impression of the T-1 transport/assault WIG vehicle. The drawing does not reveal the location of the loading door, though the same solution as on the Orlyonok was probably envisaged.

mode, or over a distance of 2,000 km (1,243 miles) at an altitude of 4,000 m (13,120 ft). Design performance of the T-1 included a service ceiling of 7,500 m (24,600 ft) which places it into the C category according to the modern IMO classification.)

A published drawing of the T-1 shows a machine featuring an aircraft layout. The wings fitted with endplate floats had a fairly high (for a WIG vehicle) aspect ratio; the craft had a T-tail. The powerplant comprised two booster engines in the forward fuselage arranged in the same fashion as those of Orlyonok, and two cruise turboprop engines. The latter were located in an unorthodox manner – they were mounted at mid-span on the leading edges of the swept stabilisers which was fitted with small endplates.

In May 1966 the Air Force formulated their conclusion on the T-1 project. It took into account the critical remarks made by TsAGI and stated that the project on the whole met the requirements, but a number of drawbacks had to be eliminated in accordance with an annexed list. But the Design Bureau did not get a chance to improve the project. In June 1966 the Ministry of Shipbuilding shut down the funding for the T-1 project on the pretext that it 'had not been accepted by the customer'.

Patrol WIG vehicle

This machine of moderate size featured an aircraft layout and was powered by two turbojets mounted in the forward fuselage. They performed the dual role of booster engines during take-off and cruise engines in forward flight.

Project 905 troop-carrier *ekranoplan*

The Russian reference book Russia's Armament (Vol. III, the Navy, 1996-97), says the Russian state armament programme envisaged at one time the development of strike, ASW and troop-carrier WIG vehicles (Projects 903, 1133 and 905 respectively). Of these, only the Project 903 (Loon') was built. No additional information on the Project 905 is available.

Project 09031

This 'project of a patrol ekranoplan ship' is mentioned in an internet source without any further particulars. The 903 digits in the number may point to a 'family relationship' with the Loon' (project 903).

Ballistic missile transporter WIG vehicle

A project bearing this description (designation not cited) was tailored specially for the transportation of ballistic missiles in an open cargo hold atop the fuselage. The vehicle, comparable in size to an IL-76 transport, basically shared the traditional layout of the CHDB designs in having low-set wings with endplate pontoons (floats) and the use of power-augmented take-off. Its powerplant comprised two turboprop engines mounted on horizontal pylons on each side of the forward fuselage shaped like a boat hull. The engines could be swivelled to direct the air stream under the wings during take-off and were then placed in a horizontal position for cruise flight. The tail unit comprised two swept splayed fins and rudders topped by the horizontal tail.

The open cargo hold occupied the whole length of the top fuselage behind the forward-located flight deck, so that the missile could be loaded and unloaded from the rear between the vertical tails. It appears that the vehicle was expected to be suitable for operation also from flat stretches of land.

Joint Project of the Central Hydrofoil Design Bureau and the Aerocon Company (USA)

In early 1992 negotiations took place between the Alekseyev Central Design Bureau of Hydrofoils and the Aerocon company of the USA on joint development of a new WIG vehicle. The Aerocon company had been set up at the initiative of DARPA (Defense Advanced Research Project Agency) – an agency working for the US military. Aerocon was tasked with establishing co-operation with the Russian organisation holding leading positions in WIG vehicle construction, with the intention of borrowing advanced Russian technology. Aerocon had received from DARPA a contract worth US$ 546,000 for investigating the concept of a WIG vehicle.

At that time the experts of the US Central Command (CENTCOM) seriously considered the possibility of employing a WIG vehicle in combat. To bring down the cost of creating the WIG machines, US military specialists made a provision for the development of a civil version.

The project envisaged the construction of a giant machine possessing an all-up weight of 5,000 t (11,000,000 lb) and a cargo-carrying capacity of 1,500 t (3,310,000 lb), which would be able to transport 3,000 passengers or 2,000 troops with full military equipment and materiel. The vehicle's dimensions included a span of 170 m (557 ft). a length of 100 m (328 ft) and a height of 35 m (115 ft). The powerplant comprising 20 turbojets with a static thrust of 395 kN each was expected to give the machine a cruising speed of 800 km/h (497 mph) and a range of 16,000 km (9,900 miles) in cruise flight at a height of 2-10 metres (6-33 ft) above the water surface.

This cooperation did not progress far and was terminated without resulting in the emergence of a detailed project.

An artist's impression of a projected fast patrol craft using WIG technology – one of several projects developed by the Central Hydrofoil Design Bureau which never reached the hardware stage.

Chaika-2 (Seagull II), four-engined version

This is a project of a sea-going multipurpose WIG vehicle. Its baseline model was to be developed into a family of shore- or water-based WIG vehicles intended for various duties. Their possible missions include border control, patrolling the 200-mile maritime economic zone, SAR work, passenger and cargo transportation, ecological and legal maritime monitoring.

The machine shares the 'aircraft' layout characteristic of the progeny of the Alekseyev Design Bureau, a novel feature being the composite layout wings with swept outer wing panels of narrower chord outboard of the stabilising floats. The powerplant comprises two 4,500-kgp (9,900-lbst) Gavrilov (Tumanskiy) R-195 booster turbojets in the nose and two 2,500-ehp Klimov (Izotov) TV7-117S turboprop engines driving SV-34 six-blade propellers for cruise. The booster engines used for blowing under the wings during take-off are arranged in a fashion similar to that of the Orlyonok. The cruise engines feature an unusual arrangement: instead of being placed on the fin, they are mounted on small foreplanes with flaps mounted on top of the forward fuselage. Specifications include an all-up weight of 40 to 50 tonnes (88,200-110,250 lb), a payload of 4 tonnes (8,800 lb), a seating capacity of 100 passengers, a speed of 350 km/h (218 mph) and a range of 3,500 km (2,175 miles).

Chaika-2 (Seagull II), twin-engined version

This project bearing the same designation as the preceding one was obviously developed to the same specification, but merits being treated as a separate project due to substantial differences. It shares with the preceding Chaika-2 a basically similar hull (fuselage) and tail unit, but features a totally different powerplant and an unusual wing layout. Instead of a combination of two turbojets and two turboprops, it is powered solely by two turbofans mounted on the forward fuselage sides. They act both as cruise engines and as booster engines during take off; for the latter purpose the engines are fitted with deflector vanes above the nozzles to direct the jet efflux under the wings, thus creating a static air cushion. The nose of the hull, being free from the buried booster engines, is suitably redesigned.

As for the wings, the 'normal' low-set wings similar to those of the four-engined Chaika-2 are supplemented by a pair of wings mounted high on the fuselage above the trailing edge of the main wings. The wingtips of the two sets of wings are joined by vertical endplates with auxiliary floats, creating a biplane wing box with backward stagger. This project exists in several versions intended for both military and civil duties. A model representing a military version of the twin-engined Chaika-2 shows it to be fitted with a peculiar superstructure above the fin in a fashion similar to the Loon' missile-carrying *ekranoplan*. This superstructure is absent in a drawing which apparently shows a civil version. This project apparently failed to reach the hardware stage.

In 1996 mention was made in the Russian press of a baseline project of a sea-going WIG vehicle weighing some 50 t (110,250 lb) which was being developed in the Central Hydrofoil Design Bureau with a view to subsequent construction on its basis

An artist's impression of a twin-turboprop ballistic missile transporter *ekranoplan* for which no designation is known.

of various versions intended both for state agencies and for commercial operation (this may well be a reference to the Chaika-2 design).

Blue Shark

This was a project of an ekranoplan intended for maritime patrol duties related to the 200-mile economic exclusion zone. An available three-view drawing shows this craft to resemble a scaled-down Orlyonok. Like its bigger brother, it has one cruise turboprop engine mounted at the junction of the fin and the high-set horizontal tail. The drawing gives no definite clue as to whether nose-mounted buried booster engines are present (no nozzles are shown, albeit there is something resembling air intakes). The low-set wings, basically similar in proportions to those of the Orlyonok, are supplemented by outer wing panels of higher aspect ratio having a marked sweepback and noticeable dihedral.

The military role of the craft is clearly evidenced by six weapons pylons attached to a kind of a small wing mounted atop the fuselage amidships. However, there was a possibility of commercial applications, too. In 1997 this project was mentioned in a Russian publication as *'a WIG boat intended for export'*.

Projects for Passenger and Transport WIG Vehicles

In addition to passenger versions of the baseline Orlyonok design described above the Central Hydrofoil Design Bureau prepared several more projects of sea-going passenger *ekranoplans*. Details follow of some of these projects.

Chaika (Seagull)

This project of a river-going passenger *ekranoplan* is described as 'the first passenger WIG vehicle design' of the Alekseyev Design Bureau. It was developed in 1970 (incidentally, with the participation of Rostislav Alekseyev's daughter Tatyana, a marine engineer) and was intended to carry 70 passengers at a speed of 250-300 km/h (155-186 mph) over a distance of more than 700 km (435 miles).

The machine is generally similar in its layout to the SM-6 and the Orlyonok with its low-set wings and a T-tail. A notable difference is the absence of a cruise engine on top of the fin. It appears that two engines buried in Chaika's forward fuselage are intended to serve both as booster engines at take-off and as cruise engines, their nozzles rotating to suit the flight mode.

Construction of the prototype started in 1974, but the machine was never completed. The reason was simple: everything pertaining to the design of *ekranoplans* fell into the 'Top Secret' category, which gave those responsible for counter-intelligence a pretext for objecting to the transfer of this technology to the civilian sector. Looking back at this project nowadays, some experts express the opinion that it was unlikely to gain acceptance anyway because its safety level was insufficient and the speed of 250 km/h was clearly too high for the river traffic.

MPE

The Central Hydrofoil Design Bureau worked on a number of projects bearing a common designation MPE (*mor**skoy** passa**zheer**skiy ekrano**plahn*** – sea-going passenger *ekranoplan*). They include a pro-

An artist's impression of the four-engined Chaika-2 in military form with a gun barbette at the base of the fin.

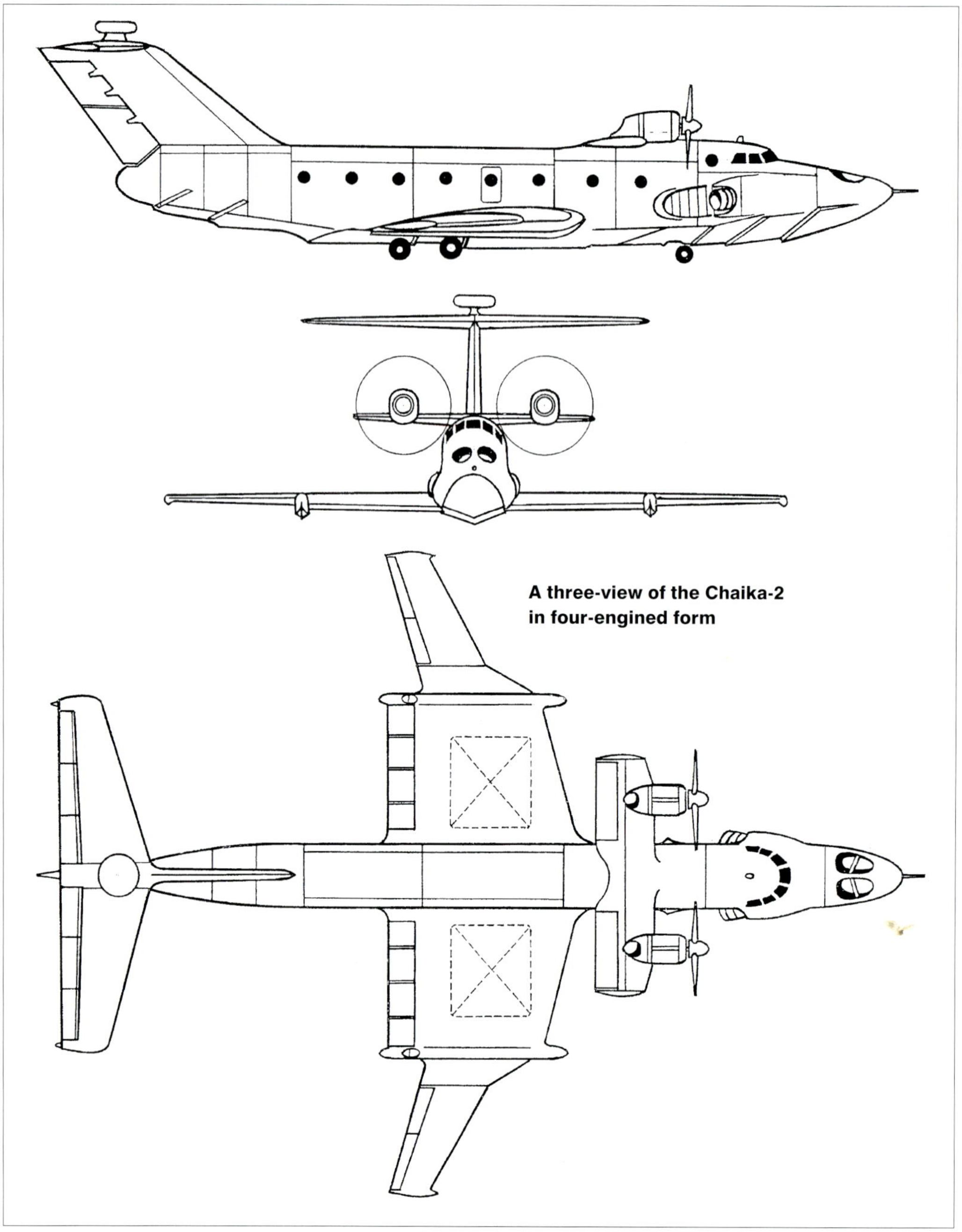

A three-view of the Chaika-2 in four-engined form

ject of a machine designed to carry 250 passengers and adaptable to various uses; also envisaged was the development of a 450-passenger machine possessing a speed of 550 km/h (342 mph), a range of 6,000 km and a capacity for operating at a sea state with waves 3 m (10 ft) high.

It appears that some of these projects were 'inherited' by a new design bureau, known initially as 'Technology and Transport' which broke away from the 'mother' organisation in 1993. Projects developed now under the name of this new organisation include MPE-100, MPE-200, MPE-300, MPE-400 etc. (see Chapter 6), a section dealing with this company under its new name 'Amphibious Technologies and Transport').

WIG craft for use in northern areas

'A WIG craft intended to be operated in the conditions of the North' is the description given to a project (no designation cited) which makes use of a layout reminiscent of Roberto Bartini's designs. This *ekranoplan*, presumably intended for cargo transportation, has a very thick wide-chord wing centre section of rectangular planform which doubles as the fuselage with a large internal volume. It is flanked by sidewalls (skegs) which turn the vehicle into a catamaran and form a space in which the ram air creates a dynamic air cushion. Mounted on the aft ends of the sidewalls are two large swept fin-and-rudder assemblies topped by a horizontal tail, the span of which exceeds the distance between the fins. Attached to the sides of the wing centre section (fuselage) are unswept outer wing panels of a fairly high aspect ratio and normal (aircraft-type) relative thickness. The flight deck is located close to the leading edge of the wing centre section. The powerplant comprises two high-bypass turbofan engines mounted on pylons above the root sections of the outer wing panels. Two flush air intakes in the front upper part of the wing centre section suggest that there may be a provision for auxiliary engines creating a static air cushion during take-off. The vehicle is obviously intended for operation both above the sea surface and above ice and snow-covered stretches of land.

Type A WIG Vehicles (*Ekranoplan* Boats, DAC Boats) designed by the CHDB

In the late 1970s Rostislav Alekseyev realised that for a number of reasons it was not possible to launch series production of full-fledged ekranoplans (Type B and C craft, in modern classification) for commercial service. Instead, he suggested to his associates that they take up design work on simpler craft – dynamic air cushion (DAC) ships which, as distinct from the 'true' WIG vehicles, are intended for motion only in the horizontal plane, their vertical motion being reduced to the barest minimum (in modern classification they are designated Type A WIG vehicles). The work on this class

A towing basin model showing the twin-engined biplane version of the Chaika-2 project. Note the two pairs of stabilising floats (at mid-span and at the wingtips). The nose shape is non-representative, as a blower is incorporated to feed air to the engine emulators. The Orlyonok-like model in the background probably represents one of the vehicles in the MPE series; note the winglets and the unswept horizontal tail.

A display model of the twin-turbofan biplane version of the Chaika-2. Note the cannon barbette on top of the fin. Oddly, the model is painted in an Air Force style camouflage instead of blue or grey colours suitable for overwater operations.

A provisional three-view drawing of the twin-turbofan version of the Chaika-2.

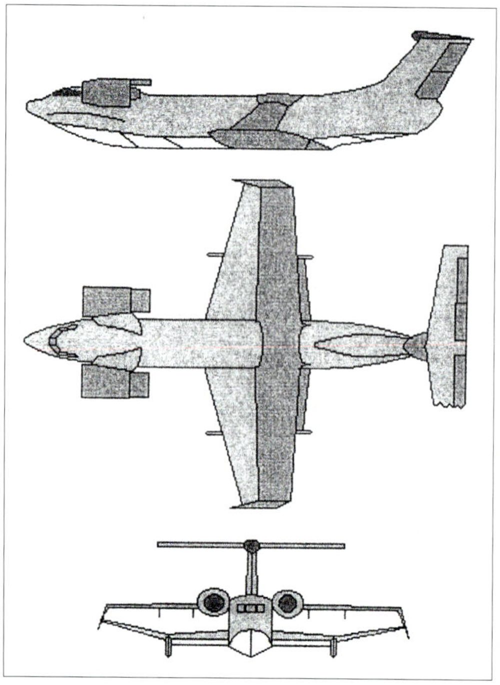

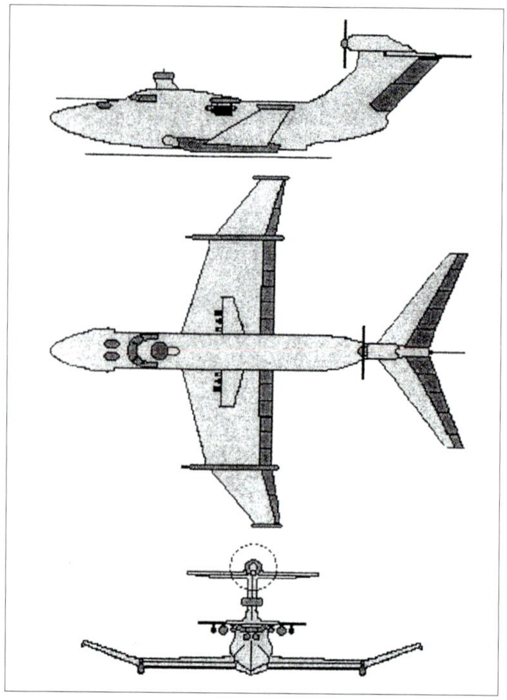

Far right: A provisional three-view drawing of the Blue Shark.

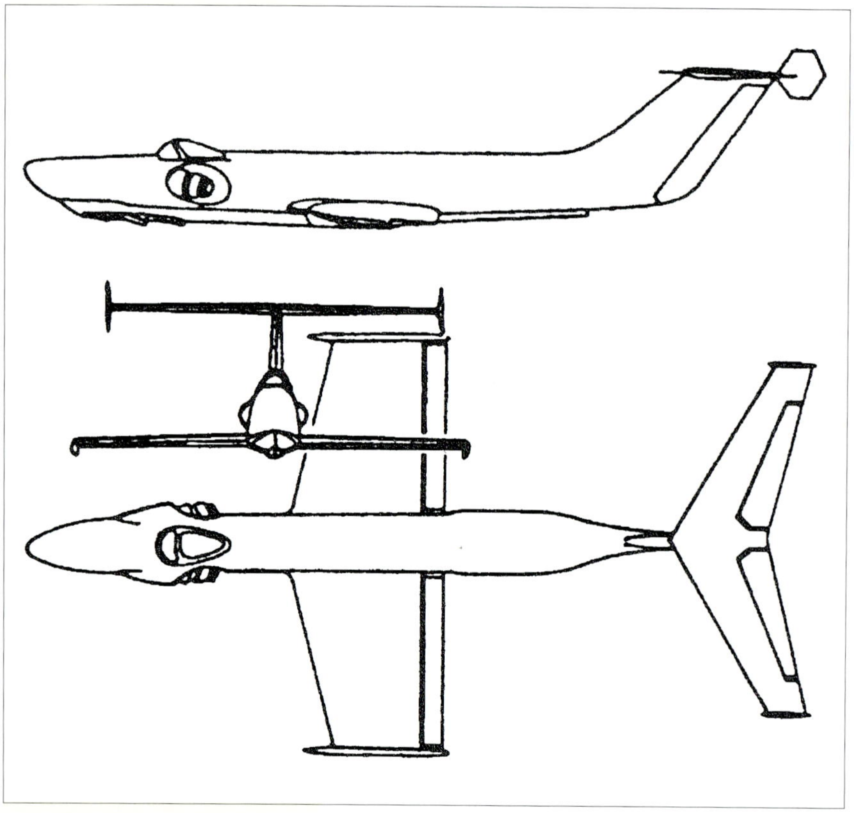

A very early preliminary three-view drawing of the Chaika passenger WIG vehicle. The fuselage ahead of the wings bears a strong similarity to the SM-6.

of WIG craft resulted in several projects, such as the Volga-2, Meteor-2, Kometa-2 and Vikhr'-2. The designations call for some explanation. The digit 2 signifies the second use of a designation that was previously borne by Alekseyev's passenger hydrofoil boats built in series; he obviously wished to emphasise continuity between the two classes of his creations.

LAVP-02

To study some basic questions pertaining to vehicles of this type, Alexeyev designed a small two-seat craft which was in fact a platform flanked by inflatable pontoons. It was designated LAVP-02 (***lyoh**kiy appa**raht** na voz**doosh**noy po**doosh**ke* – light air cushion vehicle). The use of inflatable pontoons was a novel design feature which had some advantages as compared to rigid skegs or the flexible 'skirt' employed by ACVs.

The machine was propelled by a tractor airscrew mounted ahead of the driver's seat. The air stream created by the propeller was partly directed under the platform to form the air cushion. The vehicle with an all-up weight of 360 kg (790 lb) had a length of 5.5 m (18 ft $0\frac{35}{64}$ in) and was powered by a 30-hp RMZ-640 engine from a snowmobile which permitted it to attain a speed of 65 km/h (40 mph) and to negotiate a slope with a gradient of 15° when beaching. There were a further three similar vehicles in the LAVP series, differing in detail.

Design specifications of the Blue Shark (civil version)

Take-off weight	22.5 tonnes (49,600 lb)
Length	27.6 m (90 ft $6\frac{39}{64}$ in)
Wing span	21.4 m (70 ft $2\frac{33}{64}$ in)
Speed	300-400 km/h (186-248 mph)
Range	2,000 km (1,242 mils)
Crew	2
Passenger capacity	about 30
Seaworthiness	sea state 3

Volzhanochka

One more small research vehicle was used in the experiments. Bearing the name *Volzhanochka* ('little girl from the Volga region'), this was also a two-seat vehicle configured as a platform mounted on two inflatable pontoons. A piston engine placed amidships drove a tractor propeller which was placed on an outrigger ahead of the platform, serving the double purpose of forward propulsion and creating a dynamic air cushion. Some sources referred to this little craft as the LAVP-E.

Volzhanka-1

Yet another machine intended purely for research purposes was required in connection with the design of WIG vehicles certified as ships (Type A). To study the basic layout of such a vehicle, a machine dubbed Volzhanka-1 (*volzhanka* means girl or woman from the Volga region) was built. Photos show this single seat vehicle to have rectangular wings of very low aspect ratio fitted with inflatable floats at the tips. Placed above the wings was the open cockpit protected by a nose fairing and a windshield. It was flanked by two engines buried in the wings and transmitting their torque through extension shafts to tractor airscrews placed ahead of and above the wing leading edge. The propellers had annular shrouds with movable vanes directing the air stream under the wings during take-off. The twin fins were topped by a horizontal tail.

A display model of the Chaika as a passenger *ekranoplan*. Here the horizontal tail lacks endplates. The painting on the wall depicts a three-turboprop river-going passenger *ekranoplan* (see page 98).

In the course of the tests the Volzhanka-1 was modified. The fins were slightly altered and a third fin was added between them. It was placed in the slipstream of a propeller driven by a small engine. The vehicle made a series of successful flights.

Volzhanka-2

This was yet another research vehicle. Judging by the available photo, it was a single-seat machine featuring an unusual location of the cockpit in the

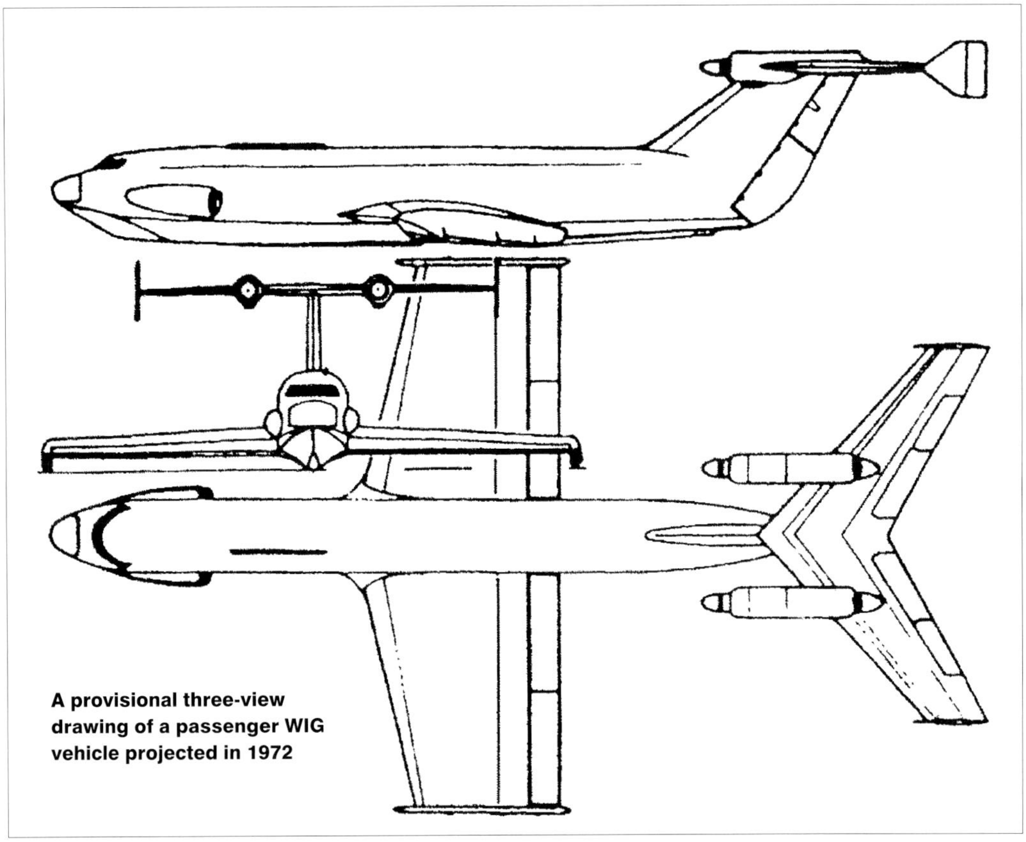

A provisional three-view drawing of a passenger WIG vehicle projected in 1972

An artist's impression of a large ocean-going passenger craft with a double-deck hull similar to the Loon' in general arrangement – the WIG equivalent of the Boeing 747.

fin leading edge. Two tractor propellers are discernible in the front part of the fuselage ahead of the low-aspect-ratio wings. The fin-and-rudder assembly is topped by the horizontal tail.

SM-10 (forerunner of the Volga-2)

The concept of the Volzhanka-2 was developed into a bigger WIG craft designated SM-10, intended for research in connection with plans for the construction of some specialised ekranoplans. Upon completion of these research programmes it was modified into passenger vehicle accommodating eight passengers and a driver. Completed in 1985, it became an analogue of the future production model – the Volga-2. Its specifications include: length, 11,43 m (37 ft 6 in); wing span, 7.63 m (25 ft); height, 3.32 m (10 ft 11 in); all-up weight, 2,200 kg (4,850 lb); cruising speed, 120 km/h (75 mph); range, 300 km (186 miles).

Volga-2 *ekranoplan* boat

This eight-passenger dynamic air cushion amphibious boat designed in the Central Hydrofoil Design Bureau and built at the Volga Shipyard in Nizhniy Novgorod in 1986 featured only minor differences from the SM-10. The vehicle is powered by two engines placed on the wings on both sides of the hull. These are series-produced 140 hp VAZ-413 Wankel-type gasoline engines with a mixed air/water cooling system. They transmit their power through extension shafts to four-blade shrouded propellers. The shrouds are fitted at their rear plane with remote-controlled horizontal deflector vanes which direct the airflow under the wings in the take-off mode.

The vehicle features rectangular wings of low aspect ratio (1.0) fitted with endplates and inflatable pontoons at the tips; the pontoons are provided with an inflation system and a pressure control device. Thanks to these pontoons the vehicle can be operated all year round: in the summer it operates from water and in the winter from splintered ice and sludge. The vehicle is capable of coming out from the water surface on to a shore with a gradient of slope up to 7°.

A T-tail serves for control and stabilisation of the vehicle. As distinct from the prototypes, the strut-braced stabilisers have small swept extra fins installed at approximately three quarters of the span on the production model. The wings are provided with flaps and spoilers.

The streamlined hull houses a cabin with seats for eight passengers and a driver; the seats are of aircraft type.

The Volga-2 has the same dimensions as the SM-10 (see above). Specifications initially quoted for the Volga-2 included an all-up weight of 2,500 kg (5,500 lb), a speed of 120 km/h (75 mph) and a range of 500 km (310 miles). These figures underwent some revision in the course of production.

The production model of the Volga-2 is powered by two standard 131-hp ZMZ-406 four-cylinder 2.3-litre automobile engines manufactured by the Zavolzhskiy Engine Plant (ZMZ). The ZMZ-V.4602.10 is also mentioned as the engine type used on the Volga-2.

The Volga-2 entered production at the 'Sokol' aircraft factory in Nizhniy Novgorod to meet an order from RAO Gazprom (a gas industry concern in Russia). By March 2003 seven machines had been delivered. Two machines were sold to China, another two to Kyrgyzstan where they were operated on Lake Issyk-Kul' and the Syr-Dar'ya River. One example was sold to Montenegro. At one time it was reported that the sales of the Volga-2 had totalled eight machines. In 2006 there were reports about an expected delivery of two Volga-2 craft to the Russian shipping company Inmortrans Ltd; that would add up to a total of ten machines sold. From 1996 onwards the Central Hydrofoil Design Bureau was engaged in designing various versions of the Volga-2, including sea-going and tropicalised variants. One of them is described below.

Volga-2MT

Encouraged by the sale of two Volga-2 craft to China and the prospect of further sales to that part of the world, the CHDB undertook development of the Volga-2MT version tailored for operation in tropical climates (hence the MT for *modifi**tsee**rovannyy, tro**pich**eskiy*). Work on this version was in progress in 2003. No particulars concerning the differences from the baseline version are available, except for the more powerful engines.

Operational service of the Volga-2 proceeded in a generally satisfactory way from the technical point of view, but was marred by at least one accident which took place in 2003. On 19th July that year a Volga-2 WIG vehicle collided with a *Vos**khod*** (Sunrise) hydrofoil boat near the river terminal of Nizhniy Novgorod and capsized as a result. Seven of the passengers escaped unscathed, while one passenger and the mechanic (ie, driver) of the craft were taken to a hospital with injuries, the passenger subsequently dying in hospital. The Volga-2 sank, but was recovered soon after the accident.

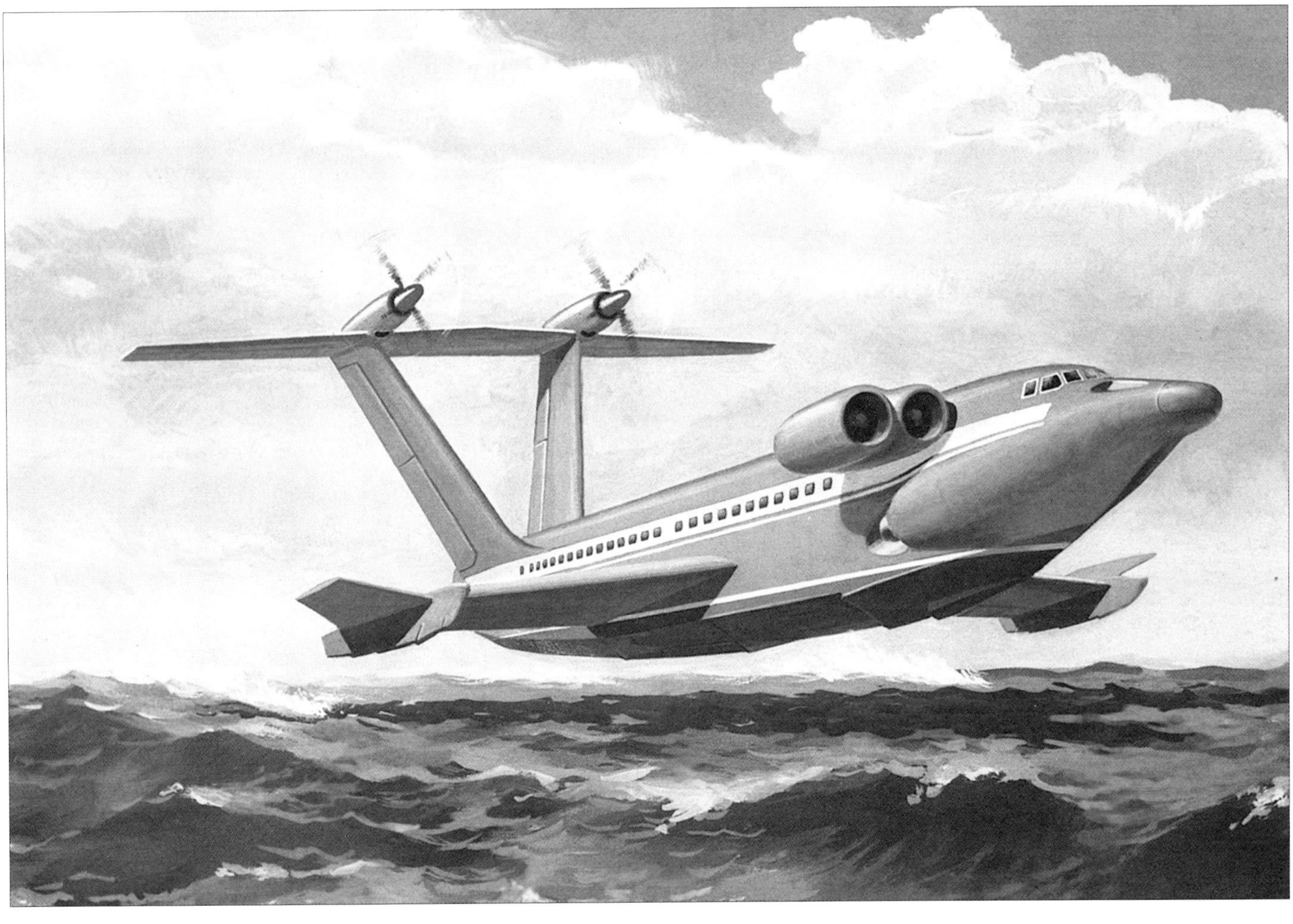

This projected 'WIG airliner' has an unusual arrangement, combining Orlyonok-type buried cruise engines and fin-top cruise turboprops with additional nose-mounted turbofans similar to those of the Loon'.

An artist's impression of a projected WIG vehicle intended for operation in the Arctic. Note the intakes of the booster engines creating an air cushion. As the picture shows, the craft was to be capable of operations out of ground effect.

Unfortunately, for various reasons (not least financial ones) the Sokol plant failed to obtain a sufficient backlog of orders to justify further production, and the manufacture of the Volga-2 appears to have been discontinued, at least for the time being.

SM-13

This experimental WIG vehicle was created for the purpose of studying the basic layout of a bigger design, the *Raketa-2 ekranoplan* boat, for which it served as a kind of subscale demonstrator (quarter-scale model). The SM-13 had rectangular wings of low aspect ratio with endplate floats at the tips. Sitting atop the low-set wings was the hull with a passenger compartment and a T-tail. The powerplant consisted of three piston engines, two of which were placed on both sides of the hull and one was mounted on the fin approximately half-way up. They were fitted with two-blade propellers. The machine successfully passed its test programme.

Raketa-2 (Rocket II)

In 1990, using the Volga-2 layout as a basis, the Central Hydrofoil Design Bureau prepared the project of a bigger DAC ship called Raketa-2. This river-going vehicle was intended for transporting 90 passengers at a cruising speed of 120-130 km/h (75-81 mph) to a distance of up to 800 km (500 miles), the maximum speed being 150-180 km/h (93-112 mph). Its powerplant comprises three Klimov TV7-117 turboprops delivering 2,500 ehp (1,785 kW) each; two of them are mounted on the forward fuselage sides and serve as booster

Two views of the LAVP-02 (alias LAVP-87) DAC vehicle during tests on snow-covered ground.

One more view of the LAVP-02 during trials on the Volga River. This craft was intended to test features developed for commercial DAC vessels.

Here the LAVP-02 is seen skimming the water surface. The exposed engine cylinder and the propeller guard are visible.

engines for take-off, while the third engine (for cruise) is mounted on the leading edge of the fin. Revised performance figures include a maximum speed of 190 km/h (118 mph) and engine power of 3 x 1,840 kW.

It has also been described as a Class B sea-going WIG vehicle in the IMO system, intended for passenger and cargo transportation between sea-side cities and islands. It can perform cruise flight with waves up to 1.3 m (4 ft 3 in) and stay afloat with waves up to 1.5 m (5 ft). The vehicle is capable of negotiating a gently sloping bank with a gradient up to 5° for the purpose of taking on and disgorging passengers or undergoing maintenance, which considerably simplifies its operation. The vehicle is capable of moving above flat stretches of land, ice and snow-covered fields. Its maximum all-up weight is 33 t (72,770 lb).

Due to lack of funding this project remains on the drawing board to this day.

The rather rickety-looking Volzhanka-1 test vehicle. Note the twin engines and propellers driven via extension shafts.

Here the Volzhanka-1, seen about to enter the water of the Volga River, is shown in modified form.

Raketa 2.2 (?)

This designation can be found in some Western publications; it purports to refer to a three-engine 90-passenger version of the vehicle as distinct from an original two-engine 50-passenger version (neither the two-engine version, nor the 'Raketa-2.2' designation are mentioned in available Russian sources which refer to the 90-passenger vehicle simply as 'Raketa-2'.

Meteor-2, Kometa-2

These projects of river-going DAC ships have been only briefly mentioned in Russian sources. According to some Western publications, the Meteor-2 is a vehicle intended to transport 120 passengers at a speed of 170 km/h (106 mph) to a distance of 800 km (500 miles), while the Kometa-2 can carry 150 passengers at a speed of 185 km (115 mph) to the distance of 930 km (578 mph). The Kometa-2 was to be powered by a single (?) 6,500-kgp (14,330-lbst) Lotarev D-36 turbofan.

Vikhr'-2 (Whirlwind II)

This is a project of a large sea-going Type A WIG vehicle, about which little is known, apart from its general appearance (see drawing). According to a Western source, it has a seating capacity for 250 passengers, a speed of 280 km/h (174 mph) and a range of 1,500 km (930 miles). It was to be powered by two Lotarev D-36 turbofans.

The Volzhanka-1 in cruise flight. Note the increased-area fins, the aft-mounted extra engine and the pipes behind the Nos. 1 and 3 propellers – presumably bleeding off part of the prop wash for inflating the tip floats.

Another view of the modified Volzhanka-1; note the small extra fin aft of the centre engine.

UT-1 Trainer and Strizh Family of Light WIG Vehicles

The Central Hydrofoil Design Bureau has developed and, in part, brought to the hardware stage a number of projects of light WIG vehicles intended for various duties which carry the common designation *Strizh* (Swift, the bird) with varying sequence numbers. Their forerunner was the UT-1, a two-seat training ekranoplan designed and built in 1968.

UT-1

The UT-1 (*oo**cheb**no-treni**rov**ochnyy*– trainer, used attributively) was intended for familiarising the pilots with the special features of WIG vehicle control and for providing instruction and training in all operational modes: during the take-off run and unstick, cruise flight in surface effect and alighting on water or a snow-covered even surface.

The prototype UT-1 was built in 1968. The first phase of the testing was conducted in February and May of that year. The vehicle displayed satisfactory pitch and roll stability, as well as good controllability. In the opinion of the test pilots, the machine's performance fully met the technical requirements, making the UT-1 suitable for use in its intended role. The testing was continued in the subsequent years.

This machine with a wing span of 9.8 m (32 ft 2 in) used the aircraft layout with a T-tail and was powered by a single Czechoslovak-built Walter M-332 six-cylinder in-line engine delivering 120-140 hp. It

A prototype of the Volga-2 WIG craft on the bank of its namesake, the Volga River. Note the exposed engines.

A Volga-2 – possibly the prototype – in cruise flight. Note the cowled engines and the boomerang-shaped aerial above the cockpit.

Another prototype of the Volga-2 (or the same craft following modifications), featuring recontoured engine cowlings, though this is not yet the definitive shape. The tail unit is still unmodified.

A fine shot of a production Volga-2 in cruise mode. Note the auxiliary fins on the stabilisers; the fin bears a Russian flag.

was Alekseyev's first machine to be provided with a water-ski impact-absorbing device. Testing of the UT-1 fitted with this device was conducted in 1973. It showed a considerable improvement of the craft's seaworthiness – the UT-1 could perform a take-off with a wave height up to 0.4 m (1 ft 4 in).

The UT-1 was used not only for training flights but also for investigating the out-of-ground-effect flight mode ('aircraft mode'). The results of these experiments were incorporated in the design of the Strizh (swift, the bird) described below.

Strizh

This small WIG vehicle was conceived as early as 1981 (the work was headed by chief designer V. Boolanov) and was intended to meet the needs

As these photos show, the Volga-2 can operate both from water and from ice or snow-covered ground.

Right and below: The driver's seat and instrument panel of the Volga-2. Note the side-stick, the rubber-bladed cooling fan, the overhead handle for training the roof-mounted searchlight and the triple windscreen wipers. The latter are a must because a lot of spray is flung up on the windscreen when the craft enters the water.

of the Navy, training the crews for the full-size WIG vehicles taken on strength by the Navy. (According to some sources, it also bore the designation Project 19500).

The technical project was completed in 1985, and the prototype made its first flight in 1991. Flown by project test pilot Yu. A. Chirkin, it successfully passed manufacturer's tests on water and then, during the winter season, in flights above snow-covered fields.

The Strizh has two cockpits in a stepped-tandem arrangement with dual controls and identical sets of instruments. Thanks to the vehicle's special aerohydrodynamic layout it has proved possible to ensure stable movement close to the supporting surface without making use of automation. The Strizh possesses good manoeuvrability and controllability.

A cutaway drawing of the Volga-2

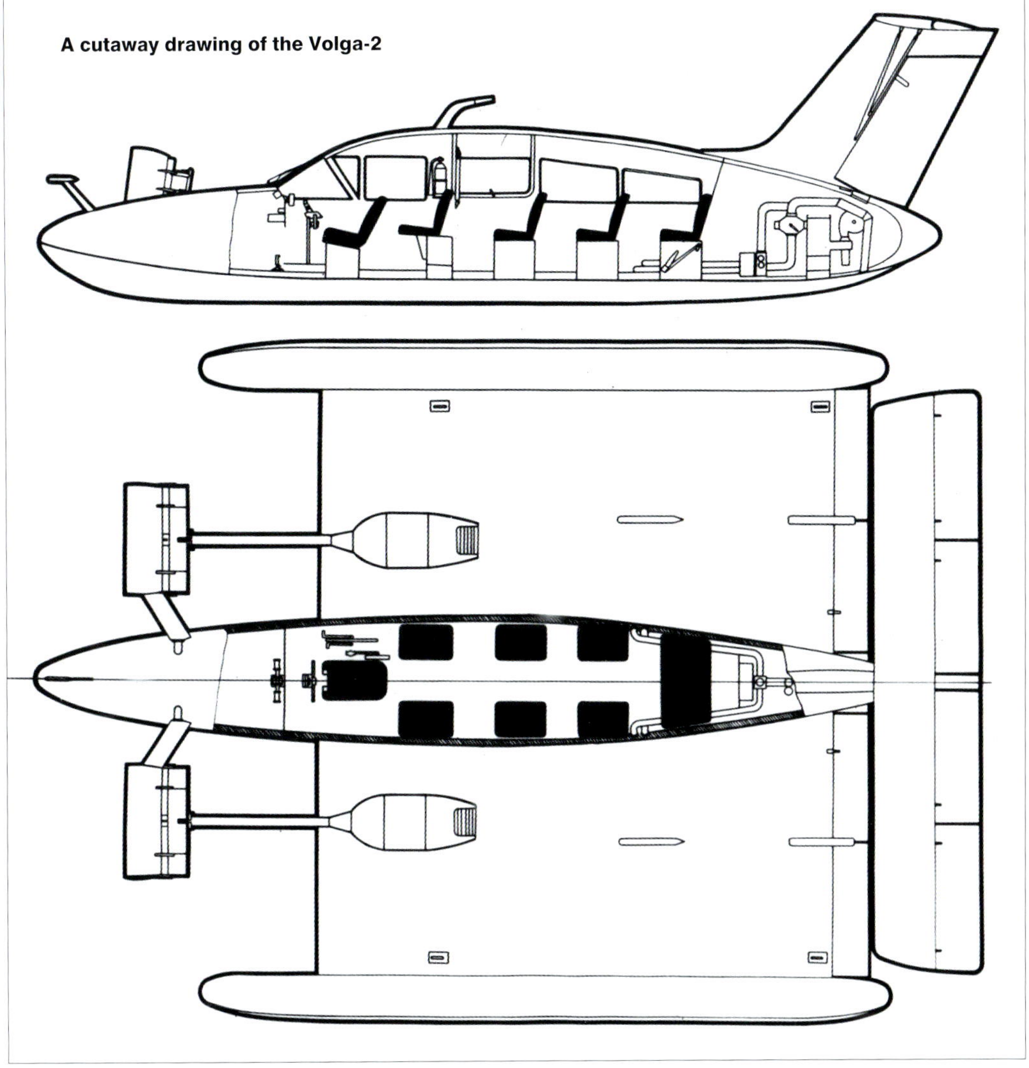

Pages 110-111: 07 Red, a production Volga-2, 'parked' on the bank of the Volga River in 2001 (note the Russian flag on the fin). The production version has additional vertical tail surfaces and reshaped engine cowlings.

Here are some specifications. The machine has a length of 11.4 m (37 ft 4¾ in), a wing span of 6.6 m (21 ft 7¾ in) and a height of 3.6 m (11 ft 9¾ in). It is powered by two 160-hp VAZ-4133 water-cooled Wankel engines mounted on the wings. The five-bladed fixed-pitch propellers have a diameter of 1.1 m (3 ft 7 in); they are driven by shafts with universal joints via a single-stage reduction gearbox and an automatic coupling.

With an all-up weight of 1,630 kg (3,600 lb) the Strizh has a maximum speed of 200 km/h (124 mph) and a cruising speed of 175 km/h (109 mph) in the WIG mode. Range with a passenger is 500 km (310 miles), the ferrying range is 800 km (500 miles). Flight altitude in ground effect is 0.3-1.0 m (1-3 ft). When flying out of ground effect, the vehicle can rise to an altitude of 800 m (2,620 ft) and reach a speed of 200 km/h (124 mph).

In addition to training, the Strizh can be used for patrol duties, liaison and business flying. The vehicle is placed in the Experimental Class R of the Russian River Fleet Register.

Strizh-M and Strizh-S

A production version designated Strizh-M is to be powered by Voyager 300 engines delivering 220 hp apiece or by 175-200-hp Bakanov M-17 flat-four engines of the Voronezh Engine Design Bureau

Manufacturer's specifications of the Volga-2 and the Volga-2MT

	Volga-2	Volga-2MT
Register class	Experimental R class of the Russian River Fleet Register	Type A in the IMO classification
Displacement, kg (lb)	2,900 (6,395)	3,000 (6,615)
Draught, m (ft)	0.3 m (1 ft 0 in)	0.3 (1 ft 0 in)
Speed, km/h (mph)	120 (75)	120 (75)
Range, km (miles)	300 (186)	300 (186)
Crew	1	1
Number of passengers	8	8
Seaworthiness (wave height), m (ft)		
at take-off and in cruise	0.3 (1 ft 0 in)	0.5 (1 ft 8 in)
when afloat	0.75 (2 ft 5 in)	0.75 (2 ft 5 in)
Engines – number x kW	2 x 114	2 x 147

07
ВОЛГА-2

07
ВОЛГА-2

A production Volga-2 in cruise mode, with propeller vane deflection clearly visible.

(VOKBM). The latter engine, though, has failed to reach production status so far.

Judging by the available three-view drawing, the Strizh-M differs from the prototype Strizh in having two seats in tandem under a common canopy instead of two staggered separate cockpits. However, CHDB advertising materials also mention the Strizh-M with two staggered cockpits which are presumably the standard arrangement for training purposes, while the common two-seat cockpit may be intended for liaison and similar duties. In WIG mode cruise flight the Strizh-M would fly at a height of 0.5-1.2 m (20 in – 3 ft 11 in) above the water surface, with a capacity for making 'hops' to a maximum of 50 m (164 ft) if required.

Mention has been made in the press of a Strizh-S version offered for export. No details are available.

Despite good test results, the Strizh did not go into production. The reason was the curtailment of the Navy's WIG craft procurement programme. The sole prototype was turned over to the CHDB which used it for training test pilots and for demonstration flights at various exhibitions in Russia and abroad. On 5th October 1994 the pilots had the audacity to demonstrate the flying qualities of the Strizh on the Moskva River right in front of the Russian Government building on Krasnopresnenskaya Embankment (popularly known as the 'White House').

The basic layout and main design features of the Strizh were used in developing a family of small WIG vehicles for civil purposes with an all-up weight ranging from 1.6 to 5 t (3,530-11,000 lb). It includes the following machines:

In defiance of superstition this vehicle, a subscale analogue of the projected Raketa-2 passenger WIG, was designated SM-13 and marked 013 accordingly. The three engines are well visible here.

An artist's impression of the 90-seat Raketa-2 passenger dynamic air cushion vehicle travelling along one of the inland waterways.

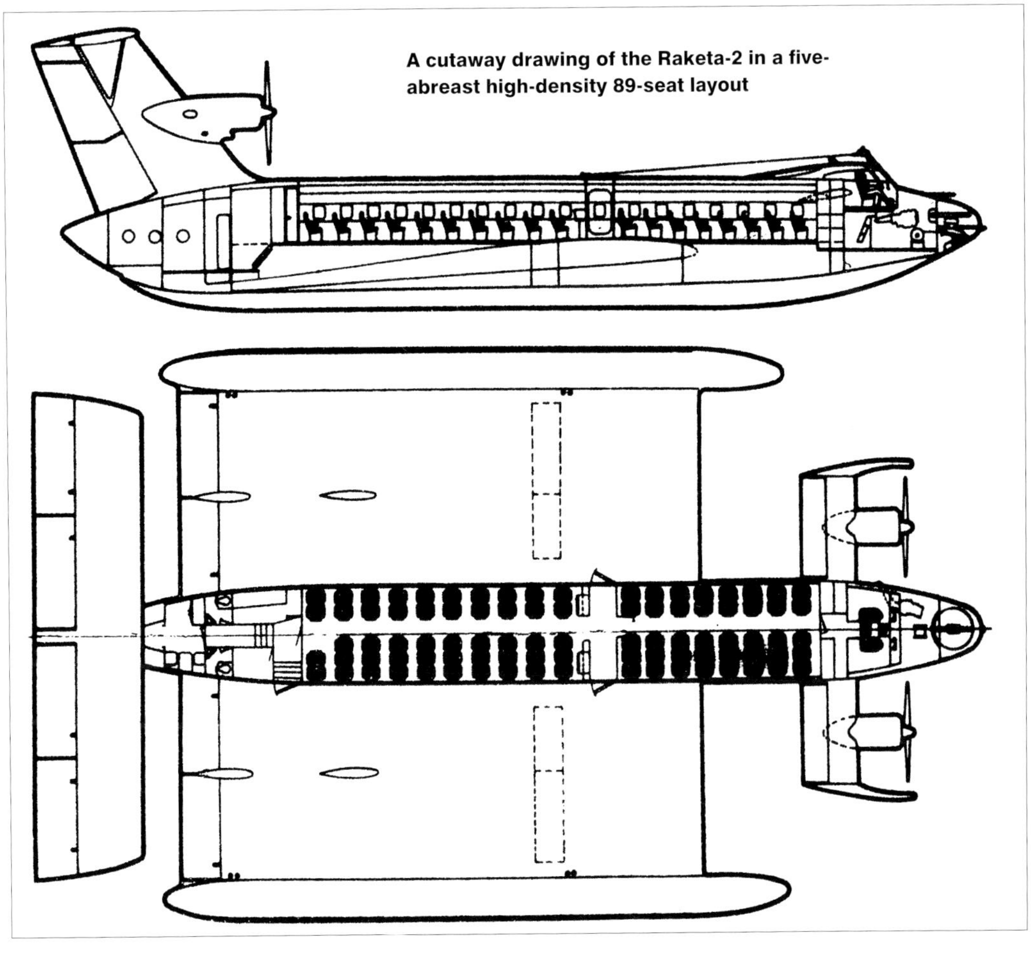

A cutaway drawing of the Raketa-2 in a five-abreast high-density 89-seat layout

This artist's impression from the mid-1970s shows how a river port would have looked, had WIG craft operations reached the intended scale. The type of craft is unknown (it is similar to, but obviously smaller than, the Raketa-2).

An artist's impression of the 250-seat Vikhr'-2 sea-going DACV.

Strizh-3 (aka Kulik – Snipe)

The Strizh-3 looks like a scaled-up Strizh-M and differs in having small outer wing panels added outboard of the wingtip floats/endplates (the so-called composite layout wings). The powerplant comprises two engines with an output of 280-300 hp apiece. Several engine types have been considered in the course of development. For example, the Strizh-3 could be powered by two Zoche Munich aircraft diesel engines of 300 hp each, or by two identically-rated VOKBM M-16 eight-cylinder engines (the latter type failed to reach production status). Another option was the use of engines manufactured by Teledyne Continental Motors.

The Strizh-3 was designed as a sea-going cargo/passenger *ekranoplan* which could transport a maximum of six passengers with one crew over a distance of up to 800 km (497 miles). The pilot was accommodated in a common cabin with the passengers. There was a project version with two pilots seated in a staggered-tandem arrangement. The machine was to have a cruising speed of 210-230 km/h (131-143 mph) and a maximum sped of 240-250 km/h (149-155 mph). In WIG mode cruise flight the

Above: The diminutive UT-1 WIG vehicle which served for training pilots in operational procedures. It is seen here flying over a frozen river.

Below: The UT-1 was the first Alekseyev design to feature a hydroski, which is clearly visible in this view as the craft rises out of ground effect.

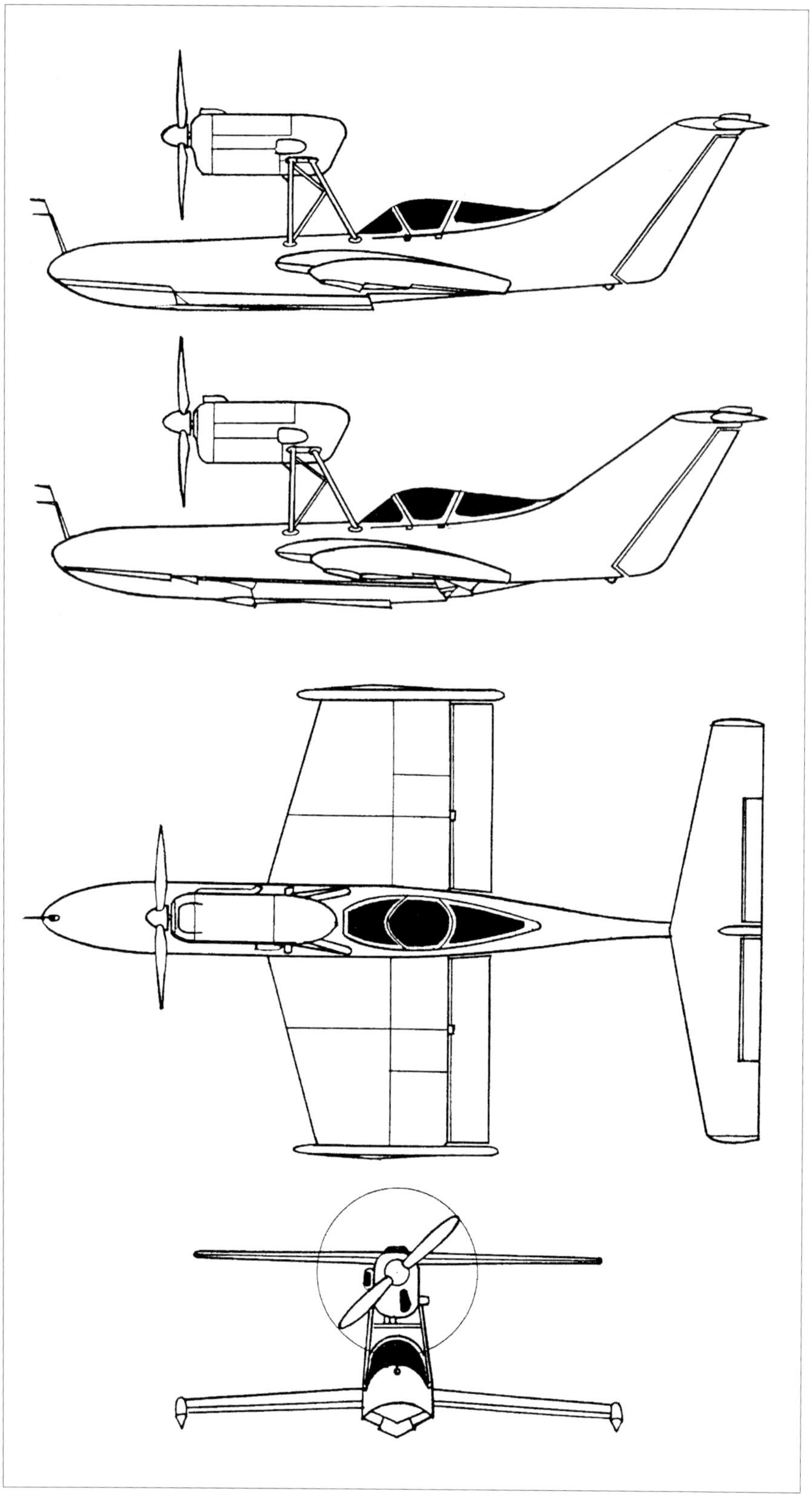

A three-view drawing of the UT-1 in definitive configuration. The upper side view shows the early version without a hydroski.

ekranoplan would fly at a height of 0.6-1.5 m (2-5 ft) above the water surface, with a capacity for making 'hops' to a maximum of 50 m (164 ft) when needed. The Strizh-3 was to have a capacity for cruising flight in the WIG mode with a sea state of 3 (wave height 1.25 m/4 ft), and a capacity or staying afloat in a sea state of up to 4.

Strizh-4 (aka Baklan – Cormorant)

This machine is powered by two Lycoming TIGO-541E flat-six piston engines of 450 hp each or two TDA-450 engines.

Judging by the available three-view drawing, the Strizh-4 looks like a scaled-up Strizh-3 and differs in having a roomier fuselage with an increased seating capacity. Like the Strizh-3, it features the added outer wing panels.

Strizh-5

This type is powered by two Merlin aircraft diesel engines of 650 hp apiece.

This WIG craft was projected in both military and civil versions. The military version was intended for patrolling the 200-mile economic exclusion zone. Being slightly larger and heavier than the Strizh-4 and repeating its basic layout, the military version did not have the extra outer wing panels (at least in one of the project configurations) and was fitted with armament. The latter comprised a remote-controlled turret with a small-calibre cannon mounted atop the fuselage just aft of the pilot's cockpit and two launch rails for anti-ship missiles installed further aft on the fuselage.

The proposed civil version would have the armament deleted and the fuselage adapted for accommodating passengers. Different sources give slightly differing specifications for the Strizh-5; in one of the versions it is credited with the following dimensions: a length of 16.4 m (62 ft 5¾ in), a wing span of 10 m (38 ft 1¼ in) and a height of 5.2 m (19 ft 9¾ in). Other figures are to be found in a table on page 107 dealing with all the Strizh types.

Strizh-6

This was a project, under development in 1997, of a small sea-going WIG vehicle intended to carry 20 persons.

None of the Strizh projects was implemented. (The table is based on information published by P. P. Yablonskiy. Some figures in the table may differ from those in the text because they refer to different version of a given project)

Transport Amphibious Platforms (TAP)

Description of the activities of the Alekseyev Design Bureau would be incomplete without mentioning the projects of vehicles designated collectively as TAP (***trahns**portno-amfi**biy**naya plat**for**ma*, transport amphibious platform). Since 1989 the design bureau had developed a series of projects of this kind which embody the concept of a 'ship lifted out of the water' through the use of a dynamic air cushion. They utilise a gas dynamic cushion effect obtained by directing the efflux of forward-mounted jet engines beneath the platform hydrofoil flanked by vertical walls (skegs, boat hulls or pontoons). Unlike the traditional WIG vehicles, the TAP has no airfoil-shaped lifting surfaces (the platform creating the lift is flat); it remains in contact with the water or ice at all times and belongs to the ship class. They are intended for year-round operation on rivers and littoral sea areas, including shallow-water areas. TAP vehicles can also be operated on routes in ice-covered areas.

TAP vehicles have high cruising speeds (up to 250 km/h; 155 mph) and a high cargo-carrying capacity reaching 40-50% of the full displacement. They can perform transport operations over distances of up to 1,500 km (932 miles) without refuelling, both on inland waterways and in the open sea at sea states of 4-5; they are capable of landing on a shore without berthing facilities and negotiating a slope of up to 5°.

Such craft displacing up to 800 tonnes (1,753,600 lb) are intended for both civil and military duties. The possible military roles will be dealt with below. As for the civil applications, the TAP craft can be used for passenger and cargo transportation, as well as for some special duties, such as car ferries, refrigerator vessels, fire-fighting, SAR, geological prospecting, offshore loading and unloading, as well as the transportation of oversize equipment units and structures weighing up to 350 tonnes (771,750 lb).

TAP-30

This is a project of a vehicle with a displacement of 30 tonnes (66,150 lb) and a cargo-carrying capacity of 10 tonnes (22,050 lb). It features an open cargo platform resting on inflatable pontoons, with the crew cockpit occupying the front part of the platform. No aerodynamic tail surfaces are fitted. The cargo platform is flanked by longitudinal bodies

A three-view of the Strizh

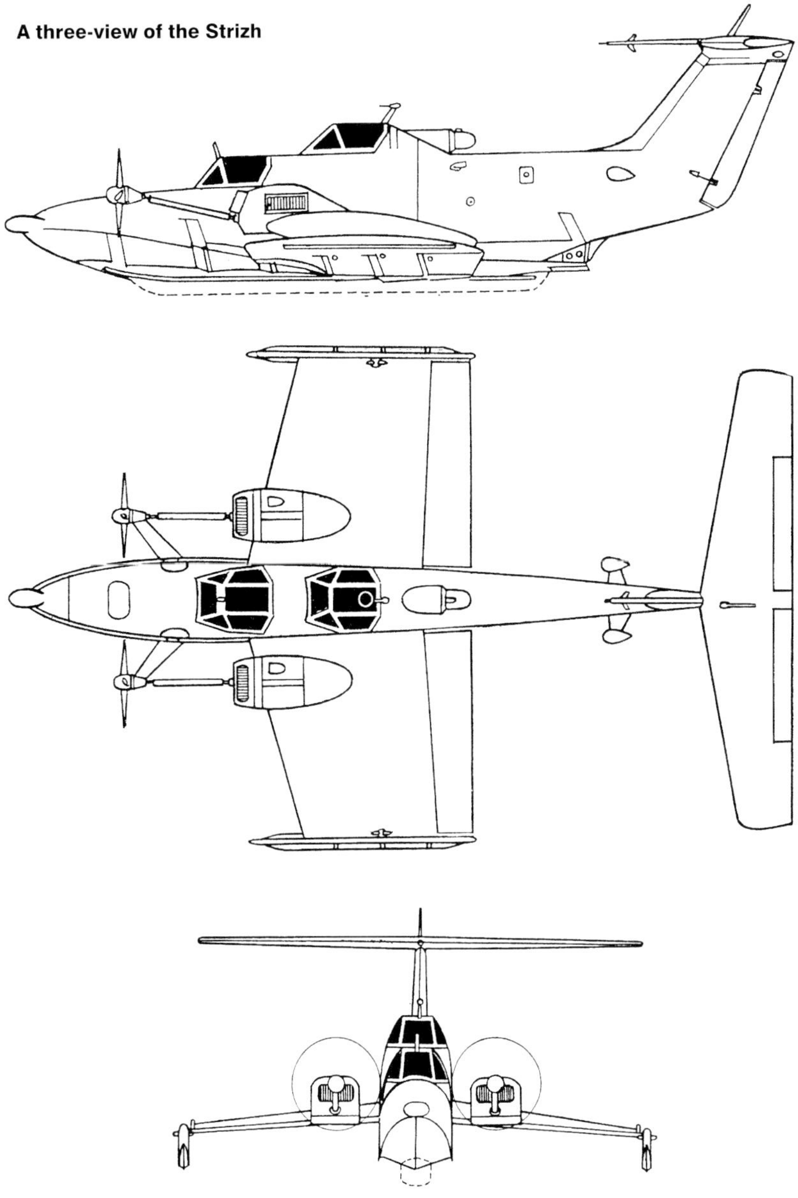

The Strizh training WIG vehicle in cruise flight above the Volga River. The vehicle wears its original grey colour scheme.

The Strizh trainer shared the powerplant arrangement of the Volga-2, except for the shrouded propellers with movable vanes. The fairing aft of the rear cockpit is a flight data recorder housing.

Here the Strizh is shown in a later civil-style colour scheme.

These views illustrate the vehicle's new colours and also show the water rudder.

Here the Strizh is shown during winter tests on a snow-covered surface.

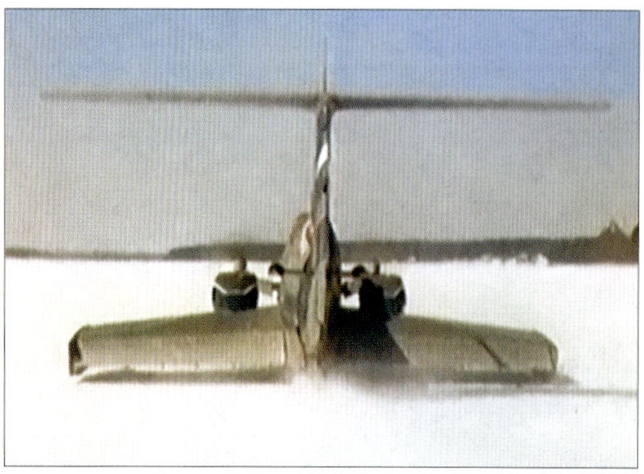

The smartly painted Strizh training WIG vehicle in cruise flight. The legend added to the fuselage reads *AO TsKB SPK* (Central Hydrofoil Design Bureau Joint-Stock Co.).

(side skegs) which, apart from providing protection for the cargo, house the engines. Four turbojets are placed in pairs on each side of the platform with aft-facing air intakes. The jet efflux of the engines is directed under the bottom of the platform and creates a static air cushion, in addition to providing the thrust for forward propulsion.

TAP-150, TAP-300, TAP-500

The displacement of these three TAP vehicles roughly corresponds to the designation numbers, their cargo-carrying capacity being 60, 120 and 200 tonnes (132,300 lb, 264,600 lb and 441,000 lb) respectively.

Another view of the Strizh prototype in later guise as a company demonstrator. The FDR fairing is painted orange to facilitate location in the event of a crash.

The Strizh makes a demonstration flight on the Moskva River in front of the Russian Government building.

The pilots of the Strizh occasionally make daredevil manoeuvres during demo flights, as seen here.

An artist's impression of the Strizh-M, showing the common canopy over the two seats.

TAP-700

One of the projects in this series bears the designation TAP-700 referring to the displacement of 700 tonnes (1,543,500 lb). The cargo platform dimensions are 40 x 25 m (13 x 82 ft). The hull of boxy contours with an open deck has nothing aircraft-like about it, save for the two swept-back fins-and-rudders, one on each side of the stern, with their tips bridged by the horizontal stabiliser and elevator. Two turboprop engines with tractor propellers are mounted at the junctions of the fins and the stabiliser. Six turbojet engines mounted on a kind of foreplane ahead of the bow serve the purpose of creating an air cushion under the bottom of the craft, which is further augmented by ram air during cruise.

The open deck permits the carriage of outsize cargoes. The crew compartment and the pilot's cabin form a structure joining the foreplane and the bow.

Military versions of the TAP-700 and TAP-500

The inherent advantages of the TAP layout did not escape the attention of the military who duly appreciated the possibility of accommodating all sorts of war materiel on the spacious open platform. Coupled with the high speed, good seaworthiness and amphibious qualities of the TAP designs, this prompted the military to study the possibility of using TAP craft as high-speed manoeuvrable carriers of high-power missiles. Two types were singled out for this purpose: the TAP-500 and TAP-700 with

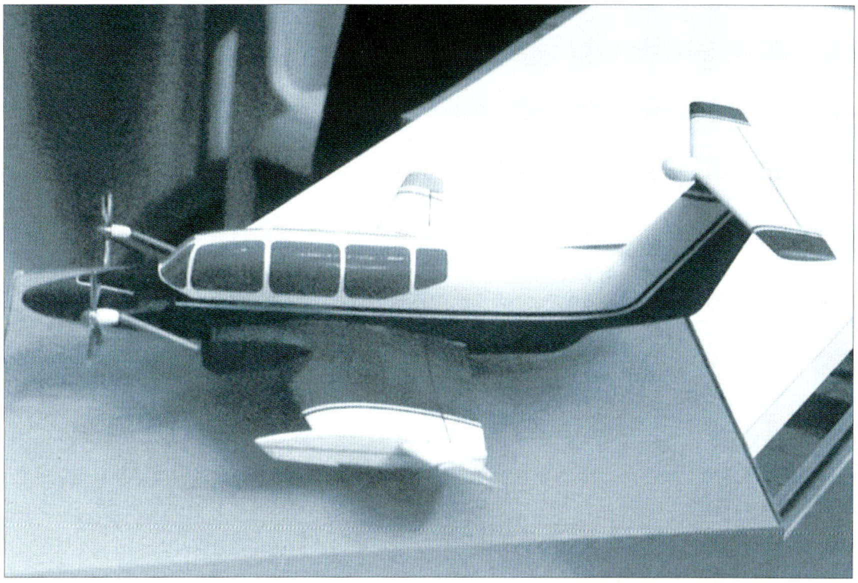

This display model apparently represents the projected Strizh-3 with a larger cabin and composite layout wings.

An artist's impression of the Strizh-3 passenger *ekranoplan*.

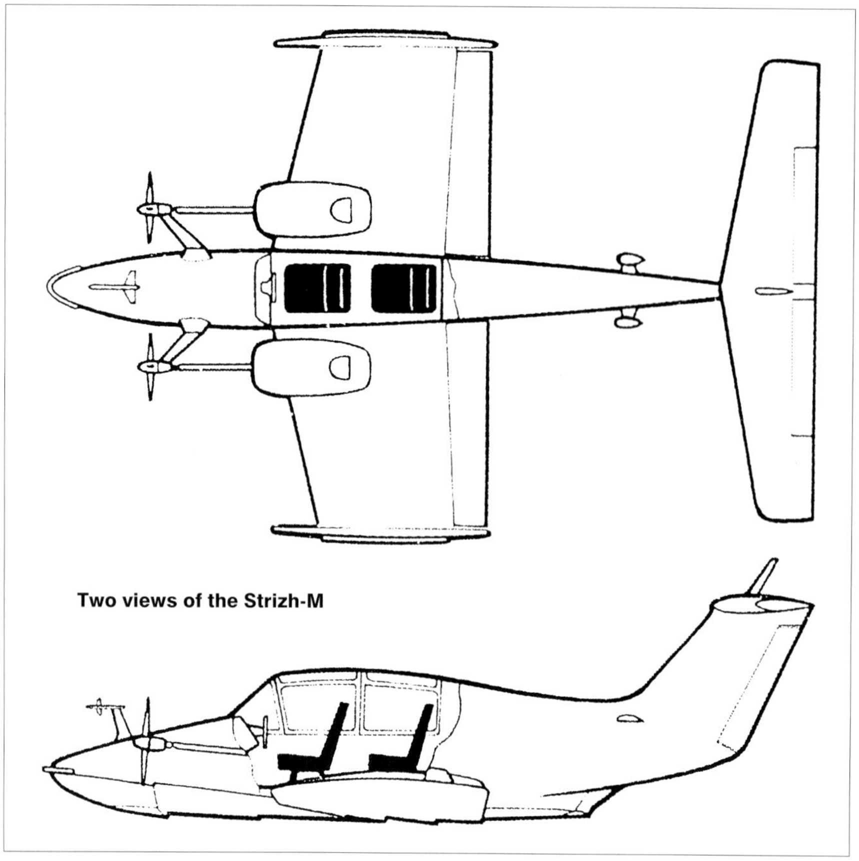

Two views of the Strizh-M

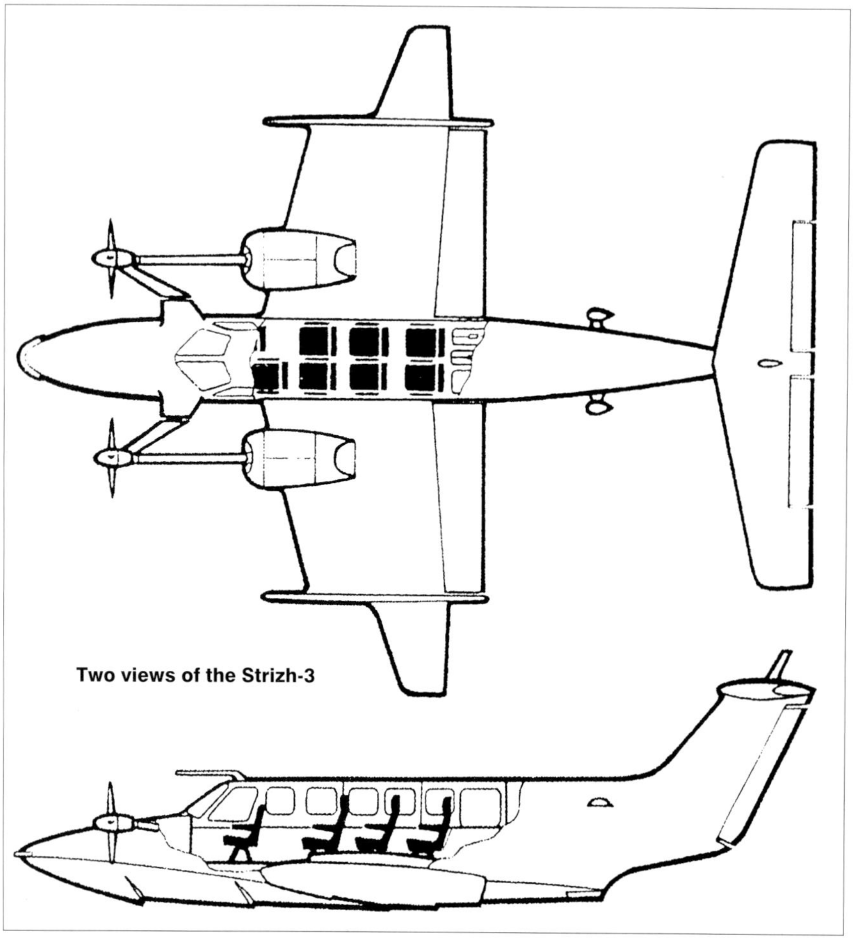

Two views of the Strizh-3

a load-carrying capacity of 200 tonnes (132,300 lb) and 250-300 tonnes (551,250-661,500 lb) respectively.

Several options of the missile weapon complement to be carried by the TAP craft were considered. The results of these studies boiled own to four possible versions of TAP-borne missile strike systems. They included:

1. 12 anti-ship cruise missiles with a range of 150 km (93 miles), to be mounted on the TAP-500;
2. 24 small-size theatre tactical anti-ship missiles with a range of 350 km (218 miles), to be mounted on the TAP-500;
3. 20 anti-ship cruise missiles with a range of 150 km (93 miles), to be mounted on the TAP-700;
4. 16 anti-ship cruise missiles with a range of 150 km (218 miles) and a multi-role helicopter, to be mounted on the TAP-700.

The TAP-class craft also appeared to be eminently suitable for use as assault transport means. They could ensure speedy delivery to combat areas of all sorts of military vehicles and their crews, including tanks, armoured personnel carriers, self-propelled air defence systems, self-propelled howitzers, multiple-launcher rocket systems (MLRS) etc.

STP-600

This craft is essentially similar in layout to the TAP-700. The figure 600 signifies a displacement of 600 tonnes (1,323,000 lb). The vehicle was tailored for the carriage of the *Buran* (Blizzard) space shuttle, an ill-fated Soviet counterpart of the US Space Shuttle. In this case, too, the powerplant comprised two turboprop cruise engines and six turbojets for blowing under the bottom of the craft. The side bodies had a more pronounced likeness to flying-boat hulls, with several planing steps distributed along their length.

A combined WIG vehicle

In a highly unorthodox project from the CHDB a vehicle of the TAP class served as a carrier for a smaller WIG craft, resembling in layout some of Bartini's projects. It had a rectangular wing centre section flanked by boat hulls and outer wing panels with two turbojets mounted above the latter. Apparently the smaller WIG craft was of the C-class in the present IMO classification. The drawing depicting this combination does not provide a clue to the role intended for it.

Projects of this kind developed by the Alekseyev Central Hydrofoil Design Bureau never reached the hardware stage. Some of them were inherited and further developed by the company ATT whose activities are described in Chapter 6.

The CHDB in the post-Soviet period

The demise of the Soviet Union and the radical transformation of Russia's political scene and economic structure has had a profound effect on the activities of enterprises engaged in defence-associated industries. The CHDB was affected by these changes – first and foremost due to the virtual disappearance of state funding and defence orders, and, secondly, as a result of the tendency towards privatisation of state enterprises and turning them into joint stock companies.

In the early 1990s the CHDB underwent two major transformations. Firstly, it was privatised, that is, turned into a joint-stock company in which a certain amount of shares was owned by the personnel, while the rest was acquired by other business enterprises. Secondly, the loss of government funding and orders led to a drastic reduction of personnel. Large groups of engineers and designers chose to part company with the CHDB and formed their own new design bureaux with a status of JSCs, taking much of the design work on the *ekranoplans* previously handled by the CHDB with them (more about this in Chapter 6).

The CHDB in its new shape became a part of a group of companies, known as the 'High-Speed Ships' Financial & Industrial Group. This group was formed in 1994 with the declared purpose of uniting Russia's oldest shipbuilding enterprises with a view to ensuring the full cycle of designing and manufac-

Three views of the Strizh-4 (aka Baklan)

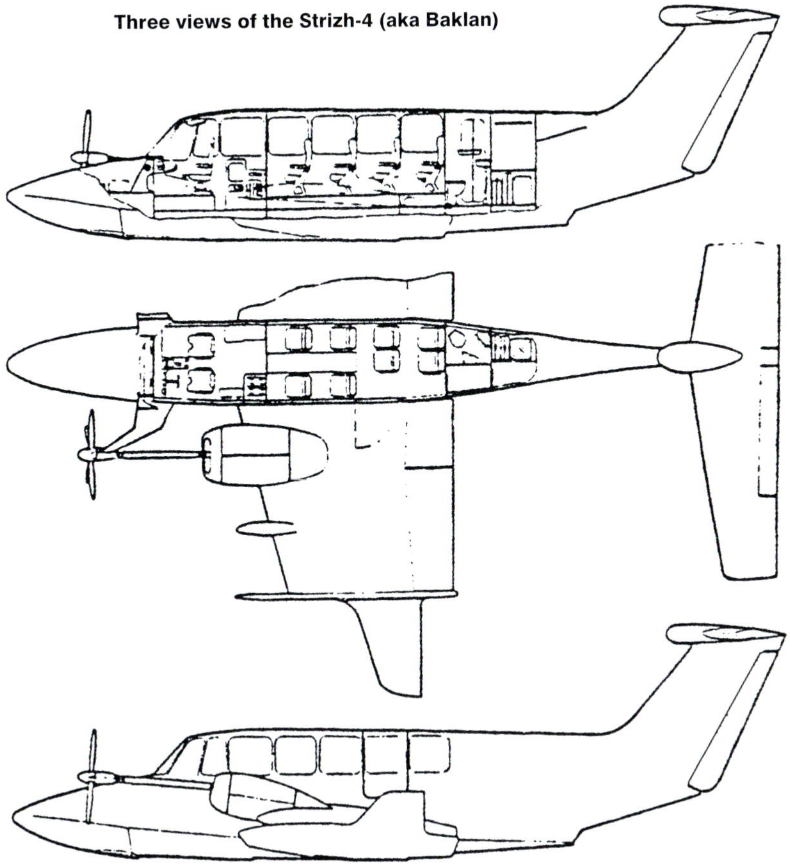

Specifications of ekranoplans of the Strizh family

	Strizh	Strizh-M	Strizh-3	Strizh-4	Strizh-5
Crew	1	1	1	1	1
Passengers	1	1	5-7	7-9	10-12
Length	11.4 m (37 ft 4 3/4 in)	11.4 m (37 ft 4 3/4 in)	13.4 m (43 ft 11 9/16 in)	15.4 m (50 ft 6 19/64 in)	17.0 m (55 ft 9 19/64 in)
Wing span	6.7 m (21 ft 11 49/64 in)	6.7 m (21 ft 11 49/64 in)	11.2 m (36 ft 8 15/16 in)	13.0 m (42 ft 7 13/16 in)	14.0 m (45 ft 11 3/16 in)
Height	3.6 m (11 ft 9 47/64 in)	3.6 m (11 ft 9 47/64 in)	4.0 m (13 ft 1 31/64 in)	4.7 m (15 ft 5 1/32 in)	5.2 m (17 ft 0 47/64 in)
All-up weight, kg (lb)	1,650 (3,640)	1,800 (3,970)	2,700 (5,950)	4,300 (9,480)	5,200 (11,470)
Cruising speed, km/h (mph)	180 (107)	180 (107)	n.a.	210 (131)	220 (137)
Max speed, km/h (mph)	200 (124)	200 (124)	n.a.	240 (149)	270 (168)
Lift-off speed, km/h (mph)	85-90 (53-56)	n.a.	n.a.	n.a.	n.a.
Landing speed, km/h (mph)	115 (71)	n.a.	n.a.	n.a.	n.a.
Engine power, hp	2 x 155	2 x 220	2 x 300	2 x 450	2 x 650
Range	200 (124)	400 (249)	800 (497)	800 (497)	800 (497)
Max wave height, m (ft):					
on take-off	0.4 m (1 ft 0 5/16 in)	0.4 m (1 ft 0 5/16 in)	0.5 m (1 ft 11 in)	0.6 m (2 ft 3 in)	0.7 m (2 ft 8 in)
on landing	0.7 m (2 ft 3in)	0.7 m (2 ft 3 in)	0.8 m (2 ft 7 in)	1.0 m (3 ft 3 in)	1.2m (3 ft 11 in)
In cruise over sea surface	0.8 m (2 ft 7 in)	0.8 m (2 ft 7 in)	1.0 m (3 ft 3 in)	1.2 m (3 ft 11 in)	1.4 m (4 ft 7 in)

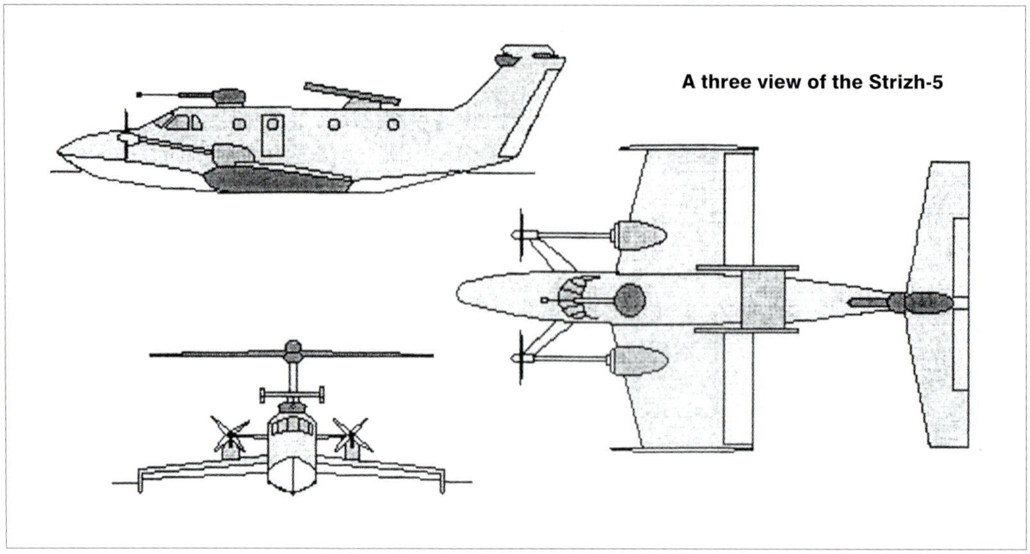

A three view of the Strizh-5

An artist's impression of the TAP-30 craft carrying a load of containers.

A towing basin model of the TAP-700. The blower at the front creating an air cushion is not representative of the projected full-size craft.

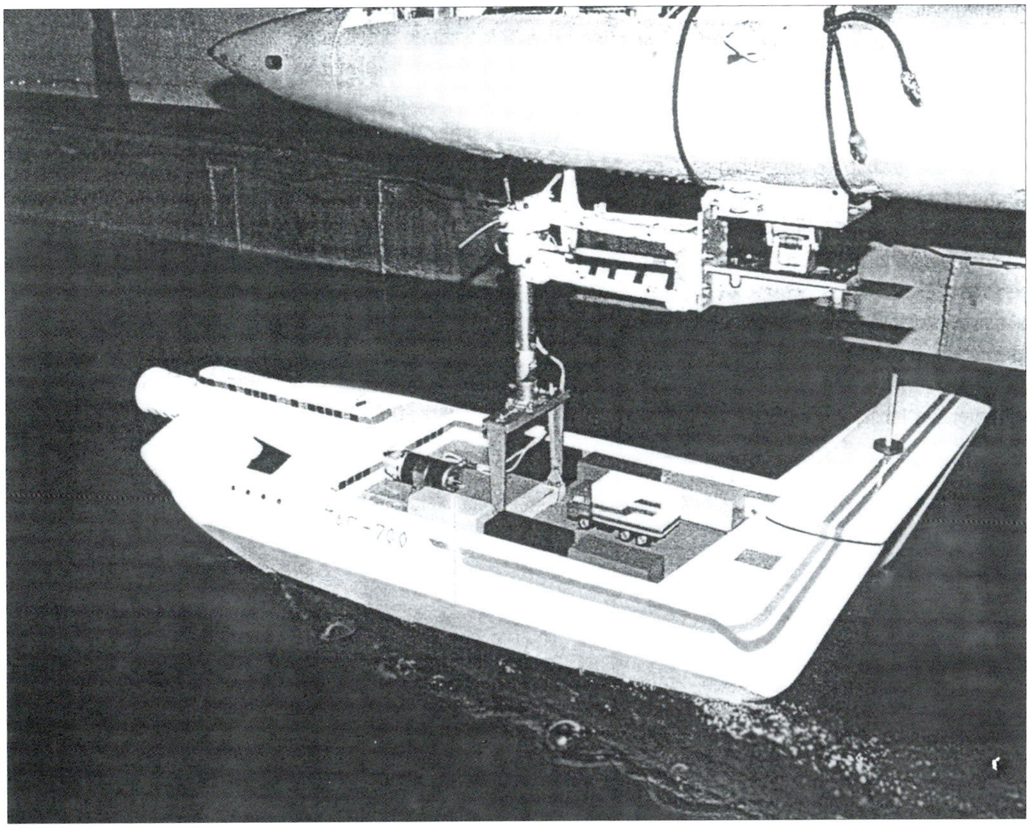

A model of the TAP-700 on test in the towing basin.

A larger radio-controlled model of the TAP-700 used for tests on open water.

turing high-speed ships. In addition to the CHDB, it comprised several other enterprises (shipyards, an engine plant and a design bureau), one of which was the Volga Shipyard closely associated with the CHDB. An official list of the products of the High-Speed Ships group included ships of various types and, nominally, 'multi-purpose *ekranoplans*'. In practice, the latter were not regarded a matter of priority and eventually were struck off the list.

The latest development in these matters occurred in June 2009 when the High-Speed Ships group sold its share holding in the CHDB to the St.

An artist's impression of a civil TAP-700 coming ashore of offload outsize cargo. Note the foreplanes carrying the blower engines.

This artist's impression depicts the TAP-700 as a car ferry. Note the lateral cranes for autonomous cargo handling and the 'danger' markings in the area of the latter.

This model depicts a pure jet craft in the TAP series armed with 16 anti-ship missiles.

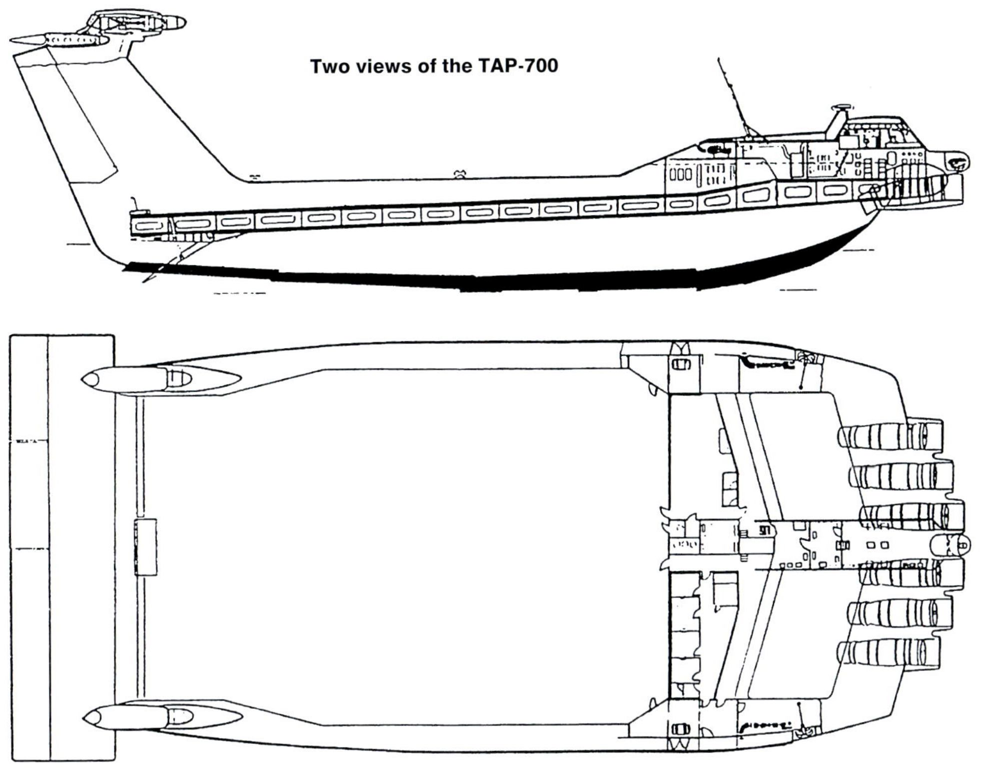

Two views of the TAP-700

Petersburg-based company Radar-MMS engaged in the design and manufacture of avionics. The consequences of this change of affiliation remain to be seen. The management of Radar-MMS has already declared its willingness to facilitate a revival of the CHDB's activities in the field of ekranoplan design.

In the period since 1992 these activities have been drastically curtailed, no new projects having

Design performance characteristics of the Transport Amphibious Platform family

	TAP-30	TAP-150	TAP-300	TAP-500	TAP-700
Displacement, tonnes (lb)	30 (66,150)	150 (330,750)	330 (727,650)	525 (1,157,615)	700 – 750 (1,543,540 – 1,653,750)
Cargo-carrying capacity, tonnes (lb)	10 (22,050)	60 (132,300)	120 (264,600)	200 (441,000)	250 – 300 (551-250 – 661,500)
Speed, km/h (mph):					
on still water	100-110 (62-68)	170-180 (106-112)	210-220 (131-137)	240 (149)	250 (155)
on waves	60-80 (37-50)	90-140 (56-87)	110-160 (68-99)	120-200 (75-124)	140-200 (87-124)
on land	90 (56)	100 (62)	100 (62)	100 (62)	100 (62)
on ice or snow	90 (56)	180 (112)	200 (124)	200 (124)	200 (124)
Range, km (miles)					
on still water	125 (78)	480 (298)	750 (466)	1,400 (max) (870)	1,500 (max) (932)
on waves	80 (50)	350 (218)	340 (211)	400 – 1,100 (249 – 683)	700 – 1,100 (435 – 683)
on land	180 (112)	320 (200)	420 (261)	450 – 800 (280 – 497)	500 – 700 (311 – 435)
on ice or snow	180 (112)	580 (360)	850 (528)	900 – 1,100 (559 – 684)	600 – 1,500 (550 – 932)
Crew	3	3	4	4	4

An artist's impression of the STP-600 vehicle in Soviet navy colours hauling the Buran space shuttle.

An artist's impression of a two-component transport system developed by the CHDB – a WIG-type transporter carrying a twin-hull WIG craft with front loading. Note the inflatable balloons on the carrier on which the smaller craft rests.

An artist's impression of a double-deck ocean-going passenger WIG craft. There are two booster engines and two booster/cruise engines in the nose. The cruise engines on top of the tail appear to be shrouded profans.

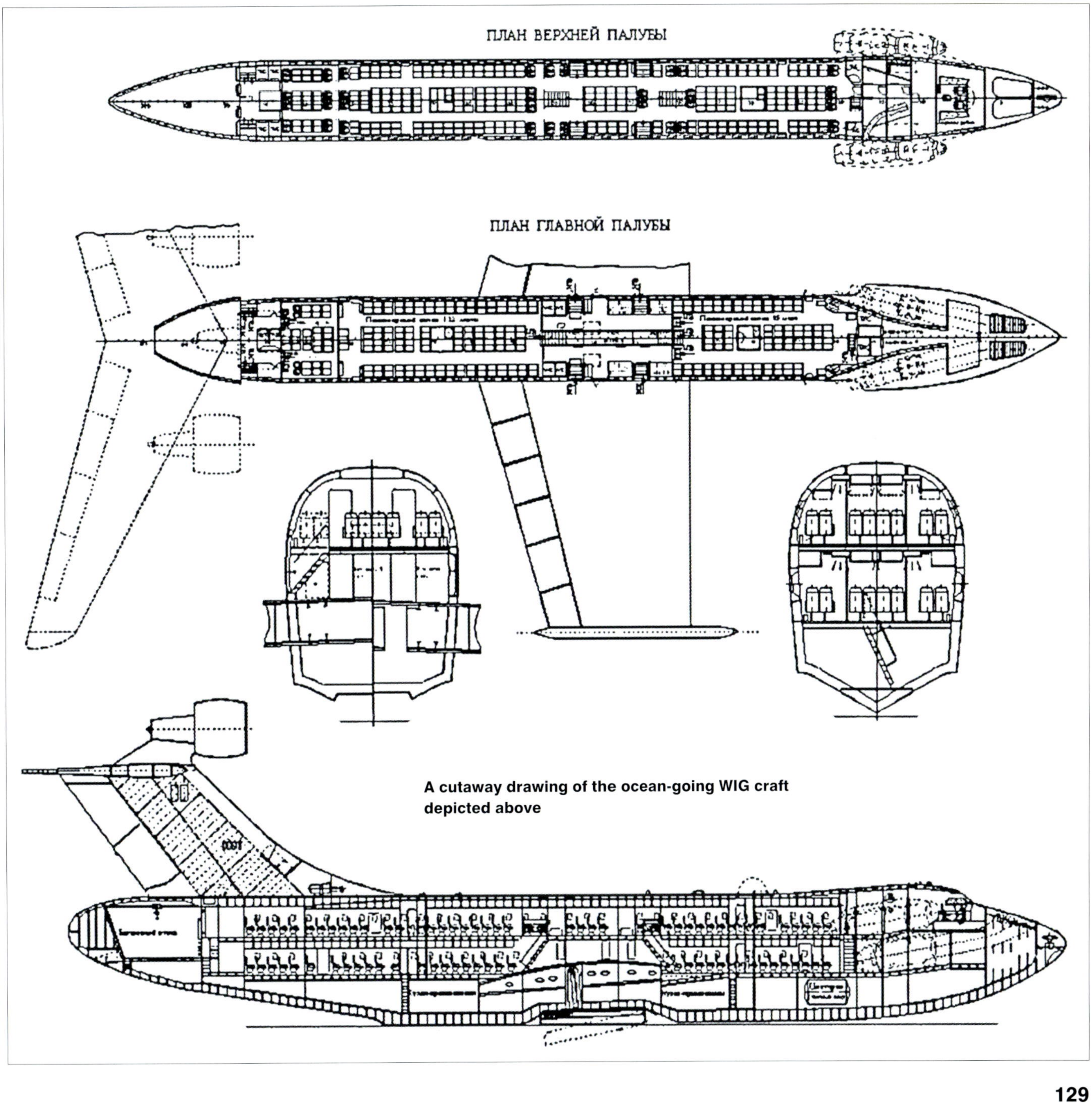

A cutaway drawing of the ocean-going WIG craft depicted above

progressed to the hardware stage. No new designs of military *ekranoplans* from the CHDB (or from the High-Speed Ships financial and industrial group whose affiliate the CHDB had become) have come to the public knowledge and are probably non-existent. As for the WIG craft intended for civil duties, some projects have been kept afloat, apparently without any serious effort for putting them into practice. Here are two such projects, as advertised by the High-Speed Ships holding company.

Sea-going passenger *ekranoplan* for 200-250 passengers

Apart from this generic description, no special designation was given. A photo of a model accompanying the advertisement showed something that was virtually a demilitarised Orlyonok, albeit the main design performance figures quoted differed from those cited for the formerly known passenger versions of the Orlyonok. The figures are given in the table on this page.

Sea-going passenger *ekranoplan* for 550 passengers

Again, no special designation is given, apart from this title to the description which is accompanied by an artist's impression and general arrangement drawings. The pictures show a WIG vehicle featuring an aircraft layout. Basically it is a scaled-up Orlyonok, with a flying-boat hull, low-set wings of low aspect ratio, and a large-span swept horizontal tail placed atop the fin. Yet there are some differences in the layout. The booster powerplant comprises four turbofan engines, two of which are installed on short horizontal pylons on both sides of the front fuselage just aft of the pilots' cockpit, while the other two are buried in the forward fuselage in the Orlyonok fashion, with flush air intakes and splayed exhaust nozzles. As for the cruise powerplant, it comprises two propfans placed above the horizontal tail halves, instead of a single centrally mounted turboprop on the Orlyonok. The booster engines are Kuznetsov NK-87 turbofans rated at 13,000 kgp (28,665 lbst) for take-off, while the cruise engines are Kuznetsov NK-93 contra-rotating integrated shrouded propfans delivering 18,000 kgp (39,690 lbst) for take-off. The NK-87 was put into limited production and used on the Loon' WIG vehicle, while the NK-93 is still undergoing tests, with uncertain prospects for series production.

The powerplant described above (with two cruise engines) can be seen in the artist's impression and the general arrangement drawings. Apparently this is just one of several project configurations; the text of the advertising material describes the vehicle's powerplant as comprising *'two or three cruise NK-93 propfan engines and four NK-87 turbofan booster engines designed by the Kuznetsov SNTK [Samara Science and Technology Complex]'*.

Design features of this project include a double-deck layout of passenger cabins furnished with airliner-type seats (mostly eight abreast with two aisles) and provided with an in-flight entertainment system, as well as with electronic communication means. The cabins are housed in the central part of the hull. The front part of the hull houses the flight deck and crew compartment, two of the four booster engines, and avionics, including a radar with an antenna in a thimble radome. The aft part of the hull houses the luggage compartment, APUs and hydraulic and electric equipment. The wings incorporate integral fuel tanks. Both the wings and the fuselage are watertight and ensure buoyancy of the machine when afloat. For extra safety the lower part of the hull and the wings are divided into watertight sections.

The main systems of the *ekranoplan* (control system, hydraulics, electrics, life support system, radio and navigation equipment etc.) are of the type used in aircraft and feature the necessary degree of redundancy to ensure safe operation of the machine.

Design specifications of the 200-250-seat passenger WIG vehicle based on the Orlyonok

Normal AUW	approx. 90 tonnes (198,450 lb)
Maximum AUW	approx. 110 tonnes (242,550 lb)
Cruising speed	up to 400 km/h (249 mph)
Range	1,000-1,500 km (622-932 .miles)
Flight crew	3
Cabin crew	6
Passengers	appr. 200-250
Seaworthiness for take-off and landing	Sea state up to 4
Seaworthiness when afloat and in flight	Sea state 4-5
Booster engines	2 x NK-8-4K
Cruise engines	1 x NK-12MK

Del'fin (Dolphin) passenger WIG craft

In September 2006 the Russian magazine *Expert-Volga* (a business publication) carried an article dealing with the prospects of shipbuilding in Russia. A paragraph of this article reads as follows: *'Furthermore, the Alekseyev CHDB appears to face gleaming prospects of the development of WIG craft construction both for export and for the home market. [...] A technical project of the Del'fin passenger ekranoplan powered by aircraft engines envisages the transportation of 570 passengers over a distance of up to three thousand kilometres [1,865 miles] at a speed of 600 km/h [373 mph]'*.

*Del'**fin*** may well be the designation for the unnamed project described above.

CHAPTER TWO

BARTINI: BOLD IDEAS

ITALIAN-BORN DESIGNER'S PROJECTS

Robert L. Bartini is a well-known aircraft designer of Italian descent who worked in the Soviet Union. In the 1930s he designed the Stal'-6, Stal'-7, Stal'-8 and DAR aircraft which were built in prototype form; the Stal'-7 passenger aircraft served as a starting point for the Yermolayev Yer-2 bomber which saw service during the Second World War. Bartini authored a whole range of bold and unorthodox transport and combat aircraft projects, many of which were far ahead of their time. In addition to practical design work, he devoted much attention to scientific work in the aeronautical field, in which he achieved noteworthy results. At the final stage of his creative work Bartini devoted much attention to aerial vehicles making use of the ground effect; he studied and evolved the theoretical basis for this new kind of means of transportation. It was Bartini who introduced into the Russian aeronautical terminology the term *ekrano**lyot*** – a vehicle capable of flight not only in ground effect but also at considerable altitude over ground or water. The word *ekranoplan* was from the outset regarded as referring to vehicles flying at close proximity to a supporting surface. Bartini designed a number of flying vehicles which can be classed either as WIG vehicles proper (*ekranoplans* and *ekranolyots*), or as aircraft possessing certain features of WIG vehicles. This part of his design work, as well as his work in designing traditional aircraft, was to a large extent geared to military applications.

In late 1950s Bartini together with a group of associates was working at Plant No. 938 in Lyubertsy, a suburb of Moscow. (This plant was later known successively as the Ukhtomskaya Helicopter Plant, the Kamov Helicopter Scientific and Technical Complex and, finally, as the Kamov JSC.) His activities had nothing to do with helicopters; he was working on a series of projects of long-range supersonic bombers and reconnaissance aircraft. In parallel, during that period he evolved a theory which he called 'The Theory of the Earth's Intercontinental Transport'. The basic conclusion of this theory boiled down to the following: the best means of transport would be an amphibious vehicle capable of vertical take-off (in helicopter mode or with the help of an air cushion, endowed with a cargo capacity of large marine vessels and similar to aircraft as regards speeds and equipment. Further work on this concept led Bartini to the idea of creating heavy vehicles capable of alighting on a sea surface in sea states of 4 and more. One of the main directions of Bartini's work was based on the so-called contact-free take-off and landing when the aircraft would first lift off from the water or ground surface to a small height and then, supported by an air cushion (dynamic or static, or both), would perform a take-off run without resistance or shocks from waves.

The work along these lines concentrated on two projects – the giant '2500' VTOL amphibian (to be dealt with later in this chapter) and the relatively small MVA-62 multi-purpose vehicle intended for supporting naval task forces.

The background for the latter work was a crash programme launched in the Soviet Union in the early 1960s in the field of anti-submarine warfare due to the need to counter the threat posed by the US Navy's nuclear-powered missile-carrying submarines. Several comprehensive studies were conducted with a view to defining the basic approach to the problem. The results of one of these studies touched off the work by Bartini on the VVA-14 VTOL amphibian which was preceded by the MVA-62 project described below.

Chief Designer Robert Lyudvigovich Bartini, the creator of many unorthodox aircraft designs.

MVA-62

This aircraft incorporating certain features of WIG craft was intended primarily for ASW duties. Projecting of the MVA-62 was completed in 1963. This machine, with a normal AUW of 34 tonnes (74,970 lb) featured a flying wing layout with a wing of a fairly complex

A model of the MVA-62 maritime VTOL amphibian. Note the inflated landing devices (floats) with the waterline marked on them.

Another view of the same model with the floats retracted. Note the swept wings, the chin-mounted radar and the nose boom carrying a reaction control nozzle.

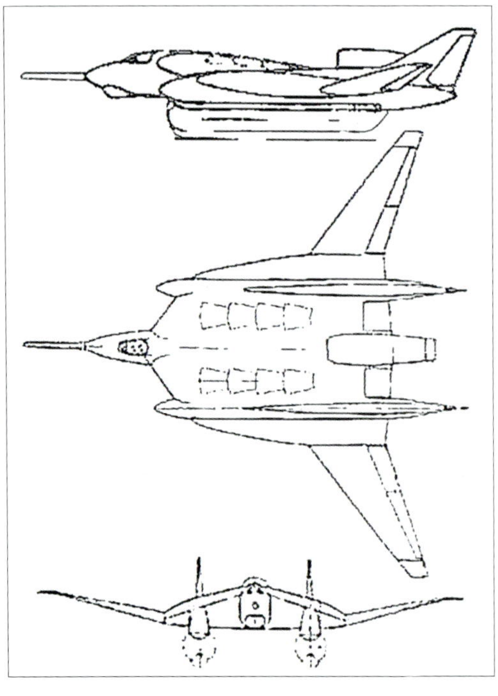

A three-view of the MVA-62, showing the inverted-gull wings with leading-edge root extensions, the trailing-edge flaps and the eight lift engine intakes with double doors.

configuration. It comprised a very wide chord centre section of high relative thickness with a nearly straight trailing edge and sweptback leading edges. Mated to the wing centre section at its aft end were sweptback outer wing panels of high aspect ratio, having marked dihedral. The fuselage merged with the wing centre section into a sort of integral layout. Two streamlined bodies located beneath the wing centre section on both sides of the fuselage carried two vertical tails at their aft ends; they also housed the inflatable pontoons which enabled the aircraft to take off from water (or from ground) and alight or land on any surface. The thick wing centre section provided accommodation for eight vertically placed lift engines which were intended to lift the aircraft just above the water during take-off and thus enable it to make the take-off run without making contact with the sea surface. At the same time the ram air would add to this a dynamic air cushion which would be formed in the space under the wing centre section between the pontoons. Propulsion for horizontal flight during take-off and in cruise flight would be provided by a single turbojet mounted above the aft part of the wing centre section between the vertical tails. Flight control at low speeds was to be effected with the help of puffer jets. Implementation of this project would have given birth to an ASW aircraft capable of making a landing anywhere on water or ground surface, operating at high sea states, performing ASW missions when afloat with the help of a dipping sonar etc.

The MVA-62 project served as a basis for designing the VVA-14 amphibian.

VVA-14 VTOL amphibian

In 1965 Bartini came up with the idea of building a VTOL amphibious ASW aircraft designated VVA-14 (*verti**kahl'**no vzle**ta**yuschaya am**fib**iya* – vertical take-off amphibious aircraft; 14 was the number of engines). He envisaged the VVA-14 as 'having take-off and landing devices enabling it to operate without dependence on airfields, including operation from water and snow-covered surfaces, and permitting it to stay afloat for an unlimited duration with the engines shut off, because drifting objects can be more easily camouflaged and are more difficult to detect'. In accordance with the official specification laid down in joint directive No. 935-320 of the Soviet Council of Ministers and the Communist Party Central Committee dated 11th November 1965, he was to create an aircraft with two 8,700-kgp (19,180-lb st) Solov'yov D-30M turbofan cruise engines fitted with devices for thrust vectoring in the vertical plane, and 12 Kolesov RD36-35PR lift turbojets fitted with turbofan attachments. The vehicle was to possess a cruising speed of 650-750 km/h (404-466 mph) and a service ceiling of 10-12 km (32,810-39,370 ft). The practical range with a weapon load of 2,000 kg (4,410 lb) was to be within 4,000-4,500 km (2,490-2800 miles). The mentioned directive was entitled 'On the creation of new aviation assets for combating missile-carrying submarines'. It was followed by the order No. 371 issued by the Ministry of Aircraft Industry on 26th November 1965 and somewhat later by the tactical requirements for the VVA-14 amphibian which had been endorsed by the Air Force and Navy Commanders-in-Chief on 7th June 1966.

One of the specification points stipulated that the flying vehicle was to be capable of movement in ground effect for the purpose of achieving both greater range and greater concealment.) This places the VVA-14 into the modern category of Type C WIG vehicles (ekranolyots), although Bartini

An early wind tunnel model of the future VVA-14 built in 1967. Two cruise engines are mounted fairly high at the base of a single vertical tail. Note the chin radome and the open intakes of the lift engines. There is apparently no horizontal tail.

A later model of the VVA-14 (also built in 1967). It still has one fin and rudder but tailplanes have been added, and the cruise engines are set lower and inclined nose-up, featuring elliptical intakes.

One more wind tunnel model of 1967 similar to the one depicted above, except that the main vertical tail has been augmented by two smaller ones. Note the shape of the engine nacelles' rear ends. The shape of the wings is close to the actual aircraft.

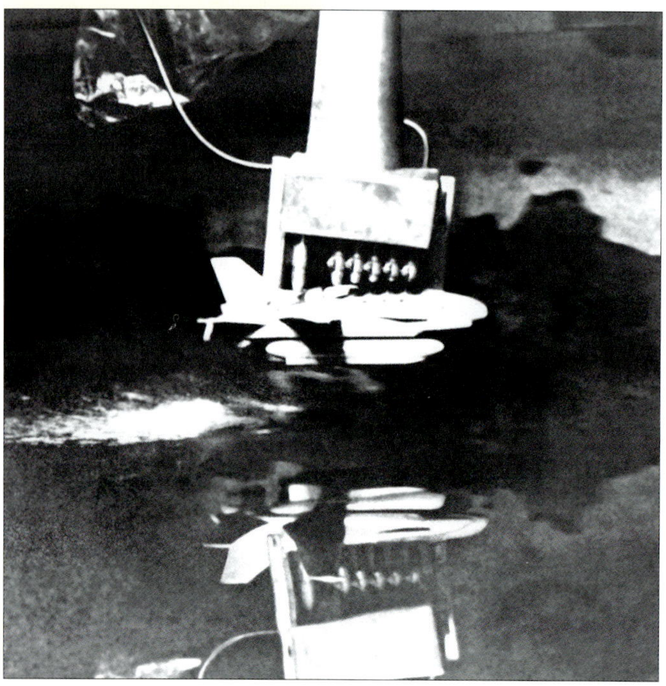

A model of the VVA-14 (in the configuration shown at the top of this page) in the towing basin; the inflatable floats are shown deployed.

A display model of the VVA-14 (again built in 1967) in take-off/landing configuration. Here the floats swing into position on four sets of parallel arms.

The same model 'hovering above the water'. Note that the rearmost pair of lift engines is separated from the other five by the wing spar carry-through structure.

This view shows the all-movable tailplanes, the small horizontal strakes ahead of the wings (called deflectors and not present on the actual aircraft) and the cranked wing trailing edge.

The same model in cruise configuration with the floats retracted.

Lower view of the VVA-14 model, showing the weapons bay amidships and the teardrop radomes under the rear ends of the sponsons.

did not use this term with reference to the VVA-14, and the aircraft mode was the main operative mode for it. Bartini and his associates chose for the VVA-14 a layout which differed very much from the aircraft layout adopted by the Alekseyev Design Bureau. Using modern terminology, one might call Bartini's layout the composite wing layout. The wings comprised a centre section of large thickness and chord (low aspect ratio) coupled with high aspect ratio outer wing panels placed outside the ground effect height. The wing centre section was flanked by sponsons which housed the take-off and landing device – inflatable pontoons affording the aircraft the ability to stay afloat. Thus, the water-based aircraft resembled a catamaran vehicle. The designer visualised his creation as capable of performing a prolonged flight with a high lift/drag ratio in ground effect and a flight with an acceptable lift/drag ratio at high altitude.

The VVA-14 was designed as a vehicle requiring no airfields for take-off. For this purpose it was to be fitted with twelve RD36-35PR lift engines, then under development in the Rybinsk Engine Design Bureau (RKBM) led by Pyotr A. Kolesov. The exhaust gases of these engines not only created vertical thrust but also formed an air cushion in the space beneath the wing centre section. The use of the air cushion effect made it possible to limit the

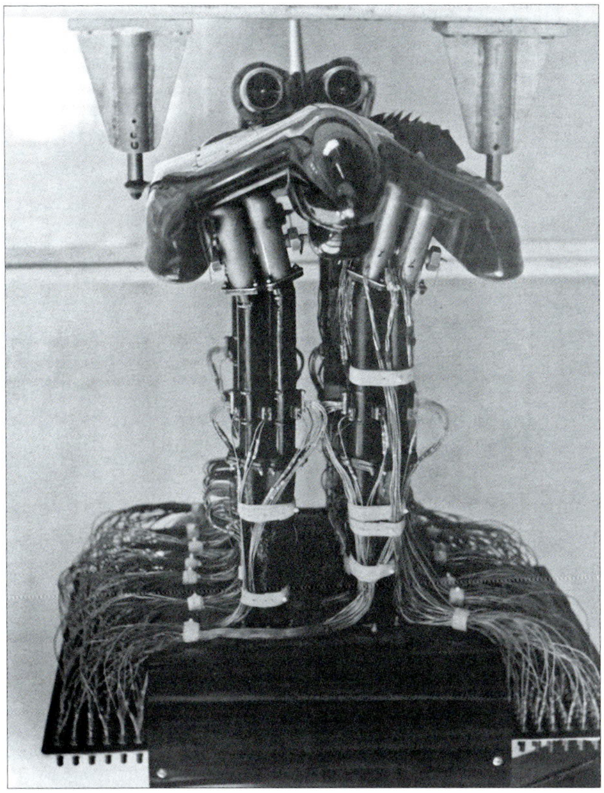

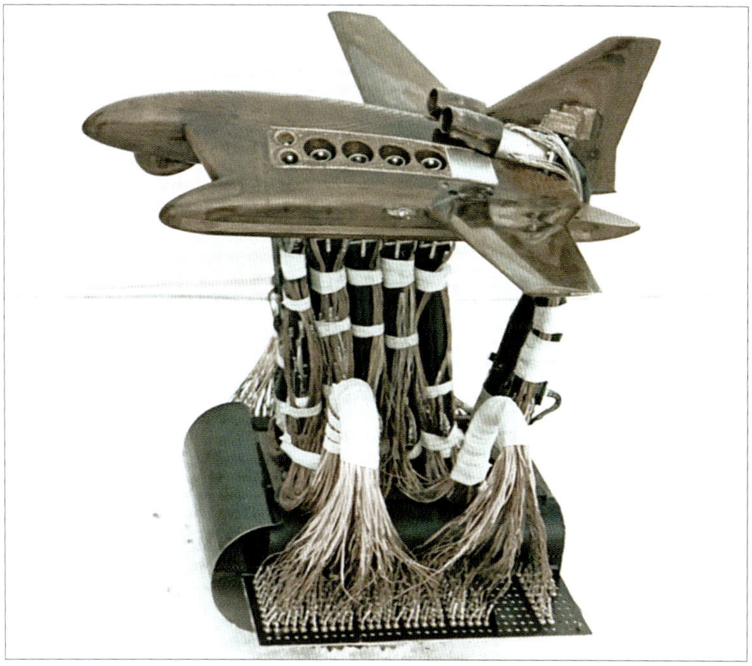

Top left, top and above: A test rig representing the original tailless version of the VVA-14; it features electric fans representing the cruise and lift engines.

Left and above left: A display model representing the final configuration with aft-mounted twin vertical tails and a dorsal package of two cruise engines.

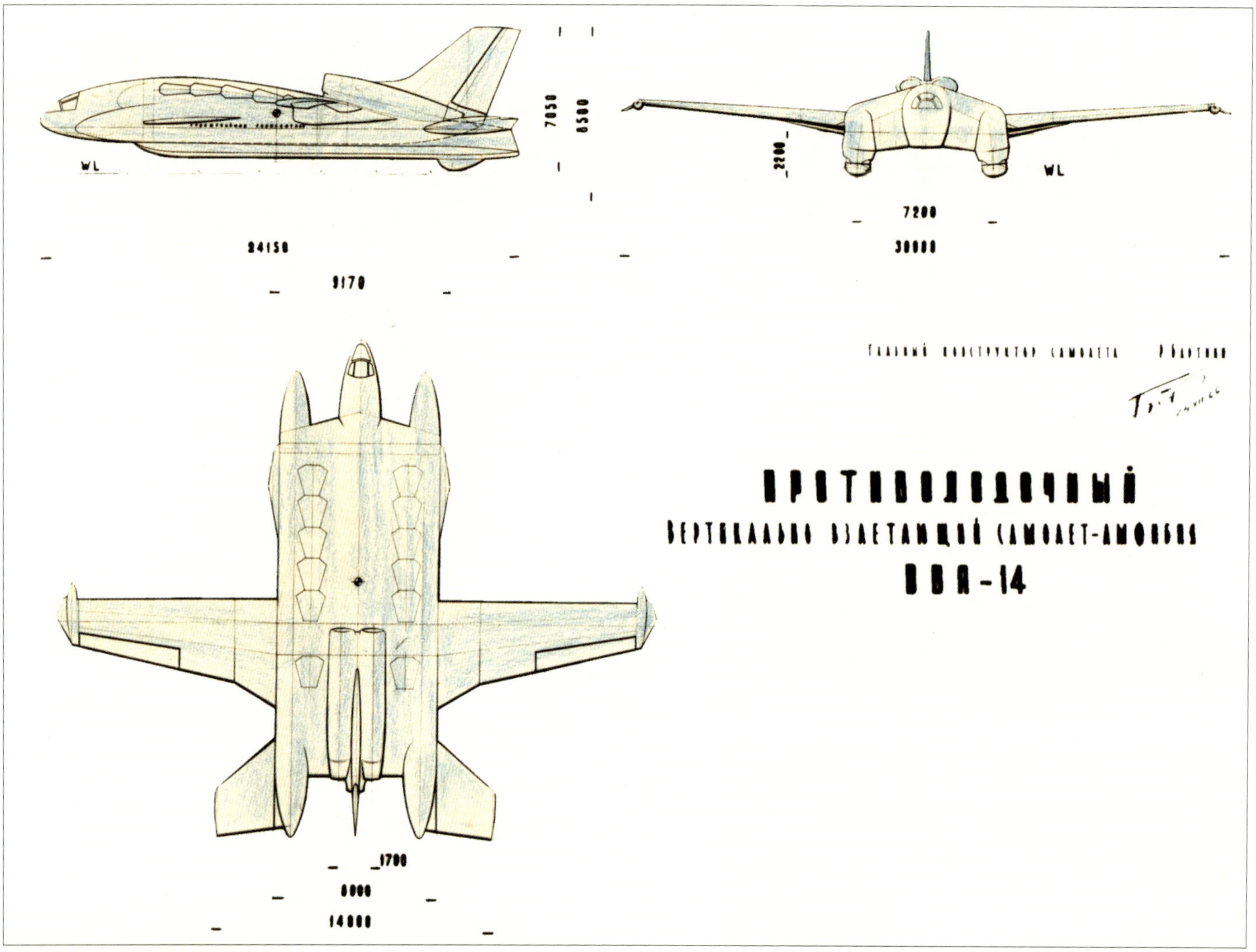
WL
24150
7050
8500
9170
2200
7200
30000
1700
14000
ПРОТИВОЛОДОЧНЫЙ
ВЕРТИКАЛЬНО ВЗЛЕТАЮЩИЙ САМОЛЕТ-АМФИБИЯ
ВВА-14

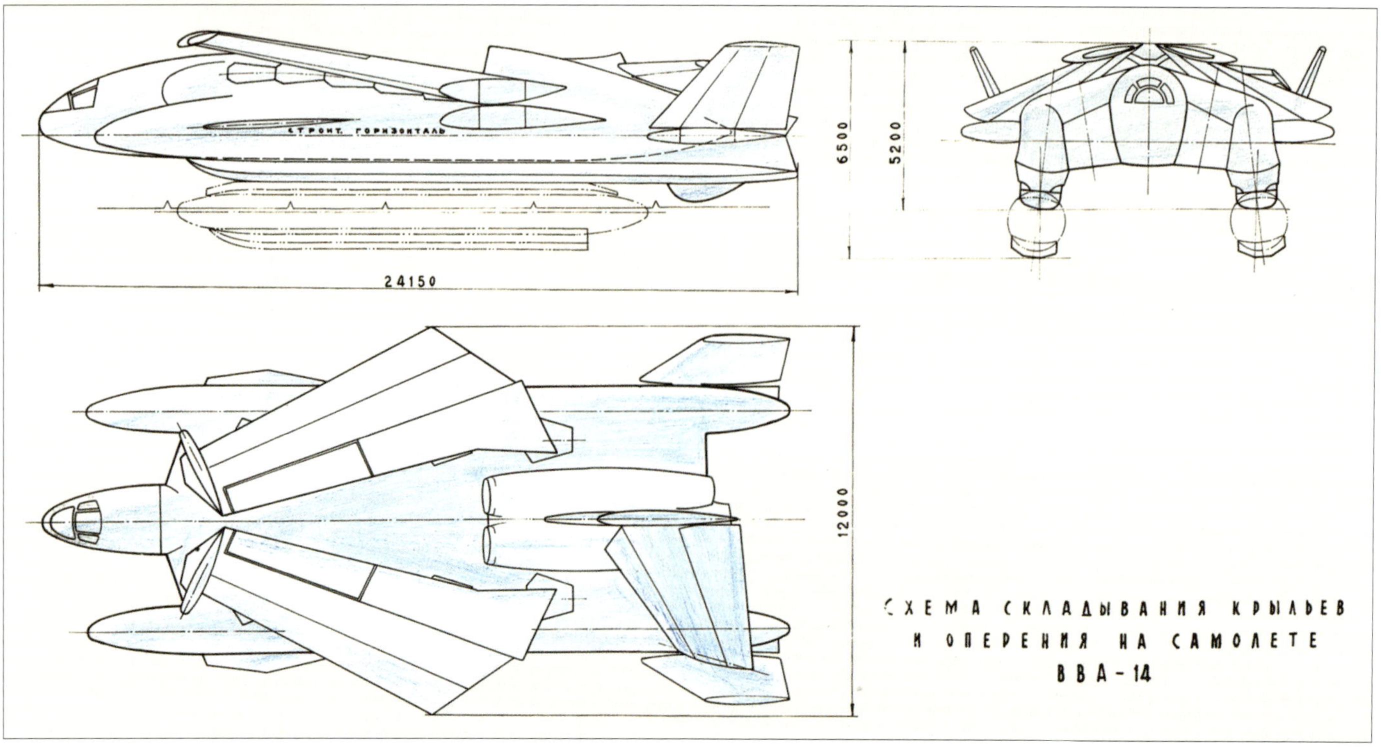
СТРОИТ. ГОРИЗОНТАЛЬ
24150
6500
5200
12000
СХЕМА СКЛАДЫВАНИЯ КРЫЛЬЕВ
И ОПЕРЕНИЯ НА САМОЛЕТЕ
ВВА-14

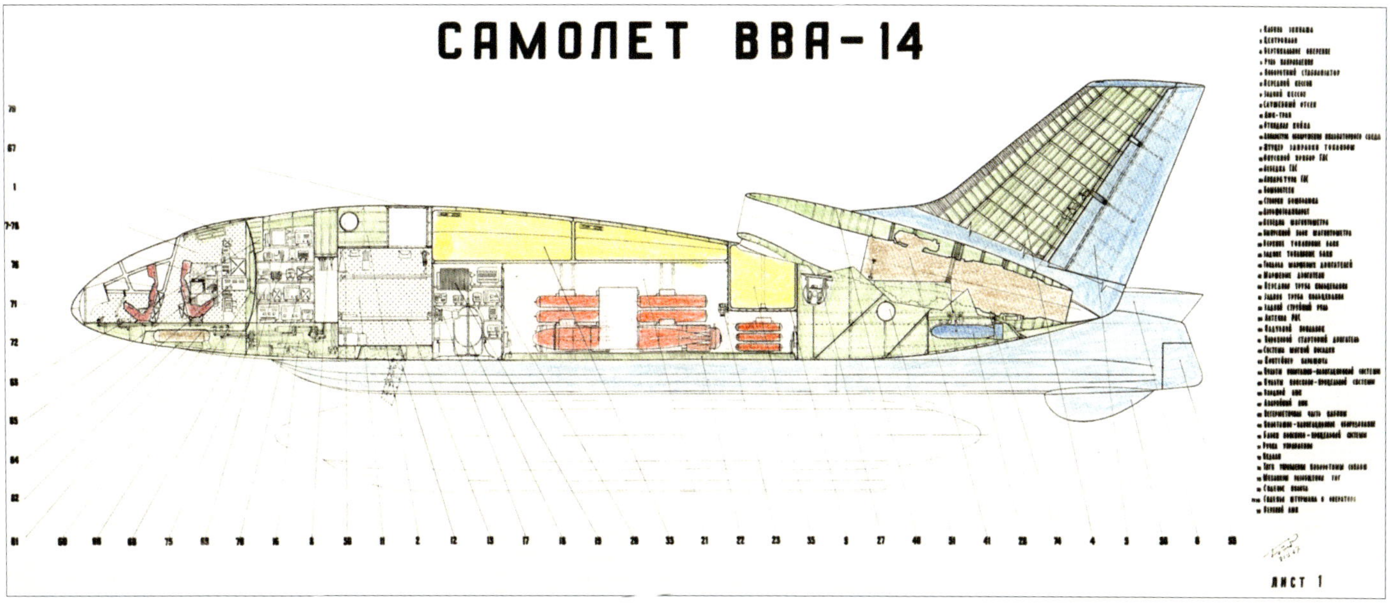

thrust required for vertical take-off and landing to a value less than 1 in relation to the take-off weight.

In 1967 the design team led by Bartini completed an advanced development project of the VVA-14 – a VTOL amphibian with two cruise engines and 12 lift engines. As distinct from later configurations, actually built or projected, this initial project version of the VVA-14 featured a single vertical tail. Dimensions and design performance figures were as follows: length 24.15 m (79 ft 2¾ in), wing span 29.98 m (98 ft 4⅜ in), maximum AUW 50,000 kg (110,250 lb), maximum useful load 2,000 kg (4,410 lb), maximum speed 790 km/h (491 mph), cruising speed 670 km/h (416 mph), loitering speed 350-375 km/h (218-233 mph), service ceiling 9,500 m (31,160 ft), range with maximum fuel load 5,200 km (3,232 miles), time on ASW mission at a distance of 100 km (62 mph) from base – 4.3 hours, crew – 3 persons.

The baseline version was presumably intended to be operated from ground airfields or from sea surface and had non-folding wings. In parallel, a shipboard version of the VVA-14 was projected in 1967. An advanced development project of this version envisioned folding wings and fin that would enable the VVA-14 to be based aboard Type 1123 ASW cruisers (SNS *Moskva* and SNS *Leningrad*) carrying Kamov Ka-25 *Hormone* helicopters, or specially modified large cargo vessels and tankers, or ASW cruisers built specially as VVA-14 carriers.

It was envisaged that the VVA-14 would be operated in three versions differing in equipment

Opposite page, top: A three-view of the VVA-14 in single-fin configuration from the project documents.

Opposite: This is how the VVA-14's wings and tail unit were to fold for deck storage.

Above: Two cutaway drawings of the VVA-14, showing the lift engines with fan attachments and the weapons bay.

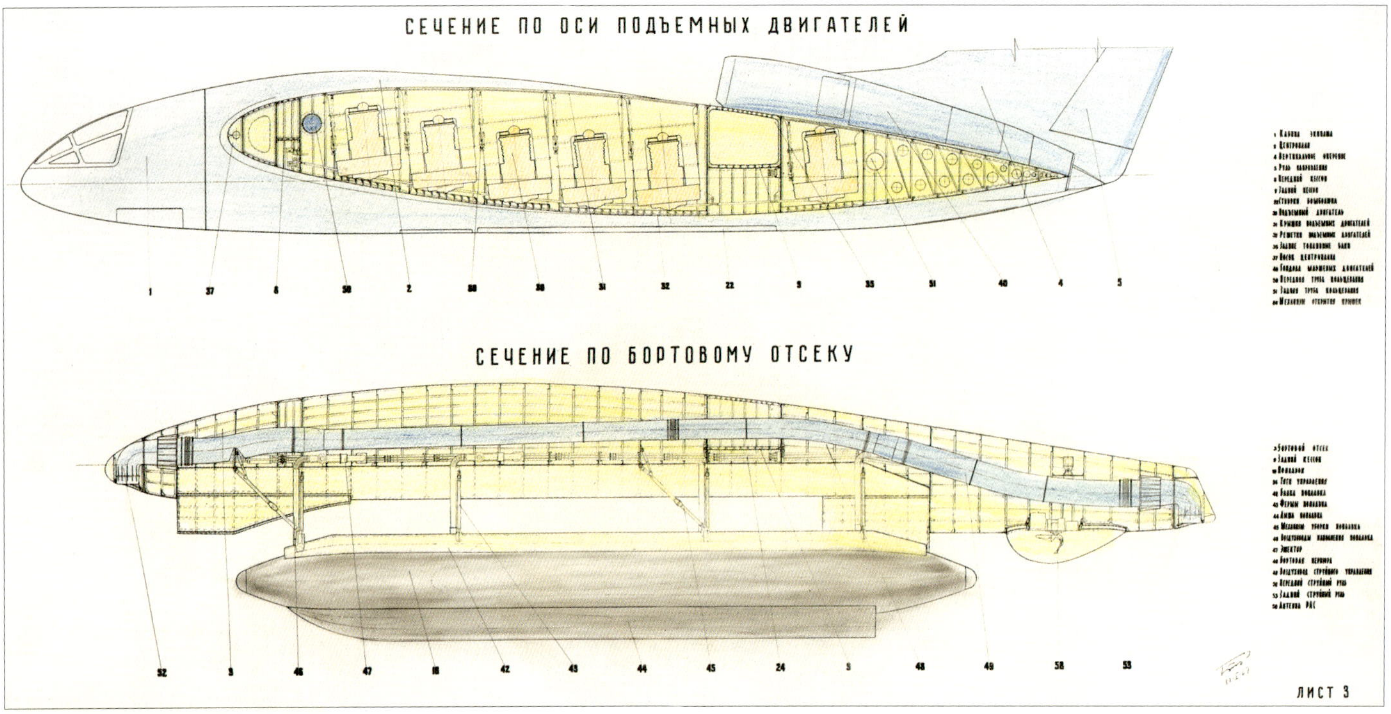

Two more drawings showing sections along the lift engine axes and along the sponson.

and armament: a search version, a search-and-strike version and a dedicated strike version. In one of the configurations of the latter, studied in 1967, the VVA-14 was to be fitted with the prospective ***Po**lyus* (Pole) search-and-strike system enabling it to deal strikes against missile-carrying submarines at a distance of not less than 200 km (124 miles) from the aircraft. In this version the VVA-14 was to carry under the fuselage a large air-to-surface missile weighing 3,000-4,000 kg (6,615-8,820 lb) and measuring 9.5 m (31 ft 2 in) in length. Additional equipment comprised a radar ranging device, an

One of the ground test rigs used in the VVA-14 programme.

A floating model of a late project configuration of the VVA-14. Note the strong anhedral on the inner wings, the circular cruise engine intakes and the deflector strakes ahead of the wings.

A large scale model of the VVA-14 in the towing basin.

infrared direction finder and a panoramic radar. This project did not go beyond the stage of a technical proposal submitted to the customer.

Bartini's design bureau had no production facility of its own, therefore it was initially planned that the construction of the VVA-14 would take place at Plant No. 938 (the Kamov Design Bureau's prototype production facility in Ukhtomskaya). However, Kamov's engineers lacked expertise in the construction of heavy aircraft. In consequence, a decision was taken to transfer Bartini to Plant No. 86 in Taganrog where he was placed at the head of a new design bureau specially set up for dealing with the VVA-14 project. Viktor I. Biryulin was appointed Bartini's deputy. In late December 1968 this design bureau was tasked with preparing a detail project of the VVA-14. This task proved to be a major challenge for the newly established OKB, and in 1970 the Taganrog-based Beriyev Design Bureau (headed by Aleksey K. Konstantinov from 1968)

A flight simulator rig developed for the VVA-14; note the projection screen.

A reaction control nozzle test rig for the VVA-14 converted from a lighter. Note the jet engine at the bows and its fuel tank amidships.

The same rig afloat on the Black Sea, the test engineers and the Kazanka speedboat providing scale. Note the outboard motor on the left.

The reaction control system test rig in action: the air jet directed downwards creates a fountain of spray.

Here the rig is moving under its own power; the jet engine is running at full throttle, causing the lighter to assume a nose-up attitude.

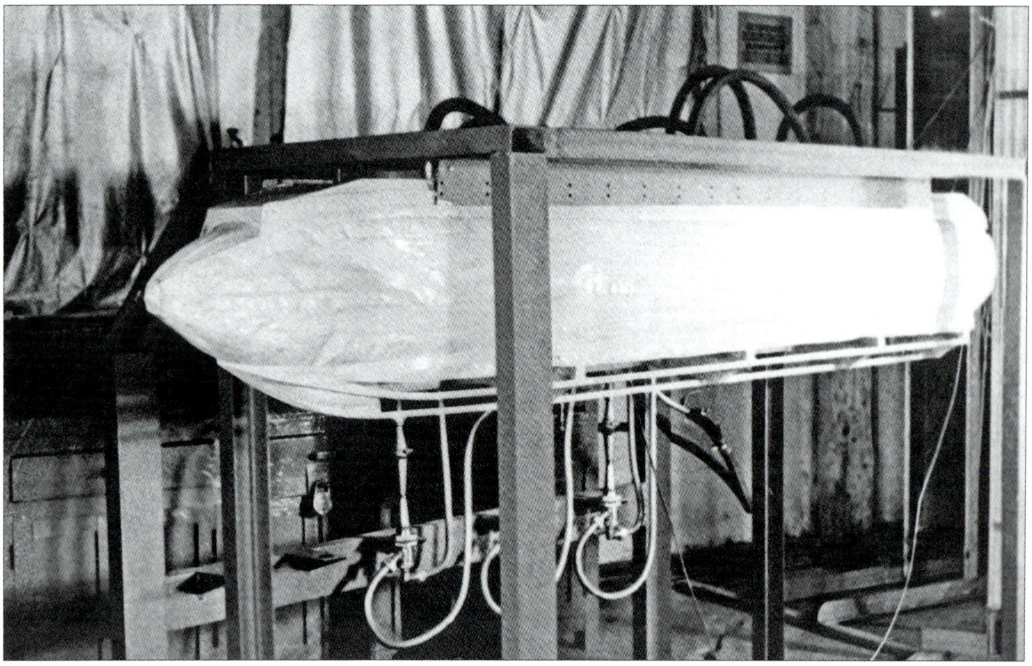

This rig was built for testing the VVA-14's inflatable floats. Here the float is shown in inflated condition; note the rigid 'skid' at the bottom.

Here the float is shown in deflated (retracted) condition.

Opposite page, top: The first VVA-14, CCCP-19172, at Taganrog. The bicycle landing gear is clearly visible.

Centre: The machine was initially flown minus inflatable floats and lift engines.

Bottom: A three-quarters rear view of the VVA-14, showing the ventral strakes at the rear of the sponsons. Interestingly, these leave no room for the rear reaction control nozzles.

was instructed to join in and take part in the preparation of the technical project. Construction of the prototypes of the VVA-14 was to take place at the experimental production facility of this design bureau.

Bartini was appointed Chief Designer for the VVA-14, with N. D. Leonov as project designer. In actual fact, the construction of the prototype was effected under the direction of Deputy Chief Designer Pogorelov (who had replaced Biryulin in this capacity) because Bartini lived in Moscow and came to Taganrog from time to time.

Plans were in hand for building three prototypes of the VVA-14. Construction of two machines was launched simultaneously, the first and the second examples being designated 1M and 2M respectively (only the first of them was eventually completed). The project had been considerably reworked in comparison with the 1967 configuration and featured two vertical tails instead of the single fin and rudder. The cruise engine installation was revised accordingly.

The three prototypes were earmarked each for its special part of the test programme. The first pro-

CCCP-19172
АЭРОФЛОТ

CCCP-19172
АЭРОФЛОТ

CCCP-19172

The VVA-14 after the addition of inflatable floats; here the machine sits on the floats with the gear retracted.

The VVA-14 rests on its wheels; the floats are stowed. Note the Be-12 Chaika ASW amphibian in the background.

totype (the 1M) was to be flown without lift engines and to be used for testing the aerodynamic qualities and flight performance of the machine in all flight modes except vertical take-off and landing; the second prototype was to be fitted with lift engines and pass tests in all VTOL modes, while the third prototype, at a later stage, was to be used for testing the systems and armament and developing the combat application techniques.

By the summer of 1972 the 1M prototype had been completed. The RD36-35PR lift engines were not available at the stipulated time, nor were the floats; in consequence, a decision was taken to conduct initial testing with a wheeled undercarriage

– the machine was fitted with a retractable bicycle undercarriage with outrigger struts (the latter were taken straight from the Myasishchev M-4 *Bison* bomber). Registered CCCP-19172 (a civilian 'disguise'), the VVA-14 performed its maiden flight from a concrete runway on 4th September 1972. In the first flight the machine displayed satisfactory stability and controllability. The first tests corroborated the viability of the aerodynamic layout chosen; it came as a pleasant surprise that the ground effect made itself noticeable already at the height of 10-12 m (33-40 ft) with the MAC measuring 10.75 m (35 ft 3¼ in), and became quite pronounced at a height of some 8 m (26 ft).

During the winter of 1973-74 the inflatable pontoons were finally fitted and the machine was tested afloat. The VVA-14 performed flights with the pontoons deflated and retracted, as well as with the inflated pontoons. By mid-1975 the machine had made as many as 107 flights. In 1974-75 the deployment and retraction of the inflatable pontoons was performed 106 times, including 11 operations of this kind in flight.

Even before the trials with the pontoons began, Bartini realised that the promised lift engines would most probably never be delivered; this would mean the end of the whole project. To save his creation from that fate, already at that stage Bartini took the decision to rework the 1M (VVA-14) VTOL amphibian into a WIG vehicle. Project work in this direction started immediately, but this idea was put into practice somewhat later, already without Bartini's participation (he died in December 1974).

A tall ladder was required for cockpit access via an oval hatch on the starboard side.

A test pilot in the cockpit of the VVA-14.

The Navy lost interest in the VVA-14; the programme was closed down. The almost completed second prototype, the 2M, was never flown and the third example was not built at all.

Before going on to the story of the 14M1P WIG vehicle based on the VVA-14, a few words must be said about the various project versions of the latter.

The VVA-14 taxies on the grass airfield at Taganrog, creating a local dust storm.

The VVA-14 on the slipway at Taganrog; the wheels are already up. Note the portside entry hatch and the blanked-off air intakes.

The VVA-14 afloat at Taganrog Bay. As these photos show, the ventral strakes have been removed.

One more view of the VVA-14 waterborne at Taganrog. The starboard entry hatch is open.

Here CCCP-19172 is seen in flight with the floats deployed. Interestingly, the ventral strakes are in place.

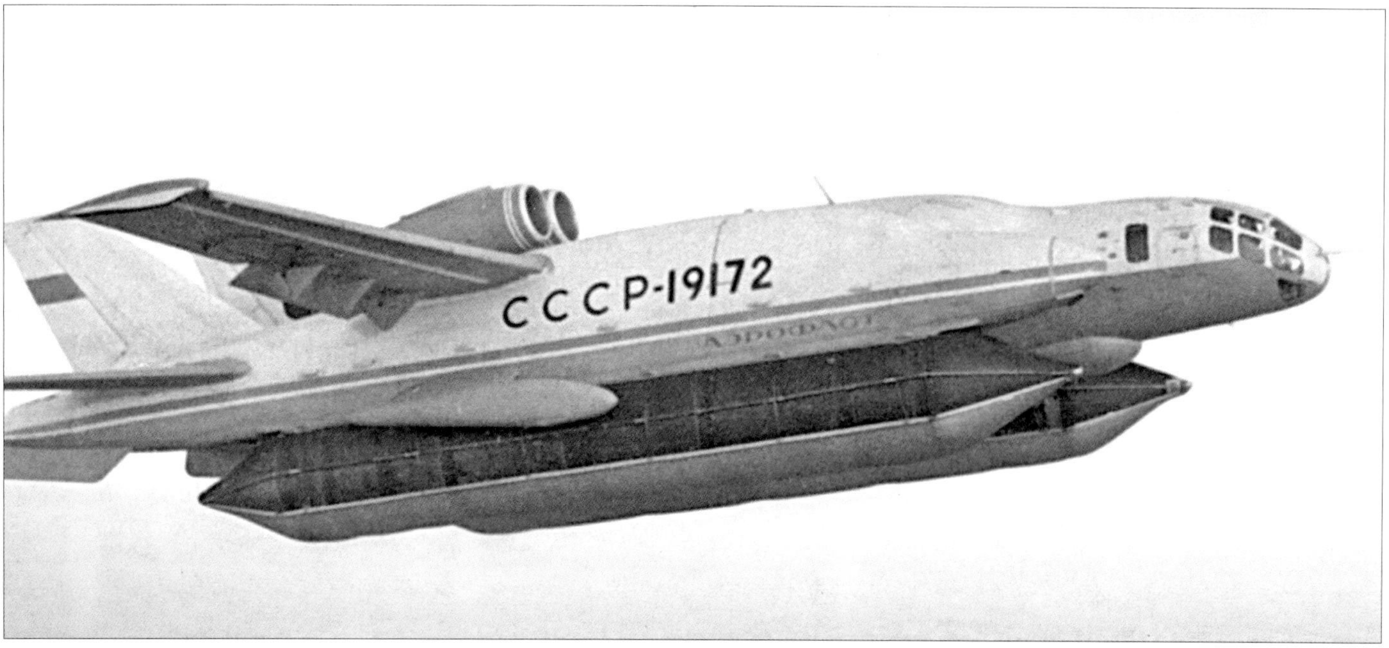

Above: One more view of the VVA-14 flying with the floats deployed. Note the characteristic nose-up attitude in level flight.

VVA-14 – shipboard version (project)

The initial project of the VVA-14 ASW aircraft from 1967 existed in the basic (water- or ground-based) version and the shipborne version. The latter differed in being provided with folding wing panels and tail surfaces; it was intended for being based aboard Type 1123 ASW cruisers, specially adapted large-capacity bulk cargo ships and tankers, or ASW cruisers designed with the VVA-14 in mind.

VVA-14 – transport version (project)

A transport version of the VVA-14 would be able to carry 32 passengers or 5 tons (11,025 lb) of cargo over a distance of up to 3,300 km (2,050 miles).

VVA-14PS – SAR version (project)

The VVA-14 ASW amphibian provided the basis for a project of search-and-rescue version, the VVA-14PS (*poiskovo-spasatel'nyy* – SAR, used attributively) which was studied in the Beriyev Design Bureau in 1973. The aircraft, having all the operational qualities of the baseline version with regard to take-off and landing, was intended for spotting and recovery of spacecraft and reentry modules of manned spacecraft after splashdown in the world ocean. It was also expected to conduct the search and rescue of aircraft, surface ship and submarine crews in distress at sea. In the space programme support version the fuselage of the

Below: Here CCCP-19172 is seen with the floats stowed for high-speed flight.

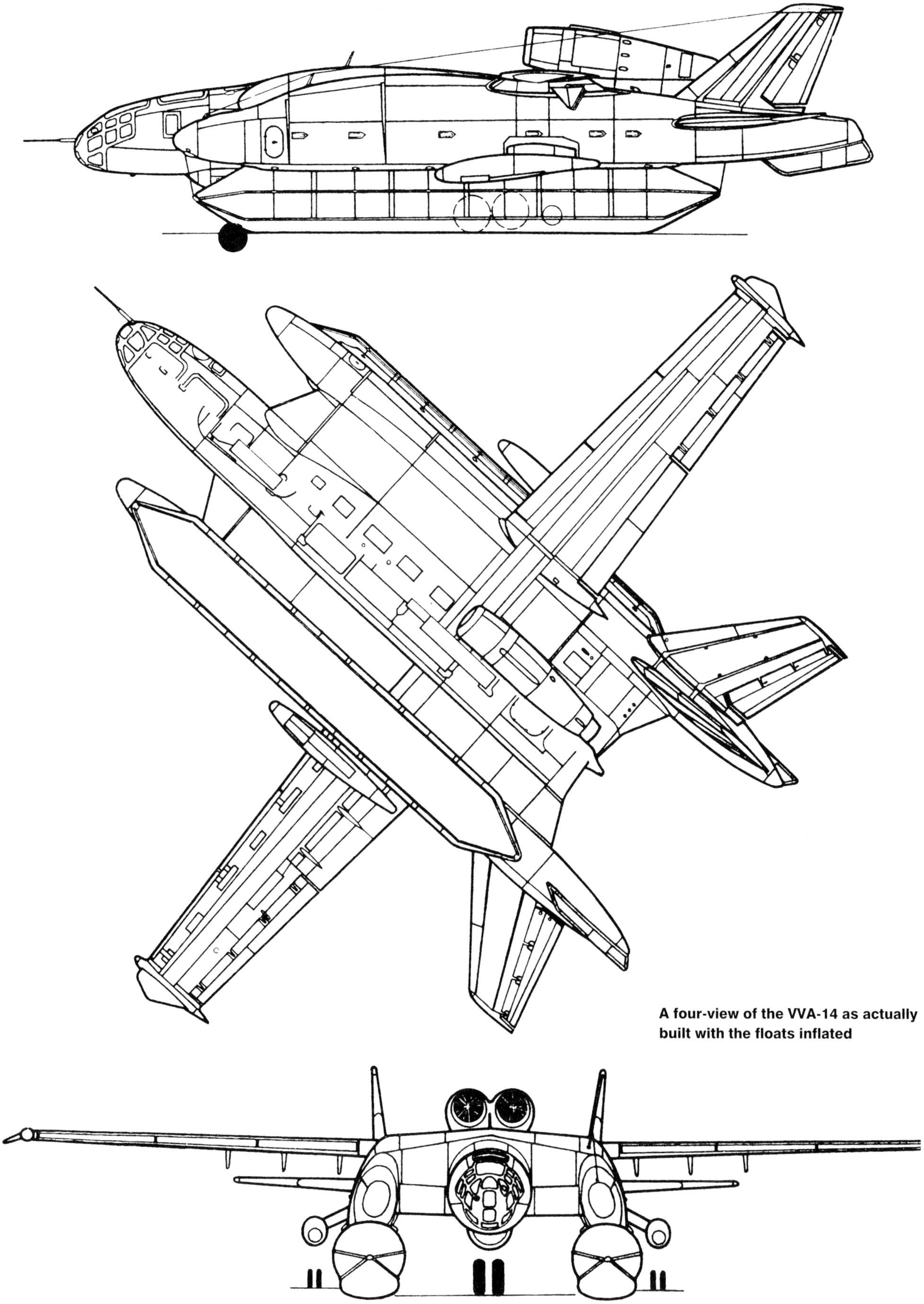

A four-view of the VVA-14 as actually built with the floats inflated

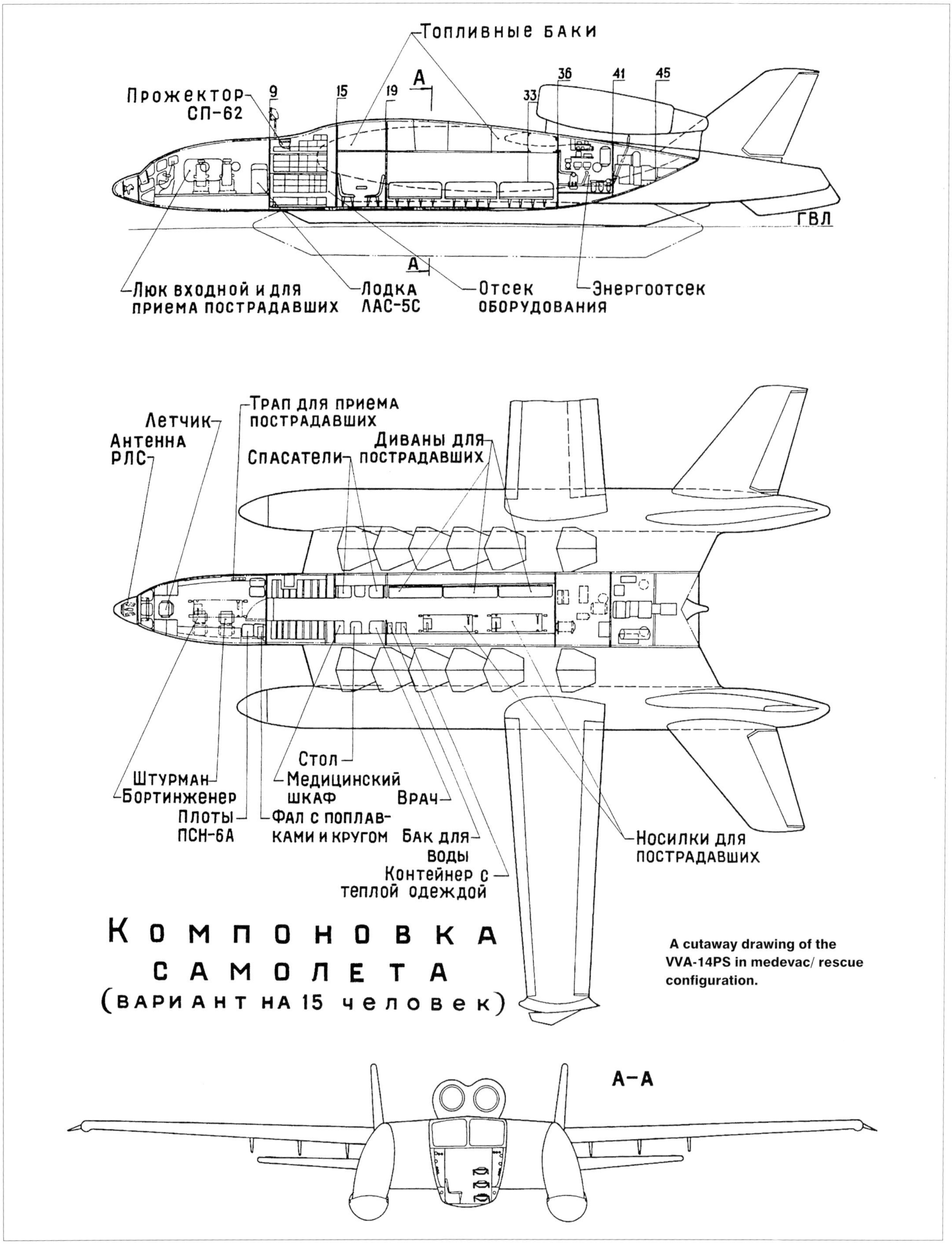

A cutaway drawing of the VVA-14PS in medevac/ rescue configuration.

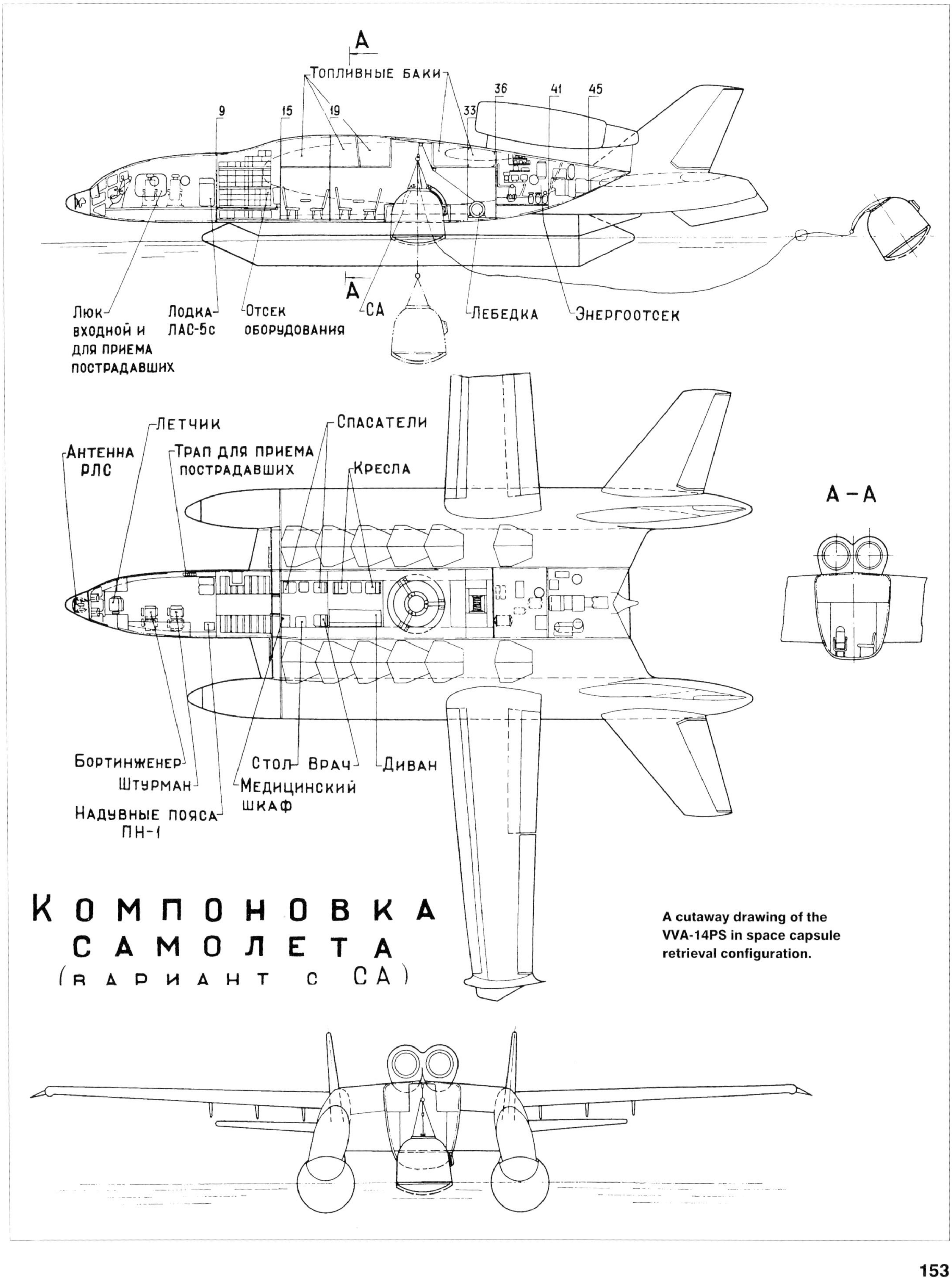

A cutaway drawing of the VVA-14PS in space capsule retrieval configuration.

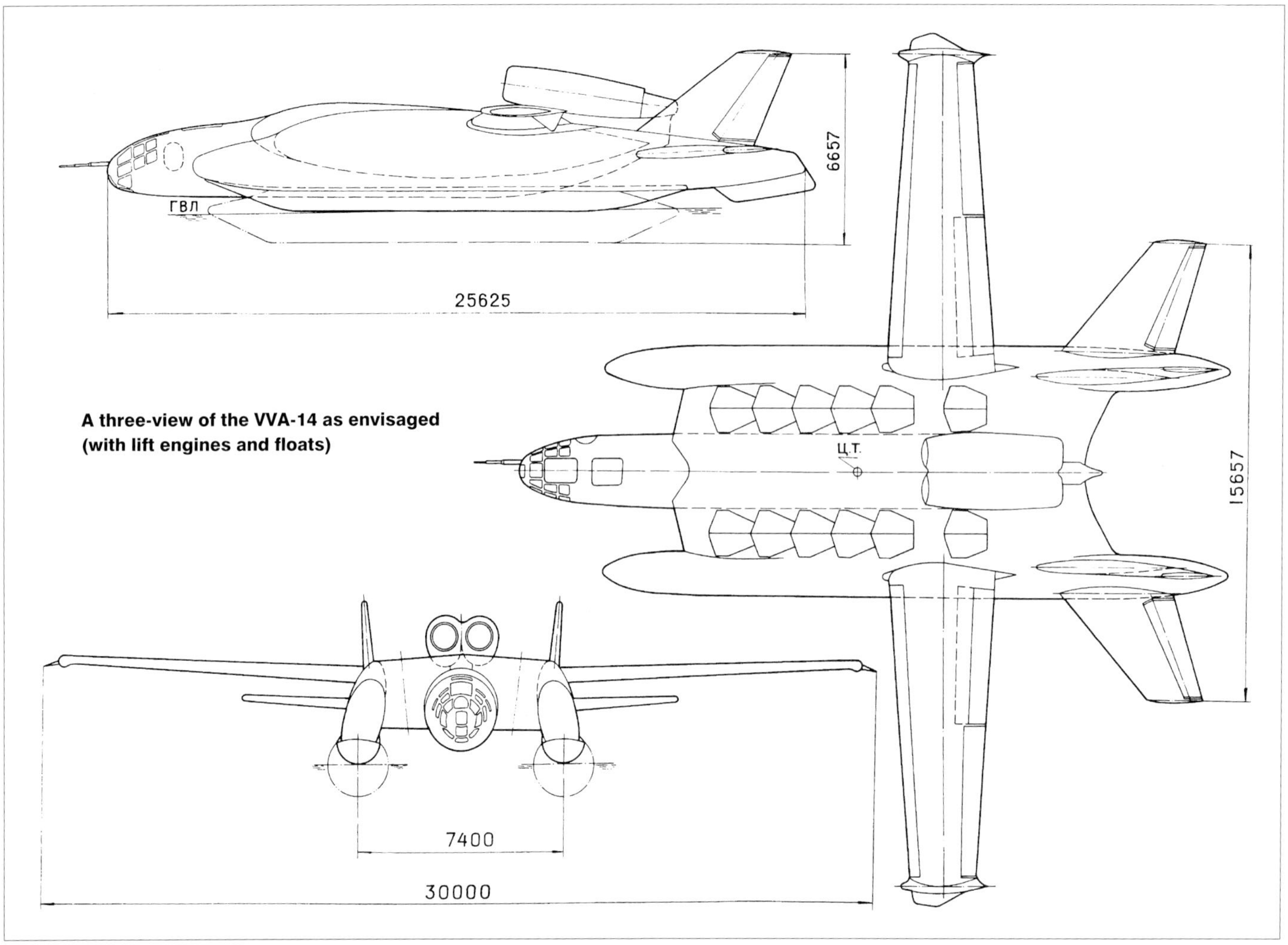

A three-view of the VVA-14 as envisaged (with lift engines and floats)

VVA-14PS housed a compartment with medical equipment where cosmonauts could be accommodated upon recovery. There was a special compartment for the reentry module and a system for its pickup and loading. The aircraft was provided with a hoist and carried life boats and life rafts. The 'normal' SAR version differed in having the spaceship pickup and loading system deleted and accommodated 15 rescued persons, including 6 wounded on litters. The VVA-14PS carried a complement of search equipment, including a radar, and a flight and navigation suite enabling it to fly over water areas devoid of landmarks at any time of the year, day or night, in good and adverse weather.

Termination of the VVA-14 programme led to the work on the VVA-14PS project being halted at an early stage.

VVA-14 – radio relay version (project)

There were plans for outfitting the VVA-14 with a special radio relay antenna and a device for raising it to a height of 200-300 m (660-990 ft) with the aircraft afloat.

A towing basin model of the 14M1P WIG vehicle. The number 7311 does not denote '1973, experiment No. 11', as the vehicle was developed in 1976.

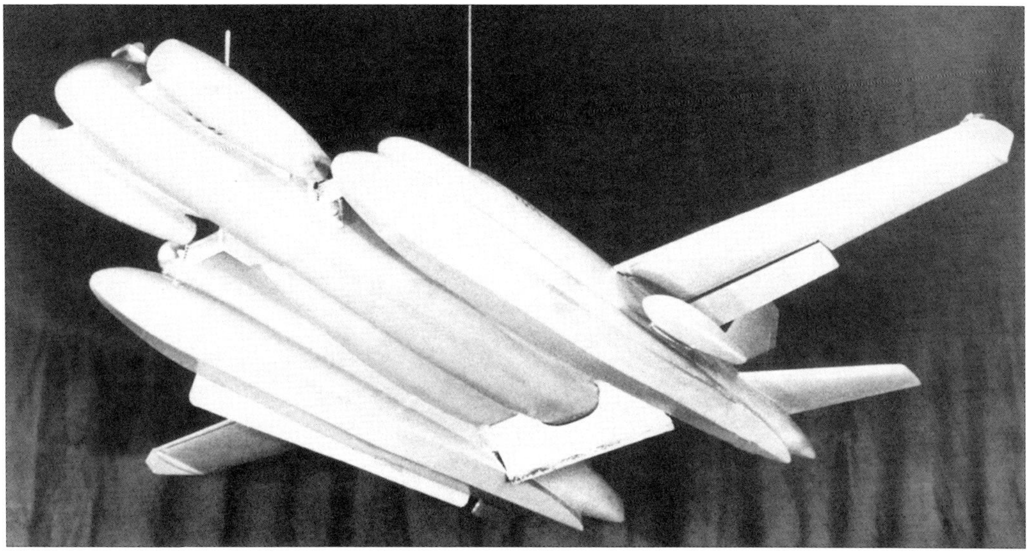

A lower view of the same model, showing the canted strakes on the floats and the rear flap between the floats forming a dynamic air cushion.

The same model in the towing basin, with a measurement scale attached to the forward fuselage.

Opposite page:
An artist's impression of the VVA-14PS picking up a reentry capsule after splashdown.

One more view of the same model during high-speed tests in the towing basin.

A different model of the 14M1P attached to a speedboat for open-air towing tests.

Opposite page, top: The real 14M1P being towed on the water at Taganrog.

Below and opposite: The 14M1P parked at Taganrog, showing the nose-mounted booster engines. The purpose of the boxy structure underneath is unknown.

N3440

Top and above: The 14M1P had a 'plug' inserted into the forward fuselage to enable installation of the booster engines. Note the new rigid floats and the fixed gear with no outrigger strut fairings. The pod under the port wing houses a cine camera.

The 14M1P on the slipway. Note that the cruise engines have been retrofitted with cascade-type thrust reversers.

Opposite page: Three more views of the machine afloat at Taganrog.

CCCP-19172

CCCP-19172

The 14M1P begins its high-speed run. Note the boarding ladder attracted to the starboard booster engine nacelle.

The craft accelerates, assuming a nose-up attitude as it tries to become airborne.

The forward engines created a huge amount of spray in take-off mode.

14M1P WIG vehicle

As noted above, in 1974 Bartini conceived the idea of turning the VVA-14 into a WIG vehicle. This idea was put into practice in 1975-76, after the termination of the VVA-14 programme. Dispensing with the use of the lift engines, the team of designers (already without Bartini) installed two more D-30M turbofans as booster engines flanking the forward fuselage of the 1M machine in similar manner to Rostislav Ye. Alekseyev's WIG vehicles. The forward fuselage had to be suitably stretched for this; the nozzles of the D-30Ms were provided with jet efflux control vanes.

The flexible floats were replaced by rigid ones. The trailing edge of the wing centre section was fitted with flaps which, together with the wing centre section and the side sponsons, formed a kind of 'scoop' in which the exhaust gases of the booster

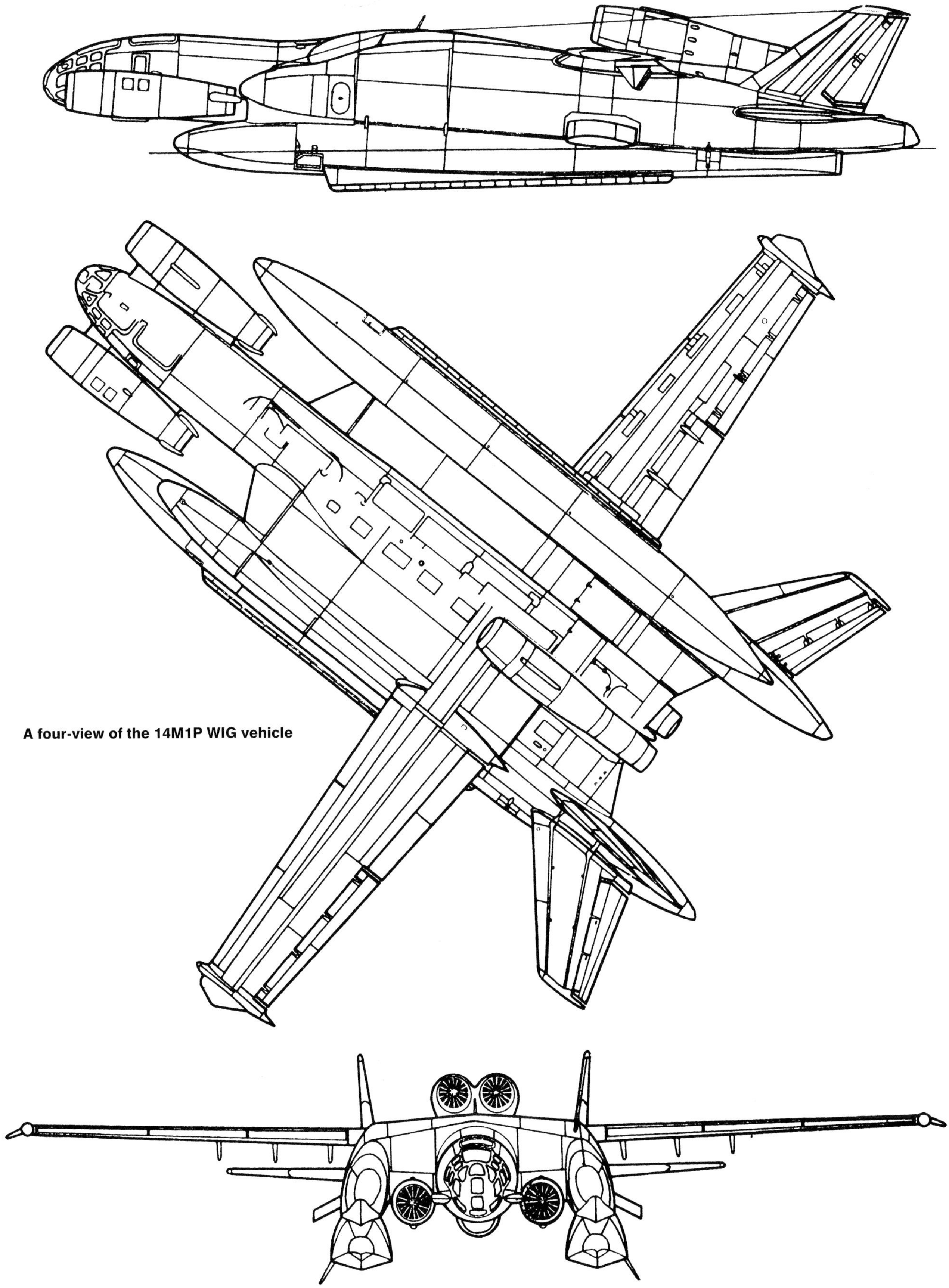

A four-view of the 14M1P WIG vehicle

The disassembled 14M1P at the Monino museum with the fake registration CCCP-10169.

This view shows the ejection hatches. Parts of the airframe are lying beside the vehicle.

turbojets created an air cushion. To enhance the effectiveness of the take-off and landing device, half-submerged skegs were mounted on the floats. The undercarriage was also modified. The original bicycle undercarriage was retained, but it could not be used because of the damage that would be inflicted by the jet efflux of the nose-mounted engines. Therefore the nose and main units were retracted and their wheel well doors were sealed; the outrigger struts were removed. Instead, four non-retractable units of a beaching gear were mounted on the floats, the front units being of a castoring type with a locking mechanism to fix them in flight. Available photos show the 14M1P prior to this modification, with the bicycle undercarriage extended and the original outrigger struts attached to anhedral pylons, but without the streamlined fairings into which they previously retracted.

All the modifications were completed in 1976. The modified aircraft was no longer a VTOL machine, and the letters VVA were deleted from its designation; now it was called 14M1P. It was, in effect, a WIG vehicle in its own right. In Russian sources it is styled as an *ekranolyot*, that is, a vehicle capable of flight both in the WIG mode and in an aircraft mode. The modified machine was subjected to testing which was conducted under the direction of project test engineer I. K. Vinokurov, with the original test crew comprising pilot Yu. M. Kupriyanov and navigator L. F. Kuznetsov (later replaced by pilot V. P. Dem'yanovskiy and navigator E. V. Vedel'). The 14M1P was not intended for fully fledged flight testing; it was, in fact, a full-scale test rig for verifying the viability of the concept.

Testing of the new machine started as pure frustration. The aircraft stubbornly refused to leave the

Close-up of the forward fuselage, showing the booster engine pylon attachments.

Many years after arriving at Monino, the 14M1P still has not been reassembled and is in a pitiful state.

ground during attempts to take off from a runway. This was attributed to dust ingestion by the front engines (the runs were performed on a grass airstrip).

Trials on water proved troublesome as well. The machine was unwilling to make turns, because the turning moments from the differential thrust of the engines were too small. Seagoing trials showed that movement in the dynamic air cushion mode was stable and the use of blowing from the front-mounted engines was a viable solution. The experimental material thus obtained was sufficient for the creation of a flyable example of the machine, but this required a thorough reworking of the design. This was clearly unrealistic, given the lukewarm attitude of the customer.

The work on the 14M1P was abandoned, not least because the Beriyev Design Bureau was overburdened with other current projects, such as the Tupolev Tu-142MR *Bear-J* communications relay aircraft and the A-50 *Mainstay-A* – the AWACS version of the IL-76MD *Candid-B* transport. The 14M1P

Two artist's impressions of the 'aircraft T' in a steep climb.

The 'T' had several versions; this one had a single fuselage and compound-type wings.

A desktop model of the 'aircraft T' showing the two pairs of booster engines under the nose and the aft-mounted pair of cruise engines located between the twin tails.

Another model of the 'aircraft T' with slightly different booster engine nacelles and forward sweep on the centre section leading edges.

was turned into a floating laboratory, and in 1987 it was sent to the Soviet Air Force Museum in Monino. The machine was delivered by barge to Lytkarino, a small settlement near Moscow. There it was unloaded from a ship to the bank of the Moskva River from where it was to be transported by a helicopter. While awaiting the arrival of the helicopter, the machine remained unattended, with lamentable consequences – it was badly damaged and partly plundered by unknown persons. The damaged aircraft was ferried by a Mi-26 helicopter to the Monino Museum where it remains to this day in a pitiful condition. Incidentally, the vehicle, as shown in Monino, wears the registration CCCP-10687, as distinct from the registration CCCP-19172 which was worn by the VVA-14 (1M) and the 14M1P during tests. One might suppose that this is the second example of the VVA-14, the 2M. However, this sup-

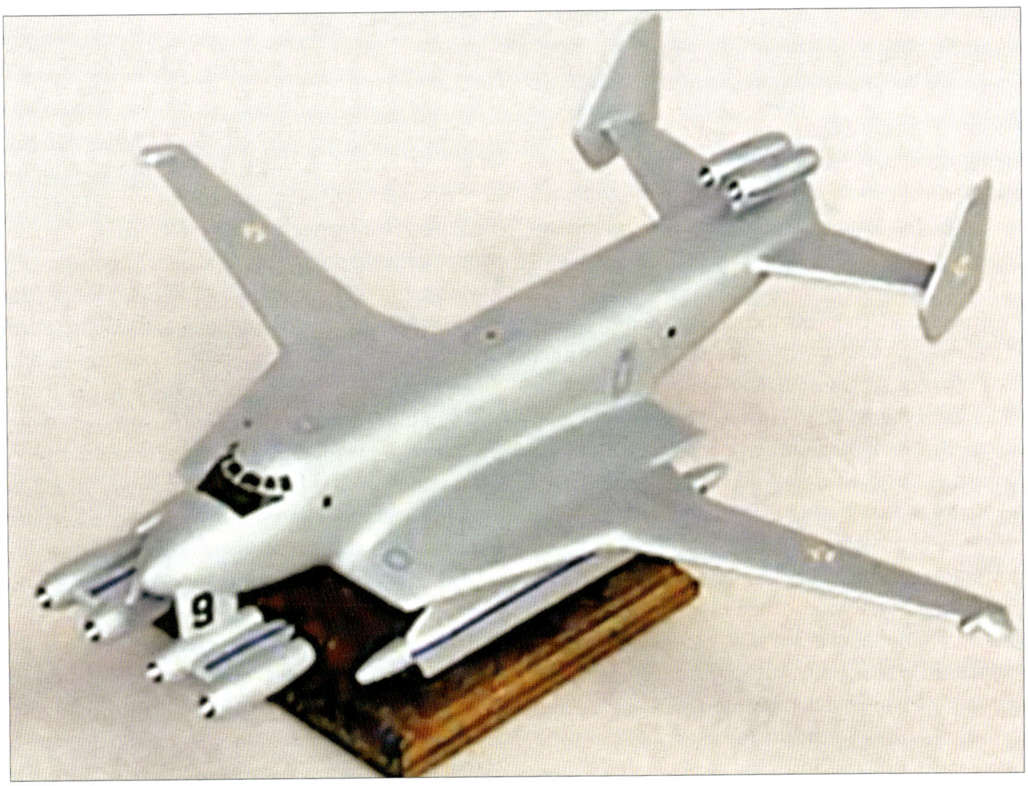

The floats of the 'aircraft T' and their pylons formed a cavity in which the forward engines were to create an air cushion.

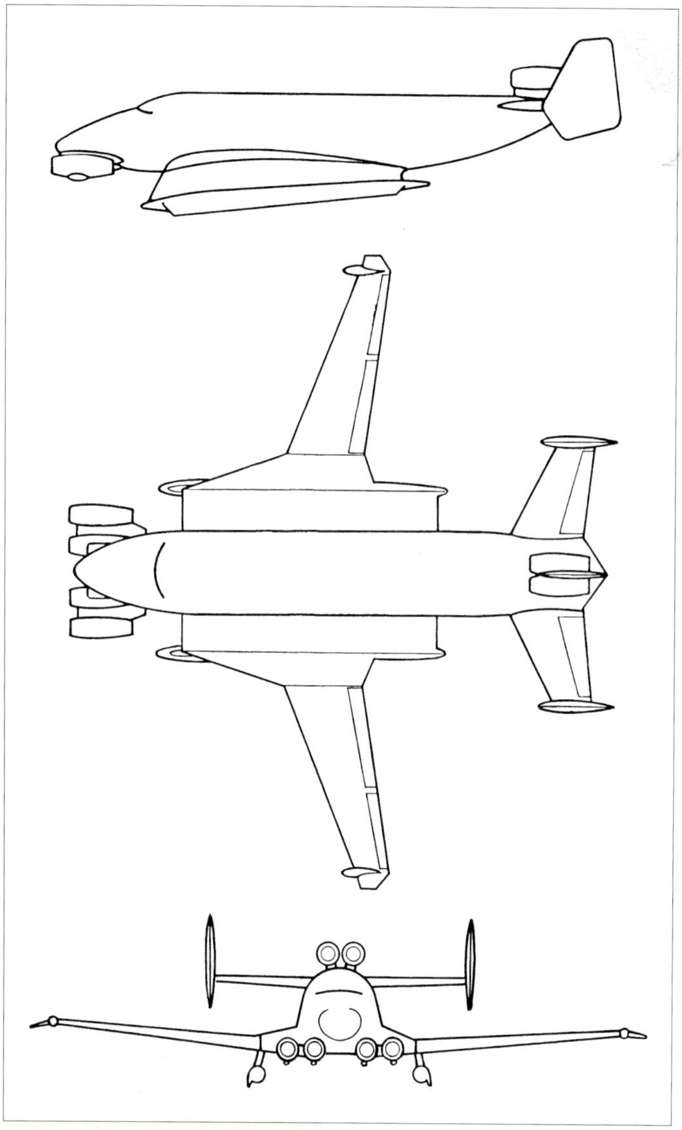

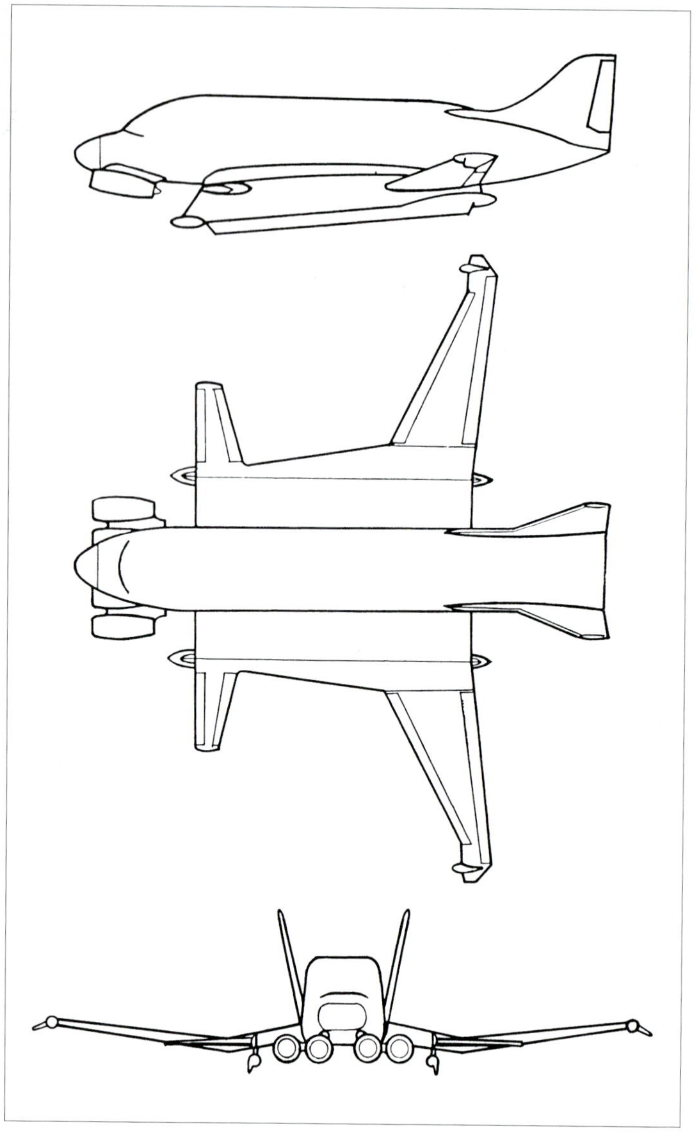

Above: A three-view of the 'aircraft T' in the traditional layout with twin tails and six engines.

Right: This three-view presumably shows the T-20A project.

position is belied by the fact that the Monino exhibit sports the attachment interfaces for the pylons carrying the front engines (the engines themselves are missing); this means that the exhibit is indeed the 14M1P.

Project T. That was the designation of a WIG vehicle design which was evolved by R. Bartini after the commencement of testing of the VVA-14. Project T was created on the basis of research associated with developing an aerodynamic layout of a future sea-going *ekranoplan*. Two versions of models were tested in the TsAGI towing basin. Work was in full swing on both a military and a civil version. In the latter version the passenger compartments were placed at a good distance from the engines and accommodated in the wing centre section and in the two boat-like hulls flanking it; these provided buoyancy for the machine when afloat and helped form the air cushion for fuller use of the ground effect.

As can be seen from an available drawing, the Project T *ekranoplan* was a vehicle of catamaran configuration with composite layout wings comprising a thick, low aspect ratio centre section coupled with outer wing panels of usual aircraft proportions having moderate sweepback. The outer wing panels featured leading edge root extensions. Four booster turbojets were mounted in pairs on pylons ahead of the centre section leading edge on both sides of the flight deck. Two cruise turbojets were placed on a pylon above the rear part of the wing centre section (the layout had obviously much in common with that of the VVA-14). Attached on the outside of the aft ends of the hulls were twin tail surfaces comprising horizontal tails and endplate fins and rudders.

The machine's basic specifications are as follows: wing span, 30.5 m (100 ft); length, 48 m (157 ft); all-up weight, 50 t (110,000 lb); payload, 20 t (44,100 lb); maximum speed, 550-650 km/h (342-404 mph), cruising speed, 370 km/h (230 mph).

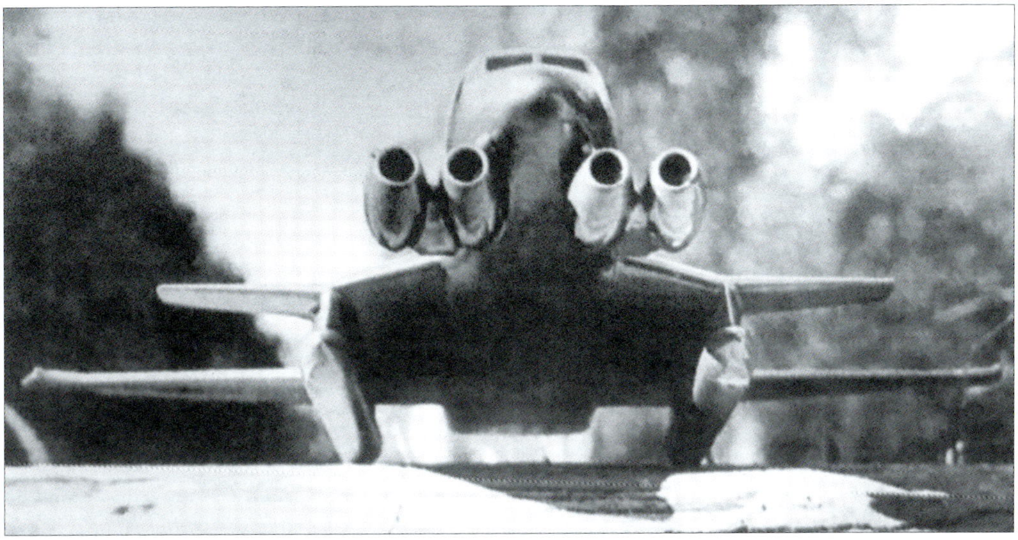

A model depicting what is probably the T-20A *ekranoplan*. The canard foreplanes flanking the wing centre section are visible here.

The machine had a wide fuselage with two low aspect ratio vertical tails mounted directly on it.

Another aspect of the same model. Note the anhedral on the wing centre section and the nose-up angle of the engine packs.

A model of a projected Bartini *ekranoplan* utilising the same layout as the 'T' but powered by three turbofans.

There was also a version of the Project T which was based on a traditional single-fuselage aircraft layout. In common with the catamaran version described above, it had a powerplant comprising two cruise turbojet engines and four engines acting both as cruise engines and booster engines during take-off. The four engines, mounted in pairs on horizontal pylons on both sides of the aircraft's nose, directed their efflux under the wing centre section which had a very large chord. Attached to the lower surface of the wing centre section at its ends were two full-length vertical pylons with elongated floats which helped form a cavity in which the air cushion was formed during take-off. High aspect ratio outer wing panels were added on both sides of the wing centre section, with leading-edge root extensions. The two cruise turbojets were mounted above the rear fuselage between the twin fins attached to the tips of the horizontal tail. Judging by the Red Star insignia on the model, this was a project of a military version (note also the absence of cabin windows).

Bartini's death in December 1974 prevented the work on this machine, as well as on several other designs, from being completed.

Bartini considered WIG vehicles to be a very promising kind of aerial vehicles for use over the expanses of seas and oceans. Gheorgiy S. Panatov, the then leader of the former Beriyev Design Bureau (TANTK named after Beriyev) (now headed by Viktor I. Kobzev) noted in his report at a symposium dedicated to the 100th anniversary of Bartini's birthday: *'Bartini worked with enthusiasm on projects of giant ekranoplans and ekranolyots weighing several thousand tonnes and featuring the same basic layout as the VVA-14, on such projects as the OVA-62, PVA-70, SONA, OVA-120, on contact-free take-off and landing vehicles* (i.e. vehicles with an air cushion undercarriage – *Auth.*) *– the T-2000, T-500, T-14, T-6, AER, EKhO-50 and others'*.

Concerning the T-500 and T-2000 we have the following evidence: *'In the course of the rapid development of design and construction of combat ekranoplans in our country in the 1960s and 1970s the concept of composite layout wing coupled with the use of booster engines found its worthy realisation (the 14M1P* ekranolyot *was designed and built, a contest was won for the creation of the T-500 and T-2000 heavy ekranoplans), and only Bartini's death and the subsequent perestroika and reforms in our country prevented these large-scale projects from being implemented'* (an excerpt from an article by V. Kolganov, a former associate of Bartini's, in the May 2000 issue of the *Kryl'ya Rodiny* (Wings of the Motherland) magazine.

Here is some information on some of Bartini's abovementioned projects involving the use of ground effect (sometimes in combination with an air cushion undercarriage):

A model of a projected twin-hull *ekranoplan* (possibly the OVA-62) having four large fans built into the wing centre section to form a static air cushion.

OVA-62

This was a project of an ocean-going amphibious aircraft with an AUW of 52 tonnes (114,660 lb). Its powerplant comprised two 5,400-kgp (11,900-lbst) Solov'yov D-20P cruise turbofans and four lift engines driving large-diameter fans.

T-6

T-6 was an agricultural aircraft powered by one Izotov TV3-117 turboshaft delivering 2,200 shp. The vehicle is similar to the VVA-14 in having composite layout wings with a wide-chord centre section and narrow-chord outer panels. The centre section housed six large fans enabling the vehicle to take-off with a zero run: the T-6 was to lift off thanks to a static air cushion and then accelerate without contact with the ground, the take-off distance being 120-138 m (390-450 ft). The machine measuring 22 m (72 ft) in wing span and 14.2 m (46 ft 7 in) in length had a design all-up weight of 6,500-7,500 kg (14,300-16,500 lb) and a payload of 2,700-3700 kg (5,950-8,160 lb). The service ceiling was to be 3,000 m (9,840 ft). Presumably, when being operated for crop spraying it could make use of ground effect.

T-14

T-14 was a project of a cargo/passenger aircraft powered by three 1,750-kgp (3,859-lb st) Ivchenko AI-25T turbofans. Its layout was basically that of a WIG vehicle, featuring composite layout wings with a wide-chord centre section, the lower surface of which, together with a pair of 'skegs', forms a kind of scoop for an air cushion created by blowing from two nose-mounted engines and then by forward movement of the aircraft. The third engine (a cruise engine) is mounted above the aft fuselage between the surfaces of the 'butterfly' tail unit. The cruise altitude is 6,000 m (19,700 ft), but ground effect mode is used for take-off and landing. The aircraft was supposed to lift-off with a zero run and then accelerate at a distance of 500 m. The all-up weight was 15,000 kg (33,000 lb). Other particulars include the wing span of 23,9 m (78 ft 5 in) and length of 19.7 m (64 ft 7⅝ in), the empty weight of 8,800 kg (19,400 lb), a maximum speed of 600 km/h (373 mph) and a cruising speed of 515 km/h (321 mph) at altitude.

T-20A?

This unconfirmed designation featured in a caption to a photo of model of one of Bartini's designs featuring basically the same layout as the T-14 with its V-tail, but of larger dimensions (a wing span of 29.5 m/96 ft 9½ in is cited in one source). Four cruise/boost engines of unknown type are installed under the forward fuselage. A special feature of this design is the installation of foreplanes near the leading edge of the wing centre section. The layout of this machine seems to have much in common with the single-fuselage version of the Project T, apart from the foreplanes and the V-tail. Rather fulsome cylindrical bodies (a kind of floats) mounted on long-chord pylons under the wings are noteworthy.

Ekranolyot

This machine is depicted in an artist's impression which was once published with the generic name 'Ekranolyot' in the caption instead of the proper

A model of the huge '2500' aircraft carrier ekranoplan. Note the foreplanes carrying the boost.cruise engines and the radomes on top of the fins.

designation. The drawing shows a machine of apparently huge dimensions, judging by the relative size of the crew cockpit and the provision of as many as eight turbojets for propulsion. The aerodynamic layout has much in common with that of the MVA-62 described earlier in this chapter. It features a wide-chord rectangular wing centre section flanked by two fuselage-like side bodies which carry vertical tail surfaces. Attached to the wing centre section well aft are the swept-back outer wing panels of high aspect ratio. The crew cockpit is located in a sort of fuselage protruding from the leading edge of the wing centre section. What makes this project differ in layout from the MVA-62 is the foreplane joining together the fuselage and the front ends of the side bodies protruding ahead of the leading edge. The foreplane carries eight turbojets arranged in four pairs; they obviously perform the double role of cruise and boost engines whose efflux can be directed under the wing centre section. In some publications this picture was captioned as T-500, but this identification remains unconfirmed. It is also tentatively identified as the DLK (*dozvukovoye letayushcheye krylo* – subsonic flying wing). The DLK layout was studied by Bartini from 1962 as a part of his work on heavy transport WIG vehicles in the *ekranolyot* category.

T-2000

Unfortunately, no information is available about this project of a WIG vehicle, apart from the fact that it was going to be of gigantic dimensions and weight.

SVVP-2500 (project 2500)

Information on this project is rather vague, creating the risk of misinterpretations. In its original form it was visualised as a giant STOL vehicle making use of lift engines (SVVP means *samolyot vertikal'novo vzlyota i posahdki*, VTOL aircraft). According to one interpretation, Bartini *'started the work on a WIG craft equipped with hydrofoils which subsequently was developed into the project of the SVVP-2500* ekranolyot', that is, a WIG vehicle capable of flying also in the aircraft mode. It was to have an AUW of 2,500 tonnes 5,512,500 lb) and had the layout of a 'flying wing' with a square-shaped centre-section and outer panels. The powerplant was to comprise lift engines and cruise engines.

Another source describes the '2500' vehicle as an amphibian which had a wing centre section *'the size of a football field'* which *'could well serve as the landing deck of a flying aircraft carrier'*. The wing centre section was flanked by fuselage-like bodies. Attached to their underside were elastic cylindrical pontoons. The aft ends of the fuselage-like bodies carried twin vertical tails and outer wing panels (which might well be described as horizontal stabilisers). A model of the craft shows the fins to be topped by saucer-like bodies. The fuselages protruded well forward of the wing leading edge.

The cruise turbojets were initially to be located on vertical pylons above the aft part of the wing centre section where they would be protected from sea spray and dust ingestion. After getting acquainted with Rostislav Alekseyev's experience in the use of turbojet efflux for augmenting the dynamic air cushion during take-off, Bartini decided to relocate the engines. A package of four turbojets was mounted under a foreplane which was attached to the starboard fuselage nose. This made it possible to direct the efflux into the space under the wing. The trailing edge of the wing centre section was fitted with a flap which could be deflected during take-off. The efflux gases accumulated in the chamber, thus creating an air cushion which helped the vehicle raise itself out of the water and enter the ground effect flight mode.

Bartini studied different options of the powerplant for this monster. One of these options was a nuclear powerplant which could be used during

A model of the T-500 tail-first *ekranoplan*. The double-deck fuselage gives an indication of the machine's huge size.

A model depicting the Ekranokhod monorail passenger transport with aerodynamic offloading.

cruise flights of long duration; in this case the take-off was to be effected with the engines running on the usual chemical fuel.

The elastic pontoons were designed to ensure a safe landing both on the water surface and on the ground. They were suitably shaped hydrodynamically, being provided with chines and steps. The underside of the pontoons incorporated skids.

Bartini predicted that the '2500' craft, with its MAC of 250 m (820 ft), would be capable of performing a flight in ground effect mode at an altitude of 150-200 m (490-660 ft). The test results obtained with the VVA-14 amphibian, described above, reinforced his belief in this. This would significantly increase the safety of operation of large-size WIG vehicles above the sea surface.

This project was clearly ahead of its time, but some of its technical features were implemented on a smaller scale in the VVA-14 amphibian .

EKV-600

EKV-600 was a 'ground-effect speedboat' (presumably for sports use). Judging by the available drawing, this single-seat machine had wings of low aspect ratio with a straight leading edge and forward sweep on trailing edges. Two floats are attached to wingtips and protrude ahead of the leading edge. The noses of the floats are connected by a foreplane. Attached to the main wing centre section are outer wing panels featuring marked dihedral. The hull has a fin at its aft end. Flaps are presumably mounted at the trailing edge of the main wings. The drawing gives no clue to the type of the powerplant.

EKhO-50

EKhO-50 was described – presumably by Bartini himself – as an '*ekranokhod*', which can be broadly translated as a vehicle for movement (*khod*) in ground effect (*ekrahn* – here, supporting surface). The vehicle features a 'flying wing' layout (in the sense of this term as applied to WIG craft), i.e., a rectangular platform possessing an airfoil section is flanked with endplate floats. The front part of the platform houses the crew compartment, the aft part carries a tail unit comprising two surfaces inclined at an angle of 45°. The vehicle is powered by four TV3-117 turboshafts delivering 2,200 shp each (no propellers are visible in the available drawing).

Basic specifications include: overall length, 36.0 m (118 ft); overall width, 21 m (69 ft); air cushion area, 330 m^2 (3,550.sq ft); all-up weight, 50 t (110,250 lb); payload, 29 t (64,000 lb); draught when afloat, 1.25 m (4 ft); height above the surface at cruising speed, 0.165 m (6 _ in); cruising speed, 130 km/h (80 mph); maximum speed, 150 km/h (93 mph); endurance, 8 hours; crew, 8 persons.

(Drawings of the T-6, T-14, EKV-600 and EKhO-50 described above have been redrawn from poor-quality originals and should be regarded as provisional).

An artist's impression of the Ekranokhod in action.

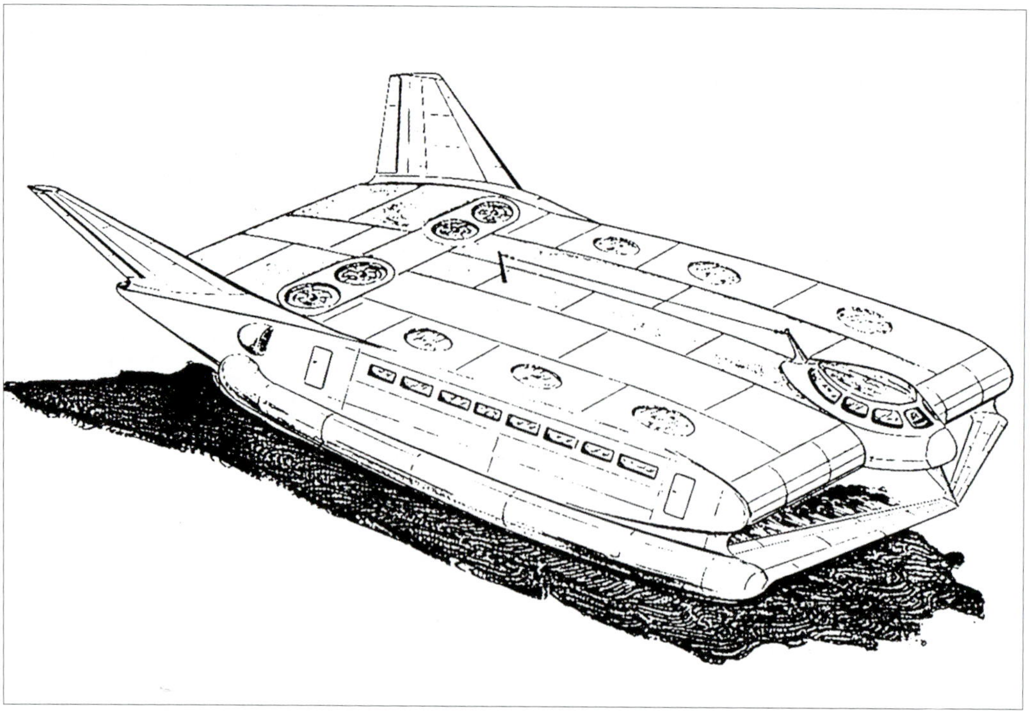

An artist's impression of an altogether different Ekranokhod similar in concept to the hovercraft that used to operate on the English Channel service.

The results of the pioneering work conducted by Bartini in the field of WIG vehicles were 'inherited' by the Beriyev Design Bureau (currently TANTK named after G. M. Beriyev) under whose auspices he worked during the last years of his life. His ideas are being followed up by this design bureau (see next chapter).

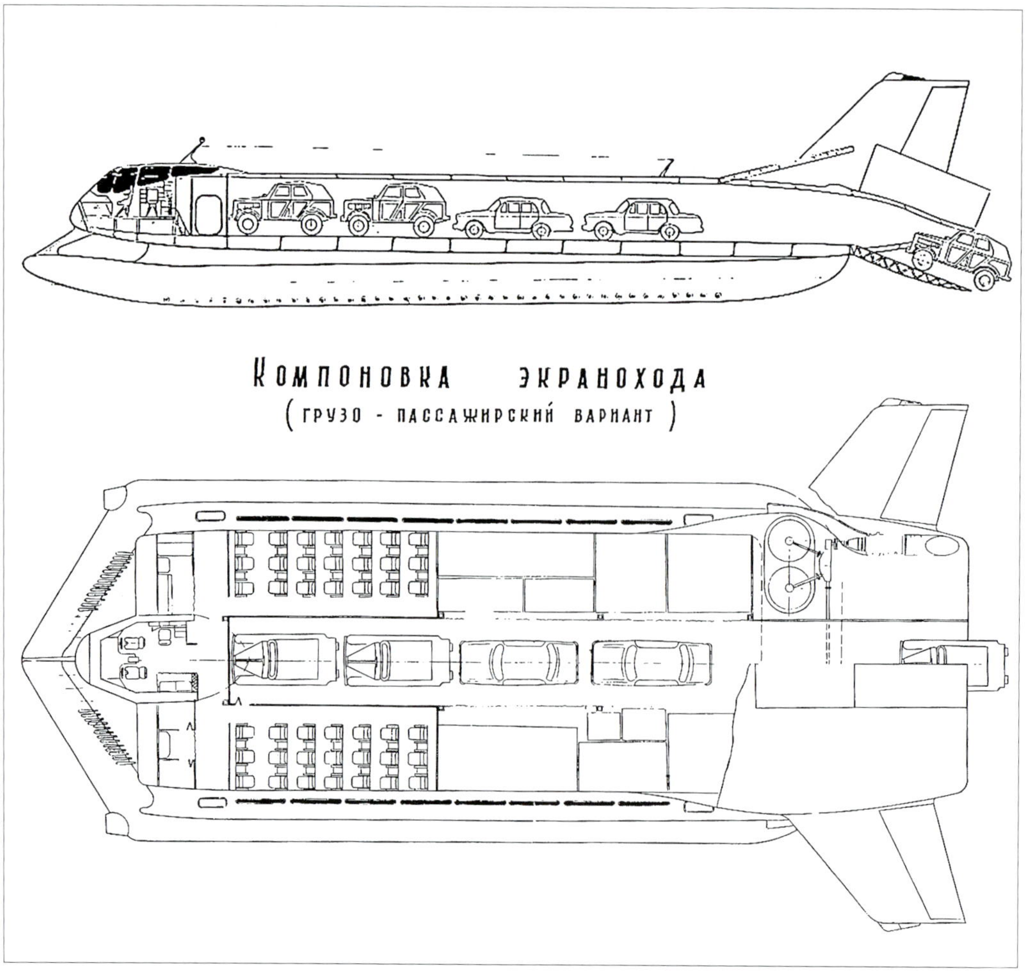

A drawing of the Ekranokhod in combi configuration, with two passenger cabins flanking a cargo hold big enough for five saloon cars or jeeps. Note the rear loading ramp.

CHAPTER THREE

BERIYEV'S ACTIVITIES

HYDROPLANE VERSUS EKRANOPLAN

Gheorgiy Mikhaïlovich Beriyev's design bureau, later transformed into the TANTK (*Taganrogskiy aviatsionnyy naoochno-tekhnicheskiy kompleks* – Taganrog Aviation Scientific and Technical Complex) named after G. M. Beriyev, is well known for its predominant role in the design of Soviet and Russian seaplanes (mainly flying boats). The Beriyev TANTK (also known as TASTC in the English-language abbreviation) initiated its work on WIG vehicles in the early 1960s. This work comprised both scientific research in this field and practical design work. The latter included the development of several projects of super-heavy WIG vehicles and a project of an aircraft-carrier based on the use of ground effect (*ekranoplan* aircraft-carrier). These projects were evolved under the direction of A. G. Bogatyryov who worked in the Beriyev Design Bureau in the capacity of a leading designer. Artist's impressions are available of four of these projects. Two of them are based on the use of Lippisch-type reverse-delta wings of giant dimensions in combination

The Be-1 (alias GL-1) *ekranoplan* research vehicle afloat at Taganrog.

An artist's impression of a projected super-heavy *ekranoplan* designed by A. G. Bogatyryov. The machine uses the Lippisch layout and has six nose-mounted boost/cruise engines and canard foreplanes. Note the four dorsal loading hatches.

with a V-shaped tail unit comprising two surfaces that were canted outwards approximately 45°. As is usual in the Lippisch layout, in both cases the wings had marked anhedral and were provided with floats at the tips. At the same time the two projects differed in some respects. One of them was powered by six turbojets, two of which were installed above the wins well aft, just ahead of the tail surfaces. The remaining four engines formed a package mounted on an outrigger boom attached to the wing leading

Another WIG craft project by Bogatyryov, again using the Lippisch layout but with canted wingtips and aft-mounted cruise engines. Note the triple vertical tails. The four boost engines have deflector vanes and there are six loading hatches.

The EA-1200 *ekranoplan* project by Bogatyryov, showing the disc-shaped fuselage, the three booms carrying the foreplanes mounting the booster engines, the aft-mounted cruise engines, the wingtip-mounted T-tails and six dorsal loading hatches

edge on the centreline (it also accommodated the flight deck). Being thus placed ahead of the wings, the engines could direct their jet efflux under the wings, augmenting the ram air cushion during take-off. This project also featured additional surfaces attached to the wingtip floats at an angle – again, in keeping with the traditional Lippisch layout. The vehicle apparently had no fuselage, the wings providing the space to accommodate the useful load. The other of the two projects, on the other hand, had a sort of fuselage protruding ahead of the wing leading edge. The forward fuselage was flanked by two packs of turbojet engines, each of them comprising three engines in a common nacelle with separate air intakes. The engines apparently were intended to act in the double role of cruise engines in cruise flight and booster engines during take-off. The engine packs, in turn, were flanked by swept-back foreplanes whose tips were joined to the wing leading edge by special booms. In this case there were no additional aerodynamic surfaces on the wingtip floats.

Another pie-in-the-sky *ekranoplan* project by Bogatyryov with forward-swept anhedral tailplanes tipped by floats. The nose-mounted booster engines appear to be way too low above the water.

Front view of the Be-1 on its beaching gear at Taganrog, showing the float design and the angled forward hydrofoils.

Opposite: This three-quarter view shows well the V-shaped rear hydrofoils. The hydrofoils necessitated a tall beaching gear; all three units were equipped with floats to facilitate installation and removal.

The other two projects by Bogatyryov were altogether different. One on them was a kind of a flying wing of an unorthodox shape. The main part of the wing was nearly circular in planform, and was supplemented by sweptback outer wing panels at the rear. Placed at the tips of these were two T-tails featuring sweepback on all surfaces. A third vertical tail was mounted on the centreline at the wing trailing edge. The powerplant included four booster turbojets placed on the upper surfaces of the foreplanes which were carried by three booms protruding from the wing leading edge (the centre one incorporated the flight deck). A further four turbojets were placed in pairs at the wing trailing edge near the roots of the outer wing panels.

Finally, the fourth project featured, in fact, a tail-first layout with the wings sharply swept back, while the canard foreplanes were swept forward and pro-

Side view of the Be-1, showing the wing endplates, the wing/float junction and the water rudders.

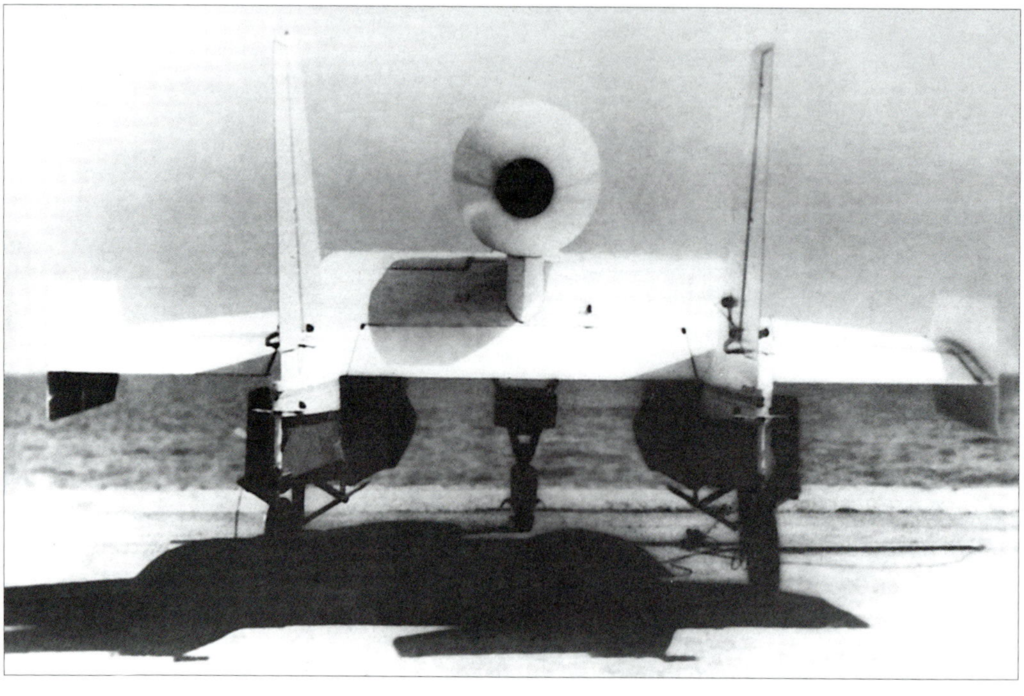

Rear view of the Be-1, showing the three trailing edge flaps and the engine pylon.

01

01

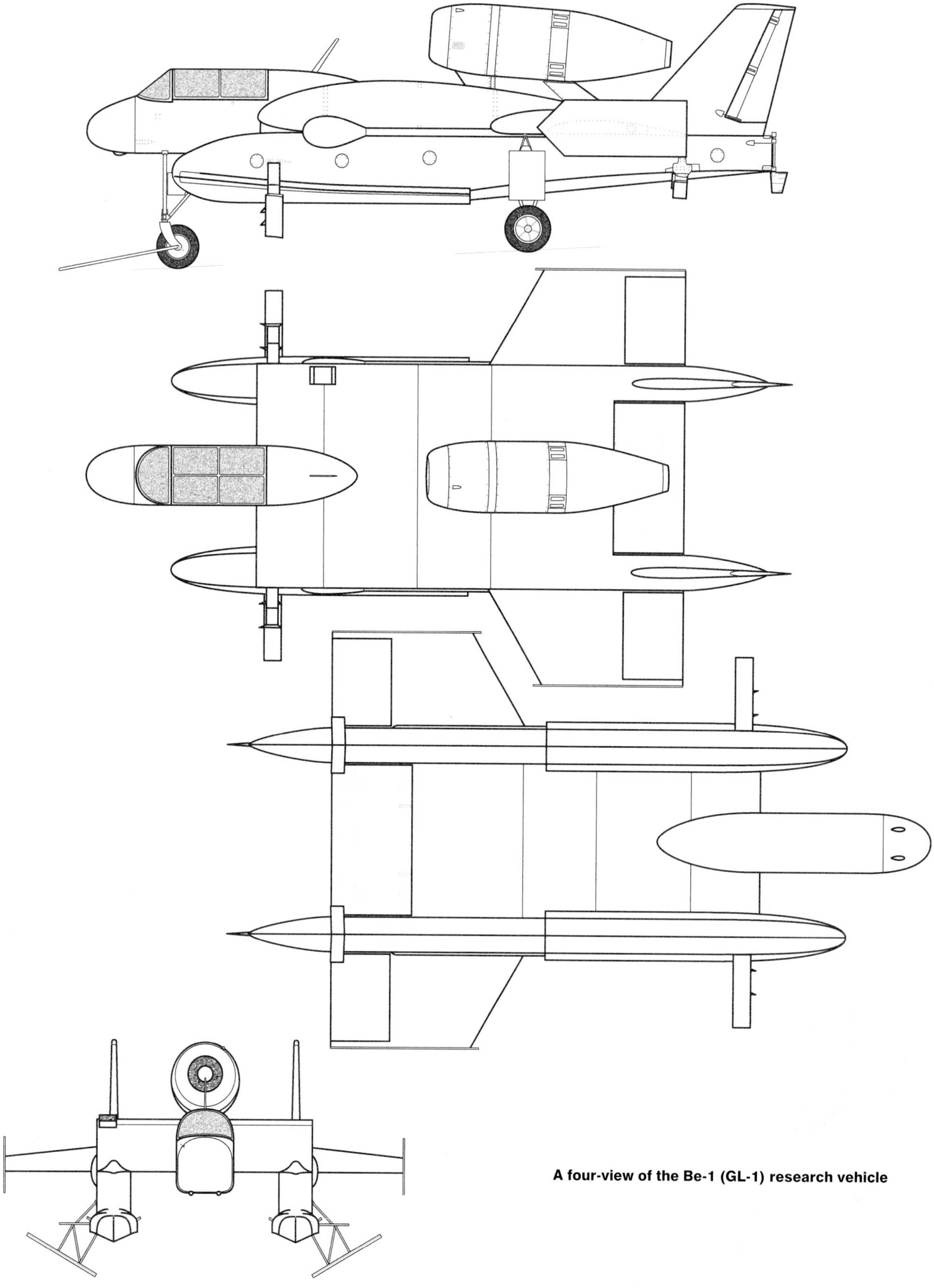

A four-view of the Be-1 (GL-1) research vehicle

vided with what appears to be floats at the tips. As in the previous case, there were two T-tails placed at the wingtips. Four cruise turbojets were mounted above the trailing edge of the wings close to the fuselage. In addition, two booster turbojets were carried on a pylon protruding from the nose between the forward-swept foreplanes. All four projects described above must have had military applications, the exact nature of which is unclear. The external appearance of the last two of these projects makes one wonder how they could alight on a sea surface (if they could at all) without plunging their forward-mounted engines into the water.

As described in the previous chapter, Bartini's activities in the field of WIG design were to a large extent geared to the Beriyev Design Bureau. The story of the VVA-14/14M1P, is justifiably included into the official history of the Beriyev TANTK as one of its salient points.

Interestingly, several WIG designs of this OKB, including the aircraft-carrier project mentioned above, envisaged a combination of ground effect achieved on an airfoil wing with the use of hydrofoils. Enlisting assistance from TsAGI, the OKB studied a catamaran (twin-hull) layout with hydrofoils for this aircraft-carrier project. From 1963 onwards TsAGI specialists conducted a series of experiments on this subject.

In the OKB parlance, a vehicle combining in its cruise flight mode the use of aerodynamic lift and ground effect on an airfoil wing with the lift created by hydrofoils was called ***ghid****roekrano****plan*** (hydro-WIG vehicle). In the case of the twin-hull layout the hydrofoils were located according to the so-called four-point arrangement (each of the boats had a pair of hydrofoils – one at the bows and one at the stern). The forward hydrofoils were located ahead of the centre of gravity and the aft ones behind it.

In cruise flight mode the *ghidroekranoplan* was supposed to be supported by the forward-mounted hydrofoils and the airfoil wings, while the aft-mounted hydrofoils left the water and became airborne. One of the stages in the investigation of this layout envisaged the testing of a self-propelled model of the ekranoplan aircraft-carrier; the purpose of this testing was to evaluate the adopted layout of hydrofoils, as well as the controllability, stability and seaworthiness of the craft.

G. M. Beriyev was entrusted with the construction of the self-propelled model, while TsAGI undertook the studies involving the use of towed models in the towing tank. In Beriyev's OKB the piloted model was officially designated Be-1 and was more commonly known as *Ghidro****lyot*** (*ghidro* = hydro, *lyot* = flyer).

The Be-1 skims the sea, kicking up plumes of spray from the forward hydrofoils. That was all it could do; it never became truly airborne.

01

01

Be-1 (GL-1, 'Ghidrolyot')

Sometimes referred to as the GL-1 or G-1, this machine can be described as a WIG vehicle of a catamaran layout. When afloat, the vehicle rested on two floats; these supported low aspect ratio wings comprising a centre section and small outer panels with endplates. The outer panels had smaller thickness than the centre section. The open cockpit was installed at the leading edge of the centre section. The Be-1 was provided with hydrofoils attached to the floats in a four-point arrangement. The hydrofoils' incidence was 4° for the angled forward pair and 0° for the V-shaped rear ones. The rear hydrofoils were mounted higher up relative to the forward ones and were expected to be lifted out of the water during cruise. The tail unit comprised twin fins, the role of the horizontal tail being performed by flaps installed on the aft part of the wing centre section and outer wing panel trailing edges. The vehicle was of predominantly wooden construction; it was powered by a Walter M-701C-250 turbojet (imported from Czechoslovakia) mounted on a pylon above the wing centre section.

In the course of testing the vehicle put to sea twelve times. It made eight runs in the displacement mode, forty runs in the hydrofoil mode, and another forty in the airfoil-supported mode with flaps set at 20-25°. To reduce the gap between the wing trailing edge and the water surface, the chord of the flap mounted on the centre section was doubled, which resulted in a marked increase of the wing-generated lift. According to the designers' calculations, the thrust of the engine was presumed to be sufficient to accelerate the Be-1 into a flight in ground effect when the hydrofoils would become inoperative. However, the testing failed to produce this result, and the vehicle moved in all cases with the hydrofoils submerged, albeit the floats were lifted out of the water.

Be-11

This was a project of a 100-seat passenger *ghidroekranoplan*, the work on which was conducted in the Beriyev OKB on the basis of the results of the work on the Be-1. Judging by the available artist's impression, the vehicle featured a twin-hull (catamaran) layout. The hulls were joined by an airfoil-shaped rectangular platform, a sort of wing of very low aspect ratio. The space beneath this wing, flanked by the hulls, formed a cavity in which an air cushion was created by ram air during the craft's movement. Presumably, there must have been a flap at the wing trailing edge to assist in building up the air cushion during take-off. The main wing placed between the hulls was supplemented by smaller lifting surfaces outboard of each hull. The powerplant in one of the versions was to comprise two Ivchenko AI-20 turboprops driving AV-68 four-bladed propellers (well-known for their use on the Il'yushin IL-18 airliner and the Antonov An-12 and An-32 transports). The propellers were enclosed by annular shrouds. Each of the two hulls housed a

Opposite: The Be-1 at rest on the Black Sea at the Beriyev OKB's flight test facility. Note the cooling air intake above the starboard float.

Opposite, bottom: Another view of the Be-1 in skimming mode. Note the different spray pattern.

An artist's impression of the Be-11 sea-going passenger WIG craft. The centrally mounted cockpit and ducted propellers are noteworthy.

An artist's impression of the Be-105 *ekranoplan*.

passenger compartment; the flight deck was accommodated in a separate nacelle attached to the wing leading edge.

Be-105

This project of a WIG craft was one of a series of similar projects developed by the Beriyev TANTK in 1990 on a commercial basis in 1990, when the curtailment of military orders forced this design bureau to seek new fields of activities in order to survive. These projects were developed to meet the requirements of Samsung Aerospace company of South Korea. This particular machine, the Be-105, was a multi-purpose surface-effect vehicle which, in addi-

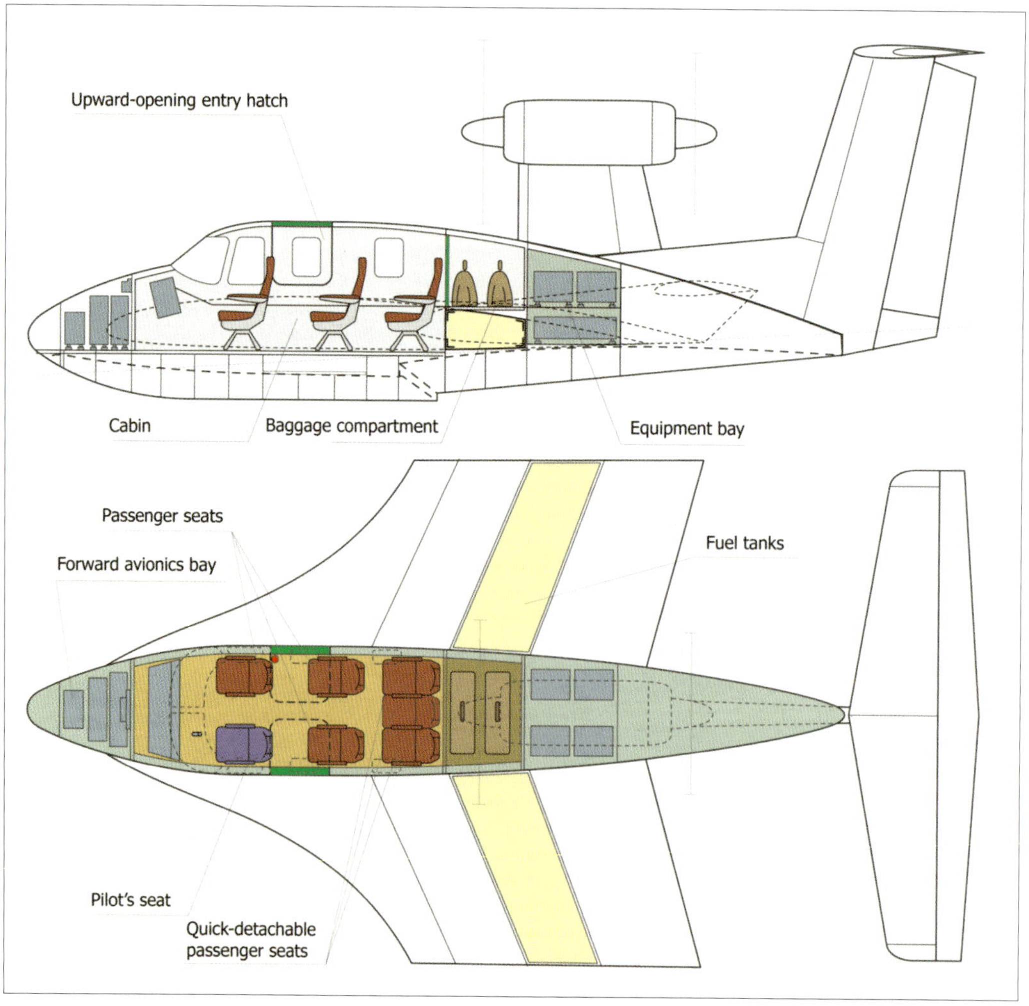

A drawing from the project materials showing the Be-105's internal layout.

An artist's impression of a Be-105 moored at a quay; an inflatable raft is used to take the passengers ashore.

tion to cargo transportation in littoral areas, could be used for tourist travel, search and rescue, smuggling prevention (coast guard patrol duties), urgent medical aid and so on.

In its general layout the Be-105 had much in common with the well-known Be-103 amphibian whose development was started at about the same time. Both machines featured moderately swept low-set wings of normal aspect ratio with prominent leading-edge root extensions. When the vehicle was afloat, the wing centre section rested on the water surface for added buoyancy, the dihedral outer wing panels rising above the surface (Beriyev was experimenting with the concept of the so-called displacement-type wings for its prospective large flying boats and amphibians).

An impression of the Be-105 being hoisted out of the water and placed on a ground handling dolly by a crane.

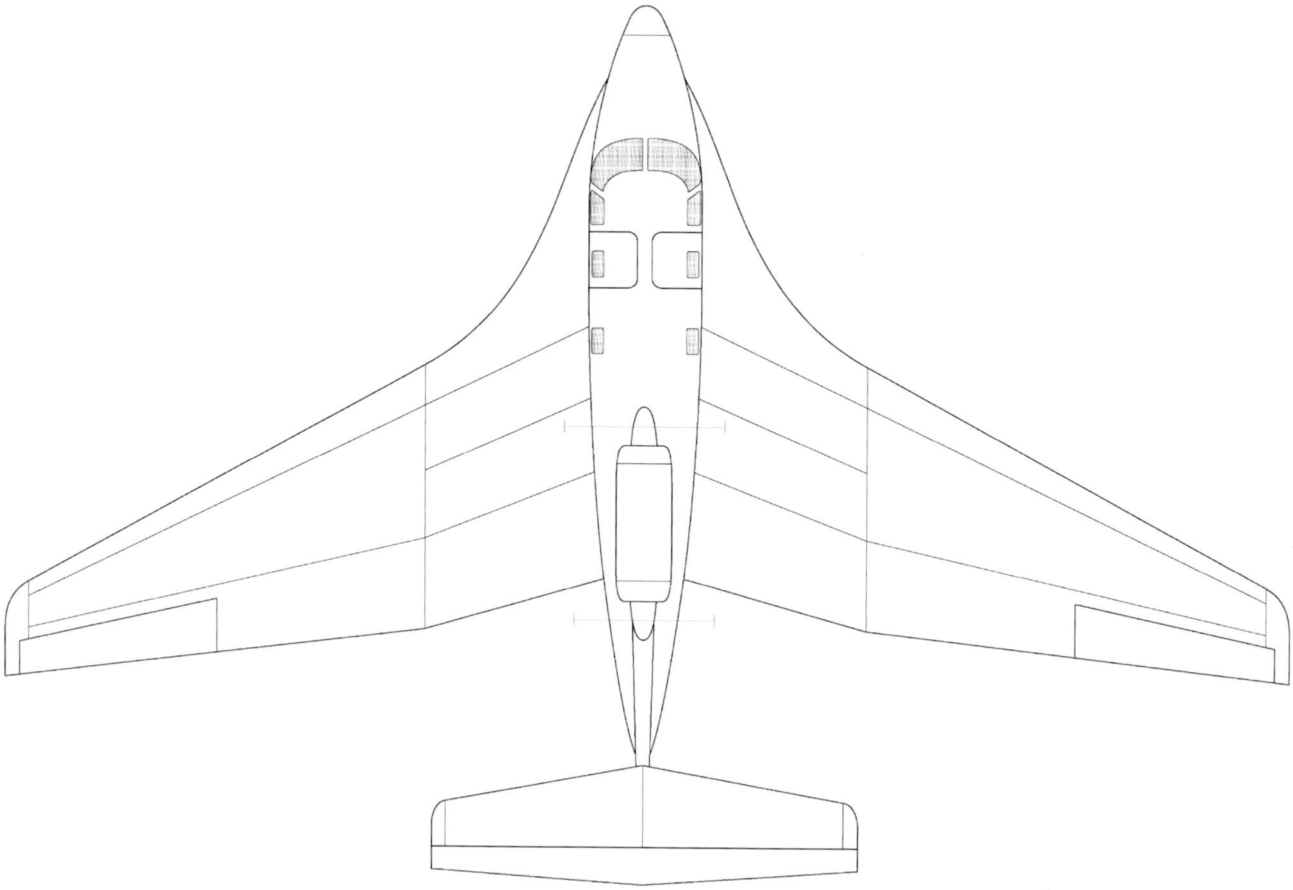

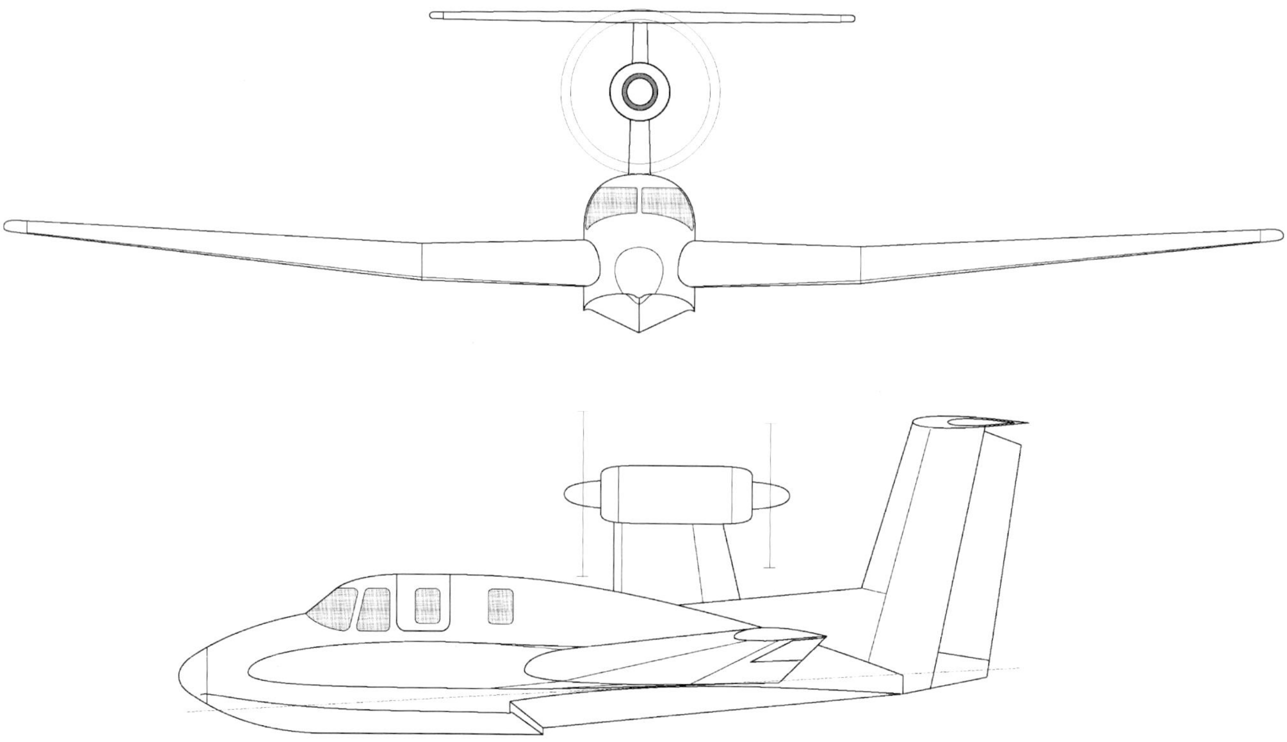

A three-view of the Be-105; note the different propeller diameters

An artist's impression of the Be-107 in cruise flight. It appears to have strakes at mid-span assisting in the formation of an air cushion.

The cabin accommodating a pilot and six passengers could be easily adapted for cargo carriage and patrol duties. In the latter case two of the passenger seats were replaced by swiveling seats for two gunners who could fire pivot-mounted 7.62-mm Kalashnikov PKM machine-guns through hatches.

The powerplant was to comprise two 300-hp M-16 radial engines mounted back to back on a pylon atop the fuselage to drive three-blade tractor/pusher propellers. (The M-16 engine was under development at the Voronezh OKBM in early 1990s but never reached production status.) Optionally, the Be-105 could be powered by Teledyne Continental Motors IO-550B flat-six engines.

The rear fuselage carried a T-tail with a gently swept fin-and-rudder and unswept stabilisers with inset elevators. Lateral control was effected by ailerons. Thus, the Be-105 was a WIG vehicle coming as close as possible to the traditional aircraft layout and was classed as ekranolyot by its designers (presumably in the B or even C category by the present IMO classification). However, design performance figures published by Beriyev contain no mention of high-altitude flying. This vehicle with a maximum AUW of 2,700 kg (5,950 lb) and a maximum payload of 500 kg (1,102 lb) was expected to reach a maximum speed of 275 km/h (171 mph) and a cruising speed of 220 km/h (136 mph).

The work on the Be-105 project continued until 1991; in parallel, a similarly configured aircraft based on the Be-105 and having the same powerplant was projected. However, due to the lack of orders the Be-105 did not reach the hardware stage.

An impression of the Be-107 at rest; a floating landing stage is used for embarkation/disembarkation.

Overleaf, top: An impression of the Be-107 in Russian colours in cruise mode. No mid-span strakes are visible here.

Bottom: A drawing from the project documents showing the Be-107's internal layout.

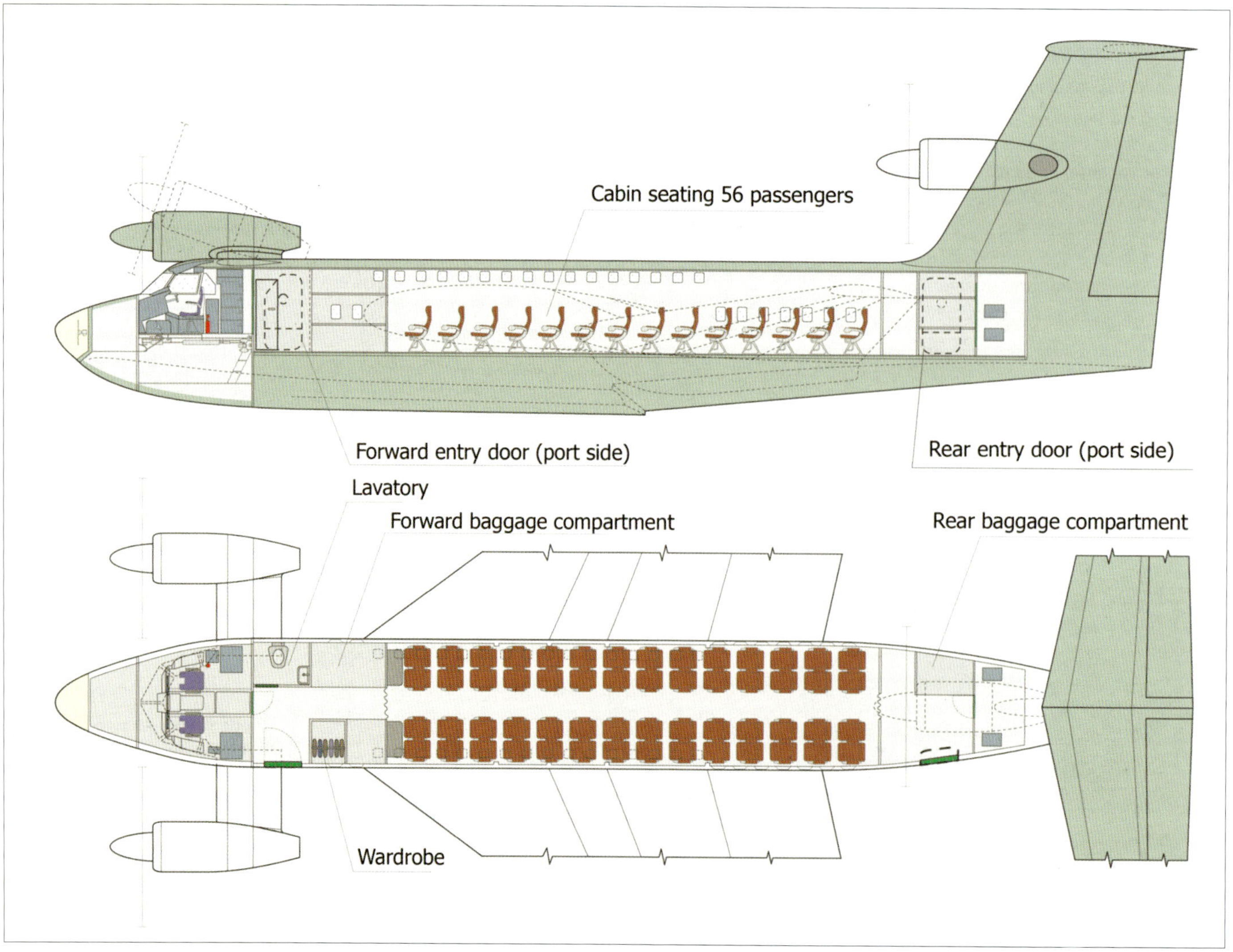
Cabin seating 56 passengers
Forward entry door (port side)
Rear entry door (port side)
Lavatory
Forward baggage compartment
Rear baggage compartment
Wardrobe

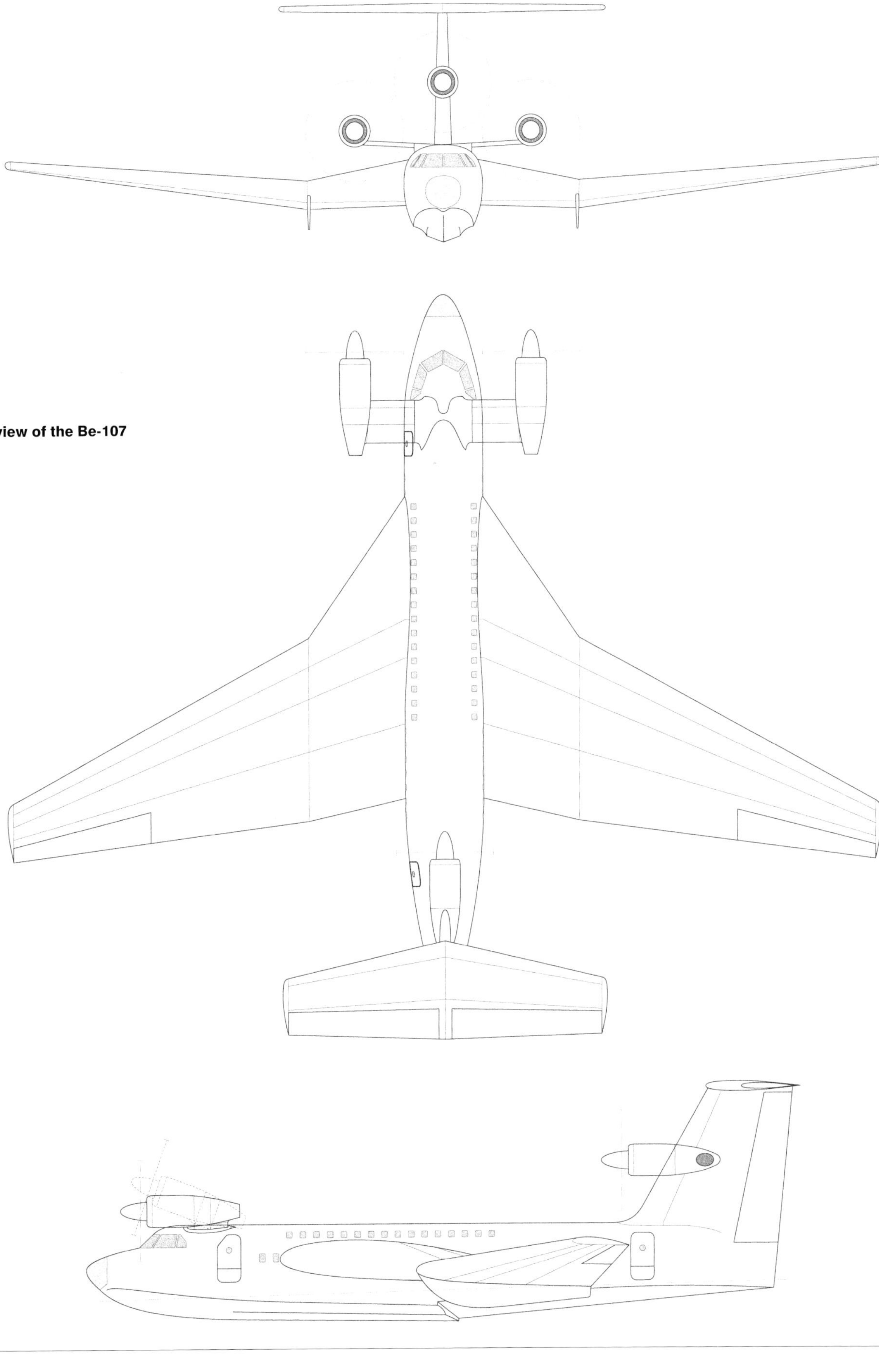

A three-view of the Be-107

Opposite: A radio-controlled model of the A-70 ('D') afloat.

Opposite, below: The same model in flight, showing the planing step and water rudders.

Be-107

This project, also developed to meet a specification submitted by Samsung Aerospace, resembled a scaled-up Be-105, sharing with it the basic aerodynamic layout. Notably, it had roughly the same wing planform and a similar T-tail. But there were important differences, too. To begin with, the Be-107 was intended to carry 60 passengers, and its AUW was 25,000 kg (55,125 lb) – almost ten times that of the Be-105 (2,700 kg). The wings had a centre section of greater relative thickness which almost blended into the fuselage (this necessitated moving the windows of the passenger cabin higher up, almost to the level of the ceiling). The fuselage, measuring 26.50 m (87 ft 0 in) in length was of the traditional flying-boat hull type, with a single step on the planing bottom amidships.

The powerplant featured a completely different engine arrangement. It comprised three 2,500-ehp Klimov TV7-117S turboprops, two of which were mounted on swivelling pylons placed high on each side of the forward fuselage. At take-off they could be swivelled to direct the prop wash under the wings, thus creating an air cushion. Incidentally, the wing centre section was provided with deep strakes on its underside at the junction with the outer wing panels. They formed a chamber in which the air cushion was produced thanks to the prop wash and the slipstream. The third engine was mounted on the fin leading edge. This arrangement is similar to the one used in several WIG craft projects of the Central Hydrofoil Ship Design Bureau (Alekseyev Design Bureau). The difference is, of course, the combination of this engine layout with wings of very low aspect ratio (Alekseyev) or relatively high aspect ratio (Beriyev). In the latter case the wing span was 32.30 m (106 ft 0 in)

The vehicle's design performance included a maximum speed of 375 km/h (233 mph), a cruising speed of 250 km/h (155 mph) and a range of 2,180 km (1,355 miles) with a maximum payload.

The Be-107 was intended for use primarily for tourist travel and passenger transportation in archipelagos and littoral areas. This project shared the fate of the Be-105 described above. In 1991, when all attempts to find investors and procure the necessary funding proved futile, the work on the project was terminated.

Projects of super-heavy flying boats and amphibians with WIG features

In the 1980s and 1990s the Beriyev Design Bureau (Beriyev TANTK) devoted much effort to research and practical design work in the field of developing hydroplanes of different classes endowed with extra-high load-carrying capacity. This line of research was based on the assumption that seaplanes of large dimensions would possess far better sea-going properties enabling them to operate in world ocean areas of southern latitudes 80 to 95% of the time. A whole series of projects was developed, comprising machines in the weight class ranging from over 500 tonnes (1,102,500 lb) to 2,500 tonnes (5,512,500 lb) and even more. A common feature of these projects was the use of the WIG effect either for take-off or for operation in WIG mode, as a supplement to normal aircraft-type operation. These designs were classed as ekranolyot; they fall into the present C class of WIG vehicles.

Listed below are some of these projects.

P-2

This project of an amphibious aircraft was used for studying the basic design features of the above-mentioned super-heavy machines. Its general layout is known from a photo of a model published in a collection of reports from a symposium held at the Ghelendzhik-98 hydro aviation show. The photo (unfortunately, too poor to be reproduced) shows a large vehicle with four turbojets mounted on the forward fuselage in a fashion similar to Alekseyev's *ekranoplans*. The machine has wings with a wide-chord centre section and outer wing panels of greater aspect ratio. Placed on the underside of the wings, at the junction of the centre section and the outer wing panels, are vertical walls (a kind of skegs) obviously intended to create a chamber under the centre section for building up an air cushion with the help of blowing from the nose-mounted engines.

A wind tunnel model of the P-2 amphibian.

A model of the A-70 (A-2500) amphibian in the towing basin.

A-70 ('D')

This project, sometimes referred to as the Be-70, was presumably similar to the P-2 and served the same purpose. Precise configuration is unknown. Interestingly, two designations – A-70 and A-2500 – accompanied one photo of a towing-basin model of an 'ultra-heavy amphibious aircraft' published in the same source as above. The configuration of the model corresponds to that of the Be-2500 project with aft-mounted engines (see below). Apparently, the A-2500 and the Be-2500 are two designations of the same project. The relation between the A-70 (Be-70) and the A-2500 (Be-2500) is not clear (these may be projects sharing a common layout but differing in dimensions).

Be-750 seaplane/WIG craft (project)

This project was revealed for the first time (without designation) as a drawing published in the materials of a Ghelendzhik symposium on hydro aviation. The designation became known in 2002 when this drawing appeared in a book on the activities of the Beriyev Design Bureau. Described as 'a super-

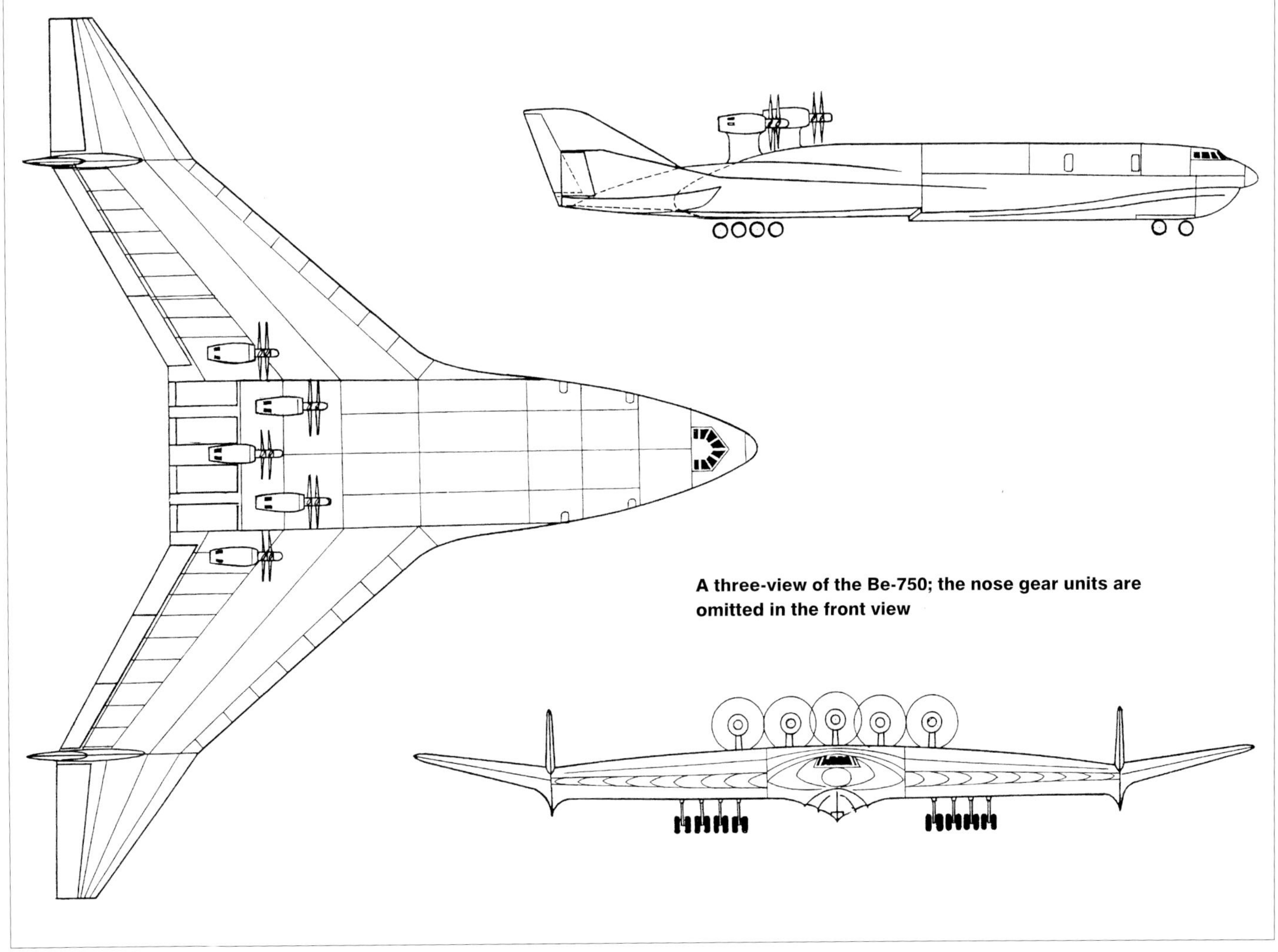

A three-view of the Be-750; the nose gear units are omitted in the front view

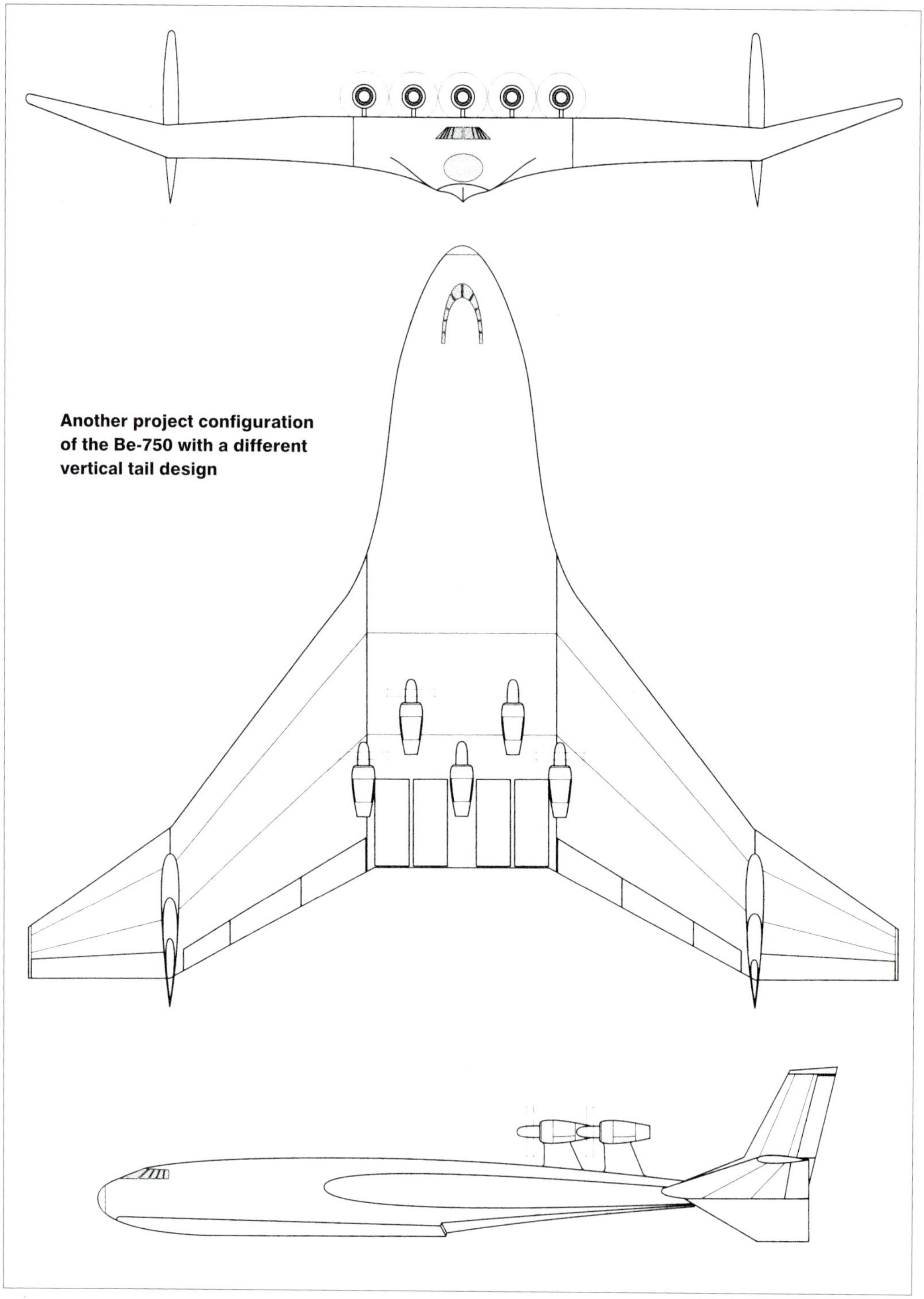

Another project configuration of the Be-750 with a different vertical tail design

heavy seaplane', this is a vehicle of the flying wing type with wings featuring double sweepback on the leading edges and blending smoothly into a boat-type fuselage (integral layout). It is powered by five turboprops mounted on pylons above the aft fuselage to drive contra-rotating propellers. Directional stability and control is ensured by two vertical tails mounted on the wings close to wing tips. The wings are provided with ailerons outboard of the fins and elevons (flaps) inboard of them. Other particulars are unknown. Presumably this design makes use of ground effect in the take-off and landing mode.

Be-750 version powered by three turboprops (project)

A Beriyev TANTK exhibition stand at one of the Ghelendzhik hydro aviation shows carried a drawing of a hydroplane (no designation was given) which was identical in plan view to the Be-750 as described above, the only visible difference being the powerplant. In this case it comprised only three turboprop engines, also driving contra-rotating propellers. The drawing was accompanied by the following particulars: take-off weight 750 tonnes (1,653 lb); payload 300 tonnes (661,500 lb); cruising speed 800 km/h (497 mph); range 7,800 km (4,848 miles). The take-off weight of 750 tonnes (the same as the designation digits in the previous case) makes it reasonable to surmise that it is actually the same project, probably with the same designation, in which the number of engines was reduced to three due to their greater power (no engine type was indicated in either case). This pattern of providing powerplant options with a different number of engines is also in evidence in other Beriyev designs.

Be-800 seaplane/WIG craft (project)

This *ekranolyot* features a highly unorthodox layout. In addition to the main boat-hull fuselage, it has two smaller boat hulls making the vehicle a sort of trimaran. The vehicle features a joined wing of high aspect ratio. It comprises the high-set swept-back forward wing resting on the central part of the fuselage and the swept-forward aft wing mounted on the twin-fin tail unit and joined to the forward wings at 70% of their span.

The powerplant comprises six Kuznetsov NK-62M turbofans with an aggregate take-off thrust of 35 tonnes (77,175 lbst). Four of these engines are mounted on the aft fuselage and the other two on the upper surface of the forward wing. The flight deck is located in the front part of the main fuselage; the central pressurised part of the fuselage houses six cargo compartments which can be converted into passenger compartments. The fuel is stored in the centre section of the forward wing and in the hulls. Unfortunately, no illustration is available.

Be-1000 amphibian (project)

Broadly similar in layout to the Be-750, this amphibious aircraft an integral type flying wing layout with the wings blending smoothly into the fuselage. The latter is shaped as a boat hull with transverse and longitudinal steps. The thick wing roots are partly submerged when the aircraft is afloat. The wings have a leading-edge sweepback of 50° and are fitted with large winglets serving as twin vertical tail surfaces. Seven Kuznetsov NK-62M turbofans are mounted above the central part of the wing. The aircraft's undercarriage comprises a nose unit, main units and supporting units with six-wheel bogies. The forward fuselage houses the flight deck, while passengers are accommodated on two decks in the pressurised front section of the hull. Volumes in the wing and fuselage aft of the passenger compartments are used for cargo holds. The Be-1000 has a design cargo carrying capacity of up to 600 tonnes (1,323,000 lb) and a maximum cruising speed of 600 km/h (373 mph).

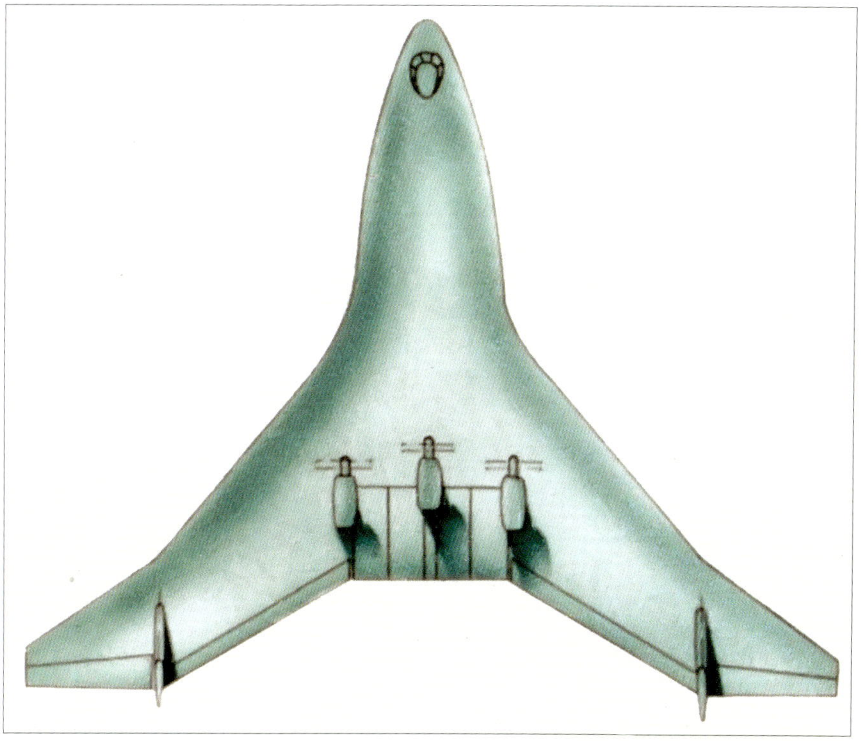

A drawing of a three-engined version of the Be-750.

Be-? – WIG craft in the 1,000-tonne AUW class (project)

The Beriyev TANTK exhibition stand mentioned above also carried a plan view of another prospective hydroplane for which the following particulars were cited: take-off weight 1,000 tonnes (2,205,000

A drawing of the Be-1000 project with eight forward-mounted engines.

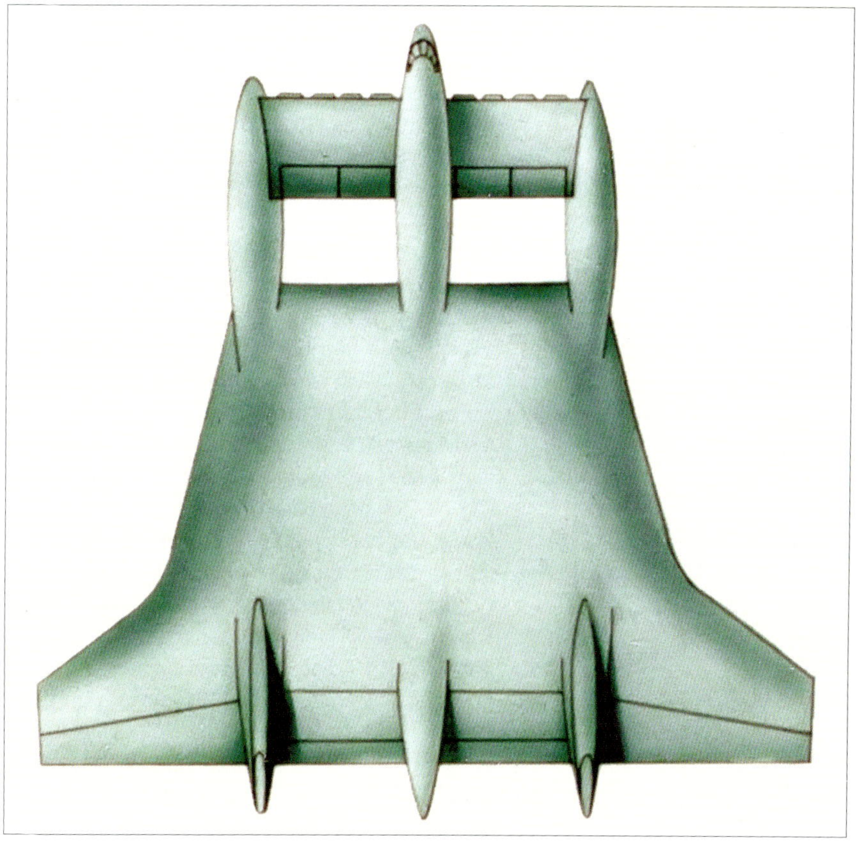

An artist's impression of the Be-1200 at its landing stage with the loading doors in the rear fuselage and wing trailing edge open. Passengers embark through landing gantries at the front.

lb); payload 400 tonnes (881,830 lb); cruising speed 660 km/h (410 mph); range 8,000 km (4,970 miles). The layout of this huge machine was unorthodox indeed. It was a 'flying wing' (tailless aircraft) with three fuselages blended into a rectangular wing centre section of very low aspect ratio and wide chord. The wing centre section was supplemented by outer wing panels with a compound sweepback on the leading edges. The trailing edge of the outer wing panels was occupied by ailerons, while the trailing edge sections located between the fuselages carried control surfaces that might perform the role of elevators or flaps. Vertical tails were mounted on the aft ends of the two outboard fuselages. The front parts of the three fuselages were linked by foreplanes. The drawing showed four turbofans mounted under each foreplane (eight in all). Quite obviously, their efflux could be directed under the wing for creating an air cushion during take-off. This feature, reminiscent of Alekseyev's and Bartini's designs, makes it possible to class this vehicle as having much in common with WIG vehicles proper, even though it may have been intended to be operated mainly in the aircraft mode.

Be-1200 (Be-2000)

This is a project of an amphibious flying boat which was presented in model form by the TANTK at the Ghelendzhik hydro aviation show in 1996 as Be-1200; at Ghelendzhik-98 the same model bore the designation Be-2000. The layout of this gigantic machine powered by six powerful jet engines clearly places it in the category of Type C WIG vehicles, or ekranolyots, in Russian parlance. In its general configuration it comes close to a flying wing, though it features an empennage in the shape of two wing-mounted vertical tail surfaces topped by separate horizontal stabilizers. The wings have considerable sweepback; a thick, wide-chord centre section with a straight trailing edge blends into the fuselage. Outer wing panels of smaller thickness are attached to the centre section, producing what is known as composite layout wings. Large pylons acting as stabilising floats are attached to the underside of the wings at the junction of the centre section and the outer panels; they also act as walls forming a closed space under the wing into which the exhaust of the four nose-mounted engines is directed at take-off,

A display model of the giant Be-1200 ekranoplan amphibian, showing the main cargo bay in the fuselage and one of the port wing cargo bays.

Four boost/cruise turbofans are mounted on the foreplanes, augmented by two cruise engines on the wing centre section.

The main cargo cabin of the Be-1200 is large enough to take a Kamov helicopter with its tall rotor mast, as shown here. The wing bays are intended for vehicles and the like.

An artist's impression of the Be-2500P which is similar to the model on the previous pages except for the placement of the cruise engines on the vertical tails.

in the same fashion as on Alekseyev's KM and Loon' vehicles. In cruising flight they presumably supplement the thrust of two cruise engines placed on pylons above the aft part of the wing centre section inboard of the fins.

According to the information subsequently made available by Beriyev, the Be-2000 has a take-off weight of 2,000 tonnes (4,410,000 lb). It has been projected in several versions differing in the wing planform and the number and arrangement of the engines. These versions fall into two basic groups: those featuring the assisted take-off engines and those lacking them. The Be-2000 version described above belongs to the former of the two categories and is designated the Be-2000P (P stands for *pod**doov*** – 'blowing', or power-augmented ram air cushion). In one of the configurations of the Be-2000P six NK-62M turbofans are mounted on the swivelling horizontal pylons installed on the forward fuselage. A further four engines are installed in the aft part of the wing centre section or on pylons attached to vertical tails. The swivelling pylon doubles as a foreplane; the engines installed on it act as cruise engines in cruise flight.

The Be-2000 *sans suffixe* lacking the booster engines features in one of its configurations the powerplant comprising 12 NK-12M turboprops mounted on pylons above the upper surface of the wing.

The boat hull of the aircraft has a double-deck layout, the upper deck providing accommodation for 730 passengers and the lower deck being configured as a cargo hold measuring 88 x 8 x 4 m (288 ft 8¾ in x 26 ft 3 in x 13 ft 1½ in). In a SAR version the space on both decks can be used for accommodating the survivors (544 heavily wounded and 1,214 rescuees).

Be-2500

Information on this project was presented by the Beriyev TANTK at the Hydro Aviation Show 2000 in Ghelendzhik in September 2000. This huge machine weighing 2,500 tons (5,500,000 lb) at take-off is a further development of the Be-1200 (Be-2000) layout. It combines the properties of a

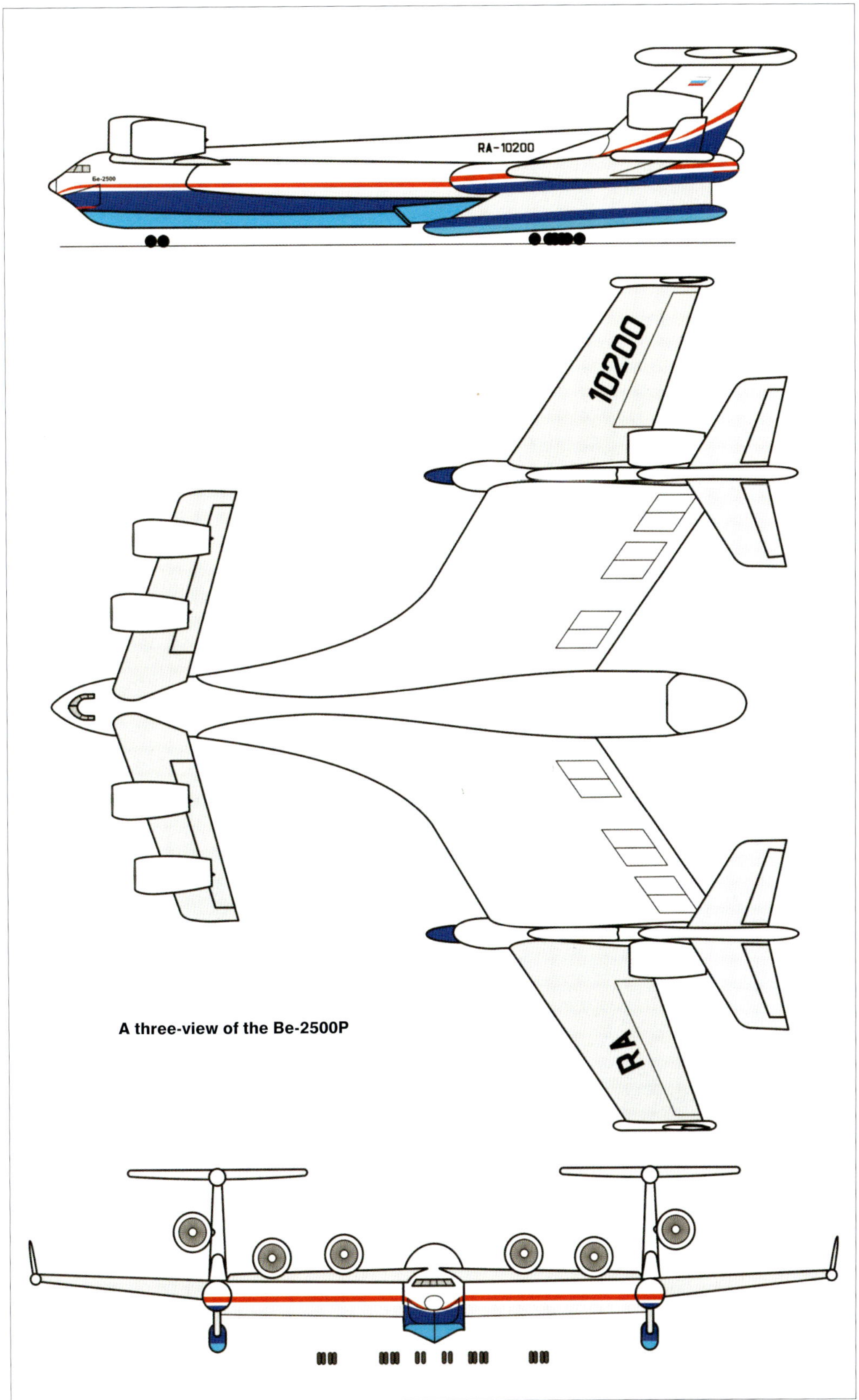

A three-view of the Be-2500P

traditional seaplane (flying boat) and a WIG vehicle, being capable of flying both in ground effect at a height of 4-10 m (13-33 ft) and at a high altitude of 8,000 to 12.000 m (26,240 to 39,360 ft). The vehicle features a 'flying wing' layout, the wings blending smoothly into the fuselage (integral layout). During take-off the mutual position of the boat-type fuselage and the wings with a large-area

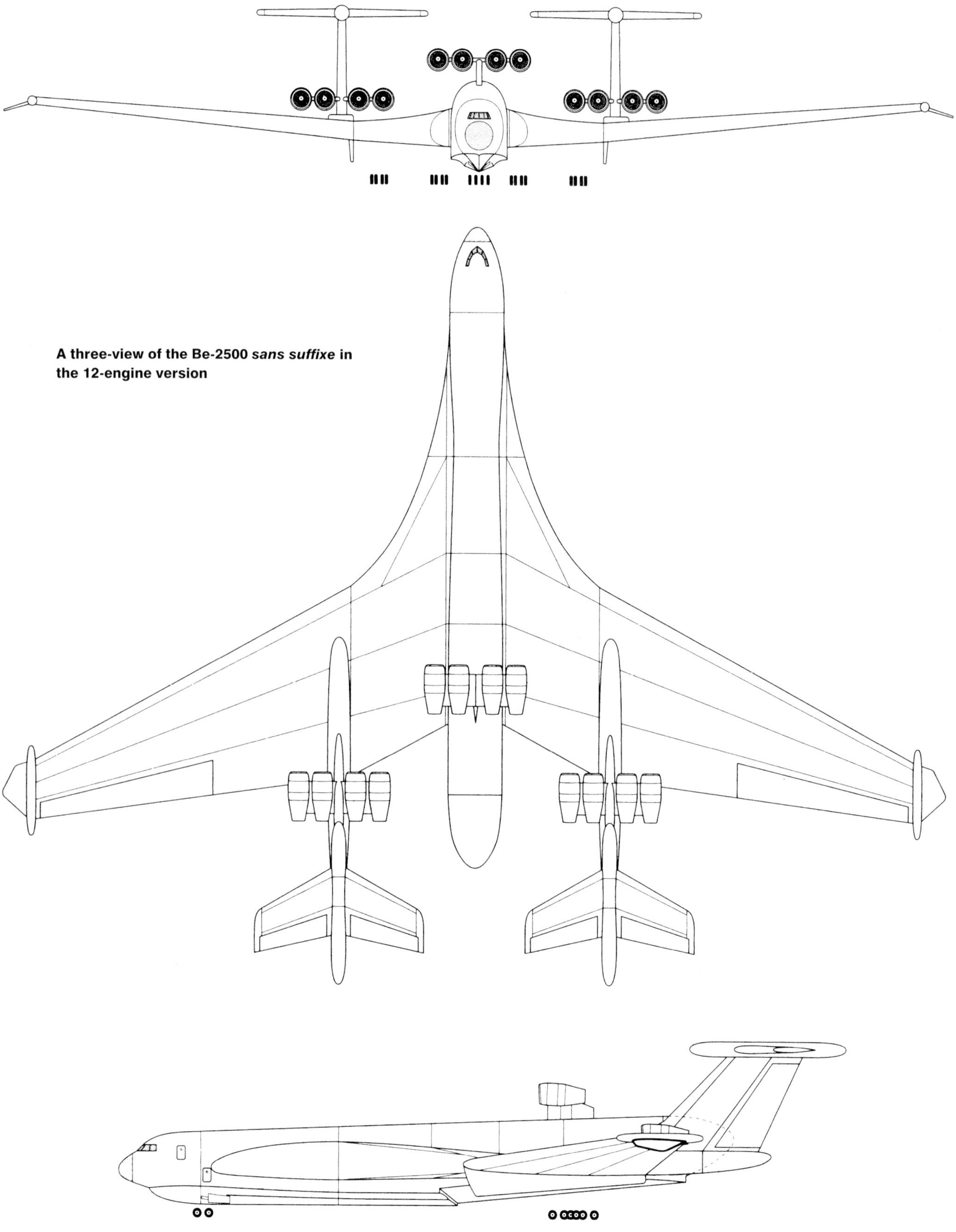

A three-view of the Be-2500 *sans suffixe* in the 12-engine version

Specifications of the Be-2500 and Be-2500P				
	Be-2500		Be-2500P	
All-up weight, t (lb)	2,500 (5,500,000)		2,500 (5,500,000)	
Length	123 m (403 ft 6¾ in)			
Wing span	156 m (511 ft 10 in)			
Wing area, m^2 (sq ft)	3,428 (36,900)		3,184 (34,275)	
Engine type	Kuznetsov NK-116 turbofan		Kuznetsov NK-116 turbofan	
Take-off thrust, kgp (lbst)	6 x 105,000 = 630,000 (6 x 231,500=1,389,000)		6 x 105,000 = 630,000 (6 x 231,500=1,389,000)	
Maximum payload, t (lb)	1,000 (2,200,000)		1,000 (2,200,000)	
Cruise flight mode	High altitude (H = 10 km/32,810 ft)	In ground effect	High altitude (H = 10 km/32,810 ft)	In ground effect
Cruising speed, km/h (mph)	800 (497)*	450 (280)	800 (497)	450 (280)
Payload, t (lb), at stage length of:				
7,000 km (4,350 miles).	700 (1,540,000)	450 (990,000)	700 (1,540,000)	630 (1,390,000)
10,000 km (6,210 miles)	480 (1,060,000)	80 (177,000)	460 (1,014,000)	300 (660,000)
Ferrying range, km (miles)	17,000(10,600)	10,700(6,650)	15,800(9,800)	12,700(7,900)
Safe take-off speed, km/h (miles)	420 (260)	420 (260)	360 (224)	360 (224)
Take-off run, m (ft)	15,000 (49,200)	15,000 (49,200)	9,300 (31,500)	9,300 (31,500)

*700 km/h (435 mph) in another source

centre section enables the aircraft to perform hydroplaning with the step of its hull and the trailing edge of the wing centre section touching the water surface.

The machine has been designed in two versions: Be-2500 and Be-2500P, which differ in their aerohydrodynamic layout in a fashion similar to the Be-2000 and the Be-2000P. In the case of the Be-2500 *sans suffixe* all six engines are aft-mounted (two of them are installed above the fuselage and the other four in pairs on both sides of the two fins. Thus, there is no provision for using the engine exhaust as a means of building up an air cushion under the wing during take-off. The number of engines can vary in different versions. One of the sub-types of the Be-2500 *sans suffixe* has 12 smaller engines in the same arrangement as the one described above, except that each of the six engines has been replaced by a pair of engines. The outer wing panels are blended smoothly into the wing centre section, the chord and thickness decreasing gradually from root to tip.

As for the Be-2500P, its layout is almost identical to that of the Be-2000, the only difference being the shape of the wing centre section trailing edge (which has sweepback instead of being straight) and the location of aft-mounted engines which are placed outboard of the fins, not inboard, in a published drawing (however, there were models showing the aft-mounted engines placed inboard of the fins). Thus the Be-2500P, unlike the Be-2500 *sans suffixe*, can use its nose-mounted engines for power-augmented take-off, directing their exhaust under the wings.

The Be-2500 is to be provided with a retractable undercarriage designed to sustain only the minimum take-off weight. It is intended to be used only when ferrying the machine to factory airfields for repairs, and for beaching the machine. The nose gear comprises two independent units side by side, each with a four-wheel bogie, while the four main units are equipped with 12-wheel bogies having three rows of four wheels, the outer units being mounted further aft.

The powerplant of the Be-2500 needs some comment. In the opinion of the designers, an aerial vehicle of that size and weight would best be powered by engines with a trust rating in the 100-tonne

This model of the Be-2500 has all six engines mounted on the canard foreplanes. Surprisingly, the placard reads 'Be-2500', although the model represents the Be-2500P version.

Four more views of the same Be-2500 model. Note the angle at which the foreplanes (and engines) are set to direct the engine exhaust under the wings and form a static air cushion.

(2,205,000-lb) class. Such were the NK-116 turbofans rated at 105 tonnes (231,500 lbst). A preliminary project of the NK-116 turbofan, with a 5-m (16-ft) fan diameter, was studied at the Samara-based SNTK Trud ('Labour' Science and Production Enterprise, formerly known as the Kuznetsov OKB) in 1994. The engine was intended for prospective super-heavy transport aircraft, including seaplanes. Nothing has been heard about the work on this engine in recent years; at present its emergence within a reasonable time frame is quite unrealistic.

As an option to the use of the NK-116 turbofans, the designers envisaged the installation of British Rolls-Royce Trent 800 turbofans delivering a thrust of 45 tonnes (99,225 lbst) apiece without reheat and 54 tonnes (119,070 lb) with reheat (!). Obviously, the use of engines with a thrust rating of that class instead of the NK-116s would dictate an increase in the number of engines.

Be-2500 – a version with six front-mounted engines

The Be-2500 project has spawned one more variation, as evidenced by a model photographed in 2006 in Ghelendzhik. While being basically similar to the Be-2500P described above, this version sports the following alterations. The two engines previously placed on the wings (inboard or outboard of the fins) are relocated to the foreplanes, supplementing the four engines already placed there; thus, all six engines are mounted above the foreplanes. The vertical tails are no longer topped by horizontal tails which have been deleted altogether; furthermore, the fins are splayed.

Be-2500 as part of a maritime space complex

The unique potential of the Beriyev TANTK with regard to designing and producing hydroplanes in any weight category and for any duties (including WIG vehicles) called forth a very unorthodox idea of creating a maritime space complex (MSC) designed to tackle a wide range of tasks of global scope. This complex would make it possible to launch any space objects and manned space vehicles in a wide range of latitudes and trajectories and bring them back into the required point of the World Ocean covering 71% of the globe's surface. One of the projected versions of the MSC, called MSC-2500 and intended for launching payloads of more than 20 t (44,000 lb) to low orbits around the Earth envisages the use of a Be-2500 super-heavy amphibious carrier aircraft and an air/space vehicle

(ASV, shuttle orbiter) capable of performing descent and landing in stages. The idea is based on the assumption that the Be-2500, by virtue of its enormous cargo-carrying capacity (1,000 tons/ 2,200,000lb) will be able to carry the heavy ASV and a maximum fuel load, using large water areas as its base, and the ASV will comprise a manned module in the shape of an amphibious vehicle capable of performing take-offs and landings on water, land or the deck of a receiving vehicle.

* * *

It is presumed that the Be-2500 and other similar super-heavy aerial vehicles may be used for transportation on transatlantic and transpacific routes, making use of the existing port facilities. The designers think that no new, unique infrastructure will have to be created. Super-heavy seaplanes can be used in SAR operations and in offshore oil and gas prospecting and extracting activities.

The Be-2500 is a long-term prospective design not intended to be implemented in the immediate future. It is quite obvious that at present projects of that magnitude are beyond the technical and financial capacities of the Russian aircraft industry – or any single country, for that matter. They should be implemented on the basis of broad international co-operation. Viktor Kobzev, General Director of the Beriyev TANTK, is optimistic about the technical and commercial viability of the project. In 2007 he stated in a press interview that the work on studying the various aerodynamic and hydrodynamic layouts of the Be-2500 was actively pursued, involving wind tunnel and towing tank tests. He noted that some of the technologies required for the implementation of the project were not yet available but would most certainly be developed in due course of time. Earlier, in 2004, Kobzev had said: 'We have submitted this project to our military customers and we have found support from them'.

Be-5000

The designation of this project of a giant flying boat suggests that its AUW is as high as 5,000 tonnes (11,022,930 lb). Nothing is known about this project apart from a general arrangement drawing published in Ghennadiy S. Panatov's book on the history of the Beriyev Design Bureau in 2002. The drawing shows a flying boat with two hulls joined by a rectangular wing centre section of a very wide chord and big thickness. Unswept outer wing panels of relatively high aspect ratio are mounted on the outboard side of each hull, producing a wing of a very big span. The wingtips are fitted with winglets. Each of the hulls has a single transverse step amidships. The front view of the hulls shows their bottoms to represent respectively the right and left half of a normal hull with deadrise and a longitudinal step, so that the inner sides of the two hulls are vertically flat. The aft ends of the hulls carry vertical tails which support the horizontal tail (stabiliser and elevator) with a span exceeding the distance between the vertical tails. Crew cockpits are located at the front end of each hull.

Particularly interesting is the powerplant which comprises as many as 23 turbojet engines! Seven of these are mounted above the rearmost part of the wing centre section, while the rest is divided into two groups of eight engines, mounted atop the two outer wing panels and protruding ahead of the leading edges. The large number of engines is presumably due to the unavailability of turbojets of sufficiently high thrust at the time when the project was conceived; it may well be surmised that the use of the most powerful engines available at present would cut the number required by 50%. The drawing suggests that the thick wing centre section provides the main space for the carriage of a useful load and is intended to house cargo holds with access from the front.

It stands to reason to suppose that the cavity formed by the wing centre section and the two hulls serves the purpose of creating a dynamic air cushion during take-off and thus places this flying boat into the category of aircraft making use of the WIG effect at least in the take-off mode.

VTOL amphibian for ASW duties

Among the projects of large hydroplanes and amphibious aircraft studied at the Beriyev Design bureau there was a project of a VTOL amphibian intended for ASW duties. No information is available on this project, apart from the artist's impression which is published here. The drawing shows an aircraft of large dimensions, featuring a canard layout in an unorthodox configuration. The foreplanes of large area (or, indeed, the front wings in a tandem-wing layout) are joined to the main wings by the latter's leading-edge root extensions. The boat-hull type fuselage is blended into the wings, forming an integral structure aerodynamically. An interesting feature is the use of four floats mounted at the tips of both the main wings and the foreplane.

Four cruise turbojets are placed in packages of two above the main wings. The location of the lift engines is not clear, but they might well be placed in the LERXes of the main wings. The large aggregate wing area and the very long chord at the roots, creating a sort of low-aspect-ratio wing centre section, suggest that this aircraft was intended to be endowed with WIG craft properties that could come to good use at least during the take-off.

* * *

As may well be seen, the Beriyev TANTK, following up the traditions laid down by Robert Bartini during the years of his work in this design bureau, continues serious research in the direction of creating large-size seaplanes intended for transcontinental transportation and capable of being operated in the WIG mode. At present the emphasis is placed on traditional seaplanes (flying boats), such as the Be-200 and A-40/42. The projects of gigantic seaplanes/WIG craft are clearly beyond the current financial and technical resources of the Russian aircraft industry and are viewed as long-term prospective projects that might eventually become the object of international cooperative ventures.

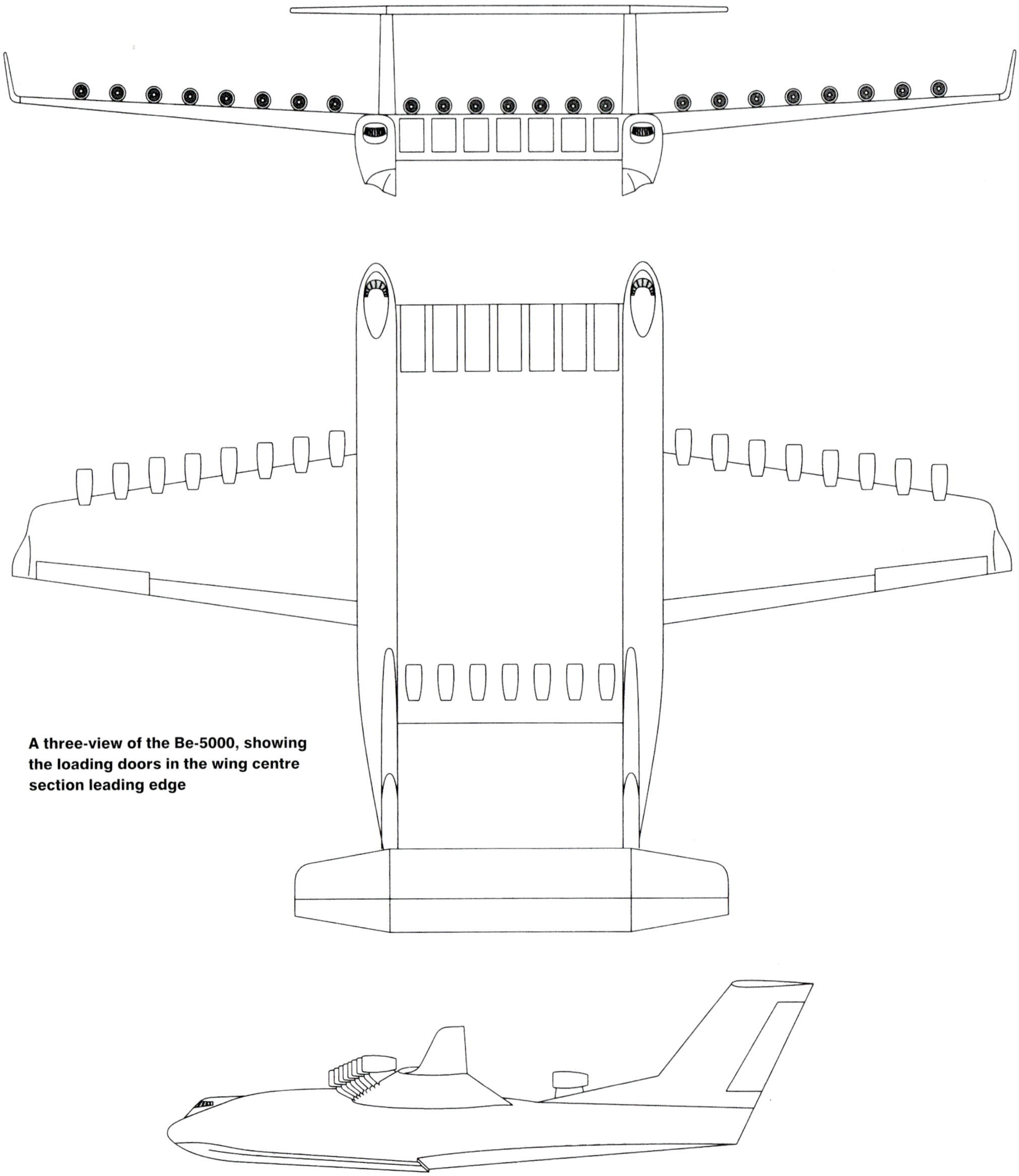

A three-view of the Be-5000, showing the loading doors in the wing centre section leading edge

CHAPTER FOUR

SUKHOI: ATTEMPT AT DIVERSIFICATION

WIG VEHICLES ON THE AGENDA

The Sukhoi OKB (at present officially known as AVPK Sukhoi – the Aviation Defence Industry Complex named after Pavel Osipovich Sukhoi) is world-renowned for its fighters, fighter-bombers and attack aircraft. In the mid-1980s it also embarked on work associated with WIG vehicles. From 1985 onwards it co-operated for several years in these matters with the Central Design Bureau of Hydrofoils named after Rostislav Ye. Alekseyev and with such organisations as TsLST (Central Laboratory for Research on Rescue Equipment) and the Krylov Central Shipbuilding Research Institute in St. Petersburg.

In 1989 the Sukhoi OKB began working on a programme to define the concept and configuration of a WIG vehicle. The following configurations were considered:

- single and twin fuselages;
- wings of various sweep, aspect ratios and dihedral angles;
- different types of vertical tail surfaces (single-and twin-finned, a V-tail, with or without a horizontal tail);
- wing centre sections of different planform and shape, and different means of air flow under the bottom surface of the vehicle;

A model of the S-90-200 passenger WIG showing the twin double-deck hulls and the push-pull engine arrangement.

One of the project configurations of the S-90-8 eight-seat WIG craft. This one is powered by a single M-601 turboprop. Note the air scoop allowing the propeller to build up a static air cushion.

- with different number and types of engines, as well as different powerplant arrangements;
- configurations of various dimensions.

By early 1992 the layouts of Sukhoi's S-90-8 and S-90-200 WIG vehicles had been frozen as the basic designs for further investigation. (For the outsider, Sukhoi confuse the picture by using the S-90 designation for a number of very different designs; the additional digits, such as the -8 and -200 in these designations, refer to the seating capacity, so that each of them may cover several related or unrelated designs.)

By 2000 ten versions of vehicles of varying dimensions had been considered. They represented variations of the composite layout wing concept developed by Bartini together with TsAGI and SibNIA (*Si**beer**skiy na**ooch**nyy insti**toot** avi**ah**tsii* – Siberian Aviation Research Institute named after Sergey A. Chaplygin in Novosibirsk) and employed in his VVA-14 vehicle. Here follows the description of Sukhoi WIG vehicle projects, some of which have been presented to the public at various aviation events at home and abroad.

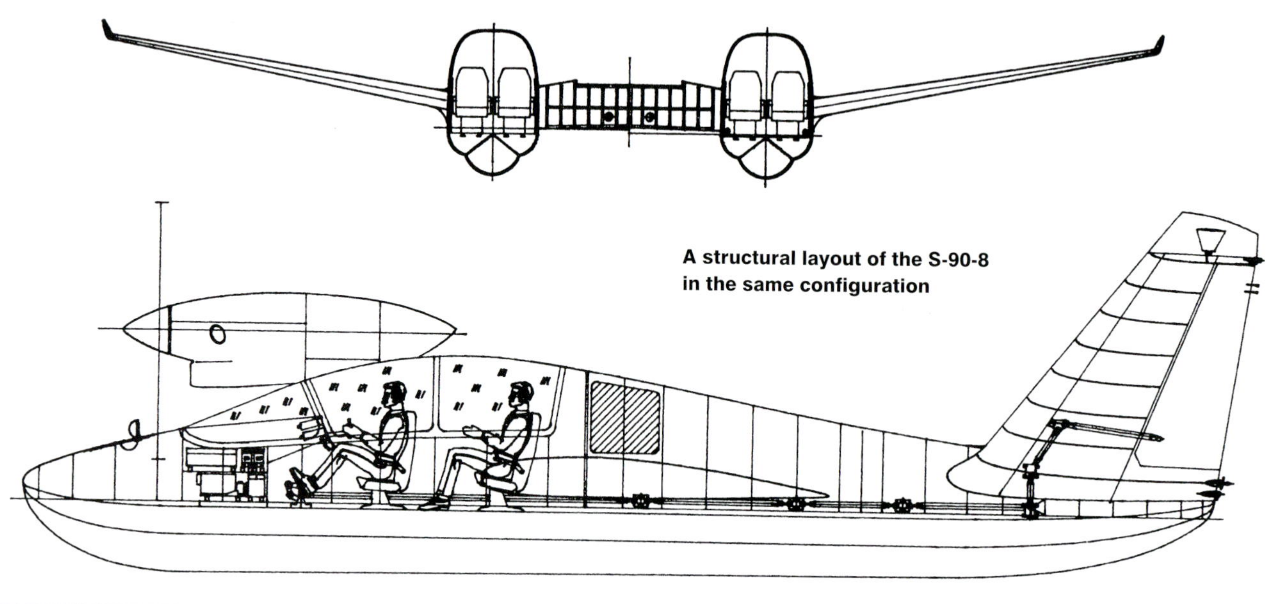

A structural layout of the S-90-8 in the same configuration

S-90-8

This is a small WIG vehicle intended for carrying eight passengers over water on short-haul routes. It is powered by a Czech-built series-produced Walter (Motorlet) M-601 turboprop engine optimised for the application. The S-90-8 features a twin-fuselage layout with a wing centre section arranged between the fuselages. The fuselages of a moderate fineness ratio are oval-section structures which have segmented rubberised fabric shells on their bottom surfaces. The nose section of each fuselage accommodates an avionics bay followed by a passenger cabin. There are a pilot's station and three passenger seats in the port fuselage and four passenger seats in the starboard one. The large glazing area of the bubble canopies affords a good view in all directions.

Flanked by the fuselages is a thick-profiled wing centre section with a cutout at the front to pass the propeller wash under the wings for creating a static air cushion. The wings, with an aspect ratio of 5, are slightly swept forward at the leading edges, the sweep angle being –1°. The wings are fitted with ailerons for lateral control. Dihedral is 10°. The tail sections of the fuselages mount a Vee tail unit, the panels of which are canted 45° outboard; each tail unit panel has a control surface.

An engine nacelle housing the single M-601 with a four-bladed variable-pitch tractor propeller is mounted on a pylon located along the line of symmetry of the wing centre section in its forward part. The engine is rated at 740 ehp (551 kW).

Here are some specifications and performance figures of the machine: length, 11.7 m (38 ft 4⅝ in); wing span, 15.1 m (49 ft 6½ in); tailplane span, 9.3 m (30 ft 6 in); wing area with centre section, 48.2 m² (518.78 sq ft); take-off gross weight, 3,700 kg (8,155 lb); maximum speed, 300 km/h (186 mph); cruising speed, 200 km/h (124 mph); maximum range, 640 km (397 miles); range with maximum

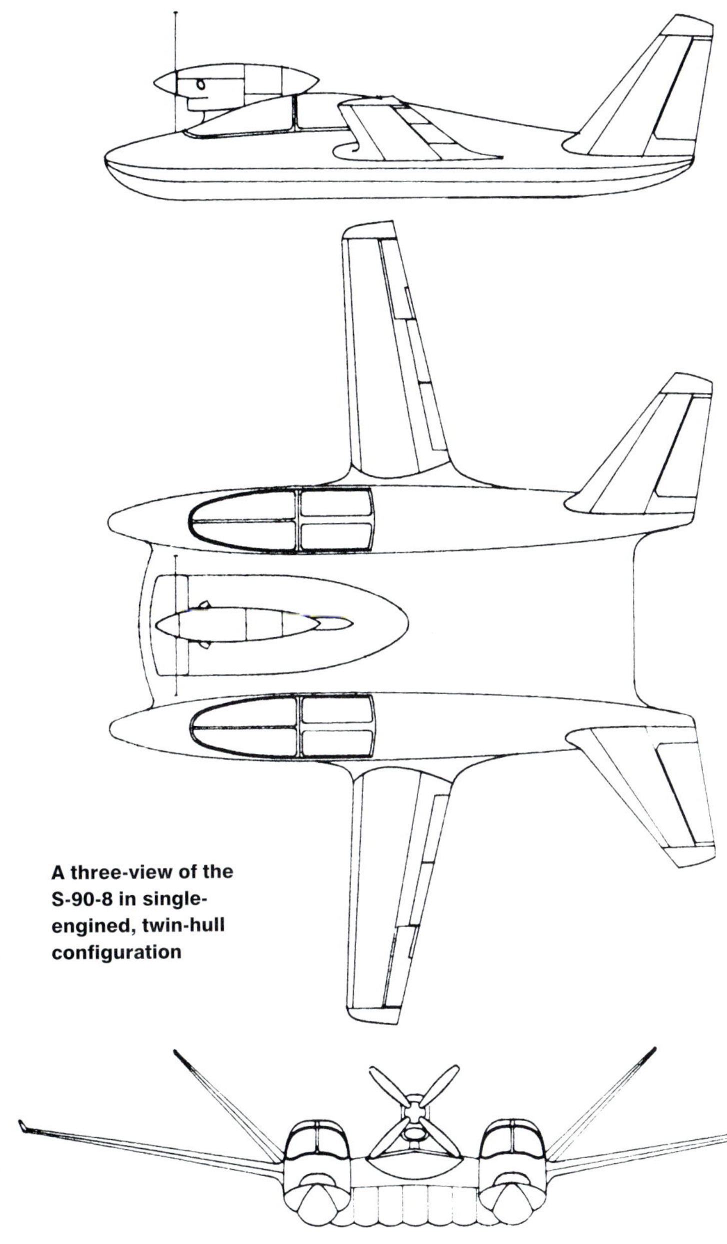

A three-view of the S-90-8 in single-engined, twin-hull configuration

A very similar configuration of the S-90-8 with two M-601s mounted in tandem in push-pull configuration.

Despite being also designated S-90-8, this version has a totally different layout with a single fuselage, twin skegs and 'semi-T-tails', plus a ducted fan as a propulsor.

A revised model of the same configuration, showing the portside entry doors. Note that the horizontal tails are strut-braced and the propeller shroud is faired into the wing centre section.

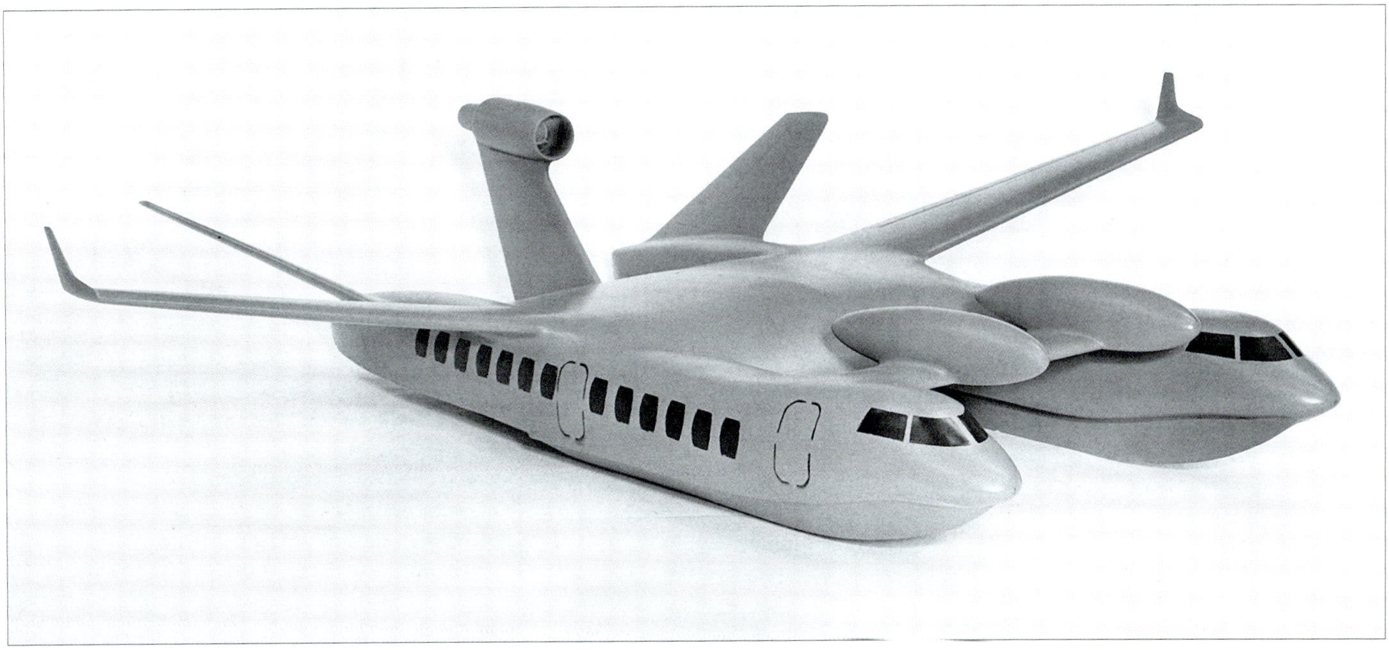

payload, 440 km (273 miles); ground effect altitude, 1.5-2 m (4.9-6.6 ft).

There was a project of a very similar version of the S-90-8 which differed in having a second M-601 engine installed between the tails in pusher configuration.

Yet another vehicle, also designated S-90-8, was, in fact, a completely different design featuring a single fuselage, twin skegs flanking a low-aspect-ratio wing centre section, and 'semi-T-tails'. The propulsion was effected by a ducted pusher propeller installed behind the cabin. The shape of the shroud surrounding the propeller varied in different model configurations.

An interesting postscript to the description of this vehicle is provided by a short notice at one of Russian web-sites. According to this report, *'the Sukhoi Design Bureau, having started co-operation with Alekseyev CHDB, later switched over to joint work with NPP (Science and Production Enterprise) Tekhnika, a small company which had seceded from CHDB and taken up the design and manufacture of ACVs.* (This small company was founded by Stanislav S. Alekseyev – *Auth.*) *One of NPP Tekhnika's products, the Sever-3 ACV powered by two [RMZ-640 two-stroke] engines from the Buran snow scooter, achieved the dynamic aircushion flight mode and attained a speed of 110 km/h [68 mph]. It was envisaged that Sukhoi and NPP Tekhnika would jointly design and manufacture the Sever-8, an eight-seat twin-fuselage ekranoplan whose layout resembled that of the T-12* (Sukhoi's project of an attack aircraft – *Auth.*)*; it was intended to play the role of a scaled-down prototype for the "big" ekranoplans'*. The description of the Sever-8 comes close to that of the S-90-8, but the story needs confirmation.

Yet another version of a passenger WIG craft designated S-90, a twin-hull design with a butterfly tail, a cruise turbojet and twin turboprops at the front.

S-90-8 specifications (provisional)

Length	11.7 m (38 ft 4⅝ in)
Wingspan	15.1 m (49 ft 6³¹⁄₆₄ in)
Height	3.5 m (11 ft 5⁵¹⁄₆₄ in)
Tailplane span	9.3 m (30 ft 6⁹⁄₆₄ in)
Wing area, m² (sq ft):	
gross	48.2 (518.78)
centre section	36.6 (393.93)
outer wing panels	11.6 (124.85)
Tailplane area, m² (sq ft)	11.0 (118.39)
Take-off gross weight, kg (lb)	3,700 (8,155)
Fuel load, kg (lb)	500 (1,100)
Wing loading at normal take-off weight, kg/m² (lb/sq ft)	77 (15.71)
Max speed, km/h (mph)	300 (186)
Cruising speed, km/h (mph)	200 (124)
Range, km (miles):	
with max fuel	640 (397)
with max payload	440 (273)
Max flight altitude, m (ft)	1,500 (4,920)
Ground effect altitude, m (ft)	1.5-2 (5-6.5)

S-90-200

This project of an amphibious passenger/cargo WIG vehicle was developed by the Sukhoi OKB on the basis of a preliminary agreement with the Aero Marine Singapore PTE Ltd. It was intended for carrying passengers and cargo on medium- to long-haul maritime routes with poorly equipped hydro-airports. The S-90-200 is a twin-fuselage (catamaran) WIG vehicle accommodating 210-220 passengers in a double-deck layout.

The most common version of the Sukhoi Design Bureau logo

Another variation on the twin-hull S-90 design with two turbofans on top of the wing centre section and two fin-mounted cruise engines.

The fuselages are oval-section structures provided with inflatable rubberised fabric shells on their bottom surfaces. Both forward fuselages accommodate crew workstations. The main fuselage space is occupied by a double-deck passenger cabin. The upper deck of each fuselage is divided into a cabin for 39 first class passengers and a cabin for 54 business class (tourist class) passengers. The lower deck houses eight one- or two-passenger state rooms. The vehicle has a crew of 14.

The fuselages are connected by a thick airfoil-shaped centre section, that is, a wing of low aspect ratio. The centre section is supplemented by outer wing panels of greater aspect ratio which enable the vehicle to move out of ground effect if necessary to avoid obstacles or overfly areas with intensive shipping. The wings with an aspect ratio of 5.0 are slightly swept forward at the leading edges, the sweep angle is −1°. Each outer wing panel is fitted with three-section flaperons and has an upward-canted tip. The vehicle has a Vee tail unit with one panel installed on each fuselage; the tails are canted 45° outwards. Each panel is provided with a control surface.

A model of the S-90-200. The wing centre section incorporates dorsal cargo loading doors.

S-90-200 specifications (provisional)

Powerplant	2 x NK-12MK
Length	40.0 m (131 ft $2\frac{51}{64}$ in)
Wingspan	60.92 m (199 ft $10\frac{27}{64}$ in)
Height	11.85 m (38 ft $10\frac{35}{64}$ in)
Wing area, m2 (ft2):	
gross	757.2 (8,150)
centre section	502.0 (5,403)
outer wing panels	254.0 (2,691)
Tailplane area, m² (sq ft)	69.9 (752)
Take-off gross weight, kg (lb)	132,000 (290,930)
Fuel load, kg (lb)	58,000 (127,830)
Max payload, kg (lb)	20,000 (44,080)
Wing loading at normal take-off weight, kg/m² (lb/sq ft)	172 (35.08)
Max speed, km/h (mph)	470 (292)
Cruising speed, km/h (mph)	380 (236)
Max range with 220 passengers, km (miles)	8,000 (4,968)
Max flight altitude, m (ft)	1,500 (4,920)
Ground effect altitude, m (ft)	2.0-5.5 (6.5-18)

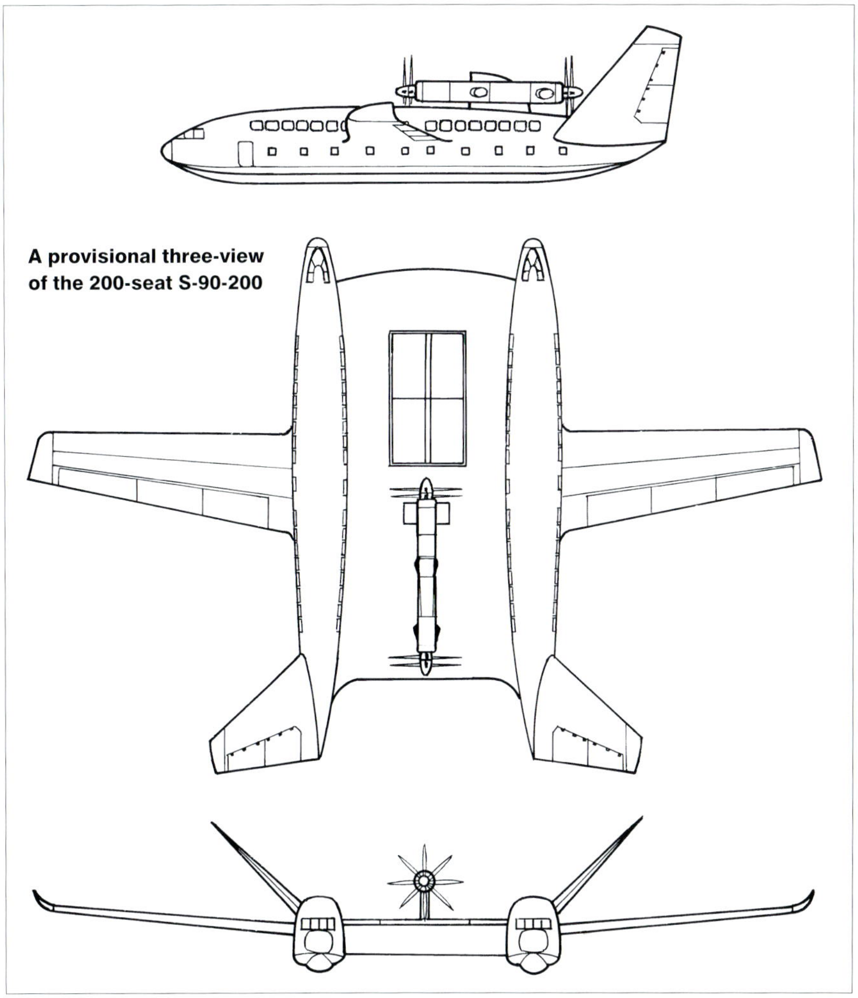

A provisional three-view of the 200-seat S-90-200

The powerplant comprises two 15,000-ehp Kuznetsov NK-12MK turboprops driving eight-blade contra-rotating propellers. The engines are installed in tandem in a pylon-mounted nacelle on the rear part of the wing centre section. During take-off and landing the propeller wash is ingested by a special device and directed through a system of air passages to be discharged under the bottom surface of the wing centre section. Thereby a static air cushion is created, supplementing the dynamic air cushion produced by ram air during cruise flight. There is a provision for a flexible skirt which is retracted during the transition from the static to the dynamic air cushion; the longitudinal segmented components of the skirt act as shock absorbers during landing.

Here are some basic specifications and performance figures: length, 40 m (131 ft $2\frac{51}{64}$ in); wing

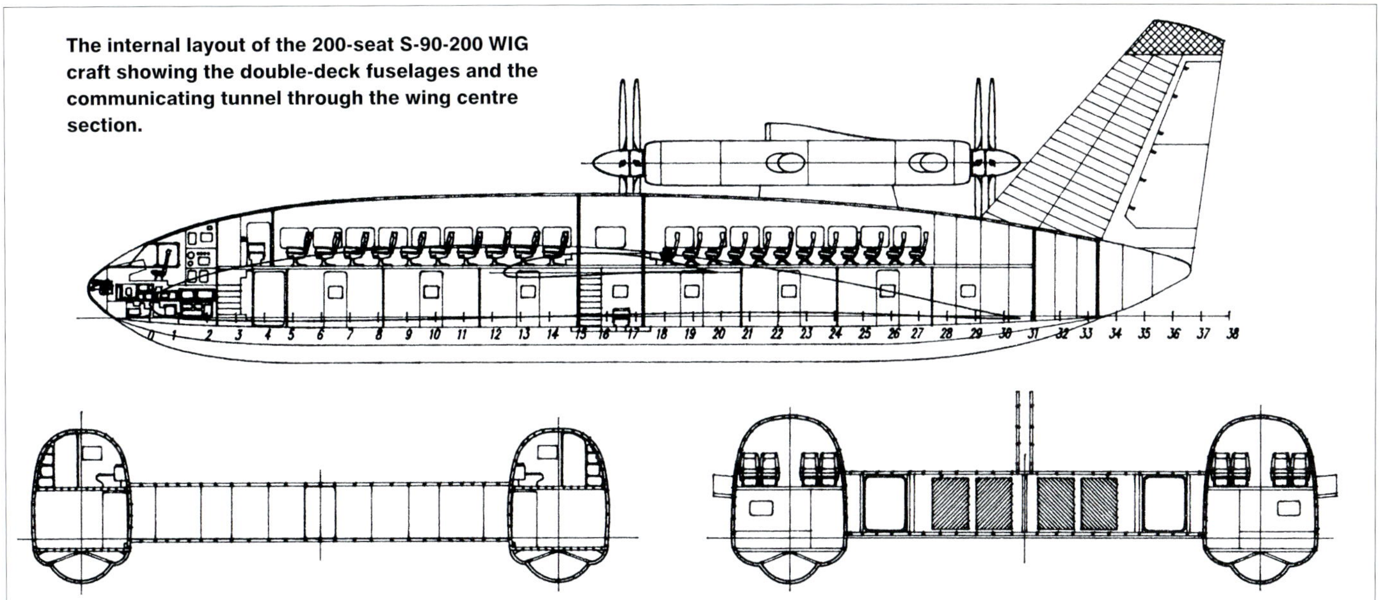

The internal layout of the 200-seat S-90-200 WIG craft showing the double-deck fuselages and the communicating tunnel through the wing centre section.

This model depicts one of the projected WIG craft known as the S-90-40. The three-turbofan craft bears a strong resemblance to the A-90 Orlyonok.

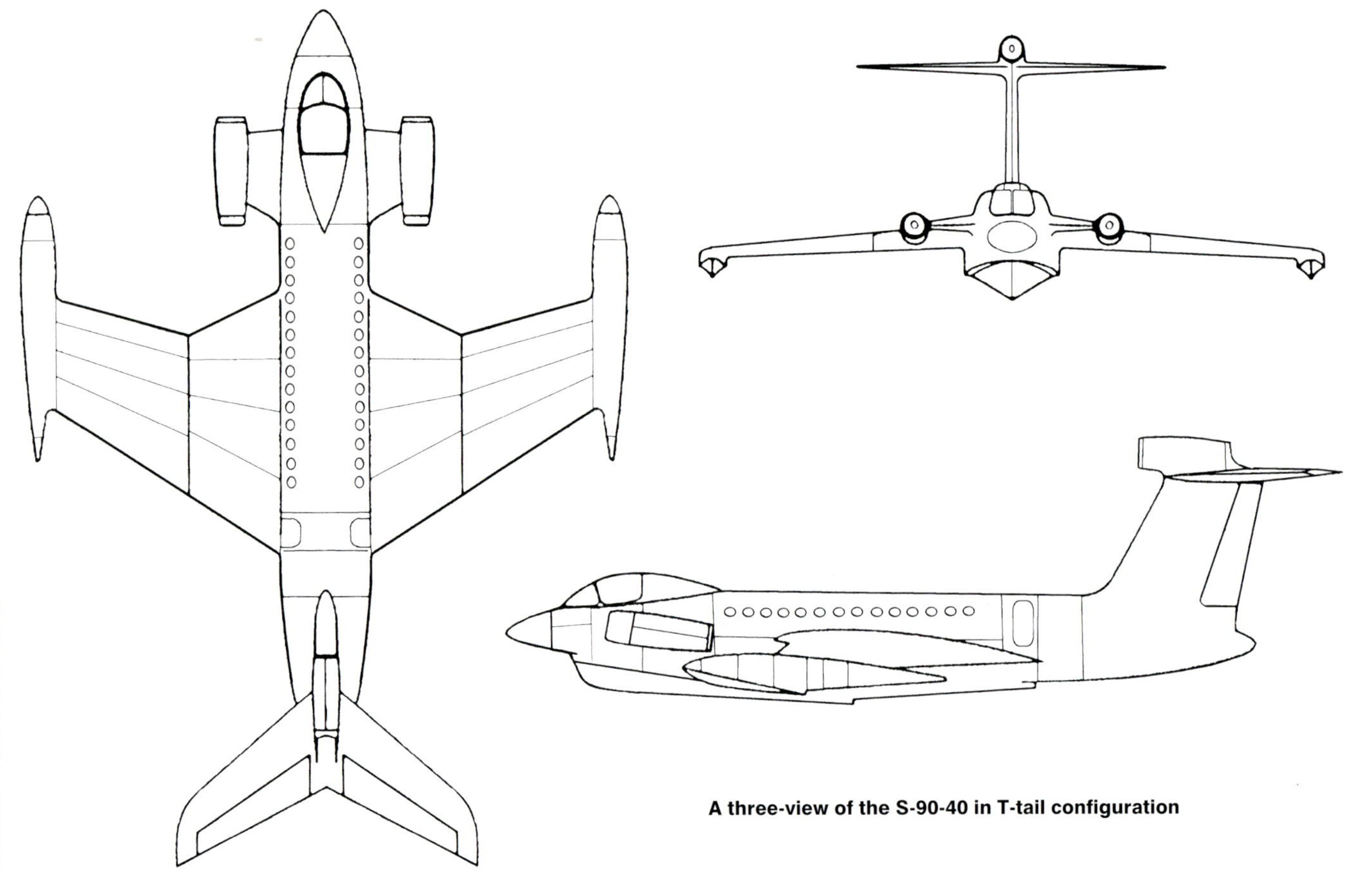

A three-view of the S-90-40 in T-tail configuration

span, 60.92 m (199 ft 10$\frac{27}{64}$ in); take-off gross weight, 132,000 kg (291,000 lb); payload, 20 tons (44,080 lb); maximum speed, 470 km/h (292 mph); cruising speed, 380 km/h (236 mph);* maximum range with 220 passengers, 8,000 km (5,000 miles); maximum flight altitude, 1,500 m (4,920 ft);* ground effect altitude, 2.0-5.5 m (6.6-18 ft).

*Note: An advertising leaflet cites the cruising speed as 470 km/h (292 mph) and the service ceiling as 2,500 m (8,200 ft).

S-90 (twin-fuselage configuration)

This S-90 project was a twin-hulled vehicle, each hull having its own crew cockpit and a passenger cabin, with an entry door amidships. The hulls were connected by a shoulder-mounted rectangular wing centre section occupying about half the length; the high-aspect-ratio outer wing panels were unswept, with strong dihedral, and small winglets. As on the S-90-8 and the S-90 200, the tail unit consisted of trapezoidal fin and rudder assemblies canted strongly outward. The craft had a mixed powerplant: an airfoil-section cross-member connecting the forward hull sections carried two turboprop engines side by side for creating a static air cushion, while the cruise engine (a turbofan) was mounted on a tall pylon at the trailing edge of the wing centre section.

S-90 (another twin-fuselage configuration)

This configuration was similar to the one described above but had an all-jet powerplant; the pylon carried two cruise turbofans side by side, and two more turbofans of a larger type were installed on top of the wing centre section near the leading edge.

S-90-40 (single-fuselage aircraft-type configuration)

This 40-seat passenger WIG vehicle powered by three turbofans was intended for medium-haul routes over sea and ocean areas. It differed from those described above in being based on a single-fuselage 'aircraft-type' layout reminiscent of Alekseyev's designs, featuring a single cruise engine at the top of the fin and two booster engines in nacelles flanking the forward fuselage. They were

A very different model of a passenger WIG craft bearing the same designation S-90-40, with twin skegs and twin tails carrying the engines.

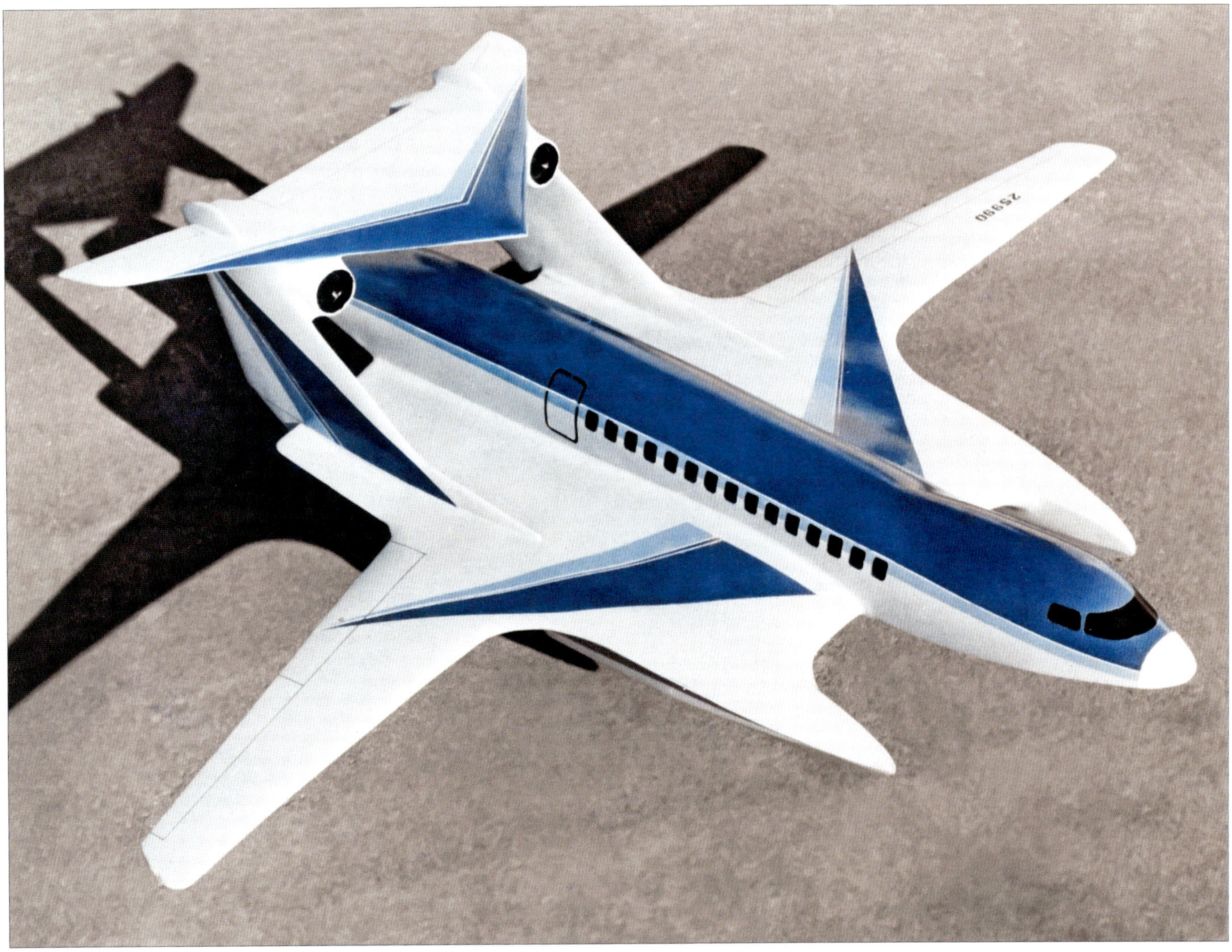

A model of the Su-2000 light passenger WIG craft.

set at an angle permitting their exhaust to be directed under the wings for creating a static air-cushion. A characteristic feature of the design was the planform of the wings which were slightly forward-swept, with a leading-edge kink at half-span. The machine had a design cruising speed of 400 km/h (248 mph) and a range of 2,000 km (1,240 miles).

S-90-40 (a different single-fuselage configuration)

A vehicle of approximately the same size, but of a different configuration had an airliner-type fuselage sitting on top of a rectangular wing centre section flanked by long floats (skegs) to which high-aspect-ratio forward-swept outer wing panels equipped with flaps and ailerons were attached. The wing centre section carried twin swept-back vertical tails connected at the top by an arrowhead-shaped stabiliser with a three-section elevator. The powerplant consisted of two turbofan engines located at the fin/tailplane junctions on the inboard side.

S-90 (Su-2000)

In 1997 the OKB started work on the S-90 project which featured a layout considerably differing from the two projects described above. Some reports mention Aleksandr Polyakov as the chief designer for this project. In several publications and advertising materials this vehicle was referred to simply as the S-90, but there was also a display model of this machine bearing the designation Su-2000.

This time the vehicle makes use of the 'Bartini layout', featuring an integral fuselage (lifting body) and an air cushion undercarriage provided with a special fan and a separate power unit. It is intended

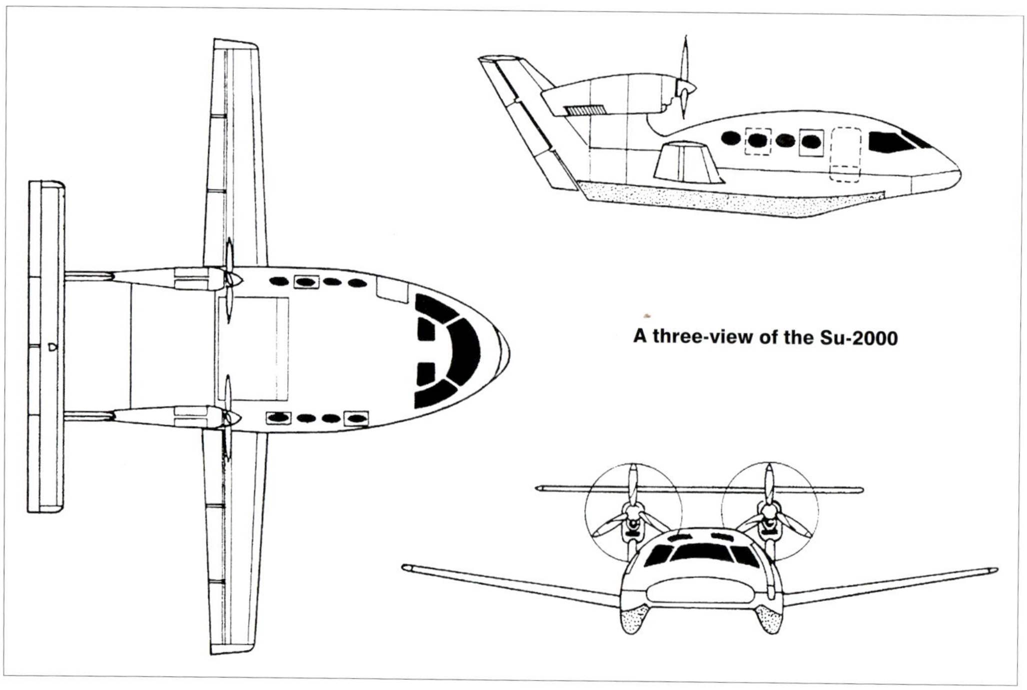

A three-view of the Su-2000

Basic design specifications of the S-90:	
Length	13.83 m (45 ft 4$\frac{31}{64}$ in)
Wing span	16.91 m (55 ft 5$\frac{47}{64}$ in)
Height	4.85 m (15 ft 10$\frac{15}{16}$ in)
Crew	2
Number of passengers	19, 26 or 31
Weights and performance figures are indicated for three operation modes: aircraft/WIG craft/ACV	
Maximum take-off weight, kg (lb)	7,900/9,500/10,500 (17,420/20,940/23,150)
Empty equipped weight, kg (lb)	4,500/4,500/4,500 (9,920/9,920/9,920)
Maximum payload, kg (lb)	2,500/3,000/3,000 (5,510/6,615/6,615)
Maximum fuel load, kg (lb)	3,000/3,000/3,000 (6,615/6,615/6,615)
Cruising speed, km/h (mph)	400/400/80 (248/248/50)
Flight altitude, m (ft)	0.5 – 4,000/0.05 (1 ft 7 in – 13,120 ft/0 ft 2 in)
Take-off/landing speed, km/h (mph)	120/120/n.a. (74.5/74.5/n.a.)
Range, km (miles):	
with a maximum fuel load	3,100 (1,925)
with 19 passengers	1,260/2,400 (782/1,490)
with 25 passengers	760/2,450 (472/1,521)
with 31 passengers	1,870/1,970 (1,161/1,223)
Take-off/landing run, m (ft)	230/240 (755/790)

for passenger and cargo transportation both in aircraft mode at high altitude and in ground effect mode. In the latter case it can fly over water surface in sea states up to 2 and over flat areas on the ground with hummocks up to 0.5 m (1 ft 7$\frac{11}{16}$ in) high. Initially the designers studied a layout featuring a hydrodynamically shaped displacing hull with planing steps on the bottom and endplates at the wingtips; it was to have booster engines placed ahead of the centre section leading edge and injecting an air stream under the wing (Alekseyev's layout).

A model of the S-90-4 light amphibious WIG craft powered by a four-cylinder piston engine.

These views of the S-90-4 show the retractable quad landing gear. The main units retract into the inboard faces of the floats.

The S-90-4 is characterised by a 'horizontal triplane' layout and triple vertical tails.

However, as the work progressed, the engineers decided to abandon the hydrodynamic take-off; instead, they adopted a layout featuring an air-cushion undercarriage with retractable skirts fore and aft and with streamlined inflatable pontoons instead of rigid endplates incorporating steps on the underside. The use of a special fan building up the pressure in the static air cushion made it possible to reduce by half the planform area of the wing centre section and accordingly the planform area of the machine as a whole , while retaining the same all-up weight. In addition, the smaller size of the wing centre section and reduction in the airframe weight made it possible to increase the seating capacity and to switch over from a traditional lifting wing centre section to an integral lifting fuselage which is shaped as a low fineness-ratio structure formed by high-thickness airfoils with an ogival forward portion. The aerodynamic layout of the S-90 features wings of composite configuration comprising a low aspect ratio fuselage/wing centre section which is intended for creating lift in the ground-effect flight mode and for accommodating the payload, and aircraft type outer wing panels (with a high aspect ratio). A 350-shp Allison 250-C20R turboshaft engine (which powers various helicopters, including the Kamov Ka-226 helicopter) is used for driving the air cushion fan; it also doubles as an APU. The cruise powerplant comprises two 960-ehp PZL-10S (Glushenkov TVD-10B) turboprops mounted on the fins which serve as pylons. The fins are topped by the 'bench-shaped' tailplane.

Three operational modes were envisaged for the S-90: it could be operated as an aircraft, as a WIG craft or as ACV.

Research showed that the flight altitude in ground-effect mode should not exceed 0.5 m (1.6 ft) and that flights at this height should be performed over an ideally flat surface (the surface of rivers and lakes in calm weather). According to

This unusual amphibious WIG craft with tandem wings and ducted propellers was developed by Yevgeniy P. Groonin's design team at the Sukhoi OKB (later known as the T-2072).

some calculations, flights of this kind I would make up not more than 5-10 % of the total flight time in the course of, say, a year. Therefore a view was held that the S-90 could be constructed and operated as a Type C WIG vehicle, or an aircraft operating independently of airfields, with the 'aircraft' flight mode as the principal one, while the flight in ground effect is reserved as a supplementary function for short-distance flights or for carrying out special tasks.

S-90-4

Little is known about this four-seat craft, which features a 'horizontal triplane' layout with two floats flanking a rectangular wing centre section to which dihedral outer wing panels and dihedral canards are attached. The fuselage pod attached at the front of the centre section accommodates a pilot and three passengers under a large bubble canopy, The tail unit comprises three fins connected at the top by a tailplane; the centre fin carries a four-cylinder inverted in-line engine driving a three-blade tractor propeller. A retractable quad landing gear is provided.

S-?? amphibious WIG craft, later redesignated T-2072 (project)

This vehicle was developed by Yevgeniy P. Groonin's design team at the Sukhoi OKB to meet

As this view shows, the vehicle was to have folding wings and a quad landing gear similar to that of the S-90-4. The extremely large lateral doors and rear door are noteworthy.

Three-quarters rear view of the T-2072

the technical requirements submitted by the Navy. This was an *ekranolyot*, that is, a type C vehicle, capable of free flight at altitude and of movement in the WIG mode. The aerodynamic layout was similar to the 'horizontal triplane' layout of the S-90-4 described above. It was intended to be used by the Marines. The fuselage provided accommodation for 15-20 troops who could disembark through side hinged doors or through a rear hatch. There was a provision for a hatch at the bottom of the fuselage, permitting the disembarkation of frogmen. The vehicle with an AUW of 6800-7000 kg (14,990-15,430 lb) was to be powered by two 1,400-ehp TVD-20 turboprops with ducted pusher propellers. The vehicle was to be provided with a device for creating a static air cushion that would facilitate breaching. In one version this was to be effected by a separate lift engine, in another version – by bleeding the air from the cruise engine. In both cases the air stream thus obtained was to be injected into the space under the wing centre section through nozzles located on the foreplane. Provision was made for the installation of two 30-mm cannons in the floats.

When Groonin left the Sukhoi OKB and started his activities as a leader of his own design bureau, he retained this project and eventually took some steps to revive it in a modified form (see Chapter 6).

The T-2072 features large winglets and inverted-gull shaped foreplanes. The striped areas are walkways.

This is how the T-2072 would look when waterborne.

S-919 and other projects

In addition to the projects described above, the Sukhoi Design Bureau is known to have worked on a number of other projects of ekranoplans which have not been widely publicised. These included the S-92, S-94 and S-919 projects on which no information is available, apart from the fact that the S-919, S-90 and presumably some other Sukhoi projects, underwent wind tunnel tests at SibNIA. There is a photo of a wind tunnel model from SibNIA on the institute's official web site which may well represent one of the designs mentioned above.

At present the Sukhoi Design Bureau is no longer engaged in the design of ekranoplans.

CHAPTER FIVE

ENTHUSIASTS
MAKE THEIR CONTRIBUTION

Research in the field of ground effect and practical design of WIG vehicles in the USSR were not the exclusive domain of big design bureaux tasked by the government. Enthusiastic individuals, both specialists and amateur designers, were also engaged in this work, as were enthusiast design teams set up in various institutions of higher learning (student design bureaux, or SKB – *stoo**dench**eskoye kon**strook**torskoye byu**ro***). In addition, a number of scientific institutions did theoretical studies in this field, sometimes supplemented by practical design work. This chapter contains a brief review of the designs created by such enthusiasts. It covers the designs related to the whole of the Soviet Union including those republics (the Ukraine, Lithuania) which later, after the break-up of

Upper row: A remote-controlled model – probably representing the T-310 *ekranolyot* designed by Yevgeniy P. Groonin at the TsLST. Above: An early model of the ESKA-1 craft; note the fin fillet. Right: The rather different actual ESKA-1 with Groonin in the cockpit.

The ESKA-1 taxies on the water; unlike the photo on the previous page, the cockpit canopy is in place. The digits 0673 are the first flight date (June 1973). The legend under the cockpit reads *Eksperimental'nyy*.

The ESKA-1 (with uncowled engine and no spinner) in flight, showing the angled wingtip aerodynamic surfaces.

Here the ESKA-1 is seen on display at the NTTM-74 exhibition at the VDNKh fairground in Moscow. Note the cowled engine and the propeller spinner.

the USSR, became independent states. Similar design activities in the Russian Federation after 1992 are also included.

TsLST and educational institutions

TsLST

A prominent place in the work under review belongs to the TsLST OSVOD RSFSR (*Tsen**trahl'**naya labo**rato**riya spa**sah**tel'noy **tekh**niki **Ob**schchestva spa**sen**iya na **vod**akh* – Central Laboratory of New Types of Rescue Equipment under the Rescue Agency of the Russian Federal Soviet Socialist Republic). Enlisting the support of several SKBs and young designers, this organisation produced a whole range of designs of light WIG vehicles in the 1970s and 1980s.

A rare colour photo of the ESKA-1 during tests.

ES-1

This machine of wooden construction was developed in 1971 as an *ekrano**lyot**nyy stend* (*ekranolyot* test vehicle), hence the ES. It was intended for studying the stability and controllability of a wing of circular planform during movement close to the supporting surface, as well as for investigating the possibilities of using an ultralight ekranoplan for rescue purposes. The test vehicle was designed by Yu. V. Makarov. The ES-1 had a water-displacing hull in the shape of a boat with small chines and a flat bottom. The outer rim of the wing was made flexible. The rigid central part of the wing was surrounded by a flexible ring-shaped surface made of sheet polyethylene 0.5 m (1 ft 7¾ in) wide; it increased the diameter of the wing to 3.6m (11 ft 9¾ in). The rigid part of the wing had an incidence of 10°, while its flexible leading edge had zero incidence. Thus, the rigid wing with an elastic rim had a concave profile. At the wingtips the elastic rim was bent downwards at an angle of 30°, producing the effect of endplates.

The ekranolyot had a T-tail unit and a slab stabiliser. There being no ailerons, the rudder was used as the means for lateral control. Placed behind the cockpit was an M-107 two-stroke motorcycle engine driving a two-blade pusher propeller. The ES-1 was tested on the Moskva River.

ESKA-1

This *ekranolyot* (Type B WIG vehicle) based on the Lippisch configuration was designed and constructed in the TsLST by a group of young designers under the guidance of A. V. Gremiatskiy who was chief designer of the project. Yu. S. Gorbenko, Yu. V. Makarov and Yevgeniy P. Groonin (the latter is referred to in several sources as the author of the

The ESKA-1 in modified form with a one-piece curved windshield. Note how the canopy is hinged to the windshield frame. The legend on the nose appears to read *R. Elektron*.

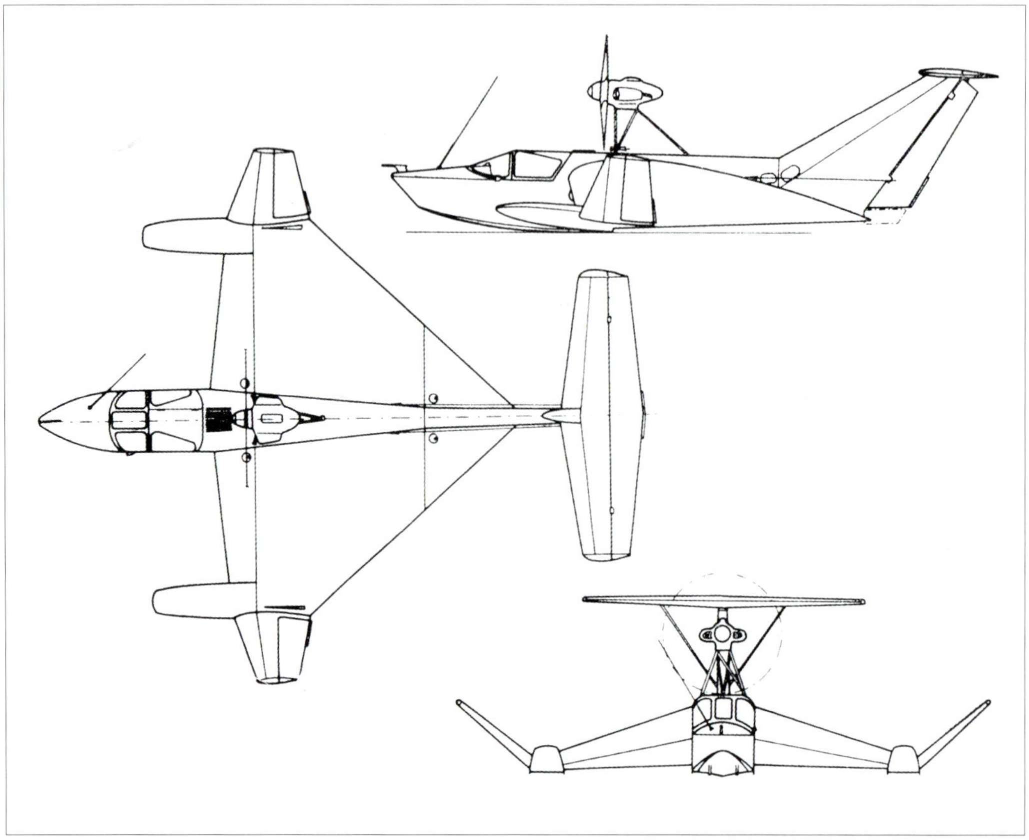

A three-view of the ESKA-1 as displayed in 1974 (with cowling and spinner.

ESKA-1 design) also participated actively in the design and construction work.

The ESKA-1 was designed as a rescue vehicle intended for rendering urgent aid at a distance of up to 50 km (31 miles) from a coastal rescue station. It was a two-seat machine of wooden construction. Simple and easily available materials were used, such as pinewood, aviation plywood, Styrofoam and fibreglass. It utilised the classic Lippisch layout. The reversed-delta wings with anhedral on the leading edges created a dome-shaped cavity enhancing the ground effect. The wing trailing edge was slightly submerged when afloat and acted as a step during the take-off run. The airfoil section of the delta wings with a flat undersurface ensured high longitudinal static stability. Lateral stability and control were ensured by small detachable aerodynamic surfaces fitted with ailerons and attached at an angle to the tips of the main wings. The strut-braced tailplane was mounted at the top of the sharply swept fin.

The vehicle was powered by a 32-hp M-63 flat-twin motorcycle engine with reduction gear driving a two-blade fixed-pitch wooden tractor propeller of 1.6 m (5 ft 3 in) in diameter; the engine was mounted above the hull on a cabane made of steel tubes. The all-up weight of the machine was 450 kg (992 lb), the payload being 220 kg (485 lb).

A drawing of the projected ESKA-4 four-seat ekranolyot developed by the TsLST. Note the separate water rudder.

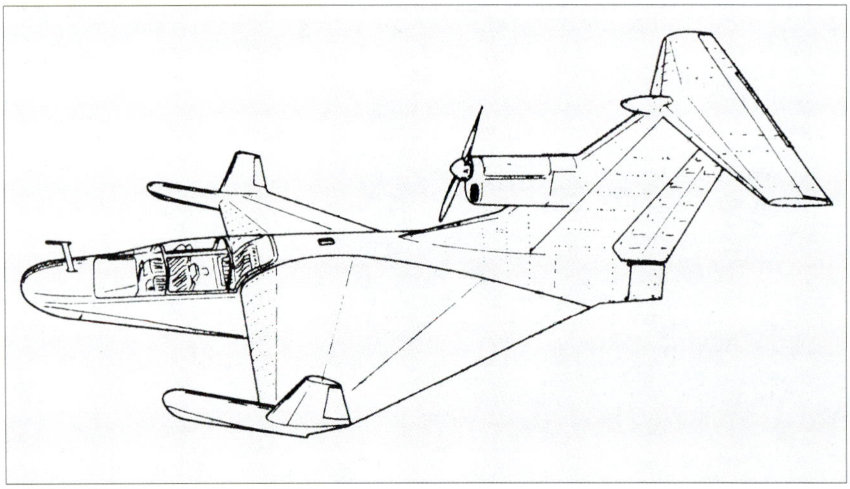

The first flights took place in the summer of 1973. All flight modes were tested: hydroplaning, flight in ground effect and free flight at an altitude of more that 2 m (6.5 ft). The most effective height of flight in ground effect was between 0.3 and 1.5 m (1 and 5 ft). With a 50 per cent payload the ESKA-1 could soar to 50 m (164 ft) to surmount obstacles. In ground effect mode with a full payload the ekranoplan could work up a maximum speed of 122 km/h (75 mph). Range with maximum fuel was 300-350 km (186-217 miles). The single example built was used as a shuttle transport on the Volga River for more than ten years.

Further developments of the ESKA-1 proposed by Yevgeniy P. Groonin were designed in the TsLST. They included:

ESKA-4

This was a four-seat *ekranolyot* of the Lippisch configuration powered by a single Walter M-332 Minor inverted in-line six-cylinder air-cooled engine with a two-blade tractor propeller mounted on the fin leading edge. Two rows of seats were accommodated under an extensively glazed canopy.

T-301

Sharing the same basic layout with the ESKA-4, the T-301 was a single-seat machine having two 18-hp engines with two-blade pusher propellers mounted on pylons above the fuselage in a V arrangement.

T-302

Being a further development of the T-301, the T-302 differed in having two 18-hp engines replaced by one 50-hp Wankel-type engine.

LP-901

This four-seat machine is also a Lippisch-style vehicle, but a twin-fuselage design with boat hulls and twin fins topped by a horizontal stabiliser. It was to be powered by an engine with a pusher propeller mounted on a pylon above the wing centre section.

T-503

The T-503 was a WIG vehicle with twin floats and dome-shaped (anhedral) wings topped by a sailplane-type cockpit seating two persons in tandem. The engine with a two-blade pusher propeller was installed behind the cockpit. A monowheel undercarriage was provided for beaching.

ES-2 (E-0773 Shmel')

This was yet another ekranoplan test vehicle intended for investigating the properties of a flexible wing and for studying its stability and controllability during flight in ground effect. It is referred to variously as ES-2, Shmel' (Bumblebee) or E-0773. The machine was built by the same team as the ESKA-1. To save costs, it was produced by converting a Czechoslovak-built Orličan L-13 Blanik sailplane. The control system, undercarriage and equipment of the glider were retained. An M-63 flat-twin motorcycle engine was installed above the fuselage. The sailplane's wings were removed and replaced by new ones featuring a rigid profiled leading edge with bracing struts and flexible lifting surface made of two layers of rubberised fabric. The ES-2 had large 'armpits' between the wings and the fuselage, the spars and supporting struts were in the air flow.

Initially the engine was not available, only the engine mount being fitted. Therefore the first flights had to be performed with the ES-2 towed by a Moskvich-412 saloon car. The WIG vehicle was piloted by Valeriy Goobin. Non-powered flights took

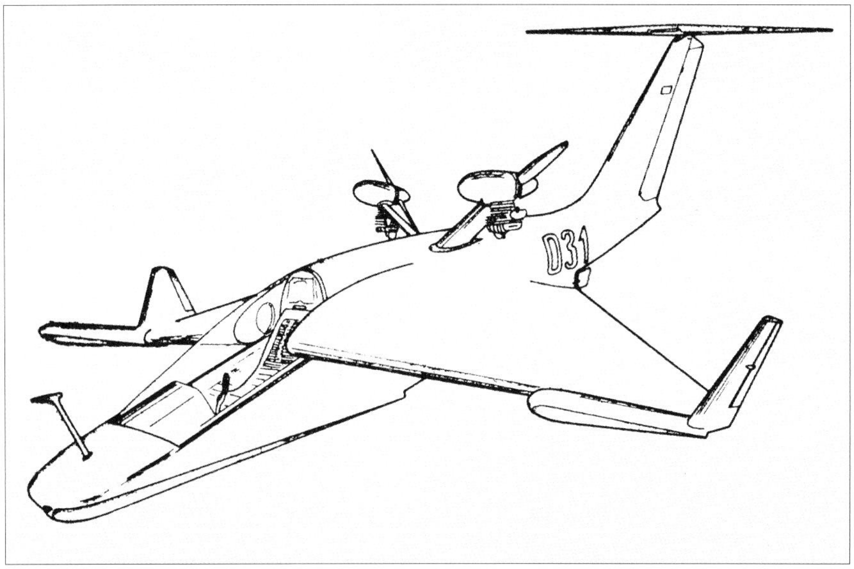

A drawing of the T-301 *ekranolyot*.

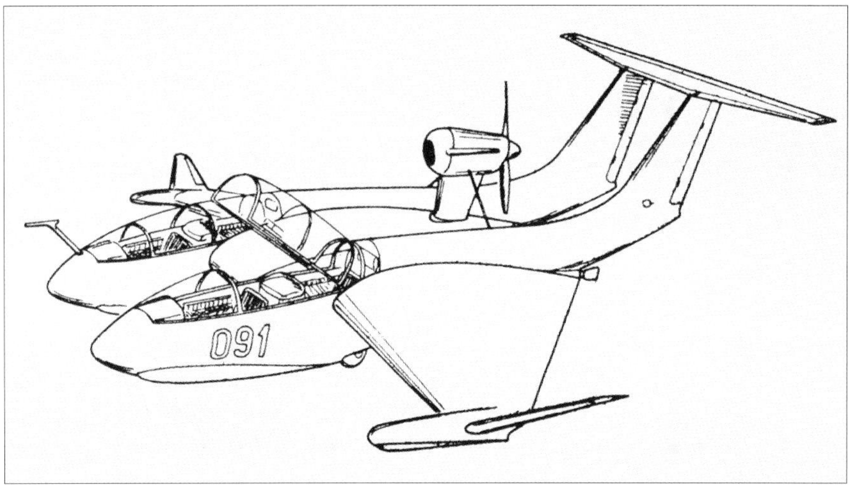

Another Groonin project developed at the TsLST – the twin-hull LP-901 *ekranolyot*.

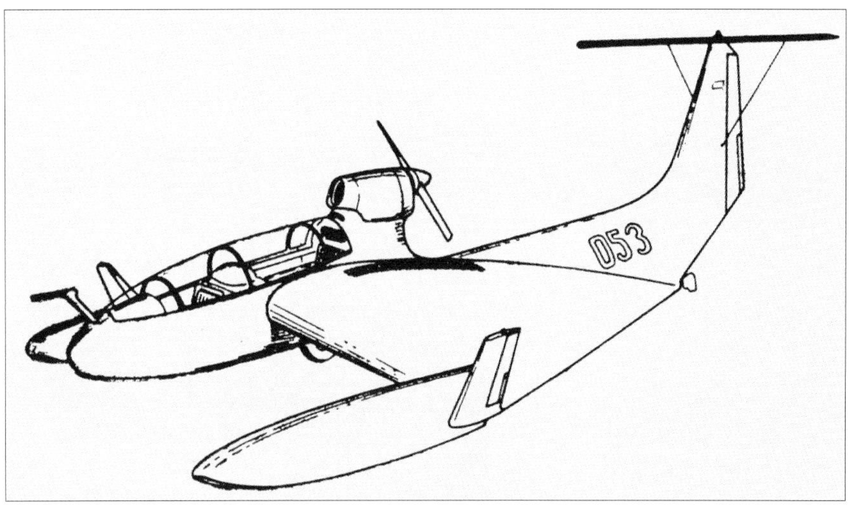

One more project from the same team – the more conventional T-503.

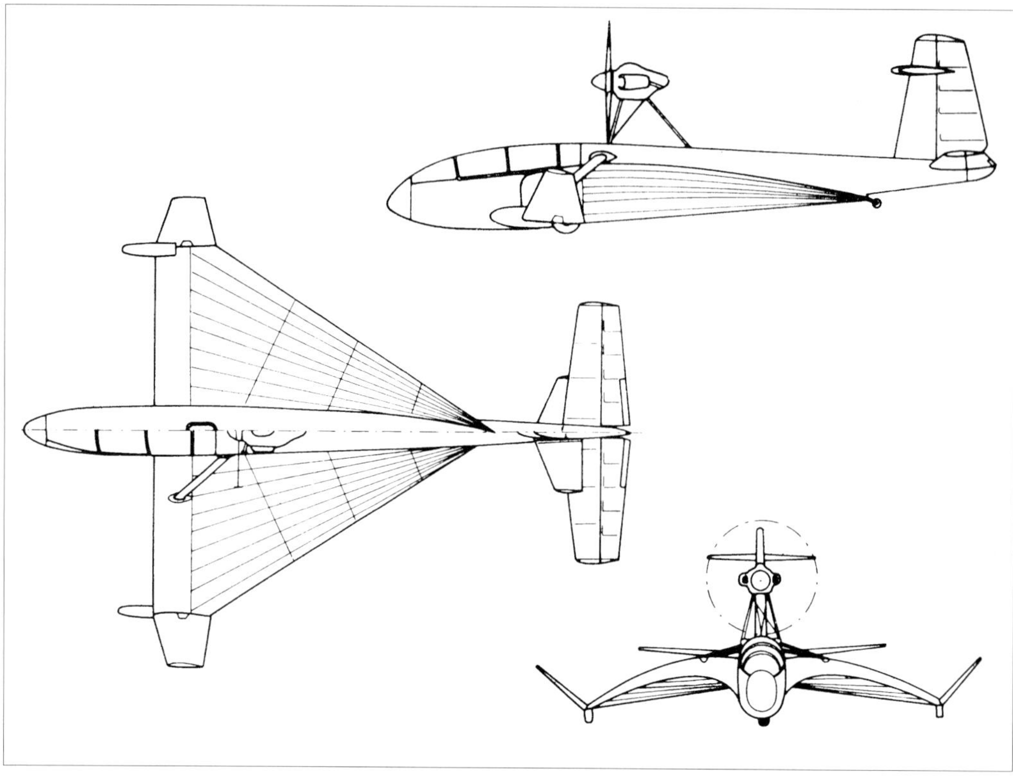

A four-view of the ES-2 flexible-wing *ekranolyot*. Note the extra stabiliser on the fin.

place in the spring of 1974; four months later the ES-2 was completed and tested.

Tests conducted in Liubertsy near Moscow revealed satisfactory stability and controllability. The aerodynamic characteristics obtained could also be regarded as sufficiently high. In some drawings this machine is shown with an additional small stabiliser mounted near the top of the fin.

ES-2M

In 1975 a further development of the vehicle described above resulted in the ES-2M with rigid Lippisch-type wings which was built in the SKB of MVTU (Moscow Higher Technical College named after Nikolay E. Baumann, now known as MGTU – Moscow State Technical University) jointly with the TsLST. The main design and construction work was performed by V. A. Akinin, Yu. V. Makarov, A. B. Sobolev and Yu. S. Gorbenko. The ES-2M based on the L-13 sailplane had an all-metal construction. The fuselage and the tail unit were strengthened by installing two additional frames designed to carry the engine mount and attachment points for two wing spars. The central unit of the control system was completely reworked and considerably simplified. Like the original version,

The ES-2M WIG vehicle with rigid wings on show at the NTTM-76 exhibition; its L-13 Blanik origins are patently obvious.

the ES-2M was powered by a 32-hp M-63 engine driving a two-blade wooden tractor propeller of 1.6 m (5 ft 3 in) diameter.

For operations from water, the *ekranolyot* was provided with a detachable boat hull which was attached to the fuselage in four points. In that case the undercarriage monowheel was enclosed in a vertical niche placed along the axis of the boat. When extended, the wheel enabled the vehicle to go out onto a gently sloping bank, taxi and perform a take-off from land while being fitted with the flotation gear. Thanks to the thin airfoil section of insignificant curvature, the clean wings and slender fuselage this *ekranolyot* had better aerodynamic characteristics, improved stability and easier handling compared to the original ES-2.

After testing conducted in the summer of 1976 the ES-2M was shown at the Exhibition of Scientific & Technical Achievements of Young Enthusiasts (NTTM-76 – *Na**ooch**no-tekh**nich**eskoye* ***tvor****ch-estvo molo**dyo**zhi*) in Moscow where it won a gold medal.

An-2E (first use of designation)

This WIG vehicle project based on the An-2V floatplane version of the well-known Antonov An-2 *Colt* utility biplane was prepared in the TsLST in 1973 by a group of young specialists led by Yevgeniy P. Groonin. The new machine inherited from the An-2 the fuselage and the Shvetsov ASh-62IR radial engine with an AV-2 four-blade variable-pitch propeller. These components were mated to new low-set wings of the reversed delta type having marked anhedral and fitted with large wingtip floats; the latter carried small dihedral outer wing panels with ailerons. The vehicle was also given a new T-tail of large span. Since the new wings obstructed the normal portside cargo door, a dorsal loading hatch was provided where the upper wing centre section used to be. Two vanes were installed on the sides of the engine cowling to direct part of the prop wash under the wings, assisting take-off.

The An-2E (*ekranoplan*) was to be provided with a retractable wheel undercarriage which would enable it to operate from land, as well as from the surface of lakes, rivers and littoral areas.

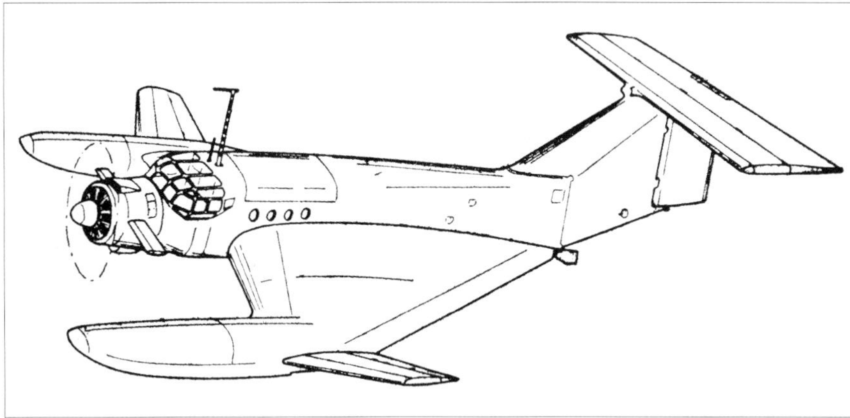

A drawing of the first WIG vehicle to be designated An-2E. Note the dorsal loading hatch and the deflector vanes on the nose.

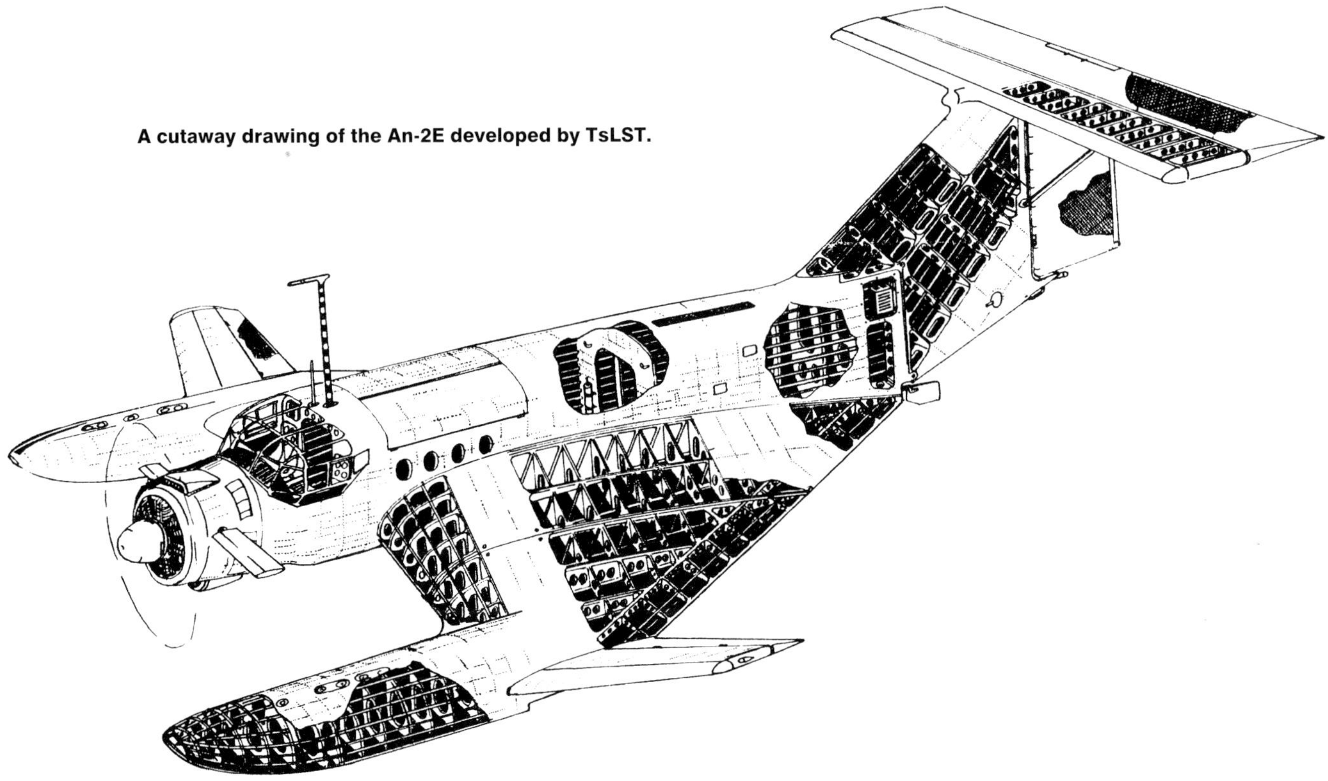

A cutaway drawing of the An-2E developed by TsLST.

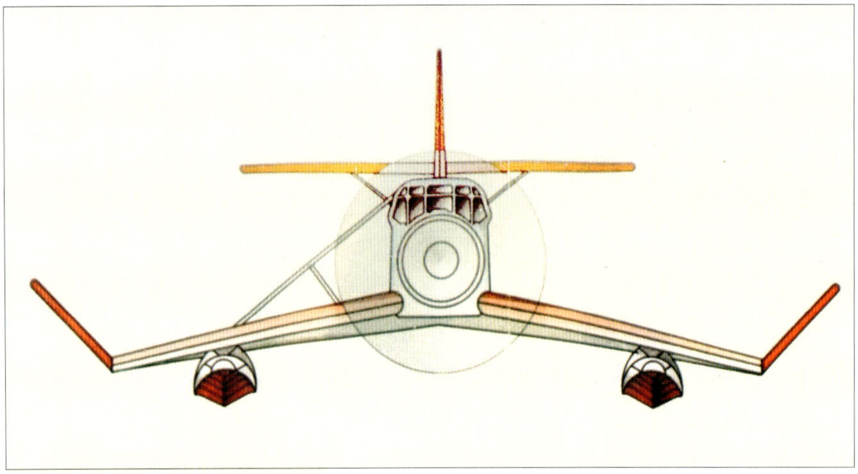

Front view of the An-2E developed by the Moscow Aviation Institute.

One more ekranoplan derivative of the An-2V proposed by the Groonin team.

An artist's impression of the Groonin E-0974 Parawing *ekranoplan*. The large elevator trim tab is noteworthy.

An artist's impression of the TsLST R-1001 Manta. Note the front and rear loading doors.

An-2V converted into a WIG vehicle with flexible wings

Another project of an *ekranoplan* based on the An-2V was proposed by a group of young designers in the TsLST. As distinct from the An-2E described above, this project retained practically the whole of the floatplane's airframe – except the wing box, which was replaced by a flexible fabric lifting surface of reversed-delta planform. The rigid leading edges were formed by special outrigger structures attached to both sides of the fuselage and also carrying small surfaces with ailerons, like those used in vehicles of the Lippisch layout.

E-0974 Parawing

This WIG vehicle was designed at the initiative of Yevgeniy P. Groonin. The machine featured an unusual configuration with wings of reversed-delta planform, shaped like a semi-circle when viewed from the front. The wing planform, coupled with the wingtip floats and the aileron-carrying surfaces attached to them, is reminiscent of the Lippisch machines. Originality lies both in the semi-circular front-view shape of the leading edges and in the fact that each of the wings is attached to the fuselage only at the front, while the aft parts serve as booms carrying the twin fins topped by horizontal tail. The vehicle is powered by a 42-hp Czechoslovak Java M-150 motorcycle engine with a pusher propeller of 1.1 m (3 ft $7\frac{5}{16}$ in) diameter.

R-1001 Manta

In 1974 a group of young specialists in the TsLST developed a two-seat *ekranoplan* intended for liaison with the Soviet fishing fleet. The project was designated R-1001 Manta. The machine's configuration was reminiscent of some Lippisch designs. That was seen, among other things, in the asymmetrical location of the cockpit pod which was placed on the port side of the airfoil-shaped body housing a cargo compartment. The outer wing panels followed the Lippisch layout, the tail unit had twin fins linked by an arrow-shaped horizontal tail. The 210-hp Walter Minor VI engine with a tractor propeller was mounted above the body. The vehicle had an AUW of 1,460 kg (3,220 lb). The Manta did not progress further than the drawing board.

E-120

Built in 1971, that was one of the experimental WIG vehicles designed in the TsLST. This single-seat machine was noteworthy for its wing of circular planform. Such a wing possesses some unique qualities, including the ability to preserve the lift without stalling at very high angles of attack right up to 45°. Such a wing is also capable of using efficiently the ground effect for lift increase and may prove promising for WIG vehicles, provided the controllability issues are solved successfully.

EMA-4

The EMA-4 vehicle, developed and built at TsLST, underwent tests in 1972. It was classed by its

The circular E-120 WIG vehicle, marked '02'. Confusingly, some sources refer to it as the ES-1, though the inscription 'Э-120' can be seen on the starboard wing. The legend on the tail reads *Ispytaniya* (Tests).

Another example of the E-120 marked '03' with the tail unit and powerplant yet to be fitted. Note the lateral strakes. Test pilot Baluyev is shown in the cockpit in the right-hand photo.

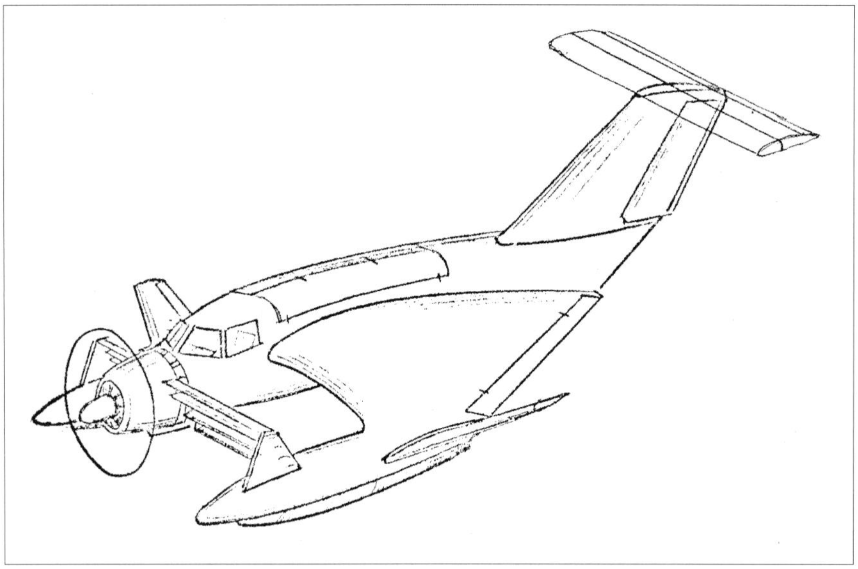

designers as an 'amphibian with aerodynamic off-loading'. The vehicle was a tiny boat of boxy contours whose hull was flanked by aerodynamic lift surfaces forming a disc-shaped wing. A piston engine installed behind an enclosed cockpit drove a ducted two-blade pusher propeller. An all-movable fin located behind the propeller presumably could serve as a rudder. The vehicle apparently could be operated on water in the hydroplaning mode, making use of the WIG effect, and on snow.

E-400

According to an article in the Polish magazine *Skrzydlata Polska*, an experimental WIG vehicle with that designation was designed in the TsLST in 1972. No further details are available.

ESKA EA-6A

This is an improved four-seat version of the ESKA-1. In its contours it is nearly identical to its forerunner, featuring a wider cabin with a curved panoramic windshield and a slightly raised aft fuselage. A scaled-strength model of the EA-6A to 1/4th scale was tested in September 1973. It had a span of 1.75 m (5 ft $8\frac{57}{64}$ in) and was powered by a 1.8-hp

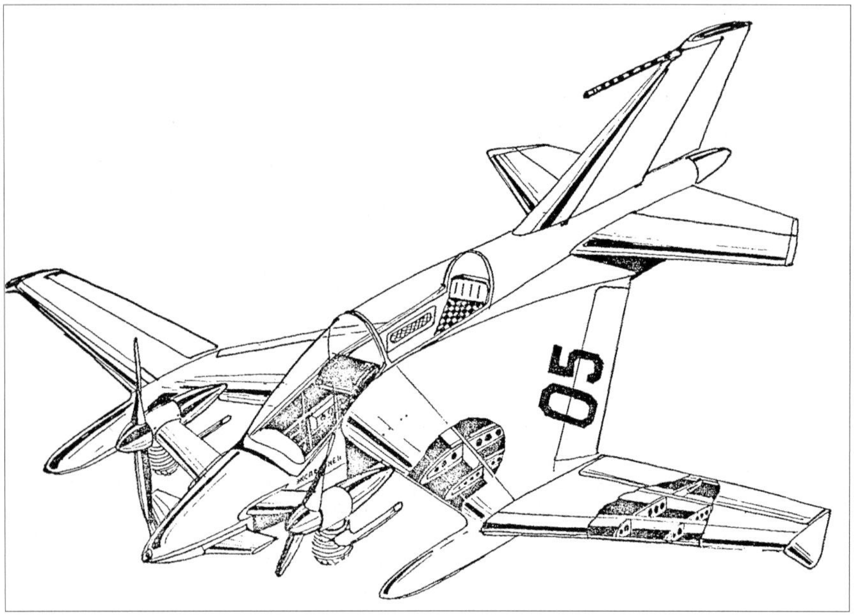

One of Groonin's WIG vehicle projects resembling a scaled-down version of the An-2E.

A diminutive WIG vehicle developed by Groonin with two motorcycle engines flanking the nose.

Below left: An artist's impression of the Groonin E-0874 with its unusual propeller placement.

Groonin's projects included even an ekranoplan in the form of a human-powered aircraft (HPA).

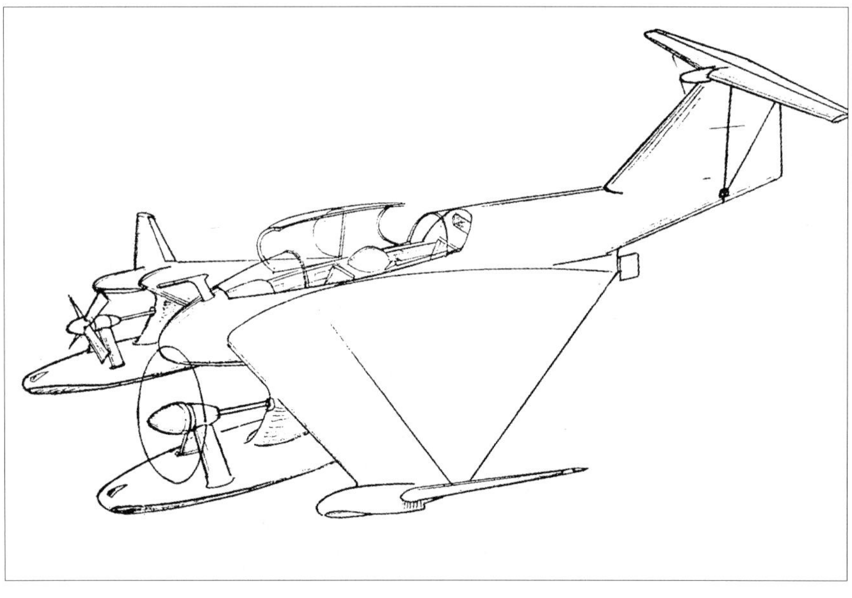

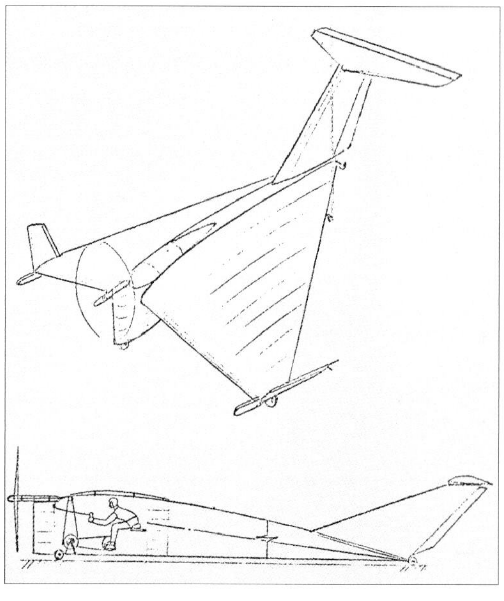

two-cylinder engine driving a propeller of 300 mm (11.8 in) diameter.

TsLST projects for converting aircraft into WIG vehicles

In 1974, at the initiative of Yu. V. Makarov, employees of TsLST in co-operation with specialists from RIIGA (Riga Civil Aviation Engineers Institute) started design work aimed at converting series-built aircraft types into WIG vehicles. They enlisted support from the Section of Ground Use of Aircraft Hardware at the Riga branch of GosNII GA (State Research Institute of Civil Aviation) which dealt, among other things, with converting time-expired aircraft into other types of transport – such as ACVs, aero-sleighs etc.

The TsLST studied the possibility of converting some aircraft types about to be phased out from Aeroflot service (An-2, Lisunov Li-2) and the Be-12 *Mail* ASW amphibian into WIG vehicles. It was presumed that the Be-12 powered by less powerful and, consequently, less fuel-consuming piston engines (as compared to the turboprop-powered baseline aircraft) could find widespread use in the national economy. A project designated Be-12E is described elsewhere in this chapter. Studies involving the An-2, Yak-12 and Yak-40 were conducted by RIIGA (RKIIGA, see below).

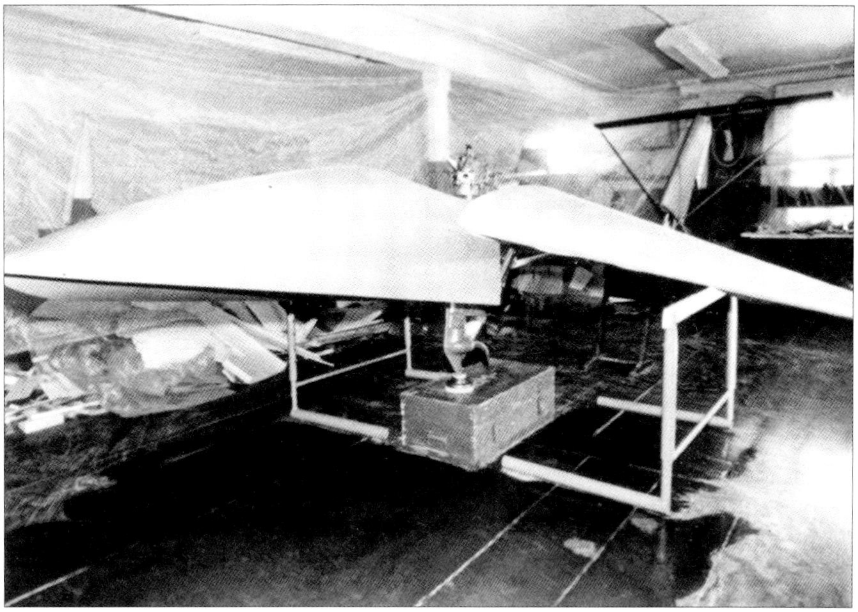

A speedboat (hydroplane) with aerodynamic offloading developed by Groonin.

In addition, projects of WIG conversions based on the Il'yushin IL-14 *Crate* airliner and the An-12 *Cub* transport were developed at TsLST on the level of student graduation projects.

Groonin's projects from 1974-75

During his work in the TsLST Yevgeniy Groonin tprepare a big number of interesting projects of WIG

Three-view/structural drawings of Groonin's hydroplanes with aerodynamic offloading – the K-550 (left) and MS-298.

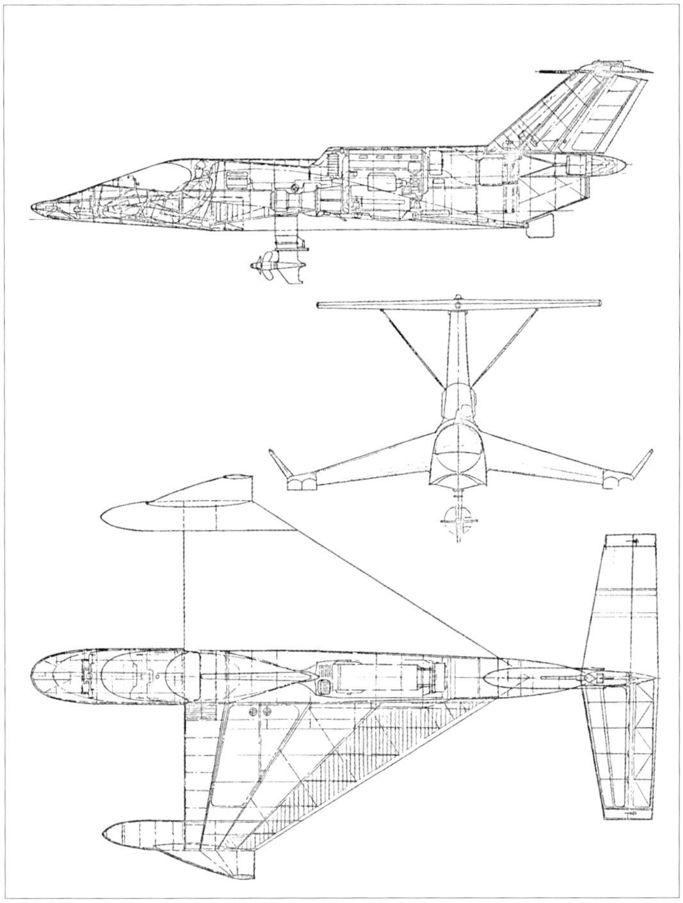

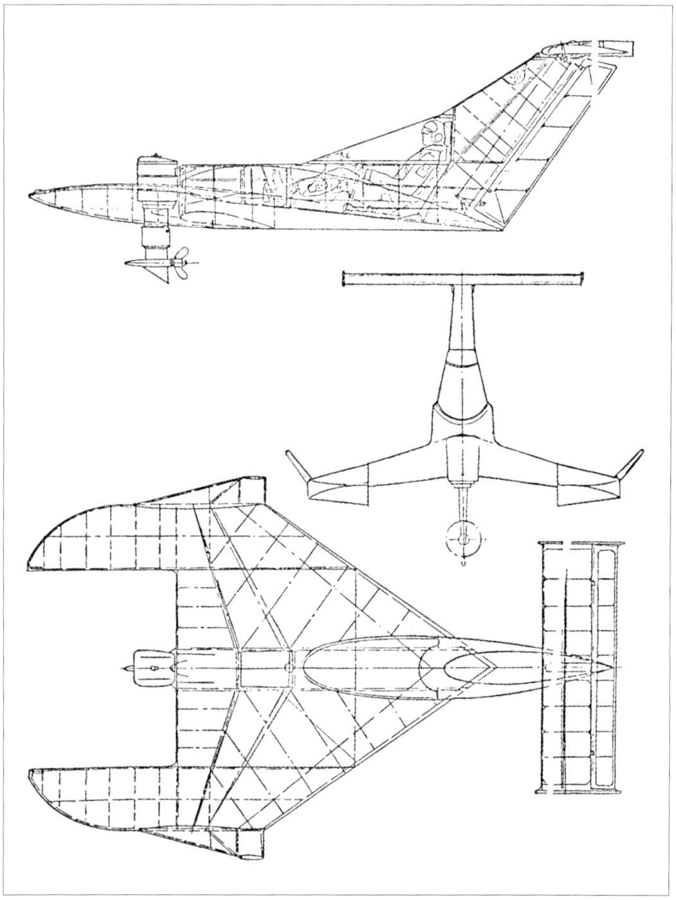

vehicles, most of which were based on his favorite reversed delta wing configuration The E-0874 project from 1974 was a two-seater with two underwing floats mounted on pylons. Propulsion was ensured by two small propellers installed on inverted-V pylons at the front ends of the floats; they were driven through extension shafts by engines housed in the wings.

Another project from 1975 incorporated movable vanes intended to direct the air stream from the nose-mounted propeller into the space under the dome-shaped reversed delta wing. This was the power-augmented take-off in combination with the Lippisch layout. A further variation on this subject was provided by a project of a two-seat light craft in which two single-cylinder piston engines were mounted on horizontal pylons on both sides of the fuselage nose. The propeller wash was partly directed into the space under the wing centre section to create a static air cushion.

A more radical idea was to use a turbojet engine whose efflux could be directed through internal ducting to nozzles mounted on a foreplane; the hot gases would thus be ejected under the wings to create a static air cushion, in addition to providing horizontal thrust for cruise. However, the most radical project was that of a single-seat human-powered (!) ekranoplan using the Lippisch layout.

Groonin's projects of speedboats using ground effect

During his work in the TsLST Yevgeniy Groonin devoted some attention to designing speedboats with WIG properties which were based on the use of his favourite Lippisch layout. Characteristic for all of them was the use of water propeller as a means of propulsion, with the craft just slightly rising above the water surface in ground-effect flight. At least one vehicle of this kind was actually built. A picture

The ELA-01 WIG vehicle on snow-covered ground during tests. An M-332 engine with a two-bladed propeller is fitted here.

The ELA-01 skims along the water with the flaps deployed. Note that the cockpit canopy has been removed.

The ELA-01 afloat, clearly showing the 'aerodynamic chamber' formed by the floats and the wing centre section.

The ELA-01 on its beaching dolly. The craft is in later guise with an M-337 engine and a three-bladed propeller.

shows it to be a single-seat craft with reversed-delta wings, T-tail and an outboard motor protruding from the underside of the hull in its centre section.

There was also a project of a light single-seat WIG speedboat, the MS-298, with an outboard engine mounted in the bows and the pilot's cockpit blended into the contours of the triangular vertical tail. This time the fuselage was lifted out of the water, the vehicle resting on two wingtip floats in a sort of catamaran configuration.

Yet another project of a single-seat racer, the K-550, distinguished itself with the use of an inline (or perhaps V-type?) engine of high output located inside the centre section of the hull and transmitting its torque to the water propeller through an extension shaft and two pairs of bevel gears.

Moscow Aviation Institute (MAI)

(currently Moscow Aerospace University)

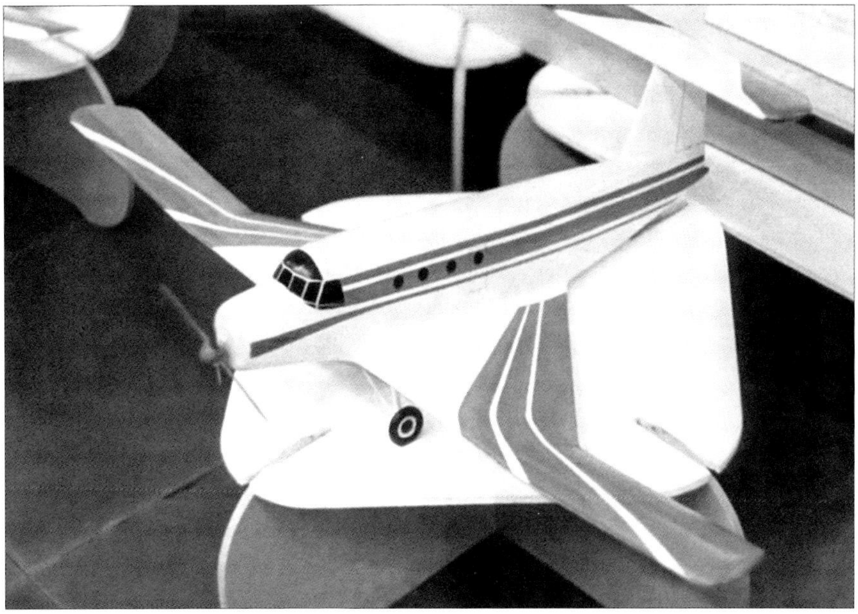

A model of the MAI Grach-2 agricultural WIG craft displayed at the NTTM-82 exhibition, clearly showing the craft's An-2 origins. Note the compound wings and T-tail.

ELA-01

In 1976-1978 the student design bureau (SKB) of this institute jointly with the SKB of the Riga Institute of Civil Aviation Engineers (RIIGA, later RKIIGA, still later Riga Aviation University), guided and assisted by professors and engineers of these institutes, designed and built an experimental vehicle designated ELA-01; the ELA presumably stood for *eksperimen**tahl'**nyy le**tah**tel'nyy appa**raht*** – experimental aerial vehicle. The vehicle was designed under the direction of A. A. Badiagin (MAI) and V. Z. Shestakov (RKIIGA), with F. A. Mukhamedov (a senior research worker at MAI) as project designer. The machine was built at the experimental sports aviation factory in Prienai (the then Lithuanian Soviet Republic).

The ELA-01 can be classed as a Class C WIG vehicle (*ekranolyot*), although it was sometimes described as a 'light rescue hydroplane'. The very word *ekranoplan* was taboo for reasons of secrecy at that time; moreover, the ELA-01 featured wings of composite layout which in itself was considered secret. The vehicle had a wing centre section resting directly upon two floats. These floats, together with the underside of the wing centre section, formed an air chamber so characteristic of WIG vehicles. Attached to the leading edge of the wing centre section was a cockpit nacelle; behind it, a 140-hp Walter Minor (M-332) six-cylinder air-cooled inverted in-line engine was mounted on a truss-type pylon. It drove a two-blade tractor propeller with ground-adjustable pitch.

The ELA-01 is sometimes described as a vehicle with a *micro-vertical take-off*. It was an ekranolyot which could lift itself vertically to an altitude of a dozen centimetres above the supporting surface with the help of a static air cushion, and then make a transition to horizontal flight in a ground effect mode above water or an even land surface.

To perform the micro-vertical take-off, the ELA-01 made use of an auxiliary six-cylinder engine driving a fan; the air flow from the fan was directed into the space beneath the wing via a curved duct. The space for the static air cushion was fenced off by the two floats and by flaps on the leading and trailing edges of the wing centre section. Therefore during the take-off and landing the ELA-01 became an ACV, turning into a WIG vehicle in cruise flight.

The Grach-3 displayed in model form at the same event used a compound-wing/tailless layout with large flaperons.

The floats had a V cross-section on the outer side, the inner side of each float being flat. There were transverse steps on the bottom of the floats.

The vehicle successfully made its first flight on 4th November 1978, piloted by factory test pilot R. Pivnickas. The testing was conducted on the Neman River in the vicinity of Kaunas. The vehicle's AUW was about 1,000 kg (2,200 lb). To allow for an

The MAI-designed An-2E *ekranoplan* at the MAKS-2005 airshow in Zhukovskiy. Note the strake connecting the wing trailing edge to the fuselage.

The logo of the Moscow Aviation Institute (MAI).

expected increase of the AUW in the course of testing it was decided to replace the M-332 with the more powerful 210-hp M-337 engine driving a three-blade variable-pitch propeller. The re-engining, effected by 1st December 1978, permitted the AUW to be increased to 1,250 kg (2,760 lb).

In 1979-1983 the ELA-01 was fitted with an automatic control system and with a flight recorder intended to accumulate information about the vehicle's behaviour in different flight modes. This permitted the vehicle to be an effective tool in researching the questions of controllability and stability of WIG vehicles. In addition to that, a considerable amount of work was done between 1981 and 1985 to develop and perfect the retractable flaps fencing off the static air cushion and the variable geometry floats. The work conducted on the ELA-01 was completed in the winter of 1984-85. In the summer of 1985 it was transported from Lithuania to MAI. Comprehensive information on the results of the work was submitted to the customers of this project.

Grach-2 and Grach-3

In 1980 the students of MAI under the direction of A. A. Badiagin were working on the design of several agricultural aircraft making use of ground effect during crop dusting. Two layouts were considered: a 'flying wing' and a low-wing monoplane with a T-tail. The wings of the agricultural aircraft had a broad-chord centre section of low aspect ratio and wing outer panels of greater aspect ratio which, in addition to improving the lift/drag ratio, increased the width of the strip covered by chemicals (the wings had a span of 22 m/72 ft 2⁹⁄₆₄ in). The projects dubbed Grach-2 and Grach-3 (Rook) were based on the An-2R agricultural aircraft and made use of its fuselage, undercarriage, engine and agricultural equipment. The Grach-2 and Grach-3 carried a load of chemicals 200 kg (440 lb) greater than the An-2R; they promised a lower cost of agricultural work per hectare and a better payload-to-weight ratio at a lower all-up weight (5,300 kg/11,680 lb). Models of the Grach-2 and Grach-3 aircraft were demonstrated at the NTTM-82 exhibition of technical achievements of young specialists in Moscow in 1982 and were awarded medals and diplomas.

A WIG vehicle of a twin-fuselage flying wing layout

This project was proposed by MAI students; in 1968 it was demonstrated in model form at the All-Union Exhibition of Economic Achievements (VDNKh – ***Vy**stavka dostizheniy narodnovo khozyaistva*) fairground in Moscow. In this machine two fuselages flanked a thick wing of very low aspect ratio. The wing housed a rotor (fan) designed to provide the vehicle with vertical take-off capability. In cruise flight the rotor was disengaged and faired over by movable vanes forming a smooth wing surface. In the forward movement the wing created lift augmented by ground effect. The model was intended for research of aerodynamics and structural layouts of aircraft.

A WIG vehicle based on the fuselage of the Mi-8 helicopter (project)

This project of a 40-seat *ekranoplan* utilising the fuselage of the Mil' Mi-8 *Hip* medium-lift helicopter was developed at MAI. No details are available, apart from a brief mention in a report at a web site.

An-2E (second use of designation; MAI-designed, MARZ-built)

During the recent years a project of converting the An-2 biplane into a WIG vehicle was put into effect by MAI students. In 2003 the design work on this machine dubbed An-2E was started by students working in OMKB Aerocar, one of the institute's two Student Design Bureaux (*Obyedi***nyon***noye molo***dyozh***noye kon***strook***torskoye byu***ro** – Joint Youth Design Bureau; the other one is OSKBES – Branch Student Design Bureau for Experimental Aircraft Construction). OMKB is headed by chief designer M. A. A Tetiushev, but some sources indicate that the design work was led in this case by Yuriy V. Makarov, an MAI graduate known for his work on light aircraft and WIG vehicles. The An-2E (one of several projects bearing this designation) was built at the ROSTO paramilitary sports organisation's Moscow Aircraft Repair Plant (MARZ – *Mos***kov***skiy* **a***viare***mont***nyy za***vod**) in July-August 2003 by converting a Polish-built An-2R, c/n 1G 192-10. The resulting *ekranoplan* was conceived as a multipurpose vehicle capable of transporting 20 persons. In late August, prior to the commencement of testing, the An-2E with the unusual registration ЭA-00078 (that is, EA-00078 in Cyrillic characters) on the fuselage was exhibited at the MAKS-2003 air show in Zhukovskiy.

The standard wing box of the An-2 was replaced by single wide-chord, low-set wings having the same area and measuring 15.6 m (51 ft 2¼ in) in span. The wings had a straight leading edge and an ogival trailing edge. They were provided with winglets installed at an angle of 45°. The wings had a marked anhedral. In effect, this was a modification of the well-known Lippisch layout.

The An-2E, as shown in Zhukovskiy, retained the standard wheel undercarriage of the An-2, but provision was made for replacing it with floats – either on struts, as on the An-2V floatplane, or by attaching the floats directly to the wing undersurface at mid-span, with a distance of 8 m (26 ft 3 in) between the floats. In this case the dome-shaped wing and the floats created a chamber into which a part of the propeller wash was injected, creating a static air cushion. The floats were to be fitted with retractable wheels, thus turning the An-2E into an amphibian.

The example shown in Zhukovskiy retained the ASh-62IR radial, but that was regarded as a temporary configuration. After the testing the vehicle was to be fitted with a 580-hp YaMZ automotive diesel (apparently a Vee-12 YaMZ-850.10 or YaMZ-8502) or with similarly rated diesel engines of foreign manufacture (MAN, Mercedes). The following design performance was cited for the An-2E: empty weight 2,900 kg (6,395 lb); AUW 5,600 kg (12,350 lb); cruising speed 200 km/h (123 mph); minimum speed 50 km/h (31 mph); range 2,000 km (1,230 miles); seaworthiness – sea state 4; fuel consumption (diesel fuel) – 48 lit./hour (10.56 Imp gal/hour), or 24 lit./hour (5.28 Imp gal/hour).

After the MAKS-2003 airshow the An-2E was to start the test programme, but there is no evidence

An-2 RA-2366K following modification as a WIG 'triplane'.

of it ever being flown. The subsequent story of the vehicle is veiled in mystery. Despite the claim that orders had come for similar conversions from eight customers in Russia and abroad, the example shown in Zhukovskiy does not appear to have been flown at all, to say nothing about putting it into production. In 2009 the An-2E was photographed sitting at the MARZ airfield (Chornoye) in a dismantled condition without wings. A sad story, indeed.

An-2E triplane WIG vehicle

A very interesting conversion of an An-2 into a WIG craft was effected some time before the An-2E described above. Information concerning the year and place of construction is missing, as well as the identity of the person and/or organisation behind the project. It may well have been Yuriy Makarov and MAI, as in the previous case. This time a very unorthodox solution was chosen. The An-2 (registered RA-2366K), retaining its normal wing box, was fitted with a third pair of wings which was installed above the existing lower wings with a small gap between them The root chord of the new wings was about three times bigger than the chord of the lower wings. On the photo the third wings appear to have straight leading edges and, possibly, ogival trailing edges. The normal powerplant and undercarriage of the An-2 were retained. There is no information about the testing.

An-2 converted into an ekranoplan at Ul'yanovsk (MAI design?)

Yet another conversion of an An-2 into a WIG vehicle (possibly also masterminded by MAI and Yu. V Makarov) was effected at the Aviastar aircraft plant in Ulyanovsk in 2002. There is no information about its aerodynamic layout and other design features, apart from the fact that it was fitted both with wheeled undercarriage and floats. It was reported that the vehicle was tested in the ground effect mode and in all flight modes at altitudes up to 2,000 m (6,560 ft), displaying excellent stability and controllability.

Be-12E and Be-12ED (projects)

This design was offered in 1979 at MAI by Yu. V. Makarov, a well-known designer of ultra-light aircraft and a participant of the development of several WIG vehicles in the TsLST. The Be-12E (*ekranoplan*) was a WIG vehicle based on the conversion of the Beriyev Be-12 Chaika ASW amphibian; it was to be fitted with two 1,000-hp ASh-62IR radials instead of the normal 4,250-ehp Ivchenko AI-20M turboprops. The gull wings of the amphibian gave place to reversed-delta wings of low aspect ratio. The tail unit of the Be-12 and its control system were retained. The transformation of the Be-12 into a WIG vehicle reduced its empty weight to 14,000 kg (30,860 lb) and the all-up weight to 23,500 kg (51,810 lb). Therefore the 2,000 hp delivered by the ASh-62IR piston engines were quite sufficient for overcoming the 'drag hump' during acceleration at take-off and for ensuring a rate of climb of 0.5-0.7 m/sec (98-137 ft/min) required for making the vehicle capable of manoeuvres over the supporting surface at altitudes up to 50-100 m (164-330 ft). The designer regarded the project as possessing good fuel efficiency, but difficulties with providing gasoline for piston engines led him to the idea of making use of diesel engines in WIG vehicles.

In 2010 this project, with a new designation Be-12ED and somewhat revised specifications, cropped up at a web site of a Russian company bearing the name ZAO 'SI' (that is, 'SI' JSC). The company declares its intention to promote various innovative technical projects, including *ekranoplans*, but apparently has nothing to do with aviation. In the Be-12ED version the ASh-62IR engines can, as an option, be replaced with two 1,000-hp 12ChN15/16 tank diesel engines (this may account for the D suffix). In the present version the vehicle is to have an empty weight of 19,000 kg (41,890 lb), a useful load of 16,000 kg (35,280 lb), an AUW of 36,500 kg (80,480 lb), a maximum speed, of 350 km/h (218 mph), a landing speed of 60 km/h (37 mph) and a range of 6,000 km (3,730 miles). The Be-12ED is intended to carry 60-80 passengers and to be operated at sea states of up to 5.

A 40-seat WIG vehicle based on the Mi-8 airframe (project)

According to a press report, the MAI student design bureau developed a project of a WIG vehicle making use of the fuselage of the Mi-8 helicopter. No details are available, apart from the mention of its 40-seat capacity, which is more than one could expect from the Mi-8's passenger cabin.

Conversion of the Renault Twingo car into a WIG vehicle (project)

In 1994 the students of MAI developed a project of converting a small French car – the first-generation Renault Twingo – into various transport vehicles,

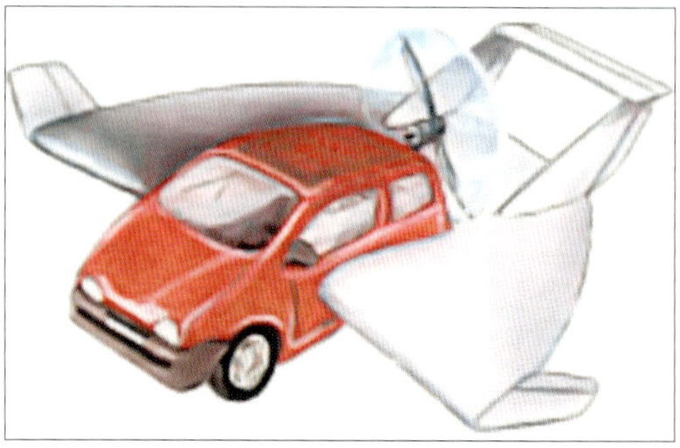

An artist's impression of a first-generation Renault Twingo car turned into a WIG 'aerocar'.

Stills from a cine film showing the T-501 *ekranolyot* with the original powerplant (two Neptoon-23 engines) being towed by an ACV.

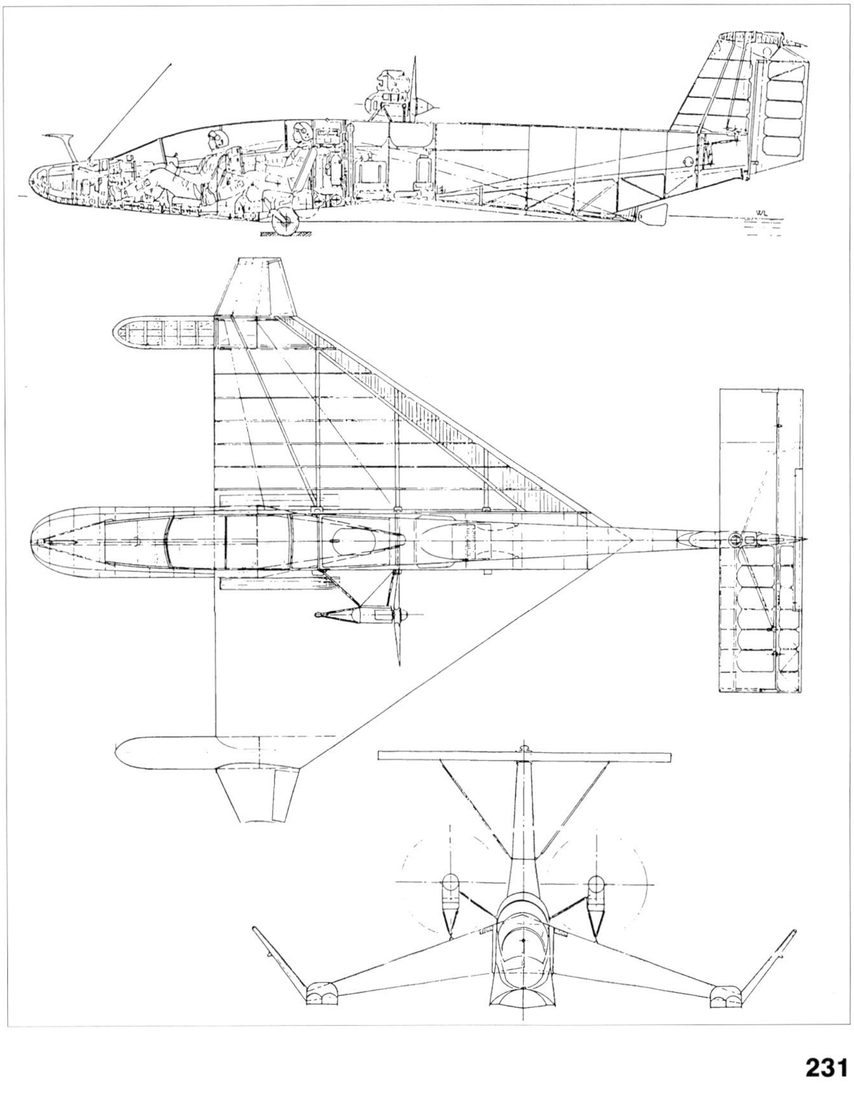

A three-view/structural drawing of the T-501. The engine supports do not match the actual craft.

including a 'flying car' and a hydroplaning boat. Among the conversions proposed was also a WIG vehicle. In this variant the car, driven by a 65-hp engine, was to be fitted with a wing measuring 6.7 m (22 ft), with an area of 20 m^2 (215 sq ft). With a maximum AUW of 1,100 kg (2,425 lb), the vehicle was expected to attain a maximum speed of 120 km/h (75 mph), the landing speed being 45 km/h (28 mph). The project was not put into practice.

MIIGA (Moscow Institute of Civil Aviation Engineers)

(currently Moscow State Technical University for Civil Aviation – MGTU GA)

T-501

This institute provided the framework for the activities of a group of young enthusiasts who created the T-501 WIG vehicle. This two-seat machine was classed as an *ekranolyot* and was intended for flight both in ground effect and at high altitude. It was designed and built in 1976-1983 by a group of young aircraft designers led by Yevgeniy Groonin who started their work at a Youth Technical Club in Kaliningrad (now Korolyov) near Moscow. The airframe was produced by adapting the Czechoslovak L-13 Blanik sailplane. Its fuselage was modified to feature the hydrodynamic contours of a speedboat with a planing step on the bottom. The wings of wooden construction featured a reversed-delta planform (Lippisch layout) and anhedral on the leading edge. The craft had an unswept T-tail. Two modified Neptoon-23 (Neptune) outboard motors with a total output of 46 hp were mounted on a horizontal beam above the fuselage, driving pusher propellers. The T-501 had a wing span of 9 m (29 ft 6⅜ in) and an AUW of 650 kg (1,430 lb).

MIIGA students took an active part in the design work, and in 1980 the group fully transferred its activities to the MIIGA. Testing conducted in 1982 showed that the power of the two Neptoon-23 engines was insufficient. In consequence, this powerplant was replaced by a Lyul'ka TS-21 gas turbine APU engine, initially driving a two-blade wooden propeller. The TS-21 mounted on a cabane above the fuselage developed a static thrust of 240 kg. Some sources claim that this engine, too, proved insufficient and failed to enable the T-501 to reach its design objective – flight in ground effect mode. This was allegedly due to imperfect hydrodynamic

contours of the boat hull, but this is contested by Groonin who regards the vehicle's design as basically sound. According to other sources, the vehicle did make a single flight in ground effect mode, lifting itself above the water surface. The testing was discontinued after an incident caused by a peculiar feature of the TS-21 engine (which, as already men-

Two views of the T-501 afloat in later guise (with a single TS-21 engine).

Top right: The T-501 on its beaching dolly.

The logo of the Moscow State Technical University for Civil Aviation (MGTU GA).

One more view of the turboprop-powered T-501 during tests.

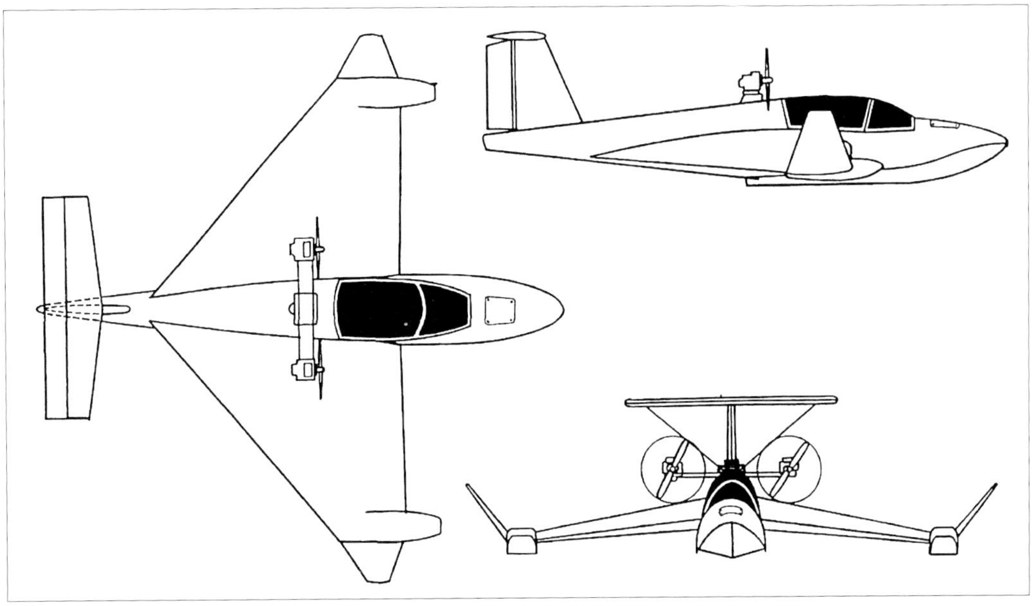

A three-view of the T-501 in original form.

tioned, was a jet fuel starter for an afterburning turbojet). In its original application it was programmed to shut down automatically when the loading on the shaft disappeared as the turbojet fired up. During the flight of the T-501, as the speed grew, the propeller became less loaded, and at a certain point the TS-21 cut automatically. This brought about a change of trim with a strong pitch-up. The *ekranolyot* 'jumped' to an altitude of 7-8 m (23-26 ft), reaching an angle of attack of 30°, and then pancaked and alighted on the surface, sustaining minor damage.

Under all circumstances, this work gave useful experience to those engaged in it. Yevgeniy Groonin graduated from MIIGA in 1983 with an engineer's diploma, his graduation thesis being the design of a WIG vehicle for use in the national economy

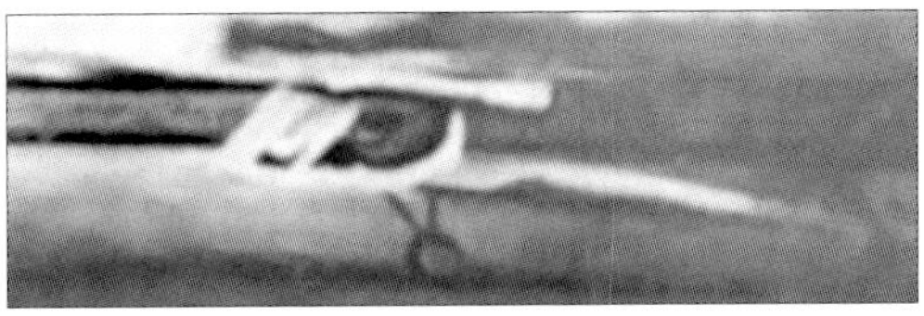

A poor but interesting shot of the EMA-1 research vehicle during tests.

Moscow Aviation Technical School named after Godovikov

EMA-1

In 1967 the students of this technical school designed and built an ultralight WIG vehicle designated EMA-1 and featuring a canard layout. The project was prepared by Yu. V. Makarov. The vehicle had a three-spar wing of circular planform. Placed ahead of the wing was a lifting stabiliser, also of circular planform, fitted with large-area elevons. The engine delivering a mere 4 hp was placed behind the pilot's cockpit. The EMA-1 featured a wooden construction with fabric skinning, an enclosed cockpit and a tailwheel undercarriage with a tail skid. The vehicle, described as ekranolyot, was tested at the Khodynka airfield in Moscow in 1968-69. It showed good stability and

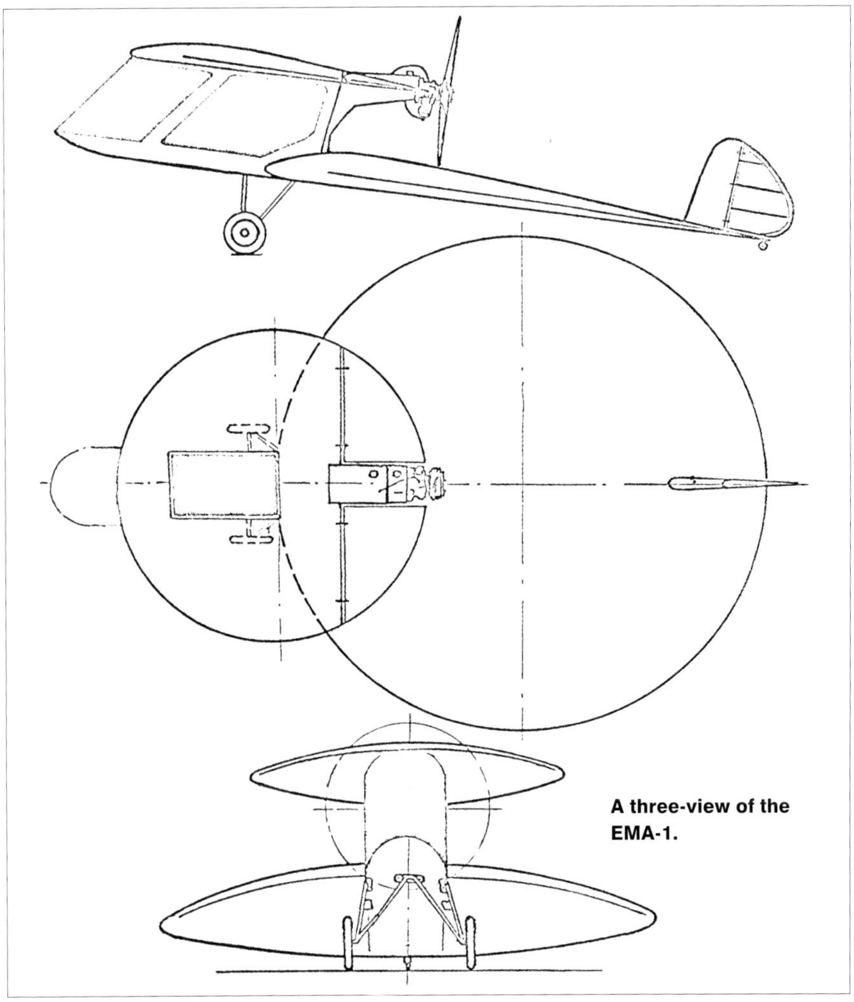

A three-view of the EMA-1.

controllability and accelerated to 50 km/h (31 mph) but failed to enter the ground effect flight mode due to being underpowered.

Passenger WIG vehicle designed by Skvortsov and Gorshunov

In 1995 two young designers, Konstantin Skvortsov and Yevgeniy Gorshunov, designed at the MATI (Moscow Aviation Technology Institute) a passenger WIG vehicle intended for use over land. The vehicle had two fuselages flanking a wing of large dimensions. It was to be equipped with a highly unorthodox powerplant in the shape of a huge flywheel placed in the wing. The flywheel actuated two propelling devices fitted with usual airscrews. It was to be spun up, using electric power from a ground power unit, and was expected to rotate for several hours, ensuring a flight speed of no less than 300 km/h (186 mph) at an altitude of 1.5 to 3 m (5-10 ft). The vehicle was to make a halt every 200-300 km (124-186 miles) in order to give a booster charge to the flywheel with the help of compressed air. The vehicle with its double-deck fuselages was expected to take on board as many passengers as a usual train. In 1996-97 the work on the project was still going on, but nothing was heard about it later.

Nikolayev Shipbuilding Institute (NKI)

(at present National Shipbuilding University named after Admiral Makarov)

Chaika and Albatross WIG vehicles

In 1971 senior year students of the Nikolayev Shipbuilding Institute in the Ukraine began their work on ekranoplans. Eventually a project of a WIG vehicle prepared by students Yu. V. Fed'ko and G. S. Durmashkin was endorsed as a project for their graduation thesis. Construction began of the prototype which was dubbed Chaika (Seagull). It was a single-seat ekranoplan featuring a typical Lippisch configuration with a reversed-delta wing and a T-tail. The fuselage was given the shape of a boat hull of a very small cross-section. The wings were of flexible type, reminiscent of a hang-glider. The fabric was attached to arches forming the leading edge. The arches, in their turn, were attached to a transverse member, a kind of a spar, which also carried upturned winglets at its ends. There was no cockpit, the pilot occupying an open seat atop the boat hull.

The Albatross WIG craft (speedboat with dynamic offloading) developed by the NKI.

The vehicle had a span of 4.2 m (13 ft 9⅜ in), a length of 6 m (19 ft 8_ in) and a wing area of 11 m² (118.4 sq ft); its design speed was 80 km/h (50 mph).

The boat hull for this vehicle was completed in 1975; further work was conducted in the institute's student design bureau by younger students who took over from the graduates. In 1976 the testing began; it was confined to runs on tow behind a motorboat. During one of these runs the Chaika vehicle suffered an accident.

The student design bureau designed and built one more vehicle, called Albatross, which was completed by the autumn of 1976. It was in fact a two-seat speedboat with aerodynamic off-loading afforded by the wings which flanked the boat hull. The wing area was 4.0 m² (43.0 sq ft), with the hull measuring 4.5 m (14 ft 9 in) in length. Propulsion was ensured by a Vikhr' (Whirlwind) outboard motor driving a water propeller. During the tests the vehicle attained a speed of 45 km/h (28 mph); the aerodynamic lift compensated for about 80% of the vehicle's weight

OIIMF (Odessa Institute of Marine Fleet Engineers)

In 1963-1966 a group of students of this institute (OIIMF – ***O**des**skiy **i**nsti**t**oot **i**nzhenerov **mor**skovo **flo**ta*) working under the direction of Yu. A. Boodnitskiy, designed and built the OIIMF-1 WIG vehicle and its subsequent versions – the OIIMF-2 and OIIMF-3. All of them featured a 'flying wing' layout with two wings spaced apart both longitudinally and in height. The wing chord was 1 m (3 ft 3⅜ in) on the front wings and 3 m (9 ft 10 in) on the aft wings. They were attached to end-plate floats (skegs). The single-seat open cockpit was placed on top of the main wings.

The first of the vehicles was powered by one 18-hp Izh-60K motorcycle engine, the second model had two such engines mounted on the leading edge of the main (aft) wings. Their propellers drove the air under the main wings, thus creating an air cushion retained with the help of flaps hinged at the wings' trailing edge. At a speed of 35-40 km/h (22-25 mph) the lift, including that produced by ram air pressure, reached 80% of the vehicle's weight. The power of the two engines proved insufficient for reaching the design speed of 100-120 km/h (62-75 mph), and the OIIMF-3 model received two K-750 engines of 26 hp each. The airframe was lightened and the front wings were fitted with flaps. Testing was planned for the summer of 1967, but failed to take place due to some technical problems.

KnAPI

(KnAPI – Komsomol'sk-on-Amur Polytechnic Institute (*Komso**mol'**skiy-na-**Amoo**re politekh**nich**eskiy* *instit**oot***; currently KnAGTU – Komsomol'sk-on-Amur State Technical University)

The KnAPI ELA-7 Albatross WIG vehicle on a lake near Komsomol'sk-on-Amur during tests. The tail unit design is well visible.

ELA-7 Albatross

In 1968-1971 the participants of the student design bureau of the Polytechnical Institute in Komsomolsk-on-Amur created an experimental flying vehicle dubbed ELA-7 Albatross. This was a 'seaplane with a lifting fuselage' – actually a WIG vehicle. It had a wing centre section of rectangular planform and substantial area, supplemented in its rear part by small outer wing panels fitted with ailerons. The wing centre section was flanked with two floats which had a keel surface at the centreline of their bottom. A 32-hp MT-8 flat-twin engine from a Dnepr motorcycle driving a tractor propeller was mounted on the leading edge of the wing centre section. The engine cowling blended into a fairing of the open cockpit. A flap attached to the trailing edge of the centre section, together with the floats, formed a cavity for an air cushion under the wing. The ELA-7 was provided with Vee tail surfaces attached to tail booms linked by a horizontal tail.

The propeller wash served in part for injecting the air under the wings. A small steerable vane mounted behind the propeller on the leading edge of the wing centre section deflected the airflow, increasing the portion of the airstream directed under the wings.

The ELA-7 was tested in the summer of 1971 at a lake near Komsomol'sk-on-Amur. Due to insufficient propeller thrust the vehicle developed a speed of a mere 36 km/h (22 mph). The testing was concentrated mainly on investigating the effect of off-loading the wing by means of injecting (blowing) the air under its surface. The off-loading amounted to 100 kg (220 lb) at the propeller's maximum static thrust. The designers of the vehicle came to the conclusion that the chosen layout was quite satisfactory as far as the aerodynamic off-loading was concerned.

ELA-8

This was a further development of the ELA-7 featuring changes in aerodynamic layout. These included installation of a single-fin empennage and refinement of the hydrodynamic shape of the floats. The horizontal empennage of the ELA-8 was installed in the front part of the floats and had no dihedral. The outer wing panels mounted on the aft sections of the floats had 5° dihedral. Thus, the seaplane featured a tandem-wing aerodynamic layout with a lifting fuselage. The forward set of wings was fitted with elevators, while the aft set of wings, as distinct from the ELA-7, had no control surfaces and was fitted with small endplates. To increase the air blowing effect the propeller axis was moved downward, closer to the leading edge of the wing centre section; the prop was driven via an extension shaft. The foreplane directing the airstream downward was shaped as a multi-slot deflector. The flap installed on the trailing edge of wing centre section received spring loading and was deflected automatically, as the pressure under the wing decreased.

The all-up weight of the vehicle powered by the same 32-hp MT-8 engine was brought down to 380 kg (840 lb).

The ELA-8 was tested at a lake near Komsomol'sk-on-Amur in the summer of 1974. Several runs were made, the speed reaching 50 km/h (31 mph). The blowing produced an aerodynamic off-loading of up to 280 kg (620 lb).

In 1975 the ELA-8 was modified and redesignated ELA-8M; it appears that the foreplane mentioned above was installed in the process of this modification.

The logo of the Komsomol'sk-on-Amur State Technical University (KnAGTU, ex KnAPI)

ELA-13

This WIG vehicle built in the SKB of the KnAPI in 1977-78 was, in effect, a research vehicle for investigating the influence of the proximity of the water surface on the take-off and landing performance of

The ELA-8, showing the repositioned engine driving the propeller via an extension shaft, the redesigned fuselage and tail surfaces.

The ELA-13 research vehicle. The apparent boxy shape is due to the sidewalls flanking a 'lifting body'.

seaplanes. It had a lifting fuselage, an open cockpit, a T-tail and was powered by a 32-hp MT-8 flat-twin engine from a Dnepr motorcycle driving a pusher propeller of 1.6 m (5 ft 3 in) in diameter. Two floats were attached to the sides of the fuselage. Attached to the centre part of the fuselage were two outer wing panels with ailerons. The ailerons doubled as flaps, their deflection being geared to the movement of the elevator. This ensured the functioning of a direct wing lift control system which performed well in the course of the ELA-13's flight tests. Endplates installed at the tips of the outer wing panels helped cut induced drag.

The vehicle's all-up weight was 250 kg (551 lb), markedly less than that of the ELA-7 and ELA-8.

Seen during towing basin tests, this model of a strike WIG craft developed by KnAPI bears a striking resemblance to Bartini's VVA-14.

During the tests, which commenced on the Amur River in July 1978, the vehicle suffered a crash after pitching-up on take-off. Repairs made in the winter of 1978 were accompanied by modifications, including an increase of the floats' displacement in their nose parts, shifting the centre of gravity forward and selecting a propeller with a static thrust increased to 100 kg (220 lb). The modified vehicle was designated ELA-13M. During the testing conducted on the Amur River in July 1979 the ekranolyot made 32 successful flights, displaying good stability and controllability in different flight modes both in and out of ground effect. The maximum flight speed was in excess of 90 km/h (56 mph). The flight altitude out of ground effect reached 10-12 m (33-40 ft). The vehicle won the first prize at the All-Union contest of scientific work performed by students, held in Leningrad in 1981.

Combat WIG vehicles (projects)

Approximately in the late 1960s or early 1970s the Student Design Bureau of KnAPI conducted work on projects of WIG vehicles intended for attack missions (presumably in response to tactical requirements submitted by the military). One of the project configurations was very similar in layout to Bartini's VVA-14. It featured a wide-chord, low-aspect-ratio wing centre section and narrow-chord, high-aspect-ratio outer wing panels. The wing centre section was flanked by slab-sided sponsons apparently fitted with inflatable pontoons on the underside. The crew cockpit was mounted on the leading edge of the wing centre section, blending into its contours. The tail unit was, in fact, a V-tail with the two surfaces set wide apart and mounted outboard of the aft end of the wing centre section. Experiments were conducted with models, but no actual prototypes were built.

Komsomol'sk-on-Amur State Technical University (KnAGTU, formerly KnAPI)

In 1996 design work was conducted there aimed at creating a double-purpose transport means. It was envisaged as combining the features of a hydrocycle and a light WIG vehicle, the one being easily transformed into the other. It was to be a WIG vehicle of Type A, requiring no aircraft-type certification.

RKIIGA (formerly RIIGA)

(Riga Red Banner Institute of Civil Aviation Engineers; now Riga Aviation University)

From 1975 the Student Design Bureau of this institute conducted research and development work on transport means intended for use in areas with difficult terrain and no roads. This work encompassed ACVs and vehicles based on dynamic air cushion, that is, vehicles using ground effect. This work was conducted under the direction of V. Z. Shestakov and R. V. Shchavinskiy.

Apart from the ELA-01 (a joint project with MAI, see above), the SKB of this educational institution developed a project of the ELA-3 *ekranolyot*. Its scale model was presented at the Exhibition of scientific and technical work of young specialists in Moscow in 1984 (NTTM-84); further details of the vehicle are not available.

It may be surmised that the following 'anonymous' description contained in the institute's official history referred to the ELA-3. The vehicle was a flying machine with an air cushion undercarriage. Its powerplant drove a propeller creating horizontal thrust in cruise flight, and a fan which was engaged on take-off for creating a static air cushion under the fuselage. The low pressure exerted by the undercarriage on the supporting surface enabled the vehicle to operate from flat stretches of land, as well as from ice, snow and water. In cruise flight it could make use of a dynamic air cushion, that is, ground effect.

Students of the RKIIGA prepared a number of graduation designs of WIG vehicles of various categories. These included some projects prepared at the initiative of the TsLST (as mentioned above) on the basis of the An-2, Yakovlev Yak-12 light cabin monoplane and Yak-40 *Codling* short-haul airliner. In all cases the reversed-delta wing layout was used.

Interestingly, a project based on the An-2 envisaged converting the machine into a WIG vehicle by fitting it with rigid monoplane low-aspect-ratio wings while retaining the floats of the An-2V hydroplane. The 1,000-hp ASh-62IR radial was to be replaced by a 420-hp YaMZ-7511 Vee-8 automotive turbo diesel engine.

The conversion of the Yak-40 was based on using Lippisch-type wings with pronounced anhedral and wingtip floats lifting the fuselage above the water. A similar layout was chosen for the Yak-12 conversion.

Irkutsk Polytechnical Institute (IPI)

EVP-1

In 1982-83 a group of students and engineers under the direction of S. V. Trunov working in the SKB of the aviation faculty of this institute developed a design of the EVP-1 WIG vehicle. The machine featured aircraft layout with a T-shaped tail unit and slab stabiliser. The wings of trapezoidal planform had anhedral on the leading edges. The trailing edge section of the wing behind the rearmost spar was made elastic. The 18-hp Izh-P3 cruise engine (from an Izh Planeta motorcycle) with a pusher propeller was installed on a pylon ahead of the fin. The EVP-1 was also fitted with a 2-hp Sh-52 lift engine which drove a fan producing a static air cushion. The wings with a total area of 5 m² (53 sq ft) and a span of 4.5 m (14 ft 9 in) ensured aerodynamic off-loading of the vehicle amounting to 90% of its all-up weight at speeds of 65-70 km/h (40-43 mph). The ekranoplan had an empty weight of 100 kg (220 lb) and an all-up weight of 180 kg (397 lb). In the course

This unorthodox vehicle is one of the projected configurations of the M-6 passenger *ekranoplan* created in Irkutsk in the mid-1990s. The model shown here was displayed at the MAKS-95 airshow.

An early artist's impression and three-view of the RT-6 (alias Ikar) light WIG vehicle developed by the Kazan' State Technical University. The actual vehicle was somewhat different.

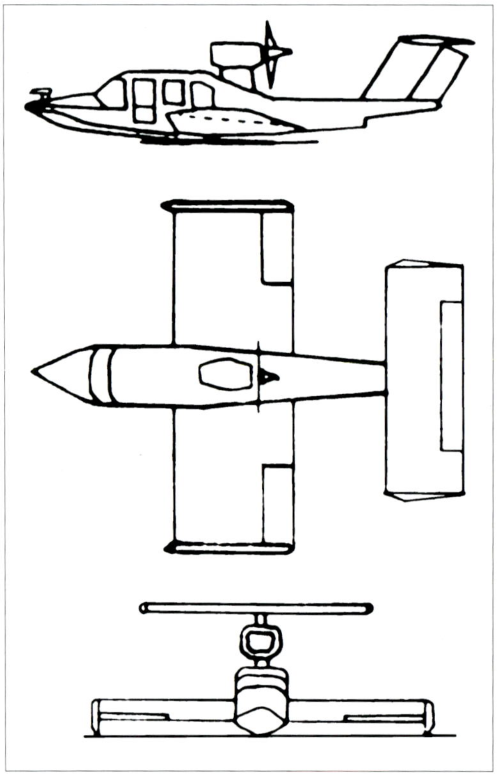

The logo of the Kazan' Aviation Institute (KAI)

of testing conducted at the Irkutsk water reservoir in 1983 the EVP-1 displayed excellent manoeuvrability and stability in all flight modes in ground effect.

M-6

This light ekranoplan was built under the auspices of the IPI in the NPS Scientific Development and Production in the mid-1990s. The machine featured a canard layout with a foreplane that was diamond-shaped in planform. The foreplane was split into two halves, their edges forming a 'reverse slot'; the designers claimed that this layout helped ensure stability in ground-effect flight mode through auto-stabilisation without resorting to the automatic control system. The vehicle was powered by a Rotax engine driving a three-blade tractor propeller, the air flow being directed under the wings during take-off via a large chin intake.

Kazan' State Technical University named after Andrey N. Tupolev (KGTU)

(formerly KAI – the Kazan' Aviation Institute)

RT (RT-6, RT-X, River Taxi, Ikar)

In the early 1990s several KAI graduates who had worked on WIG vehicles at the Alekseyev CHDB suggested to their alma mater that it should take up the summing up of the research data on this subject that had been accumulated by that time. In 1993 a programme, aptly named 'Ekranoplan' and supported by state funding, was initiated; KAI became the leading organisation co-ordinating the efforts of 15 higher learning and research institutions. The work on the systematisation of research data was successfully conducted; in particular, all aerodynamic and structural layouts of WIG vehicles that had existed in the world were carefully studied. KAI researchers came to the conclusion that it was not

The actual prototype of the RT-6 (Ikar) in the assembly shop at KAI. Note the original two-bladed propeller. The shape of the glazing differs from the drawing above.

The Ikar skims the water in a test flight. Note the new six-bladed propeller.

possible to single out a layout that would have a decisive advantages over the others; therefore, it would be wise to stake on a simple layout involving no high costs.

In 1996, despite dwindling state funding, it was found expedient to build a research vehicle. It was to be a small six-seat machine. Its layout was suggested to KAI by the Nizhniy Novgorod-based branch of the Krylov Central Shipbuilding Research Institute (TsNII) where a series of light ekranoplan projects was being developed under the common name of RT (*rech**noy**e tak**si*** – river taxi). Accordingly, the KAI project also received the RT name, sometimes spelt as RT-6 (six passengers) or RT-X. Alternatively, it was known as ***Ikar*** (Icarus). Its chief designer is Aleksey Moiseyev. In August 1999 this project was presented at the MAKS-99 air show. Construction of the machine took quite some time due to financial difficulties. As a result of the efforts of KAI students and professors, the vehicle was completed in 2005. In 2006 it was launched and entered the stage of preparations for flight testing, with a few runs on water. In September 2007 the vehicle performed its first demonstration flight. According to test pilot Sergey Stepanov, the machine displayed good handling qualities – it was stable on ruffled water surface, easily controlled at low and high speeds, and, importantly, capable of lifting off from the water. The RT-6 became airborne after attaining a speed of 120 km/h (75 mph).

The RT-6 (Ikar) features an aircraft layout with a boat-type hull, low-aspect-ratio wings of rectangular planform and a T-tail. It is powered by a single 265-hp piston engine with a six-blade pusher propeller mounted on a truss above the fuselage (early drawings showed a pylon; a data sheet from 1999 cited 165 hp which obviously proved insufficient). Other design performance figures include an all-up weight of 1,500 kg (3,300 lb), a cargo-carrying capacity of 400 kg (880 lb), a range of 1,000 km (622 miles), a flight altitude of 0.2-1.0 m (8 in – 3 ft) and a cruising speed of 150 km/h (93 mph).

The RT is intended for operation over the surface of water reservoirs, large rivers, lakes and coastal areas of seas and oceans, as well as above ice- and snow-covered expanses. Possible uses include river-going taxi services, transportation of small cargoes, patrol duties and search & rescue work. The possibility of putting the machine into series production depends on whether investors can be found. It was reported that there was some interest from both mainland China and Taiwan in this machine.

Khar'kov Aviation Institute (KhAI)

Reshetnikov's WIG vehicle

In 1963 V. V. Reshetnikov, a student of the Khar'kov Aviation Institute (KhAI, now renamed National Aerospace University), designed and built a control-line model of a WIG vehicle which incorporated a device for creating a static air cushion during take-off and landing. The vehicle featured a wide-chord wing centre section supplemented by narrow-chord outer wing panels and a T-tail. A small engine drove a shrouded propeller mounted above the

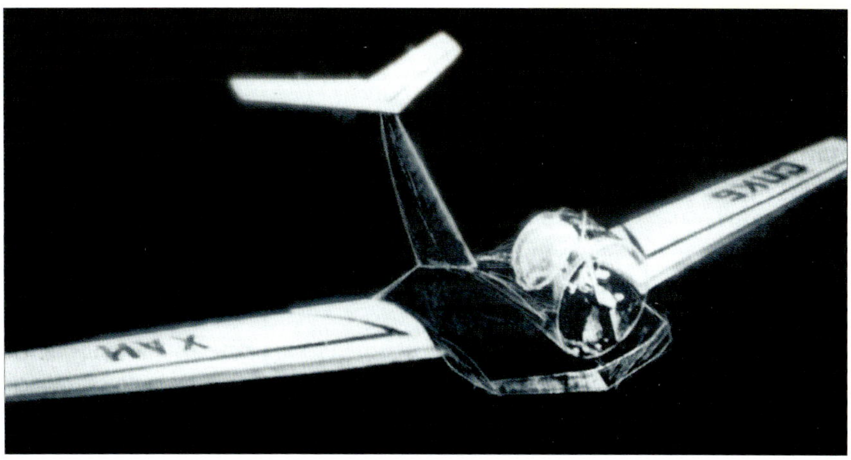

A control line model of the *ekranoplan* developed by V. V. Reshetnikov at KhAI.

A control line model of the KhAI-25 WIG vehicle. The bar between the 'semi-T-tails' is added for rigidity only.

A large model of the KhAI-26 flying wing WIG vehicle powered by a pulse-jet engine. Note the horizontal tail linking the vertical tails.

The real KhAI-26 on the Oskol Reservoir during tests. The actual craft has a different tail unit – the twin fins are not topped by the stabiliser.

leading edge of the wing centre section; part of the propeller's slipstream could be deflected to form the air cushion under the wings.

KhAI-25

In 1966 S.V. Yelistratov, a student of KhAI and an active participant of the Student Design Bureau, defended his graduation thesis, the subject of which was 'An experimental WIG vehicle' – something fairly exotic at that time. After that he headed the work of a group of enthusiasts aimed at studying the various layouts of *ekranoplans* and eventually building a full-scale vehicle. In 1967 they completed the project of the KhAI-25 WIG vehicle based on the use of composite layout wings – that is, comprising a wide-chord centre section and narrow-chord outer panels. This layout ensured high aerodynamic efficiency during flight near the supporting surface and during flight out of ground effect as well. The wing centre section of the KhAI-25 was flanked by floats whose aft ends carried twin vertical tails topped by horizontal tails on the outer side. A control-line model built by the students displayed stable flight close to the ground, in the transition mode and in the out-of-ground-effect mode.

KhAI-26

In 1969 the KhAI Student Design Bureau started the design and construction of the KhAI-26 two-seat WIG vehicle. The work proceded under a contract with the Almaz Central Design Bureau (a shipbuilding design bureau which also devoted some effort to research and design work on *ekranoplans*). Prior to testing the real thing, the students built a flying

Left and far left: The Khar'kov Aircraft Factory (KhAZ) ME-1 radio-controlled *ekranoplan* model on the ground and in flight; note the wheel undercarriage.

far left: The broadly similar KhAZ ME-2 RC model; note the vertical tail design.

KhAZ workers prepare the ME-5 RC model for a flight. Note the engine placement.

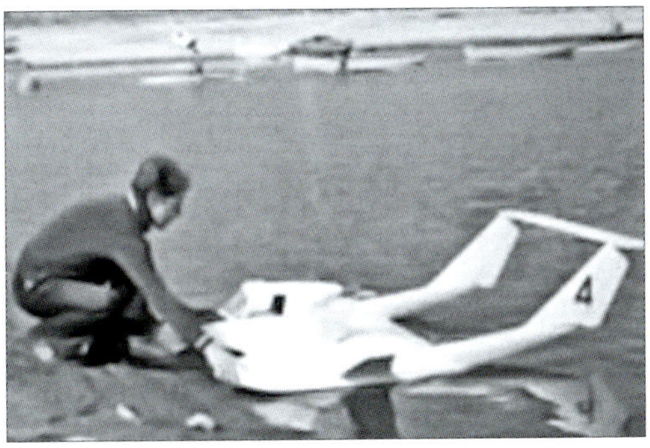

Two views of the KhAZ ME-4 RC model at different points in time.

model of the KAI-26, using a model aeroplane pulse-jet for propulsion. The KhAI-26 became the first piloted WIG craft built at KhAI. It was a two-seat vehicle of wooden construction. It featured a flying wing of rectangular planform and very low aspect ratio, flanked by two floats, the aft ends of which carried the vertical tails. The front parts of the floats housed open cockpits (for the pilot and the researcher. The floats were provided with steps on the bottoms. The wing was fitted with a flap. Forward propulsion was ensured by a Vikhr' (Whirlwind) outboard motorboat engine delivering 30 hp.

The testing of the KhAI-26 was conducted on the Oskol Reservoir in 1970. The vehicle attained a speed sufficient for hydroplaning, but failed to progress to the flight in ground effect. A more powerful engine delivering 45-50 hp was needed, but it was hard to procure. The test programme had to be curtailed before conclusive results could be reached.

Khar'kov Aircraft Plant, enthusiast design bureau

ME-series WIG models

From 1974 a group of enthusiasts – employees of the Khar'kov Aircraft Plant was studying the problems of WIG craft. In January 1975 the group's members formed a voluntary design bureau which was given the name *Gorizont* (Horizon). The group's organiser and leader was V. V. Matyushin,

The logo of the Khar'kov Aviation Institute

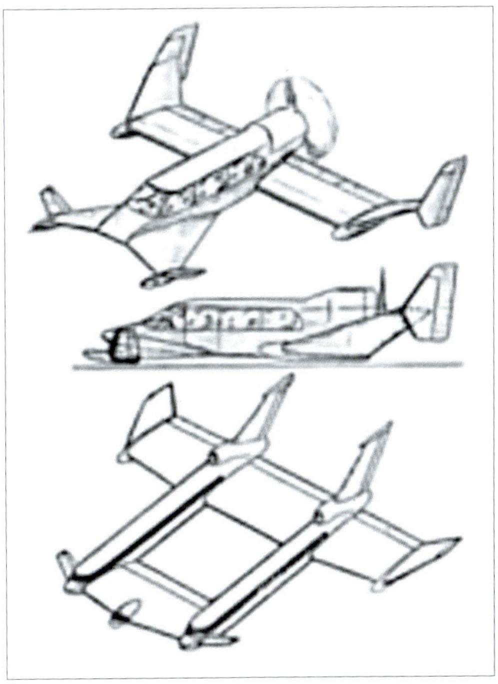

Provisional drawings of two *ekranoplan* projects prepared by KhAI.

This model represents a KhAI project of an *ekranolyot* intended for seismic monitoring.

a young aircraft designer. Together with his colleagues he started projecting WIG vehicles which were based on the layout of ground effect craft created by A. Lippisch – the X-112, X-113 and X-114.

A model of their first design was tested in KhAI's wind tunnel. At the same time they built a large-size control-line model dubbed ME-1 (*mo**del'** ekranopla**na*** – WIG craft model) for flight testing. The model featuring a classic Lippisch configuration with a fin-mounted engine was successfully tested in July and August 1975. It displayed satisfactory stability and controllability and attained a lift/drag ratio of 30 in flight close to the supporting surface. The wooden model weighing 4 kg (8.82 lb) was powered by a 0.7-hp engine.

The next model, tested in 1976, was the ME-2, constructed from Styrofoam and powered by a 0.35-hp engine. Featuring the same layout, it had a T-tail with a sharply swept fin to increase the arm of the horizontal tail. This helped achieve satisfactory pitch stability. A lift/drag ratio of 25 was registered in the ground effect flight mode.

In the same year of 1976 the ME-3 control-line model was tested. It differed from the preceding designs in having two rectangular wings placed in tandem with and adjustable slot between them (5-10 mm; 0 13/64 to 0 13/32 in). The incidence of each wing set could be adjusted before flight. The wings were flanked by endplates, whose extensions were given the shape of twin fins topped by a horizontal tail. Additional wing panels were mounted outboard of the endplates. The vehicle measuring 1.48 m (4 f 10¼ in) in span and weighing 3.8 kg (8.38 lb) was powered by a 0.5-hp engine. The tests produced good results. The lift/drag ratio in free flight was 11, rising to 26-28 in ground effect mode.

In late 1977 the ME-5 *ekranoplan* model was designed and built. Featuring a classical aircraft layout of a low-wing monoplane, it had wide-chord rectangular-shaped wings with upturned swept wingtips and a T-tail. The engine driving a tractor propeller was mounted on a pylon above the forward fuselage.

The ME-4 radio-controlled *ekranoplan* model was built in June 1979. It featured a twin-float (catamaran) layout, slotted wings of low aspect ratio and a twin-boom, twin-fin tail unit with the horizontal tail on top of the fins. Small upturned 'winglets' were added outboard of the floats. The crew cockpit was located on the centreline. This was virtually a scaled-down (1/5th scale) two-seat *ekranoplan*. With a length of 1.96 m (6 ft 5⅛ in) and a span of 1.91 m (6 ft 3¼ in) it weighed 9.5 kg (21.0 lb) and was powered by a 1.4-hp engine driving a pusher propeller behind the cockpit. The model was tested at the Tbilisi Water Reservoir in October 1979. The vehicle displayed a lift/drag ratio of 7 in free flight and 20 in flight close to the supporting surface.

Troop-carrier WIG vehicle (project)

In the spring of 1981 members of the voluntary design bureau at the Kharkov aircraft factory prepared an advanced development project of a troop-carrier WIG vehicle. V. V. Matyshin was the Chief Designer. The machine with a AUW of 16,500 kg (36,380 lb) was intended to carry 29 persons and was to be powered by three Ivchenko AI-25 turbofans rated at 1,500 kgp (3,307 lbst) apiece. The project was submitted for consideration to the Minister of Defence Dmitriy F. Ustinov. The reaction was quick – in July 1981 an interdepartmental commission visited the Khar'kov aircraft plant to have a closer look at the project. This was followed by discussions in the Ministry of Aircraft Industry and the Ministry of Shipbuilding. The designers were tasked with building scale models for wind tunnel tests at TsAGI. However, the attitude of the authorities proved half-hearted. No funding was forthcoming, and the hopes of building a prototype at the Khar'kov aircraft plant were frustrated by the uncooperative attitude of the latter. Thus, the project came to naught.

Canard WIG vehicle projects

Nevertheless, the voluntary design bureau continued for some time the work on the WIG subject, pursuing theoretical studies of different layouts. These studies lasted until 1986. They resulted in several patent applications, which were granted. One of the applications was concerned with the *ekranoplans* featuring the canard (tail-first) layout. Several small models featuring this configuration were built and successfully flown. Projects tentatively studied included vehicles of differing dimensions, from single-engined 6-8-seaters to twin-hulled machines comparable to large airliners in seating capacity.

Work on WIG vehicles Conducted by Scientific Institutions

WIG research in TsAGI (Central Aero-Hydrodynamics Institute)

The world-renowned Central Aero-Hydrodynamics Institute named after Nikolay Ye. Zhukovskiy, based in Zhukovskiy near Moscow and better known by its Russian abbreviation of TsAGI (*Tsen**trahl'**nyy **a**ero**ghid**rodina**mich**eskiy insti**toot***), has played an extremely important role in all aspects of aeronautical research in the Soviet Union and in present-day Russia. This research encompasses, among other things, the WIG vehicles. Working in close co-operation with such design bureaux as the Alekseyev CHDB, Beriyev, Bartini and Sukhoi, TsAGI specialists conducted thorough theoretical studies and numerous wind tunnel and towing basin tests to help develop the most rational aerodynamic and hydrodynamic layouts of WIG craft. In addition to backing up the design work on specific projects in the mentioned design bureaux, TsAGI was engaged in evolving advanced layouts for prospective WIG vehicles that might one day be embodied in practical design.

WIG designs of the Krylov Central Shipbuilding Research Institute

Speedboats with aerodynamic off-loading (Kramaryov's designs in the MS series)

The St. Petersburg-based Central Research Institute of Shipbuilding named after Academician Aleksey N. Krylov (known by its Russian abbreviation of TsNII) has long been engaged in work associated with WIG vehicles. Emphasis is placed on theoretical studies, but some attention is devoted also to practical design. Several small machines designed by Ye. A. Kramaryov reached the hardware stage.

These were speedboats with aerodynamic off-loading, making use of outboard motors with water propellers. This allowed them to be lifted out of the water in cruise flight to a height of a few centimetres above the surface, with the water propeller remaining submerged. Four single-seat vehicles of this kind were successively developed by Kramaryov; they were designated MS-01 through MS-04. They were fitted with short-span wings carrying endplate floats. Such was the MS-02 which successfully performed test runs in the ground effect mode. This was the first speedboat of the series to 'fly'; the preceding MS-01, powered by a 30-hp Vikhr'-30 outboard motor, had failed to lift off, but corroborated the soundness of the hydrodynamic layout.

The MS-02 powered by a German-made König outboard motor had a displacement of 230 kg (507 lb); it had a length of 4.33 m (14 ft 2½ in) and a width of 2.20 m (7 ft 2½ in). The vehicle attained a speed of 157.5 km/h (97.9 mph).

The MS-02 speedboat with aerodynamic offloading designed at the Krylov Central Shipbuilding Institute in ground effect mode. The legend reads *ispytaniya* (tests).

The next model, the MS-03, was basically similar to the MS-02; it was the first WIG speedboat of the MS series to take part in official contests. A speed of 157.5 km/h (97.8 mph) was attained at a measurement mile. The vehicle proved very stable; it could make hops to a height of 0.5-1.0 m and alight without problems.

The MS-04 vehicle following modifications with a new twin-fin tail unit.

Another craft in the series, the MS-04, was intended exclusively for racing. Pictures of this craft were circulated by the TASS News Agency in 1990. This single-seat vehicle featured an 'aircraft' layout with low-set stub wings and a swept T-tail. The latter had anhedral on the horizontal stabiliser and was manufactured as a single all-movable unit without control surfaces; it was mounted on the cowled outboard engine and moved together with it around two axes (this feature had its shortcomings, making the whole structure less rigid). The boat-shaped hull accommodated an open cabin in its front part. The wings of trapezoidal planform, fitted with endplate floats, had prominent root fillets. It is presumably

Above: The MS-04 as originally built. Note the unusual all-movable T-tail with anhedral stabilisers hinged at the fin root. The outboard motor is provided with two large silencers.

this vehicle that is referred to in the text to the TASS pictures, where mention is made of a TsNII-designed WIG vehicle with a 350-cc engine produced by König GmbH (West Germany), capable of developing a speed of 160 km/h (99 mph).

The MS-04 took part in international speedboat races – for example, the one in Milano in 1988. After testing in its initial configuration the MS-04 was fitted with a new tail unit featuring twin fins.

Kramaryov and his associates started work on the MS-05 two-seat WIG craft intended for training; its model displayed fine behaviour in flight. Unfortunately, the full-scale craft was not completed.

In the early 1990s further work on vehicles of this type at TsNII was discontinued due to lack of funding,

Passenger WIG craft (project)

The official caption to a TASS photo mentioned a TsNII-developed project of a WIG vehicle *'bearing a superficial resemblance to a modern airliner and powered by engines with propellers'* (presumably turboprops). The project had been demonstrated at international exhibitions in New York, Tokyo and Munich and patented in 15 countries.

WIG vehicle for a WIG Sea Launch system (project)

In the course of some years the Krylov Shipbuilding Institute (TsNII) has been studying the feasibility of using large ekranoplans as a means of launching aerospaceplanes into orbit and ensuring their return to Earth from orbit. In a number of publications E. A. Aframeyev, PhD, a senior researcher of the Krylov TsNII, presented a project of a WIG vehicle intended to be a part of the WIG Sea Launch system and designed to serve for the launch and retrieval of shuttle space vehicles.

Implementation of such a system would make it possible to launch space vehicles into orbit from ocean areas close to the Equator which would reduce the amount of energy required for orbiting space payloads and cut the costs associated with such operations. This would also obviate the need for reserving special land areas for the fall of the spent rocket boosters.

The whole concept is based on the assumption that the use of a WIG vehicle in procedures associated with the launch and retrieval of space shuttle vehicles will make it possible to ensure an aircraft-type horizontal landing of the shuttle, just like a landing on a conventional airstrip (which is singularly difficult to find in equatorial latitudes). As pointed out by Aframeyev, such projects are usually based on the use of huge WIG vehicles with an all-up weight of 1,500-2,000 tons (3,300,000-4,400,000 lb) and space shuttles weighing 600-800 tons (1,320,000-1,760,000 lb) but their emergence is a matter of a remote future. However, there is no need to wait that long, says he. The solution of the problem of horizontal launch from an ocean surface and landing on it can be found much earlier if it is based on the use of WIG vehicles weighing up to 750 tons (1,650,000 lb) and space shuttles weighing up to 300 tons (660,000 lb).

The system is supposed to function as follows. Immediately prior to launch the shuttle orbiter is loaded onto the WIG vehicle and both of them are refuelled. Then the WIG vehicle with the shuttle mounted piggy-back takes off. When the required speed is reached, the shuttle ignites its engines and separates from the carrier vehicle. In the case when a two-stage shuttle vehicle is used, separation of the stages takes place at the altitude of some 30,000m (98,400 ft) and the stage which has fulfilled its mission makes a landing on the airborne WIG vehicle and then is re-loaded onto the delivery ship.

A model of the WIG Sea Launch space system proposed by TsNII showing the bizarre WIG launch/retrieval vehicle and the space shuttle mounted piggy-back. The Nos. 2 to 5 engines have thrust reversers and, apparently, deflectors direct in the jet under the wings for take-off.

The same procedure is repeated by the shuttle orbiter upon its return, after which it can be re-used.

The WIG vehicle, as presented in the published illustration, is a gigantic machine with a wingspan of some 80 m (260 ft), featuring a twin-fuselage layout with a wide-chord thick wing centre section and outer wing panels of trapezoidal platform. The two boat hulls each carry their own set of tail surfaces located on the outboard side of the hulls, thus affording free access to the wing centre section from the rear and the transfer of a space vehicle to and from the *ekranoplan*. Placed on a crosspiece connecting the front parts of the boats are six turbofans performing the double function of boost engines (during take-off) and cruise engines. The shuttle orbiter is placed above the wing centre section. The WIG vehicle is provided with retractable diesel-driven water propellers at the stern and transverse thrusters at the bows for low-speed manoeuvring when afloat. The front parts of the boat hulls incorporate raised flight decks and compartments for the transported personnel.

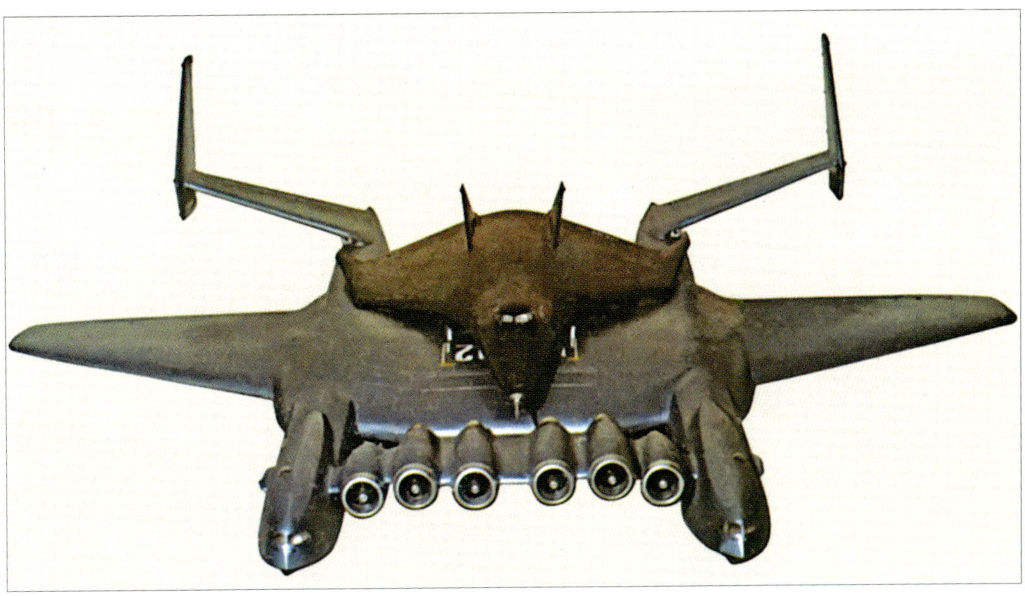

Front view of the same model. The *ekranoplan*'s tails are widely spaced to prevent damage by the blast of the orbiter's engines.

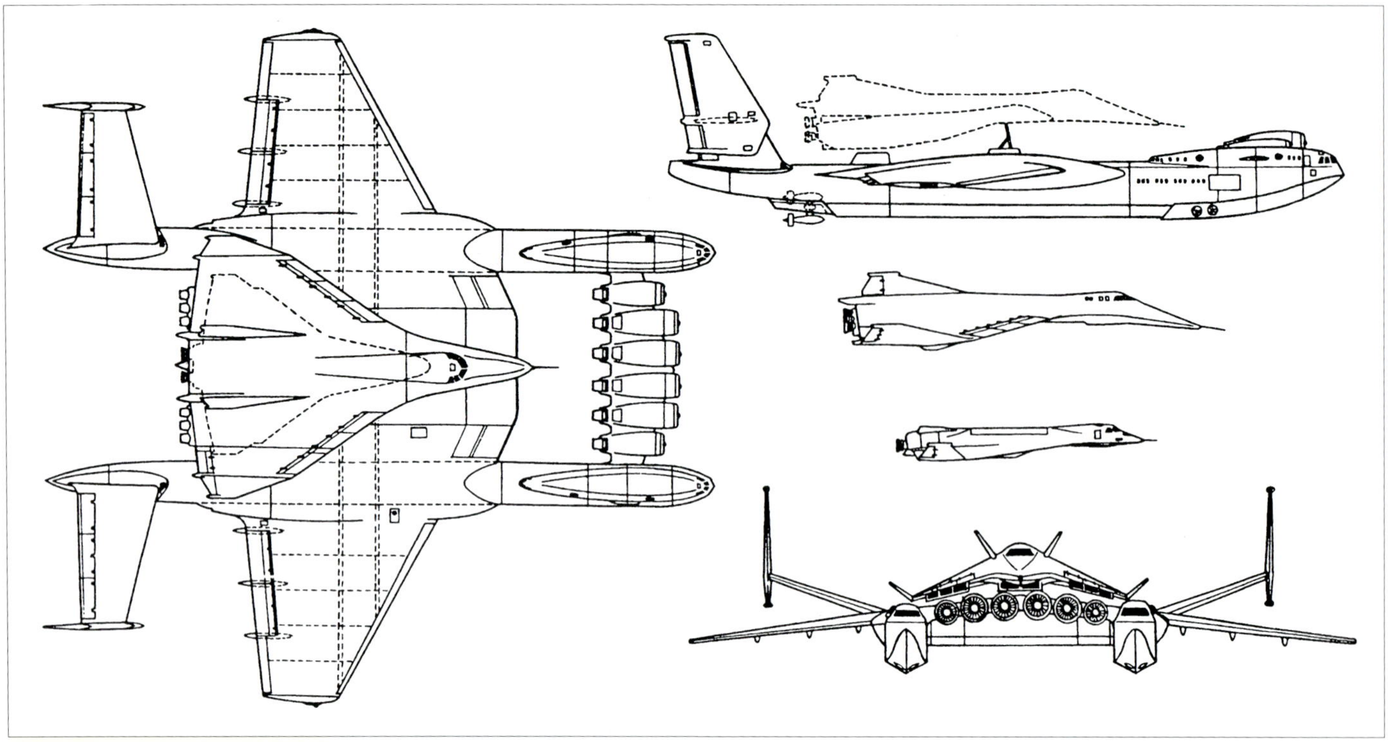

A three-view drawing of the Krylov TsNII's space launch system with two alternative shuttle orbiters. Note the retractable water propulsors and transverse thrusters for manoeuvring when afloat.

Here are some basic specifications. The full take-off weigh with the space shuttle on board is 750 t (1,650,000 lb), the main powerplant comprises six turbofans rated at 30,000-35,000 kgp (66,000 to 77,000 lbst) apiece, the powerplant for slow movement on water comprises two high-rpm diesel engines. Cruise flight speed is 550 to 600 km/h (342 to 373 mph), low speed for manouevring when afloat is 25 km/h (16 mph).

Burevesnik

The *Burevesnik* (Storm Petrel) appears to be yet another of the Krylov TsNII's projects of aerospace systems based on the use of a WIG vehicle as a carrier for a spaceplane, on the same lines as in the project described above. A photo of a model shows this to be a giant *ekranoplan* of a similar twin-hull configuration, with the wide-chord wing centre section serving as a platform for a space vehicle

A model of the broadly similar Burevesnik WIG vehicle (marked as such on the hulls). The shuttle orbiter is marked *Aviatsionno-kosmicheskaya sistema* (Aerospace system).

A model of the SSS twin-hull WIG vehicle. The engines are carried on cross-members ahead of the wing centre section.

mounted on top of it. A transverse structural member joining together the front sections of the hulls carries six high bypass ratio turbofans whose efflux presumably can be partly directed into the space under the wing centre section during take-off. No further information is available.

SAR *ekranoplan* for the SSS (Sea Safety System)

In the course of the last two decades the Krylov Shipbuilding Institute has devoted much attention to investigating the possibilities of creating a global international sea safety system, the last three words forming the SSS acronym. This system is called upon to ensure speedy and effective assistance to crews and passengers of ships, aircraft, submarines, oil rigs and other technical means who happen to be in distress at sea. Large *ekranoplans* with an AUW of about 750 tonnes (1,653,400 lb) and a radius of action of 3,000-4,000 km (1,860-2,490 miles) from their bases constitute the main element of this system, which can comprise 12-13 ports located in the Far East, South-East Asia, Africa, Europe. North and South America, and Australia and 50 heavy *ekranoplans* stationed at these ports.

The Krylov Shipbuilding Institute has also prepared an advanced design project of a heavy WIG vehicle weighing some 750 t (1,653,400 lb) and intended to be a part of this global safety system. It is referred to in some sources as the 'SSS' (a display model of this vehicle wears the SSS inscription). The vehicle is capable of taking off and alighting in sea states up to 5 inclusive, staying afloat and drifting for a long time and reaching a port of refuge at low speed if it is prevented from normal flight for some reason. The WIG vehicle can reach speeds of 400-500 km/h (249-311 mph) and operate within a radius of 3,000-4,000 km (1,860-2,490 miles) from a port. The *ekranoplan*-ship can deliver to the scene of an accident a large number of rescue means ranging from life rafts and motorboats to special boats for setting up floating barriers (used for containing oil spills), a deep sea diving vehicle and a helicopter. On board the WIG vehicle the survivors are provided with the necessary medical aid without waiting for arrival at a seaport. The safety of operation of such a WIG vehicle in sea conditions is far superior to various types of aircraft-based means.

To substantiate the project, the Krylov Institute (TsNII) has conducted a vast amount of design studies and research in wind tunnels, towing basins, on test rigs and on the open water surface. The design of the heavy WIG vehicle was developed on the basis of using available engines, structural materials, onboard equipment and with due regard to the state-of-the-art level of technology and production methods in the construction of high-speed ships and aircraft. It was presumed that further development of the project, construction and operation of the rescue WIG vehicles and of the system as a whole could be put into effect by an international consortium of shipbuilding and aircraft companies with financial support from nations having an interest in maritime rescue operations.

The SSS *ekranoplan* developed by the Krylov TsNII is a catamaran vehicle with two boat hulls and a composite wing layout. Placed between the hulls is a wing centre section of large chord and relative thickness; outboard of the hulls it is supplemented by outer wing panels of higher aspect ratio and lesser relative thickness. The twin-fin tail unit includes a horizontal tail resting on top of the fins. The crew stations are housed in a nacelle attached to the leading edge of the wing centre section and two foreplanes joining the nacelle and the hulls. Suspended under the foreplanes are four turbojets

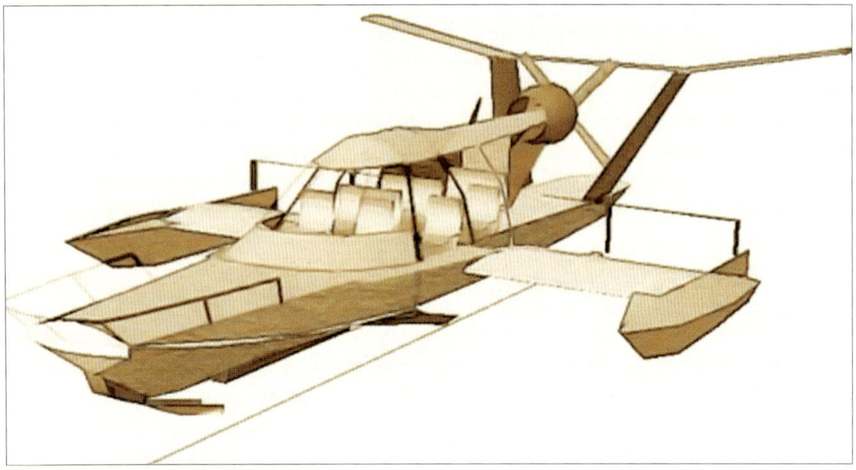

A computer-generated image of the RT1-360 with tandem wings, hydrofoils and tractor propellers driven by a single engine via reduction gear.

The basic project version of the RT1-360 with single wings, hydroskis and an M-14PT engine driving a single pusher propeller. Note the yacht-type handrails.

which act both as booster engines at take-off and as cruise engines. For slow-speed movement when afloat the vehicle is fitted with diesel engines driving water propellers in the aft parts of the hulls. The vehicle can carry a Kamov Ka-27PS *Helix-C* SAR helicopter on top of its wing centre section.

Krylov TsNII branch in Nizhniy Novgorod

A branch of the Krylov Central Shipbuilding Research Institute was set up at Gor'kiy (now Nizhniy Novgorod) on the basis of the CHDB test facility. In the subsequent years this organisation developed a series of projects of small WIG vehicles. The designer behind these projects was E. V. Vasil'yev. Some of them are described below.

KEP-6 (KEP-6A)

This was a project of a passenger WIG vehicle (KEP = ***kah**ter-ekrano**plahn*** – WIG speedboat) designed to carry four to six persons. Its wings had a composite configuration in planform and consisted of a centre section and outer wing panels with endplates. According to some sources, the KEP-6A had a twin-fin tail unit and a powerplant with two propellers that could change their plane of rotation. The project was presented at the 'Ekranoplan-96' international conference held in Kazan' in 1996.

WIG vehicles in the RT series

The TsNII's Nizhniy Novgorod branch also prepared a technical proposal for a series of business-class light amphibious WIG vehicles powered by indigenous automobile engines from the VAZ (Lada) and ZMZ enterprises and by the production 360-hp Vedeneyev M-14P aircraft radial engine. They were known under the common designation RT (*rech**noy**e tak**si*** – river taxi) with sequence numbers. They featured an 'aircraft' layout (like that of the SM-6). The programme included such vehicles as the RT-2, RT-2M, RT-4, RT-5, RT-6MA, also presented at the 'Ekranoplan-96' conference.

But the series started with the RT-1 project, which served as a basis for the further projects evolved by modifying and scaling up the basic 'aircraft' layout. In one source, four projects developed at the branch are singled out. These were the RT2-760 and RT-360 cargo/passenger craft and the RT1-360 and RT1-150 passenger WIG vehicles. They all shared the same basic layout and featured a modular construction. The boat-type hull had a superstructure which could be built of composite materials. The powerplant consisted of series-built automobile and aircraft-type piston engines. The craft were provided with a wheel/hydroski undercarriage enabling them to be operated from water, snow-covered ground and ice.

It remains to be added that the basic RT-1 project was recommended by the TsNII branch to the student design bureau of the Kazan' Aviation Insti-

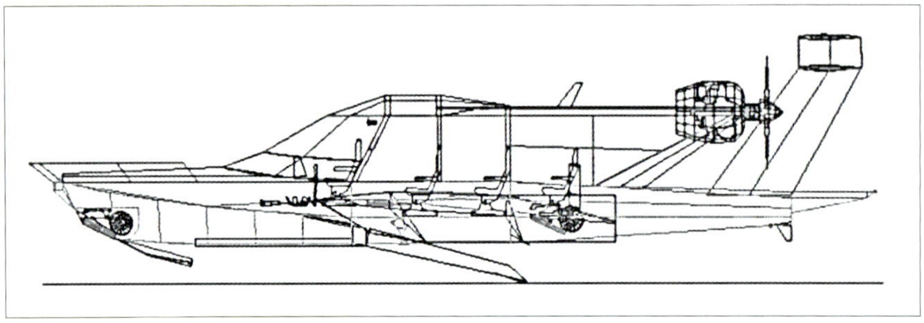

A cutaway drawing of the RT1-360 in M-14PT-powered pusher configuration. Note the retractable beaching gear.

Performance figures on some of the RT series projects

	RT2-760	RT2-360	RT1-360
Number of passengers	30	21	12
Engine power, hp	2x540	2x195	1x195
Operational speed, km/h (mph)	193 (120)	161 (100)	152 (94)
Range with max fuel load, km (miles)	1,500 (932)	1.500 (932)	1,000 (622)

tute (KAI) as a starting point for their work on a small river-going WIG vehicle, later to be known as RT, RT-X or Ikar (see above in the KAI section).

SLEP-2

This was a project of an ultra-light two-seat ekranoplan (SLEP-2 = *sverkh**lyokh**kiy ekrano**plan** dvukh**mes**nyy*) designed by E. V. Vasil'yev at the Gor'kiy branch for the purpose of studying and testing technical features for the RT-series *ekranoplans* described above. The SLEP-2 was not built.

Sigma series of light WIG craft

Several projects bearing a common name Sigma were developed at the Gor'kiy branch of TsNII. Here are some facts on the Sigma-6 project. Developed from the preceding Sigma-5 design, this vehicle was a high-speed passenger WIG boat intended to carry six passengers over a distance of up to 1,000 km (622 miles). The vehicle featured an aircraft layout with a composite configuration of the wings which had an aspect ratio of 2.3. The tail unit consisted of two fins topped by a horizontal tail. A single M-14P radial engine ensured propulsion in cruise flight. There was also a special installation for power-assisted take-off which comprised an M-18 piston engine and an OV-23 axial blower. The vehicle was expected to be operated all year round at major rivers, inland water reservoirs and on routes along coast lines. It would be capable of moving above water, ice, snow, areas of shallow water, and above even solid surface at an altitude of 1 m (3 ft), with short hops to a greater altitude to clear natural obstacles.

The vehicle's high speed made it advisable to operate it at rivers with a width in excess of 500 m (1,640 ft) in the following versions: a route taxi on routes between cities; a vehicle for various duties such as mail delivery, ambulance work, SAR duties etc.; an executive transport for business tours; transportation of small-size cargoes and perishable foodstuffs.

A. N. Panchenkov's WIG vehicle designs

Anatoliy N. Panchenkov, an enthusiast of WIG craft, started his career of a researcher and designer as a young member of the staff of Alekseyev's CHDB. At a certain moment he left this organisation to pursue scientific studies in Kiev, where he worked for several years in the Hydromechanics Institute. In 1968 he moved to the Irkutsk Polytechnic Institute. These two stages of his work and the associated WIG craft designs are described below.

Hydromechanics Institute of the Academy of Sciences of the Ukrainian SSR

Anatoliy N. Panchenkov started his research and experiments with WIG craft in the abovementioned scientific institution in the early 1960s. A series of experimental vehicles was built under his direction in Kiev. It comprised three projects designated successively as K-1, K-2 and K-3 (K stands for ***Kiy**evskiy* – originating from Kiev). In many sources these designs are referred to as the ADP-1, ADP-2 and ADP-3 respectively; ADP stands for *appa**raht** na dina**mich**eskoy [vozd**oosh**noy] po**doosh**ke*, dynamic air cushion vehicle. However, some sources state that the ADP prefix made its appearance later, starting with Panchenkov's fourth design (in Irkutsk). This leaves the impression that the ADP prefix was assigned by some authors to the first three designs retroactively. Furthermore, the ADP prefix is used in some publications for scale models that were built by Panchenkov's group in parallel with the piloted craft.

Theoretical research and experimenting led Panchenkov to the conviction that the required stability of flight in ground effect could be achieved in a WIG vehicle featuring a canard layout. In consequence, his vehicles had an elongated fuselage with a stabiliser mounted in its front part. The first such vehicle was the K-1 (ADP-1) built in 1965 (1964, according to other sources). It was a cross between a planing boat and a hydrofoil boat fitted with a single flat lifting hydrofoil under the bows sec-

Designer A. N. Panchenkov.

Below: The Panchenkov K-1 as originally built with a two-blade propeller.

Bottom: The K-1 in modified form with a four-blade propeller and endplates on the foreplanes.

A model of the ADP-01 super-heavy passenger ekranoplan developed by Panchenkov at the Hydromechanics Institute.

endplates on the main wings. The latter were fitted with flaperons. Placed on top of the wings, in the propeller wash, was the fin and rudder assembly. During trials the vehicle showed a maximum speed of 110 km/h (68 mph) in flight at the height of 0.25 m (10 in). Stabilisation of the flight altitude over the surface was ensured by the front wings (lifting stabilisers) mounted on the forward fuselage. Increasing the stabilisers' angle of attack caused them to lose lift due to stalling at supercritical angles, and the vehicle lowered the nose, restoring the working AOA of the stabilisers. However, the area of the front wings proved insufficient and had to be increased; the front wings were fitted with endplates.

The logo of the Ukrainian Academy of Sciences' Hydromechanics Institute

A scale model of the ADP-01 was tested, using a Volga hydrofoil speedboat as a tug.

A model of the K-3 configured as a heavy passenger *ekranoplan* with a double-deck fuselage and six turbojet engines.

tion of the hull. It had a K-750 flat-twin motorcycle engine with a pusher propeller placed behind the cockpit. The vehicle was subjected to modifications in the course of testing; pictures show it with a two-blade and a four-blade propeller, with and without

In 1965-66 the K-1 WIG vehicle was fitted with a tricycle wheeled undercarriage; the main wing endplates were deleted. The two-blade propeller was replaced by a four-blade one. The fuselage acquired streamlined contours and was fitted with a windshield. The airframe weight rose to 380 kg (840 lb). In this guise the vehicle was allegedly re-designated ADP-2. Tests were conducted at an airfield near Kiev. The ADP-2's design performance included a flight altitude of 0.25 m (10 in) and a maximum speed of 150 km/h (93 mph. Other sources mention the K-2 as the successor of the K-1 and describe it as fitted with a modified hydrofoil which suffered a failure during one of the test runs, necessitating repairs to the craft.

Concurrently with the testing of the piloted vehicles, Panchenkov and his colleagues tested several scale models featuring the same canard layout; they were towed by a motorboat, reaching the flight in ground effect in the process. One of the models had a twin fuselage layout. The models represented the layout of future large-size *ekranoplans*, including prospective machines of gigantic dimensions. One of the models, designated K-3, displayed a remarkable lift/drag ratio of 30 during the towing tests. This model was repainted to represent a scaled-down ocean-going passenger *ekranoplan* and was displayed at various exhibitions.

After the demonstration of the K-3 model Panchenkov's experiments attracted attention in certain quarters responsible for maintaining secrecy in the area of WIG research and design activities. At that time the CHDB in Gor'kiy enjoyed virtual monopoly on WIG design, and competition was not encouraged. One fine day Panchenkov was told by 'men in black' that he and his colleagues were no longer permitted to work on the design of *ekranoplans*. A stroke of luck helped overcome the ban. Panchenkov chanced to meet Academician Melent'yev, the leader of the Siberian Energetics Institute (affiliated to the Siberian section of the Russian Academy of Sciences). Melent'yev invited Panchenkov and his group to Irkutsk where he promised to provide for them the necessary conditions for further work on *ekranoplans*. He was as good as his word. In 1968 Panchenkov and 14 members of his team moved together with their families to Irkutsk (see a sequel to this story below).

Irkutsk Polytechnic Institute

(at present Irkutsk State Technical University)

ADP-04 – ADP-07 series of WIG vehicles

At the Irkutsk Polytechnic Institute Anatoliy Panchenkov resumed the work on ekranoplan design, sticking to his favourite canard layout. His first machine designed in Irkutsk was designated ADP-04 (first use of the ADP prefix for 'dynamic air cushion vehicle'; the digit 4 was a tribute to the three preceding designs of the Kiev period). The testing of the vehicle started in April 1970 on the ice of Lake Baikal. The first runs showed that the vehicle was underpowered and unable to lift off. Faced with this problem, Panchenkov hit upon the idea of testing the vehicle without a pilot. With just enough fuel for a few minutes' flight and with the rudder fixed for circular motion, the craft was allowed to begin its take-off run and soon became airborne, making one circle after another until it ran out of fuel. This was considered a success. Later the machine was fitted with a more powerful 32-hp M-63 engine; redesignated ADP-04M, it performed a series of piloted test flights over Lake Baikal.

The results of these tests permitted to start preparations for the construction of a new vehicle, the ADP-05, the prototype of which was to be manufactured at the Irkutsk aircraft plant. The vehicle was later dubbed ***Orfey*** (Orpheus). In its first version (Orfey-1) it looked like a catamaran vehicle with two ADP-4 fuselages mated to a rectangular platform on which an eight-seat passenger cabin from a Kamov Ka-30 aerosleigh was placed. The 260-hp AI-14RS radial mounted behind the cabin and driving a pusher propeller served for propulsion.

The ADP-04M in flight over a snow-covered surface.

A model of the ADP-06 is towed by a Volga hydrofoil speedboat, using a special outrigger.

Despite the assistance from the aircraft plant, manufacture of the ADP-5 proceeded slowly and was not completed before 1975. In the meantime, Panchenkov took pains to organise a test facility on the shore of the Bratsk Reservoir. In 1975 the ADP-5 was moved to this facility, and a further five years were spent in developing and modifying it prior to flight testing. The first flights showed that the bulky cabin from the Ka-30 created excessive drag. It was replaced by the forward fuselage from a Yak-18 with a nose-mounted engine, but an unfortunate mishap led to a fire which destroyed this cabin (this was the unlucky Orfey-2). Eventually the designers procured a passenger cabin from a Yak-12 lightplane. In this configuration, dubbed Orfey-3, the *ekranoplan* was successfully flown until 1985.

The logo of the Irkutsk State Technical University

The Orfey-1 WIG vehicle making use of the complete body and powerplant of a production Ka-30 aerosleigh.

The design team with the Orfey-2 WIG vehicle. Anatoliy Panchenkov is second from right. The guy on the left is fooling around; giving someone a jolly pair of 'horns' during a photo session is an all-time favourite joke.

The Orfey-3 making use of the cabin and powerplant of a Yak-12 light aircraft.

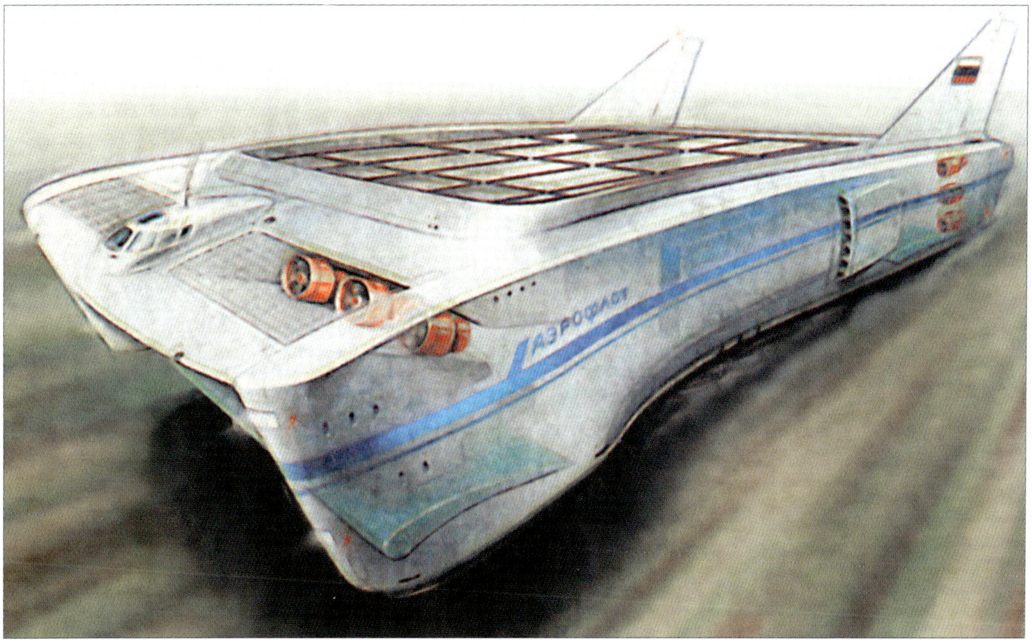

An artist's impression of Panchenkov's huge cargo *ekranoplan* with 12 buried engines and freight containers in the hold. The craft wears Aeroflot titles.

Panchenkov's last project from the Irkutsk period was the ADP-06 which was under development between 1979 and 1981. A test scale model was successfully flown, towed by a motor boat. However, the work on the ADP-06 gradually lost impetus and was eventually abandoned. In 1983 Panchenkov moved to Gor'kiy where he took up a position at the city's Polytechnic Institute.

After Panchenkov's departure his followers from the Irkutsk Polytechnic Institute designed and built the ADP-7 two-seat ekranoplan powered by a 210-hp Walter M-337 engine. Its testing was started in 1985 and looked promising, but the lack of funding sealed the fate of the project.

Panchenkov's giant ekranoplan (project)

In June 1992, after Anatoliy N. Panchenkov's visit to the USA, the magazine *Popular Mechanics* published an artist's impression illustrating a project of a gigantic WIG vehicle proposed by Panchenkov. Weighing 4,000 tonnes (8,820,000 lb) in the flight configuration, this machine had two fuselages shaped like flat and relatively thin endplates; they were joined together by a deck of rectangular planform which was, in fact, an airfoil-section wing intended to provide lift while accommodating passengers and cargo. This lifting surface was supplemented by a further two, located at a lower level in tandem between the side bodies. The vehicle measured 120 m (394 ft) in length and 50 m (164 ft) in width. According to the magazine, this vehicle was intended to be operated over the expanses of tundra along specially prepared routes, carrying passengers and cargo at a speed of 550 km/h. There is some evidence that Panchenkov did, in fact, contemplate a project of that magnitude, but the work did not proceed further than the initial studies.

Irkutsk State University jointly with IAPO

(Irkutsk Aviation Production Association)

In 1993 a laboratory of complex studies of this university headed by B. S. Berkovskiy conducted research and design work in the framework of a programme named Skaht (ray, the marine animal). It envisaged the design of WIG vehicles with an all-up weight ranging from 1 t to 1000 t (2,200 to 2,205,000 lb) featuring an air cushion undercarriage. It was presumed that, given the required

An artist's impression of the M-5-1 experimental WIG vehicle.

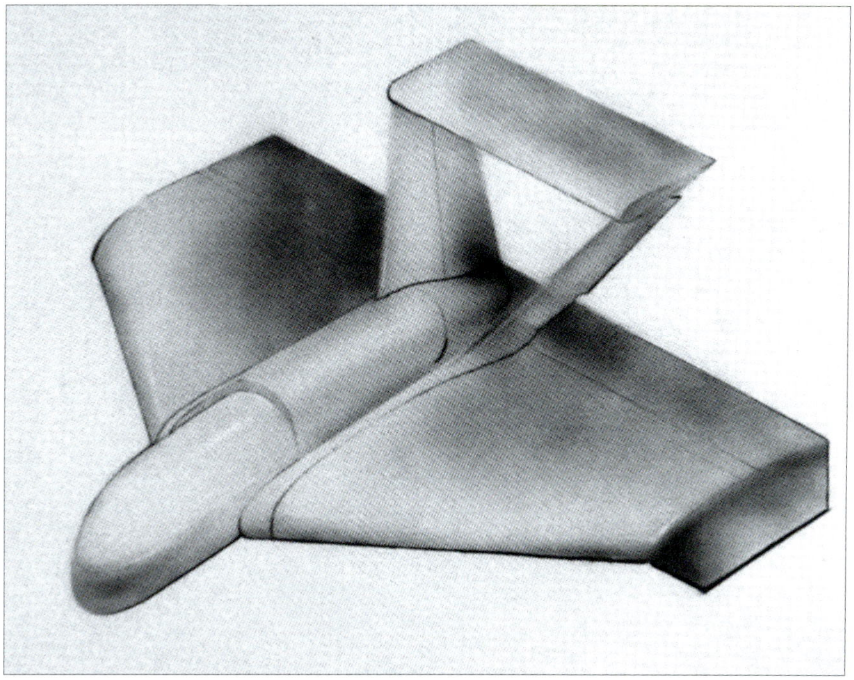

The M-5-1 nearing completion. Note the dorsal air intake and the hinged flaps under the wing leading edge.

funding, these vehicles could be developed to the hardware stage. In 1993 design studies evolved by the laboratory were presented at the MAKS-93 airshow; a model was shown of a 'flying wing' WIG vehicle with an air cushion undercarriage. The vehicle was envisaged as a means of solving transport problems in Siberia and the Far North. Such vehicles require no roads or prepared airfields and can be used all year round over any flat surface. This, in the opinion of the designers, promises a good economic effect.

The WIG vehicle can be built in two basic layouts. One of them features wings of triangular planform with a thick S-shaped airfoil and is intended for medium-haul (2,000-km/1,240-mile) cargo transportation; the second one is a flying wing shaped as a flat platform and is intended for short-haul (1,500-2,000km/930-1,240-mile) cargo routes.

The M-5-2 (evolved from the M-5-1) at MosAeroShow'92 minus tail section, showing the RU19-300 turbojet in cloth wraps. It carries the logo of the Stela Aviation Company which assisted in funding the programme. The trailing-edge flap is well visible.

Another view of the M-5-2, showing the port leading-edge flap and the port air intake.

In addition to passenger and cargo transportation, such WIG vehicles were considered to be suitable for other duties, such as fighting forest fires. The results of the laboratory's work were demonstrated at international exhibitions in Seattle (USA), Hannover (Germany) and Moscow.

Development of these projects was conducted with the participation of the Irkutsk-based Stela commercial aviation company having a research division. Some of the projects (illustrated by photos on these pages) bore the designations M-5-1, M-5-01, M-5-2.

A wind tunnel model of the M-5-01 heavy WIG vehicle utilising the flying wing layout. This model does not feature the six turbofan engines to be mounted on the upper surface near the trailing edge.

A model of the M-5-01 – again bearing the Stela logo – on display at the MAKS-93 airshow.

The logo of the Siberian Aviation Research Institute (SibNIA)

SibNIA

(S. A. Chaplygin Siberian Research Institute for Aviation)

This scientific institution based in Irkutsk is one of the most important centres of aerospace research in Russia, comparable in its status to the Moscow-based TsAGI. Apart from basic research in aerodynamics and other aspects of aeronautical science, SibNIA has made a significant contribution to the development of specific aircraft and WIG vehicle designs, making use of its T-203 and T-205 wind tunnels. The WIG craft whose aerodynamic layout was researched at SibNIA include the T-1, Orlyonok, Loon', SM-6 and Project 905 from the Alekseyev CHDB; Beriyev's A-2000 project; Bartini's T-500, VVA-14 and 14M1P; Sukhoi's S-90 and S-919 projects, LAT (Taganrog Light Aviation) T-50 project. The tests were conducted under conditions simulating the presence of a supporting surface and the use of booster engines for power-augmented take-off. They helped select the most rational features and parameters of the aerohydrodynamic layout and assisted take-off devices of the WIG vehicles and to study the stability and controllability of *ekranoplans* in different modes of flight in ground effect, including flight above ruffled water surface.

S-2 Kasatka

In the early 1990s SibNIA, struggling with financial difficulties and looking for ways to diversify its activities, embarked on the design of a highly unorthodox passenger aircraft which received the designation the designation S-2 *Kasatka* (Killer

An artist's impression of the S-2 Kasatka WIG craft developed by SibNIA.

Whale). Its distinguishing feature was a flattened airfoil-shaped fuselage creating a substantial share of the required lift. The rest of the lift would be created by two pairs of tandem-mounted wings joined at the tips and forming a diamond-shaped figure in plan view. The lower part of the fuselage was given hydrodynamic contours enabling the plane to be operated both from land and from water. Propulsion was ensured by a ducted propeller located above the fuselage. In its basic version the aircraft was intended to carry 10-12 passengers or a cargo of 1,000 to 1,500 kg (2,200 to 3.300 lb) at a cruising speed of 580 km/h (360 mph). Other possible duties included geological survey, aerial photography and monitoring flights. The lifting fuselage with its long chord imparted to the aircraft certain properties of a WIG vehicle in the take-off mode.

In 1993 wind tunnel tests were conducted with a big scale model, but the aircraft did not reach the hardware stage.

Andrey N. Tupolev

The well-respected Tupolev Design Bureau is mentioned here, among scientific institutions, entirely because WIG vehicles did not occupy any place of importance in its activities and do not merit a separate chapter. Actually, the only project from this design bureau that can be classed as a WIG vehicle is the project of an aerosleigh with a TsAGI-developed wing system. Information on this project appeared in the Russian aeronautical magazine *Kryl'ya Rodiny* (Wings of the Motherland) in 1994. Judging by the published photo of a model, the aerosleigh has a boat-shaped hull and is powered

The Tupolev AS-2 aerosleigh on snow during trials. Note the boat hull.

The logo of the Tupolev Joint-Stock Co.

As this photo of the first prototype shows, the AS-2 has what is known in the car tuning community as 'lambo doors' or scissor doors.

Two views of a homebuilt WIG vehicle built in Arkhangel'sk.

by an engine with a pusher propeller installed above the aft part of the hull. The vehicle is provided with high-set wings of normal 'aircraft' aspect ratio; two booms attached to the wings carry the tail surfaces. The wings working in ground effect are presumably intended to only partially off-load the vehicle, reducing the pressure on the snow or other supporting surface (water or marshland). There is no evidence of a prototype ever being built.

A vague reference to 'A. Tupolev's *ekranoplan*' can be found in another source where it is put into the category of vehicles intended for 'crawling on the ground' (more precisely, for moving over water, ice, snow and marshes). Presumably, it is a reference to the vehicle described above.

It is worth noting that as far back as the 1960s Tupolev's Design Bureau designed and built the A-3 aerosleigh of an unusual configuration. It had a boat-shaped hull enabling the vehicle to move on water, snow and marshland. Some reports indicate that the weight of the vehicle was partially off-loaded by the pressure of the ram air on the front undersurface of the hull in cruise. This aerosleigh was put into production and was widely used on lakes and rivers, especially in the northern areas of the USSR and in Siberia. In the 1990s the Tupolev OKB designed and built yet another aerosleigh – the AS-2 – again with a boat-hull body. It was exhibited at the MAKS-97 and MAKS-99 airshows in Zhukovskiy near Moscow.

WIG vehicles designed by individuals

R. Adomaitis

In 1982 an amphibious *ekranolyot* was built under the direction of R. Adomaitis in the then Soviet Lithuania. It was built by members of the Kaunas aviation sports club in the village of Pacunai. The vehicle, powered by a 105-hp Walter Minor engine, had a low-aspect-ratio wing of triangular planform. It underwent testing at the airfield of the Kaunas club with Adomaitis at the controls.

Arkhangel'sk-built ekranoplan

A very small single-seat WIG-vehicle resembling a scaled-down ESKA-1 was built by some enthusiasts in the city of Arkhangel'sk. No further particulars are available.

The SABAK-1M homebuilt aircraft with WIG properties. The wings could be detached, turning it into an aerosleigh. What looks right flies right, they say; unfortunately the SABAK-1M crashed in its fifth flight.

A sketch showing Dvoynikov's homebuilt WIG.

Yuriy S. Bakanov.

This enthusiast designer, assisted by his friends, designed and built a two-seat flying boat/WIG vehicle designated SABAK-1M (SABAK stands for ***sood**no amorti**zee**rovannoye Ba**ka**nova* – Bakanov's shock-absorbing vessel). It has a configuration of a normal light hydroplane powered by a single Walter M-332 piston engine with a pusher propeller installed above the fuselage. A special

Two views of an *ekranolyot* built in Oogol'nyy in the Soviet Far East (Primor'ye Region).

feature of the vehicle is its boat fuselage featuring chines shaped like skis, the space between them forming a sort of tunnel. The aircraft entered flight test on 12th January 1991 but crashed in its fifth flight, suffering serious damage, after which it was not repaired. Actual performance, including behaviour in ground effect, was not recorded, the design speed being 140 km/h (87 mph).

Blinov

In 1965 one Blinov, an employee of the Moscow Aviation Institute, evolved a concept of a cargo transport vehicle called 'Flying wing'. The amphibious design with a wingspan of 125 m (410 ft) was intended to transport a cargo of 550 t (1,200,000 lb) at a cruising speed of 400 km/h (249 mph) to a distance of 5,000 km (3,100 miles) at an altitude of 2,000 m (6,560 ft). Actually this was a seaplane making use of ground effect at take-off. Blinov noted that 'pockets' placed at the wingtips produced the surface effect reducing the take-off distance and the required engine power. To check the concept, several radio-controlled models were built and flight-tested.

A. Dvoinikov

In the 1970s a small, rather primitive WIG craft was built by A. Dvoinikov, a technician responsible for radio communication who was an employee of the Gor'kiy branch of Alekseyev's CHDB. The craft was entirely unlike any of the CDHB projects. Built mostly of plywood, it consisted of a wing with a forward sweep on the leading edges, with a light truss on top which carried the vertical tail at its aft end. Mounted at the extended forward end of the truss was a Vikhr'-M outboard motor modified to drive an airscrew. Dvoinikov, sitting astride the truss, made numerous rides on his mount, both above the water in summer and above the frozen water surface in winter, at a speed of some 100 km/h (62 mph). He used this craft for his private needs for several years until the wooden machine finally broke up due to rotting. Then he built a copy of it, this time of metal construction, and used it for a further several years. Dvoinikov was a talented person who experimented on his own with models of WIG craft featuring all sorts of configurations.

'Ekranolyot' from the Far East

In 1974 enthusiast aircraft designers from the Oogol'nyy township in the Far-Eastern Primor'ye region built an ultra-light single-seat WIG vehicle dubbed 'Ekranolyot' (a proper name, in this case). This was a typical 'home-built' job, no aviation materials, good production facilities or a really suitable engine being available. The vehicle of wooden construction featured the Lippisch configuration. Ailerons were carried by winglets set at an angle to the main wing. The T-tail featured strut-braced stabilisers. The bare airframe (less canvas skinning) weighed 350 kg (771 lb). The vehicle was powered by a 10-hp PD-10 two-stroke engine normally used as a starter for heavy tractor diesels. During tests in 1975 the machine proved to be sensitive at the controls, which was detrimental to stability in flight.

V. I. Getmantsev

Vyacheslav Getmantsev, an enthusiast inventor with a predilection for hydroplane design, developed several projects of winged water-based craft intended to combine the flight in ground effect with the use of water propeller as a means of propulsion. This means that the altitude of flight is limited by the length of the forward-located pylon carrying the water propeller, and will vary from 0.5 to 1.0 m (1.5 to 3 ft). The submerged nose pylon is to be provided with a hydrofoil whose lift will off-load 15-20% of the vehicle's weight; the rest is to be supported by the aft-mounted wings. Getmantsev built a small proof-of-concept boat and prepared preliminary projects of two much larger vehicles intended for tourism and other duties; he is advertising them in the hope of attracting investors for the purpose of implementing these projects.

Getmantsev's single-seat WIG at rest, showing the strong wing dihedral.

R. N. Kolokol'tsev

In the 1980s this enthusiast designer, a resident of Leningrad (now St. Petersburg), designed, built and tested two single-seat WIG craft (see photos).

Leonid Mironov

In 2008 L. Mironov, an employee of the Irkutsk aircraft plant (IAPO), designed a small WIG craft featuring a canard layout. The five-seat vehicle was to be powered by an automobile engine and was expected to attain a speed of 150 km/h (93 mph). According to Mironov, the cabin with its interior could well be taken straight from a rear-wheel-drive Lada (a Russian car tracing its origins to the Fiat 124 – *Auth.*).

V. F. Plotnikov and A. I. Osipov

In 1977 V. F. Plotnikov, senior engineer of Military Unit 13132, together with his colleague A. I. Osipov prepared a preliminary project of an amphibious WIG craft. He classed his project as an invention – 'a WIG vehicle featuring a basically new aerohydrodynamic layout' – and received Russian patent No. 144571 for it. The project was named ***Oplot*** (stronghold) – an obvious phonetic allusion to the author's surname. The WIG craft proposed by Plotnikov features a canard layout and swept-forward wings. The wings are fitted with slotted Fowler flaps on the trailing edge; the flaps are provided with 'hydrodampers' (Plotnikov's term, literally translated – *Auth.*) for absorbing the shocks from the wave crests. The fuselage shaped as a boat hull has a step located well aft. To facilitate the take-off, the hull's bottom is 'lubricated' by air bled from an engine's compressor. Take-off devices include aerodynamic/gas-dynamic vanes which make it possible to change the thrust vector of the turbojets for the purpose of directing the efflux under the wings and obtaining the control forces required for steering the vehicle.

The powerplant comprises four turbojets with thrust reversers. The engines are mounted high above the fuselage on the foreplane which rests on canted vertical surfaces incorporating rudders. In one of the versions the foreplane is unswept, in another one is swept back. In addition to the nose-mounted fins and rudders, directional control is effected with the help of rudders forming part of canted wing endplates (absent in some of the drawings). The canted endplates represent, in fact, a sort of butterfly tail, the rudders also acting as elevons. This layout, in the opinion of the designers, would enable the vehicle to make turns in ground-effect flight close to the sea surface without the need for banking. Provision is made for a retractable undercarriage enabling the craft to land on ground. The designers planned to provide the vehicle with an ejection capsule as a means of crew rescue.

An artist's impression of a racing hydroplane with WIG properties developed by Getmantsev. The water propeller is mounted on a strut at the bows.

The project of the Oplot WIG craft formed the basis of V. F. Plotnikov's thesis entitled 'Refinement of the aerodynamic layout and problems of development of modern WIG vehicles'. The thesis was defended at KAI (the Kazan' Aviation Institute, now the Kazan' State Technical University). Due to the absence of wind tunnel tests the thesis was deemed to be only 'a project proposal'.

In 2001 Plotnikov and Osipov published a book describing their project. In this book they say nothing about the roles envisaged for their WIG craft; its external appearance gives no clue either. A single-

Above: The MKh-2 Bahbochka (Butterfly) homebuilt WIG vehicle designed and built by R. N. Kolokol'tsev. A curious aspect of the design is the inverted-Vee ('butterfly') tail which probably accounts for the name.

Another one of Kolokol'tsev's WIG endeavours – the MBB. Note the skid landing gear which is due to the fact that the vehicle was tested from the frozen surface of the Gulf of Finland.

seat cockpit might point to some military applications, but the drawings do not show any weapon installations.

K. B. Popov

K. B. Popov was one of A. N. Panchenkov's associates from the period of his work in Irkutsk. After Panchenkov's departure from Irkutsk Popov embarked on a project of a three-seat *ekranoplan* designated Baikal-2, relying on the assistance from Nikolaus Gross, a wealthy German businessman. In 1993 Gross started financing the work on the Baikal-2, but withdrew from the project some time later. Still, K. B. Popov and his friend I. N. Gusev succeeded in completing the machine powered by a Rotax-912 piston engine. It entered the initial test phase on water and on ice, but the lack of funding did not permit to conduct a full-scale test programme. The machine was placed in storage.

Aleksey I. P'yetsukh

In 1967 Aleksey I. P'yetsukh, a former test pilot and a combat pilot during the war, designed and built the PAI-67 WIG vehicle. The machine had two sets of wings arranged in tandem, the main wings having a diamond-shaped planform. The lifting surfaces were spaced in height and featured anhedral. The vehicle was powered by a 20-hp Vikhr' outboard motor retaining its water propeller. To reduce the unstick speed at take-off, the vehicle was provided with hydrofoils which in cruise flight were lifted to a height of 10cm above the water. Directional control was effected by water rudders mounted on the pylons of the rear hydrofoil. A large-area lifting steerable stabiliser was fitted. Roll control was effected by differential deflection of port and starboard elevator halves. The water displacing hull housed an enclosed cockpit in its centre section and tapered off aft of the cockpit into a fin and a large-sized rudder. A. I. Pyetsukh himself tested the PAI-67 at the Khimki Reservoir near Moscow. The vehicle lifted itself out of the water in 12 to 15 seconds and developed a speed of 60 km/h (37 mph), far superior to the speed of boats with the same engine.

Vladimir Sedykh

In 2003 Vladimir Sedykh, a resident of the town of Bratsk in the Irkutsk Region of East Siberia, built a small WIG craft featuring the classical Lippisch layout. Dubbed Skat (Ray, a marine animal), it had a boat hull fuselage with a T-tail and was powered by a small engine mounted above the hull and driving a pusher propeller. The craft was tested on skis from a snow-covered surface and on water.

V. Sereda

This enthusiast of WIG vehicles has built several radio-controlled models of *ekranoplans* which he uses for testing his ideas concerning a rational design of light WIG vehicles. He has developed several preliminary projects of such vehicles in the A and C classes, some of which (the A-type machines) combine the features of ACV and WIG craft. For example, a five-seat vehicle dubbed Sigma Proxi (*sic*), powered by a 160-hp engine, has a design cruise speed of 140-160 km/h (87-99 mph) and can travel in ground effect at an altitude of 0.3

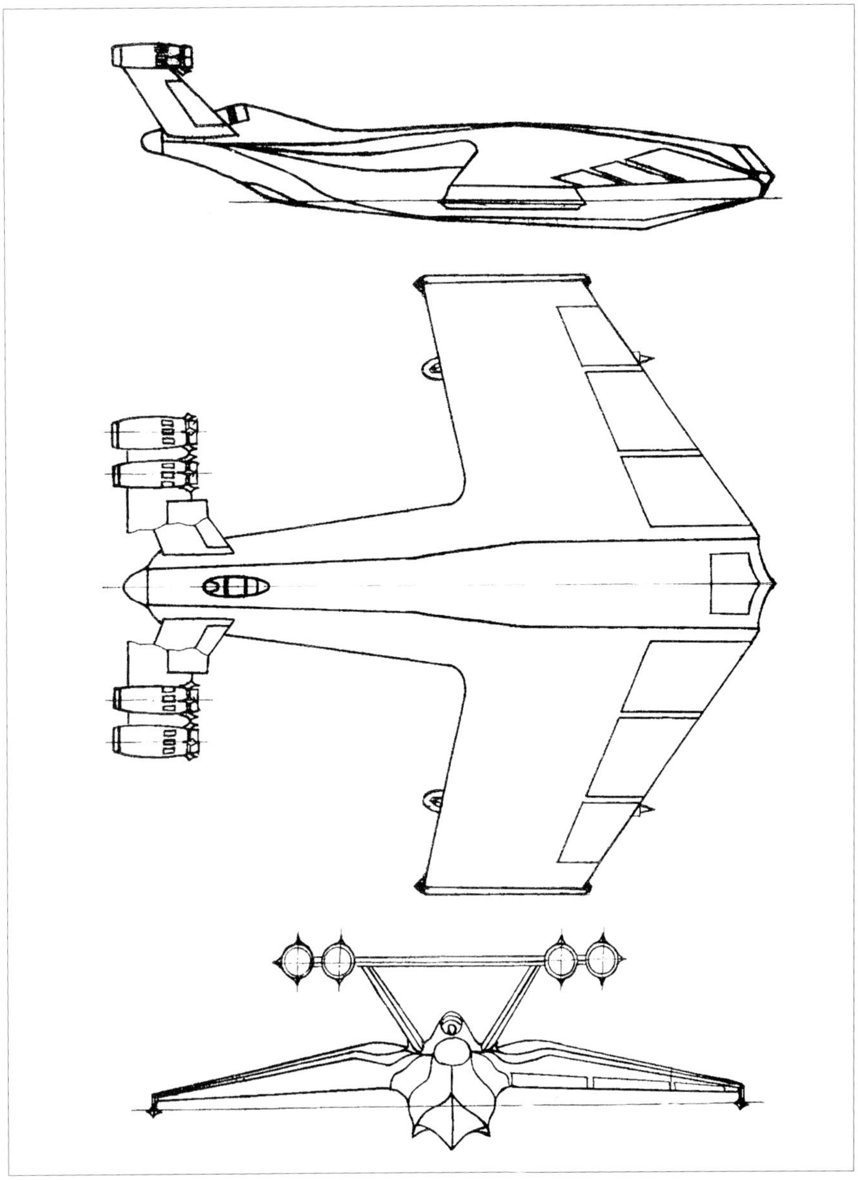

A provisional three-view of a heavy WIG designed by Plotnikov and Osipov.

The Baikal-2 WIG developed by K. B. Popov

The Skat *ekranolyot* designed by V. Sedykh. Note the open cockpit access door.

This series of pictures shows the Skat during flight tests on the Irtysh River.

– 1.2 m (1-4 ft) above the supporting surface. It combines the static air cushion produced by injecting a part of the propeller wash into the space under the hull and the lift created by stub wings at close proximity to the surface.

A provisional drawing of the Sigma Proxi WIG vehicle.

A slightly larger vehicle, called Sigma Proxima, uses an aft-mounted pusher powerplant. Class C vehicles designated Sigma-E and Sigma-J are based on the Lippisch layout with a difference: in addition to the reversed-delta wing centre section, they feature sufficiently large outer wing panels enhancing their flying qualities in the out-of-ground effect mode.

N. I. Stoyano

In 1975-1980 N. I. Stoyano, a resident of the town of Mytischi (Moscow Region), designed and built an ekranolyot called Ayans-86 (the meaning of the name remains obscure). The vehicle had two sets of wings arranged in tandem and measuring 3.6 m (11 ft 10 in) in span. The wings were joined together by floats at their tips. The 140-hp Walter Minor engine with a pusher propeller was placed behind a two-seat enclosed cockpit. The tail unit comprised a fin-and-rudder assembly and a stabiliser with an elevator. The vehicle was tested in 1985. When flown from the water it failed to reach the design speed due to the unsatisfactory hydrodynamic shape of the floats. In tests on snow with a ski undercarriage it showed a top speed of 150 km/h (93 mph). The all-up weight of the rather heavy machine was 1,100 kg (2,425 lb).

P. G. Tkachenko

In 2002 P. G. Tkachenko and Yuriy Makarov, aviation specialists known for their work in student design bureaux, were working in Moscow on a project of a small two-seat WIG vehicle basically repeating the Lippisch layout. The distinctive feature of the design was the use of the powerplant (a small piston engine driving a shrouded pusher propeller) for creating a static air cushion under the boat hull. For this purpose the engine was mounted behind the cockpit in such a way that the lower part of the propeller rotation plane was 'sunk' into the fuselage and the air flow from the propeller was driven through a slot into the space under the hull.

P. Tsymbalyuk

A group of enthusiasts in Arkhangelsk headed by P. Tsymbalyuk designed and built a vehicle called 'Ekranolyot' (again!). In this case, too, the Lippisch layout was used, with a reversed-delta wing having anhedral on the leading edges and supplemented with aileron-carrying winglets. The tail unit included all-movable strut-braced stabilisers placed atop the fin. Floats were attached under the wingtips. A 105-hp M-332 engine was mounted on a truss cabane above the wing centre section; it drove a standard propeller but with cropped blades, which resulted in a substantial loss of thrust. The boat hull was strengthened with glassfibre. The vehicle was tested in 1977, reaching a speed of more than 60 km/h (37 mph) on water and up to 80 km/h (50 mph) on ice.

I. Vorontsov

In 1977-1978 in the city of Perm' a group led by I. I. Vorontsov designed and built an ekranolyot named

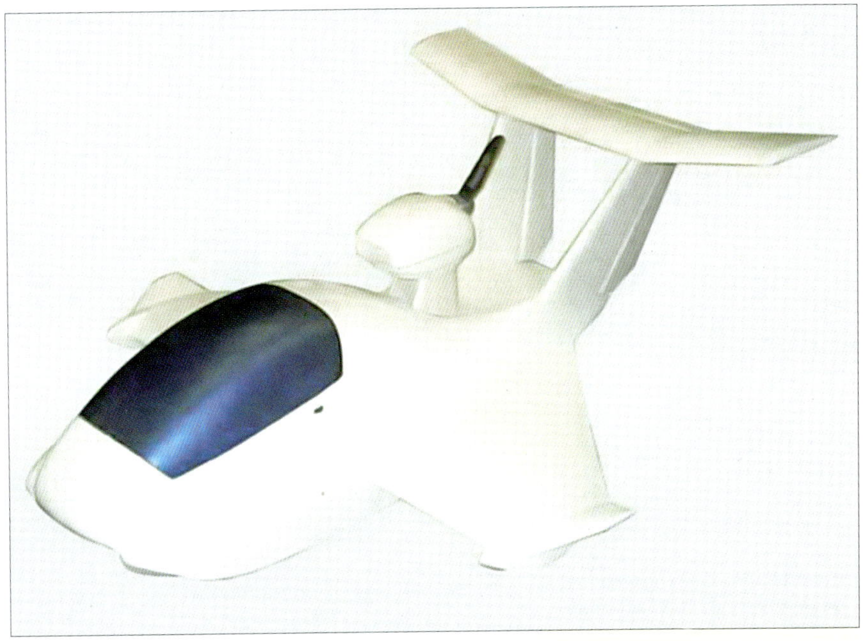

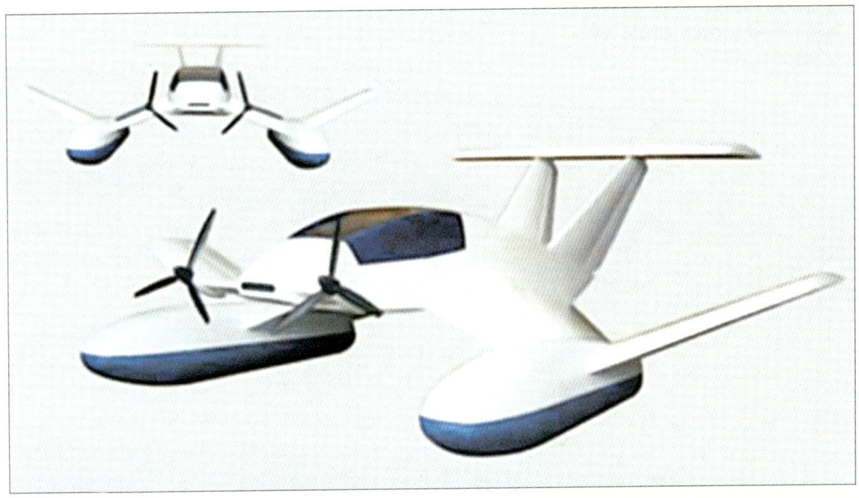

A model of the slightly larger Sigma Proxima.

A computer-generated image of the Sigma-E. The propellers are driven by a single engine via extension shafts.

An artist' impression of the Sigma-J. Note the nose-mounted prop wash deflector vanes.

A model of an ekranoplan designed by P. G. Tkachenko. Note how part of the prop wash is directed under the vehicle to form a static air cushion.

Elektron. It was of wooden construction and had a configuration similar to that of the TsLST ESKA-1. The vehicle was powered by a 32-hp engine from a Ural motorcycle driving a wooden propeller of 1.7 m (5 ft 7 in) in diameter through reduction gear. Initially it was powered by an engine from a Czech-built CZ motorcycle (pronounced 'chezet'), but its output proved insufficient for a vehicle weighing 400 kg (880 lb).

In March 1979 the ekranolyot was flight-tested, making take-offs and landings on snow. Tests revealed good stability.

P. P. Yablonskiy

In 1985 P. P. Yablonskiy, then a student of the Zhukovskiy Military Engineering Air Academy, submitted a graduation project of a transport WIG vehicle. It had two fuselages joined together by a low-aspect-ratio wing centre section. To reduce the outward air flow from beneath the wing centre section, strakes were fitted to the underside of the fuselages in the area of the wings. A high-set horizontal tail was used. Wind-tunnel tests simulating the ground effect were conducted with models. Test results corroborated the design characteristics of the WIG vehicle.

A computer-generated image of the Manta WIG designed by A. Yukayev.

Nikolay V. Yakubovich

A design belonging to Nikolay V. Yakubovich is mentioned in his article Between two elements published in the July 1998 issue of the *Kryl'ya Rodiny* magazine: *'In 1975 this author submitted a project of a transport WIG vehicle intended for transporting cargoes of up to 365 t to a distance of up to 9,000 km [5,590 miles] at a cruising speed of 410 km/h [254 mph]. It featured a wing centre section with an aspect ratio of 0.5, flanked by boats of a planoconvex shape ./…/ When the vehicle was loaded, special elastic floats were inflated on the sides. /…/ To create an air cushion, a stream of air from turbofan installations was pumped into the cavity formed by the underside of the wing centre section, and the front and rear flaps. As the cruise engines accelerated the vehicle, the front flap was retracted and a transition from the static to the dynamic air cushion took place. The powerplant consisted of two high-output NK-12 turboprops'.*

Al. Yukayev

This enthusiast designer has put forward a project of a 10-seat passenger WIG vehicle dubbed Manta (that is, the manta ray). The vehicle weighing up to 19 tonnes (41,890 lb) in flight configuration has a length of 21 m (68 ft 11 in) and a wing span (including the endplate floats) of 18 m (59 ft). It is a vehicle in the C class, capable of free flight at altitude in addition to the flight in ground effect. Its performance includes an economical cruising speed of 180 km/h (112 mph) in ground effect. The designer claims that fuel consumption in this mode will be 7-8 times smaller in comparison with a yacht with similar dimensions and payload. In free flight at altitudes up to 5,000 m (16,400 ft) the vehicle is expected to attain a cruising speed of nearly 500 km/h (310 mph) at the cost of much greater fuel consumption.

CHAPTER SIX

FREE ENTERPRISE

ENTER NEW COMPANIES

The beginning of the 1990s was characterised by the break-up of the Soviet Union. It gave place to the Russian Federation and new independent states, former Soviet Republics which, together with Russia, formed the Commonwealth of Independent States (CIS). The construction of WIG vehicles as a branch remained virtually 100% within the boundaries of the Russian Federation (apart from Russia, only the Ukraine could boast some scientific work in this field during the Soviet period).

Sweeping market reforms giving full reign to private enterprise in the Russian economy had their effect on the situation also in the aircraft industry and associated branches. Unfortunately, the consequences were mostly on the negative side. The drastic reduction of state funding and of state orders placed many enterprises on the brink of bankruptcy and severely curtailed the scope of their activities. In these circumstances the WIG craft design and construction could hardly be a matter of priority.

The early 1990s saw the emergence of a large number of private companies (design bureaux) which declared their intention to engage in aircraft design. Among these were several firms whose plans encompassed the design and construction of WIG vehicles. These were small enterprises which, as a rule, had no production facilities of their own and possessed very limited financial resources. Their activities only rarely resulted in producing real hardware even in prototype form, to say nothing of series production. However, they produced a number of 'paper designs' which merit some attention because of their innovative spirit.

In addition to new private enterprises, this chapter will touch upon the activities of two design bureaux, whose activities in the field of ekranoplans date back to the Soviet period – simply because they do not merit a separate chapter.

As mentioned in the Introduction, the late 1980s and early 1990s saw a gradual disintegration of the Alekseyev CHDB. Several groups of engineers, having abandoned this design bureau, set up nearly a dozen small companies which declared their intention to continue design work on transport means based on dynamic principles of sustentation. In actual fact, only a few of them remained true to *ekranoplans* – many of the new-born enterprises switched over to work on air cushion vehicles, a line of business that seemed more lucrative, or reverted to the construction of small hydrofoil boats (this was the case with Transall-AKS, for example).

Among the new companies engaged in the design of WIG vehicles only two can boast construction of prototypes intended for series production. These are the Amphibious Transport Technologies Joint-Stock Society (JSC) – initially known as Technology and Transport – and the KOMETEL JSC. Both of them subsequently underwent transformations and changes of name and affiliation. It stands to reason that the following review of designs produced by new firms should start with these two enterprises.

Amphibious Transport Technologies (ATT, Joint Stock Company)

(now a subsidiary of the ATTK – Arctic Trade and Transport Company)

This company was founded in 1992 in Nizhniy Novgorod under the name Technology and Transport (TET) JSC. It was formed by about 130 engineers who, until then, had worked in the Central Design Bureau of Hydrofoils named after Rostislav Ye. Alekseyev. Gradually the staff rose to about 200 employees. The new company was headed by D. N. Sinitsyn, with Aleksandr I. Maskalik as his deputy. The company declared its intention to pursue the design of WIG vehicles for civil duties, making use of some projects which were taken over from the CHDB (this caused a dispute over intellectual property rights which was eventually settled).

The basic problem of finding an investor was solved by establishing co-operation with a businessman from Taiwan who actually became the owner of the bulk of the company's stock. He financed the work on a WIG vehicle, but became the owner of the rights to the design and of all the machines produced, as well as of the right to sell them. In response to his order the newly formed design team embarked on the design of a small WIG boat named Passat (Tradewind); in 1996 it was renamed Amphistar

Amphistar

The Amphistar belongs to the category of small Type A WIG vehicles – high-speed craft intended for operation only within the height of ground effect, powered by an engine of more than 55 kW, carrying not more than 12 passengers, operated only in daytime within 20 miles from the coast and within 100 miles from a place of refuge, and having an all-up weight of not more than 10 t (22,045 lb). The five-seat Amphistar is intended for maritime

An all-white Amphistar moves along a snow-covered field, showing the two large side windows.

pleasure rides and tourism. It is a dynamic air cushion speedboat with an enclosed cabin, featuring a forward location of the engine.

Here are the main specifications and performance figures of the machine: overall length, 10.44 m (34 ft 3 in), overall width (wingspan), 5.9 m (19 ft $4\frac{9}{32}$ in); overall height, 3.35 m (10 ft $11\frac{57}{64}$ in); maximum all-up weight, 2,720 kg (6,000 lb); operating empty weight, 2,200 kg (4,850 lb); crew and equipment weight, 117 kg (258 lb); payload, 300 kg (660 lb); fuel load, 100 kg (220 lb). Range with 100 kg of fuel is 350-400 km (217-248 miles) depending on the weather (wind force, wave height). The vehicle is amphibious – it can negotiate shallow places, come out onto an unprepared bank with a gradient of up to 5°, move on the ground at speeds of 10-15 km/h (6.2-9.3 mph) and go back to the water. The airframe of the Amphistar is made of corrosion-proof composite materials.

The Amphistar's wing set of rectangular planform and low aspect ratio is fitted with flaps and provided with endplates in the shape of inflatable pontoons which ensure the vehicle's stability when afloat and form the sidewalls of the 'scoop' in which the air cushion is created (there is also a retractable inflatable support pontoon on the centreline). A compartment placed amidships in the hull accommodates four passengers and a driver. The aft bay of the hull houses equipment, while the forward part of the hull is occupied by a 300-hp Mercedes-Benz engine which transmits its torque through a central gearbox and two side gearboxes to two AV-110 tractor propellers with ground-adjustable pitch. The propellers can swivel their plane of rotation and direct the air stream under the wings for take-off.

The tail unit comprises twin fins and rudders mounted on the rear fuselage in a V arrangement, with the horizontal tail placed atop the fins. Directional control is effected by the rudders during movement in ground effect and by a retractable water rudder when afloat.

A more colourful example of the Amphistar. Note the curved 'bumper' (propeller guard), another distinctive feature of the early model, and the inflatable centreline pontoon.

Probably the same Amphistar is seen here travelling over water.

In 1997 the Amphistar was certified in the Russian Shipping Register in accordance with the IMO rules (adopted somewhat later) for type A vehicles designed for flying only in ground effect and regarded as boats for certification purposes. The ATT company prides itself on having obtained this certificate, which had required a lot of effort and entailed considerable expenses.

In all, 12 machines of the Passat/Amphistar type were built between 1992 and 1997. This machine was demonstrated in Düsseldorf in 1996 and 1997. At that time a Russian company called Pacific Technique Development handled the marketing of the machine.

Efforts were undertaken to promote sales of the Amphistar in North America. For this purpose a company named Amphistar USA Ltd was formed in 1998. This company began to market the machine in the USA under a new name – Xtreme Xplorer. Yet another company, Amphistar Bahamas Ltd, was established in 1999 to promote the vehicle in the Bahamas. Trial operation and demonstration flights of the Xtreme Xplorer were undertaken in the USA and in the Bahamas; they gave the machine much-needed publicity.

However, in April 2000 the project was closed down at the insistence of the Taiwanese partner who had lost his enthusiasm for the project. At his insistence the Amphistar vehicles belonging to him were withdrawn from operation and placed in storage. Amphistar USA Ltd ceased all activities.

After that Sinitsyn and his partners took out a patent on all designs developed after the Amphistar and now rely on their own resources in the production of prototypes.

Three years prior to that, in 1997, the Technology and Transport company had entered into co-operation with the Russian company named ATTK (*Ark**tich**eskaya tor**govo**-**trahns**portnaya kom**pah**niya* – Arctic Trade and Transport Co.) which is engaged in transportation of goods into regions of the Russian Far North. The ATTK undertook the marketing of TET designs and funding of the design team's work. Practically, since 2000 the ATTK has been acting as financial sponsor for this design team based at Nizhniy Novgorod which in that year changed its name to Amphibious Transport Technologies JSC (ATT). The leader of ATTK Ruben Nagapetyan had become an enthusiast of the idea of using ekranoplans as a transport means in northern areas and made substantial investments into the ATT company. By April 2003 ATTK acquired a production and test facility for the manufacture of *ekranoplans* in the Nizhniy Novgorod (formerly Gor'kiy) Region. The company bought the former branch of Alekseyev's CHDB in Chkalovsk and started its reconstruction.

An Amphistar in cruise mode. Apart from the twin fins and powerplant arrangement, the vehicle is similar to the larger Volga-2.

Aquaglide series of WIG vehicles

The ATT company turned a new page by introducing the Aquaglide programme replacing the

This overhead view of two Amphistars shows the narrow fuselage, short wing span and raked stabiliser tips. Note that the red and black markings on the right-hand example form the letter X (signifying the US marketing name Xtreme Xplorer).

Two views of the prototype Aquaglide-5, an updated version of the Amphistar, showing the additional roof pillars (there are four windows per side instead of two).

The Aquaglide 5 afloat. Note the lack of the 'bumper' at the front; instead, small L-shaped guards are attached directly to the propeller reduction gear housings.

defunct Amphistar programme. The new programme includes the Aquaglide 5 WIG speedboat and a project of a multi-seat passenger WIG craft designated Aquaglide 50 (the two machines have a seating capacity for 5 and 48 passengers respectively). There are also other designs in this series.

Aquaglide 5

The Aquaglide 5 is a somewhat reworked Amphistar. The changes include introducing four smaller windows instead of two large ones on each side of the passenger cabin (which makes the hull more rigid). The front parts of the pontoons have been shortened, and a protective bar ahead of the propellers has been deleted. In 2002 one example of the Aquaglide 5 was built and another was under construction; the machine was ready for series production which depended on finding a customer that would be prepared to make a financial contribution to the project. In the autumn of 2002 ATTK reportedly received the first ten orders for the Aquaglide 5: China and Malaysia ordered three machines each, the remaining four being destined for Italy. However, there is no confirmation of the orders having been fulfilled.

In 2008 Ruben Nagapetyan told a journalist that ATTK did not intend to organise the manufacture of the whole range of subassemblies of the Aquaglide 5 at its own facilities – it would be engaged primarily in the final assembly, relying heavily on outsourcing and letting its partners produce various units of the craft. He also stressed that ATTK could not fund all its programmes on its own and was badly in need of partners and investors.

Here are the specifications and performance figures for the Aquaglide 5.

Specifications of the Aquaglide 5

Length, m (ft)	10.7 (35)
Width, m (ft)	5.9 (19)
Height, m(ft)	3.4 (11)
Displacement, t (lb)	2.4 (5,290)
Seating capacity, persons	5
Cruising speed, km/h (mph)	150 (93)
Range, km (miles)	up to 400 (248)
Seaworthiness, wave height m (ft)	0.35 (1)

Since 1997 the ATT company, along with the passenger craft of the Aquaglide series, has been working on a series of vehicles of various sizes, initially known under the common designation TAP (***trahns**portno-amfi**biy**naya plat**for**ma* – transport amphibious platform) which are intended for transporting cargo in the regions of the Far North. (Apparently there is some kinship between these projects and the TAP projects developed by the Alekseyev CHDB.)

These vehicles, now bearing designations in the Aquaglide range, look like elongated flat platforms flanked along the whole of their length by endplate floats. Placed in the front part of the platform is the enclosed crew workstation (cockpit). Most of the flat upper surface of the platform is used for open carriage of various cargoes. Since the upper surface of the platform is not shaped like an airfoil section, the lift during cruise is created solely by the dynamic air cushion created by ram air in the cavity which is formed by the bottom of the platform and the floats.

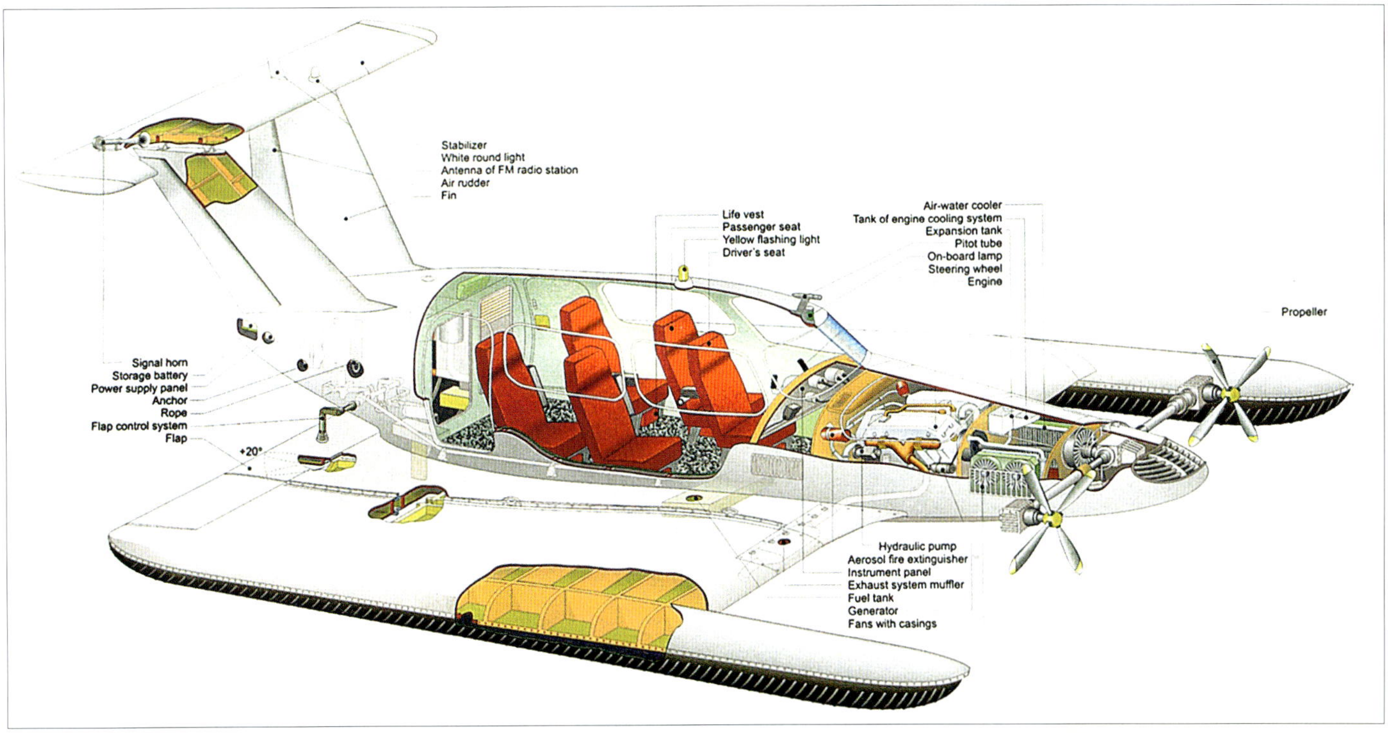

A cutaway drawing of the Aquaglide 5.

Two views of the Aquaglide 5 on display at the ILA-2006 airshow in Berlin-Schönefeld with ground handling wheels attached. The craft was shown alongside an IL-76TD transport aircraft and an MBB Bö 105CBS-5SF-SAR helicopter belonging to EMERCOM of Russia, implying possible future use by this civil aid agency.

The instrument panel and control wheel of the Aquaglide 5.

In the Aquaglide 5 the driver sits on the centreline.

The cabin is fitted out with four comfortable passenger seats. Life vests are stowed under the seats.

Here, the door leading into the baggage compartment is visible at the back of the cabin.

The powerplant of these vehicles comprises four turbojets arranged in tandem pairs in each float. While the aft-positioned engines act as cruise engines only, the front engines are mounted back to front, discharging their jet exhaust through special ducts beneath the bottom of the platform, thus creating static air cushion at take-off and landing. The platforms are amenable to producing derivatives with enclosed accommodation for the carriage of cargo or passengers – they have simply to be 'crowned' with a suitably shaped superstructure. All of these craft belong to the A category in the IMO classification.

Rear view of the Aquaglide 5 seen at one of the Hydro Aviation Shows in Ghelendzhik.

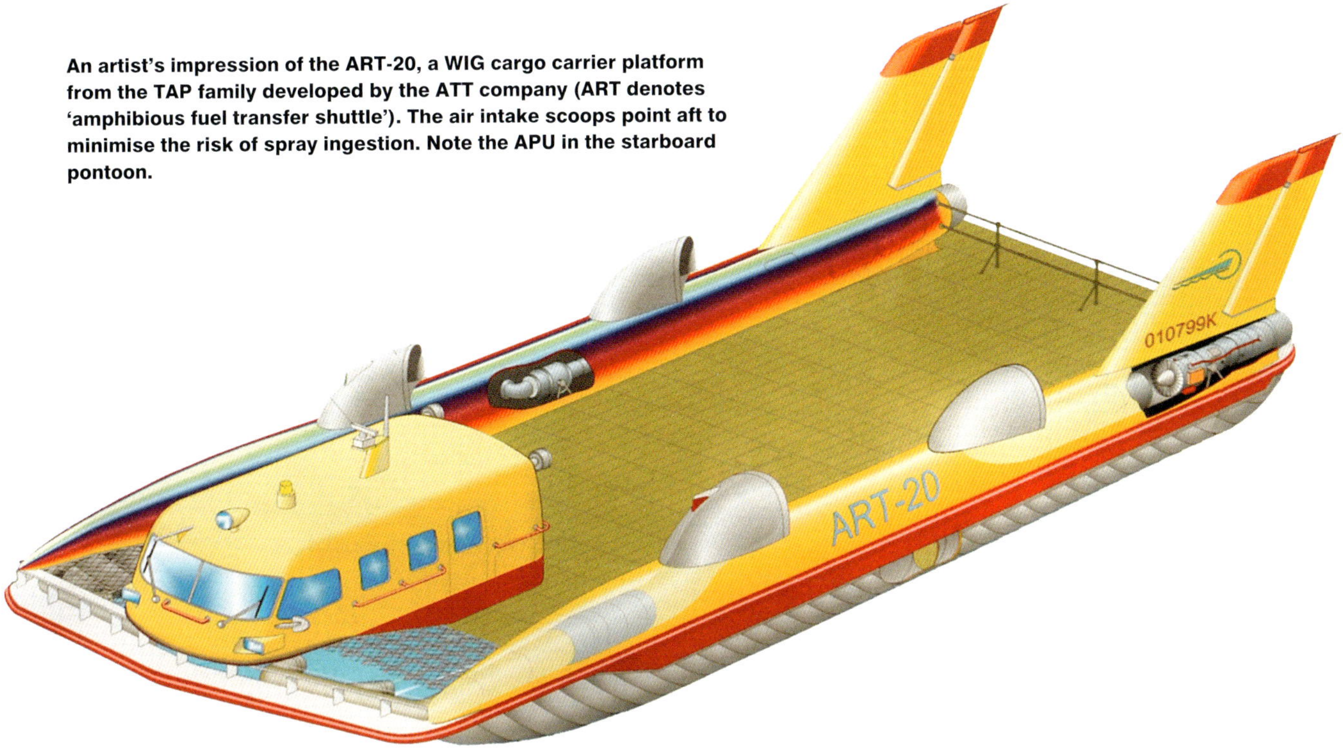

An artist's impression of the ART-20, a WIG cargo carrier platform from the TAP family developed by the ATT company (ART denotes 'amphibious fuel transfer shuttle'). The air intake scoops point aft to minimise the risk of spray ingestion. Note the APU in the starboard pontoon.

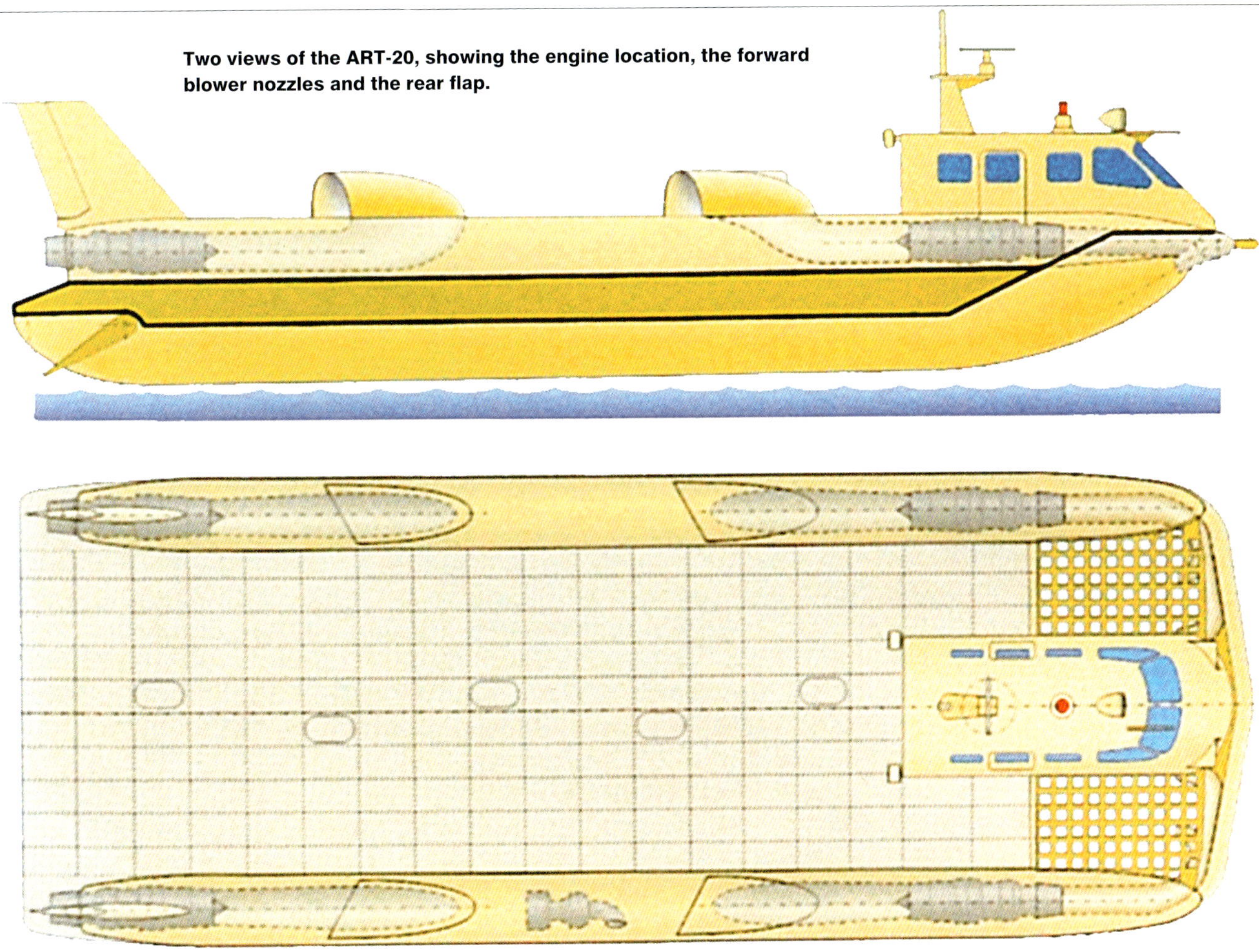

Two views of the ART-20, showing the engine location, the forward blower nozzles and the rear flap.

The logo of ATT (Amphibious Transport Technologies JSC)

The logo of the ATTK (Arctic Trade & Transport Co.)

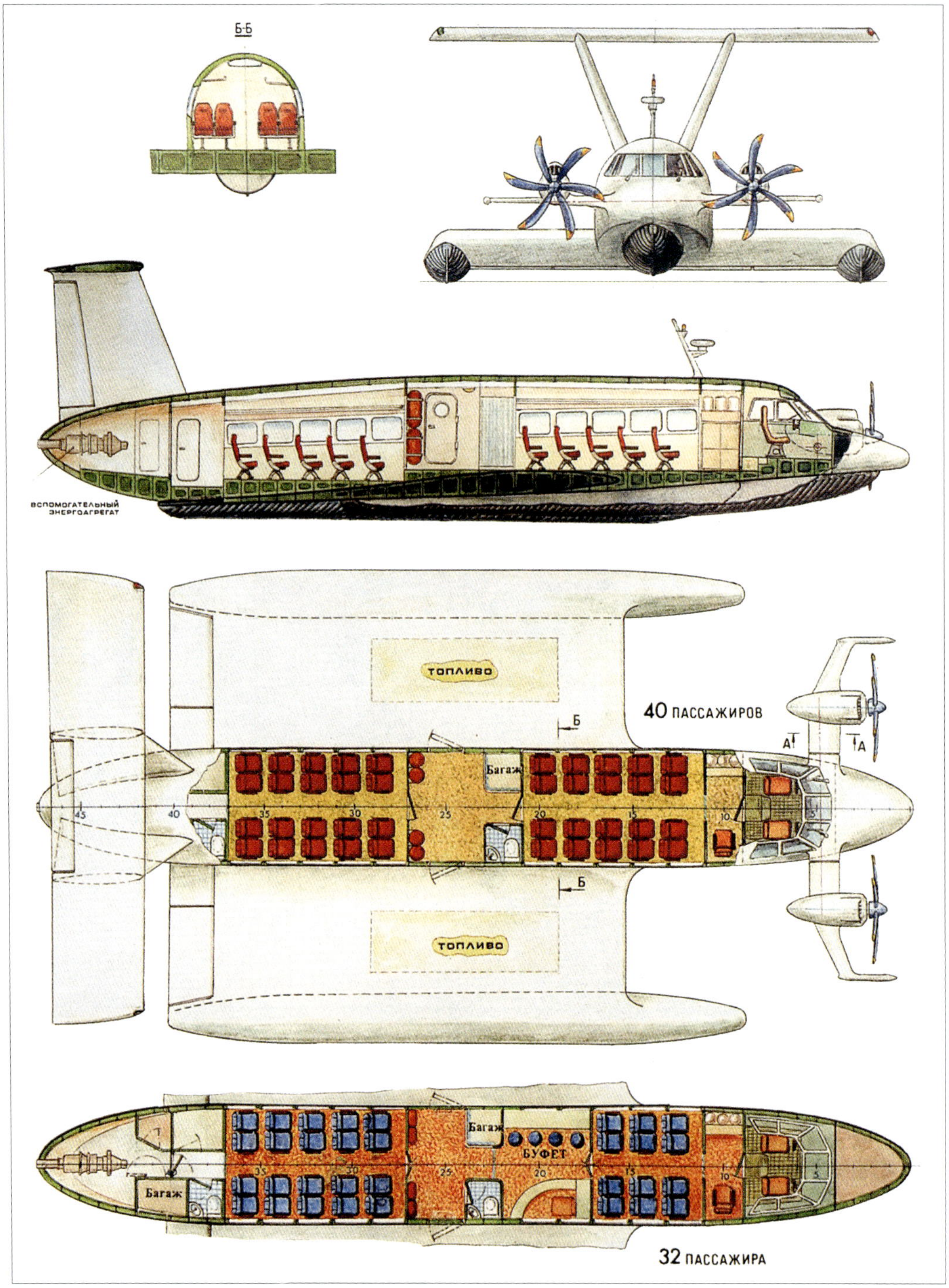

A cutaway drawing of the Aquaglide 40 in a 40-seat layout, with an additional view of a 32-seat configuration with a galley/buffet amidships.

An artist's impression of the Aquaglide 40 in ATTK colours.

Listed below are the current projects in the Aquaglide range.

Aquaglide-20F (ART-20)

The Aquaglide-20F represents a vehicle in the class of ships on a dynamic air cushion and is roughly equivalent to the Class A WIG vehicles because it makes use of ground effect in close proximity to the supporting surface and always retains contact with the surface. The dynamic air cushion greatly reduces the craft's pressure on the supporting surface. The craft is designed as a platform intended for the delivery of cargoes, which are accommo-

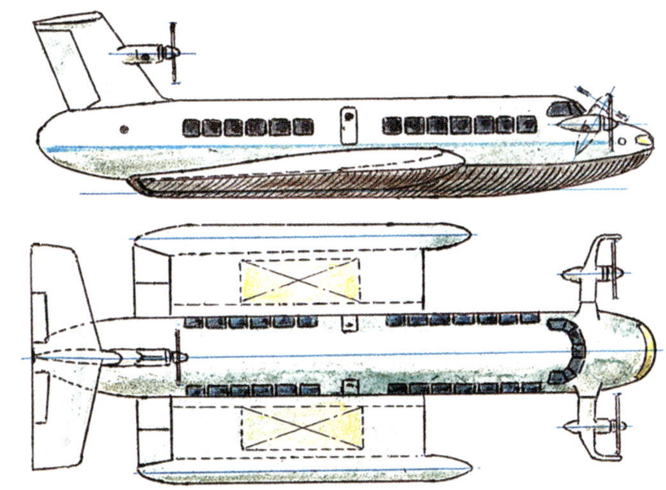

A three-view drawing of the projected Aquaglide-50 with the forward engines in take-off and cruise positions

dated on an open deck, from a ship to a pier and vice versa. The powerplant comprises four 1,500-kgp (3,310-lbst) Ivchenko AI-25 turbofans installed in pairs on each side of the platform. The Aquaglide-20F has a displacement of 20-23 tonnes (44,100-50,710 lb) and is capable of transporting a cargo with a total weight of 7-10 tonnes (15,430-22,050 lb). Its cruising speed is 90 km/h (56 mph) on water and 65 km/h (40 mph) at a height of 1 m (3 ft). This vehicle was previously designated ART-20 (*amfi**beey**nyy razgroozchik* ***top**liva*, amphibious fuel offloader) because it was intended for delivering fuel from a tanker to the shore, while being able to handle other types of cargo.

Aquaglide-30

This is a project of a passenger WIG vehicle. With 28 passengers on board, it will be able to develop a maximum speed of 200-220 km/h (124-137 mph) and cover a distance of nearly 700 km (435 miles) without refuelling. According to R. Nagapetyan, ATTK was going to seek a strategic investor willing to spend 20 million euro for the purpose of implementing this project.

The vehicle resembles a scaled-up Aquaglide 5, featuring the same kind of twin-fin tail unit with a horizontal stabiliser atop the fins and a low-set wing with endplate floats at the wingtips. However, the dimensions of the wings and the fuselage are

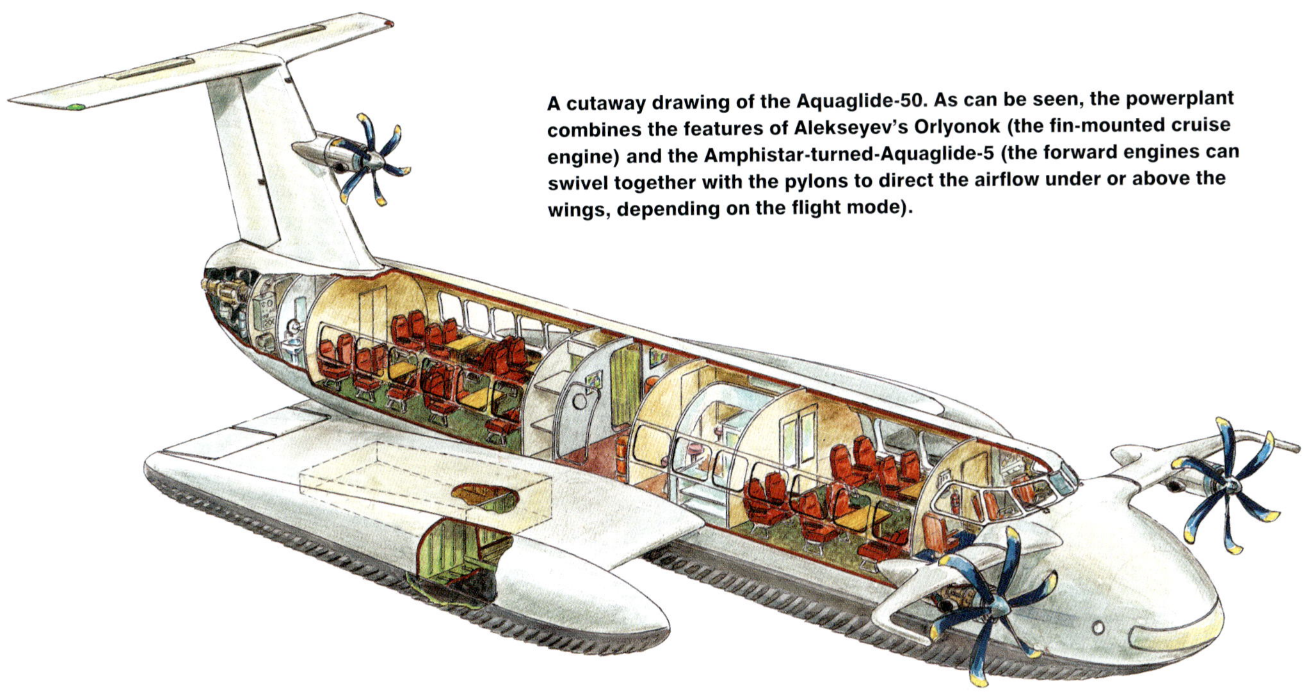

A cutaway drawing of the Aquaglide-50. As can be seen, the powerplant combines the features of Alekseyev's Orlyonok (the fin-mounted cruise engine) and the Amphistar-turned-Aquaglide-5 (the forward engines can swivel together with the pylons to direct the airflow under or above the wings, depending on the flight mode).

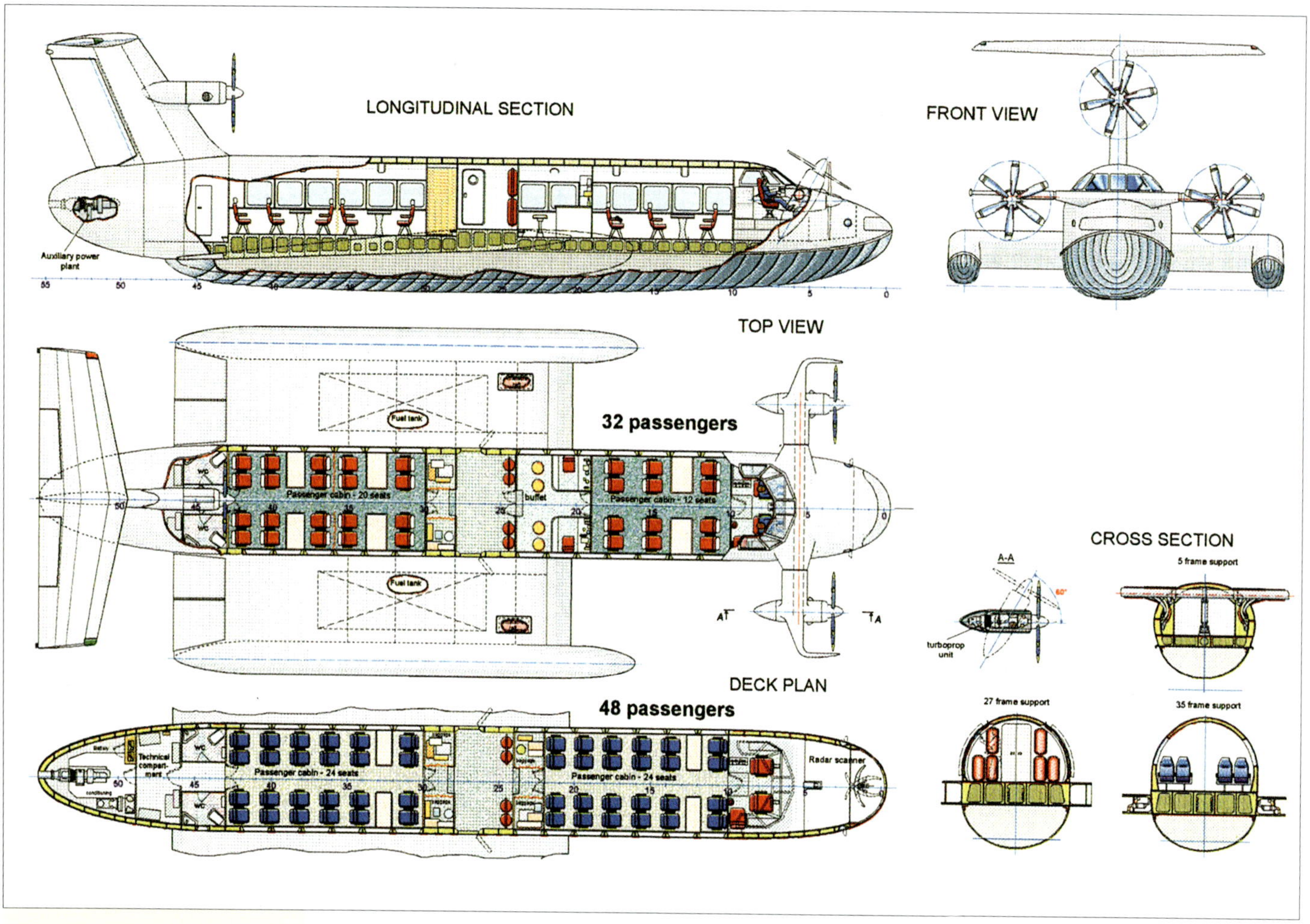

A cutaway drawing of the Aquaglide 50. The main drawing shows a 32-seat layout with a galley, with an additional view of a 48-seat version.

appropriately increased. The powerplant comprises two engines, presumably turboprops, with an aggregate output of 2,400 hp for take-off. The engines are mounted on pylons on both sides of the front fuselage.

Aquaglide-40

The Aquaglide-40 represents a further development of the concept embodied in the previous design. It follows closely the layout of the Aquaglide 30, with suitably increased dimensions to provide accommodation for 40 passengers in the maximum seating capacity arrangement. Passengers are accommodated in two compartments, each having 20 seats. Apart from a toilet and a baggage hold, there are no special amenities. A cabin arrangement for 32 passengers differs in having two rows of seats in the forward compartment deleted. The space thereby saved is used to arrange a galley with seats for four persons. In a fashion similar to the Aquaglide-30, the engines are mounted on swivelling horizontal pylons flanking the forward fuselage; in this case the six-blade propellers with scimitar-shaped blades are provided with guards on the outboard side. The rear fuselage section aft of the passenger compartment houses an extra baggage hold, a second toilet and an APU. The two fuel tanks are accommodated in the wing panels.

Aquaglide-50

This is a project of a passenger WIG craft in Class A, designed to carry 32-48 passengers. The vehicle's notable feature is the absence of an elevator; at the same time the machine is inherently stable as regards the altitude, pitch and roll. The altitude of cruise flight in ground effect is 1 m (3 ft) above the water surface.

The vehicle is powered by three Allison turboprops with six-blade propellers, two of which are mounted on outriggers on the forward fuselage sides ahead of the wings and slightly above them; they can be tilted 60° nose-up to direct the prop wash into the space under the wings during take-off. The third engine, solely for cruise propulsion, is mounted on the fin leading edge, about half-way up. The multi-spar low-aspect-ratio wings have endplates resembling seaplane floats in cross section. The lower part of the endplates is manufactured of a soft material and absorbs shocks when coming into contact with the water surface, in addition to providing buoyancy. The craft has a T-tail. The vehicle's structure is made of aluminium and glass fibre. Directional control in

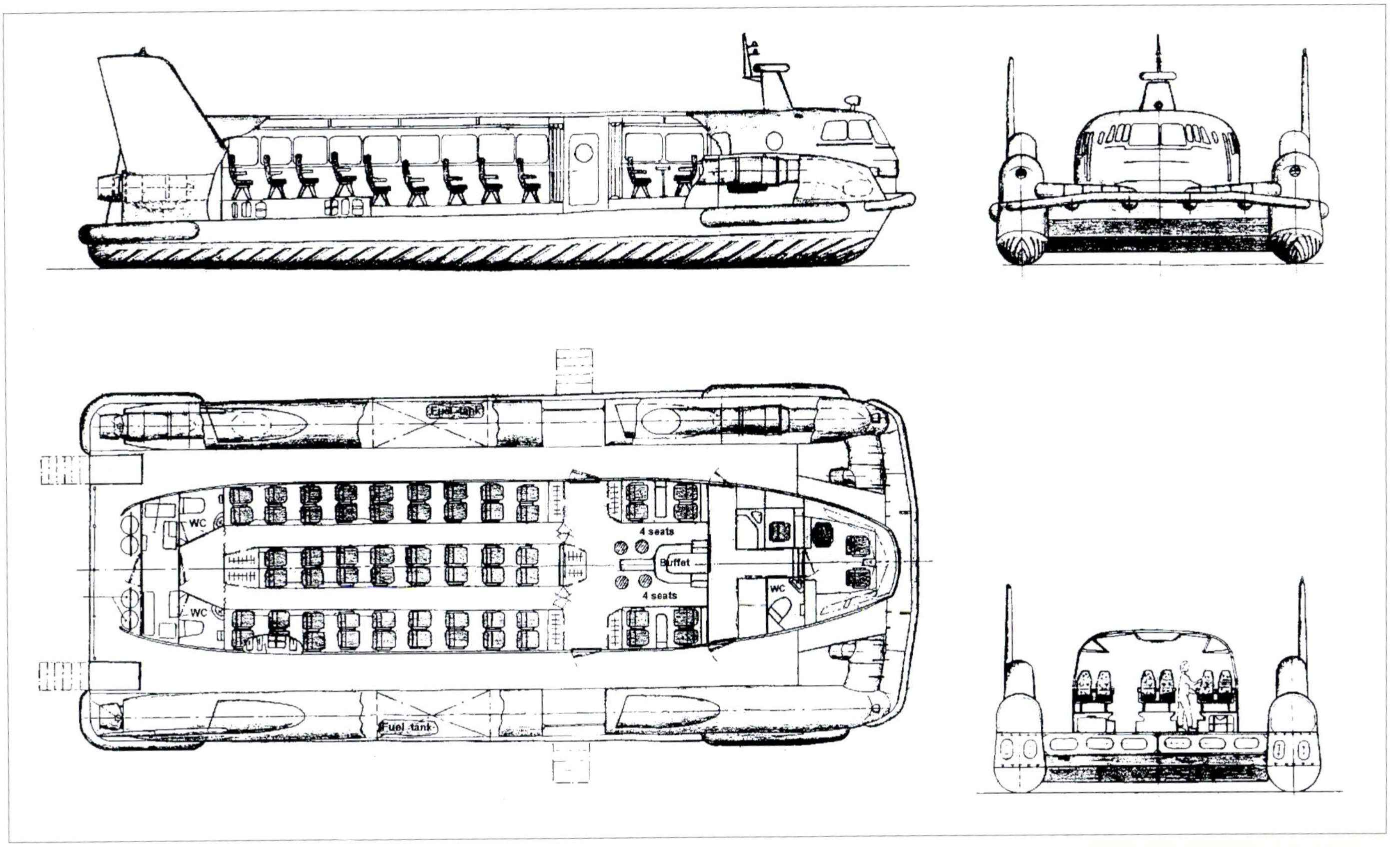

flight is effected with the help of an aircraft-type rudder. During low-speed movement on the water a retractable water rudder is used, in addition to the differential pitch of the Nos. 1 and 3 propellers.

Aquaglide-60

This designation covers a family of Class A transport WIG vehicles intended to carry 60 passengers or 10 tonnes (32,800 lb) of cargo at a speed of

Cutaway drawings of the passenger-configured Aquaglide 60 (above) and the Aquaglide 60F combi version with minimum seating.

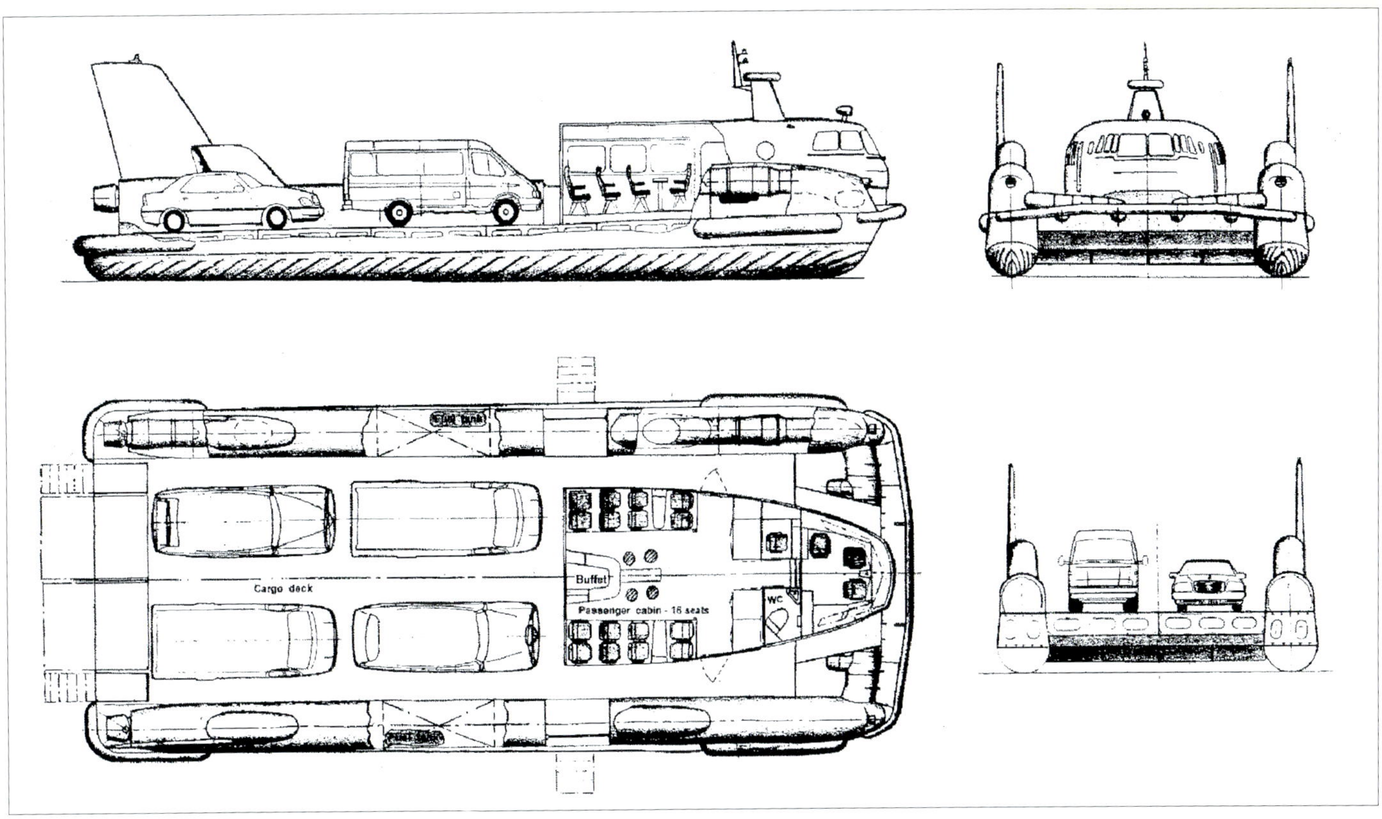

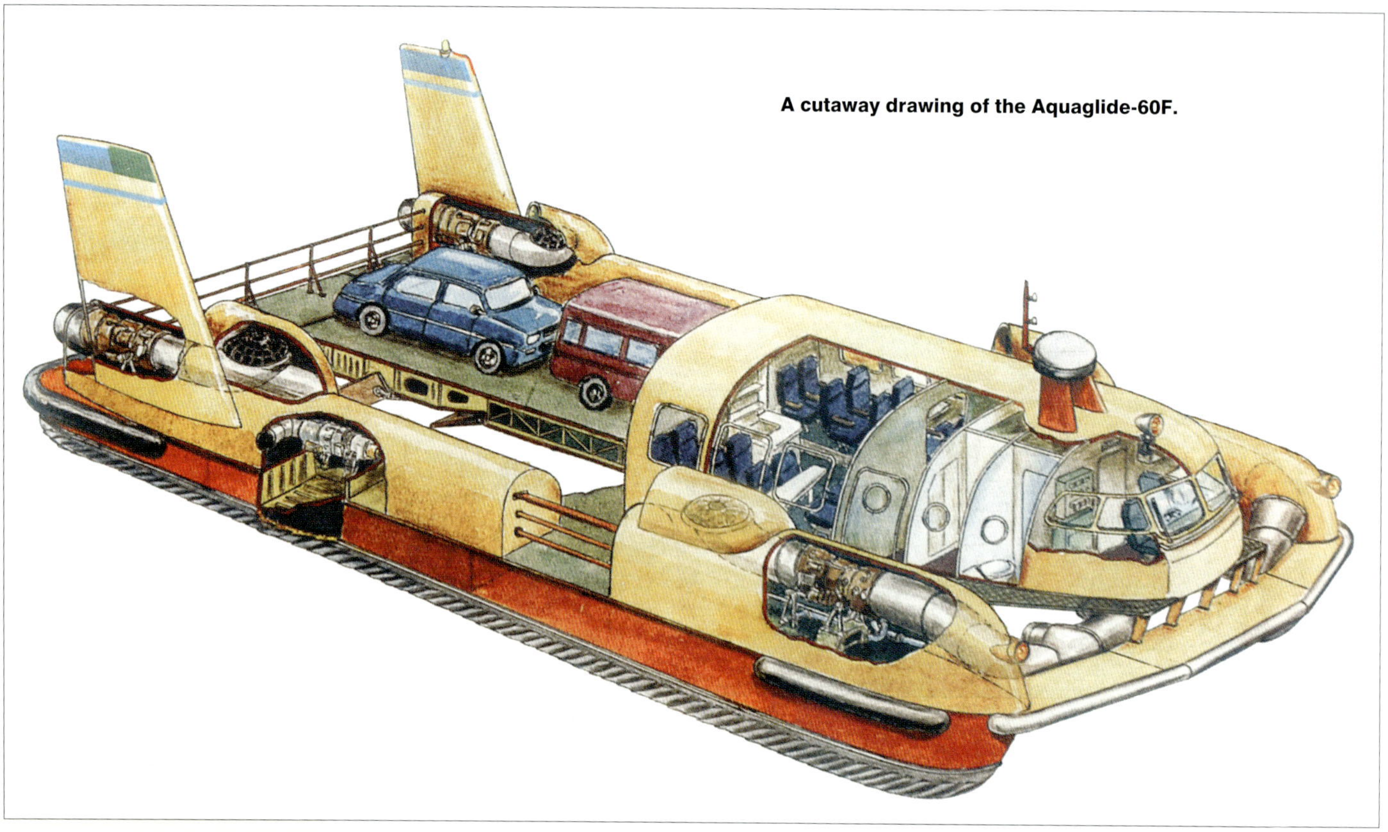

A cutaway drawing of the Aquaglide-60F.

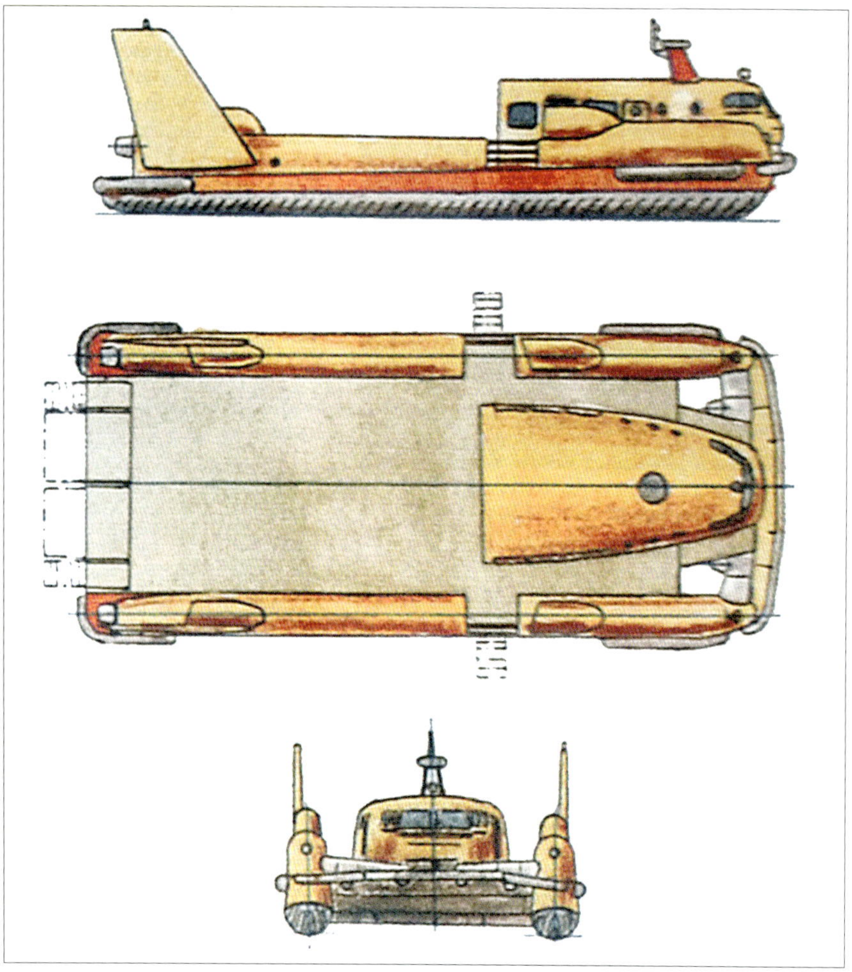

A three-view of the Aquaglide-60F, showing the vehicle loading ramps and boarding ladders.

120 km/h (75 mph) over a distance of up to 500 km (310 miles), with a wave height in cruise mode up to 1.25 m (4 ft). In their general layout they look like a scaled-up Aquaglide-20; passenger versions differ in having the open cargo deck replaced by an enclosed passenger cabin. In the mixed passenger/cargo version the front part of the platform is occupied by an enclosed cabin for passengers, while the aft part of the platform remains open and can be used for cargoes (for example, cars). The cargo or combi version with an open deck is designated Aquaglide-60F.

Aquaglide-200

This is a project of a Class A sea-going passenger WIG vehicle designed to carry up to 200 passengers and seven crew at a speed of 150 km/h (93 mph) over a distance of up to 600 km (373 miles) with a wave height in cruise mode up to 2 m (6 ft). The vehicle with a displacement of 100 tonnes (330,000 lb) has a cargo carrying capacity of 35 tonnes (77,170 lb). The vehicle's dimensions are as follows: length 43 m (141 ft), width 16 m (52 ft 6 in), height 9.5 m (31 ft 2 in). In its general layout the machine resembles the Aquaglide-60, having no wings (the lift is generated entirely by the bottom of

A cutaway drawing of the Aquaglide-200 with a combined powerplant (cruise propfans and booster turbojets)

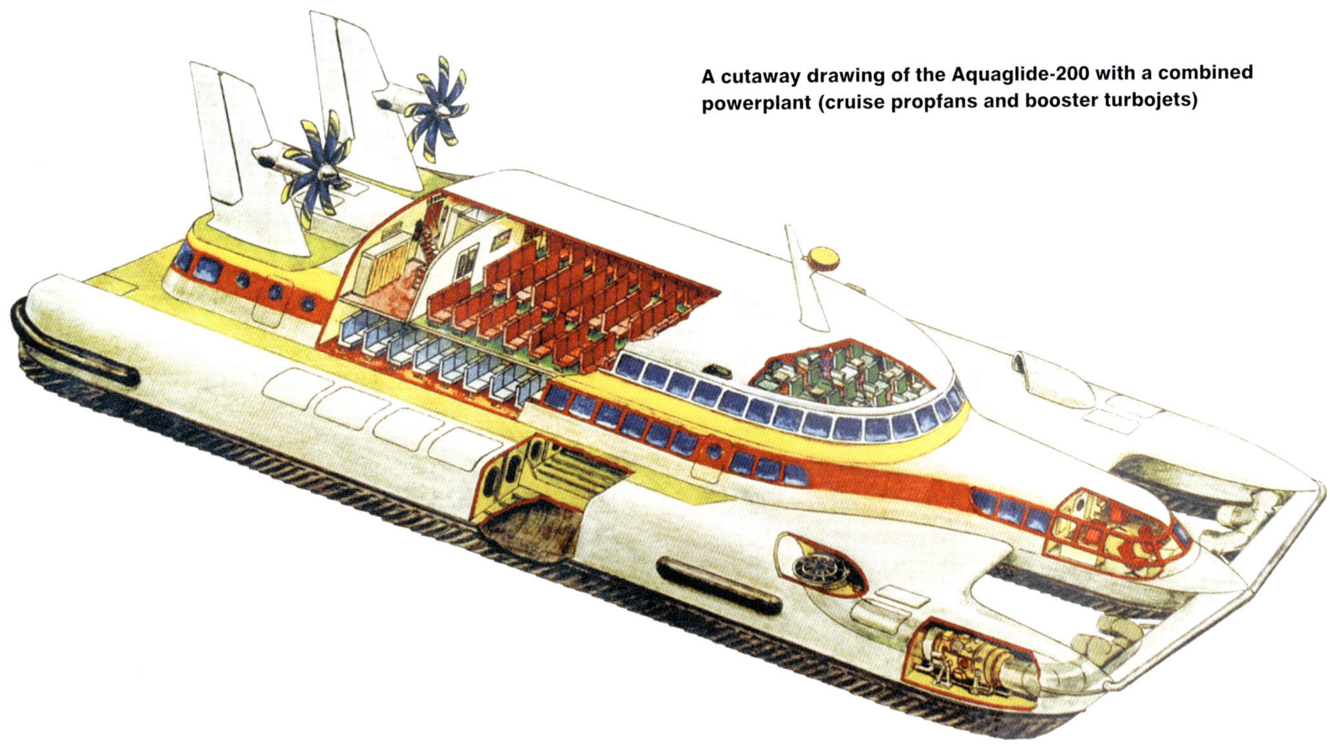

the platform). The powerplant comprises two propfan cruise engines mounted on the leading edges of the two fins, plus two blower jet engines buried in the forward parts of the floats, with nozzles located on a foreplane linking the floats. An all-turboprop version is also contemplated.

Among the Aquaglide projects described above it is the Aquaglide 30 that enjoys priority at present. According to some reports, construction of the prototype has already started.

MPE model range

The MPE acronym stands for *mor**skoy** passa**zheer**skiy ekrano**plahn*** – sea-going passenger WIG vehicle. This was a common designation for a series of projects of passenger ekranoplans evolved originally in the Central Hydrofoil Design Bureau and taken over for further development by the TET (later ATT) company when it separated from the mother organisation. This series includes machines of different weight and seating capacity, ranging initially from the 10-ton (22,045-lb) MPE-10 to the 470-ton (1,036,155-lb) MPE-400,with a seating capacity from 20 to 475 passengers. Later the range of projects was revised and extended to include the MPE-2 and MPE-3 light machines. The Alekseyev lineage

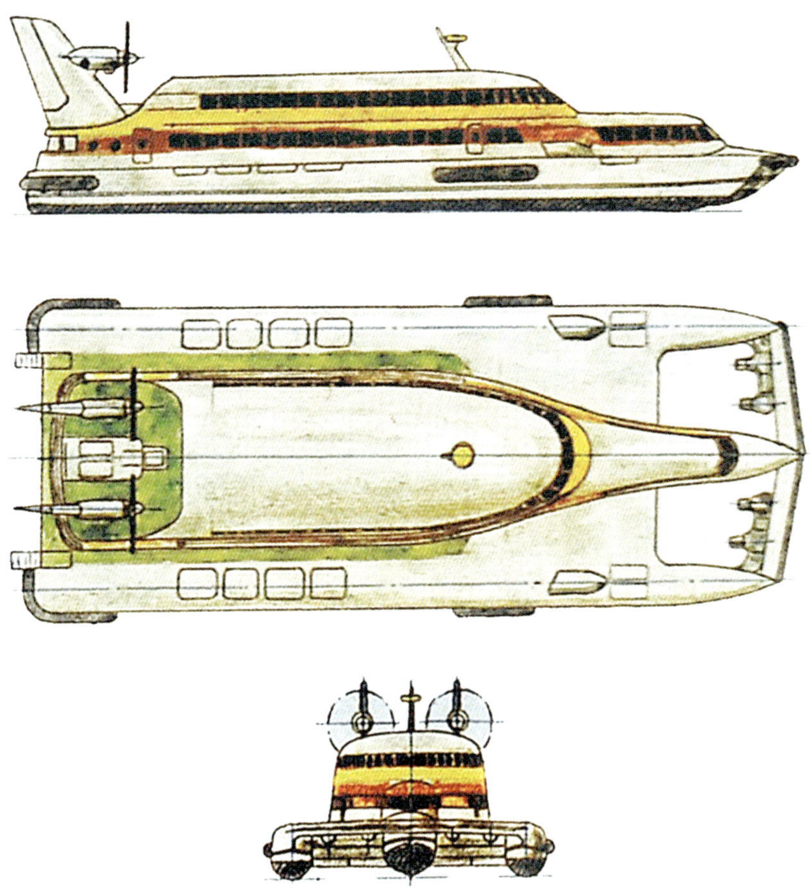

A three-view of the Aquaglide-200 with a combined powerplant.

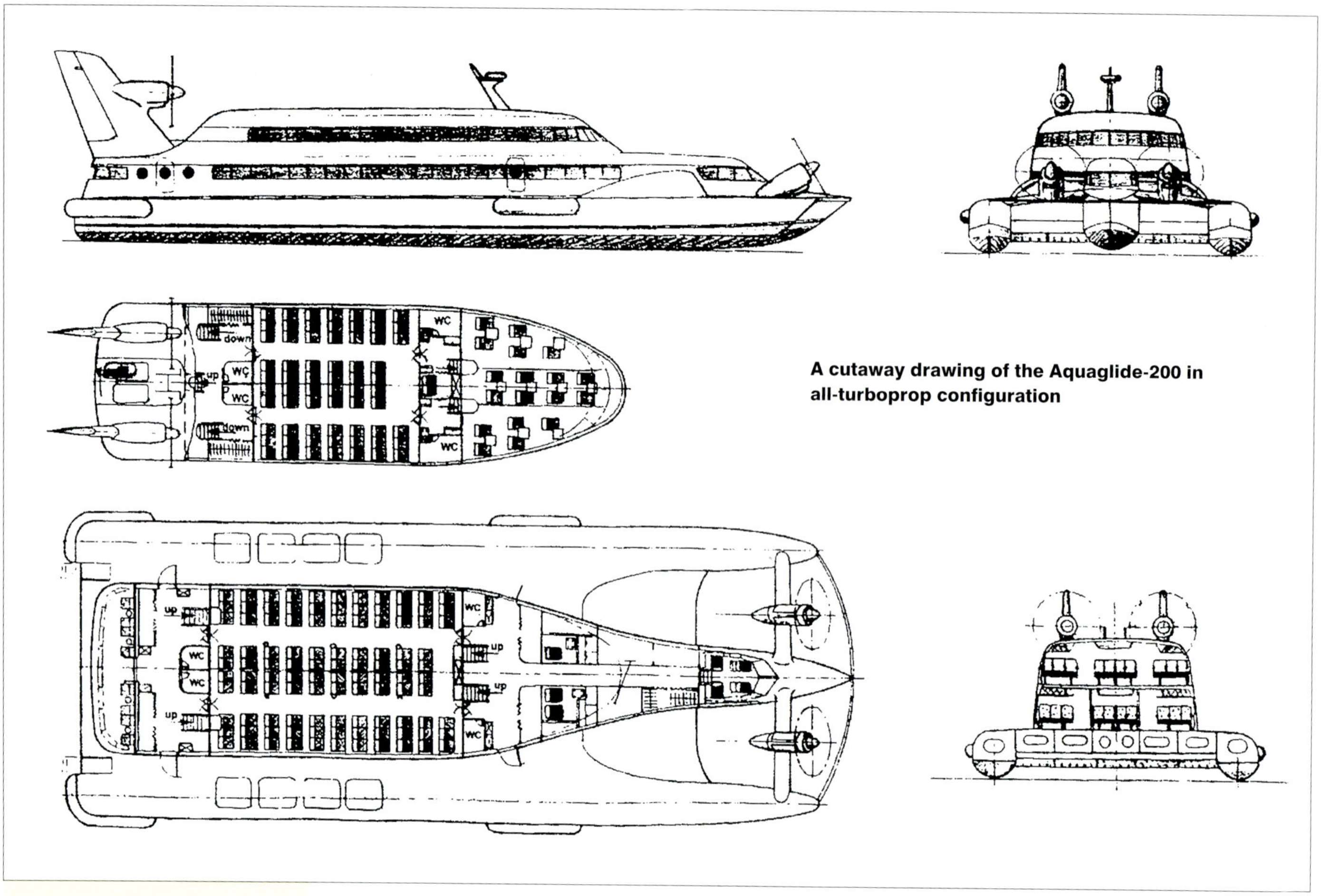

A cutaway drawing of the Aquaglide-200 in all-turboprop configuration

of the heavier MPE vehicles is reflected in their general configuration similar to that of the Orlyonok, Loon' etc., with booster engines buried in the forward fuselage and cruise engine(s) placed high on the tail unit. A distinctive feature of these designs is the use of composite layout wings with high-aspect-ratio outer wing panels added to the main wings outboard of the endplate floats. Equally characteristic is the tail unit consisting of two fins and rudders canted slightly outwards, with the horizontal tail placed on top of the fins; the latter carries one or two turboprop engines. An example of this

An artist's impression of the MPE-2 light WIG vehicle. The craft looks like a cross between the Aquaglide-5 and the Strizh-M project.

An artist's impression of the larger MPE-3 similar to the Strizh-3, except for the tail unit.

Design specifications of the ATTK MPE family					
Designation	Displacement, t (lb)	Cruising speed, km/h (mph)	Seating capacity, crew/passengers	Range, km (miles)	Maxi wave height at take-off, m (ft)
MPE-2	1.8 (3,970)	180 (112)	1+1	500 (311)	0.5 (1.6)
MPE-3	3.0 (6,615)	210 (131)	1+8	800 (497)	0.8 (2.6)
MPE-10	10 (22,045)	250 (155)	3+18	800 (497)	1.25 (4.1)
MPE-23	25.0 (55,110)	300 (186)	3+48	1,000 (622)	1.25 (4.1)
MPE-55	55.0 (141,240)	300 (186)	3+70	1,500 (933)	2.0 (6.6)
MPE-200	210 (462,962)	400 (249)	250	3,000 (1,865)	3.5 (11.5)
MPE-400	470 (1,036,155)	475 (295)	460	6,000 (3,730)	6.0 (20)

An artist's impression of the MPE-10 showing obvious Orlyonok lineage. Note the gull-wing outer wing panels.

An artist's impression of the 200-seat MPE-200. Again, its Alekseyev origins are obvious – apart from the twin tails and two cruise engines, the MPE-200 is very similar to the Orlyonok.

configuration (with two cruise engines) is the MPE-200 project.

The MPE-2 and MPE-3 projects differ from the bigger craft in the series in having a layout reminiscent of the Strizh vehicles developed by the Alekseyev CHDB, with wing-mounted engines driving nose-mounted propellers via extension shafts. However, this layout is combined with splayed twin fins topped by the horizontal tail – a configuration common to all vehicles in the MPE series.

A three-view of the MPE-200.

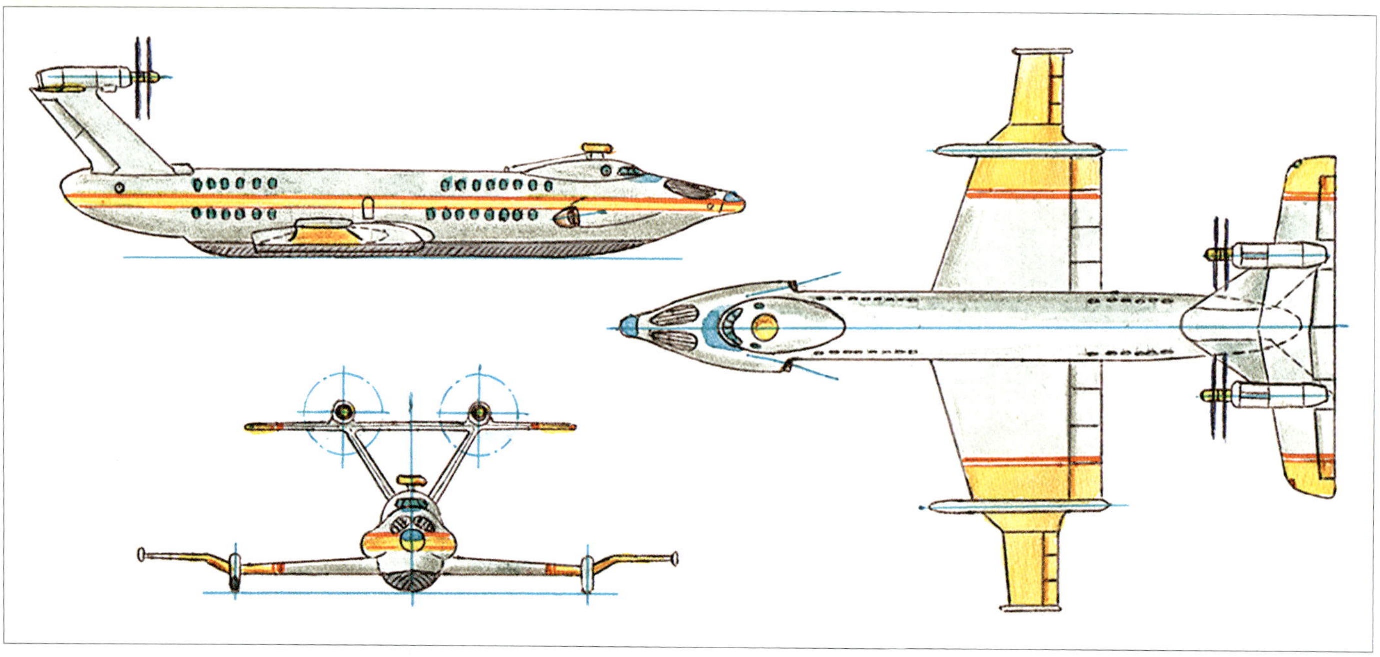

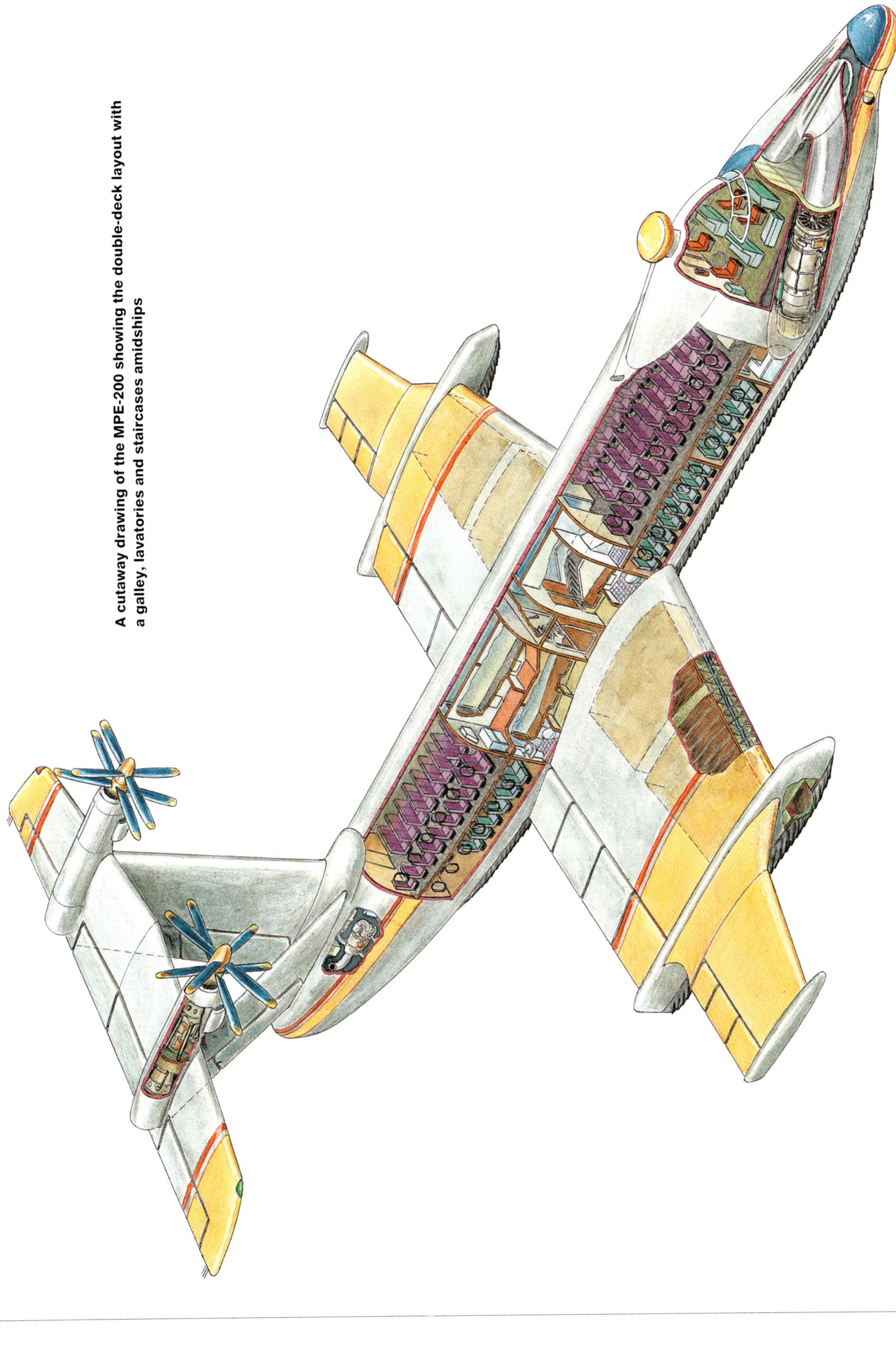

A cutaway drawing of the MPE-200 showing the double-deck layout with a galley, lavatories and staircases amidships

A desktop model of the MPE-200.

The table on page 279 provides information on the current of MPE projects under development by ATTK. These projects belong to Type B according to the IMO classification.

Not included in this table are projects of MPE-100 and MPE-300 vehicles which are no longer cited in the company's advertising materials.

A model of the EL-7 Ivolga unveiled at the MAKS-99 airshow in Moscow. Note the six-bladed propellers and unswept horizontal tail.

WIG vehicles designed by enterprises under the direction of Vyacheslav Kolganov

In 1996 the community of Russian firms and organisations engaged in design and manufacture of *ekranoplans* was joined by the KOMETEL JSC set up in Moscow. Under the guidance of its Director and Chief Designer Vyacheslav V. Kolganov it developed several projects of WIG vehicles which, in the firm's advertising materials, were classed as *ekranoplans* and *ekranolyots* (i.e Type A and Type B vehicles). Subsequently the enterprise headed by Kolganov underwent some changes of name and structural changes. By 2001 a larger science and production company (NPK) bearing the name TREK (an acronym for ***Tr**ahnsport **ek**ologichnyy* – environmentally friendly transport) was set up. This company established co-operation with the Omsk-based aerospace enterprise Polyot (Flight) where series production of Kolganov's machines was to be started. In 2002 Polyot and TREK jointly set up the Start-TREK JSC intended to handle the manufacturing of the *ekranoplans*.

The next stage in the reorganisation took place after 2005 when TREK became a part of the Industrial Financial and Production Group (IFPG). Kolganov again headed this enterprise as general director and chief designer. The IFPG positions itself as an enterprise whose activities comprise the design, manufacture and post-sale servicing of ekranoplans, as well as the training of personnel. Two of Kolganov's designs – the EL-7 and the EK-12 – have reached the hardware stage; in addition, there are several projects, all of which are described below.

EL-7 Ivolga (Golden Oriole)

This is the first design of this company that has been developed as far as the hardware stage. It is a Type B vehicle intended for the transportation of 8 to 11 passengers or small cargoes. The EL-7 features a composite wing aerodynamic layout well suited for a vehicle intended to be operated both in and out of ground effect. The wings comprise a centre section of high relative thickness and low aspect ratio with a straight leading edge and forward sweep on the trailing edge, and folding outer wing panels of greater aspect ratio (taken from the Yakovlev Yak-18T cabin monoplane) attached to it. The wing centre section has a dome-shaped configuration in front view and rests upon large floats, producing a kind of catamaran with the fuselage (passenger cabin) placed on the centreline atop the wings. The wing centre section is equipped with front and rear flaps which, together with the floats, form a cavity where an air cushion is created; the cavity assists the machine's take-off and can be used as a thrust reverser to shorten the landing run.

The powerplant comprises two car engines installed in bays in the centre section on both sides of the fuselage. Other types of engines, including diesels and aircraft engines, can be installed.

The engines transmit their power through shafts with universal joints to two propellers in annular shrouds installed on each side of the forward fuselage. The shrouds enhance the propellers' thrust at low speeds, protect them from foreign objects, serve as a safety device for people coming close to the propellers and reduce the noise level. Depending on the flight mode, the propellers can alter the direction of their thrust. In the take-off mode the air flow created by the propellers is directed into the cavity formed by the wing centre section, the aft flap and the floats; during cruise flight it is directed above the wing centre. The propellers are deflected in concert with flap deployment, but in other flight modes they can be deflected independently of the flap.

The static air cushion thus created enables the vehicle to move without contact with the underlying surface at heights up to 0.3 m (1 ft) at a speed of up to 80 km/h (50 mph). During further acceleration the ram air pressure makes it possible to change the direction of thrust of the propellers and enter into the dynamic air cushion (ground effect) mode.

The EL-7 is an amphibious craft capable of coming out onto a gently sloping bank under its own power and returning to the water. When taxiing on water, differential use of the front centre section flaps enables the machine to make a full 360° turn literally on the spot.

The vehicle has a strut-braced T-tail. Its control system comprises a rudder, elevators, ailerons, controls for the devices governing the air cushion (devices for rotating the axles of propellers and deflecting the wing centre section flaps). Directional control can be effected not only by the rudder but also by using differential thrust of the propellers through changing their rpm, disengaging one propeller by means of a clutch or changing the propellers' pitch.

Testing of the EL-7 was initiated in Moscow in September 1998; it started with checking out the control system during taxiing on water, including the air injection ('blowing') mode. In January 1999 the WIG vehicle was tested in Irkutsk under the conditions of the harsh Siberian winter. The first flight in air injection mode was performed at the Irkutsk water reservoir on 16th February. Four days later Vyacheslav V. Kolganov, General Director of the KOMETEL company and of the TREK concern, performed a flight on the EL-7 powered by 150-hp 2.3-litre ZMZ-4062 four-cylinder in-line engines of the Zavolzhskiy Engine Factory (as fitted to the GAZ-3110 Volga saloon car) and tested the surface effect mode in cruise configuration (with flaps retracted and propellers in the cruise position), at speeds of 80-110 km/h (49-68 mph).

With two 150-hp ZMZ-4062-10 engines the EL-7 proved to be underpowered when flying with a full payload. There were plans to re-engine the EL-7 with turbocharged 210-hp ZMZ-4064-10 engines, but they were not available in time, and the machine had to be equipped with 286-hp BMW S38 six-cylinder in-line engines as fitted to the BMW M5 and BMW M6 saloons; this version was designated EL-7S. In August 1999 Kolganov, flying the machine equipped with BMW engines, demonstrated the vehicle descending from the river bank to the water, flying in ground effect in cruise configuration and coming out onto dry land again. In December 1999 another pilot, D. G. Shchebliakov, demonstrated a flight at an altitude of 4 m (13 ft), including changes of heading. Somewhat later the vehicle rose to an altitude of more than 15 m (50 ft) and demonstrated

The as-yet unpainted prototype of the EL-7 in flight during initial flight tests. Note the gently swept stabiliser.

Above: The outer wings can be folded for manoeuvring beside the pier and docking. Note the four-bladed propellers of the actual craft.

Below: Here the EL-7 prototype flies at fairly high altitude, demonstrating its ability to operate out of ground effect.

The KOMETEL EL-7S Ivolga in the static park of the MAKS-2001 airshow in Zhukovskiy. This was the first time when a WIG vehicle intended for production and commercial operation was displayed publicly. The Cyrillic VLRP titles denote the launch customer, the Upper Lena River Shipping Co.

Three shots of a still-unpainted EK-12 Ivolga. Note the new outer wings and the small extra fins. The floats have three planing steps each.

its ability to fly out of ground effect. In February 2000 the first long-distance flight took place. In the autumn of 2000 the vehicle confidently made a lift-off from and alighted on waves more than 1 m (3 ft) high.

The EL-7 proved to be simple in handling, forgiving even grave piloting errors. 'Aircraft' flight modes were successfully tried out. Banking turns in the proximity of the water surface were performed with 15° bank at altitudes beginning with 3 m (10 ft) and up to the altitude where the vehicle left the ground effect zone (above 10 m/33 ft); turns above the ground effect zone were performed with bank angles of 30-50°.

During flight close to the supporting surface the lift/drag ratio of the EL-7 Ivolga WIG vehicle reached 25, which is more than twice the corresponding figure for aircraft in a comparable category. When operation is limited to altitudes of up to 3 m (10 ft), the EL-7 is certified in the Registers for River-going and Sea-going Ships. When equipped with aircraft engines, avionics and piloting and navigation systems, the vehicle can also be certified in the Aviation Register, including 'aircraft' flight modes. In these, the vehicle will have a performance comparable to that of aircraft of the same dimensions. It will retain the ability to operate from unprepared dirt airstrips, ice, deep snow and water, including swamp areas.

In its baseline version the EL-7 WIG vehicle has a passenger cabin with easily removable folding seats making it possible to transform the cabin into a cargo compartment or a mixed cargo/passenger cabin. The *ekranolyot* can be supplied to customers in the following versions: cargo/passenger version; a version for tourism and excursions; border guard version; patrol version for use by law enforcement and nature protection agencies; SAR version; fire-fighting version; ecological monitoring version; VIP/executive and other versions to cater for the customer's special needs.

For the purpose of production and operation of WIG vehicles the design bureau (the KOMETEL company) and the launch customer, the Upper Lena River Shipping Agency (VLRP – ***Verkh**ne-**Len**skoye **r**echnoye **p**arokhodstvo*), as well as some other organisations, have formed the above-mentioned consortium named TREK Joint-Stock Company. At the end of 2001 it was reported that the concern had already launched production of the 14-seat EK-12 WIG vehicle similar to the Ivolga and incorporating refinements based on the testing of the original model. Here follows a description of this and other designs of the KOMETEL.

EK-12 Ivolga

This machine is closely similar to the EL-7 and differs mainly in the design of the folding wing outer panels, which have moderate sweepback and no taper and are attached to the floats via sections with an extended leading edge. The EK-12, intended for carrying 12 passengers and one or two crew, is powered by two 286-hp BMW S38 engines. The EK-12R version of somewhat smaller cargo capacity (the R refers to Russian engines), intended to carry eight passengers and one pilot and powered by two 210-hp ZMZ-4064-10 engines, was also studied. Interestingly, the EK-12 shares the layout and basic parameters of the EL-7 *ekranolyot* (Type B vehicle) but is classed as a Type A vehicle – obviously with a view to simplifying the certification procedure.

In April 2005 an agreement was reached on launching series production of the EK-12 *ekranoplan* in Omsk at the production facilities of the Polyot aerospace association. It was reported that by that time one machine had already been completed and delivered to a private person, a further three were being completed for customers from Chukotka and Arkhangel'sk.

By mid-2005 preliminary negotiations were held with the Federal Border Guard Agency, the Ministry of Emergency Situations (EMERCOM of Russia), the administration of the Arkhangel'sk Region and the Belomor'ye Shipping Company concerning the deliveries of EK-12 *ekranoplans*.

In August 2007 an example of the EK-12 was displayed at the MAKS-2007 airshow as an exhibit from the IFPG; it was announced that the machine was produced for the Border Guard Troops of Russia's Federal Security Service (FSB – *Fede**rahl'**naya **sloozh**ba bezo**pahs**nosti*). The second example tailored to Border Guards specifications was designated EK-12P (*pogra**nich**nyy* – border, used attributively). The evaluation process had been started. Between 2005 and 2008 two EK-12 *ekranoplans* successfully passed a series of tests in the

'001 Black', an EK-12 Ivolga intended for the FSB Border Guards, at the MAKS-2007 airshow. Note the absence of the auxiliary fins.

The same machine seen taxiing on water. Here the lower halves of the auxiliary fins are on place; note also the navigation radar on top of the fin.

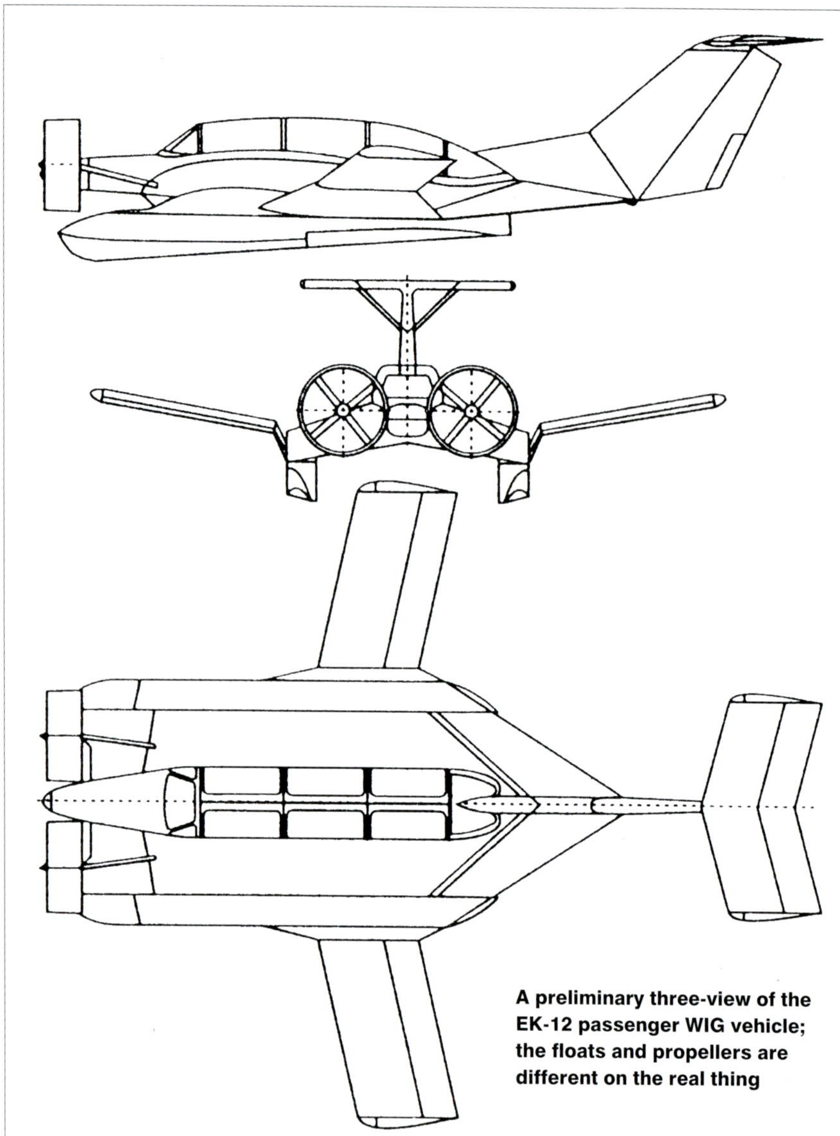

A preliminary three-view of the EK-12 passenger WIG vehicle; the floats and propellers are different on the real thing

Below: The EK-12 with the wings folded on a ground handling dolly.

Moscow region, on Siberian rivers, on Lake Baikal, on the Caspian Sea and on Lake Ladoga. In November 2008 the Chairman of the Board of Directors of the IFPG JSC Oleg Volik said that only the testing in northern areas remained to be conducted to meet the customer's demands, and, according to the plans then in hand, the EK-12 was to be introduced into operational service by the FSB's Border Guard Agency in the autumn of 2009. Representatives of the Border Guard Agency noted that the machine met the requirements for the protection of the state border and especially for the protection of biological resources at rivers and lakes, while a larger machine was needed for performing similar duties over sea areas. It would seem that the machine has fairly good chances of being introduced into service in the near future, despite all the delays that are plaguing it.

Several versions of the EK-12 for various duties have been announced. Civil versions include the appropriately equipped EK-12Med (medical, that is, ambulance) and the EK-12S (*spasatel'nyy* – rescue, used attributively).

Combat versions of the EK-12, now under development, include:

• a troop-carrier vehicle, intended to transport and land small detachments of troops (marines) for various tasks, such as anti-terrorist operations, reconnaissance etc.;

• an armed vehicle for rendering fire support to coastal army units and marines during combat activities;

• an armed patrol vehicle for the protection of naval base areas;

• an *ekranoplan* for combat engineer support, such as engineer reconnaissance, mining and mine clearance.

EK-20

This is a pure Type A WIG design based on a 'flying wing' layout. It has much in common with the EL-7, featuring the same twin-float configuration with a dome-shaped (inverted V) wing, topped by the cabin for the crew and passengers. Also similar is the arrangement and design of the powerplants with propellers in annular shrouds. The main difference is the absence of outer wing panels and a revised tail unit design. The tail unit comprises two fins and rudders mounted on the aft ends of the floats and slightly canted outwards; the horizontal tails are attached to the tops of the fins on the outboard sides (this places the horizontal tail outside the influence of the downwash over the rear part of the wing).

Powered by two 300-hp BMW M10 automobile engines, the vehicle was expected to carry a payload of 1,980 kg (4,365 lb) to a distance of 1,370 km (850 miles) when flying at 0.5 m (1.6 ft) over the surface and 1,120 km (695 miles) when flying at an altitude of 1 m (3 ft). Information on this project was

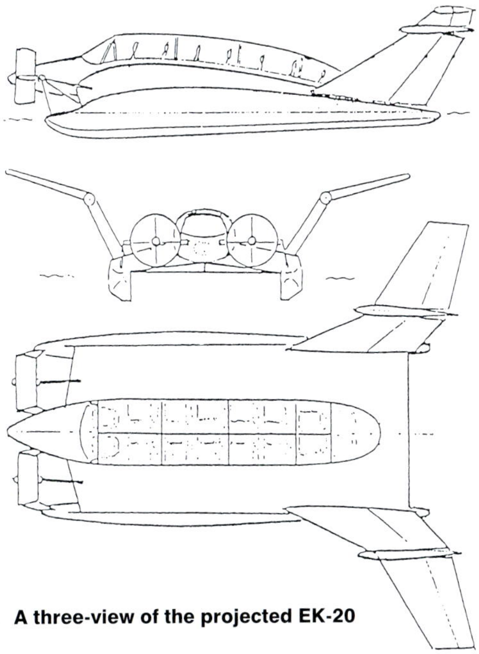

A three-view of the projected EK-20

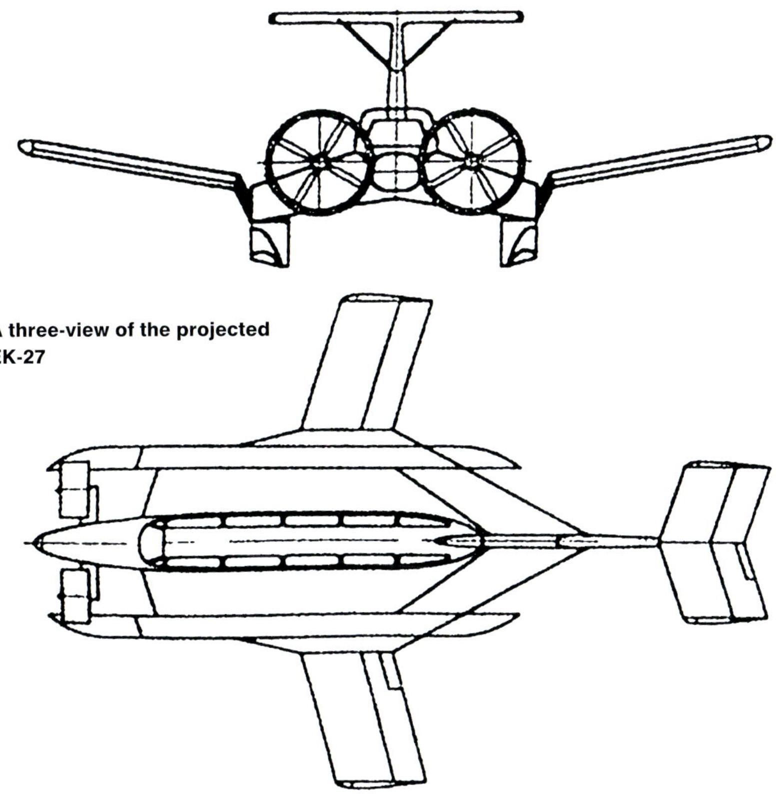

A three-view of the projected EK-27

presented at the MAKS-99 airshow in August 1999. No prototype has been built so far, and the type appears to be withdrawn from the production programme.

Specifications of the KOMETEL WIG vehicle family

Type	EL-7 prototype	EL-7S prototype modified	EK-12 prototype	EK-12R project	EK-20 project	EK-25 project
All-up weight, kg (lb)	3,300 (7,275)	3,600 (7,936)	3,600 (7,936)	3,100 (6,834)	4,900 (10,802)	5,500 (12,125)
Crew (passengers)	1 (7)	1 (10)	1-2 (12)	1 (8)	2 (19)	2 (25)
Payload, kg (lb)	700 (1,543)	1,000 (2,204)	1,200 (2,645)	850 (1,873)	1,980 (4,365)	2,500 (5,511)
Engines	automobile	automobile	automobile	automobile	automobile	automobile
Type	ZMZ-4064.10	BMW S38	BMW S38	ZMZ-4064.10	BMW M10	BMW S73
Number/power, hp.	2 x 210	2 x 286	2 x 286	2 x 210	2 x 340	2 x 400
Fuel load, kg (lb)	160 (352)	160 (352)	250 (551)	200 (440)	300 (661)	300 (661)
Range, km (miles):						
at 0.8 m (2 ft 7½ in)	1,150 (714)	1,210 (751)	1,210 (751)	1,150 (714)	1,120*(695)	1,120 (695)
at 0.3 m (11 13/16 in)	1,480 (919)	1,520 (944)	1,520 (944)	1,480 (919)	1,370** (850)	1,370 (850)
Speed, km/h (mph):						
cruising	150-175 (93-108)	180 (111)	180 (111)	160-175 (99-108)	150-175 (93-108)	160-175 (99-108)
maximum	200 (124)	210 (130)	210 (130)	200 (124)	195 (121)	205 (127)
Sea state, Beaufort scale	3-4	3-4	3-4	3	3-4	4
Taxying height, m (ft)	n.a.	n.a.	0,1 (0'3 15/16")	0,1 (0'3 15/16")	0,1-0,2 (0'3 15/16"-0'7⅞")	0,1 (0'3 15/16")
Draught, m (ft)	0.45 (1'5 23/32")	0.45 (1'5 23/32")	0.35-0.45 (1'1 25/32"-1'5 23/32")	0.35-0.45 (1'1 25/32"-1'5 23/32")	0.55 (1'9 21/32")	0.55 (1'9 21/32")
Overall dimensions, m (ft)	n.a.	n.a.	15.6 x 12.7 x 3.7 (51'2 11/64"x41'8"x12'1 39/64")	15.6 x 12.7 x 3.7 (51'2 11/64"x41'8"x12'1 39/64")	n.a.	20.1 x 18.2 x 5.1 (65'11 21/64"x59'8½"x16'8 25/32")
Dimensions with outer wings folded, m (ft)	n.a.	n.a.	15.6 x 4.8 x 4.0 (51'2 11/64"x15'9"x13'1½")	15.6 x 4.8 x 4.0 (51'2 11/64"x15'9"x13'1½")	n.a.	20.1 x 8.3 x 5.6 (65'11 21/64"x27'2 49/64"x18'4½")

*at 1.0 m (3 ft) altitude
** at 0.5 m (1.6 ft) altitude

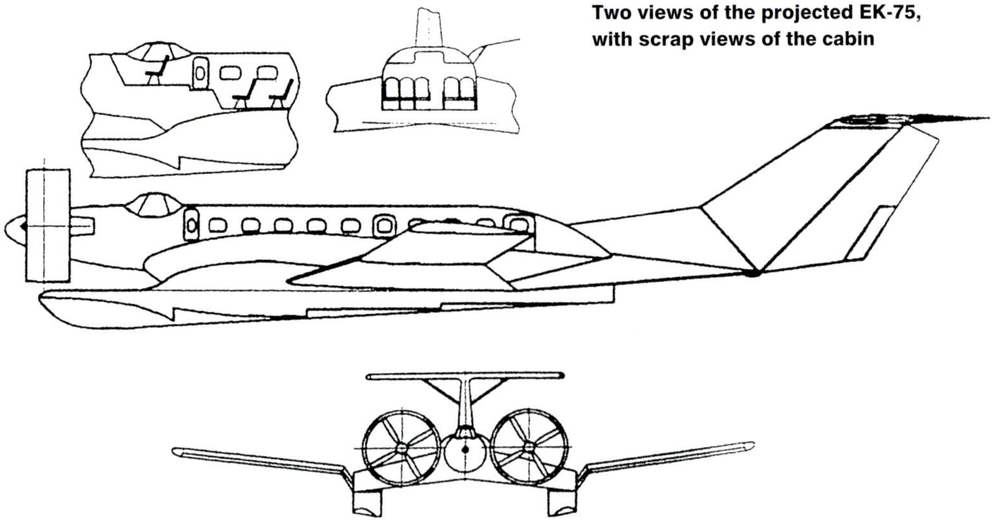

Two views of the projected EK-75, with scrap views of the cabin

EK-25

This WIG vehicle is a scaled-up version of the EK-20 powered by two 400-hp BMW S73 automobile engines. It is intended for transporting 25 passengers and two crew at a cruising speed of 160-175 km/h (99-108 mph) to a distance of 1,120-1,370 km (696-851 miles). Like the EK-20, it has been deleted from the current advertising materials of the IFPG. It has obviously been sacrificed in favour of the EK-27 design (see below) which, while having the same passenger-carrying capacity, differs in having a layout similar to that of the EK-12.

EK-27

The 25-passenger EK-27 differs from the preceding EK-25 design in being provided with outer wing panels, thus resembling a scaled-up EK-12. It features the same 'greenhouse' canopy over the cabin. The original project version was to be powered by two V12TDI diesel engines rated at 500 hp;

Specifications of the EK-series WIG vehicles (continued)

	EK-12 production	EK-27 project	EK-75 project	EK-130 project
Maximum AUW, kg (lb)	3,900 (8,600)	6,700 (13,735)	25,300 (51,865)	130,000 (286,650)
Crew/passengers	1-2/12	2/25	4/75	4-10/500
Useful load, kg (lb)	1,200(2,645)	3,000(6,615)	10,000(22,050)	50,000 (110,250)
Unrefuelled range:				
@ altitude	0.3 m (1 ft)	0.7 m (2 ft 3½ in)	1.0 m (3 ft 3⅜ in)	1.5 m (4 ft 11 in)
range, km (miles)	1,560 (970)	1,580 (982)	3,200 (1,989)	4,500 (2,797)
@ altitude	0.8 m ()	2.0 m (6 ft 6¾ in)	3.0 m (9 ft 10 in)	4.0 m (13 ft 1 in)
range, km (miles)	1,120 (696)	1,120 (696)	2,460 (1,530)	2,700 (1,680)
Speed max/cruising, km/h (mph)	220/170(137/106)	240/180(149/112)	320/410(199/255)	500/600(311/373)
Engines: type/number x power, hp	BMW M70 2 x 326	Audi Q-10 2 x 600	Klimov VK-2500 2 x 2500	Muravchenko D-436TP 4 x 7,500 kgp (16,540 lbst) take-off thrust
Fuel grade/fuel load, kg (lb)	AI-95 automotive petrol/ 270 (595)	Diesel fuel/ 360 (790)	TS-1 jet fuel/ 1,600 (3,530)	TS-1 jet fuel/ 28,000 (61,740)
Seaworthiness, sea state	3	3-4	3-5	5-7
Wave height	1.5 m (4 ft 11 in)	2.0 m (6 ft 6¾ in)	3.0 m (9 ft 10 in)	5.0 m (16 ft 4 27/32 in)
Dimensions:				
length	15.6 m (51 ft 2 11/64 in)	22.4 m (73 ft 5 57/64 in)	33 m (108 ft 4¼ in)	65 m (213 ft 3 5/64 in)
wing span	13 m (42 ft 7 13/16 in)	15.4 m (50 ft 6 19/64 in)	22.6 m (74 ft 1 49/64 in)	58 m (190 ft 2 9/32 in)
height	3.7 m (12 ft 1 39/64 in)	4.2 m (13 ft 9 23/64 in)	6 m (19 ft 8 7/32 in)	10 m (32 ft 9 45/64 in)

it had a design AUW of 5,900 kg (13,000 lb) and a useful load of 2,500 kg (5,510 lb). Later the powerplant was changed to two Audi Q-10 engines rated at 600 hp, with a corresponding revision of performance (see table on the previous page).

EK-75

The 75-seat EK-75 looks like a scaled-up EK-27, but differs in having an airliner-type fuselage placed atop a wide-chord anhedral wing centre section. The latter rests on two floats provided with several planing steps. The outer wing panels are also similar to those of the EK-12 and EK-27, featuring a moderate sweep and dihedral. The T-tail has the same configuration as in the previous designs. Two ducted propellers flanking the forward fuselage are driven by turboprop engines. The initial project version was to be powered by two Pratt & Whitney Canada PW-127H engines rated at 2,750 ehp. Later this was changed to two Klimov VK-2500s rated at 2,500 ehp.

EK-130

This much larger vehicle is intended to carry as many as 500 passengers and is to be powered by four turbojets. No illustrations are available, nor any information apart from the figures in the table below. The sheer difference in size may well require a considerable revision of its layout in comparison with the other types in the series.

In the spring of 2010 the IPFG group of companies took a decision to rename all the types in its present production and development programme. Instead of the EK prefix the designations have received the name Orion, retaining the same digits. Thus, the EK-12 has become Orion-12, the EK-27 was renamed Orion 27 et cetera. This renaming reportedly reflects some changes in the relations between the partners within the IPFG.

The following description of designs of other companies is arranged in alphabetical order of the names of the relevant firms. In some cases designs originating in one company were taken over by other companies due to changes of name or affiliation. To avoid confusion, in such cases all the relevant companies are grouped together to provide a compact description of projects having a common origin.

Stanislav S. Alekseyev's designs

(Plast JSC and other companies)

Sever-2, Sever-3, Sever-4 series of air cushion (ground effect) vehicles

Stanislav S. Alekseyev (no relative of Rostislav Alekseyev), an engineer on the staff of the CHDB, was responsible for the design and construction of the small LAVP-02 (LAVP-87) vehicle which was used for research associated with the Volga-2 and other similar WIG vehicles (see Chapter 1). In 1989 he quit the CHDB and set up his own small enterprise at the Nizhniy Novgorod-based ***Sokol*** (Falcon) aircraft factory. His intention was to start the design and manufacture of air cushion vehicles based on the concept of the LAVP-87. This vehicle was, in fact, a cross between a true WIG vehicle and a true ACV. It used the front-mounted propeller both for horizontal propulsion and for creating a static air cushion, but lacked the separate engine driving a fan for his purpose.

The Sever-2 (left) and Sever-3 air cushion vehicles.

A production example of the Sever-4 ACV.

The LAVP-02 (LAVP-87) proved to be a good design which was further developed by Stanislav S. Alekseyev into the Sever-2 (= North-2), Sever-3 and Sever-4 small ACVs (this is how they were classed officially, although they may be regarded as a cross between an ACV and a WIG vehicle). The Sever-3 flew in the ground effect mode with a speed of 100-130 km/h (62-81 mph). The Sever-3 and Sever-4 vehicles were put into production. Subsequent designs by S. S. Alekseyev were true ACVs incorporating the all-round skirt and a separate engine for driving a fan designed to create the air cushion.

The enterprise set up by Stanislav S. Alekseyev bore different names at different times; at one time it was known as the Plast JSC (see below for another project).

A display model of the PE-40 *ekranoplan* developed by the Alien Group.

Alien Group

(with Alien-Chkalovsk subsidiary)

PE series passenger *ekranoplans*

This company was set up in mid-2000s as a subsidiary of the St.-Petersburg-based Alien Group which operates high-speed passenger ships on local routes. The group's Chairman of the Board of Directors, Aleksey Gakkel', came to the conclusion that the hydrofoil ships used on these routes ought to be replaced by Class A WIG vehicles and decided to make a contribution to their development. Gakkel' and his associates established a design bureau in Chkalovsk, the town where the Alekseyev Design Bureau had had its experimental base at one time. The new design bureau, under the name of Alien-Chkalovsk, was set up on the basis of the Science and Production Enterprise for Experimental Shipbuilding that had gone bankrupt. The core of the new design bureau was formed by experienced engineers who had worked together with Rostislav Alekseyev and later in the Gor'kiy branch of TsNII. Somewhat later the Alien group formed a managing company named Ekranoflot JSC to coordinate the group's activities in WIG design and eventually to operate the fleet of *ekranoplans*. Ekranoflot JSC unites the efforts of several partners: the Krylov Central Shipbuilding Research Institute (TsNII), Klimov Engine Plant (St.-Petersburg), Sokol Aircraft Plant (Nizhniy Novgorod) and Aerosila JSC (Stoopino, Moscow Region; the latter company designs and manufactures propellers and APUs).

A cutaway drawing of the PE-40 showing the two cabins (seating 16 and 24 passengers), the VK-2500 engine and AI-9V APU in the nose etc.

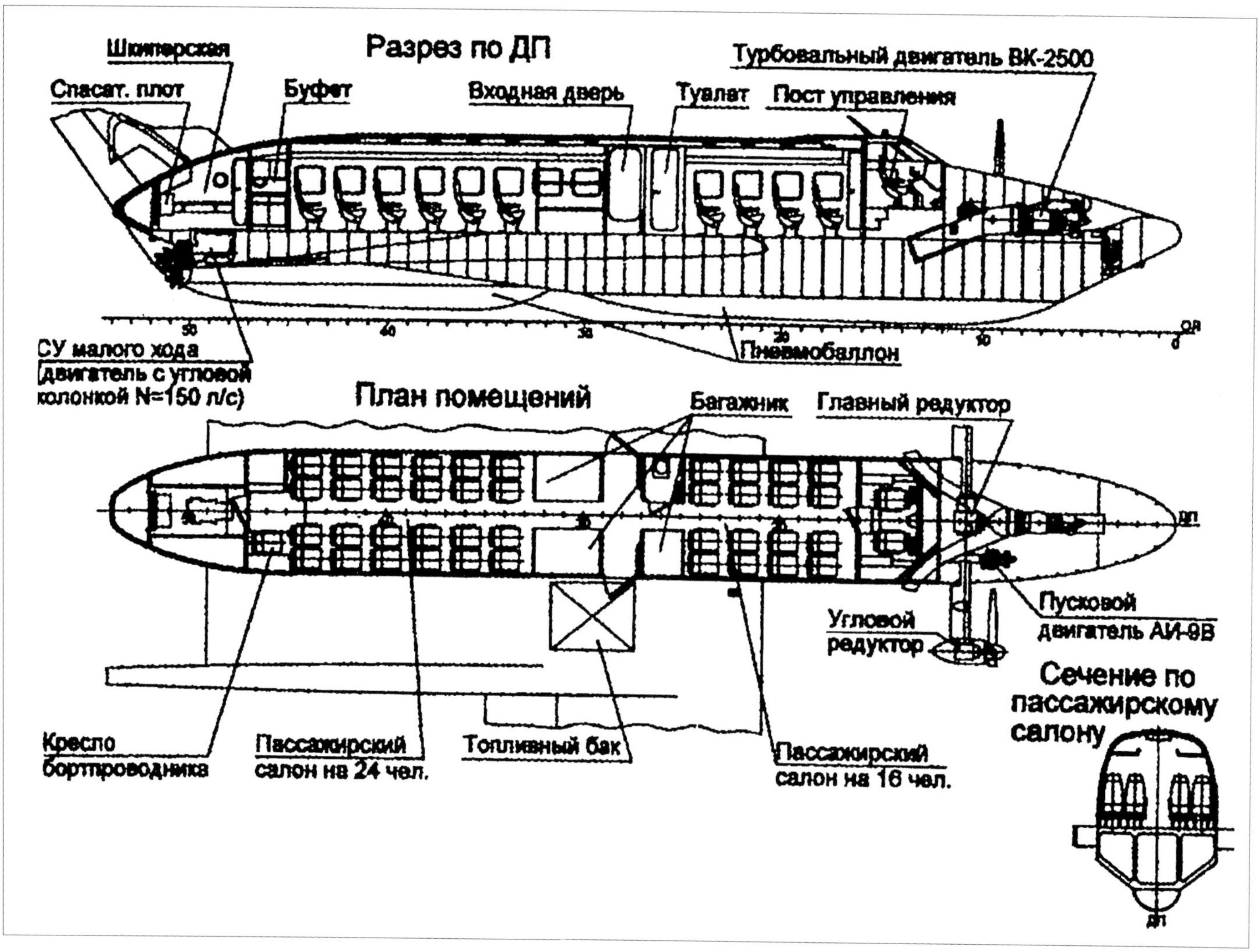

Basic specifications of the PE-series ekranoplans:

Type	PE-8	PE-12	PE-40	PE-80
Number of passengers	8	12	40	80
Length	13.5 m (44 ft 3½ in)	15.4 m (50 ft 6¼ in)	26.0 m (95 ft 3¾ in)	31.95 m (104 ft 10 in)
Wing span	8.8 m (28 ft 10 29/64 in)	10.0 m (32 ft 9 45/64 in)	16.0 m (52 ft 6 in)	20.2 m (66 ft 3¼ in)
Height	3.1 m (19 ft 7 in)	3.7 m (12 ft1¾ in)	5.7 m (18 ft 8⅜ in)	9.4 m (30 ft 10 in)
All-up weight, kg (lb)	3,350 (7,166)	5,500 (12,127)	15,000 (33,075)	31,500 (69,457)
Engine type and power, hp	VAZ-426 Wankel engine 2 x 270	Klimov VK-800 turboshaft 1 x 800	Klimov VK-2500 turboshaft 1 x 2,400	2 x Klimov TV7-117 turboprop 2 x 2,500
Speed, km/h (mph)	190 (118)	200 (124)	240 (149)	280 (174)
Maximum wave height, m (ft)	0.6 (2.0)	0.8 (2.6)	1.25 (4.1)	1.5 (4.9)
Range, km (miles)	500 (311)	800 (497)	1,000 (622)	1,200 (746)
Crew, persons	1	2	3	3

By 2006 the Alien-Chkalovsk design bureau under the direction of V. I. Baryshev had prepared projects of sea-going WIG craft for 8, 12, 40 and 80 passengers. The intention was to operate the 8- and 12-passenger vehicles on internal waterways and coastal sea areas, while the 40- and 80-passenger ekranoplans could be put on sea routes on the Baltic Sea and the Black Sea.

The projects mentioned above are designated respectively PE-8, PE-12, PE-40 and PE-80 (PE presumably stands for *passa**zheer**skiy ekrano**plan*** – passenger *ekranoplan*). Of the four designs the PE-40 is considered to be of special interest. An artist's impression shows a vehicle with a rather fat boat-hull fuselage and wings of composite layout. The low-aspect-ratio centre section extends well aft and is flanked by two swept-back fin-and-rudder assemblies topped by the horizontal tail. Outboard of the fins the wing centre section is supplemented by narrow-chord outer wing panels carrying end-plate floats at their tips. The single Klimov VK-2500 turboshaft transmits its torque via angle drive gearboxes and extension shafts to two propellers mounted on outriggers on both sides of the nose. A part of the prop wash is ejected into the space between the wings and the supporting surface. An interesting feature of the design is the provision of two inflatable pontoons forming the keel of the hull. The PE-40 has been designed as a passenger *ekranoplan*, but it can be modified into an executive (VIP) transport, a SAR craft and a vehicle for the transportation of small-size cargoes. It is to be based on paved parking sites on the shore.

An important advantage of the PE-40 is its ability to move at low speed when afloat, making use of a 150-hp piston engine installed specially for that purpose. This enhances operational safety and facilitates the mooring and the passage from a parking area to the take-off and alighting area.

Other designs in the PE series feature the same basic configuration, scaled up or down.

The resources of the Alien Group and the Ekranoglot JSC are not sufficient for manufacturing the prototypes of the proposed designs. Hence the company is looking for investors and pins its hopes on government support.

Almaz (TsMKB Almaz)

In the mid-1960s the Ministry of Shipbuilding of the Soviet Union decided to break the virtual monopoly of Rostislav Alekseyev in the design of large WIG craft and tasked the Leningrad (St. Petersburg)-based Almaz Central Marine Design Bureau (TsMKB Almaz – *Tsen**tral**'noye mor**skoy**e kon**strook**torskoye byuro*) with the design of ekranoplans. The Ministry even nurtured the idea of subordinating Alekseyev's CHDB to Almaz , but this idea was eventually abandoned. TsMKB Almaz pursued the studies of *ekranoplan* projects for some three to four years. Engineers of this organisation proposed several WIG craft projects of different layouts. Some of these projects underwent wind tunnel tests and tests with models in free flight close to the water surface.

Apparently, this work failed to yield significant results that could be regarded as an improvement upon the results produced by CHDB. The work on *ekranoplans* was terminated in TsMKB Almaz in the early 1970s. In July 1974r the top officials of the Ministry of Shipbuilding Industry officially took a decision to halt the work on ekranoplans in the Almaz Design Bureau and instructed the latter to pass all the results of research and design work to CHDB.

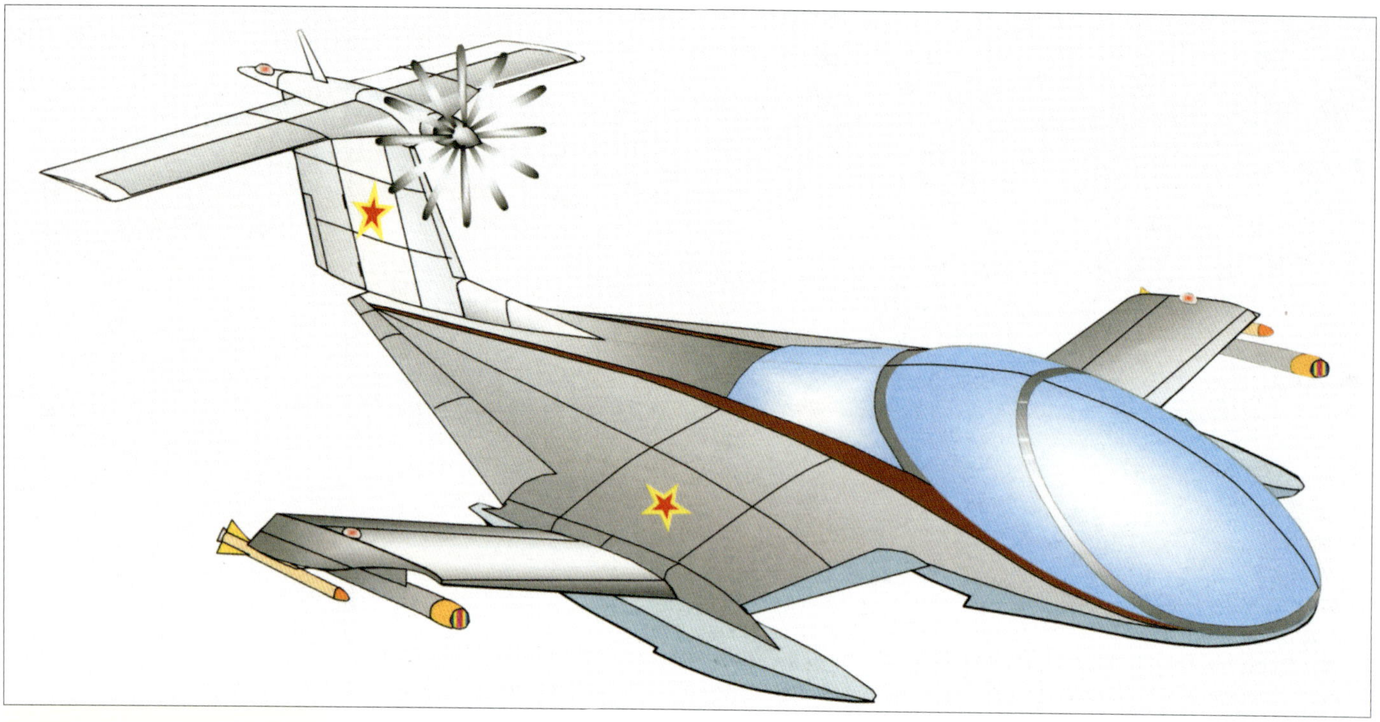

An artist's impression of the Delaero Globus-1 as an armed WIG craft.

Amphibia JSC and NPTK – see NVA projects

Amphicon – see NVA projects below

AMS – see after Wingships Company

1st Central Research Institute of the Ministry of Defence of the Russian Federation

Naval WIG craft with a displacement of 50 tonnes (under development)

In 2008 it was announced that the First Central Research Institute of Russia's Ministry of Defence (1st TsNII MO) was planning to design and build an ekranoplan with an AUW (displacement) of 50 tonnes (110,250 lb) for the Russian Navy. A statement to that effect was made by Viktor Denisov, the institute's representative, during a discussion at the Interpolitech-2008 police equipment exhibition in Moscow in October 2008. He noted that the EK-12 *ekranoplan* ordered by the Border Guard Service was suitable for operations only on inland waterways, while a craft with greater seaworthiness was required for sea operations. The 1st TsNII, he said, was in possession of expertise in these matters and was in a position to undertake the design of a large ekranoplan.

No new reports on that score have been published in the mass media since then.

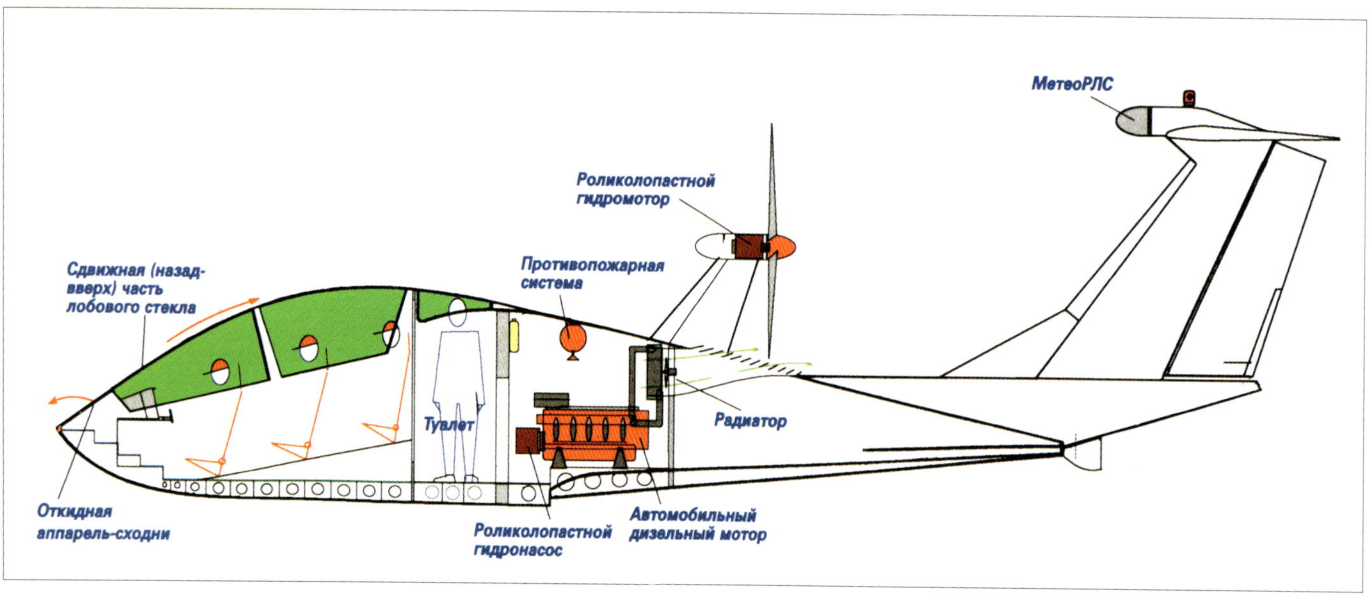

A cutaway drawing of the Globus-1, showing the unusual powerplant – an automotive diesel driving a hydraulic pump, which feeds a hydraulic motor driving the propeller (in this case a pusher prop). Part of the windshield slides upward and aft to give access to the boarding steps. A weather radar is mounted on the tail.

Delaero JSC

Globus-1 light WIG vehicle

In 1994 this small company produced a design of a multi-purpose WIG vehicle named Globus-1 (Globe-1), intended for cargo and passenger transportation, as well as for ambulance, patrol and liaison duties, to be operated mainly above water. Since then the project underwent protracted development; in 2005 it was publicised by the company's general designer Vladimir Nagornyy in a magazine article which is the source for the following description.

The Globus-1 is an eight-seat multi-purpose vehicle with a boat-hull fuselage blended into the wing centre section. The latter's planform is a reversed delta in the fashion of Lippisch designs; the wing centre section is supplemented by outer wing panels of small chord and higher aspect ratio, designed to ensure sufficient lift-to-drag ratio in the case of short-time out-of-ground-effect fly-overs (Type B vehicle). Two floats are located at the junctions of the wing centre section and the outer panels. The crew/passenger cabin is roomy enough for the passengers to stand upright. There is a provision for a toilet and a small galley. These features enable the vehicle to perform flights of long endurance and to stay afloat with passengers on board for a long time (for patrol duties or tourism).

The vehicle's powerplant originally included the following options: two DV-4 piston engines of 130 hp apiece, or two Wankel-type engines of 140 hp each, or one MKB Granit TVD-400 turboprop delivering 400 ehp. In 2005, instead of the use of two piston engines, a single 250-hp diesel engine was planned as the basic option, retaining the TVD-400 as an alternative. The engines are buried in the fuselage, transmitting their torque to a tractor propeller located at the junction of the fin and the horizontal stabiliser (the craft has a T-tail). Power transmission is effected with the help of a new type of hydraulic power train incorporating high-speed roller-blade hydraulic pumps and motors. This design feature has made it possible to obtain a low CG position and to permit the running of the engine with the propeller immobilised. Another advantage is the possibility of servicing the engine from inside the craft.

The avionics were to include a satellite navigation system and (optionally) a radar. Interestingly, the Globus-1 could carry lightweight missiles, presumably in a patrol version.

In 2005 the project seemed to have good prospects of being implemented. It received approval from TsAGI, from the Aircraft Industry Department of the Russian Ministry of Transport, and was included into the Comprehensive Programme of Development of Russia's General Aviation. Potential customers included the Administration of the Sakhalin Region and the Kurile Islands and the Border Guard Service which requested the materials on the project for consideration. However, nothing has been done in practical terms so far, and the vehicle has not reached the hardware stage.

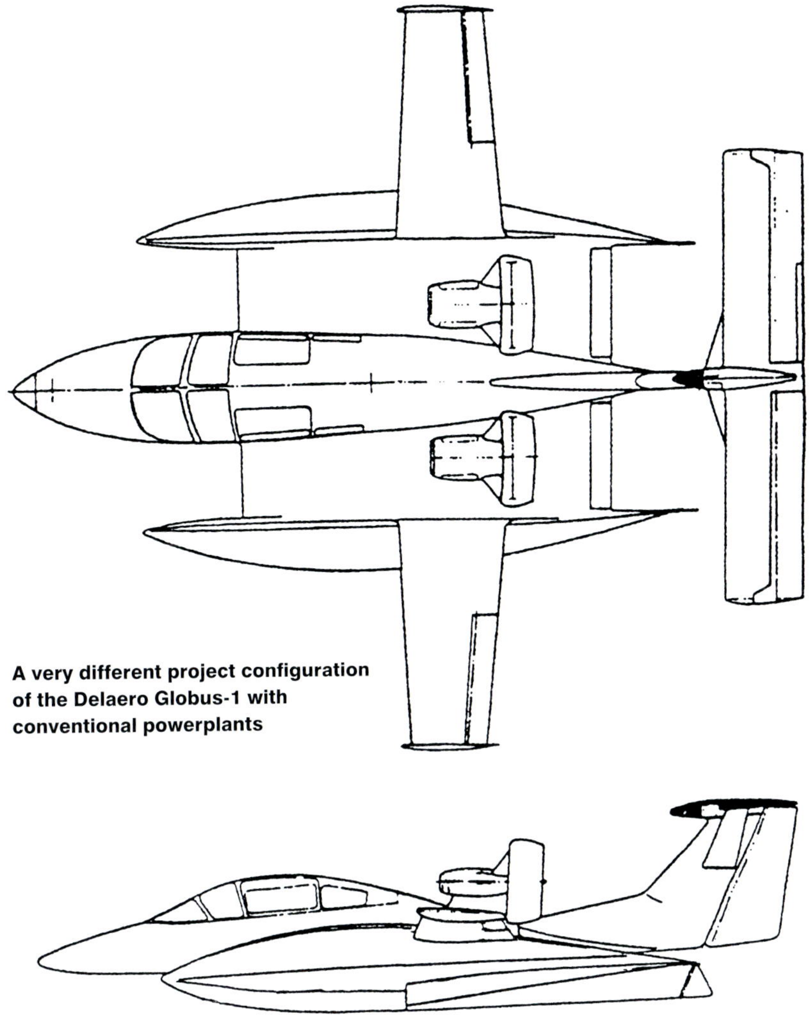

A very different project configuration of the Delaero Globus-1 with conventional powerplants

Since 2005 the project has undergone some modification. In one of the new project versions the propeller has been relocated from the top of the fin to a pylon mounted above the fuselage behind the

Basic specifications of the Delaero Globus-1

Take-off weight	2,200-2,400 kg (4,850-5,290 lb)
Payload	up to 800 kg (1,760 lb)
Altitude of high fuel efficiency flight	1.0-1.5 m (3-5 ft)
Maximum altitude	1,500 m (4,920 ft)
Cruising speed	120-180 km/h (75-112 mph)
Maximum speed	200 km/h (124 mph)
Maximum range	up to 2,000 km (1,240 miles)

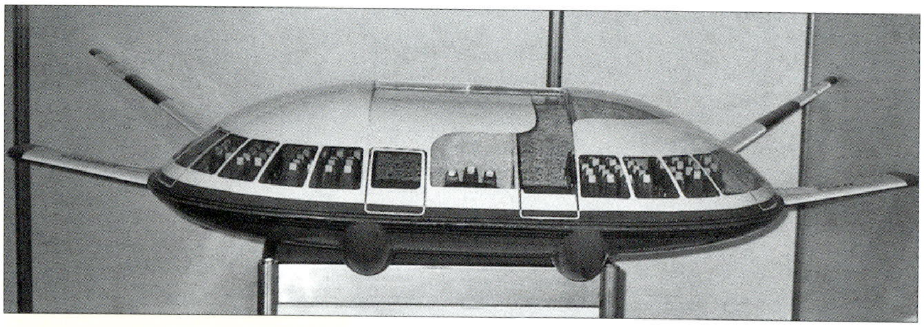

This cutaway model of one of the EKIP designs was displayed at one of the Moscow airshows.

cabin, close to the engine located inside the fuselage. As in the previous case, the propeller (a pusher this time) is to be driven by the engine via a hydraulic power train. Yet another project version of the Globus-1 represents actually a new machine under the same name. Instead of Lippisch-style wings, it uses the composite wing layout with a long-chord, low-aspect-ratio centre section flanked by floats; the wing centre section is supplemented with outer wing panels of small chord and higher aspect ratio. The powerplant comprises two flat-six engines mounted on pylons above the wing centre section, driving ducted pusher propellers.

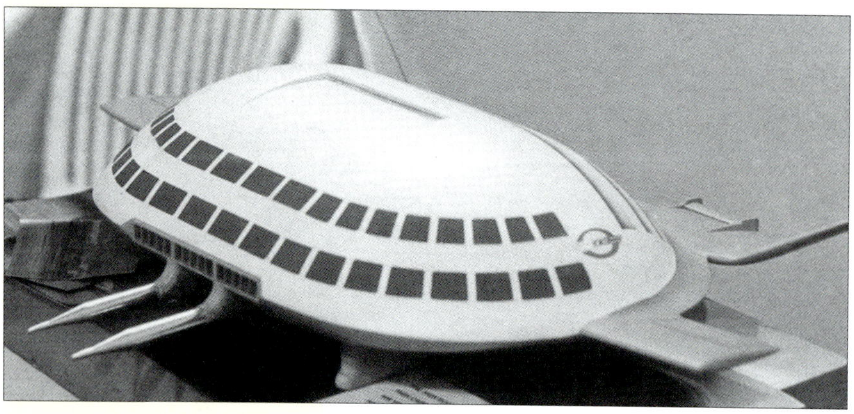

One more EKIP model sharing the same 'flying saucer' looks. The extensive glazing is noteworthy, as is the flat dorsal air intake for the cruise engines. The long probes on the nose may carry puffer nozzles.

EKIP flying vehicles

During the last two decades, unusual airborne vehicles capable, among other things, of flying in ground effect, have been under development within the framework of the EKIP company (EKIP stands for *Ekologiya i Progress* – Ecology and Progress). The post of general designer of the EKIP was occupied by Dr.Sc., Professor Lev N. Shchookin until his demise in August 2001. Previously he had worked for many years in Sergey P. Korolyov's OKB-1 renowned for its leading role in the Soviet rocketry and space research programmes. It was there that he conceived his idea of creating a new flying vehicle with an air cushion undercarriage which was originally intended for ensuring the mobility of strategic missile launch systems. Such vehicles requiring no prepared airfields could, in his opinion, find useful employment on the expanses of Siberia. However, the problem of missile mobility was solved by other means (wheeled mobile launch platforms), and Shchookin decided to use his concept for other purposes.

Under Shchookin's guidance fundamental principles and specific design features were evolved for a radically new type of aerial vehicles characterised by a highly unusual appearance. Their cushion-like lifting fuselage profiled like a very thick-section airfoil combines the functions of a fuselage and a wing (lifting body). It is fitted with small stub wings required for placing ailerons on them, and with aerodynamic surfaces acting as a tail unit. The powerplant of the EKIP vehicles is accommodated inside the vehicle's body and comprises turbofan cruise engines and auxiliary turboshaft engines driving fans which produce an air cushion during take-off and landing. One such design has two cruise engines and two auxiliary engines.

The air required for the engines is taken up through a slot on the upper side of the centre wing (fuselage) section. The efflux of the cruise engines is emitted through flat nozzles placed along the whole span of the wing centre section in the plane dividing the air streams coming from the upper and lower surfaces. Control vanes are installed in the nozzles. According to calculations, if an EKIP vehicle weighing 120 t (264,550 lb) is powered by two ZMKB (Lotarev) D-18T turbofans rated at 23,400 kgp (51,590 lbst) each the power-to-weight ratio of the vehicle will amount to 0.38-0.40, which will enable it to perform a take-off from a ground strip or water surface of not more than 500 m (1,640 ft) long – which is outstanding short-field performance. EKIP vehicles with a cargo capacity of several hundred tonnes will not necessitate the construction of special airports with 5,000-m (16,400-ft) concrete runways as required, for example, for the Airbus Industrie A380 wide-body airliner.

The air cushion take-off/landing device featuring a combined air jet and chamber layout is placed well within the contours of the body and beneath the whole of the body, making it possible to ensure a low level of pressure both on the body itself and on the supporting surface (ground or water). In addition to this static air cushion, EKIP vehicles are able to make use of a dynamic air cushion characteristic for WIG vehicles; there is a provision for operating these vehicles in the ground effect mode in addition to the basic high-altitude ('aircraft') flight mode. In fact, the EKIP vehicles combine the qualities of the ACV, WIG vehicle and aircraft. They can move in close proximity to the ground or water on an air cushion at speeds of up to 160 km/h (99 mph), perform a flight in ground effect like WIG vehicles at speeds up to 400 km/h (248 mph) and fly like aircraft at altitudes up to 10 km (32,810 ft) with speeds up to 750 km/h (465 mph).

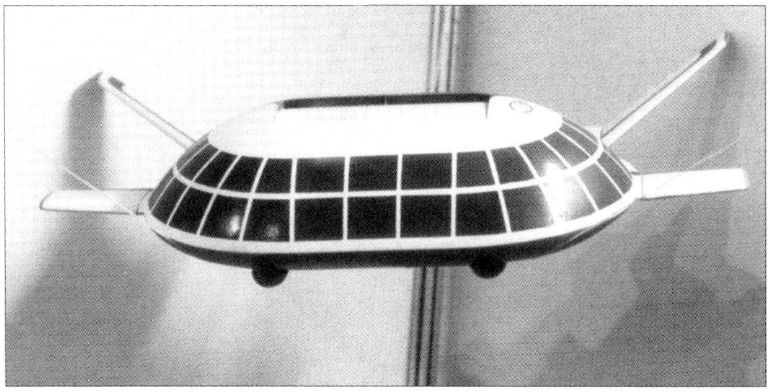

Above: A display model of the EKIP seen at one of the MAKS airshows in Zhukovskiy. Note the flat dorsal air intake.

Left: Yet another cutaway model of an EKIP displayed at the MAKS-95 airshow, showing the flat nozzle located between the canted fins.

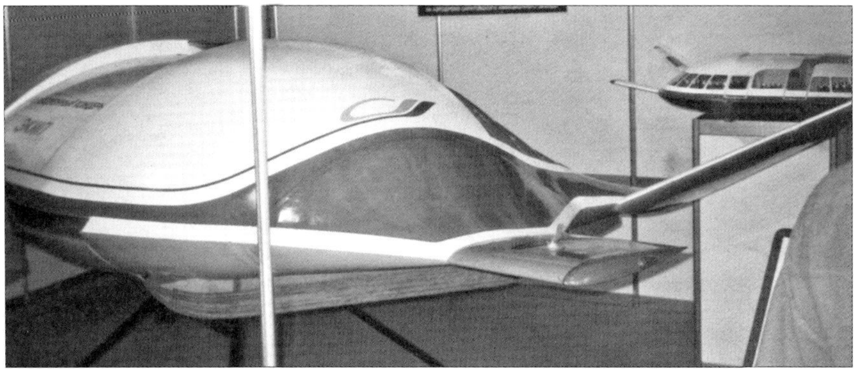

Another MAKS-95 exhibit – the L2-3 radio-controlled model. The very first L-1 RC model featured a T-tail.

As envisioned by the author of the idea, the EKIP vehicles should possess a number of advantages over traditional aircraft. EKIP vehicles require no airfields and are designed to be able to land not only on airfields of any category, but also on unprepared ground strips and water surface. The high thickness ratio of the body affords internal volumes for the accommodation of passengers and cargoes that exceed by a factor of several times the volumes available in traditional aircraft of the same cargo lifting capacity. The weight of the EKIP vehicle's airframe in relation to the all-up weight, according to estimates of specialists, is 30% lower than that of the existing aircraft, which makes it possible to increase the payload accordingly. The big volume of the body makes it easier to adapt these vehicles to the use of natural gas or hydrogen as fuel.

EKIP vehicles offer enhanced flight safety. Take-off and landing are performed at speeds which are 2 to 2.5 times lower than those of the present-day cargo and passenger aircraft; EKIP vehicles with an all-up weight of 300 t (661,375 lb) will have a take-off speed of not more than 140 km/h (87 mph) and a landing speed of not more than 100 km/h (62 mph).Even when three of the four engines have cut, the power of the remaining engine is sufficient to ensure a safe landing mode. Provision is made for active boundary layer control so as to ensure a smooth air flow around the thick body and reduce drag, which also enhances flight safety.

The main technical feature of the EKIP aircraft is the vortex-based boundary-layer control system (BLCS) controlling the airflow at the aft-facing surface of the vehicle. Creating a multitude of consecutively placed transverse vortices, the BLCS ensures separation-free flow around the body of the vehicle and a reduction of aerodynamic drag. The system is actuated by auxiliary engines which run at an economic rating in cruise flight. Operating in the maximum rating mode on take-off, they also ensure the functioning of the air cushion undercarriage.

The company effected a large volume of experimental work involving the use of the L-1 and L2-3 radio-controlled flying models. Construction was initiated of the L2-1 automatically controlled full-scale demonstrator vehicle weighing 9 t (19,840 lb), the testing of which was expected to pave the way to creating a whole range of type of such machines with an all-up weight ranging from 9 t to hundreds of tonnes.

A project was prepared of an EKIP-type vehicle for fighting forest fires. Called *Lesnik* (Forester), this vehicle was to have an all-up weight of 12 tonnes (26,455 lb) and to carry a 5-t (11,020-lb) load of water or fire retardant. Its performance included a maximum speed of 600 km/h (372 mph), a speed of 140-150 km/h (87-93 mph) during fire-fighting, a ceiling of 10 km (32,810 ft), a range of 2,000 km (1,240 miles) and a take-off/landing distance of less than 500 m (1,640 ft). Series production of this and other vehicles in the EKIP range was expected to be launched at the Saratov aircraft plant. There were plans to enlist the services of the Yakovlev Design Bureau for the detail design of the EKIP airframes.

The L2-1 automatically controlled full-scale flying demonstrator is the closest the EKIP programme has yet come to fruition. The unfinished L2-1 is seen here in the assembly shop of the Saratov aircraft factory No. 292.

By the end of 1993 the Triumph company which is a part of the EKIP concern completed design work on the EKIP L-3 120-tonne vehicle. There was an even bigger design, the L4-2, with an AUW of 600 tonnes (1,322,770 lb), which would carry a 200-tonne (440,920-lb) load over a distance of 8,600 km (5,345 miles). It was hoped that by 1997 the L-3 would reach the stage of series production. These hopes proved unjustified, yet in 1998 Lev N. Shchookin spoke optimistically in a magazine article about the chances for a relatively speedy implementation of his concept. It seemed that the ball was set rolling. Construction of the abovementioned L2-1 was proceeding at the Saratov aircraft factory No. 292. The authorities of the Saratov Region pledged their support for the project; it was endorsed by the Russian Academy of Natural Sciences and by the then President Boris N. Yel'tsin.

Unfortunately, as it often happens in the present situation in Russia with its persistent financial and economic problems and meagre financial outlays for research, the funding of the project came to a halt, it ceased to attract interest and the work all but stopped. Shchookin began to encounter all sorts of hindrances, including false promises of funding; these vicissitudes seriously affected his health.

In August 2001 Lev N. Shchookin passed away. The duties of General Designer were taken over by Semyon M. Zel'vinskiy. The EKIP company went on struggling for access to the necessary financial resources which would make it possible to implement the envisaged projects.

In the early 2000s the programme of the EKIP concern included the L2-3, L3-1 and L3-2 vehicles with an all-up weight of 12, 45 and 360 t (26,455; 99,200; and 793,650 lb) respectively and a passenger seating capacity of 40, 160 and 1,200 persons respectively. All the three vehicles have a speed of 700 km/h (434 mph) at altitude and a take-off run of 450 to 600 m (1,480-1,970 ft).

In addition to the heavy manned vehicles, the company's programme includes development of small unmanned vehicles – the EKIP-2 and EKIP-AULA L2-3 (AULA stands for *avtoma**tich**eski oopravl**ya**yemyy le**tah**tel'nyy appa**raht*** – automatically controlled aerial vehicle). Both of them are intended for monitoring and surveillance duties.

The EKIP-2 has an AUW of up to 850 kg (1,875 lb), a useful load of 70 kg (160 lb) and a cruising speed of 250 km/h (155 mph). The vehicle can be flown at altitudes between 20 m (65 ft) and 5,500 m (18,040 ft). The EKIP-2 can serve as a basis for a two-seat piloted vehicle, the EKIP-2P with an AUW of 1,000 kg (2,200 lb).

The EKIP AULA L2-3 has an AUW of 280-350 kg (618-772 lb), a useful load of 20-50 kg (44-110 lb), a cruising speed of 180 km/h (112 mph), a maximum flight altitude of 3,000 m (9,840 ft) and an endurance of 2 hours.

Confronted with the lack of interest for the EKIP programme at home, the management of the Saratov aircraft plant began to look for potential investors abroad. In 2000 Aleksandr Yermishin, the then director of the plant, went to the USA where he had meetings with the military and with representatives of the aircraft industry. The US side displayed much interest for starting the manufacture of EKIP vehicles in a pilotless version in the USA, but wished to obtain exclusive rights to the EKIP, which was unacceptable for Yermishin. From 2003 the work on EKIP at the Saratov plant was stopped because the plant was in dire straits financially. Eventually a compromise was reached. It was reported that the Saratov plant, the EKIP concern and the US Naval Aviation Research Center would undertake joint production of EKIP vehicles. US agencies were interested in using the EKIP as pilotless vehicles for combating forest fires and eliminating the consequences of natural disasters.

It was expected that in 2007 the testing of a Russian-US vehicle based on the EKIP design should start in the state of Maryland, USA, with a prospect of starting series production five years later. However, these plans obviously failed to be put into practice. At present the future of the programme is uncertain.

Eurasia JSC in co-operation with Latvian institutions

MF-17

In the mid-1990s co-operation between Russian and Latvian institutions resulted in the emergence of this project of a light WIG vehicle designated MF-17. It was developed as a joint venture with the participation of the Russia-based Eurasia JSC (headed by F. Mukhamedov), the design group of the Riga Aviation University (formerly RKIIGA) and the 'Latvijas Laivas' ('Free Latvia') Experimental Sports Shipbuilding Centre based in Jurmala, Latvia. This was a two-seat vehicle featuring a typical Lippisch layout with the reverse-delta wings. Upturned winglets with ailerons were mounted on the wingtip floats; the T-tail incorporated a rudder and elevators. The cockpit accommodating two persons in a side-by-side arrangement had a large streamlined transparency; it could be fitted with single or dual sets of controls. Mounted on a pylon behind the cockpit was an Austrian (presumably Rotax) engine driving a shrouded pusher propeller of Russian manufacture. The avionics included US-manufactured satellite navigation and communication equipment.

The vehicle's principal mode of operation was flight in ground effect, but it was capable of performing short flights at low altitude to avoid obstacles.

A model of the MF-17 light WIG vehicle co-developed by Russia and Latvia.

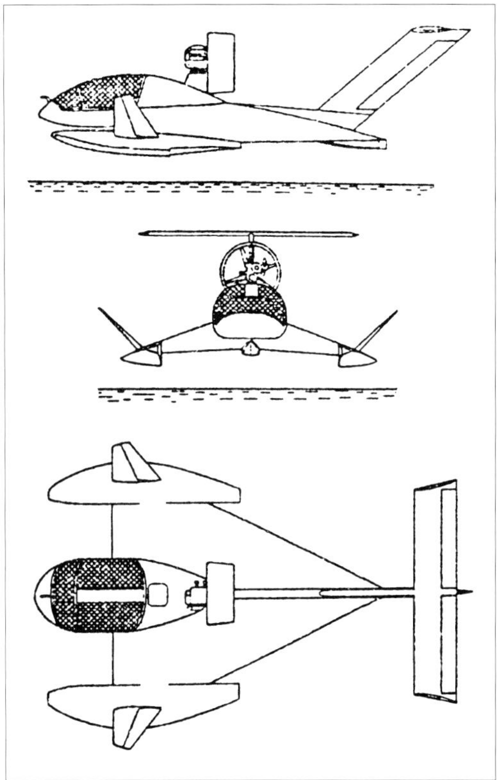

A provisional three-view of the MF-17, showing the 'taildragger' float arrangement.

With an empty weight of 250 kg (551 lb) and an AUW of 450 kg (990 lb), the vehicle had a design speed of 100 km/h (62 mph) and a range of 250 km (155 miles). The admissible wave height was 0.5-0.6 m (1 ft 8 in – 2 ft).

The participants of the project announced their plans for building ad certifying the prototype of the MF-17 in the course of 1996-97, whereupon it was to be put into production in Jurmala and sold to customers at a price of approximately US$ 30,000. All this hinged upon finding investors to back up this venture, but apparently the necessary funding could not be procured and no production ensued.

LAT

LAT (***Lyoh**kaya Avi**ah**tsiya Tagan**rog**a* – Light Aviation of Taganrog). This joint stock company which styles itself as Science and Production Enterprise (*na**ooch**no-proiz**vod**stvennoye predpri**yah**tiye* – NPP) came into existence as a result of activities of a group of young designers who, to begin with, worked within the framework of the ***Kras**nyye*

The LAT R-02 Robert on a ground handling dolly at the Hydro Aviation Show-2000 in Ghelendzhik. The aircraft is registered by the Aviation Enthusiasts' Federation of Russia (FLA RF) as FLA-RF 02558.

Kryl'ya (Red Wings) Centre of aviation enthusiast work. Later this centre transformed itself into a small private enterprise under the same name; inside this enterprise the LAT company was organised. In 1992 it became an independent structure, headed by Yuriy Usol'tsev.

Under Usol'tsev's guidance several light aircraft designs were developed first by the abovementioned Centre and then by the LAT company. These were the R-01, R-01M, R-02 and R-50 light seaplanes which bore a common name, Robert (in honour of Robert L. Bartini). Owing to some special features of their design they possessed pronounced WIG vehicle properties. All of these machines have low-set wings with a wide-chord centre section which rests on the water surface when the machines are afloat, thus ensuring their stability and buoyancy. During take-off and landing the ram air creates a dynamic air cushion under the wing centre section.

R-01, R-02

The R-01 aircraft weighing 350 kg (771 lb) for take-off was a single-seater with an open cockpit; its outer wing panels had pronounced forward sweep. It was successfully test-flown in 1989. The improved R-01M version powered by a 44-hp Robin-140EC piston engine had a take-off weight of 440 kg

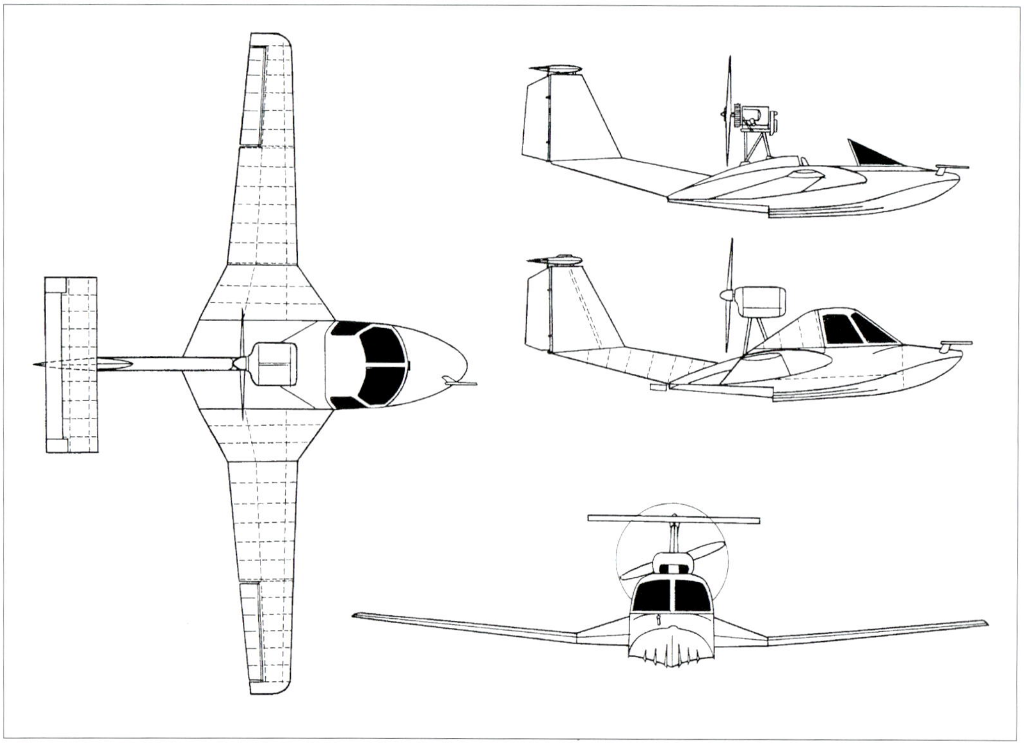

A three-view of the R-02, with an additional side view (top) of the forward-swept wing R-01M Robert.

(970 lb). The R-02 differed in having an enclosed two-seat cockpit and straight wings with an extended-chord centre section. It was intended for use as an executive, patrol and trainer aircraft.

The aircraft was powered by an 80-hp Rotax 912A3 engine installed behind the cockpit and driving a tractor propeller. The R-02 was provided with a quick-action parachute rescue system. Here are some basic figures for the R-02: wingspan, 10.0 m (32 ft 9.7 in); length, 6.3 m (20 ft 8 in); wing area, 12.4m^2 (133.3 sq ft); all-up weight, 560 kg (1,234 lb); speed, 165 km/h (103 mph).

R-50

In 1992-94 the LAT designers prepared an advanced development project of a multi-purpose amphibian designated R-50 Robert. In its baseline version it was a cargo and passenger aircraft with a cabin accommodating a pilot and five passengers; the passenger seats could be easily removed for the carriage of cargo. The basic version could also be used for patrol and liaison duties. Other versions under development included ambulance, fire-fighting, agricultural, SAR, ecological survey and other versions. The baseline version was to be powered by two Czech 140-hp Motorlet (Walter) M-332AR engines which could eventually be replaced by the indigenous MKB Granit TVD-400 turboprops (the definitive version was expected to deliver 500-560 ehp) or 250-hp VOKBM M-17 piston engines. Provision was made for the installation of the MIKBO-43 multi-function integrated avionics suite permitting the aircraft to fly in adverse weather conditions and at night.

In common with its predecessor, the R-50 has a wide-chord wing centre section creating a WIG effect during take-of and landing. In ground effect the lift/drag ratio of the wings rises to 19-20 as against 11-13 in normal cruise flight. One can also use the ground effect mode for cruising flight, but a prolonged flight close to the supporting surface is possible only on condition of prior installation of an automatic pitch stability augmentation system which can be done at the customer's request.

In 1995 there were plans for creating the R-50M version with a cabin lengthened by 0.75 m (2 ft 5.5 in) and twin engines. Design specifications for it included a take-off weight of 2,700 kg (5,950 lb), a payload of 560 kg (1,234 lb) for a range of 600 km (370 miles) with two 210-hp engines or 650 kg (1,433 lb) for a range of 750 km (465 miles) with two 240-hp engines. Its dimensions were: wingspan, 15.40 m (50 ft 6.3 in); wing aspect ratio, 8.227; length, 11.40 m (37 ft $4\frac{51}{64}$ in); height, 4.30 m (14 ft $1\frac{19}{64}$ in). Series production of the R-50 was to be launched at an aircraft plant in Doobna, Moscow Region, but financial difficulties prevented these plans from being implemented.

An artist's impression of the huge twin-hull WIG vehicle designed by Marengo JSC as a space shuttle transporter.

Marengo JSC

This little-known joint stock company is engaged in developing a project of an *ekranoplan* intended as a carrier for an air-launched aerospace vehicle. The configuration of this huge twin-fuselage machine is apparent from an artist's impression published here. It is in many respects similar to the twin-hull *ekranoplan* proposed by the Krylov TsNII for the same purposes (see the preceding chapter). However, the Marengo project has some special features. In addition to the five cruise/boost turbofans mounted on the crossbar between the hulls forward of the wing centre section, there area two pairs of turbofans mounted on horizontal pylons outboard of the forward sections of the hulls. Their efflux presumably can be deflected into the space below the outer wing panels to create a static air cushion for take-off. It is apparently for this purpose that the wing outer panels carry endplates at their tips – together with the hull and the flap they create a

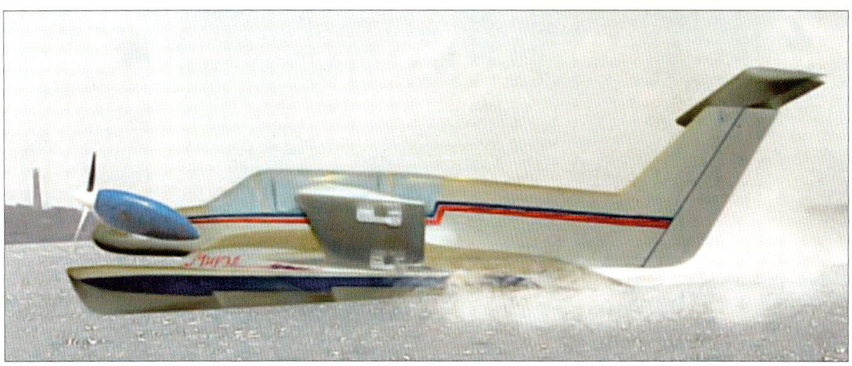

'Doctored' images of a model of the Mirel light WIG vehicle showing the machine on a beach and in flight.

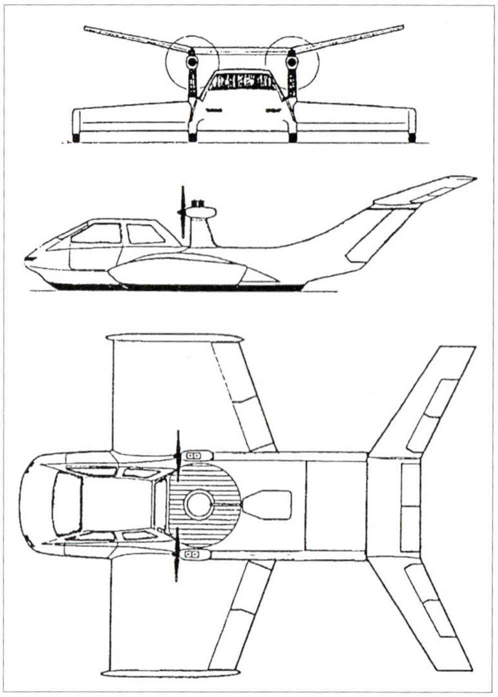

A three-view drawing of the NVA-1SM light WIG vehicle showing the horizontal fan creating a static air cushion.

chamber into which the efflux is injected. Unfortunately, no further information is available.

Mirel

This is presumably the name of a company about which no information has been published. Two artist's impressions of a WIG vehicle wearing this name on the fuselage are practically the only materials available at present on this design. The pictures show a vehicle whose layout is basically similar to that of the EK-12 Ivolga. A fuselage resembling that of a 6-8-seat lightplane and featuring a T-tail is flanked by wide-chord, short-span wing sections the tips of which rest on floats. The wing centre section has anhedral. High-aspect-ratio outer wing panels are attached to the wing centre section. Two horizontally opposed piston engines flanking the front fuselage drive three-blade propellers whose wash can be directed under the wing centre section.

NVA projects by N. N. Nazarov (Ekolen, Amphicon and other companies)

A series of highly original WIG vehicle projects was developed on the basis of a concept evolved by N. N. Nazarov, an engineer who had worked at one time in a branch of Alekseyev's CHDB which from 1976 became a Gorkiy-based branch of the Krylov TsNII. He started his work on NVA projects already during his work at the TsNII branch. Later he left this organisation and founded his own company – Science and Production Association (NPO) Ekolen JSC in St. Petersburg. (Ekolen is an abbreviation for *Eko**logi**ya* ***Len**skovo* *reghi**on**a* – Ecology of the Lena River Region, indicating that the projects were to be tailored to the needs of that region in East Siberia.) It was there that he started formulating his comprehensive programme of *ekranoplan* con-

A model of a heavier cargo WIG vehicle in the NVA series, showing the cargo bays inside the wings.

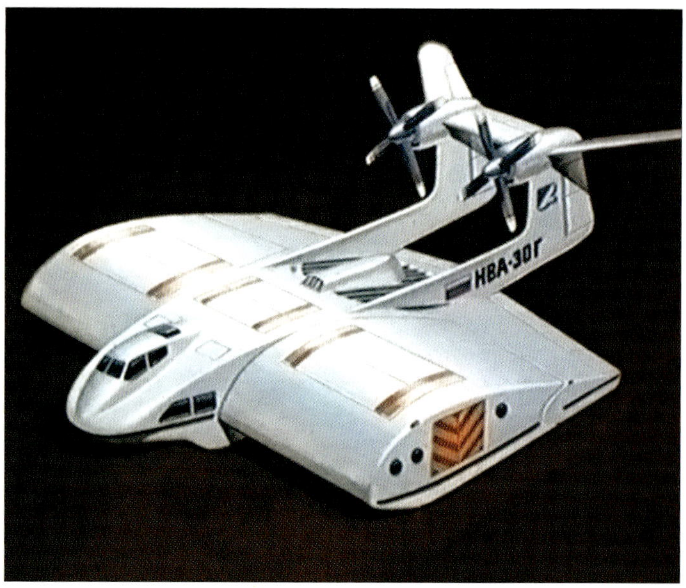

These artist's impression of the NVA-30G show the unusual wing design with detachable full-span cargo modules. Note the loading doors in the tip ribs and upper surface of the centre section and the outer wing modules.

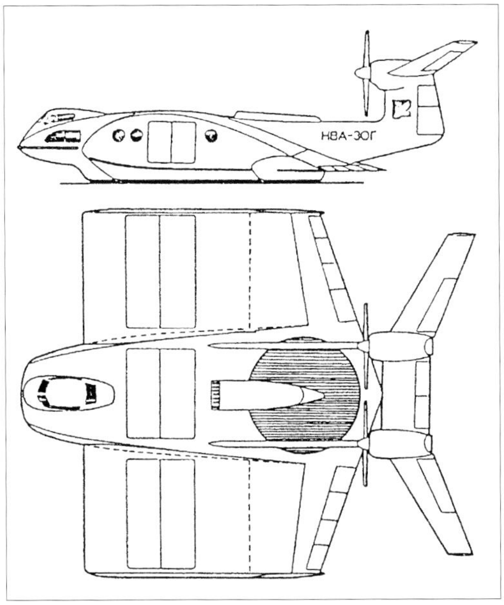

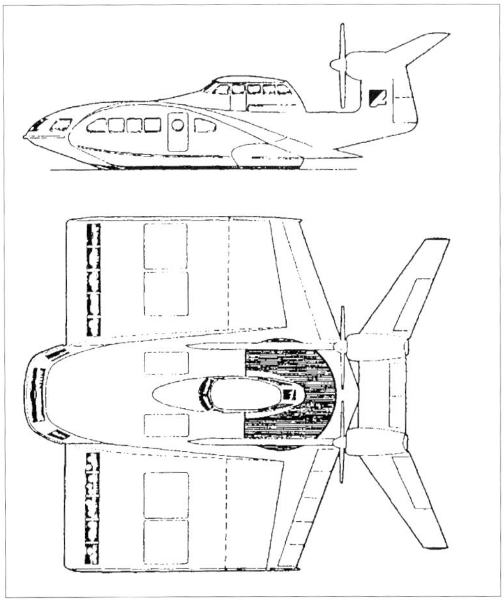

Far left: Two views of the NVA-30G with the wing cargo modules attached.

The NVA-30P passenger version is rather different, having a cockpit located well aft (on top of the fan creating the static air cushion).

struction based on the NVA concept. This work was carried on by Nazarov in a successor company, named Amphicon, which was set up in Nizhniy Novgorod. Amphicon is an abbreviation for Amfibiynye konstrooktsiï (amphibious designs). The full name of the company is NPF Amphicon, NPF is deciphered as naoochno-proizvodstvennaya firma – Science and Production firm. N. N. Nazarov was its General Director and Chief Designer.

Owing to various vicissitudes Nazarov had to change his place of work and move to Siberia where he worked in the Baikalenergotrans (BET) company based in Ulan-Ude, Buryatia, and in the Amphibia JSC company based in Abakan, Khakassia, in co-operation with a number of other companies and institutions. During a short period some work on Nazarov's designs was conducted at the Krasnoyarsk Machine-building Plant – one of Russia's major enterprises in the field of missile and space technology. N. N. Nazarov passed away in Abakan after a serious illness on 6th July 2008. His work is being continued by his associates. Some of Nazarov's projects are described below.

In the early 1990s the Amphicon company presented a national development programme of means of transportation in Russia based on a new generation of WIG vehicles – the so-called Ground-and-Air Amphibious Vehicles (GAAV), the Russian abbreviation being NVA (*na**zem**no-voz**dooshnyye** am**fib**ii*). The programme covered a 15-year period up to 2008. The range of projects envisaged in the programme represented a gradual transition from a 3-tonne (6,610-lb) vehicle of 'aircraft' layout to a 'flying wing' vehicle weighing 5,000 t (11,022,930 lb). In all, by 1993 Amphicon had developed ten baseline projects, each in several versions. Information about them was presented in the catalogue of the

An artist's impression of the NVA-60P – a scaled-up version of the NVA-30P with turbofan cruise engines.

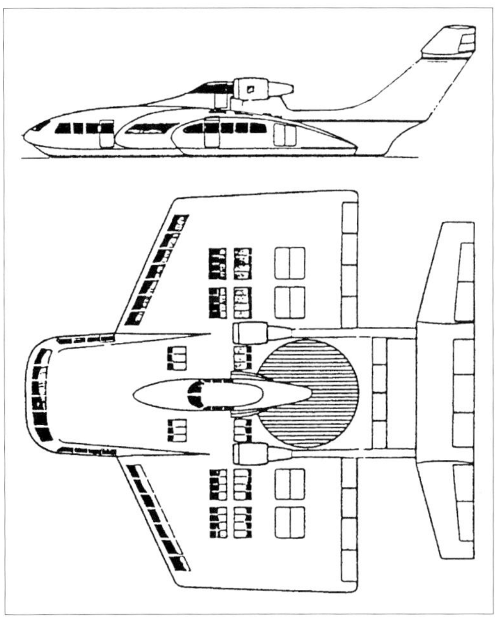

A three-view drawing of the NVA-60P. Note the 'skylights' in the wing upper surface; without them the cabins would be too dark.

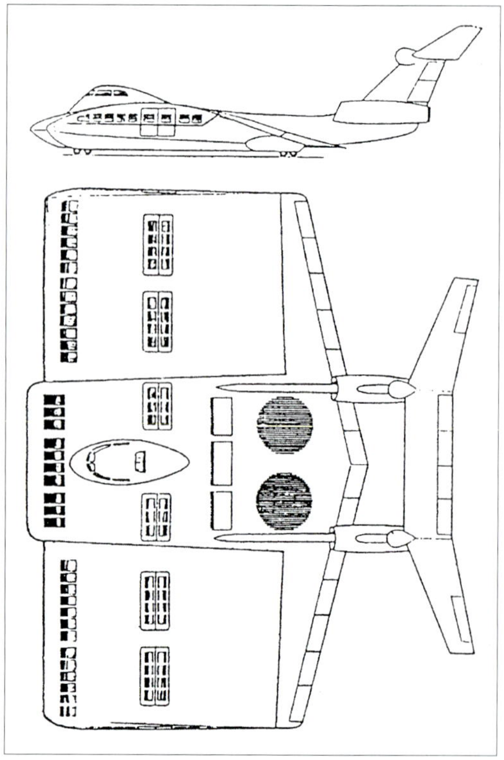

An artist's impression of the huge NVA-120 *ekranoplan* using the 'flying wing' layout.

Right: The passenger-configured NVA-120P featuring a revised tail with swept dihedral outer portions. Again, it has 'skylights' in the wing upper surface.

MAKS-93 air show (September 1993); every project was accompanied by the planned year of construction (between 1996 and 2008). The machine to be built in 2008 was to have the all-up weight of 5,000 t. Drawings of the following six projects were published in the catalogue: NVA-1SM (1996), NVA-30P (1997), NVA-30G (1997), NVA-120P (1997), NVA-60P (1997), NVA-600 (2003). The G and P suffixes mean *groozo**va**ya* (cargo) and *passa**zheer**skaya* (passenger) versions respectively. Other sources mention such projects as the NVA-60G, NVA-120GP (***groo**zopassa**zheer**skaya* – combi), NVA-600TP, NVA-900, NVA-2000, NVA-5000 (this list is not exhaustive). In English-language advertising materials the abbreviation NVA is replaced by GAAV. As witnessed by the drawings, many of the projects envisage the use of powerful fans for creating a static air cushion during take-off, making these craft a combination of ACV and WIG vehicle. The company advertised such an 'important advantage' of the NVA vehicles as 'their load-carrying capacity amounting to 50% of the all-up weight'. A characteristic feature of almost all designs was the use of airfoil-shaped fuselages as lifting bodies. Conversely, wings of very high relative thickness provided the space for cargoes and passengers.

An artist's impression of the NVA-120P.

This artist's impression shows a huge WIG vehicle in the NVA series used as a submarine tender.

An attempt to bring one of Nazarov's designs to the hardware stage was connected with the Krasnoyarsk Machine-building Plant (Krasmash). The project selected for practical implementation was the NVA-30, a relatively small vehicle. Design work progressed to the preliminary design stage. A specially established private company named Sibiam provided the funding needed for detail design and prototype manufacture which would be followed by operational trials in the Krasnoyarsk region. In 1992 Krasmash began receiving documentation on the NVA-30 from Ekolen. Construction of the prototype was started. Yet, soon the allotted funds 'vanished into thin air'; the machine was not completed.

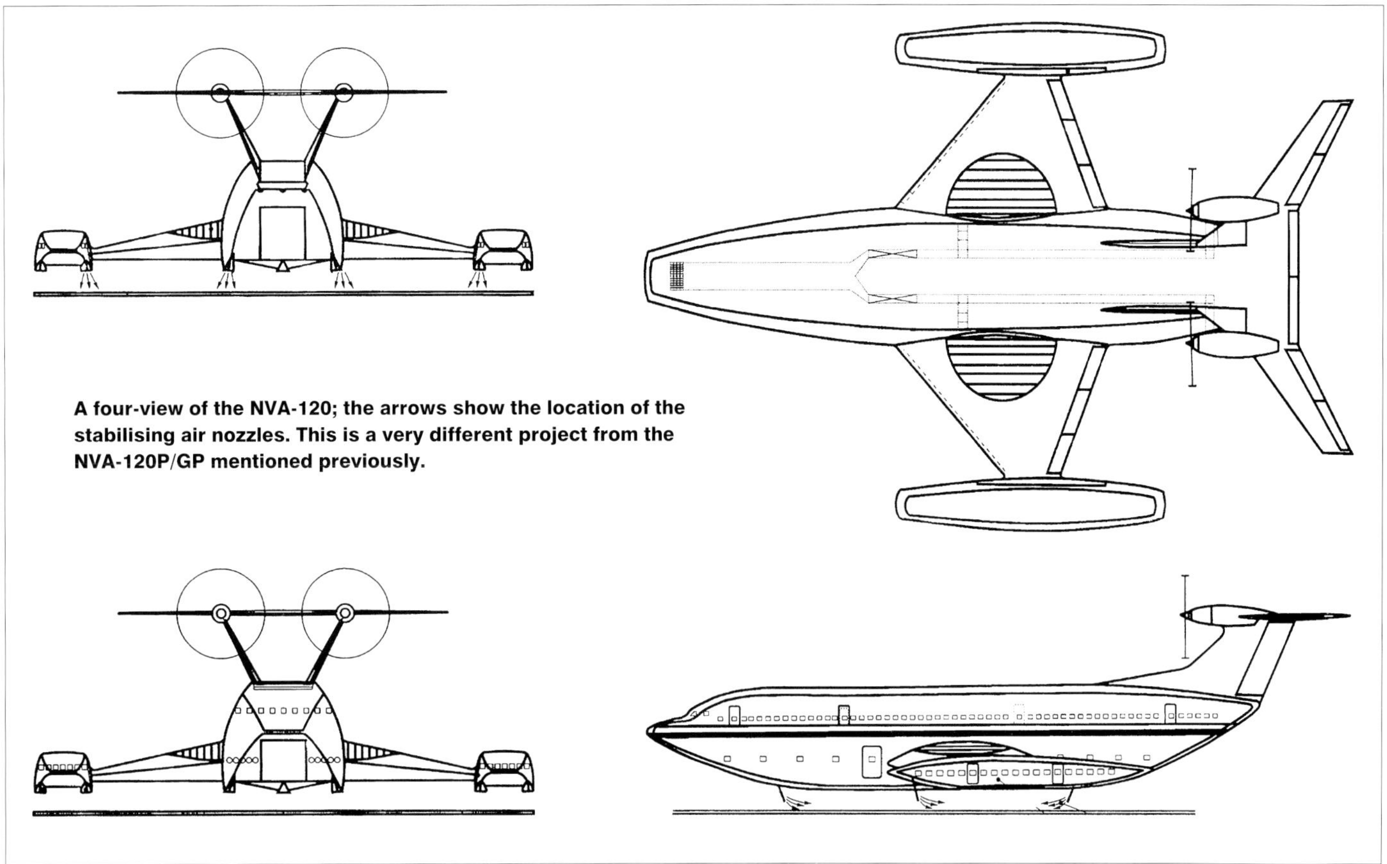

A four-view of the NVA-120; the arrows show the location of the stabilising air nozzles. This is a very different project from the NVA-120P/GP mentioned previously.

The very ambitious programme described above could be implemented only on condition of massive financial support from the Government or other sources – which was far from realistic to expect under the circumstances prevailing in Russia. To date, not a single project from the Amphicon period progressed further than the drawing board.

Nazarov's work in Baikalenergotrans resulted in the emergence of new projects differing in their layout from those described above. Some of them are illustrated by a drawing which presents three types of different size. They differ from the previous generation of Nazarov's projects in making use of the traditional low-aspect-ratio wings rather than airfoil-shaped lifting bodies. These are:

NVA-06-10 GP

This is a small river-going WIG-vehicle, presumably with an AUW of some 10 tonnes (32,800 lb). In its layout it closely resembles Rostislav Alekseyev's machines, although it is powered by a single aft-mounted turboprop, without the use of front-mounted engines for power-augmented take-off. It is intended for the transportation of cargoes and passengers, as indicated by the GP suffix.

NVA-220-300 GP

Described as a sea-going *ekranoplan*, this vehicle in the 300-tonne (661,400-lb) class embodies a trimaran layout, the side fuselages flanking a very wide-chord wing centre section. On the outboard sides they are fitted with smaller-chord outer wing panels having endplate floats. The centre fuselage is reminiscent of an airliner. Two turboprop engines

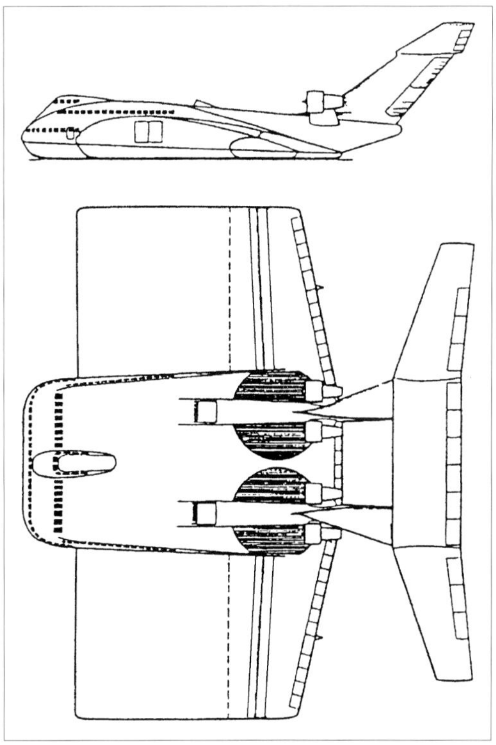

Two views of the NVA-600. Due to its large size the vehicle requires two fans to create a static air cushion.

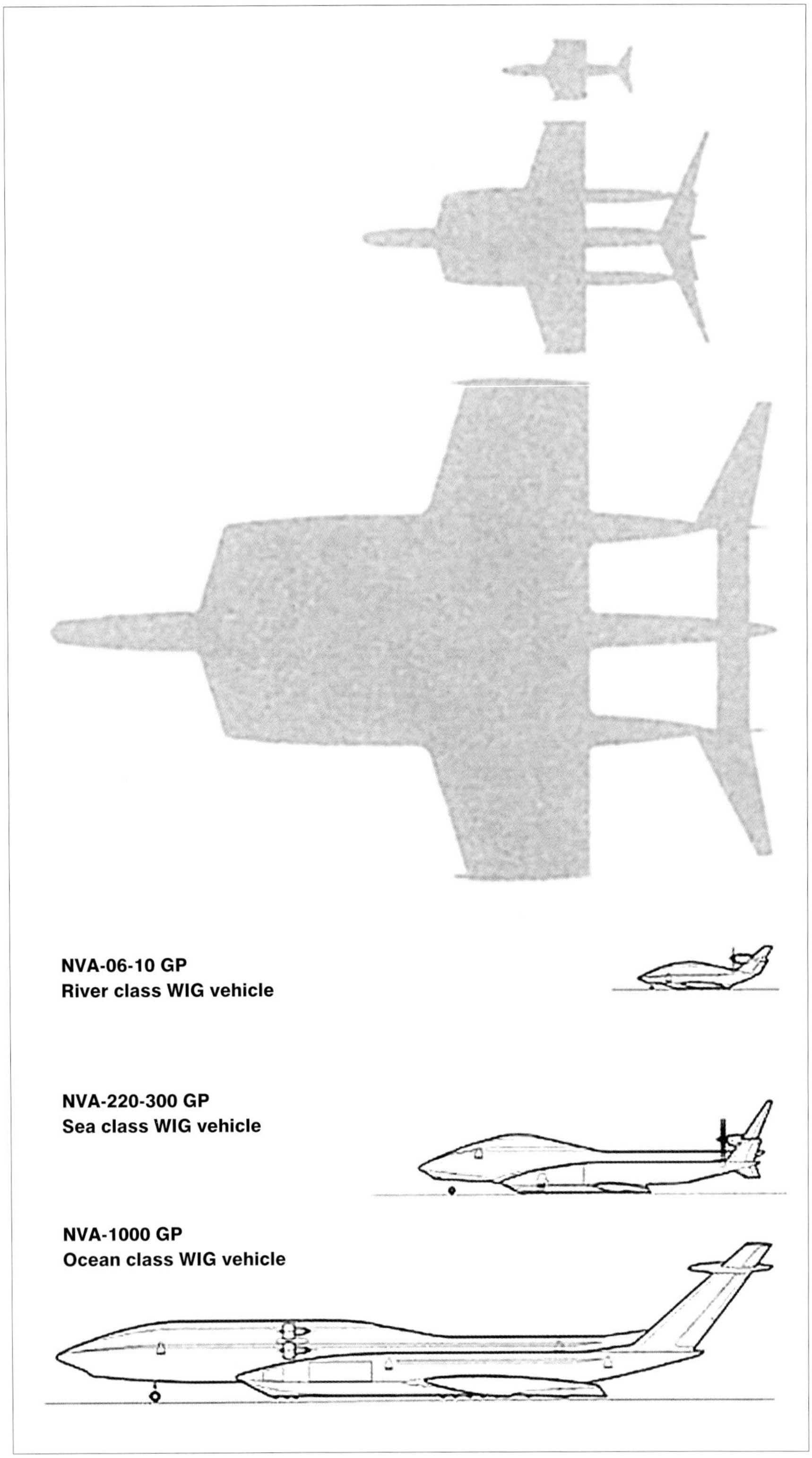

NVA-06-10 GP
River class WIG vehicle

NVA-220-300 GP
Sea class WIG vehicle

NVA-1000 GP
Ocean class WIG vehicle

are located at the junctions of the twin fins and the horizontal tail. A notable feature is the wheel undercarriage – probably for ground handling rather than for take-off and landing on a solid surface.

NVA-1000 GP

This is an ocean-going craft of truly gigantic size, presumably in the 1,000-tonne (3,280,000-lb) class, looks like a scaled-up version of the NVA-220-300 described above. It is powered by four high-bypass turbofans or propfans mounted in pairs on both sides of the fuselage.

Nazarov's demise might signify the end of the NVA line of projects. However, the Amphibiya JSC continues its work on the NVA projects, having enlisted the support from an organisation which styles itself as Noöspherical industry and transport complex (NPTK). Some of these projects were given a measure of publicity; they were presumably developed while Nazarov was still alive. This series of projects differs from the preceding one in both designations and layout. It encompasses vehicles in the NVA-07 range, such as the NVA-07-025 and NVA-07-530 GP (the last three digits referring to the vehicle's weight in tones).

According to Professor Drachov, one of the leaders of the NPTK company, the WIG vehicles developed by the two companies are to be used primarily in Russia's northern areas, Siberia and the Far East.

NVA-07-025

This vehicle of relatively small size, in the 25-tonne (55,110-lb) weight class, is intended for carrying passengers. It is apparently powered by one turboprop engine with a ducted pusher propeller. A notable feature of the design is the integration of the propeller shroud with the fins placed on the aft parts of the floats flanking the short-span wing centre section. Outer wing panels of small chord and higher aspect ratio are attached to the floats.

NVA-07-530 GP

This is a heavy WIG craft which is intended for operation in the seas encompassed by the so-called Northern Sea Route (the route along Russia's Arctic coast-line). This huge vehicle will be capable of carrying a 200-tonne (441,000-lb) cargo at a speed of 550 km/h (342 mph). An unusual feature of the design is the combination of three fuselages joined together to form an integrated structure. The outboard fuselage sections are very thick airfoils providing lift. At the same time they are provided with endplate floats on their outer sides, thanks to which the space between the floats and beneath the fuselage serves for building up a dynamic air cushion in cruise. The vehicle is provided with low-set wings of composite layout with low-aspect-ratio inboard panels and high-aspect-ratio outer panels.

Plast JSC

PE-201

The NPP Plast (NPP – *na**ooch**no-proiz**vod**stvennoye predpri**ya**tiye*, science and production enterprise) was one of a dozen small enterprises that were founded in Nizhniy Novgorod (Gor'kiy) by former employees of Alekseyev CHDB. Apparently some of the projects developed at CHDB were taken over by the new company and, in a slightly revised configuration, were advertised to prospective customers under new designations. One such project is the PE-201 which bears more than a passing resemblance to the Strizh-3 and Strizh-4 described in Chapter 1. This vehicle, carrying a pilot and seven passengers, is virtually identical to the Strizh-4 and differs primarily in having the winglets moved slightly aft, so that their trailing edge is level with the trailing edge of the wing. The vehicle was to be powered by two 450-hp diesel engines; its specifications include a length of 15.4 m (50 ft 6⅜ in), a wing span of 13,0 m (42 ft 9 in), a height of 4,7 m (15 ft 5 in), a

A computer-generated image of the NVA-07-025. The legend on the fuselage reads *Amfibiya* (amphibian).

This computer image depicts a heavy sea-going passenger WIG vehicle in the NVA series (possibly the NVA-07-530). Note the double-deck fuselage with cabins in the thick-profile wing centre section.

An impression of the same vehicle cruising over broken ice. This view shows the composite-layout wings and the four ducted propfans located side by side.

A model depicting one of the many projects demonstrated by the RosAeroprogress company at various airshows – a 'horizontal triplane' WIG vehicle. The black/yellow striped areas may indicate payload bays.

This model seen at one of the Moscow airshows represents a projected amphibious WIG vehicle of classic Lippisch layout displayed by RosAeroprogress. Judging by the shape of the engine nacelle, the vehicle was to be powered by a small turboprop.

The same model afloat with the 'engine running'. The vehicle is a two-seater.

Opposite page:

A three-view of a similar six-seat WIG vehicle powered by an M-14P radial, another RosAeroprogress (Roks-Aero) project. The mainwheels retract into the stabilising floats.

A cutaway drawing of the same vehicle. A special equipment bay is located aft of the cockpit.

maximum AUW of 4,400 kg (9,700 lb), a load-carrying capacity of 1,300 kg (2,870 lb), a cruising speed of 210 km/h (131 mph) and a range of 1,000 km (622 miles).

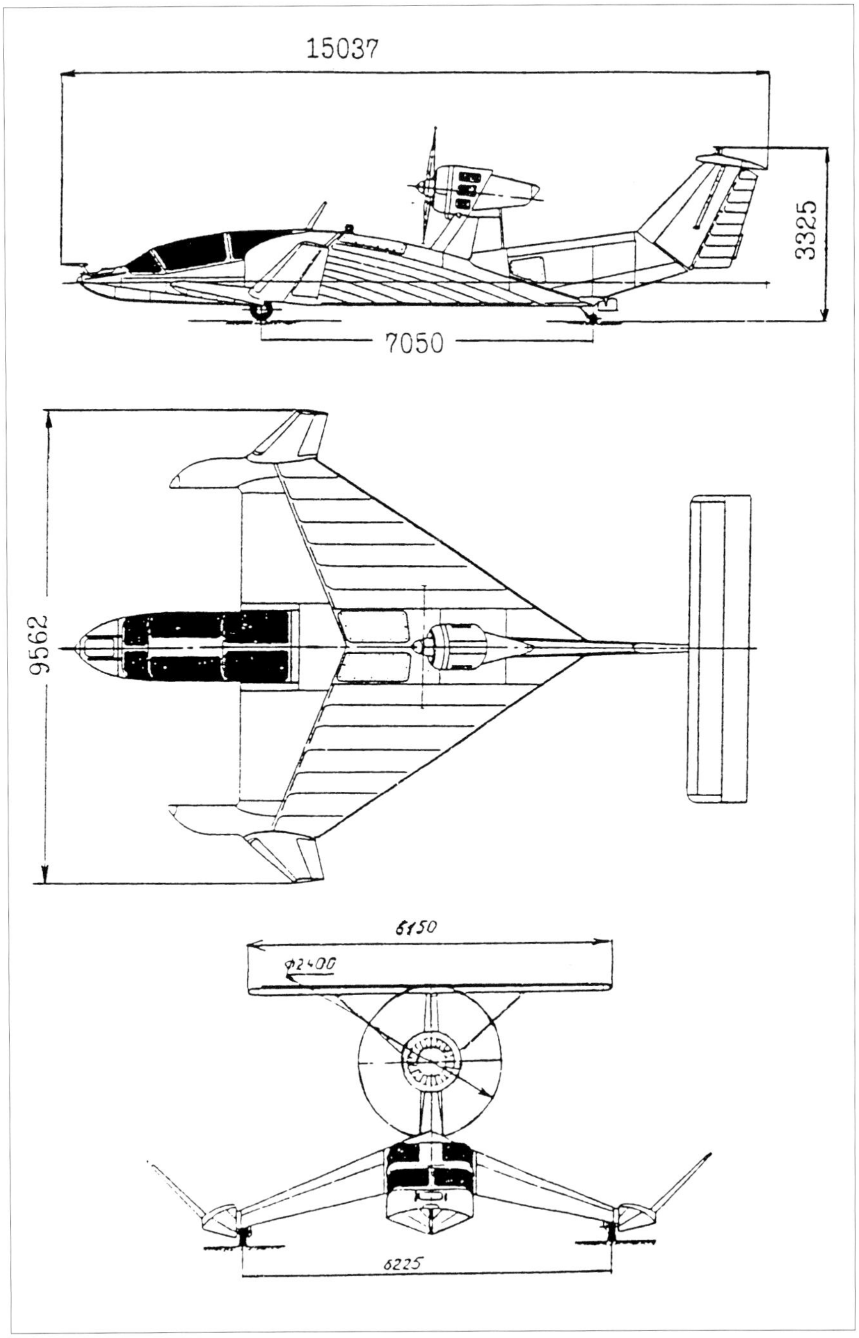

RosAroprogress, Roks-Aero JSC and other companies (Groonin's projects)

In the early 1990s Yevgeniy P. Groonin, a designer who had previously worked in TsLST and later in Bartini's and Sukhoi's design bureaux, founded a private design bureau called RosAeroprogress. In the course of the 1990s it underwent transformations, changing its name to RoksAero, then to Aeroprogress, and finally became the aeronautical subdivision of the M. V. Khrunichev State Space Research and Production Centre (this subdivision also changed its names several times).

Yevgeniy Groonin and his associates concentrated their activities on the design of light aircraft, but several WIG vehicle projects developed earlier by Groonin were kept alive. For example, a project dating back to the Sukhoi period and later reportedly designated T-2072 was shown in model form at exhibitions, as were some other models.

In 1994-95 a project of a six-seat multi-purpose amphibious *ekranolyot* (Type B vehicle) for local routes and special missions (designation unknown) was under development. It was a machine based on the Lippisch layout with reversed-delta wings and a T-tail. The wings featured anhedral and had end-plate floats at the tips to which small surfaces fitted with ailerons were attached at an angle of 45°. The wings were attached to a boat-shaped hull, the front part of which provided accommodation for the pilot and passengers under an extensively glazed canopy. The vehicle was powered by a 360-hp Vedeneyev M-14P nine-cylinder radial engine mounted on a pylon above the aft fuselage and driving a tractor propeller Another version, a two-seater, featured a small turboprop engine with a six-bladed pusher propeller. A scaled-up 16-seat machine of similar layout powered by a 960-ehp

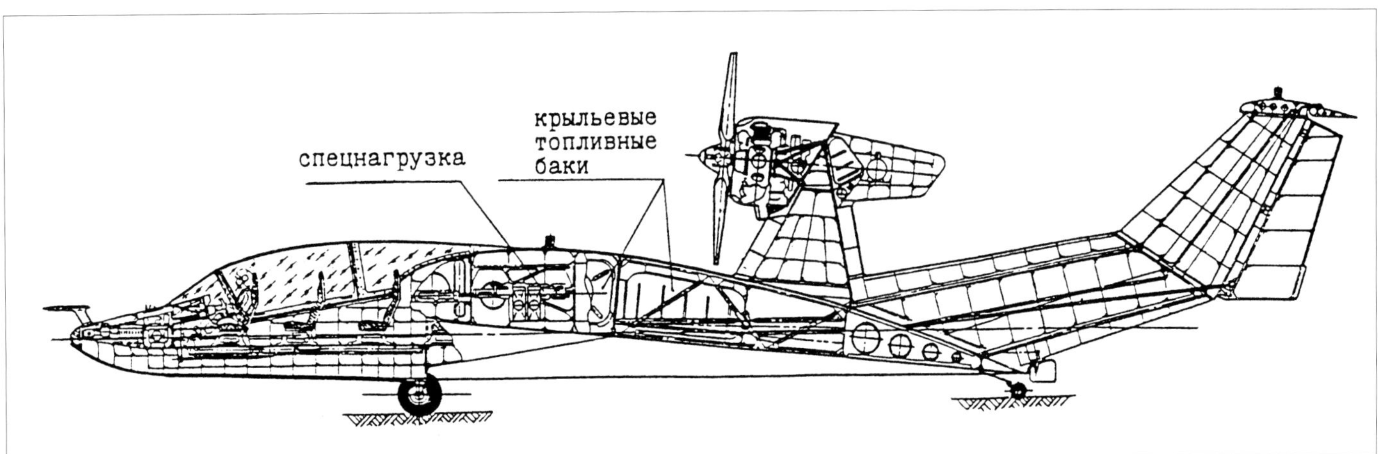

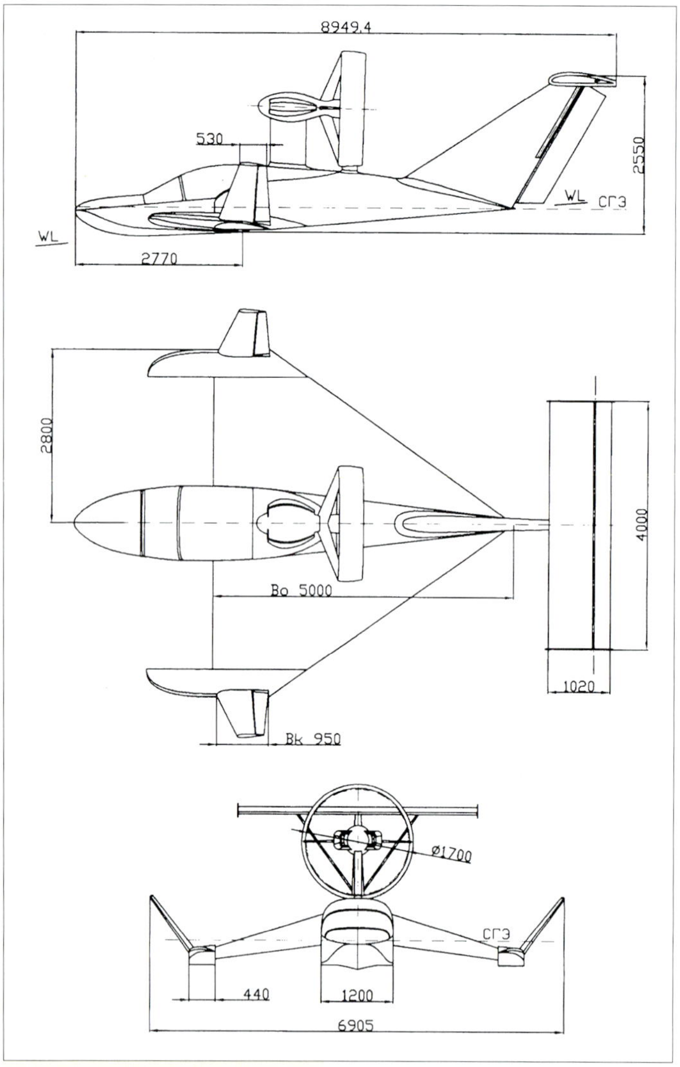

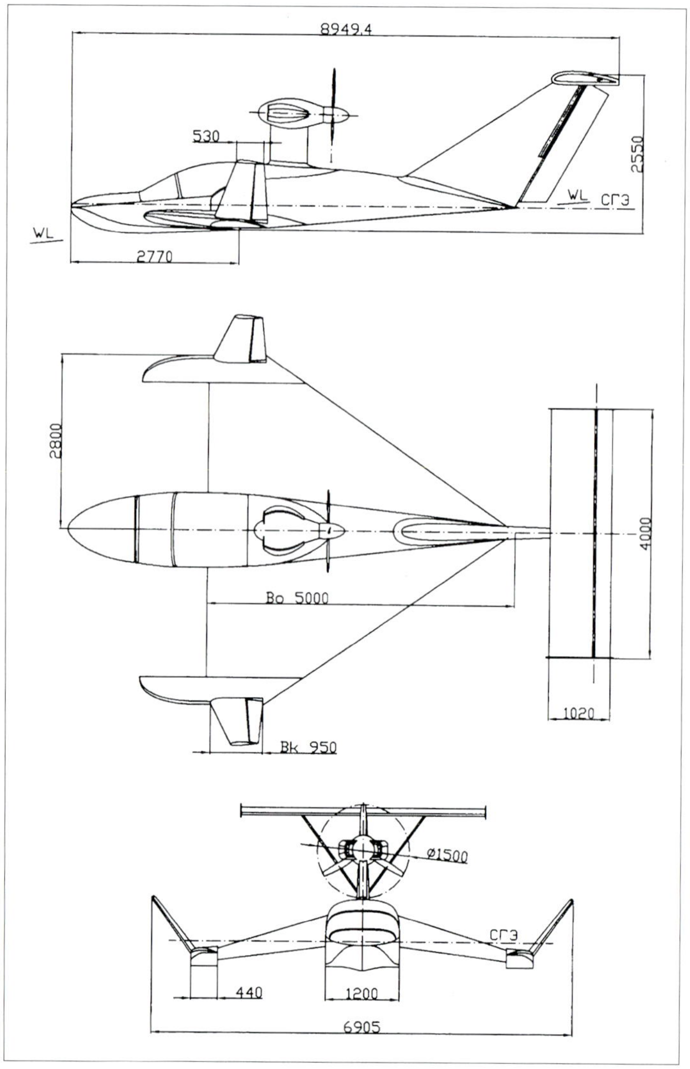

Three-views of two versions of the ESKA-2 differing only in the type of propulsor.

A three-view of the T-1001 amphibious WIG vehicle.

Glushenkov TVD-10 turboprop was also under development. There were several more projects sharing this basic configuration and differing in dimensions, powerplant type, undercarriage and onboard equipment.

During the recent years some work was done on the projects designated T-1001, T-1007, T-2001, T-2002 and others (see pictures). Of these, the T-1001 is a machine with an AUW of 1,500 kg (3,310 lb) powered by a piston engine of 210-250 hp dri-

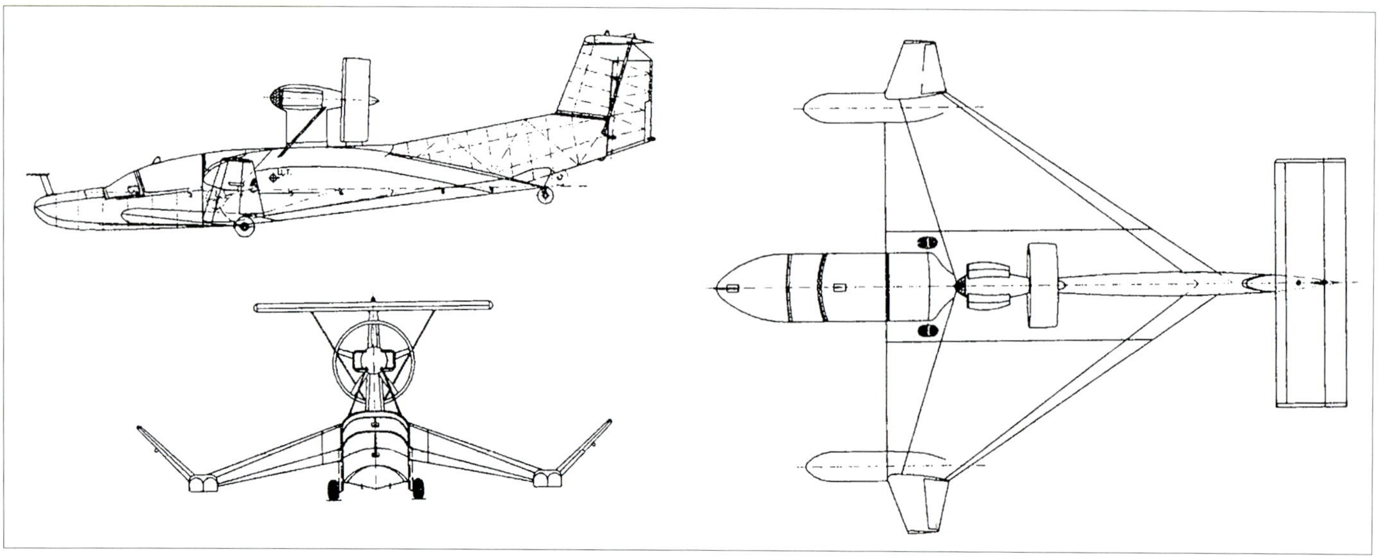

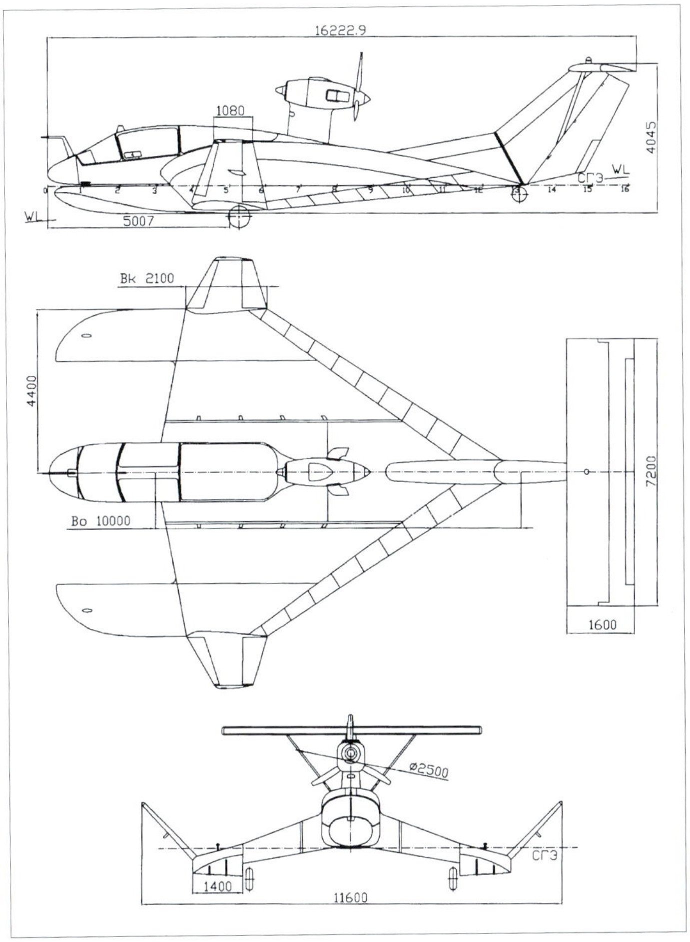

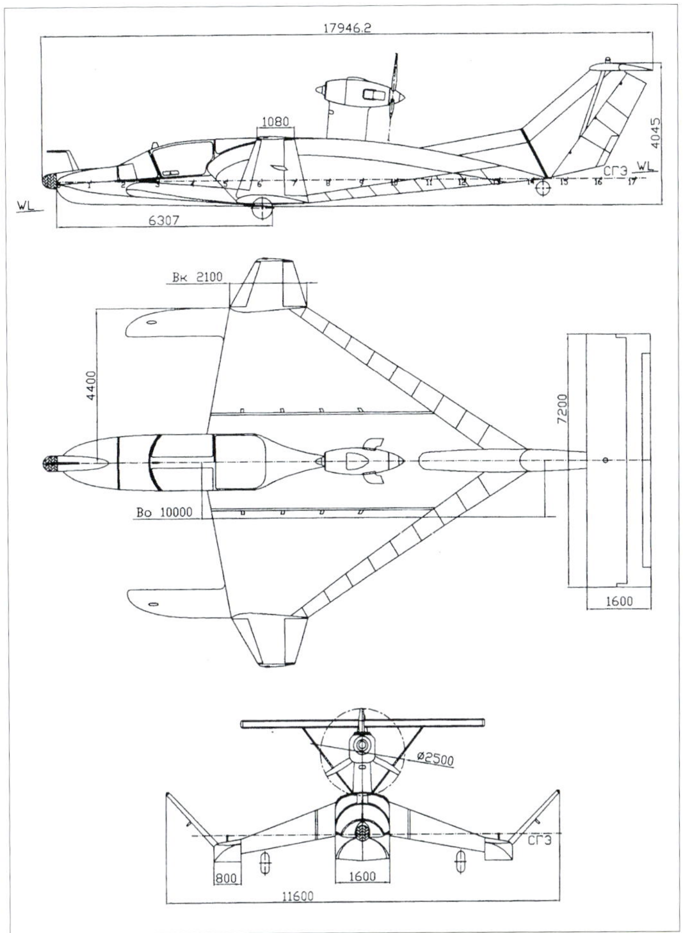

Three-views of two project versions of the T-1007 differing in forward fuselage design and float size. The one on the right is equipped with a radar.

ving a ducted pusher prop. The T-1007 is a larger machine with an AUW of 3,200 kg (7,050 lb), powered by a 700-ehp Walter M601V turboprop. Both of them are intended for surveillance, patrol and monitoring duties, as well as for SAR operations.

A project designated ESKA-2 is also under development. It is a two-seat ekranolyot which is to be powered by a 100-hp Rotax 912 engine (with a ducted propeller as an option). Featuring, again, a classical Lippisch layout, this craft is to be built entirely of composite materials.

Yevgeniy Groonin had developed several projects of light WIG craft which cannot be attributed to any organisation but merit some attention. All of them are based on the Lippisch layout. Here is a brief enumeration of these projects:

T-701 – an ultra-light WIG sailplane with flexible wings;

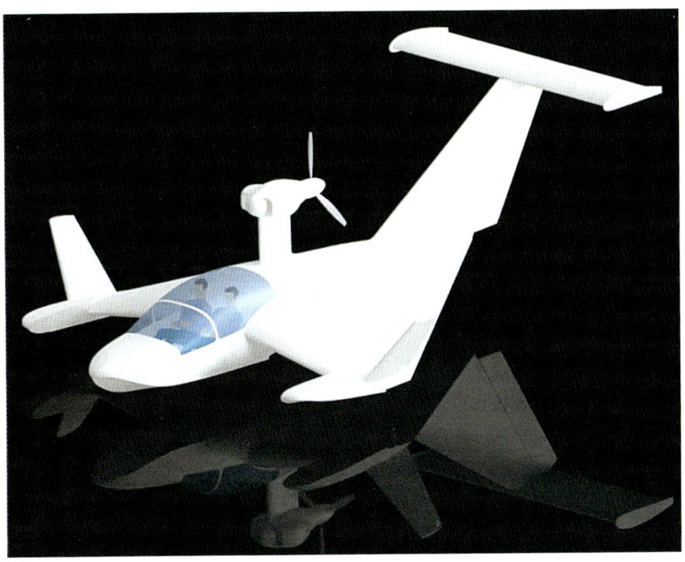

Computer-generated images of the ESKA-2 with an ordinary propeller and a ducted propeller.

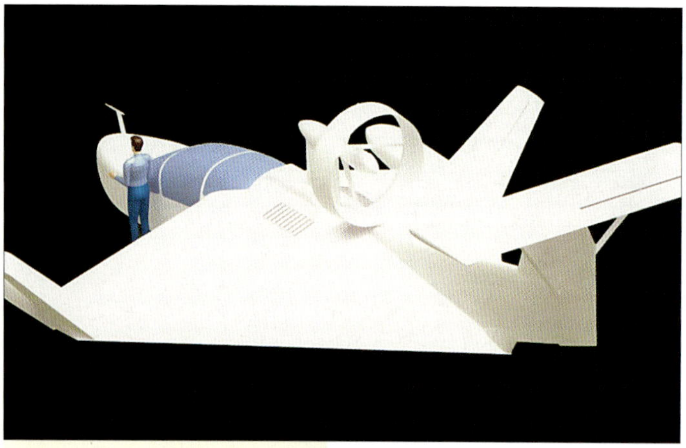

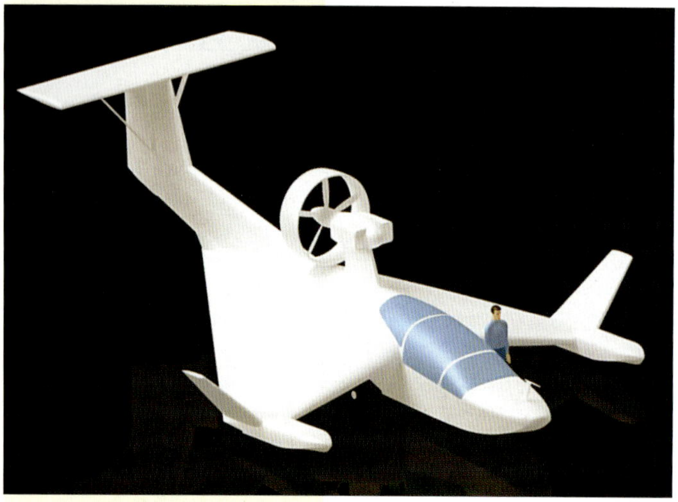

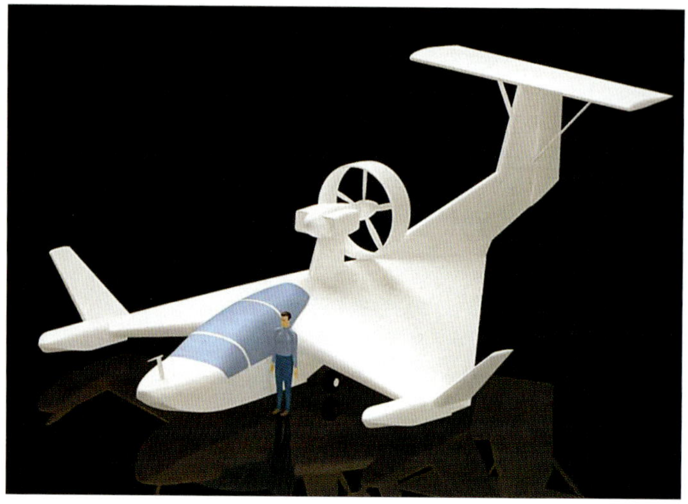

Top: A computer-generated image of the T-2001 *ekranoplan*. The engine is buried in the fuselage, driving the ducted propeller via an extension shaft and angle drive gearbox.

Top right: One of the versions of the T-2002 featuring a pylon-mounted engine with a large ducted propeller.

Lower row: A different version of the T-2002. The smaller diameter of the ducted propeller is evident.

T-702 –a development of the T-701 with a Wankel engine located in the fuselage and transmitting its torque via an extension shaft to a propeller mounted on the fin leading edge;

T-703 – a version of the T-702 with water propeller;

T-710 – a light *ekranoplan* with flexible wings and a Wankel engine on a pylon above the fuselage;

T-711 – a version of the T-710 with the engine buried in the fuselage, driving a propeller via a an extension shaft;

T-712 – a version of the T-711 with a water propeller;

T-724 – a general-purpose *ekranoplan* with rigid wings on floats, powered by an M-14P radial;

T-725 – a version of the T-724 with a power take-off to a fan creating a static air cushion;

T-726 – a version of the T-724 with the engine power distributed via a transmission to two props;

T-727 – a version of the T-725 with a water propeller and a power take-off to a fan.

Russian Ekranoplan Company JSC

Kasatka series WIG vehicles

In the early 2000s a group of enthusiasts headed by Igor' Biryukov established in the Siberian city of

Painted an ominous black (as befits a killer whale), the Kasatka-5 light WIG craft is seen here during tests on the Irtysh River.

Tobol'sk a company with a somewhat pretentious name ***Roos**skaya Ekrano**plan**naya Kom**pa**niya* (Russian *Ekranoplan* Company). Biryukov developed several designs under the common name of *Ka**sat**ka* (Killer Whale; not to be confused with the S-2 Kasatka aircraft from SibNIA described in the previous chapter). Their common feature is the special wing layout. The low-set main wings are supplemented by additional wings of smaller area located higher up and just aft of the main ones. Both wings are joined by vertical tail surfaces at mid-span of the rear wing. Piston engines with tractor propellers are mounted at the junctions of the vertical surfaces and the rear wings. Thanks to the propeller wash the lifting force of the rear wings per square m/ft is expected to be higher than on the main wings. The fuselage (or hull) has a flattened cross-section and a beaver-tail aft end and thus acquires a profile of a lifting body. The bottom of the hull has two planing steps. This layout has been used in the Kasatka-1 and Kasatka-3 vehicles with an AUW of 2.5 and 8 tonnes (5,510 and 17,640 lb) respectively having a seating capacity, including crew, of 11 and 38 persons respectively. The four-seat Kasatka-5 with an AUW of 800 kg has a basically similar layout, but is powered by one engine with a pusher propeller mounted above the rear fuselage between the fins.

The Kasatka-1, a Class A vehicle, was built in 2002-03 and tested on the Irtysh River. As far as is known, it failed to attain the flight in ground effect and made runs in aquaplaning mode at least up to 2005; further work with the original version must have been abandoned. In 2008 Biryukov publicised plans for a modified version of this craft with a single pusher propeller above the rear fuselage and changes to the wings.

The Kasatka-3 is projected as a Class B vehicle capable of short flights out of ground effect. With 36 passengers and two crew it is expected to reach a cruising speed of 250 km/h (131 mph) and a range of 3,500 km (2,175 miles). The machine is to be powered by two 360-hp engines. No prototype has been built so far.

The Kasatka-5 has been designed as a four-seat seaplane also capable of flight in ground effect. Powered by a single engine with a pusher propeller, the prototype has been built and has performed test runs on water and on snow. In the latter case it makes use of a water ski incorporated in the bottom of the hull. As far as one can judge by occasional reports, the tests have not yet yielded the expected results, no flights having been recorded.

Under these circumstances Biryukov's talk about possible military applications for his designs seems premature, to say the least.

Top: The Burevesnik-24 in the course of assembly. The yellow object underneath is a pneumatic jack.

Centre and above: Still looking somewhat incomplete, the vehicle is seen afloat during initial tests.

Sky plus Sea Design Bureau

Burevesnik-24

An interesting WIG vehicle was designed and built by the ***Ne**bo plyus **mo**re* (Sky plus Sea) Design Bureau affiliated to a technical centre headed by cosmonaut Yuriy Romanenko. The technical centre and the design bureau have their premises in the Mytishchi District of the Moscow Region. The proto-

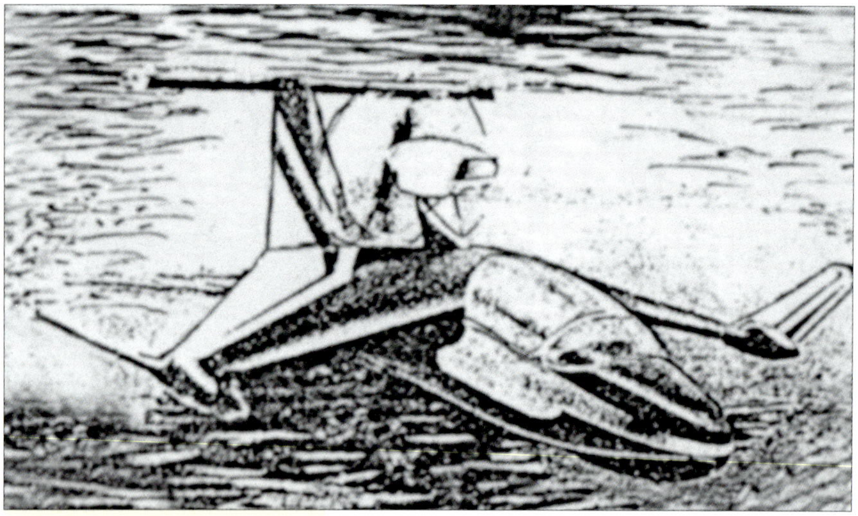

An artist's impression depicting the Ronata light WIG vehicle.

Below and bottom: The 'aeroplane boat' developed by Tekhaviakompleks seen during trials on the Moskva River. Apparently it does actually leave the water, but the pilot cannot see where he's going!

Below right: The same vehicle (minus stabilising floats) suspended from a crane to show the ogival wing planform.

type of the vehicle, dubbed *Burevesnik-24* (Storm Petrel-24), was built under the direction of Chief Designer Vladimir Bukovskiy at the design bureau's experimental production facility and underwent trials from the surface of the Pirogovskoye Reservoir, Moscow Region, in the summer of 2009. With the advent of the winter the testing was continued from snow-covered surfaces on the ground.

The Burevesnik-24 is a 24-seat amphibious vehicle which is designed to be operated in four different modes: a hydroplaning boat; an aerosleigh; a WIG vehicle; an aircraft. In other words, it is expected to fly both in and out of ground effect, which puts this vehicle into the B or C category in the IMO classification. The aerodynamic layout of the Burevestnik-24 is rather unusual for an *ekranoplan*. It is a sesquiplane with large-span strut-braced upper wings consisting of wing panels from the An-2 biplane. The lower wings of very short span and wide chord are disc-shaped; they are flanked by floats and joined with the upper wing by supporting struts. The fuselage of square cross-section had a beaver-tail rear part which carries twin fins and rudders topped by the horizontal tail. The powerplant comprises two 450-hp BMW engines driving shrouded pusher propellers. The wide-chord shrouds installed behind the upper wings, can be tilted together with the propellers to change the thrust vector. When tilted, the shrouds create additional lift thanks to their wide chord.

The empty weight of the vehicle is 3,600 kg (7,940 lb) and the AUW is 6500 kg (14,330 lb), which gives a very favourable payload-to-weight ratio. The Burevesnik-24 has a wing span of 14.5 m (47 ft 7 in) and a length of 14 m (46 ft); its top speed is claimed to be 250 km/h (155 mph).

The prototype Burevesnik-24 was preceded by three machines, of which the first was a concept mock-up. It was followed by a 16-passenger machine and then by a 20-passenger vehicle, both of which were used for researching and testing the design features of the future final project. The present 24-passenger prototype will be used to finalise the development work prior to putting the vehicle into production.

The Sky plus Sea design bureau has plans to build a 100-seat amphibian vehicle.

A computer-generated image of a proposed *ekranoplan* based on the Be-200 amphibian proposed by Tekhnologii SDP.

Technoavia JSC

Ronata

The Technoavia company (private design bureau) set up in the 1990s became fairly widely known as the developer and manufacturer of light aircraft, such as the SM-92 Finist, SM-92T Turbo-Finist, SM-94, SM-2000 and others. In late 1990s Technoavia, together with lesser known companies Delta-V and Svetlen and with the assistance from the Moscow Aviation Institute (MAI), developed a light WIG vehicle named Ronata. According to a press report, they *'were ready to conduct flight tests of the Ronata light* ekranoplan *manufactured from aluminium alloys. This vehicle was intended to carry four persons and their luggage over a distance of 1,200 km [745 miles], flying at a speed of 100-200 km/h [62-123 mph] above the water surface with waves not exceeding 0.5 m [1 ft 8 in]'*. The drawing accompanying this report showed a vehicle based on the Lippisch layout and resembling very much the ESKA-1 *ekranoplan* described in the previous chapter. There is no evidence to confirm that this vehicle was actually tested (or even completed, for that matter).

Tekhaviakompleks JSC

Aeroplane boat

The company Tekhaviakompleks JSC, based in the town of Zhukovskiy near Moscow, was founded in 2004 to handle various questions, such as the

The SDP-09 tandem-wing *ekranoplan*. The vehicle had been awaiting replacement engines for more than two years when this picture was taken.

Designer V. Surzhik in the open entry hatch of the SDP-09.

The engine bay of the SDP-009 with the cowlings removed, showing the two car engines installed back to back.

upgrading of navigation systems. It did not neglect WIG vehicles either. At the MAKS-2009 show one could sea a curious-looking little craft called ***Kater**samo**lyot*** (Aeroplane boat). It was configured as a little boat hull topped by diminutive delta wings with ogival leading edges. The wing trailing edge was provided with elevons. Stabilising floats under the wingtips and a vertical tail at the rear completed the picture. A piston engine hidden inside the hull drove a nose-mounted propeller. The pilot sat well aft, and as the vehicle had a strong nose-up attitude, he had no view forward over the nose. The craft was successfully tested on the Moskva River in August 2009; it was regarded as a proof-of concept vehicle, to be followed by larger craft of the same layout. One of them, shown in model form, featured two propellers, the second one being inserted into a slot in the vertical tail. Two- and four-seat models were under development. The vehicle is expected to be operated in three modes: as a hydroplaning boat; as a WIG craft and as an aircraft; the implementation of this bright idea hinged upon finding investors.

Tekhnologii SDP

(Dynamic Cushion Craft Technologies JSC)

Be-200 conversion into a WIG vehicle (project)

The joint-stock company bearing the name ZAO Tekhnologii SDP (SDP stands for ***sood**no na dina**mich**eskoy po**doosh**ke* – dynamic cushion craft) was founded in 2002 for the purpose of implementing several projects of WIG vehicles that had been developed in the course of the preceding years by a group of engineers from Kiev who had moved to Irkutsk together with A. Panchenkov (see Chapter 5). The group included V. V. Surzhik, P. A. Skorokhodov, V. V. Taranushenko, S. M. Remizov and G. A. Vzyatkin. Surzhik became the General Designer, with Skorokhodov, a businessman, acting as investor.

The group took out a patent for an invention the essence of which was the description of condition for the autostabilisation of a tail-first WIG vehicle during flight in ground effect. The material submitted together with the application for the patent contained a general arrangement drawing of a WIG vehicle resembling the Be-200 amphibian. In fact, this was a proposal for a conversion of the Be-200 based on the use of the latter's fuselage, engines and equipment. The high-set wings of the amphibian were to be replaced by low-set aft-mounted main wings of low aspect ratio and by smaller-area forward wings, actually a well-developed foreplane. Calculations showed that in the 'WIG version' the Be-200's AUW would reach 80 tonnes (176,400 lb) as against 43 tonne (94,815 lb), and the payload would amount to 40 tonnes (88,200 lb) instead of 12 tonne (26,460 lb). The proposal was brought to the attention of the management of the Irkutsk aircraft plant where the Be-200 amphibian was manufactured, but the response was lukewarm, and the project was not proceeded with.

SDP-09

By mid-2006 the Dynamic Air Cushion Ship Technologies JSC succeeded in building an experimental vehicle designated SDP-09 (SDP = ***sood**no na dina**mich**eskoy po**doosh**ke* – DAC ship) which was powered by two 220-hp automobile engines. The vehicle was to carry two crew and six to eight passengers. With an AUW of 2,600 kg (5,730 lb), it was expected to cover the distance of 1,500 km (932

Left: An artist's impression of the AeroMarine Systems AMS-500-4 taking off.

Above: A display model of the AMS-500-4.

miles) at a speed of 130-150 km/h (81-93 mph), flying at a height of 0.7 – 1.0 m (2-3 ft). It featured a canard layout, with aft-positioned main wings of greater span and forward-mounted wings of lesser span and area, both wings being provided with floats at their tips. The nose part of the hull was 'loaned' from the Sarepta motorboat, and the passenger cabin was an adaptation of the body of the Toyota Caldina stationcar. Two Honda car engines housed in the forward fuselage drove two six-blade tractor propellers via extension shafts with angle drive gearboxes. The vehicle was built with the assistance from A. Vzyatkin who was acting director of Plant No. 403 at that time. However, this machine proved to be ill-fated. Owing to various vicissitudes the vehicle could not begin its test programme in time, and when the tests started in March 2004 (on ice), the Honda engines failed to develop their rated power. Replacement engines proved hard to come by... The ultimate fate of this vehicle is unknown, but some reports suggest that its development was eventually abandoned

Termoplan Design Bureau, JSC

In 2007 this small private design bureau, not previously known to be engaged in WIG craft design, signified its intention to enter this field. The company's Chief Designer Yuriy Ishkov told a journalist that ZAO 'KB Termoplan' (the company's name in Russian) had started work on a WIG craft that probably would be the biggest in the world (a good start, indeed). The vehicle with a cargo-carrying capacity of 2,000 tonnes is visualised as a trimaran based on the use of three fuselages from the An-124 Ruslan super-heavy transport aircraft. The three fuselages are to be topped and joined together by a 'promenade deck' (Ishkov's term, curious enough for a vehicle designed to fly at a speed of up to 500 km/h). They house cargo holds and passenger compartments. The wings imparting WIG qualities to the craft are also borrowed from the An-124. In the passenger version the vehicle is expected to seat more than 1,500 passengers. In a military version it can be converted into a high-speed aircraft carrier capable of accommodating up to 25 aircraft in its storage holds. Needless to say, the project has slender chances of being implemented, on account of the huge investments that would be required.

WingShips Company

The WingShips Company was established in Moscow in 1998. It is the Russian branch of the WingShips International Corporation which had been established in Delaware, USA, for the purpose of developing new marine transport technology – WIG craft on the basis of Russian expertise in *ekranoplan* construction.

PM-1 and PM-2 *ekranolyots* (projects)

In co-operation with specialists from TsAGI the WingShips Company has developed two projects of multi-purpose C-type WIG vehicles intended to carry up to 8 persons. These are the PM-1 and PM-2, sharing the same fuselage and differing in the powerplant and wing span. Both of them feature a wide fuselage, composite-type wings and a Vee tail unit. The unorthodox hydrodynamic layout of the vehicle features a kind of elongated tunnel under its bottom into which the ram air is fed.

The PM-1 is powered by two 900-kgp (1,980-lbst) AMNTK Soyuz R127-300 turbofans; it has an AUW of 3,500 kg (7,715 lb) and can cover a distance of 1,200 km (745 miles) with a maximum payload of 1,000 kg (2,205 lb) at a cruising speed of up to 270 km/h (168 mph) in ground effect. In aircraft mode it can rise to 4,000 m (13,120 ft).

The PM-2 is powered by two Lycoming TIO-540F piston engines. It can cover a distance of 1,400 km (870 miles) with a maximum payload of 900 kg (1,985 lb) at a cruising speed of up to 210 km/h (131 mph) in ground effect. The maximum altitude of flight out of ground effect is again 4,000 m.

A wind tunnel model of the WingShips PM-2 featuring composite wings and aft-mounted ducted fans; the tail surfaces are just visible behind. The second photo has been altered to advertise the vehicle as the AMS-400 Odyssey; the final configuration of the latter may be rather different.

AeroMarine Systems Company

This company, founded in 2002 as a sister enterprise to the WingShips Company, closely co-operates with the latter and is engaged in the design of WIG craft and light seaplanes as well. It came up with several new designs of WIG vehicles which are listed below. The company advertises these projects in the hope of attracting prospective investors for a joint-venture manufacture of these machines,

AMS-500 Corvette

This multipurpose WIG vehicle is advertised in two versions: the AMS-500-4 patrol version and the AMS-500-30 passenger version. In actual fact, these are two different designs, the AMS-500-30 being a scaled up version of the AMS-500-4. Both of them are intended to be operated in all the three modes included into the IMO classification, that is, as a vehicle of the A. B and C type. In other words, they can fly in ground effect only sticking to the water surface (Class A); or fly at an altitude of 1 to 4 m above the surface and make occasional hops to a higher altitude (Class B); or rise to an altitude of up to 4,000 m (13,120 ft).

AMS 500-4 Patrol

This craft carrying two crew and eight passengers at a maximum TOW of 4,000 kg (8,820 lb) is based on a machine developed by Yevgeniy P. Groonin way back during his work at the Sukhoi OKB (see Chapter 4). In its present configuration it is has a length of 12 m (39 ft 4 in) and a wing span of 14 m (46 ft) and is to be powered by two M-14 radial engines. Options include two Lycoming piston engines or one M-601 turboprop. With a maximum payload of 1,400 kg (3,087 lb) it can travel at a cruising speed of 240 km/h (149 mph) in ground effect over a distance of 1,600 km (984 miles).

AMS-500-30 Passengers

This is a much larger craft with a maximum TOW of 30,000 kg (66,150 lb), having a length of 21 m and a wing span of 25 m (82 ft). It is intended to carry five crew and 44 passengers at a cruising speed of 360 km/h in ground effect mode over a distance of 3,000 km (1,863 miles). The powerplant comprises two 2,500-shp TV7-117 turboprops.

AMS-400 Odyssey

Again, this is a common name for two different projects – the AMS-400-4 Business and AMS-400-30 Sea Train.

AMS-400-4 Business

This vehicle with an AUW of 4,000 kg (8,820 lb) can carry two crew and up to eight passengers and is powered by one M-601 turboprop. Being closely comparable to the AMS-500-4 in seating capacity and performance, it has lightly smaller dimensions and a different layout looking like a refined version of the WingShips PM-1 described above. The engine is placed above the rear fuselage between the splayed fins of the V-type tail unit. The extensively glazed boat-hull fuselage is to provide comfortable accommodation for four to six VIPs.

AMS-400-30 Sea Train

This larger version with an AUW of 30,000 kg (66,150 lb) is to carry five crew and 50 passengers at a cruising speed of 390 km/h (242 mph) in WIG mode over a distance of 3,200 km (1,989 miles). It is powered by two TV7-117 turboprops.

AMS-410

Two projects bearing this designation differ in function and size and are obviously intended for military duties the exact nature of which is not revealed.

An artist's impression of the AMS-410-DF Sea hunter in Russian Navy colours.

These are the AMS-410 Transporter and the AMS-410-DF Sea Hunter.

AMS-410 Transporter

This machine with an AUW of 4,500 kg (9,920 lb) is powered by two RD-127-300 turbofans. With two pilots and eight crew onboard it can fly at a cruising speed of up to 270 km/h (168 mph) in WIG mode and 290 km/h (180 mph) out of ground effect at altitudes up to 4,000 m (13,200 ft)

AMS-410-DF Sea Hunter

The Sea Hunter has an AUW of 9,000 kg (19,840 lb) an carries a crew of two pilots seated in tandem. It can be operated in the WIG mode and as an aircraft at altitudes up to 15,000 m (49,200 ft). The fairly large machine measuring 14 m (45 ft $11\frac{3}{16}$ in) in length and 14.5 m (47 ft $6\frac{55}{64}$ in) in wingspan is powered by two TRDD-12500 turbojets (thrust rating not specified). Its maximum payload of 3,500 kg (7,720 lb) presumably comprises various weaponry. The

The ZPKB SM-16 dynamic air cushion vehicle in cruise mode. The forward hydrofoil is barely discernible.

two versions of the AMS-410 feature an aerohydrodynamic layout which is designed to endow them with natural static and dynamic stability in flight in the vicinity of the supporting surface.

Zelenodol'sk PKB (ZPKB)

The ZPKB JSC (*Zeleno**dol'**skoye pro**yekt**no-kon-**strook**torskoye byu**ro*** – Zelenodol'sk Project and Design Bureau) has been in existence for more than half a century. Its sphere of activity is the design of military and civil ships of different classes intended for a wide range of duties. Displacement vessels are the main object of design activities, but the design bureau has also accumulated much experience in the development of high-speed ships based on dynamic principles of sustentation – hydrofoils, ACV and ships with aerodynamic off-loading. The latter category comprises also some designs that can be classed as WIG vehicles proper. Here are some projects of this kind which date back to the Soviet period (the list is not exhaustive).

Tsiklon (Cyclone)

The vessel bearing this name was designed and built at ZPKB in 1973. This was an experimental vessel with aerodynamic off-loading with a displacement of some 50 tonnes (110,250 lb). It had a normal ship hull which was provided with hydrofoils under the bows and amidships. In addition, the hull was fitted with wings provided with endplate floats. No aircraft-type tail surfaces were fitted. The powerplant comprised two 5,180-ehp Ivchenko AI-20D turboprop engines mounted on pylons above the rear section of the hull.

The Tsiklon craft was submitted for trials on 24 August 1973. The vessel made its first test run on water on 1st September 1973, with the ZPKB Chief Designer Yuriy Nikol'skiy being among those on board. The vessel's captain was Pyotr Tudriy, with Viktor Kravets as the chief of the test programme. The tests were conducted in the course of several years and produced satisfactory results. In 1975, in the course of tests, the Minister of Shipbuilding Boris Ye. Butoma and Deputy Commander-in-Chief of the Navy Admiral P. G. Kotov were invited to get acquainted with the Tsiklon and the prospects of the development of this class of ships. A conference on this subject was held on board the vessel.

SM-16

This was one of a series of designs developed by ZPKB in the category of ships with aerodynamic off-loading. SM stands for *samo**khod**naya mo**del'*** – self-propelled model. The SM-16 was built in 1977-78 and successfully passed tests both on still water and on ruffled water surface with the wave height up to 0.6 m (2 ft). This vehicle with a boat hull looking like a normal ship (not aircraft) was fitted with wings equipped with endplate floats. Propulsion was ensured by two turbojet engines mounted above the rear section of the hull. The absence of visible tail surfaces suggests that a water rudder was used for directional control. During test runs on still water the aerodynamic off-loading reached 100%, both with the functioning system of automatic movement control and with this system switched off.

Different configurations of vessels with aerodynamic off-loading similar to the SM-16 were under development until 1983; there were plans for fitting a prospective self-propelled model with 1,500-kgp (3,310-lbst) Ivchenko AI-25 turbofans. In 1984 two scientific institutions – TsAGI and the Krylov Shipbuilding Research Institute (TsNII) – submitted to ZPKB the results of their basic research which were to serve as a basis for the further design work and for perfecting the hydro-aerodynamic layouts.

The SM-16 was eventually converted into a testbed for conducting various experiments on subjects of interest for ZPKB.

Strizh

This vehicle, not to be confused with the Strizh designed by the Alekseyev CHDB, was developed by the ZPKB in early 1990s. In 1991 the advanced development project was completed, followed by detail design in 1992-1993. The vehicle was classed as a seagoing flying craft (cutter, launch); it was a Type B machine in the modern classification. The Strizh was intended for the following duties:

- coastal transport;
- patrolling the littoral sea areas with a view to intercepting the fastest boats in coastal waters;
- search and rescue operations.

As a consequence of the disarray afflicting Russia's economy in the wake of the Soviet Union's demise, the work on the Strizh drastically slowed down and eventually came to a standstill. No prototype construction was undertaken. Project work was resumed with a view to designing a WIG craft of the same layout, but of greater displacement.

A picture from the heading of the ZPKB web site shows a glimpse of the Strizh. It appears to have a boat hull shaped fuselage with a large multi-seat cockpit superstructure. The wing centre section is blended into the upper decking of the hull and features a sort of leading-edge root extensions. The wing centre section is supplemented by short-span outer wing panels with endplate floats at the tips. The tail unit consists of two swept-back splayed vertical tails carrying on their tops the horizontal tail. The powerplant comprises two engines located on vertical pylons above the central part of the hull and driving ducted tractor propellers.

CHAPTER SEVEN

EKRANOPLANS OUTSIDE RUSSIA

The story of *ekranoplans* in Russia can best be appreciated if one provides a measure of comparison with similar activities in other countries of the world. The purpose of this chapter is to give the reader a broad idea of the most important achievements and general trends in WIG research and design in some countries outside Russia. lack of space does not permit to give more than a cursory treatment to a subject that merits a separate book.

To begin with, a few words about the events of the period before World War II.

In 1935 the Finnish inventor **Toivo Kaario** took out the first patent for a vehicle based on the use of ground effect (it was an aerosleigh with wings of low aspect ratio). The first vehicle built by Kaario was a small wing measuring 2 x 2.6 m (6 ft 6¾ in x 8 ft 6²³⁄₆₄ in) and weighing 90 kg (200 lb). The pilot was accommodated on the wing in a prone position. The wing was mounted on skis and was towed by a specially adapted aerosleigh. In 1935-36 Kaario equipped his vehicle with a 16-hp engine but the available engine power turned out to be insufficient. His activities were interrupted by the war; in the post-war period he returned to these experiments.

In 1949 Kaario built a new small vehicle powered by a 20-hp engine; during tests it hovered over water with four persons on board. However, again the engine power proved insufficient to enable true flight in ground effect. Yet another project of the same kind was proposed by Kaario in 1963-64. It was configured as a wing of low aspect ratio flanked by two floats doubling as skis. Mounted atop the wing were the body with a pilot's cockpit, the tail surfaces and a special take-off device consisting of two small wings provided with endplates. Deflection of these wings made it possible to direct the airflow from the forward-mounted propeller into the space under the main wing. Thus, the same engine was used for cruiser and for the take-off boost. This was the eighth model built by Kaario. The vehicle was unusual in being fitted with two booms carrying small stabilizers to enhance pitch stability.

The early experiments of T. Kaario were followed by similar experiments elsewhere in Europe and in the USA. In the late 1930s the Swedish engineer **I. Troeng** built two self-propelled piloted vehicles. Both of them were configured as 'flying wings' with endplate floats. The first of them, powered by two 100-hp aircraft engines with propellers, had a design speed of 110 km/h (68 mph). It had an AUW of 3 tonnes (6,600 lb) and carried a pilot and several passengers in an enclosed cockpit. The other vehicle, dubbed Aeroboat, was a small single-seat vehicle weighing a mere 600 kg (1,320 lb). It differed from the first one in being propelled by a water propeller and in having a hydrofoil mounted in the area of the wing trailing edge.

In 1939-40 the American engineer **D. Warner** built a vehicle which he called a 'compressor aircraft'. It featured a canard layout and a complicated wing system. Two powerful fans created a static air cushion under the wings, while forward propulsion was ensured by separate cruise engines. This was the first example of a WIG vehicle with separate booster engines and cruise engines. He developed several projects of WIG vehicles paying special attention to enhancing the take-off performance of these craft.

In 1941 another American specialist, **A. Gazda**, developed a project of a boat fitted with wings for aerodynamic offloading; it was intended for patrol duties and for combating enemy warships. The WIG boat was to be armed with a torpedo, an aircraft cannon with a high rate of fire and a heavy machine-gun. In its layout the vehicle resembled a twin-float seaplane minus the outer wing panels. The control devices of the craft were identical to those used on seaplanes and included a tail unit with a fin-and-rudder and a water rudder for steering the machine when afloat. The powerplant was to comprise one or two radial engines.

In 1939 the well-known German aircraft designer **Claude Dornier** developed a project of a flying boat capable of being flown in ground effect. In 1941 he took out a patent in the USA for this invention. The vehicle featured an aircraft layout. It had wings of high aspect ratio and a traditional aircraft tail unit. The powerplant comprised eight engines located on the wings; the engines installed on the wing's leading edge had tractor propellers, while those installed at the trailing edge had pusher propellers. The vehicle was intended for passenger transportation.

During the Second World War activities in the field of WIG craft research and practical design had to be abandoned for a while, resuming after the end of the hostilities. The following brief survey of events relating to the post-war period and the present-day situation is made on a country-by-country basis, starting with the USA and Germany where these activities were conducted on a larger scale then elsewhere. Other countries will follow in alphabetical order.

A drawing depicting the WIG craft built by I. Troeng in cruise mode. Note the rear hydrofoil.

The USA

In 1948 an American specialist, **H. Sundstedt**, built a six-seat WIG boat configured as a thick wing supported by two floats and fitted with a ducted airscrew for propulsion. The propeller was driven by a pylon-mounted aircraft engine. The vehicle proved underpowered and failed to reach the ground-effect flight without contact with the water.

In 1958-63 the engineer **W. Bertelson** built in the USA three vehicles which he called Ground Effect Machines (GEM). Designated GEM-1, GEM-2 and GEM-3, they used the same engine for take-off and for cruise flight. They were successfully tested.

Two views of the WIG craft built by D. Warner, showing the fans creating the air cushion.

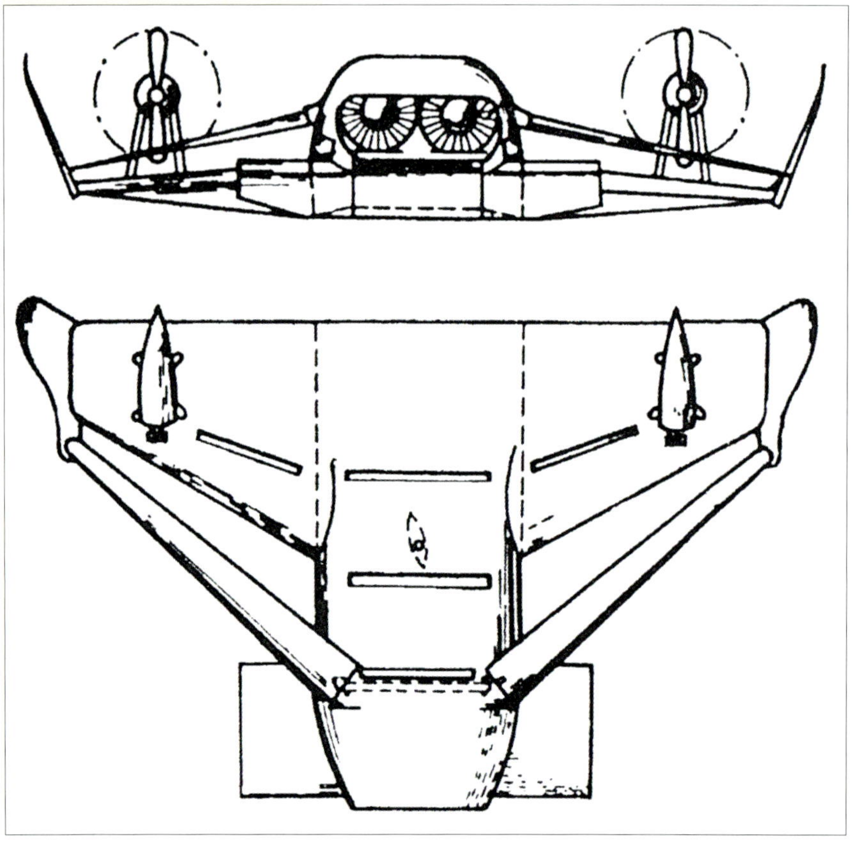

The GEM-1 was a single-seat vehicle powered by a 65-hp engine. Its wings had large endplates. It rose to a mere 5 cm (2 in) above the supporting surface in cruise flight. During take-off the airflow from the propeller was deflected by special vanes into the space under the wings.

The GEM-2 differed in having an enclosed two-seat cockpit and a single-fin vertical tail.

The GEM-3 (Arcopter) tested in 1963 differed radically from its predecessors. It had two wings mounted in a staggered-tandem arrangement. The wings had deep endplates. A four-seat cockpit was located on the forward wing, and the engine was placed behind the cockpit ahead of the rear wing. Powered by a 150-hp engine, this vehicle attained a maximum speed of 176 km/h (109 mph) and a cruising speed of 130 km/h (81 mph); it flew at a height of 45 cm (17¾ in) above the supporting surface.

In 1953 engineer **D. Welly** of German origin developed a project of a hydrofoil boat with aerodynamic off-loading. The aircraft-type wings of considerable size were intended to provide the major part of the lifting force in the cruise mode.

In 1961-62 the **Vehicle Research Corporation** (VRC) of the USA developed a project of a WIG vehicle with an AUW of some 100 tonnes (220,000 lb). Dubbed Columbia, it incorporated some features of an ACV. In 1964 this company built under the guidance of S. Rethorst the VRC-1 self-propelled single-seat model of the Columbia which was successfully tested. The proof-of-concept vehicle had the layout of a flying wing flanked by endplate floats; it weighed 2.3 tonnes (5,070 lb) and had a length of 6.3 m (20 ft 8 in). A single gas turbine engine drove two airscrews for horizontal propulsion and two fans; it had a system of jet nozzles designed to create an air cushion and was, in effect, a combination of a WIG craft and an ACV. During tests it reached a speed of 96 km/h (60 mph) in the ACV mode and 137 km/h (85 mph) in the WIG mode.

In 1962-65 a series of experiments was conducted in the USA under the guidance of the well-known Swiss inventor **Carl Weiland**. (Some sources associate these experiments with the West Coast Company, while others link Weiland's activity with Douglas Aircraft Company.) In 1964 he built a self-propelled piloted model of a WIG vehicle called Small Weilandcraft with wings in a tandem arrangement. It was a twin-hulled (catamaran) craft with the two wings in a tandem arrangement between the hulls. Each hull housed a cockpit. The vehicle was controlled by aerodynamic control surfaces which included two fins-and-rudders topped by a horizontal tail. The powerplant comprised two 260-hp piston engines. A photo depicting the craft as rolled out at the Douglas Long Beach plant shows the engines to be mounted on pylons above the hulls amidships. A description related possibly to a project version places the engines on the leading edges of the fins. Unfortunately, in March 1964 the craft suffered a crash during its initial flight tests. After a fairly stable flight at the design altitude of 1 m (3 ft) above the water the vehicle unexpectedly soared to a height of some 7.5 m (23 ft). The pilot throttled back the engines, whereupon the machine banked sharply and crashed.

At the same time the engineer developed a project of a gigantic vehicle weighing 1,000 tonnes (2,200,000 lb). Called Large Weilandcraft, it was intended for operation on transatlantic routes. This craft was intended to carry as many as 3,000 passengers. Like the smaller craft described above, it was to have two fuselages with a set of two wings in a tandem arrangement between the hulls. With the length and wing span exceeding 213 and 152 m (700 and 500 ft) respectively, the vehicle was to have a wing thickness of 3 m (10ft). This giant was to be powered by ten gas turbine engines rated at 20,000 shp apiece. Six of these engines were to be stowed away into the wings after take-off, while the remaining four turboprops mounted on pylons above the wings were to ensure propulsion in cruise flight. The vehicle's design cruise speed was 185 km/h (115 mph) in ground-effect flight at an altitude of some 6 m (20 ft) above the water.

In 1963-65 the **Lockheed Company** of the USA built two small experimental WIG vehicles developed by V. B. Koryagin, an engineer of Russian origin. The company undertook feasibility studies for civilian ferry and military transport WIG craft, but little came of it.

An important milestone in WIG design in the West was the work conducted by the well-known German aviation designer **Alexander Lippisch** who, after the capitulation of Germany, went to the USA to provide advice to Convair and NACA with their delta-wing fighter development. In the 1950s he started research on ground effect machines. Working initially with the Collins Radio Corporation, he developed the concept of the reversed low aspect ratio delta wings with negative dihedral (anhedral) which came to be known as the Lippisch layout. The anhedral gave the wings a dome-shaped configuration in head-on view. A T-tail and endplate floats supplemented by angled winglets also formed a characteristic feature of the layout. Lippisch designed the X-112, an experimental single-seat craft powered by a 25-hp engine, featuring a boat hull. It was built by Collins Radio and was successfully flown in 1963. The design proved to be stable and efficient in ground effect. The great advantage of this configuration was its inherent stability in pitch and height above the supporting surface – an important pre-requisite for the safety of operation. Subsequently it gained popularity and was widely used by WIG craft designers and constructors in many countries, especially for designs of small and medium size. Despite the satisfactory results of the testing, Collins decided to stop the project and sold the patents to a German company called Rhein Flugzeugbau (RFB) which further developed the model (for further designs by A. Lippisch, see below in the German section).

In 1975 the **NASA Langley Research Center** in Langley, Virginia, conducted tests with a model of a heavy WIG craft designated SETOL (Surface Effect Take-Off and Landing); it featured an aircraft layout. With an AUW of some 1,130 tonnes (2,490,000 lb) the craft would be able to carry a useful load of more than 450 tonnes (992,000 lb). The vehicle, featuring a T-tail and wings with an aspect ratio of 2-4, was to be provided with two types of powerplant. Eight turbofans mounted on pylons forward of the wings were to provide boost for take-off, while the cruise propulsion would be ensured by four turbofans mounted on the vertical tail under the stabiliser.

In 1966 the **Grumman Aircraft Engineering Corporation** of the USA proposed a 300-tonne

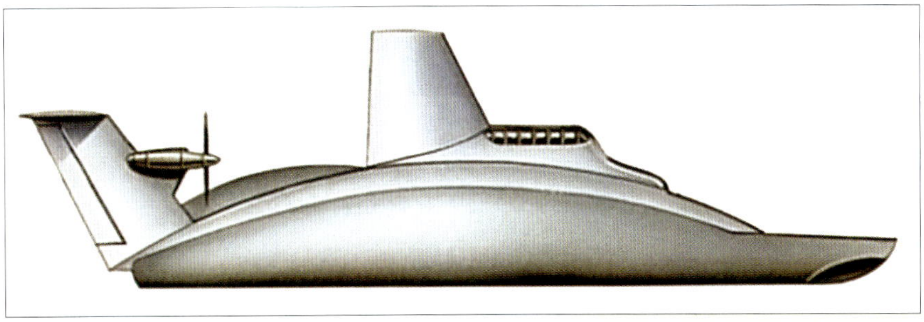

This drawing shows how the Vehicle Research Corporation Columbia would have looked.

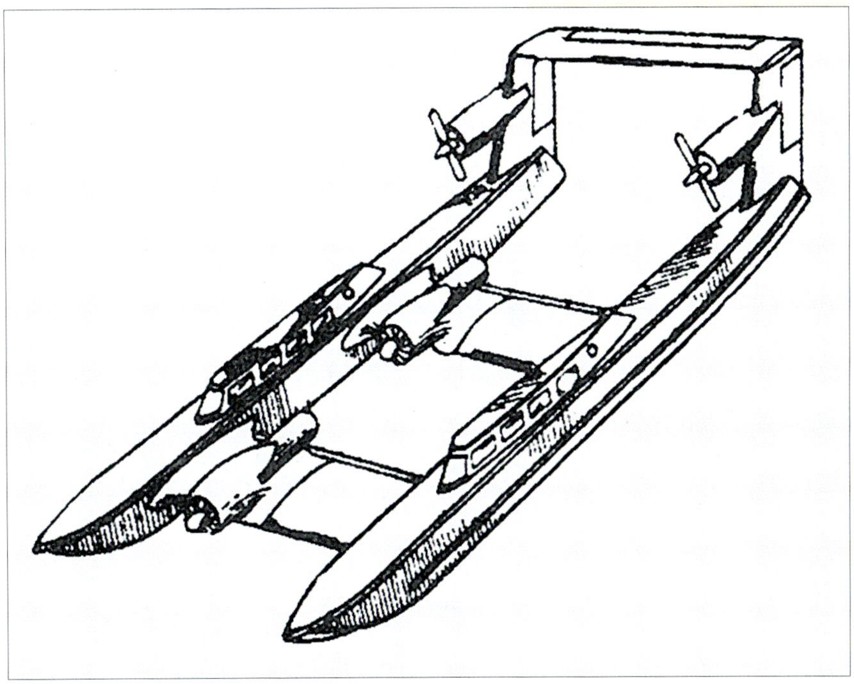

A drawing depicting the preliminary design project of the Small Weilandcraft; note the blower engines on the tandem wings. The actual craft had a different engine placement.

Registered N5691V, the Lippisch X-112 is seen during tests in the USA.

(661,375-lb) missile-carrying WIG craft configured as a flying wing with variable geometry. The latter quality was obtained by using endplate floats of special design which could be deflected upwards in flight to occupy a setting best suited for the selected flight mode.

In the mid-1960s the US company **Research Affiliates** developed two projects of combat WIG vehicles designated RAM-1 and RAM-2. While differing in size and mission type, had one thing in common – they were C-type vehicles (according to modern classification), intended to be able to fly at altitudes of more than 2,000 m (6,560 ft).

The RAM-1 was an ASW vehicle with an AUW of 89-90 tonnes (196,200-198,400 lb) which, in addition to ASW duties, was to be used as a cargo and troop transport. The vehicle was designed as a flying wing with well-developed outer wing panels to ensure a high lift-to-drag ratio and lateral stability. It was intended to carry search/targeting equipment and weapons to a total weight of 11 tonnes (24,250 lb) inside the main wing section. Two (or four) engines with a total output of 8,000 hp located in the wing panels were to expected to give the vehicle a speed of 185-240 km/h (115-149 mph) and a speed of some 93 km/h (58 mph) in the search flight mode.

An artist's impression of the Aerocon AR-1 Wingship in American Airlines colours. The two forward-mounted packs of ten jet engines give some idea of the vehicle's size.

The vehicle was to be provided with a system for jet efflux injection for the purpose of crating a static air cushion.

The RAM-2 transport/assault WIG craft (referred to in some sources as a Grumman project) was intended for transporting small groups of commandos in coastal areas when high speed and amphibious qualities were required. The vehicle had a design AUW of some 16-18 tonnes (35,000-40,000 lb) and was configured as a low-aspect-ratio 'flying wing' with large endplates which housed the powerplant and take-off devices. With an empty weight of some 14 tonnes (28,700 lb), the vehicle could carry a useful load of 2.5 tonnes (5,500 lb). The front part of the wing was hinged to serve as a ramp for the loading of troops and materiel. The WIG craft was powered by a turbojet which was expected to ensure the following performance: maximum speed, 460 km/h (286 mph); maximum speed with no load on board, 650 km/h (404 mph); minimum speed within ground effect, 65-93 km/h (40-58 mph) depending on the load. With a fuel load of 1,000 kg (2,205 lb) the vehicle was expected to have a range of 900 km (559 miles). The vehicle had good amphibious properties.

In the 1970s a team of designers headed by V. V. Koryagin (Lockheed Aircraft) developed a project of a military transport WIG craft. The vehicle featured an aircraft layout. At an AUW of 18.1 tonnes (39,910 lb) it had a length of 21.4 m (70 ft 2½ in) and a wing span of 16.5 m (54 ft 1¾ in). The wings were fitted with endplates which could be deflected in flight to an optimum angle depending on the flight's hydrodynamic conditions. A large cargo door with a ramp located in the forward part of the hull permitted the carriage of bulky military hardware, such as tanks, artillery pieces etc. The WIG craft was powered by two aircraft engines with shrouded propellers delivering a total of 2,750 hp. The engines mounted on high pylons to avoid being affected by sea spray would ensure a speed of some 315 km/h (196 mph).

In the USA, the **Aerocon Company** proposed the AR-1 Wingship – a gigantic transport ground-effect vehicle with 20 (!) engines and an AUW of 5,000 tonnes (11,022,000 lb). Apparently the company failed to obtain the necessary funding for the project which, in consequence, remained on the drawing board.

Flarecraft L-325

In the USA, a number of small companies have designed and tested a number of small recreational craft. One of them was the Flarecraft Company based in Connecticut. The company's chief Bill Russel acquired from the German company Fischer Flugmechanik the rights to distribute the Airfish 3

An example of the Flarecraft L-325 in flight.

WIG vehicle in the USA. While the Airfish 3 was there for demonstration purposes, the Flarecraft 30 was developed which was a copy of the Airfish.

Later Flarecraft produced its own design which was essentially a scaled up Airfish. In its L-324 prototype version it was designed to carry a pilot and three passengers. The machine featured the Lippisch layout with a reversed-delta wing and a T-tail. An improved production model was the Flarecraft L-325. It differed from the L-234 in providing accommodation for four passengers instead of three. Furthermore, the L-235 had a more powerful engine and was equipped with a small water jet (a 47-kW Yamaha motor) for harbour manoeuvring.

The L-325 went into limited production and was sold commercially in the USA for some time. There were plans to produce about five vehicles per month. Only a few L-325 were sold, because problems arose with the craft's stability. A short production run took place on the East coast of the USA in mid-1990s, but the machine is no longer in production.

Boeing Lowboy

During the late 1960s the Boeing Company spent much effort on the development of the Lowboy ASW WIG craft. Resembling a modern transport aircraft with low-set wings, the Lowboy was intended to be based on shore. With an AUW of 125 tonnes (275,600 lb) it was to carry mission equipment and weapons to a total weight of 6.8 tonnes (15,000 lb). The wing span of 52 m (170 ft 7 in) and aspect ratio of 12 were selected with a view to ensuring flight in surface effect above the sea at a wave height of up to 4 m (13 ft).

Boeing Pelican

In the mid-2000s Boeing Company put forward a project of a giant WIG vehicle called Pelican. Its full name is Pelican ULTRA (Ultra Large Transport Aircraft). It is, in fact, a huge high-capacity cargo plane featuring a normal aircraft layout. This would be the biggest aircraft ever built, with twice the external dimensions of An-225, the word's largest current aircraft.

The Pelican is intended primarily for airlifting US Army units with all their weaponry. During Operation *Enduring Freedom* in Iraq (2003) the redeployment of a single division required up to 30 days because its heavy armaments had to be transported by sea. The use of Pelicans would make it possible to reduce this term to five days, while 30 days would be enough to redeploy five divisions. That would signify a radical improvement in the mobility of the US Army.

Existing plans envisage the construction of a prototype not earlier than 2015, with a service introduction not before the 2020s.

The Boeing Company has studied vehicles with an AUW of 1,600 tonnes (3,528,000 lb), 2,700 tonnes (5,900,000 lb) and 4,500 tonnes (9,900,000 lb). The second version was selected for further development. Its lifting capacity is expected to exceed 1,270 tonnes (2,800,000 lb). The fuselage of rectangular cross-section, measuring 122 m (500 ft) in length, will have a double-deck layout. This will permit to accommodate 100 sea/land 20-ft containers in two tiers on the lower deck, 50 containers in one tier on the upper deck and a further 40 in the root sections of the wings. The vehicle is capable of

A computer-generated image of the Boeing Pelican. Although shown flying over the sea, the vehicle is not amphibious.

lifting 17 M1 Abrams main battle tanks (for comparison, the Lockheed C-5 Galaxy can lift not more than two such tanks at a time).

The vehicle is to feature high-set wings with a span of 152 m (500 ft), with a wing chord of up to 30 m (98 ft) and a wing area of over 4,000 sq m (43,000 sq ft). The wing outer panels have strong anhedral and downward-canted tips to enhance the ground effect. The powerplant comprises four wing-mounted engine nacelles, each housing two turboprop engines driving two co-axial propellers with a diameter of 15 m (49 ft). The engines to be used are expected to be maritime turboprop versions of the General Electric CF6 turbofans, the aggregate output of the powerplant reaching 60,000-80,000 hp.

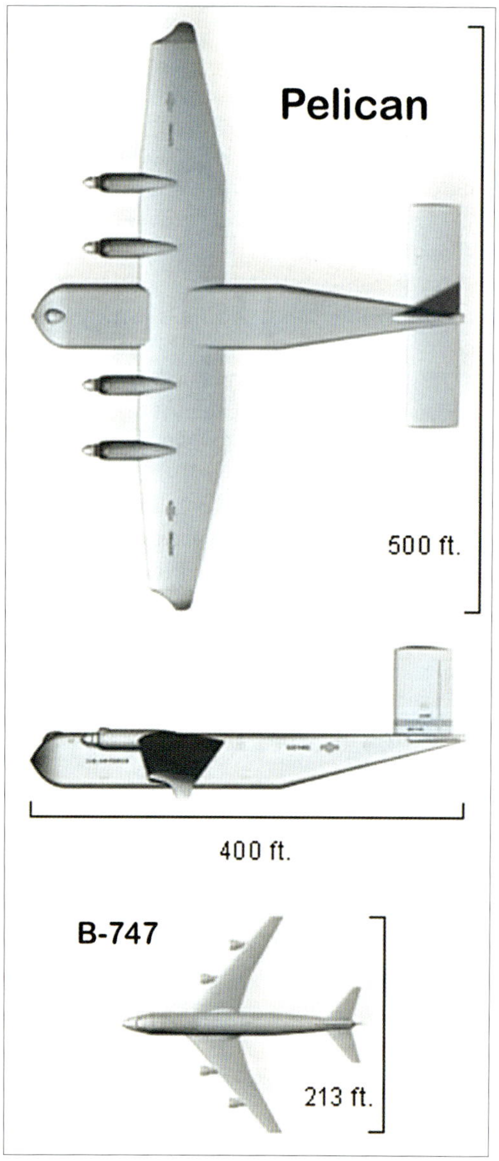

This drawing shows the Pelican's huge size, with a Boeing 747 airliner being depicted for comparison.

The vehicle will have an undercarriage comprising 38 steerable twin-wheel struts; thanks to this the specific pressure on the airfield surface will be comparable to that of modern aircraft. The take-off distance is expected to be within 2,200 m (7,200 ft).

In the WIG mode the Pelican is expected to fly at an altitude of 7 to 17 m (23 to 56 ft) above the sea surface. Yet it will be capable of rising to an altitude of up to 6,000 m (19,680 ft) for the purpose of flying over land areas or overflying the storm areas. In the surface effect mode the Pelican must be able to carry its maximum payload over a distance of 10,000 nautical miles (18,500 km); in free flight the range is reduced to 6,500 nautical miles.

A notable feature of the project is the fact that the Pelican is intended to be used from land airfields, rather than from water. This is presumably expected to reduce the required overall output of the powerplant by dispensing with the need to overcome the peak of resistance during take-off.

Germany

Dr. Alexander Lippisch and Rhein Flugzeugbau GmbH (RFB)

X-113

After his trials with the X-112 in the USA Lippisch returned to the Federal Republic of Germany, where he built the single-seat X-113 (X-113 AM). This proof-of-concept machine was manufactured by Rhein Flugzeugbau GmbH(= Rhine Aircraft Construction Co. Ltd.), a subsidiary of VFW-Fokker. Powered by a 40-hp Nelson H63-CP four-cylinder piston engine, the machine made its first flight in October 1970. The tests were quite successful, and the machine could fly out of ground effect up to an altitude of 800 m (2,620 ft). It proved remarkably stable, permitting hands-off-the-stick flight in surface effect. A constant height above the water was also maintained by the craft on its own. Yet, no commercial orders followed, and the single example built was used for sports and transport duties.

X-114

This was a further development of the X-113 – a six- or seven-seat machine featuring a catamaran configuration (the fuselage was raised above the water). Powered by a 200-hp Lycoming IO-360 air-cooled flat-six engine driving a ducted five-blade propeller, the X-114 first flew in 1977. (Dr. A. Lippisch died in 1976; all his patents had been acquired by RFB). At an AUW of 1.5 tonnes (3,300 lb) the machine attained a speed of 200 km/h (124 mph) A later version, the X-114H, incorporated retractable hydrofoils. The machine was developed under a military contract of the German government, and the prototype even sported the Luftwaffe test serial 98+29 on the fuselage, but the funding of further development was stopped. Unfortunately, the X-114 crashed due to pilot error. All further work was terminated.

Ramwing Transport

Lippisch had plans for much larger military transport and patrol craft based on his proven layout. He developed a project of a transport WIG vehicle dubbed 'Ramwing' which resembled an X-114 scaled up to the dimensions of a medium-sized cargo aircraft. The powerplant comprised four three-blade propellers in two tandem pairs on pylons above the wings. The project did not proceed further than the concept stage.

Hanno Fischer and Fischer Flugmechanik

Airfish series WIG craft

The concept of Dr. A. Lippisch was carried further by one of his associates at RFB, engineer Hanno Fischer, who later left this enterprise. In 1979 he founded his own company – Fischer Flugmechanik. Fischer decided to dispense with one of the qualities of the Lippisch designs – their capability for free flight, in addition to flight in ground effect. This quality, while affording some operational advantages, was commercially unattractive because it made it necessary to register the vehicle as an aircraft with all the ensuing expenses involved. In consequence, H. Fischer's designs were intended to be operated in ground effect only and thus could be registered as boats, entailing no need for a pilot's licence.

H. Fischer initially produced three designs of small WIG craft known as Airfish-1, Airfish-2 and Airfish-3 (the digits refer to the number of persons on board). Their performance did not include the ability for flight out of ground effect.

The Airfish-1 was successfully tested in 1987; it was followed by the Airfish-2, which had clipped wings to assist harbour manoeuvrability. In 1989 the type was licensed by German authorities as a boat. Encouraged with this success, H. Fischer produced his next design, the Airfish-3, as a pre-production two-seat recreational craft. This type was operated successfully in Germany, the Netherlands and the USA. Several further stages of development followed, and in May 1999, H. Fischer embarked on the design of Airfish-8, an eight-seat ground-effect craft.

The Airfish-8 was constructed by Airfoil Development GmbH (ADF) – a company founded by H. Fischer in 1997 for the purpose of evolving this vehicle commissioned by a foreign investor. It was designed as a prototype for commercial production. The machine, intended to carry six passengers

The Lippisch X-113 seen during tests on the Rhine as D-9568.

The X-114 nearing completion at the RFB prototype shop. Note the large floats.

Here the X-114 (98+29) is seen flying over the Rhine, showing the ducted propeller and the streamlined cabin section.

and two crew or a 760-kg 1,675 lb) payload and two crew, was based on earlier Airfish designs and featured a classic Lippisch reversed delta wing configuration.

In 1997 Fischer Flugmechanik granted a licence to the Australian company Flightship Ground Effect Pty for the manufacture of the Airfish-8 which was renamed FS-8 by the Australian manufacturer. Certification (classification) of the craft was handled by Germanischer Lloyd in Germany and later by Lloyd's Register in Australia. Under the IMO legislation, the Airfish-8 is classified as a Type A WIG vehicle, in the category of a marine vessel.

Hoverwing-2 (HV-2VT)

Fischer Flugmechanik, in conjunction with Techno Trans research institute, have been sponsored by the German Ministry of R&D to develop a second-generation WIG craft. The result was the emergence of a two-seat prototype, the HW-2VT, a scaled-down version of the targeted Hoverwing-80 with 80 seats. This flying testbed demonstrated all the required performance characteristics during testing in Holland and in the Baltic Sea. The Hoverwing concept combines the use of the classical Lippisch wings with a flat fuselage featuring a tunnel-shaped underside for enhancing the dynamic air cushion effect. Also characteristic of the projects in this series is the use of a twin-boom tail unit with the horizontal tail resting on two vertical tails. Prospective designs in this series include the Hoverwing-120 and Hoverwing-200 with the digits corresponding to the number of passengers.

Günter W. Jörg

In 1973 the German designer Günter W. Jörg developed a WIG craft based on a new tandem design. Provided the speed and weather conditions are within predetermined parameters, the design is incapable of flying out of ground effect and is inherently stable. Jörg built many different craft including an eighteen-meter version seating eight passengers. They came to be known as Tandem-Airfoil Flairboats (TAF).

Initially Günter Jörg conducted his activities within the framework of the MBB/VFW company. In 1987 he founded Botec GmbH, located near Frankfurt. Botec Company became the most important developer of WIG craft based on the tandem wing layout. A large number of WIG craft for the civilian market were developed. These TAF vehicles included a number of craft in different designs and sizes which were suitable for leisure boat application and for commercial applications. Up to 2005, 16 Tandem Airfoil Flairboats had been built and successfully tested according to all rules and regulations. The machines produced by. Günter Jörg

A model depicting the Ramwing cargo *ekranoplan* developed by Alexander Lippisch.

bore designations with the TAB and TAF prefixes, mostly TAF VIII series with additional numbers. Here are a few examples.

The **TAF VIII-1** was a two-seat machine weighing 750 kg (1,650 lb). With a 100-hp engine it attained a speed of 135 km/h and had a range of 200 km (124 miles).

The **TAF VIII-2 (Jörg-IV)** with an AUW of 1,600 kg (3,530 lb), powered by a 300-hp engine, carried a useful load of 500 kg (1,100 lb) and attained a speed of 155 km/h (96 mph).

The **TAF VIII-3** with an AUW of 3,150 kg (6,940 lb), powered by a 550-hp engine, carried a useful load of 900 kg (1,980 lb) and attained a speed of 160 km/h; the range was 400 km (248 miles).

The **TAF VIII-4** had an AUW of 4,600 kg and a useful load of 1,300 kg (2,870 lb). With a 750-hp turboprop it attained a maximum speed of 170 km/h (105 mph) and had a range of 450 km (280 miles).

The **TAF VIII-7** was project of a tandem-wing flairboat for 113 passengers. It was to be powered by two gas turbine engines of 4,250 kW each; the vehicle would cruise at a height of 1.25 m (4 ft).

In 1984 Günter Jörg in co-operation with RFB developed a project of a river bus – a flying boat measuring 60 m (196 ft $10\frac{13}{64}$ in) in length and 25 m (82 ft $0\frac{1}{4}$ in) in width which was intended to transport 400 passengers or up to 40 tonnes (88,180 lb) of cargo on the rivers of South America and Africa. It was based on a tandem-wing layout.

Techno Trans research institute

From 1993 the work in Germany on WIG vehicles for commercial use was coordinated by an organisation called Die Gesellschaft zur Förderung von Wissenschaft, Forschung und Innovation e.V. (Techno Trans) (The Society for the Promotion of Science, Research and Innovation) in Rostock in co-operation with engineers Jörg, Fischer and Matjasic. The programme was supported by some well-known companies in the aircraft construction and shipbuilding sector, as well as by the Rostock University. This programme included the design and construction, initially, of light sports and recreational vehicles, to be followed by larger craft for 30-120 passengers and cargo transportation.

One of the projects studied by Techno Trans was the **ARGE 1** large WIG vehicle for cargo transport. An illustration shows a craft with low-aspect-ratio, wide-chord wings provided with endplate floats, and a T-tail (much in common with Alekseyev's designs), powered by a tandem installation of two turboprops on a pylon above the fuselage.

Australia

In the early 1990s, a number of small enterprises, companies and individuals in Australia tried their hand at the design and construction of WIG craft. Worthy of note among these are the Radacraft and Sea Eagle International companies. They were established with the goal of developing mall commuter and recreational craft. None of the designs evolved by these companies progressed beyond prototype development stage. Nevertheless, they deserve to be mentioned here.

The **Radacraft** company produced, among others, the Radacraft G-35 – a small vehicle which resembled in its basic layout a scaled-down Russian Aquaglide-5 (see Chapter 6). The testing of the

The Airfish-8 (AF-8) is seen inside a light shelter. Note the carefully faired propeller drive shafts.

The AF-8's Australian incarnation, the Flightship FS-8, in cruise flight.

Bottom: The FS-8 on its beaching gear. Note the open portside entry door.

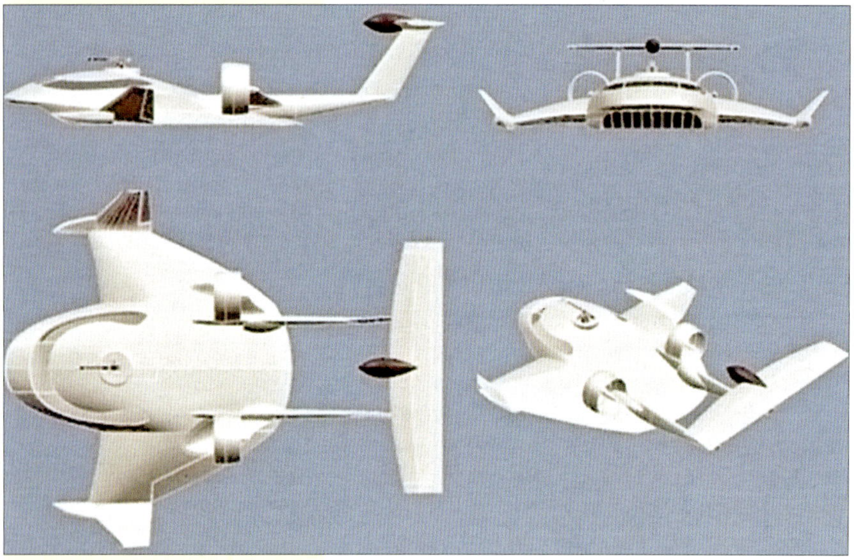

Top: A computer-generated image of a new WIG craft designed by Hanno Fischer.

Four views of the same craft, showing the wing planform and catamaran-type hull.

G-35 started in late December 1995. It was advertised as *'the only wing in ground effect craft to be designed, built and flown in Australia'*. There were plans for a more advanced vehicle, the Radacraft 850 and an even bigger machine, a 100-seat WIG vehicle which failed to be implemented (the company went out of business later).

Sea Eagle International was a company that emerged in Australia in the early 2000s; it established co-operation with a specialist company in China to develop a civilian range of Class B WIG vehicles. One of the company's designs, a six-seat vehicle designated Sea Eagle 6, became the object of this co-operation. In China it was further developed and put into production. It appears to be identical with the TSN (AD-606) – see below.

The Sea Eagle 20 project developed by the Australian company later, was a bigger machine with a hull length of 20.75 m (68 ft 0$\frac{59}{64}$ in) and an empty weight of 2,220 kg (4,890 lb). The design payload figure was 2,400 kg (5,290 lb). The vehicle powered by two 500-hp engines was expected to have a cruise speed of 230 km/h (142 mph) and to be capable of operating at a wave height of 1.5 m (4 ft 11 in) for take-off and 2.0 m (6 ft 6$\frac{3}{4}$ in) for landing. As distinct from the Sea Eagle 6 with its composite layout wings, the Sea Eagle 20 featured reversed delta wings in combination with twin vertical tails and a high-set horizontal tail. No information is available on the subsequent development.

As described above in the German section, in 1997 the Australian company **Flightship Ground Effect Pty** acquired from Fischer Flugmechanik a licence to build an eight-seat ground effect craft, the Airfish-8 which became known as the FS-8 Dragon Commuter in Australia. The first flight of the FS-8 (presumably a pre-production machine built by ADF, not by the Australian company) took place in the Netherlands in February 2001. The production model was to be powered by a 337-kW 6.2 litre Chevrolet V8 engine. Its maximum flight altitude in ground effect at full power was expected to be 3 m (10 ft). This vehicle was manufactured in limited numbers.

Canada

In 1963 the Canadian engineer **D. Coxidge** built a diminutive two-seat WIG boat. Weighing a mere 360 kg (790 lb), it measured 4.2 m (13 ft 9$\frac{23}{64}$ in) in length and 2 m in width and was configured as a trimaran with a cockpit resting on three floats. The space between the floats below the boat's hull was shielded off by front and rear flaps which were controlled from the cockpit. A 25-hp forward-mounted engine drove a propeller, whose wash was deflected by special vanes into the space below the hull. Directional control was effected by water rudders. During testing the boat attained a speed of 37 km/h (23 mph), but failed to achieve a lift-off, continuing its movement in the hydroplaning mode.

In 1972-74 the **Naval Research Center of Canada** developed a project of a multi-purpose WIG craft intended for operation primarily in Arctic areas. The range of possible mission included troop and cargo transport, landing operations, ASW and SAR duties, mine countermeasures, etc. The vehicle was configured as a catamaran with the two hulls joined by an arch-shaped structure topped by the crew cockpit. This arch-like structure was given an airfoil section and created aerodynamic lift equal to about 20% of the craft's weight in

Apart from the more streamlined cockpit section, this WIG craft designed by Fischer is similar to the one depicted above.

Artist's impressions of the Hoverwing 80 (left) and the larger Hoverwing 120.

cruise. Two gas turbines drove shrouded propellers mounted on pylons; they also drove compressors which supplied air to the air cushion chamber. The hulls were provided with a flexible skirt. Thus, this was a combination of a WIG vehicle and an ACV. The craft was to be controlled in flight by aerodynamic control surfaces, with special propellers as an option.

The craft was to be equipped with different complements of armament, depending on its mission. For self-defence it was to carry automatic anti-aircraft cannon and surface-to-air missiles. Calculations showed that this vehicle would have a 20-25% greater range in comparison with the conventional ACVs when travelling at a speed of 140-150 km/h (87-93 mph).

China (People's Republic of China)

The beginning of work in China on transport vehicles based on dynamic air cushion dates back to 1961 when China's government established the **Chinese Special Vehicles Research Institute** (CSVRI). Initially based in Beijing, it was transferred to the town of Jingmen, Hubei Province, in 1969. It was tasked with research dealing with hydroplanes and amphibious vehicles. The work performed by this institute posed a practical question: who would bear the main responsibility for the design and construction of WIG vehicles? Was it going to be the shipbuilding industry, or the aircraft industry? Eventually it was decided that the design work would be performed jointly by aviation and shipbuilding spe-

Far left: The TAF VIII-1 two-seat WIG craft in cruise mode.

The TAF VIII-4 features the same tail design, with the propeller rotating in a slit between the fin and the rudder.

The TAF VIII-3 (far left) and the projected TAF VIII-7 both feature tandem wings. The larger TAF VIII-7 has twin engines and twin tails.

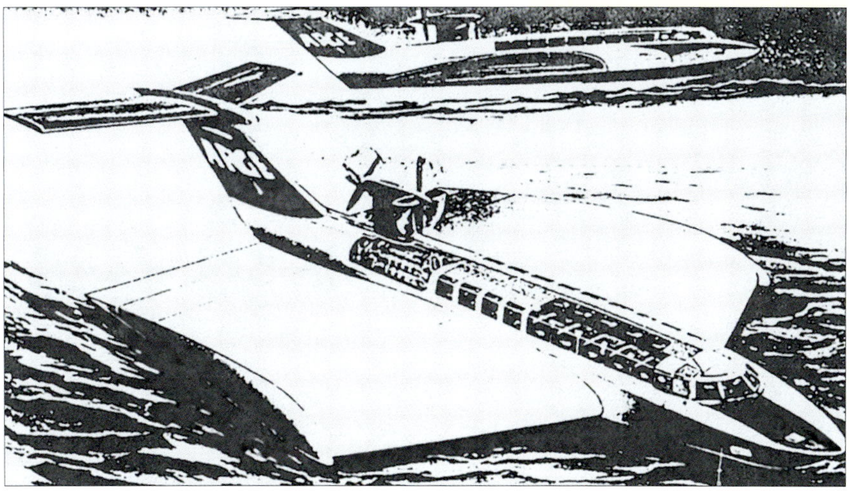

An artist's impression of the ARGE-1 developed by Techno Trans.

Front view of the Sea Eagle 6 in flight taken from a chase speedboat.

cialists, while the construction of prototypes would be entrusted to aircraft plants.

In due course several other Chinese institutions became involved in the theoretical studies and practical design of WIG craft intended for civil and military purposes. These included the **China Academy of Science and Technology Development** (CASTD) and **China Ship Scientific Research Centre** (CSSRC).

The Australian FlightShip FS-8 in cruise flight; it is identical to the German Airfish-8.

In 1967 the latter institution embarked on the design and prototype construction of the first Chinese WIG craft. The project was designated '961'.Some details on this and the subsequent types of WIG vehicles created in China are given below in the chronological succession.

The '961' WIG vehicle was built by CSSRC in Beijing in 1968. This single-seat twin-fuselage machine of purely Chinese design (not patterned on Lippisch designs) was a single-seat experimental craft with twin fuselages. It was tested amid great secrecy in 1968-69.

In the early 1970s the work on *ekranoplans* in China was temporarily halted due to political turmoil and economic complications caused by the 'Cultural Revolution'. Some ten years elapsed before CSSRC could resume its work on its next project, the '902'.

The Chinese Type 750 (aka Swan) research WIG vehicle. Note the false cabin windows painted on the side.

The '902' vehicle, featuring the Lippisch layout, was built by CSSRC in 1984 and made a series of test flights in the same year. Powered by two HS350A piston engines, it could fly over calm water only. It is regarded as a progenitor of the vehicles in the XTW series.

According to a different source, this single-seat experimental vehicle was under development from 1979 and was developed by CSVRI. It was powered by two HS350A piston engines.

In the early 1990s the Shanghai-based **708 Shipbuilding Institute** joined the work on ground-effect vehicles; it is also known as the ACV section of the **Marine Design and Research Institute of China** (MARIC).

The '750' vehicle was built by MARIC (708 Institute) in 1985 was an experimental two-seat twin-hull vehicle with triple vertical tails, powered by four ducted DT-30 piston engines rated at 22 kW apiece. A pair of engines was placed above aft sections of the hulls, while the other two engines were mounted on outriggers forward of the wing between the hulls, sending their air wash into the space under the wing and thus creating a static air cushion.

In the meantime, three ground-effect vehicles in the XTW series were designed and built by CSSRC.

The XTW-1 was built by CSSRC in 1989. This experimental three-seat machine powered by two Rotax 447 engines, featured the Lippisch layout; it had two vertical tails, canted to the sides and topped by a horizontal stabiliser. The vehicle was capable of flying in surface effect at a height of up to 10 m (33 ft) in sea state 2.

A different source states that a single example was built in1988 by CSVRI.

The XTW-2, built by CSSRC in 1990, was a scaled-up version of its predecessor. It carried two pilots and 14 passengers. The cruise flight could be performed in sea state 3, but the take-off was limited to sea state 2. The vehicle was powered by two Lycoming IO-540K1B5 flat-six engines. A different source states that a single example of the XTW-2 was built in 1988 by CSVRI.

The XTW-3, built by CSSRC in 1997, was a reworked version of the XTW-2 with a new tail unit (a T-tail). The photos also show a modified wing without the short 'shoulders' characteristic for the preceding two models.

Again, a different source states that a single example of the XTW-3 was built by CSVRI in 1996.

At about the same time a new organisation made an entry into the WIG craft design field. It was a WIG vehicle development centre (presumed to be the 605 Institute) which is known as a branch of the **China Academy of Science and Technology Development** (CASTD). In 1996 it presented its own project designated DFX-100

The DXF-100 (also referred to as DFXJ-100) was built by CASTD at an aircraft plant in Jingmen in 1998 as an experimental craft weighing 4.8 tonnes and powered by two IO-540K1B5 engines;. DXF = DiXiaoFeiji – WIG vehicle. This vehicle accommodating 12 passengers became the basis for subsequent designs in the TY (*TianYi*) series.

The TY-1 built by CASTD in. 1998 was the first in the TY series. This vehicle accommodating 14 passengers is powered by two engines of 294 kW apiece.

The development programme for the TY-1 has been aimed at commercial operation from the very beginning, so there was no prototype as such. The first craft to be built was put into commercial operation. Design work was started in June 1966 and was completed in August 1997. The TY-1 made its maiden flight on 10th November 1998. Upon completion of a 10-month test programme it was out into commercial operation on a lake in China for touristic purposes on a daily basis, sometimes up to eight runs per day.

The TY-1 was designed to carry 15 passengers, but this number had to be reduced to 11 due to a weight problem. The design weight was exceeded by 100 kg (220 lb); after adding an air conditioning system the weight and drag were such that the payloads decreased by four passengers.

The TY-1 was powered by two 224-kW Lycoming IO-450-K1B5 engines driving variable-pitch ducted propellers. The TY-1 is suitable only for lake or very flat sea operations since its maximum sea state is 3.

A second example was under construction and was to be ready by May 2000. There is no information about the actual progress of the work and the subsequent operational record of the machine.

In 1998 (?) the TY-1 was followed by the next design in the series.

The TY-2 (TianYi-2), built by CASTD, 605 Institute, was an experimental WIG vehicle powered by two ZMZ-4058 piston engines. No further details are available.

In September 1997 the 708 Institute made a come-back with new projects in the 75x series, starting with the '751'.

The '751' (DX-TE), initially known as the AF-1 and later dubbed Swan, was built by MARIC, 708 Institute, in Shanghai in 1998. This is a craft for 15-20 passengers with an AUW of 8.1 tonnes (17,860 lb) powered by three HS6 nine-cylinder radial engines (one 210-kW HS6A as a cruise engine and two 257-kW HS6E-1 forward-mounted engines that could be tilted for take-off boost.) Two years of testing corroborated the soundness of the concept. The machine was built from imported aluminium alloys and composite materials. It could be operated at sea states up to 3.

The year of 1999 saw the beginning of construction of the XTW-4 WIG vehicle – the fourth in the XTW-series.

This rather ungainly vehicle is the XTW-1 developed by CSSRC. Note the cranked wings with zero dihedral on the inboard sections; this is due to the need to provide propeller clearance.

The later XTW-3 is rather more aesthetically pleasing and features wings with constant anhedral.

Front view of the still-unpainted XTW-3 with the engines uncowled.

An artist's impression of an XTW-3 in operation.

The XTW-4 was built by CSSRC (by CSVRI, according to a different source). The XTW-4 reverted to the same tail arrangement as on the XTW-1 and -2, featuring two vertical tails canted outwards and topped by a horizontal tail. Apparently

The almost completed CASTD TY-1 in the assembly shop in primer finish.

The TY-1 taxies on the water during tests.

Here the TY-1 is seen in wing-borne flight, showing the deep endplates/wingtip floats.

the T-tail of the XTW-3 was not successful. On the XTW-4 CSSRC used for the first time turboprop engines in its WIG craft. Two PT-6A-15AG turboprops drove 5-blade propellers. The XTW-4 was launched in September 1999; by early 2000 trials on the Changjiang River were completed. No information is available on the ultimate story of the project.

Unlike the earlier XTW craft, the XTW-4 was intended for sea operation and had a boat-type hull. A new type of high-strength, corrosion-resistant aluminium alloy was used for the structure. All primary control surfaces were operated by push-pull rod and cable systems, hydraulics were used to operate the taxiing gear. This was an experimental vehicle, construction of only one example was planned.

In 1999 MARIC submitted an improved version of the '751' project designated '751G'. Modifications to the original design included relocation of the engines and of the horizontal tail. The engines were moved from the wings to pylons flanking the forward fuselage; the wing area was increased and the tailplane was raised higher on the vertical tail.

The DY-1 (known in the full-scale mock-up form as the DY-806) was presented by CASTD (605 Institute) in 2000. It was a six-seat craft powered by a single IO-540K1B5 engine The machine featured a composite layout wing with a low-aspect-ratio centre section and high-aspect-ratio outer wing panels. The vehicle could be operated in the surface-effect mode with occasional flight at an altitude of up to 30 m (100 ft).

No prototype was built; the testing was to be conducted on the first production example. This vehicle appears to be near-identical in appearance to the Australian Sea Eagle-6 and its presumed Chinese counterpart, the TSN (see below)

The SDJ-1 WIG vehicle built by CSSRC in 2000 was a six-seat craft of a catamaran layout, with the engine mounted above the wing between the fuselages. The main wing was supplemented by outer wing panels outboard of the hulls.

Two projects were reportedly developed by Hong Kong-based company **Flying Dragon Technology Ltd** by 2000.

The FLHRO-PB ('Orlyonok-2') was a project of a 150-seat passenger WIG craft, developed by the Hong Kong company on the basis of the Soviet (Russian) ekranoplan Orlyonok.

The FLHW from the same company was a project of a 50-seat passenger WIG craft (no details are available.

A notable event took place in 1999. A joint stock company named **Guangzhou Tianxiang WIGcraft Company Ltd** was set up in the Guangzhou Free Zone (the city of Guangzhou, Guangdong Province). The company, created for the purpose of developing and manufacturing ekranoplans of Chinese design, declared its intention to win leading positions on the world market. The company/s designs are described below.

The TX-2 (TY-2) or Tianxiang-2 WIG vehicle was under construction by Guangzhou Tianxiang WIGcraft Co., nearing completion in 2000. According to one source, it was powered by three 150-hp automobile engines and featured a combination of aluminium alloys and composite materials in its structure. A different source states, however, describes this vehicle was as a copy of the Russian twin-engined Volga-2 WIG vehicle, carrying two crew and eight passengers.

Development of this vehicle started in 1999. It had an AUW of 2.85 tonnes (6,280 lb).

The TX-5 (Tianxiang -5) was announced by **Guangzhou Tianxiang WIGcraft Co.** in 2001. It was a 45-seat WIG vehicle powered by two WS-11 turbofans rated at 1,720 kgp (3,790 lbst), and one WJ5E turboprop delivering 2,850 hp. The vehicle had an AUW of 19 tonnes (42,000 lb). According to the project, the vehicle was expected to be able to make short 'hops' to an altitude of up to 150 m (500 ft) for overcoming obstacles.

The TSN (AD-606) six-seat machine with a 300-hp engine was reportedly built by **Yionhe longyi Ship Co. Ltd** in Nanjing in 2002. It had composite layout wings and a T-tail.

This craft appears to be identical to a WIG vehicle developed in Australia by the Sea Eagle International company. This company worked with China's CSSRC to develop a civilian range of Class B Wing Effect Craft. The craft, also dubbed Sea Eagle, was reported to be flying in China. Quite recently, in mid-2010, there were reports stating that two Chinese WIG craft had been delivered to United Arab Emirates, and accompanying pictures showed a vehicle closely resembling the TSN (or Sea Eagle).

Development of WIG vehicles in China is conducted by Chinese scientists, designers and engineers with due regard to experience gained in other countries. In particular, China established co-operation with Russian scientific institutions engaged in researching the problems associated with WIG craft. This co-operation included contracts with Russian institutions for studying certain specific problems; Russian specialists came to China to deliver lectures on the subjects of WIG technology. The Guangzhou Tianxiang WIGcraft Co Ltd mentioned above officially acknowledged its close collaboration with the leading Russian organisations in the field of *ekranoplan* design.

In 2005 Vyacheslav Kolganov, the then general director and chief designer of the TREK Science & Production Group (at present the leader of IFPG), told journalists that a number of engineers and designers from the Alekseyev CHDB, from St. Petersburg and from Novosibirsk had been working already for several years at Chinese enterprises engaged in the development of *ekranoplans*. On the basis of the experience accumulated by these specialists, said Kolganov, the Chinese had built and were using operationally close to a hundred ekranoplans with a seating capacity for 7, 14 and 20 passengers; they were engaged in the projecting of WIG vehicles intended to carry 150 passengers and still bigger machines. Kolganov's point obviously was the much greater attention accorded in China to the WIG field as compared to Russia.

The use of Russian experience found its expression, in particular, in the construction of the YH-7, a copy of the Russian Ivolga (EL-7) WIG craft, which was built in Shanghai (in 2002?). However, generally speaking, Chinese designers have demonstrated their ability to produce designs which cannot be classed as mere copies of ekranoplans created in other countries. This was acknowledged by the abovementioned Kolganov, who, while speaking to a journalist in November 2008, said that in China the WIG vehicle construction had become a task of state importance. This subject, he said, was attracting great interest there. He noted that a shipbuilding plant in Shanghai had started the manufacture of the airframe of a 150-seat ekranoplan and there were plans for creating a WIG vehicle capable of carrying 600 passengers. Chinese specialists, noted Kolganov, were very active in studying theoretical aspects of ekranoplan construction and were actively co-operating with their Russian colleagues from SibNIA (the Siberian Aviation Research Institute).

Chinese designers are visualizing new projects of WIG vehicles of ever growing weight and dimen-

The '751' (Swan) WIG craft taxies on the water.

Two views of the '751' in cruise flight. Note the 'power egg' installation of the centre engine.

A computer-generated image of the DY-1 light WIG vehicle.

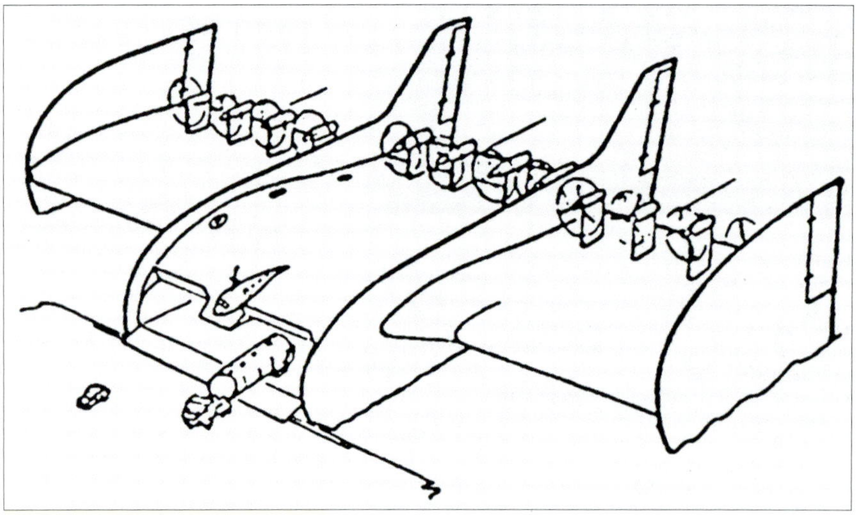

An artist's impression of the French Cygne-14 large transport WIG craft.

sions, some of which are truly gigantic machines. For example, there were reports about a vehicle called Xintianwen-4 (project Changhe-6) with a displacement of 500 tonnes (1,102,290 lb). In 2006 publicity was given to a series of projects on military WIG vehicles, including a WIG-type aircraft carrier, a missile-carrying WIG craft and other projects.

In 2007 a WIG vehicle with unknown designation was reported to be under development at Shanghai-based **Tongji University**. With a design payload of 4,000 kg (8,800 lb), top speed of 162 kt (300 km/h) and maximum altitude of 5 m (16 ft), the vehicle was claimed to consume half to two-thirds of fuel of an 'ordinary aircraft' while carrying 'more weight' and being up to six times faster than an ocean-going ship. The report said further development could lead to a 50-seat prototype by 2013, with future versions able to carry up to 400,000 kg (881,850 lb) by 2017.

Representatives of the **Shanghai Engineering and Construction University** announced in 2008 (?) that they would soon complete the work on the projects of several types of WIG vehicles with an all-up weight ranging from 10 to 200 tonnes (22,045-441,000 lb). They claimed that by 2017 more than 200 ekranoplans would be put into operation on regular routes; the machines in question were expected to carry a cargo of more than 400 tonnes (882,000 lb).

The success achieved by the Chinese industry in the design and construction of WIG vehicles was emphasized by recent reports (March 2010) according to which the Chinese company Jiangsu Hengchuan Group from Jiansu province, Eastern China, was going to deliver 17 WIG vehicles to the United Arab Emirates. The value of the contract was estimated at 'several milliard yuan'. The delivery is scheduled to take place in 2011. Unfortunately, no further details concerning this contract are available.

France

In 1977 specialists of French company Bertin developed a project of a transoceanic cargo transport WIG vehicle named Cygne (Swan). The project comprised two versions: the Cygne-10 and the Ceygne-14 with a useful load of 550 and 870 tonnes (1,213,000 and 1,918,000 lb) respectively. The vehicle was configured as a lifting body (thick-section flying wing) with outer wing panels of thinner profile. Both the wing centre section and the outer panels were provided with huge endplates which also acted as vertical tails and accordingly were fitted with rudders. The forward part of the lifting body (wing centre section) incorporated ramps which could be used for the roll-on loading of wheeled vehicles. The powerplant comprised 12 aircraft engines with tractor propellers which were mounted on pylons above the wings. Aerodynamic properties of the craft enabled it to fly at altitudes between 0 and 3,000 m (9,840 ft). It was expected to cross the Atlantic at a speed of 370 km/h (230 mph) in the course of 20 hours.

Great Britain

Several projects of heavy WIG craft for military duties were developed in Great Britain and the USA. In the late 1950s and early 1960s the British engineer **A. Pedrick** developed several projects. One of them was a project of an aircraft-carrier configured as a WIG vehicle. It was intended to provide accommodation for 20-30 light combat aircraft. The vehicle featured a flying wing layout with thin endplates. A streamlined superstructure located on the forward part of the upper deck housed the workstations for the vehicle's control. The empennage comprised two large vertical tails with rudders. The powerplant comprised ten turbojets located in the aft section of the body. The air intakes of the turbojets were located on the wing's upper surface; their suction helped enhance the lifting properties of the wing. A large part of the vehicle's body was occupied by a single-tier hangar with three deck lifts, two of which served for delivering the aircraft from the hangar to the deck and the third one was used for stowing them under the deck after landing. Two catapults were to be used for performing the take-off, while the landing involved the use of arrestor wires.

In 1972 the British designer **W. E. Walledge** took out a patent for an original design of a boat with aerodynamic off-loading. The boat had a streamlined hull with an aft-mounted pylon which carried a lifting wing and an engine with a propeller. The vehicle had an aircraft-type tail unit. Pitch trim was effected with the help of an adjustable stabiliser, ailerons served for lateral control. The vehicle's peculiar feature was the location of the wing far aft of the CG.

In 1976 the **Sunbury** company built the first British WIG boat featuring an aircraft layout. It had a tail unit consisting of twin fins topped by a horizontal tail. The vehicle was powered by a Rolls-Royce Gnome turboshaft engine. The machine underwent flight testing which reportedly was intended to provide a basis for a decision on the feasibility of larger machines of the same kind.

A poor-quality yet interesting photo showing the Iranian WIG craft in flight.

Iran

In 2006 the world mass media carried reports touching upon Iran's work in the field of WIG vehicle construction. This was sparked off by the news item according to which the Iranian military had tested during a 'war game' in the Persian Gulf 'a small propeller-driven aircraft that flies low over water surface at up to 100 knots'. A screenshot from an Iranian video showed a little craft very similar in appearance to the Russian TsLST ESKA-1 *ekranoplan* (see Chapter 5). An interesting comment on this event was published at a Russian web forum in 2009. It stated that 'some ten years ago' (that is, around 1999) a large-scale piloted model of a WIG craft had been built with assistance from TsAGI in the Iranian **Malek-Ashtar University**. It was made of aluminium/magnesium alloy (AMg) and was of riveted construction. The machine performed many successful fights in the Persian Gulf, but eventually fell victim to corrosion, despite all efforts to prevent this. Later (according to the comment) moulds were taken from the basic elements of the airframe, to be used for manufacturing two new airframes in glass fibre which were externally identical but featured internal differences. One of the two airframes was of traditional construction (framework and skin); the other one featured a 'sandwich' construction without the supporting internal framework. Both airframes were completed as piloted vehicles which were tested in the Persian Gulf in late 2005 and early 2006. At the same time the Iranian Navy conducted an exercise in the Persian Gulf, with due attention from the US mass media. It was then that one of these test vehicles was glimpsed in the news. It stands to reason to surmise that there are plans in Iran for further experiments with larger WIG craft intended for practical operation

Japan

At about the same time specialists of the Japanese company **Kawasaki Aircraft Co Ltd** built three WIG craft designated KAG-1, KAG-2 and KAG-3. They were configured as catamarans with large-size floats flanking the short-span wing. In particular, the KAG-3 vehicle had an open cockpit for two pilots located on the forward section of the wing. The vehicle powered by an 80-hp outboard engine attained a speed of 110 km/h (68 mph). The KAG-3 underwent comprehensive testing during which it was repeatedly subjected to modifications. The design was eventually abandoned because it was inherently unstable.

In 1963 engineer Shigenori from the Kawasaki Company developed a project of a heavy WIG vehicle featuring a 'flying wing' layout. It was to be powered by four aircraft engines mounted on tall pylons located in the aft part of the wing. The pylons doubled as vertical tails topped by a horizontal tail. The wing underside was provided with longitudinal strakes which were intended to prevent transverse airflow under the wings.

Yet another project prepared by Shigenori was a similar WIG craft equipped with a device for power-augmented take-off. It was fitted with a foreplane mounted higher up in relation to the main wing. The foreplane carried two engines with propellers. At the moment of take-off the foreplane was tilted, directing the propeller wash under the wing to create a static air cushion which lifted the vehicle out of the water. When the craft attained the necessary speed for cruise flight, the foreplane was set into the optimum position dictated by hydrodynamic conditions, and the craft's load.

In 1962 a team of Kawasaki designers led by M. Yatsushi developed a project of a WIG craft very similar to the one described above. It differed in having a fixed foreplane carrying booster engines which were given the proper incidence to direct the airflow from their propellers under the wings.

The Kawasaki KAG-3 WIG craft. Note the cockpit offset to port.

In 1972 the Japanese company **Shin Meiwa** built the AF-XS boat with aerodynamic off-loading. This two-seat vehicle with a hull having a length of 4 m (13 ft) was fitted with sweptback wings and with hydroskis. The boat was powered by a 25-hp Yamaha outboard engine. Tests showed an improvement of performance in comparisons with traditional boats in the same power class.

Desktop models of two unnamed WIG vehicles designed by NPO Europa in the Ukraine.

New Zealand

In 2007 it was reported that engineer Rudy Heeman residing in New Zealand had built an air cushion vehicle which, in addition, is capable of flight in ground effect mode thanks to the wings which can be extended after the vehicle has reached a speed of 100 km/h (62 mph). The two-seat vehicle has made some successful flights, but no news is available on the ultimate results of the testing.

South Korea

In September 2007 the government of South Korea announced its plans envisaging the construction of a large WIG craft intended for commercial purposes by 2012. The vehicle is expected to have an all-up weight of 300 tonnes (660,000 lb) and have a load-carrying capacity of up to 100 tonnes (220,400 lb). The machine measuring 77 m (252 ft 7½ in) in length and 65 m (213 ft 3 in) in wing span will have a speed of 250-300 km/h (155-186 mph). The government allotted US$ 91.7 million for the development of this *ekranoplan* for the nearest five years. The work on this project had been started as early as 1995.

Models of South Korean-designed *ekranoplans* were submitted for testing to the Krylov TsNII in St. Petersburg.

Taiwan (Republic of China)

A Taiwanese company built a prototype of a WIG vehicle designated HT-1. It is a medium-sized machine featuring the Lippisch layout. Propulsion is ensured by a single ducted propeller mounted above the fuselage close to the tail unit (a T-tail).

The **Chung-Shan Institute of Science and Technology** (based in Taiwan) conducting research in the field of civil and military aviation, shipbuilding and other branches associated with defence has devoted some attention to WIG technology, too. Detailed information on this score is not available. It is presumed that several relatively small craft intended to carry two to five persons were designed, built and tested.

The Ukraine

As related in the previous chapters, during the Soviet period some research and practical design work related to the WIG vehicles took place in the Ukraine (then a part of the Soviet Union). Moreover, at one time there were plans for starting a series manufacture of large *ekranoplans*, such as the Orlyonok and Loon', at the Feodosiya-based **'More' (Sea) Shipyard** in the Crimea. These plans were not put into practice, but the plant retained a potential for dealing with that sort of production. In the independent Ukraine this plant made an attempt to diversify its product range by starting the manufacture of a light WIG craft on the basis of a Russian design. Kolganov's Ivolga types (the EL-7 and the EK-12) have served as a basis for the development of the Shmel' (Bumblebee) WIG vehicle by the Feodosiya Shipbuilding Company 'More'. It appears to be a cross between the two designs, slightly differing in dimensions from the EK-12 and featuring the straight wings of the EK-7, rather then the swept wings of the EK-12. Its design seating capacity of 7-10 passengers lies between the figures for the EL-7 (seven passengers) and the EK-12 (12-14 passengers). The craft was advertised and offered to prospective customers, but there is no evidence of any results of these plans so far.

Some private companies are offering their own projects of light WIG craft and advertise them in the hope of finding sponsors and investors willing to invest into the construction of prototypes. As an example one may mention the company **NPO Europa** which has spawned two projects of passenger WIG craft, both of them having the same configuration and differing in size. The two machines, carrying four and 20 passengers respectively, have a typical Lippisch layout with the reversed delta wing, T-tail, wingtip floats and small winglets, only moderately upswept. The fuselages are configured as boat hulls. The powerplant comprises an engine buried in the aft fuselage and transmitting its torque via extension shafts to two ducted propellers above the fuselage.

Opposite page: A model of the Spasatel' SAR ekranoplan at the Army-2015 show, Kubinka, with the legend SPASATEL on the hull; note the double-deck layout with operating rooms on the lower deck.

The same model at the Army-2016 show.

CHAPTER EIGHT

NEW DEVELOPMENTS SINCE 2010

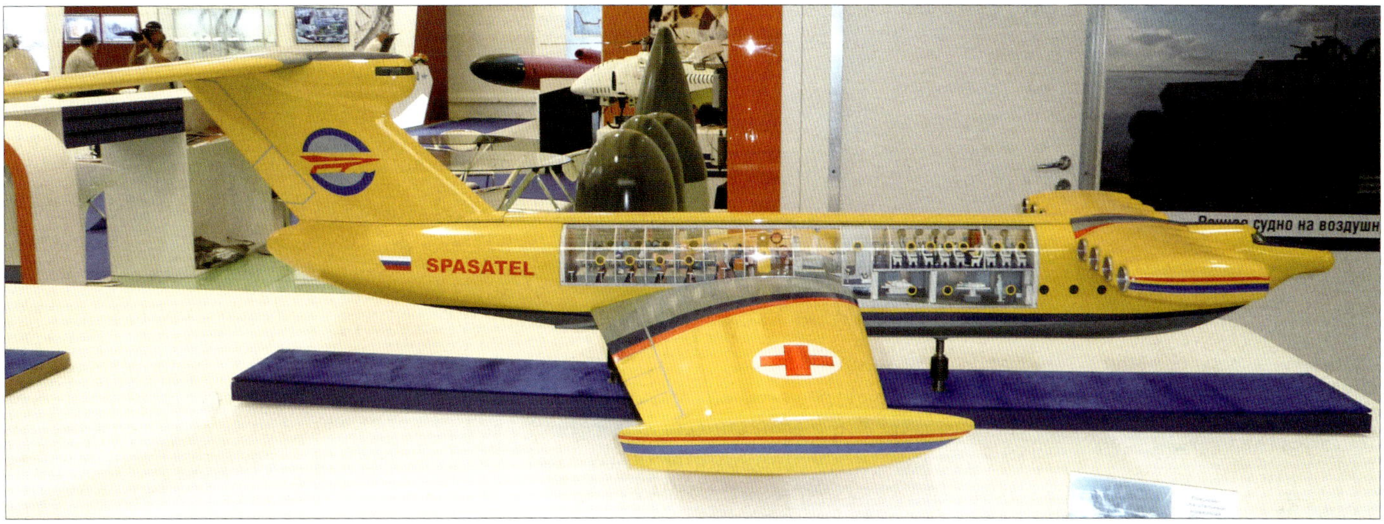

This chapter serves to update the material presented in the 2010 edition of this book and surveys new designs and construction in Russian ekranoplans since that date.

1 Comments Relating to the Text of the 2010 Book

Spasatel' SAR vehicle

(See Chapter 1, pages 77-86). This uncompleted civil offspring of the Loon' missile-carrying ekranoplan has been preserved to this day at the premises of the Krasnoye Sormovo shipyard in Nizhniy Novgorod. According to some reports, the vehicle remains in good condition; it was claimed that the vessel could be completed within a year, should the Powers That Be take an appropriate decision. Display models of the Spasatel' have been repeatedly presented at various aviation exhibitions in Russia during recent years. Interestingly, on at least one occasion – at the fifth biennial International Maritime Defence Show (IMDS-2011) in St. Petersburg – this model bore the legend Loon'-E instead of Spasatel', suggesting a would-be export version. However, many observers hold the view that resurrection of this particular machine is unlikely and it is doomed at best to become a museum exhibit. New-build WIG vehicles in the same class, now under development, are expected to fulfil the Spasatel's duties in the future.

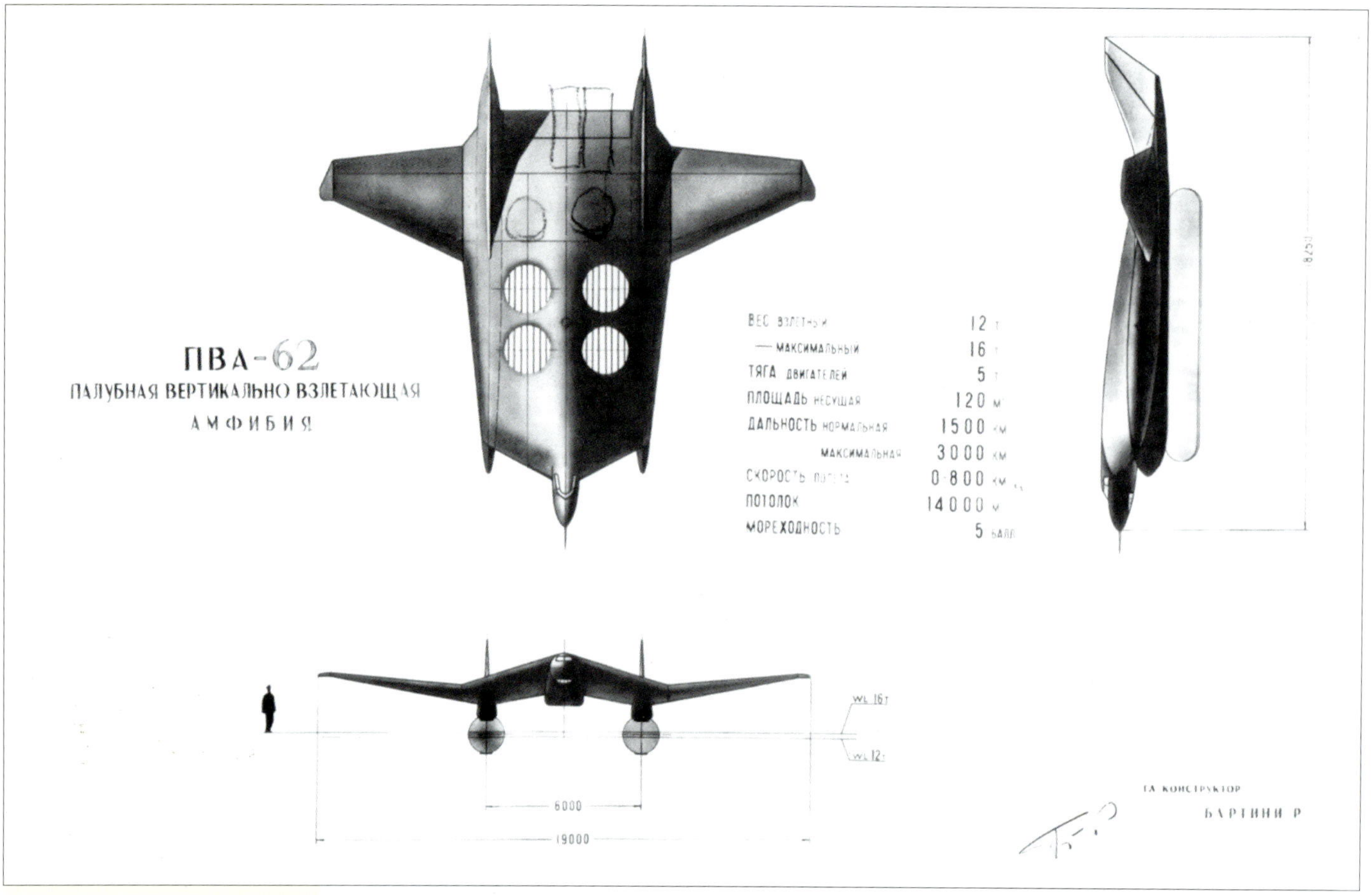

A three-view drawing of the PVA-62 from the project documents, showing the quadruple lift fans.

Bartini's projects

Supplementing and partially correcting the information in Chapter Two (pages 168-169) of this book, we can present here two projects of amphibious aircraft possessing some properties of WIG vehicles – the **PVA-62** and **OVA-62**. These projects share a common layout featuring a wide-chord dome-shaped wing centre section which, in effect, performs the role of a fuselage. It incorporates large lifting fans driven by jet efflux. The wing centre sec-

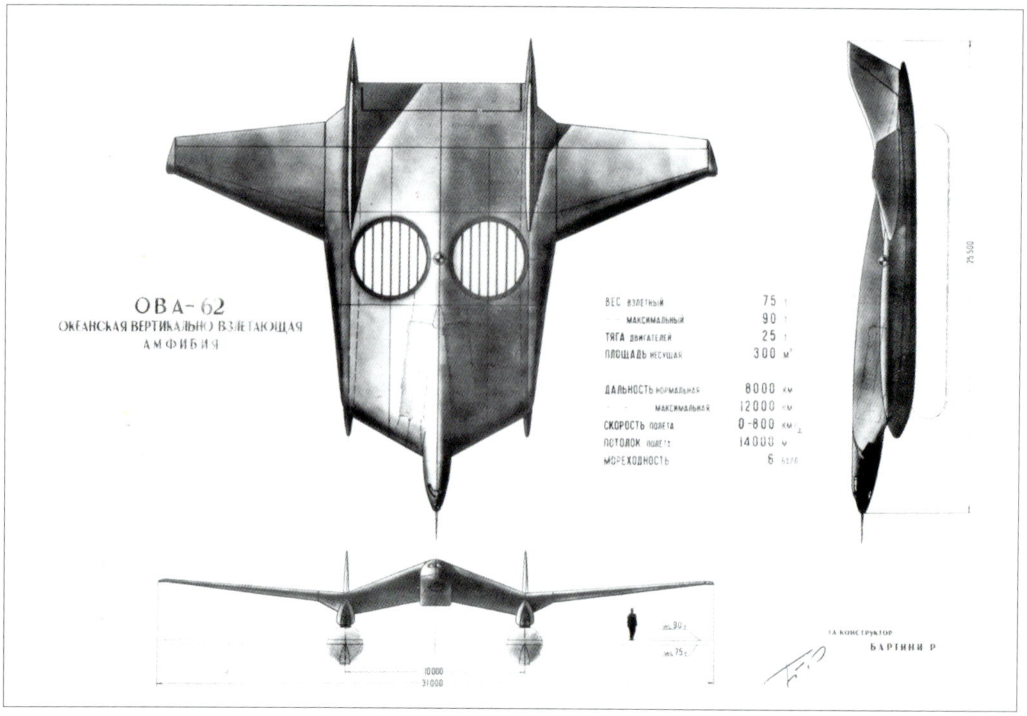

A three-view drawing of the OVA-62 from the project documents. Despite the larger size, it has only two lift fans.

tion is supplemented by strongly tapered narrow-chord outer wing panels located well aft, with marked dihedral and swept-back leading edges, and carries twin sharply swept vertical tails. The wing centre section is flanked on the lower side by two sponsons housing inflatable floats. The speed and service ceiling figures quoted below are typical for normal aircraft, yet the combination of the dome-shaped wing centre section and floats is clearly intended to form a chamber which serves to create a static air cushion during a vertical take-off and a dynamic air cushion during forward flight at low altitude. This should enable the machines to operate in WIG mode at least for brief periods.

PVA-62

The designation PVA-62 stands for ***pa****lubnaya verti****kahl'****no vzle****ta****yushchaya am****fi****biya* (shipboard vertical take-off amphibious craft developed in 1962). Basic characteristics include a TOW of 12 tonnes (26,460 lb): a maximum AUW of 16 tonnes (35,280 lb), a wing area of 120 sq m (1,291.8 sq ft), a normal range of 1,500 km (932 miles), a maximum range of 3,000 km (1,864 miles), a speed of up to 800 km/h (497 mph), a service ceiling of 14,000 m (45,930 ft), and seaworthiness enabling it to operate at up to sea state 5. Dimensions include a wing span of 19.0 m (62 ft 4 in) and a length of 18.25 m (59 ft 10½ in).

OVA-62

The OVA-62 (*oke****an****skaya verti****kahl'****no vzle****ta****yushchaya am****fi****biya* – ocean-going vertical take-off amphibious craft) is a much larger craft. Basic characteristics include a TOW of 75 tonnes (165,375 lb): a maximum AUW of 90 tonnes (198,450 lb), a wing area of 120 sq m (1,291.8 sq ft), a normal range of 8,000 km (4,972 miles), a maximum range of 12,000 km (7,458 miles), a speed of up to 800 km/h (497 mph), a ceiling of 14,000 m (45,930 ft), and seaworthiness enabling it to operate at up to sea state 6. Dimensions include a wing span of 31.0 m (101 ft 8½ in) and a length of 25.5 m (83 ft 8 in).

Activities of the Zelenodol'sk PKB (ZPKB)

The information published in Chapter Six of the book (see pp. 317-318) can be supplemented by three photos of the *Tsik****lon*** (Cyclone) experimental vessel with aerodynamic off-loading. Successful completion of the testing of this vessel was followed by a joint decision adopted by the Navy, the Ministry of Shipbuilding and the Military-Industrial Commission requiring ZPKB to start design work on the experimental **Briz** (Breeze) combat ship. Its basic layout was developed jointly by TsAGI and ZPKB and presumably reflected the experience gained with the Tsiklon.

It can be further added that during that period design work on vessels with aerodynamic off-loading was also conducted by **TsMKB** ***Almaz*** **('Diamond' Central Maritime Design Bureau)** which developed a project of the **K-1** ekranoplan; another project in the same category developed with the assistance from TsAGI was the *Bu****ran*** (Snowstorm). No details are available on these projects.

WIG designs of the Krylov Central Shipbuilding Research Institute

In addition to the pictures of the MS-02 and MS-04 craft (see Chapter Five, p. 243) we publish here a photo of the MS-03 which was designed on the same principles as a speedboat with aerodynamic off-loading.

NVA projects by N. N. Nazarov

Among the projects bearing the NVA designation the NVA-10 design stands apart, having nothing in common with the basic concept of N. N. Nazarov's other designs (see Chapter Six of this book, pages 300-305). This machine was built at the Ulan-Ude Aircraft Factory in early 2000 under the direction of N. N. Nazarov who held the post of this factory's Chief Designer at that time. This prototype was manufactured using airframe parts from the Yakovlev Yak-40 light passenger jet and two Let L-410 turboprop passenger aircraft. The front and middle sections of fuselages of the L-410 were supplemented by the rear fuselage and tail unit of a Yak-40 complete with the latter's centre Ivchenko AI-25T turbofan engine and associated dorsal air intake and S-duct forming the NVA-10's cruise powerplant. The fuselage thus obtained was fitted with low-set rectangular wings of short span and wide chord carrying at their tips a sort of large and bulky endplates which presumably can fulfil the role of floats should the vehicle alight on a water surface. However, the main role of these endplates – in combination with deep strakes beneath the wing roots and the deflectable flap on the trailing edge – is to create a space in which a static air cushion is formed during take-off. In addition to the cruise engine, the machine was equipped with a special powerplant for driving two large fans enclosed in the wings which sent compressed air into the space beneath the wings and thus ensured a vertical lift-off. After this the vehicle would begin a forward movement and accelerate to cruising speed which created a dynamic air cushion and permitted a flight in ground effect mode.

The vehicle in question was ordered by the aforementioned Upper Lena River Shipping Company; it was intended for cargo and passenger transportation and would be capable of carrying some five tonnes (11,000 lb) of cargo over a distance of 2,400 km (1,492 miles). In February 2000 a local newspaper reported that manufacturer's tests of this vehicle would begin on 1st March of that year. Plans were in hand to build a further three prototypes. In the case of successful completion of testing the machine would be put into production with a view to operation on local routes in the region. According to a newspaper article dated 5th April 2000, the beginning of the tests was delayed and was tentatively scheduled to start in the second part of April on the condition of obtaining the necessary funding. Possibly, it was precisely the lack of funds that prevented the programme from successful completion.

An interesting variation on the theme represented by the NVA-10 is the **NVA-6-10GP** (***groo**zopassa**zheer**skiy* – cargo/passenger, used attributively) WIG vehicle. Its distinctive feature is the location of the cruise turboprop engine on the leading edge of the vertical tail. No further details are available.

Chkalovsk-based company, member of Alien Group

KEP-7T WIG vehicle

This small ekranoplan was advertised in a leaflet stemming from a design bureau based in Chkalovsk, Nizhniy Novgorod Region (the title was withheld) together with the PE-40 project described in Chapter Six of this book (see p. 290). Both projects were developed by a design team working under the auspices of the Alien Group (the title ALIEN can be seen on the images of the two vehicles). Presumably it was developed before 2010. The KEP-7T appears to be a vehicle of approximately the same size as the five-seat Aquaglide-5 (see Chapter Six, p. 266) which it resembles rather closely in the basic layout. The main difference is the use of a twin-boom tail configuration instead of the fuselage-mounted splayed twin fins. The elongated forward fuselage houses a 724-hp piston engine transmitting its torque via bevel gears and angled shafts to two tractor propellers mounted on outrigger pylons on both sides of the hull. In addi-

The (apparently somewhat incomplete) NVA-10 in storage at the Ulan-Ude aircraft plant in October 2015. Note the lift fans built into the wings and the detachable rear beaching gear complementing the existing L-410 nose gear unit.

An artist's impression of the KEP-7T with the logo of the parent company, Alien Group, on the fins.

tion to ensuring forward propulsion, they obviously can be tilted during take-off to direct part of the air stream under the low-set rectangular wings provided with endplate floats. The vehicle's dimensions include a span of 8.53 m (28 ft), a length of 12.9 m (42 ft 4 in), and a height of 2.7 m (8 ft 10 in). At an AUW of 3.0 tonnes (6,615 lb) the machine can carry seven passengers and a single pilot. Performance includes a cruising speed of 190 km/h (118 mph) and a range of 550 km (342 miles). Cruising flight in ground effect can be performed with the wave height of 0.5 to 1.5 m (1.8 to 3 ft)

Quite probably it is no coincidence that the KEP-7T is reminiscent in its layout of some designs which later came to be advertised by the Orion Company (see later in this chapter)

WIG vehicles in the RT and MT series

Some projects of WIG vehicles bearing the **RT** designation and intended for river transport were described or mentioned in Chapter Five (**RT1-360** and others, see p. 248). This series emanating from the **Krylov TsNII's Nizhniy Novgorod branch** can be supplemented by several similar designs of which some details are given below. Furthermore, additional information became available on a series of projects in the **MT**-series based on the same concept (MT obviously stands for *mor**skoy trahns**port* – marine transport). They are also described below.

The RT vehicles are officially classed as 'boat-ekranoplans' (***ka**ter-ekrano**plan***). The designers' eagerness to make their machines look like boats reflected a well thought-out concept. Its central idea was to enhance the seaworthiness and stability of the craft and adapt them as much as possible to the practical requirements of ship-like operation (loading and unloading procedures etc.) at river and sea routes. The designers went as far as to provide these craft with typical 'boat-style' devices such as railings on the wings and on the 'foredeck' and fenders on the bows and at the sides of the floats.

The WIG vessels are shaped as a combination of two elements: a hull with typically boat-like nose contours and with a full-length deck from bow to stern, and a superstructure placed atop the deck and intended to house the payload and the powerplant. The boat hull is complemented by wing panels attached to it on both sides and by the twin-fin tail unit mounted on the aft end of the deck. The wing tips are fitted with endplates doubling as floats. The wing incidence is 6-8°. There are no ailerons; nor are there any high-lift devices on the wing trailing edge. A peculiar feature of the wing design is the provision of fillets at the junctions of the wing leading edge with the fuselage and the float (the designers term them as 'fixed slats'). They seem partly to overlap the wing leading edge. Their aerodynamic role, if any, is not mentioned in the official description.

The absence of ailerons is compensated by the installation of fins above the aft end of the floats; these fins incorporate moving surfaces described as rudders-ailerons, serving the double role of ensuring lateral (roll) control and directional control.

A common feature of all the designs is the tail unit which consists of two splayed vertical tails topped by the horizontal tail featuring slight dihedral on its outboard panels. The central portion of the horizontal tail (between the fins) incorporates the elevator.

Characteristic of these designs is the use of hydroskis to assist the take-off and the provision of retractable beaching gear units fore and aft in the hull.

A typical feature of the chosen layout is the location of the powerplant immediately aft of the superstructure or inside its rear part, with appropriate drive shaft(s) to propellers (one pusher propeller or two tractor propellers on outriggers). The main powerplant is supplemented by an auxiliary engine

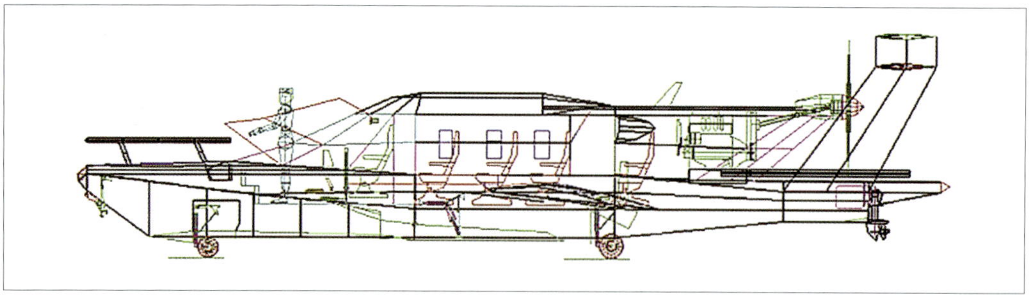

A side view drawing of the MT-1 BMW-394 passenger ekranoplan, showing the front entry hatch.

– a hydrojet engine or a piston engine with a tilting propeller shaft – for slow-speed taxying.

Described below are some of the ekranoplan projects in the RT and MT series.

MT1-BMW394

Intended to be used as a sort of 'mini-bus', this WIG vehicle was to be powered by a single BMW 3-series car engine of 394 hp; it could carry four to 12 passengers or up to 1,0 tonne (2,205 lb) of cargo at a cruising speed of 190 km/h (118 mph). The range of 1,500 km (932 miles) with full payload could be increased to 5,200 km (3,232 miles) with four passengers on board.

RT2-M14

The RT2-M14 project was a basic model for passenger and cargo WIG vehicles powered by two Vedeneyev M-14 nine-cylinder radial engines of 360 hp apiece. The engines, mounted on horizontal pylons attached to the aft part of the hull, drove four-bladed tractor propellers. At an empty weight of 3.1 tonnes (6,835 lb) and an AUW of 5.2 tonnes (11,466 lb) it was to carry two pilots and 12 to 16 passengers or a cargo of 1,500 kg (3,310 lb) at a cruising speed of 190 km/h (118 mph).

RT1-ASh62

This was a multi-purpose WIG-vehicle intended for pleasure tours, passenger and cargo transport, business travel and SAR missions. A single Shvetsov ASh-62IR nine-cylinder radial engine of 1,000 hp (used, notably, in the Antonov An-2 biplane) was installed behind the passenger compartment. It drove via angled extension shafts two six-blade propellers placed directly ahead of the twin vertical tails. The roomy cabin provided accommodation for 16 to 20 passengers at an AUW of 6.5 tonnes (14,330 lb), the empty weight being 3.8 tonnes (8,380 lb).

A very schematic computer-generated image of the RT2-M14 passenger ekranoplan, showing the bulky nacelles of the M-14 radials.

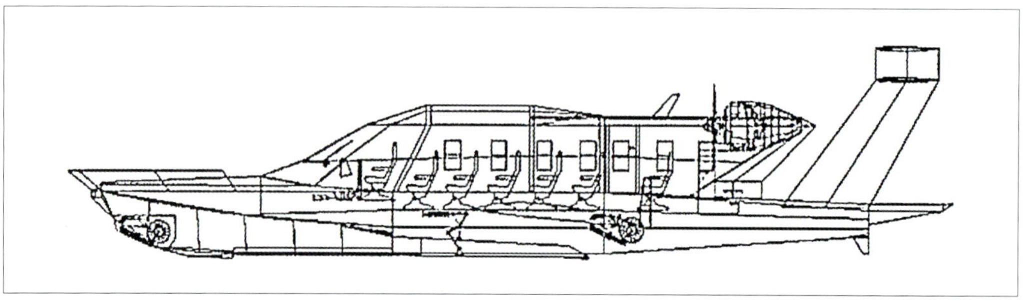

A side view drawing of the RT2-M14, showing the retracted beaching gear.

A computer-generated image of the RT1-ASh62. Note how the single radial drives two tractor propellers via reduction gear.

RT1-TV7

This 'boat-ekranoplan' powered by a single Klimov TV7-117 turboprop of 2,500 ehp is intended to carry 40 to 56 passengers. The aft-mounted turboprop engine drives two six-blade tractor propellers via angled extension shafts. An interesting feature of the vehicle's 'architecture' is the position of the crew cockpit above the passenger cabin.

RT2-TV7

This ekranoplan intended for passenger and cargo transport looks like a scaled-up version of the preceding type. It is powered by two TV7-117 turboprops mounted on horizontal pylons at the aft end of the passenger compartment. They are supplemented by a single Tumanskiy RU19-300 turbojet with a static trust of 900 kgp (1,786 lbst)

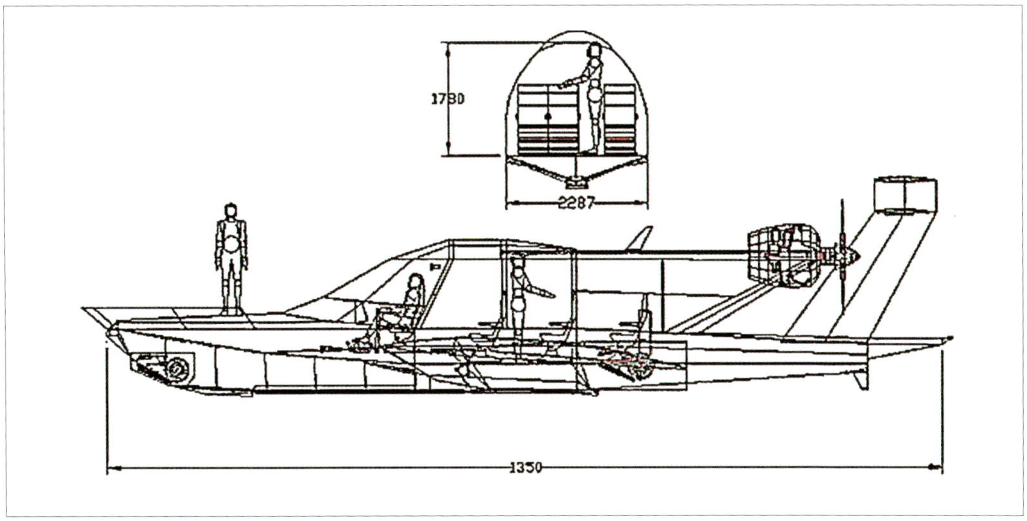

A side view drawing of the RT1-ASh62. Here, the engine appears to drive a single pusher propeller.

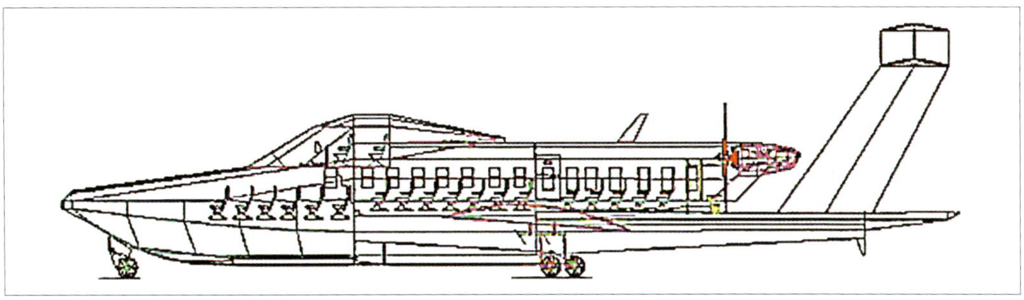

A side view drawing of the RT2-TV7 showing the raised flight deck with tandem seats and the lateral entry doors amidships.

Design performance of some WIG vehicles in the RT series				
	RT2-M14	RT1-ASh62	RT1-TV7	RT2-TV7
Length overall	n.a.	17.5 m (57 ft 5 in)	15.4 m (50 ft 6⅝ in)	30.0 m (98 ft 5 in)
Width overall	n.a.	13.5 m (44 ft 3½ in)	n.a.	23.0 m (75 ft 5½ in)
All-up weight, tonnes (lb)	5,2 (11,470)	6.5 (14,330)	9.2 (20,290)	31.0 (68,355)
Powerplant	2 x M-14P	1 x ASh-62	1 x TV7-117	2 x TV7-117 + 1 x RU19-300
Engine power or thrust	2 x 360 hp	1,000 hp	2,500 shp	2 x 2,500 shp 1 x 900 kgp (1,786 lbst)
Passengers	12-16	16-20	40-56	80-120
Payload (cargo variant), tonnes (lb)	1.5 (3,310)	2.0 (4,410)	5.0 (11,025)	9.3 (20,510)
Crew	2 pilots	n.a.	2	n.a.
Cruising speed, km/h (mph)	190 (118)	n.a.	206 (128)	242 (150)
Range in GE mode, km (miles)	n.a.	n.a.	n.a.	1,300 (808)
Maximum wave height at take-off	1.25 m (4 ft 1 in)	n.a.	1.75 m (5 ft 9 in)	n.a.

which also functions as an APU for cruise engine starting. In this case, too, the flight deck is placed above the passenger cabin capable of accommodating 80 to 120 passengers or 9.3 tonnes (20,506 lb) of cargo. The empty weight and the AUW are 17.1 tonnes (37,705 lb) and 31.0 tonnes (68,355 lb) respectively. The vehicle has a cruising speed of 242 km/h (150 mph) and can carry its payload over a distance of 1,300 km (808 miles). The beaching gear comprises two twin-wheel main units, each wheel being carried by its own strut.

EP-4

This is a four-seat light ekranoplan accommodating a pilot and three passengers for business travel in summer and winter time on rivers and lakes. The ZMZ-4062 four-cylinder inline water-cooled engine of 150 hp, loaned from a Russian GAZ car, drives a pusher propeller via an extension shaft.

A computer-generated image of the EP-4 four-seat ekranoplan. Note the handrails on the wings.

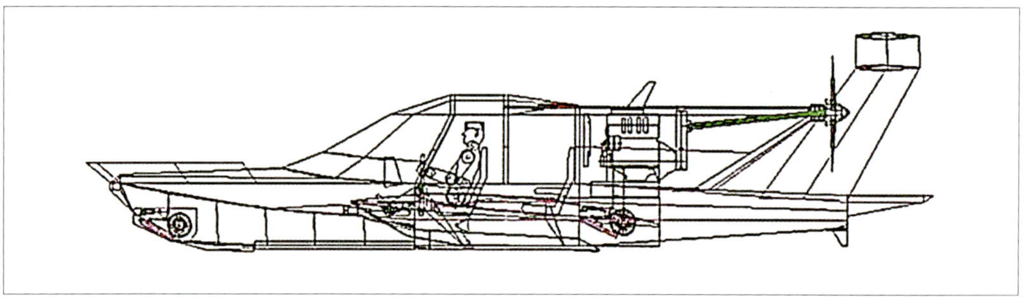

A side view drawing of the EP-4.

MT-series projects of sea-going and ocean-going ekranoplans

The RT (*rech**noy** trahnsport* – river transport) series of projects described above was supplemented by several projects pertaining to sea- and ocean-going WIG vehicles and appropriately designated with the acronym MT (*mor**skoy trahns**port* – marine transport). All of them retained the very distinctive general aero- and hydrodynamic layout of the RT series which was basically scaled up and adapted to the specific powerplant configuration. A notable feature about some of these projects was the use of industrial gas turbine units and marine gas turbines as powerplants for ekranoplans (sometimes in combination with aircraft-type turbojets). A brief description of some of these projects follows.

MT1-M90f

This ocean-going WIG craft with an AUW of 150 tonnes (330,750 lb) is powered by a single M-90fr industrial gas turbine rated at 27,500 shp. The gas turbine is mounted on a pylon-shaped rear end of the passenger compartment. The torque of the engine is transmitted to two six-bladed propellers via angled extension shafts. This powerplant arrangement was also used on other MT series designs described on this page.

MT-GTD110

A single NPO Saturn GTD-110 industrial gas turbine (also known as M-110) rated at 150,000 shp serves as a powerplant for this ocean-going WIG craft with an AUW of 720 tonnes (1,587,600 lb). The gas turbine, located aft of the passenger/cargo compartment, transmits its torque to two six-bladed propellers via angled extension shafts.

MT-GTD110U

This ocean-going WIG craft with an AUW of 1,050 tonnes (2,315,250 lb) is powered by a single GTD-110 industrial gas turbine supplemented by two Kuznetsov NK-32 turbofans delivering a thrust of 25 tonnes (55,125 lb) apiece (their location is not clear from the drawing). The NK-32 engines are intended to be used as take-off boosters.

MT-GTD110D

This ocean-going WIG craft with an AUW of 1,000 tonnes (2,205,000lb) is powered by a single GTD-110 industrial gas turbine and two NK-32 turbofans. Except for the marginally lower weight, it is identical to the preceding design.

MT1-BMW

This vehicle is intended for executive travel and can carry 12 to 18 passengers at a cruising speed of 168 km/h (104 mph). It is powered by a single 507-hp BMW S85B50 ten-cylinder Vee liquid-cooled engine from a BMW M6 sports coupe.

MT1-AI-450

This vehicle is basically identical to the previous design described above but is re-engined with a 450-hp Ukrainian ZMKB Progress AI-450 turboprop instead of the BMW M6 piston engine.

Ocean-going ekranoplan with six turbofans

This gigantic marine WIG vehicle intended for the transportation of cargo containers and a certain number of passengers is remarkable in a way. Outwardly it resembles much smaller vehicles in the RT-series, to the point of its fuselage superstructure resembling a cockpit of a small vehicle. However, this superstructure houses a passenger cabin

Design performance of small WIG craft in the MT-series

	MT1-BMW394	MT1-BMW	MT1-AI450	EP-4
Length overall	12.5 m (41 ft 0⅛ in)	16.9 m (55 ft 5²³⁄₆₄ in)	n.a.	8.8 m (28 ft 10²⁹⁄₆₄ in)
Width overall	8.6 m (28 ft 2³⁷⁄₆₄ in)	9.6 m (31 ft 6 in)	n.a.	7.4 m (24 ft 3²¹⁄₆₄ in)
Height overall	3.3 m (10 ft 9⁵⁹⁄₆₄ in)	3.6 m (11 ft 9⁴⁷⁄₆₄ in)	n.a.	n.a.
Powerplant	1 x BMW3	1 x BMW6	1 x AI-450	1 x ZMZ-4062
Engine power, hp	394	507	450	150
All-up weight, tonnes (lb)	3.2 (7,056)	3.8-4.4 (8,379-9,702)	n.a.	n.a.
Passengers	4-12	12-18	n.a.	3
Payload (cargo variant), tonnes (lb)	1.0 (2,205)	1.32 (2,911)	n.a.	n.a.
Crew	1	1	1	1
Cruising speed, km/h (mph)	190 (118)	168 (104)	n.a.	160 (99)
Max wave height at take-off	1.0 m (3 ft)	1.0 m (3 ft)	n.a.	0.5 m (1 ft 8 in)
Range in GE mode, km (miles)	5,200 (3,232)*	1,674 (1,040)** 5,240 (3,257)***	n.a.	n.a.

* with 4 passengers; ** with 1,250 kg (2,756 lb) of cargo; *** with 6 passengers

Design performance of ocean-going transport ekranoplans with gas turbine installations

	MT1-90f	MT-GTD110	MT-GTD110U	MT-GTD110D
All-up weight, tonnes (lb)	150.0 (330,750)	720.0 (1,587,600)	1,050.0 (2,315,250)	1,000.0 (2,205,000)
Engine type	M-90frgas turbine	M-110gas turbine	M-110 gas turbine +2 x NK-32 turbofans	GTD-110 gas turbine +2xNK-32 turbofans
Engine power, hpor engine thrust, tonnes (lbst)	1 x 27,500	1 x 150,000 (2 x 55,125)	1 x 150,000 +2 x 25 tonnes (2x55,125)	1x150,000 +2x25 tonnes
Propeller diameter, m (ft)	1x10.0 (1x32 ft 9 ¾ in)	2x15.0 (2x49 ft 2⅝ in)	2x13.0 (2x42 ft 7 7/16 in)	n.a.
Powerplant for slow speed, hp	Diesel engine 300 hp	Diesel engine 1,000 hp	Diesel engine 1,000 hp	Diesel engine 1,000 hp
Cargo, tonnes (lb) (passenger seats)	45 (99,225) (400)	210 (463,050)	300 (661,500)	200-400 (441,000-882,000)
Seaworthiness at take-off:				
wave height, m (ft)	3.2 (10.5)	5.2 (17)	6.0 (19.7)	7.2 (23.6)
wave force	5	5	6	6-7
Seaworthiness in cruise, sea state	up to 5	up to 5	6	n.a.
Cruising speed, knots (km/h, mph)	175320 (199)	184341 (212)	183356 (221)	365-375 (227-233)*
Range with payload				
= 0.3 of AUW, km (miles)	2,600 (1,403)	2,600 (1,403)	2,600 (1,403)	3,480 (2,163)**
= 0.1 of AUW, km (miles)	9,500 (5,130)	9,800 (52900)	9,700 (5,237)	15,200 (9,447)***

* Speed in ground effect mode and out of ground effect; ** Range with maximum payload; *** Range with minimum payload

accommodating 14 rows of seats 12-abreast with two aisles, in addition to the flight deck. But the bulk of the hull is occupied by the huge double-deck cargo compartment intended for the carriage of containers. The powerplant, as shown in the drawing, comprises six high-bypass turbofans of an unspecified type – possibly the Lotarev D-18T with a take-off rating of 23,400 kgp (51,590 lbst) – mounted on a horizontal bar between two supporting pylons above the rear part of the hull. They are supplemented by a pack of several turbojets placed directly atop the rear hull. An interesting feature of the design is its retractable multi-wheel undercarriage. Its main units comprise five wheels arranged in tandem on each side, supplemented by a twin-wheel nose unit.

Some of these conceptual projects apparently formed the basis for several practical designs publicised and promoted during the recent years by a new actor in the WIG technology field – RDC Aqualines (described elsewhere in this chapter).

2 The Period from 2010 Onwards: General Trends

In Russia the decade that has passed since the publication of the previous edition of the book has been marked by a certain revival of activities in the field of WIG design and construction after a period of stagnation that had set in since the early 1990s. Renewed interest in ekranoplans was already evident around 2009-2010. The Federal target programme 'Development of marine technology for civil purposes in the period 2009-2016' envisaged a whole range of studies, experiments and R&D work aimed at creating several aero- and hydrodynamic layouts of prospective ekranoplans in the 5 to 50 tonnes (11,025 to 110,250 lb) AUW class for domestic uses and for export. Such studies were, in fact, initiated and conducted, in particular, by the Industrial-Financial Investment Group (JSC) in cooperation with the Krylov Central Marine Research Institute in St. Petersburg.

In July 2010 Yevgeniy Meleshko, a high-ranking official of the Alekseyev Central Hydrofoil Design Bureau (head of the company's quality control section), announced that the work on design and construction of ekranoplans would be resumed in Russia in the near future. The Government, he said, had already requested the conduct of appropriate R&D and design activities. He predicted the start of practical design work for 2012.

In September 2010 the then Minister of Defence Anatoliy E. Serdyukov informed the press about the existence of plans for the development of high-capacity ekranoplans for military and civil purposes.

In 2010 an Interdepartmental working group headed by Vice-Minister of Industry and Trade of the Russian Federation was set up with the task of drafting a Concept for the development of ekranoplans in Russia. This concept, among other things, was called upon to promote the creation of appropriate legislation for the development, manufacture and practical operation of ekranoplans within the framework of the nation's transport system. Yet another of the problems to be dealt with was the development of engines optimised for use in ekranoplans. In 2011 this draft Concept was submitted to the relevant authorities and was expected to be approved by the end of that year, but the outcome is unclear.

In the meantime, the lack of such legislation hampers greatly the formation of a market for civil ekranoplans. Potential operators are reluctant to order vehicles with an uncertain legal status. A lack of orders and of state funding resulted in severe financial difficulties for the enterprises which had previously staked heavily on the development of new ekranoplan designs. Some of them were driven to bankruptcy and went out of business. This was the case, for example, with the Arctic Transport Company. Some other main actors in the field – such as the Alekseyev Central Hydrofoil Design Bureau – temporarily scaled down to a minimum their activities in the development of the WIG technology, reducing it to basic research and initial design studies.

Yet, the idea of turning WIG craft into a potent and competitive new means of transport on a par with air transport and traditional sea/river transport was kept alive and was further pursued by enthusiasts. Some of the enterprises engaged in this business underwent reorganisation and structural changes coupled with rebranding, so that new names cropped up on the scene (examples will be given below). They continued the development of some designs which had been successfully tested by 2009. This was notably the case with the Orion Company which rebranded the EK-12 as the Orion-12 and went on developing new designs in the Orion line.

Several smaller companies engaged in ekranoplan design formed a kind of coalition in the shape of the Ekranoplan Association.

New actors came on the scene – the highly successful enterprise Radar MMS in St. Petersburg joined forces with the Alekseyev Central Hydrofoil Design Bureau and became an active sponsor for the development of new and ambitious projects of passenger and transport ekranoplans (they will be described separately below).

In the middle of the present decade some changes occurred that may well promise a brighter future for the WIG technology in all its applications – civil and military alike. The Russian Government began to pay increasingly keen attention to the problems of the Arctic region, placing much emphasis on the need to safeguard Russia's security interests in this area. This involved the establishment of new military bases and outposts with the associated logistic needs (transportation of personnel, supplies etc). Furthermore, faced with the growing interest of other states to the Arctic region and the probability of a conflict of interests, the Russian government and defence authorities took a fresh look at the possibility of using ekranoplans within the structure of the armed forces for defence purposes, such as patrolling maritime areas and dealing with intruders and trespassers.

This was coupled with a growing awareness and concern about the logistic needs of the population and national economy in Siberia, the Far East and Northern regions of the country. The system of communications in this area has seriously deteriorated during the recent decades, and urgent measures are required to normalise the situation with local transport. Introduction of such a new means as ekranoplans is regarded by authorities at various levels as one of the possible approaches to solving the problem. The regions where the wide use of ekranoplans is feasible and desirable include Yakutia, Krasnoyarsk Region (the big rivers – Amur, Yenisey, Lena, Ob'), the Yamal Peninsula and Sakhalin with their oil resources, Primorsky Krai (Maritime Territory, i.e. Vladivostok region), Karelia, as well as the areas of the Black Sea, the Baltic Sea and the Caspian Sea.

An important recent development was the decision taken jointly by the Ministry of Industry and Trade and by the Ministry of Transport of the Russian Federation to set up an *Interdepartmental working group on the co-ordination of the development of ekranoplan construction in the Russian Federation*. An order to that effect was issued by the two ministries on 1st March 2018. The main tasks of the group are:

- to co-ordinate the activities of federal executive authorities, public associations, scientific institutions and other organisations in matters pertaining to the development of ekranoplans as a means of transport in the Russian Federation;
- to stimulate the formulation of proposals aimed at creating a legal basis for the development, construction and operation of high-speed amphibious (ekranoplan) means of transport in the Russian Federation;
- to stimulate the formulation of proposals concerning the development of a prototype of a high-speed amphibious craft (ekranoplan) in the interests of the constituent republics and regions of the Russian Federation;
- to stimulate the formulation of proposals for promoting the interests of the Russian Federation associated with the development of high-speed amphibious (ekranoplan) transport and WIG technology matters in international organisations – IMO and ICAO, as well as for promoting the export of production models of such transport vehicles.

Decisions adopted by the group will have the nature of recommendations.

3 The Period from 2010 Onwards: Specific Designs

New ekranoplan designs are listed in this section under the titles of the design bureaux and/or enterprises responsible for their development and manufacture. These organisations are arranged tentatively in the order of their relative importance, the last in succession being some enthusiastic individuals with their amateur designs.

Plans for the construction of ekranoplans as specified by state programmes

Official statements made during recent years testify to the revival of interest on the part of the Russian state authorities in ekranoplans in the context of defense and economic development programmes. At the MAKS-2015 Air Show in August 2015 Commander of Russia's Naval Aviation Maj.-Gen. Igor' S. Kozhin reportedly declared that the Russian Navy was expecting to obtain *'a versatile platform of ekranoplan type with a cargo carrying capacity of up to 300 tonnes [661,500 lb] in 2020'* (the date sounds unbelievable). Somewhat later the Alekseyev Central Hydrofoil Design Bureau's Chairman of the Board of Directors Gheorgiy V. Antsev told TASS news agency that the work on a prospective versatile ekranoplan for the Russian Ministry of Defence (presumably of far less ambitious capacity) had reached the advanced development project (ADP) stage.

On 30th July 2018 Deputy Prime Minister of the Russian Federation Yuriy I. Borisov made an important statement on that score (in the government, Yuriy Borisov has been responsible for matters pertaining to the defence industry since May 2018). He told journalists that Russia had not given up the idea of providing her armed forces with combat ekranoplans. According to Borisov, the state programme of armaments procurement for the period between 2018 and 2027, now in force, contains provisions for design and development work with a view to constructing a prototype of an ekranoplan. This research and development work bears the designation '*Orlan*' (Sea Eagle). Borisov did not mention specific features of the design but pointed out that the new machine would be armed primarily with missiles. He said also that the main area of operational deployment for the new vehicle would be Russia's Arctic regions, more exactly the Northern Sea Route. Apart from providing protection for the traffic, the ekranoplan could also be used for patrolling and SAR missions. At a later stage one might also envisage the use of ekranoplans in the Black Sea and the Caspian Sea.

As a sequel to this statement, ekranoplans became a subject of discussion at a round table panel arranged by the United Shipbuilding Corporation of Russia at the Army-2018 exhibition in the summer of 2018). Counsellor of the Corporation's President, former Commander-in-Chief of the Russian Navy Adm. Viktor V. Chirkov said that this shipbuilding holding company would participate actively in the development of military ekranoplans.

In September 2018 it was officially stated that appropriate institutions had started developing powerplants for prospective ekranoplans. A statement to that effect was made by Anatoliy Serdyukov, industrial director of the State Corporation Rostec

The abovementioned statement made by Yuriy Borisov provoked comments in the Russia media, including some sceptical remarks. Some of the self-appointed 'experts' call into question the validity of the idea of using an ekranoplan as a kind of strike aircraft for the protection of ship convoys and express the opinion that the WIG vehicles will be of real value primarily in the SAR role. The most radically minded opponents of ekranoplan technology flatly deny the wisdom of the whole idea, asserting that WIG vehicles offer no advantages over the existing means of transport and are inherently unsafe.

However, adherents of the new technology point out that the development of WIG vehicles is actively pursued in many countries, notably in the USA, Germany, China, Australia, Japan, South Korea, Great Britain, France, Singapore and Iran. They insist that Russia cannot afford to lose its pioneering positions in this branch of technology.

Moreover, the most outspoken protagonists of the WIG technology are convinced that Russia must make a stake on the development of super-heavy missile-carrying ekranoplans as a means of counteracting the presumed threat of a disarming nuclear strike in the not too distant future. At the same time they visualise the creation of a new potent commercial transport system based on super-heavy ekranoplans which would link South-East Asia and Europe via the Northern Sea Route.

Projects from the Alekseyev Central Hydrofoil Design Bureau under the auspices of Radar MMS

The Central Hydrofoil Design Bureau (CHDB) renowned for Rostislav Ye. Alekseyev's pioneering ekranoplan designs has preserved the legacy associated with this grand man and has kept up a certain amount of research and development effort in this sphere, albeit the company's present activities are devoted mainly to shipbuilding and manufacture of air cushion vehicles. In August 2011 an official of the

CHDB told the press that this design bureau had been approached by the Russian government with a request to resume the development of ekranoplans. According to some reports, the government tasked this design bureau with specific projects; the Orlan mentioned above may well be among them.

An important development, as mentioned above, was the establishment of cooperation between the Alekseyev Central Hydrofoil Design Bureau and the Radar MMS Company. Activities of this successful and well-established enterprise encompass the design and production of radars and associated electronic equipment, as well as the development of vertical take-off unmanned aerial vehicles (VTUAVs). Acting as a subsidiary of this enterprise, the CHDB has revealed several projects of ekranoplans of different sizes for civil and military uses; they were presented and actively advertised at various aerospace and defence industry shows over the recent years.

Described below are some of these projects.

A-005-333

This project of a multi-purpose ekranoplan for use on lakes and rivers is known at present only on the basis of a captioned picture from the product presentation section of CHDB's official web site, without any further information. It resembles closely a project described below under the designation A-020-538, leading to a suspicion that this is, in fact, the same project with two different designations.

Two artist's impressions of the A-005-333 ekranoplan for use on lakes and rivers.

A-005-514

This appears to be a derivative of an ekranoplan known as Volga-2 which dates back to 1986 (see Chapter One of this book, pages 100-101, 106-112). Advertised at present as the A-005-514, this new version incorporates some changes and improvements. The most obvious of these is the revised wing layout. In keeping with the general trend in the company's designs, the basic wide-chord short-span wings of the original Volga-2 have been supplemented by narrow-chord outer wing panels joined to the basic wing by transitional sections. This new version apparently remains a paper project to this day, since no prototypes or production machines have been reported.

Design characteristics of the vehicle capable of carrying eight passengers and a single pilot include a take-off weight of 3.1 tonnes (6,835 lb) and a payload of 0.9 tonnes (19,845 lb). The vehicle's range in ground effect is 500 km (311 miles). Dimensions are as follows: overall length 11.6 m (38 ft 0 in); overall width 11.6 m (38 ft 0 in); height 3.65 m (12 ft 0 in).

This page: Two computer-generated images of the A-005-514 still bearing the original project name Volga-2M. These views illustrate the craft's elegant lines and the new outer wing panels.

Opposite page, top left: A model of the A-020-538 displayed at the Hydro Aviation Show-2012 in Ghelendzhik.

Opposite page, top right: The same model in a slightly different colour scheme was shown at the IMDS-2018 in St. Petersburg.

A-020 (A-020-538)

This new-generation WIG vehicle was displayed in model form, together with several other designs, at the joint stand of the CHDB and Radar MMS at the Hydroaviation Show 2012 in Ghelendzhik. The same model was shown at the International Naval Show in St. Petersburg in 2017. The A-020-538 is a passenger version of the basic A-020 design which is apparently based on the layout dating back to the famous Orlyonok. The features inherited from the Orlyonok include the provision of two nose-mounted booster turbojets in combination with a cruise turboprop engine placed at the top of the fin, driving a six-blade tractor propeller. However, the A-020 differs from the Orlyonok in the wing configuration; the low-aspect-ratio main wing panels are augmented by outer wing panels of high aspect ratio and narrow chord, carrying winglets at the wingtips. Also, the flight deck is relocated forward so that the booster engines are placed aft of it rather than on the sides, with the air intakes located higher, flush with the top of the hull; this offers both better protection against spray ingestion and lower flight deck noise levels.

The vehicle has an AUW of 54.1 tonnes (119,200 lb) and can carry 50 passengers at a cruising speed of 265-290 km/h (165-180 mph) in ground effect mode over a distance of 600 km (373 miles).

Below: Artist's impressions of the A-020-538 in the livery of would-be operator Aeromost ('Aerobridge'). Note the placement of the boost engine air intakes aft of the flight deck.

An image of the A-020-533 Strizh-2 ekranoplan. The vehicle appears to be identical to the A-005-333.

A-020-533

One of the new-generation projects – a multi-purpose Class B ekranoplan for use on rivers and lakes. This machine, advertised by the CHDB at the IMDS-2017 naval show in St. Petersburg in June-July 2017, is intended for day-time passenger transportation (11 passengers and a pilot) and urgent delivery of cargoes. An information leaflet shows a vehicle with a boat hull and a swept-back vertical tail topped by large-span unswept horizontal tail surfaces. The low-set wings of low aspect ratio and short span have a trapezoidal planform with a straight trailing edge and a moderately swept leading edge. Attached to the wing-tips are floats acting as endplates. Two engines are located atop the wing leading edge close to the hull, driving six-bladed tractor propellers through long extension shafts which make it possible to direct part of the prop wash under the wings so as to create a dynamic air cushion. The rigidity of the extension shafts is ensured by horizontal struts joining the propeller hubs and the hull sides. Judging by the shape of the engine cowlings, these are turboprops (the engine type and power rating are not mentioned in the leaflet). Specifications include a length of 17.6 m (57 ft 9 in), a wing span of 11.0 m (36 ft 1 in), a displacement of 6.0 tonnes (13,230 lb), a payload of 1.3 tonnes (28,665 lb), cruising speeds in the range between 180 and 260 km/h (112-162 mph) and a range of 500 km (310 miles) in WIG mode.

A two-view drawing showing the A-020-533's cabin layout.

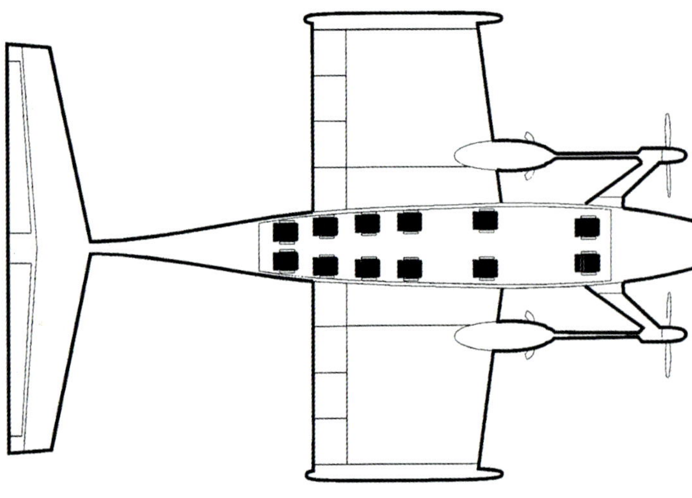

An artist's impression published in an advertising leaflet on the A-020-533 shows this machine with the inscription Strizh-2 on the side of the hull, thus revealing that we have here a case of rebranding (possibly accompanied by some further development work). In the main part of this book one can find descriptions and drawings of Strizh-3, -4, -5 and-6 (see Chapter One, pp. 114-123), but not of Strizh-2.

A-050-538

This is another new-generation project of a multi-purpose Class B sea-going ekranoplan for use on rivers and lakes. This much larger machine, which was likewise advertised by the CHDB at the IMDS-2017, is intended for day-time passenger transportation (carrying 80 passengers and a crew of four) and urgent delivery of cargoes in littoral areas. The vehicle is to be stationed afloat with a provision for entering a paved servicing pad ashore. Employment options include business travel, search and rescue missions, ecological monitoring of inland waters (large lakes) and littoral areas. In winter the machine can be operated over even snow-covered land areas or ice fields.

An information leaflet shows a vehicle with a boat hull featuring several shallow planing steps and a swept-back vertical tail topped by large-span unswept horizontal tail surfaces. The low-set wings have a 'compound' configuration. Joined to the hull are wing panels of low aspect ratio and short span. Their tips are fitted with floats acting as endplates which carry short-span sharply tapering 'transitional' sections canted upwards; attached to them

An artist's impression of the A-050-538, again in the red livery of Aeromost and wearing C80 titles. The vehicle is clearly a scaled-up version of the A-020-538, as the number of cabin windows and the size of the boost engine fairings show.

A different image of the A-050-538, this time in demonstrator (?) colours with EC-80 and 'Raketa' (Rocket) titles; the latter are mis-spelled as 'Raceta'. This view gives a better idea of the wing shape.

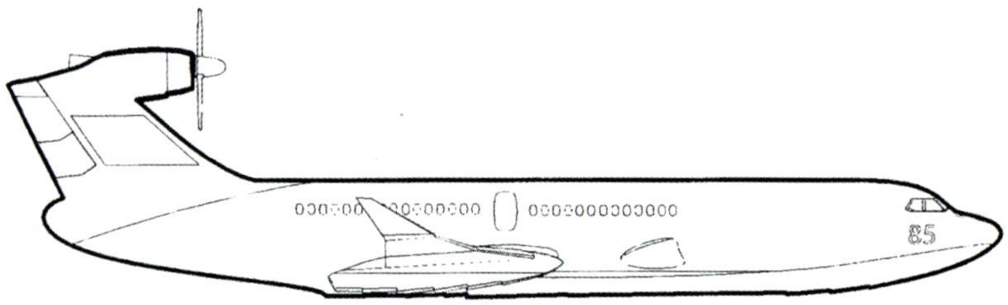

A two-view drawing of the A-050-538.

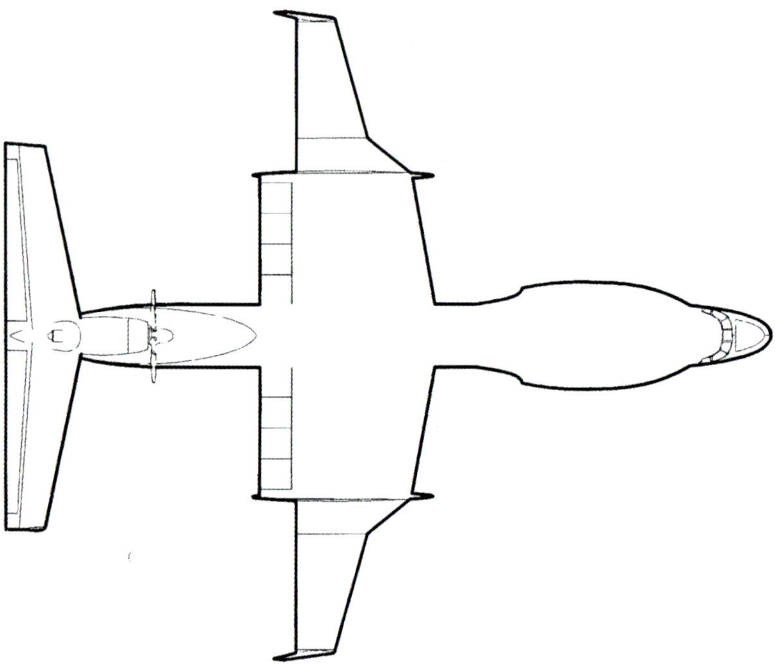

are outboard wing sections of high aspect ratio featuring winglets at the tips. A cruise turboprop engine of unknown type with a six-blade tractor propeller is mounted on the top of the fin ahead of its leading edge. Two booster turbojets are housed in the fuselage behind the flight deck; they bulge out of the hull sides, the jetpipes being angled downwards so that the jet efflux is directed into the space below the wings. The flush circular air intakes of these engines are located on the upper surface of the hull behind the flight deck.

Technical data include a wing span of 34.2 m (112 ft 2⅝ in), a length of 26.5 m (86 ft 11½ in), a brutto displacement of 38.0 tonnes (83,790 lb), a seating capacity of 80 passengers, a payload of 9.0 tons (19,845 lb), a cruising speed of 310 km/h (193 mph) in ground effect mode and 350 km/h (218 mph) in flight out of ground effect, a range of 500 km (311 miles) in out-of-ground effect mode, and a range of 1,200 km (746 miles) in ground effect. The vehicle is capable of cruising flight in ground effect with waves up to 3.5.m (11.5 ft) high.

Opposite page, top: An artist's impression of the Chaika-2 in demonstrator colour operating from a shore runway. Note the two pairs of wing-mounted floats, the inboard pair housing the outrigger struts of the bicycle landing gear.

A-050 Chaika-2

The first projects bearing the designation Chaika and Chaika-2 were developed in the CHDB at least two decades ago; they are described in Chapter One of this book (pages 95-97). The original Chaika featured low-set compound-chord wings and a powerplant combining turbojet booster engines and turboprop cruise engines on the front fuselage. The original Chaika-2 introduced a radical new feature – a biplane wing layout in which the low-set wings were complemented by high-set wings intended to endow the vehicle with the ability to fly in aeroplane mode. In addition to this new wing design, the original Chaika-2 made use of two turbojet cruise engines instead of turboprops. Both models had a T-tail.

Subsequent development resulted in several practically new projects retaining the same Chaika (Chaika-2) designation which is used separately in some cases and as an appendage to the new A-050 designation in other cases.

Here is **a description of the new-generation Chaika project** given by Ivan G. Antsev, Executive Director of Radar MMS, in an interview to the TASS News Agency in August 2017. He described the **'Chaika A-050'** (note the combination of the two designations) as a multi-purpose seagoing ekranoplan having a displacement of 54 tonnes (119,070 lb) and providing accommodation for some 100 passengers in airliner-style cabins, with a crew of two. Its payload is 15 tonnes (33,075 lb). In addition to transportation tasks, this multi-purpose craft can be used in a variety of roles, such as search and rescue, reconnaissance or surveillance, etc. He emphasised that this multipurpose platform could find employment in all spheres of activities and be used by various agencies, such as the Ministry of Interior, the Ministry of Emergency Situations, the Ministry of Defence and the Ministry of Transport. According to Antsev, detail design was already in progress, in parallel with the development work on the control systems, flight/navigation suite and radio-electronic systems. Experiments had already been carried out with models (presumably wind tunnel tests and water basin tests). He expected the emergence of a prototype in 2020-22.

In an earlier interview dated 10th July 2017, Ivan Antsev had predicted the completion of a prototype in 2019-20, but apparently he revised his time estimates to a more cautious scenario. Antsev expressed the opinion that the Chaika ekranoplan could be adapted for military roles; furthermore, it ought to possess a good export potential. He visualised the possibility of supplying these craft to India whose armed forces might well use them as platforms for the BrahMos anti-shipping cruise missiles.

Described below are some variations of the basic Chaika-2 concept.

Chaika-2 (turboprop/turbojet-powered version)

A project bearing this designation (without the A-050 appendage) was shown on a TV display at the MAKS-2017 airshow. As distinct from the original version of 2009-10, the cruise turbojets flanking the forward fuselage are replaced by turboprop engines on dihedral pylons aft of the flight deck driving six-blade propellers. Retention of the T-tail is a notable feature because other versions of this basic design have a twin-fin empennage. The vehicle's most remarkable feature is the biplane layout with backward stagger and a unique combination of swept and unswept wings in one structure. The straight upper wings are located aft of the slightly swept back lower wings and are joined tip to tip by vertical pylons with floats attached to them.

The project was presented in civil and military versions. The latter merit some attention. The vehicle was depicted in the livery of the Federal Protection Service (FSO RF – *Fede**rahl**'naya **sloozh**ba okh**ra**ny Ros**siy**skoi Fede**ra**tsii*) which provides security for the President and other top statesmen of the Russian Federation. On another picture the vehicle can be seen in a camouflage scheme with the titles of the Federal Security Service's Border Guard troops (PS FSB – *Pogra**nich**naya **sloozh**ba Fede**rahl'**noy **sloozh**by bezo**pas**nosti*). Bulges on the top of the fin and on the fuselage ahead of the fin are presumably intended for some kind of electronic equipment.

Interestingly, a picture of the civil version sporting the inscription Chaika-2 shows the vehicle on a runway with an aircraft-type undercarriage extended.

Below: An artist's impression of a camouflaged Chaika-2 in service with the Border Guard of the Russian Federal Security Service (FSB).

Bottom left and right: These computer-generated images show the Chaika-2 operated by the Federal Protection Service of Russia (FSO). Note how the craft lies on its belly when beached.

An artist's impression of the A-050 (marked as such). The craft is almost identical to the Chaika-2, the main difference being the twin-fin design of the tail unit.

A-050 (A-050-742)

One of the projects in the A-050 series is known as the A-050-742 or sometimes A-050-742d. Both versions of the designation can be seen on models displayed at different exhibitions, including several Hydroaviation Shows in Ghelendzhik in recent years, as well as at the MAKS-2017 airshow. As distinct from the Chaika-2 designs described above, they feature the tail unit with twin splayed vertical tails topped by the horizontal tail. The absence of fairings for electronic equipment is also noteworthy, indicating that passenger/cargo transport and associated roles as the primary ones. In particular, it can be used for medical evacuation, for SAR operations, for ecological monitoring of inland waterways, etc. The vehicle's powerplant comprises two Gavrilov R-195 take-off boost turbojets with a thrust of 4,500 kgp (9,920 lbst) apiece and two Klimov TV7-117SM turboprops, each delivering 2,500 ehp.

This model in virtually the same colours but wearing A-050-7420 titles was displayed at the MAKS-2017 airshow in Zhukovskiy.

A-080 (A-080-752) (Chaika-3)

One of the new-generation projects evolved in the Central Hydrofoil Design Bureau (CHDB) and pursued in cooperation with the Radar MMS company was initially presented under the designation A-080, which was changed later to A-080-752. One may also encounter yet another name for the project – Chaika-3, or Chaika III. The project was demonstrated publicly for the first time at the Hydroaviation Show in Ghelendzhik in 2012. A model sporting the A-080 designation was displayed at the joint stand (section) of the CHDB and Radar MMS. This design is notable for its very unorthodox wing layout differing from that of the A-050-752 (see below).

In 2015 the CHDB showed a virtually identical model with the designation A-080-752. The unique wing layout intended to endow the craft with the

A model of the slightly larger, all-jet A-080-752 cargo ekranoplan displayed at one of the IMDS shows in St. Petersburg.

This view of the models of the A-050 and the A-080 illustrates the difference in size and in wing design, the larger craft having short lower wings and curiously kinked interplane struts. Note also the A-080's open loading ramp.

An artist's impression of the A-080-752 wearing Chaika III titles and the flag of the Border Guard's naval element (a variation on the Russian Navy flag with a green, rather than white, background).

properties of an ekranoplan and a conventional aircraft enables it to attain an altitude of 3,000 m (9,840 ft) in the aeroplane mode and perform stable flight at this altitude. The design speed is 450 km/h (280 mph), the payload is estimated at 43 tonnes (96,750 lb). The craft will be capable of operating both from water and from airfields.

The A-080-752 project was presented once more at the IMDS-2017 show in St. Petersburg in the form of advertising leaflets describing it as a Class C sea-going transport ekranoplan (that is, capable of flights in aeroplane mode as well) intended for the transportation of urgent cargoes in littoral areas. In addition to operations over water, in winter the craft can be operated over even snow- or ice-covered areas.

The leaflet carried a photo of a model and a two-view drawing. They show a craft with a flying-boat type hull, with a V-section bottom and several shallow planing steps in the forward and aft parts. Mounted on the rear part of the hull is the tail unit consisting of two swept-back vertical tails canted outwards and topped by an unswept horizontal tail. The wings feature a complicated biplane layout with backward stagger. The moderately tapered unswept main wings located atop the hull have a large span and high aspect ratio. Located ahead of the main wings are low-set wide-chord wings of short span and low aspect ratio; their tips are joined to the main wings by specially configured angled surfaces. Two cruise turbojets of an unspecified type are mounted on short horizontal pylons at the sides of the front fuselage behind the flight deck which is blended into the hull contours and has an airliner-type stepped glazing. Two booster engines for use at take-off are buried in the extreme nose; they have lateral nozzles flanking the flight deck and flush dorsal air intakes ahead of it, in the manner of

A-080-752 Project Basic Data	
Length overall	47.6 m (156 ft 2 in)
Width overall	45.3 m (148 ft 7½ in)
Height overall	11.8 m (38 ft 8⅝ in)
Draught	1.25 m (4 ft)
Brutto displacement	100 tonnes (220,500 lb)
Crew	3
Cruising speed	410-450 km/h (255-280 mph)
Range in GE mode	5,000 km (3,108 miles)
Seaworthiness (wave height):	
on take-off/landing	2 m (6-7 ft)
in cruise flight	unlimited
when drifting afloat	up to 3 m (10 ft)

the Orlyonok. The model sported the inscription **Chaika III** on the sides of the hull, suggesting that this name is an alternative designation of the A-080-752 project.

In 2017 it was noted in the press that no investors had yet been found for the project. Its current status is not clear.

A-300-538

This WIG vehicle, advertised by the CHDB as a sea-going multi-purpose passenger/transport ekranoplan, resembles in its aerodynamic layout a scaled up A-050-538 (see above). Apart from the similarity of the hull contours and the wing layout, the bulges flanking the forward hull and housing the booster engines look distinctly alike. But here the similarity ends. The salient unique features of this design are as follows: the huge hull providing accommodation for as many as 550 passengers and a crew of eight has a double-deck structure with two rows of windows on each side. The number of booster engines is increased to four, but, as distinct from some other designs, they are semi-

As big as it gets? This artist's impression of the massive A-300-538 sea-going passenger/cargo ekranoplan shows the double-deck hull and the tandem pairs of booster engines.

buried in the forward hull and not carried on lateral sponsons. The engines are arranged in two lateral packages and stacked longitudinally in a near-tandem fashion, with the jet nozzles splayed out one after another. The flush air intakes for the booster engines are located dorsally in tandem pairs aft of the flight deck. The cruise powerplant consists of three high-bypass turbofan engines placed on the upper surface of the horizontal stabiliser, with one engine resting on the top of the fin and the other two flanking it. The C550 inscription on the hull side is presumably a purely decorative logo.

Basic specifications include a length of 72.1 m (236 ft 6 in), a span of 56.2 m (184 ft 4⅝ in), a height of 18.7 m (61 ft 4¼ in), a brutto displacement of 350 tonnes (771,750 lb), cruising speeds ranging from 500 km/h (311 mph) in ground effect mode to 610 km/h (379 mph) in flight out of ground effect. Cargo-carrying capacity (without passengers) is 64 tonnes (141,120 lb), range in ground effect mode is 3,000 km (1,865 miles). Seaworthiness (wave height) is 2.5 m (8 ft) for take-off/3.5 m (11.5 ft) for alighting and up to 6 m (20 ft) when drifting.

Transport Amphibious Platforms

Chapter One of this book contains a description of a whole range of projects in this category developed by the CHDB (see Chapter One pp. 117-128). At present they seem to have been largely abandoned as an object for active promotion. Only one design of this kind has been retained in the product presentation at the company's official web site, namely the TAP-30. However, in its present configuration it differs appreciably from the initial version (compare the picture in this section with the picture on page 124).

Performance figures for ekranoplans of the CHDB

Table 1	A-005-333	A-005-514	A-020-533	A-020-538
Length overall	13.5 m (44 ft 3½ in)	11.6 m (38 ft 0 in)	17.6 m (57 ft 9 in)	27.3 m (89 ft 6¾ in)
Width overall	8.5 m (27 ft 10⅝ in)	11.6 m (38 ft 0 in)	11.0 m (36 ft 1 in)	19.1 m (62 ft 8 in)
Height overall	3.8 m (12 ft 5⅝ in)	3.65 m (12 ft 0 in)	5.0 m (16 ft 5 in)	7.3 m (24 ft 0 in)
All-up weight, tonnes (lb)	2.7 (5,954)	3.1 (6,835)	6.0 (13,230)	54.1(119,290)
Passengers	6	8	12	50
Payload (cargo variant) tonne (lb)	0.7 (15,435)	0.9 (19,845)	1.3 (28,665)	4.5 (99,225)
Crew	2	1	1	3
Cruising speed, km/h (mph)	160-250 (99-155)	165 (103)	180-260 (112-162)	265-290 (165-180) in GE 290-340 (180-211) out of GE
Range in GE mode, km (miles)	350 (218)	500 (310)	500 (310)	600 (373)
Seaworthiness (wave height), m (ft)				
take-off/landing	0.5/0.6 (1.6/2)	0.5/0/5 (1.6/1.6)	0.6/0.8 (2/2.6)	1.2/1.4 (4/4.6)
in flight	1.25 (4)	1.25 (4)	1.25 (4)	3.0 (10)
in drifting	1.25 (4)	0.75 (2.5)	1.25 (4)	3.0 (10)

Table 2	A-050-538	A-050-742d Chaika-2	A-080-752 Chaika-3	A-300-538
Length overall	34.2 m (112 ft 2⅝ in)	34.8 m (114 ft 2 5/32 in)	47.6 m (156 ft 2 in)	72.1 m (236 ft 6 in)
Width overall	26.5 m (86 ft 11½ in)	25.35 m (83 ft 2 in)	45.3 m (148 ft 7½ in)	56.2 m (184 ft 4⅝ in)
Height overall	9.88 m (32 ft 5 in)	7.85 m (25 ft 9 in)	11.8 m (38 ft 8⅝ in)	18.7 m (61 ft 4 ¼ in)
All-up weight, tonnes (lb)	38.0 (83,790)	54.0 (119,070)	100.0 (220,500)	350 (771,750)
Passengers	80	100	na	550
Payload (cargo variant) tonne (lb)	9.0 (19,845)	9.0 (19,845)	20.0 (220500)	64 (141120)
Crew	4	4	3	8
Cruising speed, km/h (mph)	310 (193) in GE 350 (218) out of GE	360-400 (224-249) in GE 450 (255) out of GE	410-450 (255-280)	500 (311) in GE 610 (379) out of GE
Range in GE mode, km (miles)	1,200 (746)	3.000 (1,865) 1,900 (1,180) out of GE	5,000 (3,108)	3,000 (1,865)
Seaworthiness (wave height), m (ft)				
take-off/landing	1.4/1.6 (4.6/5.3)	n.a.	2.0 (6.5)	2.5/3.5 (8/11.5)
in flight	3.5 (11.5)		unlimited	6.0 (20)
in drifting	3.5 (11.5)		up to 3.0 (10)	to 6.0 (20)

WIG vehicles designed under the direction of V. Kolganov (the EK series)

Several designs developed by a team led by Vyacheslav Kolganov and bearing designations in the range between EK-7 and EK-130 have been described or mentioned in Chapter Six of this book (see pp. 282-289). Kolganov is General Director and chief designer of the TREK Science and Production Company, which is currently based in the town of Zhukovskiy (Moscow Region). Some ten years ago the TREK company entered into some kind of transactions with other actors in the ekranoplan construction business, the exact nature of which is not sufficiently transparent. It appears that, faced with some financial difficulties, the company found it expedient (or was forced) to transfer at least a part of its competence (technical documents) and know-how to another enterprise – the Orion Ekranoplan Construction Society, or simply the Orion Company, which took over production of the successful EK-12 model and its derivatives, as well as the development of further prospective designs (activities of the Orion Company are described separately below). The TREK Company, it appears, was forced by circumstances to reduce the scope of its activities which became essentially export-oriented. It has found a market niche for its products in China and some countries of South-East Asia. Kolganov and some members of his design team moved to China and assisted the Chinese authorities and organisations dealing with the WIG technology in starting **licence production of the EK-7 and then the EK-12 ekranoplans in China**. The latter deserves a more detailed treatment here.

EK-12

This ekranoplan was put into production in 2006 (see Chapter Six, pp. 285-286) and underwent a comprehensive evaluation programme. It proved suitable for year-round operation over water, ice and snow-covered areas and marshes, as well as large stretches of even dry land, the EK-12 possessed good manoeuvrability, being capable of banking turns with bank angles up to 30°. The machine obtained a certificate of the Russian marine shipping register. Quite naturally, this WIG vehicle became an object of cooperation with the Chinese.

In April 2013 the Chinese media reported that a new Chinese 12-seat WIG vehicle bearing the designation **CYG-11** had entered flight test. However, photos of the vehicle left no room for doubts: it was a reincarnation of the EK-12 ekranoplan. According to reports which appeared in April 2013, the CYG-11 had been developed by a Chinese private company known as Hainan England WIG Manufacturing Company in cooperation with foreign partners (some sources gave the name of the Chinese company as INGE, pronounced *ingeh*. In April 2015

Above: Vyacheslav Kolganov in his study, with a model of one of his ekranoplan designs on his desk.

Right: An artist's impression of the EK-17 Ivolga-2, showing the gull wings and the nose air intake.

it was reported that testing of the CYG-11 had been completed. Numerous pictures were published of two machines of this type in flight over the South China Sea. In China, Liu Guoguang, one of the leaders of the INGE company, noted in his comments that ekranoplans would be especially useful for the Chinese armed forces and law enforcement agencies. He stated that his company had finished design work on the project of the CYG-40 WIG vehicle capable of transporting 40 persons, and was engaged in projecting further models – the CEG-100, CYG-150 and CYG-200 (apparently the numbers indicate the seating capacity). It remains to be seen to what extent this work was conducted in cooperation with Kolganov's TREK Company.

In September 2013 Vyacheslav Kolganov told a journalist that his company was the author and owner of design documents on the light multi-purpose ekranoplans in the Ivolga series, namely the EL-7, the EK-12 and the EK-27 which, he said, the company was manufacturing to specific contracts. Of these machines, the EK-12 was the most well known. In August 2013 the company demonstrated at the MAKS-2013 airshow in Zhukovskiy the EK-12 number 04 which was intended for delivery to one of the countries of South-East Asia. The machine was one of a batch of ten examples which had been ordered by the customer.

Kolganov further told the journalist that the TREK Company was engaged in the development of a series of further designs which was financed by foreign investors. The designs in question were the EK-17 Ivolga-2, the EK-30, the EK-100 and the EK-150; they are described below.

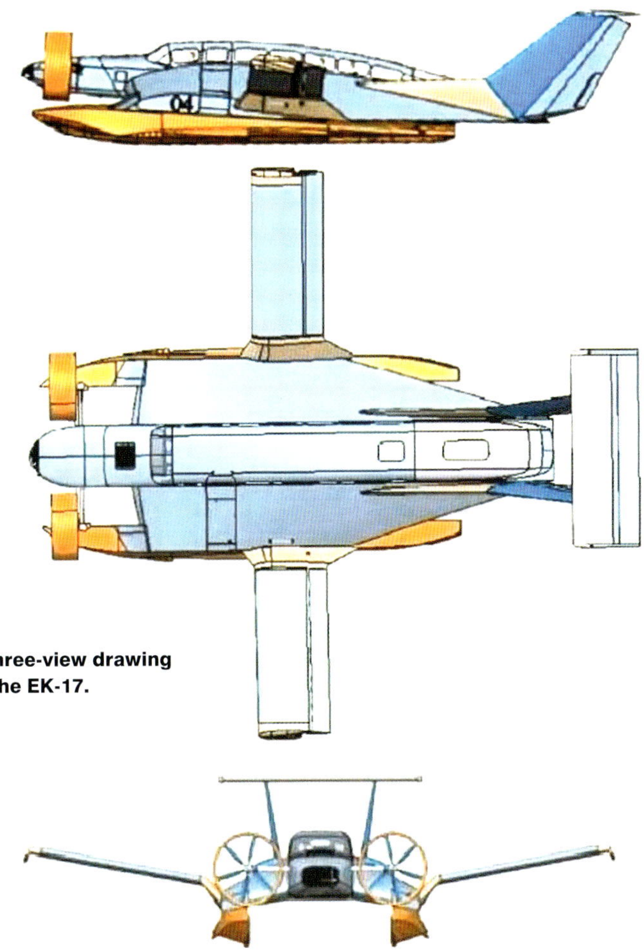

A three-view drawing of the EK-17.

EK-17 Ivolga-2

This ekranoplan having an AUW of 4,750 kg (10,470 lb) and a maximum payload of 1,600 kg (3,530 lb) represents an upgraded version of the EK-12 with a roomier fuselage accommodating 15 passengers and one or two pilots. A marked difference was the use of twin splayed vertical tails topped by the horizontal tail, as distinct from the T-tail of the EK-12. The larger passenger cabin was provided with an opaque roof replacing the all-round 'greenhouse' glazing characteristic for the preceding model. A notable feature is the 'beaver-tail' configuration of the rear fuselage with a large hatch hinging upwards, facilitating the loading and unloading of bulky cargoes. The EK-17 has retained the former type's powerplant consisting of two Chevrolet LS-3 automobile engines. Like its predecessor, the EK-17 has upward-folding outer wing panels reducing the space required for storage. Its range is estimated at 1,380 km (858 miles).

In 2013 a prototype was under construction; it was stated that production would be organised outside Russia, but the country in question was not specified. After the passage of several years no detailed information came to light on the results of this effort. In 2016 Vyacheslav Kolganov stated at a press conference in China that *'currently our company [...] has begun mastering production of the all-composite 17-seat EK-17'.*

A cutaway drawing of the EK-17 showing the lateral entry door and rear entry/loading hatch.

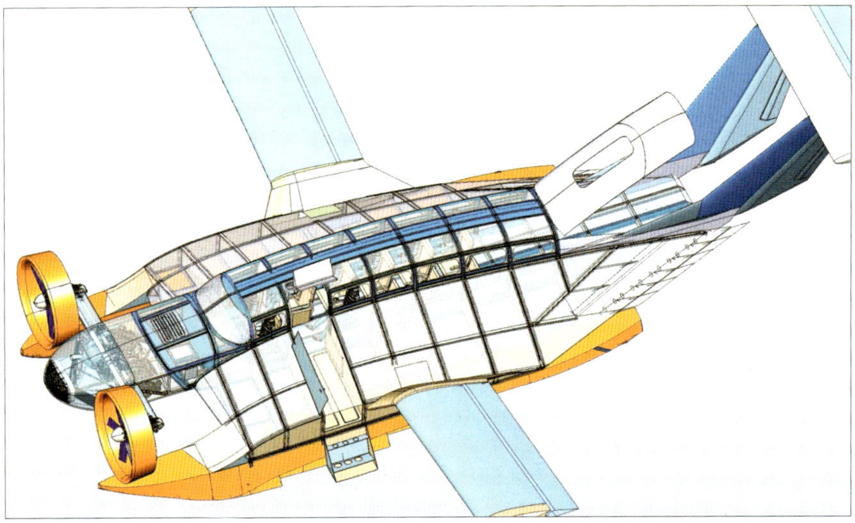

Right: A passenger version of the projected EK-30 ekranoplan showing the airstair door in the underside of the nose and the narrow rear door.

Below, top to bottom:
This image illustrates how the forward airstair door allows embarkation/disembarkation even on a beach with no landing stage. Note the full-width rear loading door (which appears to incorporate a narrow hatch).

The EK-30 parked with the tail facing the shore, the rear loading ramp allowing vehicles to be driven on/off the craft.

This artist's impression of the Ivolga-3 in flight shows the triple planing steps on the floats.

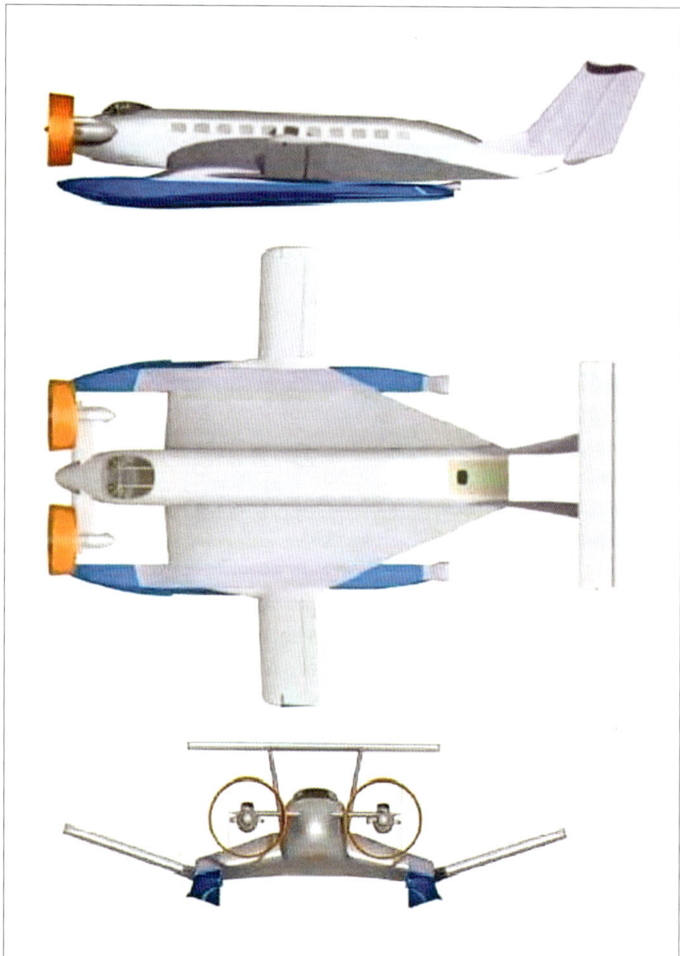

A three-view of the EK-30.

EK-30 Ivolga-3

Development of this project was also financed by an undisclosed country in South-East Asia and was undertaken to cater for the needs of that country. Likewise, it was reported that the construction of a prototype had started. A peculiar feature of the design is the flight deck with a transparent canopy standing proud of the forward fuselage contours. Another notable feature is the provision of airstairs on the underside of the forward fuselage, in addition to the upward-opening entry door in the rear fuselage between the twin tails. This door is replaced by an upward-opening loading hatch in the cargo version.

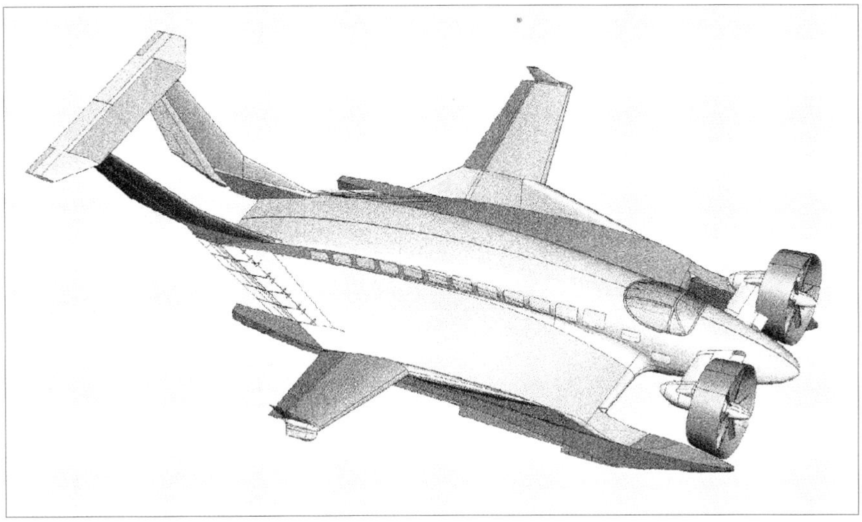

An artist's impression of a high-capacity ekranoplan developed by Kolganov.

The machine's parameters in one of the project versions included an AUW of 9 tonnes (19,845 lb) and a payload of 3.2 tonnes (7,056 lb). It was to carry up to 30 passengers and have a crew of three. The powerplant originally comprised two 785-ehp Motorlet M-601 turboprops of Czech manufacture on the forward fuselage sides driving shrouded tractor propellers. The vehicle was to have a range of 1,950 km (1,212 miles); the cruising and maximum speeds were 200 km/h (124 mph) and 260 km/h (162 mph) respectively. Performance figures were later revised in a project version with a powerplant comprising two Pratt & Whitney Canada PT6A-58 turboprops delivering 1,400 ehp apiece. The AUW rose to 9,800 kg (21,610 lb), the number of passengers to 37, other performance figures also showed an increase (see the table on page 364).

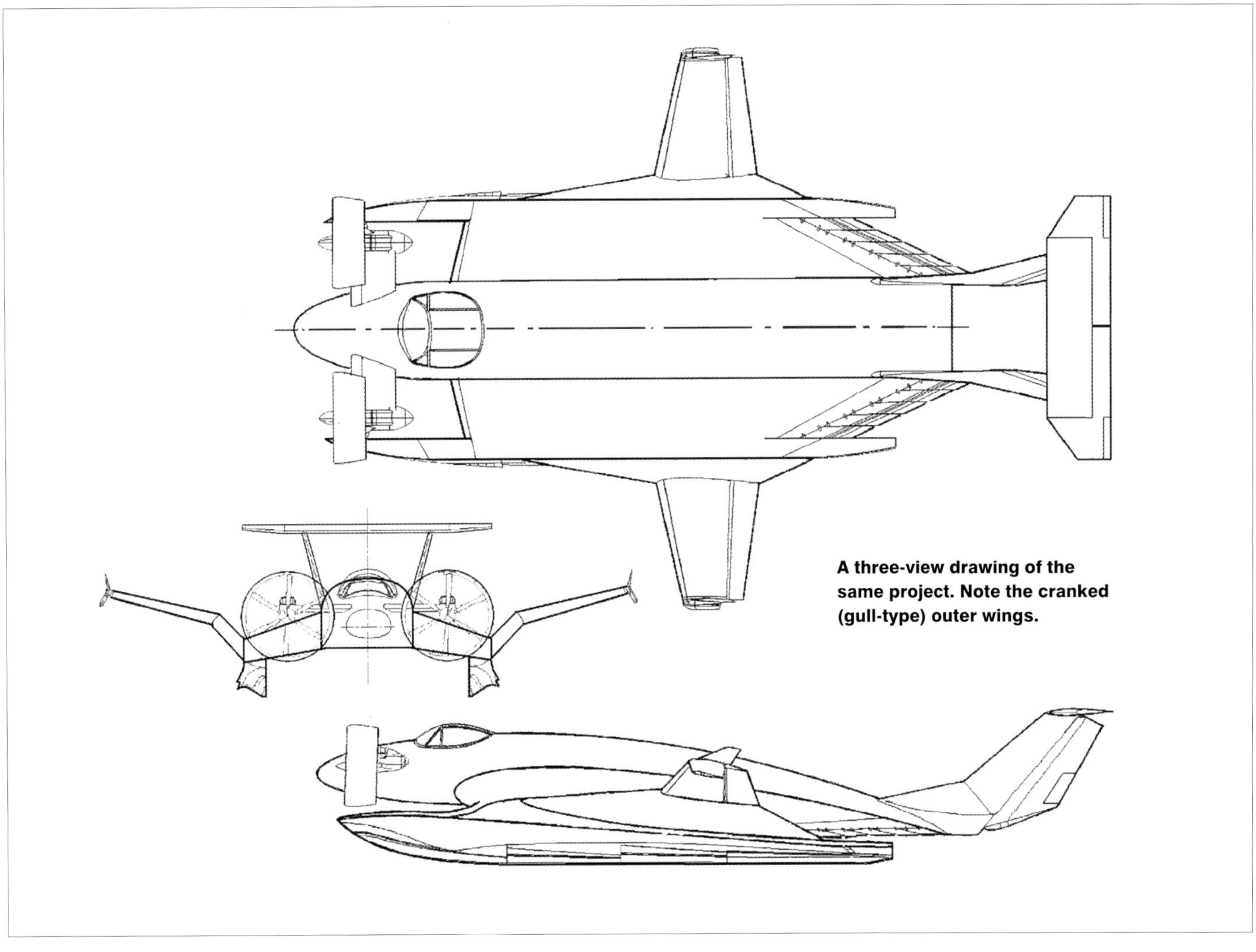

A three-view drawing of the same project. Note the cranked (gull-type) outer wings.

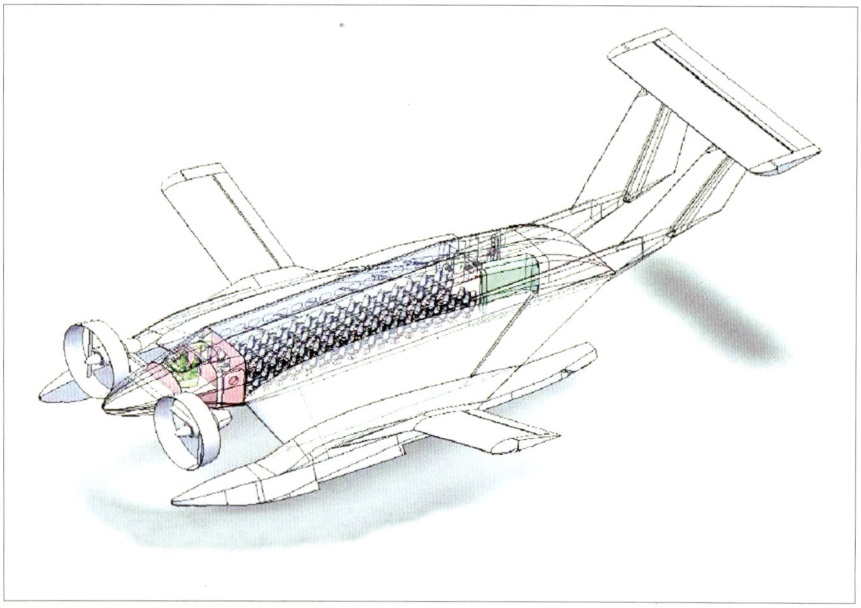

EK-100

In 2013 it was announced that design work on this river- and seagoing ekranoplan had started in response to an order from a customer whose identity was not disclosed. The vehicle shares the basic aerodynamic layout of the EK-17 and EK-30 but the fuselage of much greater size is similar to that of an airliner – both externally and as regards the passenger cabin layout. Following the pattern of the EK-30, the flight deck has a transparent canopy standing proud of the front fuselage contours. The vehicle was to have an AUW of 32 tonnes (70,560 lb) with a payload of up to 11 tonnes (24,255 lb). It was intended to carry 106 passengers and a crew of three. The powerplant comprised two Klimov TV7-117S turboprops rated at 3,000 ehp apiece. The cruising and maximum speeds were 320 km/h (199 mph) and 410 km/h (255 mph) respectively. The range was estimated at 3,200 km (1,989 miles).

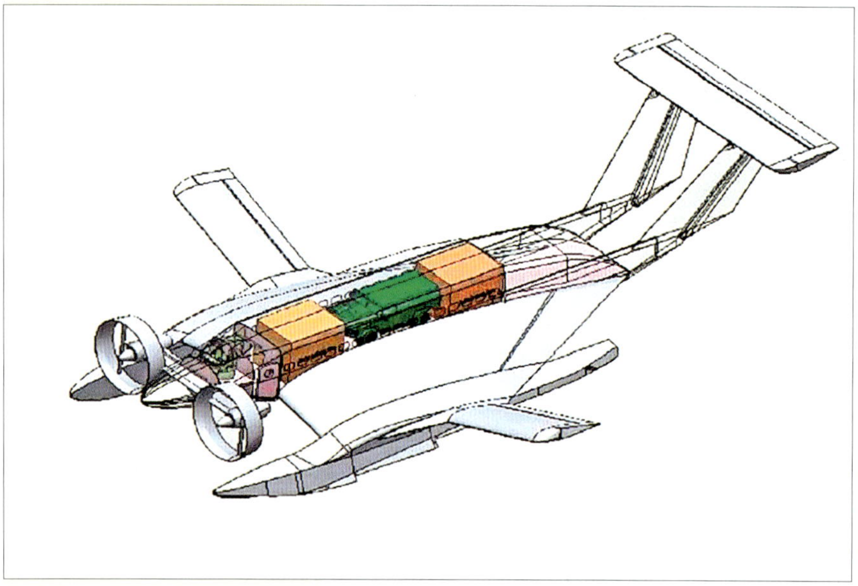

EK-150

The EK-150 is advertised as an 'ocean-going vehicle for Arctic operations'. In 2013 the work on this project was at the stage of preliminary research and initial design studies, also in response to an order from a foreign customer. The aerodynamic layout of this machine differs substantially from that of the preceding types, resembling a greatly scaled up EK-20 (see page 287). While retaining the twin-float (catamaran) configuration, the EK-150 lacks outboard wing panels and represents, in effect, a flying wing of very low aspect ratio and high thickness/chord ratio. The tail unit comprises two fins and rudders mounted on the aft ends of the floats and strongly canted outwards. The horizontal tails are attached to the tops of the fins on the outboard sides (this places the horizontal tail outside the influence of the downwash over the rear part of the wing). The thick wing provides ample

Design performance characteristics of ekranoplans of the EK family

	EK-12M	EK-17	EK-30	EK-100	EK-150
Length	15.6 m (51 ft 2¼ in)	16.7 m (54 ft 9½ in)	24.0 m (78 ft 9 in)	36.0 m (118 ft 1⅜ in)	105.5 m (346 ft 1¾ in)
Width	13.0 m (42 ft 7⅞ in)	15.0 m (49 ft 2⅝ in)	18.0 m (59 ft 0 in)	27.0 m (88 ft 7 in)	87.0 m (285 ft 5⅝ in)
Height	3.7 m (12 ft 2 in)	3.7 m (12 ft 2 in)	6.3 m (20 ft 8 in)	8.0 m (26 ft 3 in)	20.0 m (65 ft 7½ in)
Maximum take-off weight, kg (lb)	4,100 (9,040)	4,750 (10,474)	9,800 (21,609)	32,000 (70,560)	355,000 (782,775)
Crew	1-2	1-2	3	3	3-5
Passengers	12	15	37	106	1,290
Payload, kg (lb)	1,200 (2,646)	1,600 (3,528)	3,800 (8,379)	11,000 (24,255)	150,000 (330,750)
Max speed km/h (mph)	220 (137)	220 (137)	270 (168)	410 (255)	700 (435)
Cruising speed km/h (mph)	175 (109)	180 (112)	205 (127)	320 (199)	600 (373)
Range, km (miles)	1,500 (932)	1,380 (858)	2,050 (1,274)	3,200 (1,989)	6,100 (3,790)
Engine type	Chevrolet LS-3 piston engine	Chevrolet LS-3 piston engine	P&WC PT6-68 turboprops	Klimov TV7-117S turboprops	Solov'yov PS-90 turbofans
Engine power, hp/ehp or thrust, kgp (lbst)	2 x 430	2 x 450	2 x 1,400	2 x 3,000	6 x 16,000(6 x 35,280)

space for the accommodation of passengers or cargo; it is supplemented by a fuselage attached to the leading edge of the wing and blended into its contours. Two horizontal pylons (or stub wings) are mounted on the forward fuselage sides, carrying six turbojet engines (three on each side) which apparently function both as cruise engines and as take-off boosters (it can be surmised that their efflux can be deflected into the space beneath the wing during take-off to enhance the dynamic air cushion).

At an AUW of 355 tonnes (782,775 lb) this huge vehicle is to have a payload of up to 150 tonnes (330,750 lb) which enables it to carry up to 1,290 (!) passengers with a crew of three to five. Judging by an available cutaway drawing, the passengers are accommodated in large double-deck cabins occupying the fuselage proper and the central part of the wing along the axis, as well as a portion of the wing's volume on both sides between the axis and the floats. The remaining volume of the lateral parts of the wing is occupied by cargoes (presumably, hatches must be provided on the upper side of the wing for their loading and unloading).

The powerplant of the EK-150 comprises six Solov'yov PS-90A turbofans rated at 16,000 kgp (35,280 lbst) apiece. The cruising and maximum speeds are 600 km/h (373 mph) and 700 km/h (435 mph) respectively. The range is estimated at 6,000 km (3,729 miles).

Advertising materials from the TREK company contain an interesting drawing showing a variation of the aerodynamic layout embodied in the EK-150. This hypothetical version of the basic design features a revised tail unit in which the horizontal tail rests on the tops of the fins and a central pylon. Leaving aerodynamic considerations aside, one can note that this configuration has a definite advantage from the point of view of structural strength.

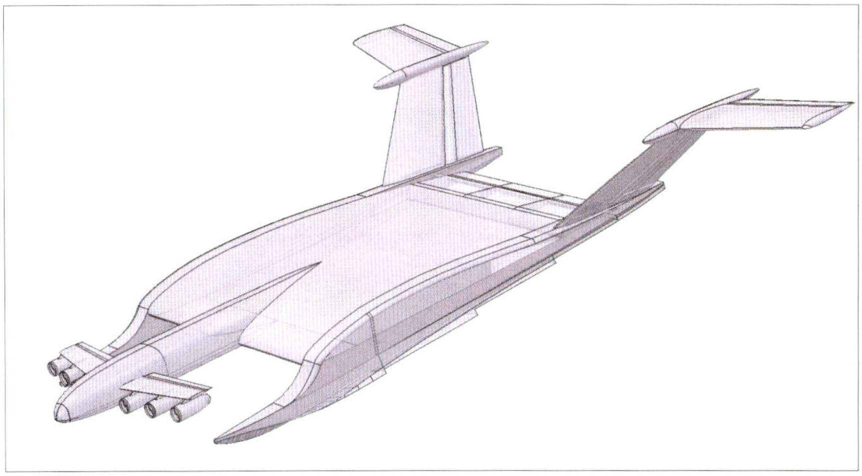

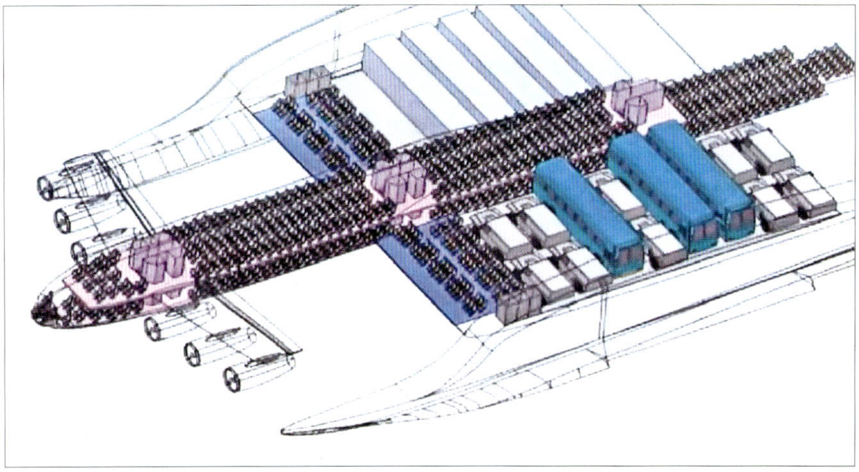

Projects from companies forming the Ekranoplan Association

The organisation which styles itself as **Ekranoplan Association** (the full title is 'Ekranoplan – Association of Designers, Manufacturers and Operators of Ekranoplans') was established in January 2010. It was formed by as many as 18 companies, of which 11 were directly involved in design and manufacture of WIG vehicles, while the rest were companies dealing with equipment, engines and transport operations.

The Ekranoplan Association has taken part in drafting the concept 'Development of ekranoplans for military and civil duties in the Russian Federation'. Teaming up with the Krylov Shipbuilding Research Institute in St. Petersburg (renamed Krylov State Research Centre in 2012), it is working on a state contract entitled 'Certification', aiming to create appropriate legislation which enables development and construction of new-generation ekranoplans. The Association has also prepared and submitted proposals concerning the draft concepts for. introducing WIG vehicles into service with the FSB's Border Guard, as well as with the Ministry of Emergency Situations (EMERCOM of Russia). Proposals were also submitted to the Ministry of Defence concerning the development of Class B ekranoplans for military applications. Finally, relevant proposals were submitted in connection with the plan for the implementation of the five-party agreement on co-operation in security matters in the Caspian Sea, which was signed on 18th November 2010 at a conference of the participating countries.

Among the member companies of the Ekranoplan Association which deserve special attention and are included in the product review below, are the following enterprises:

- Industrial and Financial Investment Group JSC (Moscow)
- Orion JSC (Moscow)
- Mirel JSC (Moscow)
- Sky plus Sea JSC (Mytishchi)

Opposite page, top: A cutaway drawing of the EK-100 in a 106-seat passenger layout with baggage space at the rear of the cabin.

Opposite page, bottom: A cutaway drawing of the EK-100 in a layout for carrying 11 tons of cargo.

This page, top: The EK-150 was to carry 150 tons of cargo or 1,290 passengers. This drawing appears to show a combi layout but was more probably meant to show in one picture how cargo (including vehicles) and passenger seats were to be accommodated.

Above: A computer-generated image of the EK-150 ocean-going heavy ekranoplan.

- Aerokhod JSC (Nizhniy Novgorod)
- Arctic Trade and Transport Company (ATTK, Chkalovsk)
- Amfikon JSC (Nizhniy Novgorod)
- Aviasystems JSC (formerly AeroMarine Systems)

As of 2012, there were six or seven companies involved to a varying extent in the ekranoplan business which were not members of the Ekranoplan Association. The biggest among them is the Alekseyev CHDB. According to the Association's Director Yuriy G. Varakosov, the CHDB has ignored repeated invitations from the Ekranoplan Association and its proposals aimed at some sort of cooperation.

Orion JSC

The full title of this enterprise is *'Orion' Ekranoplan Construction Association Limited Liability Company*. It was registered in 2002, but for several years its activities were limited to basic research and did not come to public knowledge. The company came to the fore in the ekranoplan business by the end of the first decade of this century. The Orion Company was originally headed by General Director Oleg A. Volik (succeeded by Anatoliy V. Zavgorodniy on 10th February 2015), the post of chief designer is occupied by Yuriy Varakosov (who also holds the post of Director of the Ekranoplan Association – see above). The company's central office and design bureau is located in Moscow.

The Orion Company entered into business relations with the TREK Company described above and, as a result of certain transactions, gained access to the manufacturing documents on several designs starting with the EK-12 and EK-12P which formed the starting point for a series of projects now known under the Orion brand name. They are described below.

In 2010 the Orion JSC company joined the newly established Ekranoplan Association described above. Initially the Orion Company relied on the production facilities of the Volga Shipyard in Nizhniy Novgorod, but in 2010 it decided to set up its own production base at Petrozavodsk in Karelia, in the vicinity of Lake Onega which would provide opportunities for testing ekranoplans all year round. The Orion Company acquired the production facilities of the defunct Avangard shipbuilding company in Petrozavodsk and transformed them into a site for prototype construction and series manufacture of ekranoplans. This branch of the Orion Company is known as the *'Orion' Karelian Ekranoplan Construction Association*, with Oleg Parfyonov as its leader.

Orion-12

This designation was given to production examples of the vehicle known as EK-12 (see Chapter Six, pages 285-286 of this book) when the Orion Company took over responsibility for its production. In May 2010 an example of the EK-12 previously operated by the Border Guard Service was delivered to Petrozavodsk, serving as a pattern for manufacturing two Orion-12 machines. During the autumn of 2010 the Ekranoplan Association was conducting operational testing of the Orion 12 which was to be concluded before the end of that year. In all, three examples of the Orion-12 were built. One of them was deployed at Novorossiysk and assigned to the Ushakov State Naval Academy. A centre was established under the auspices of the Academy for the purpose of training personnel engaged in the operation of ekranoplans. The EK-12 (Orion-12) was demonstrated at the Hydroaviation Show in Ghelendzhik in September 2012 and at the MAKS-2013 airshow in Zhukovskiy in August 2013.

Orion-12P

This name was given to the machine previously known as EK-12P, a version of the EK-12 developed for the Federal Border Guard Service (P stands for *pogra**nich**nyy* – in this context, border guard, used attributively). In October 2010 it was announced that in 2011 the member enterprises of the Ekranoplan Association would continue to improve and perfect the Orion-12P, rectifying defects and faults that had manifested themselves in the course of the vehicle's operational service.

Orion-14

The Orion-14 was a further development of the Orion-12P which was initially tailored for the needs of the Border Guard Service of Russia. The designers took into account the recommendations of the Service based on the experience of operating the Orion-12P; they also took into account the wishes of a foreign customer (presumably Iran).

As compared to the Orion-12, the new version featured some improvements in the power train and the engines' cooling system. It was fitted with new propellers, an auxiliary engine driving a water propeller for low-speed motion when afloat, as on a motor-boat, and had a number of other alterations. Its airframe structure incorporated new-generation composites. The vehicle's equipment contained a larger proportion of components of Russian manufacture.

A machine sporting Orion-14 titles was shown at the Hydroaviation Show in Ghelendzhik in early September 2014 where it performed demonstration flights. It differed externally from its predecessor in some details, such as the location of air scoops for the engine cooling system. The horizontal tail lacked the arrowhead-shaped auxiliary fins characteristic of the EK-12 and Orion-12.

By the end of 2014 the Orion-14 had completed the initial phase of flight tests which had been conducted in the summer and autumn over unfrozen water areas. From January 2015 they were followed by tests in winter conditions over ice-covered areas of Lake Onega. The purpose of the tests was to verify the machine's ability to be operated over ice fields with hummocks reaching a height of 50 cm (nearly 2 ft) and over slush ice, which was important for operations in the harsh conditions of the High North and the Far East.

The Orion-14 underwent certain modifications in the course of testing. It was shown on several occasions in slightly different configurations. In one of them it had **shrouded six-blade propellers**, while on another occasion this machine (or possibly a different example) had **four-blade unshrouded propellers with unusual wide-chord blades**. Yet another version was fitted with **three-blade propellers of the same kind**; this latter version was tested on the ice of Lake Onega in February 2015.

Despite apparently successful testing, the Orion-14 did not enter large-scale production and was probably manufactured in limited numbers. It attracted considerable interest abroad, notably in South-East Asia (Vietnam, Malaysia) and in Iran. According to some reports, Iran ordered a batch of 20 Orion 14 vehicles, of which at least three are known to have been delivered and tested by Iran on the Caspian Sea. Interestingly, an Iranian YouTube clip shows an example of the Orion-14 in flight over the sea and on a ground servicing platform; these examples have three-blade propellers with wide-chord blades, without shrouds. Iranian specialists came to Karelia to undergo training in the operation and servicing of the imported ekranoplans, and personnel from the Orion Company was sent to Iran to assist in the assembly and flight testing of the machines.

Orion-15

This is a passenger WIG vehicle with an AUW of 4.2 tonnes (9,260 lb), capable of carrying 15 passengers and one or two pilots at speeds up to 250 km/h (155 mph) over a distance of 1,300 km (808 miles). It is intended for operations all year round on big rivers, lakes and water reservoirs and in littoral areas. The vehicle was supposed to be powered by two Chevrolet piston engines of 480 hp apiece. Dimensions include an overall length of 13.1 m (43 ft) and a wing span of 12.3 m (40 ft 4¼ in). In addition to regular passenger and VIP transport, the machine can be used for cargo transport, medevac and SAR missions and ecological monitoring; it is also suitable for use as a mobile command post. In its layout it resembles the Orion-20 described below.

In September 2010 it was stated that a model of the Orion-15 had passed wind tunnel tests at TsAGI and the vehicle 'was being readied for production'. In June 2016 the Orion Company's representative in Karelia intimated that plans were in hand for producing a prototype of this machine which 'would at the same time be the first production machine'. This plan has not yet been implemented.

In 2017 it was reported that an organisation in Yakutia displayed some interest in adapting the Orion-15 project to Arctic conditions.

Orion-20

This machine in the 20- to 30-seat class is the biggest WIG vehicle in the Orion series which has been built to date. It is portrayed as symbolising the start of a series of Orion WIG vehicle types of different sizes.

Initial studies envisaged a configuration combining the twin-float (catamaran) layout with a twin-boom tail unit. Pictures from design documents show the Orion-20 in this shape with minor variations as regards the attachment of floats and outboard wing panels to the wing centre section of short span and wide chord. One of these variations is designated **Orion-20A**. It differs from other simi-

Computer-generated images of the Orion-20 in its early project form with a twin-boom tail unit.

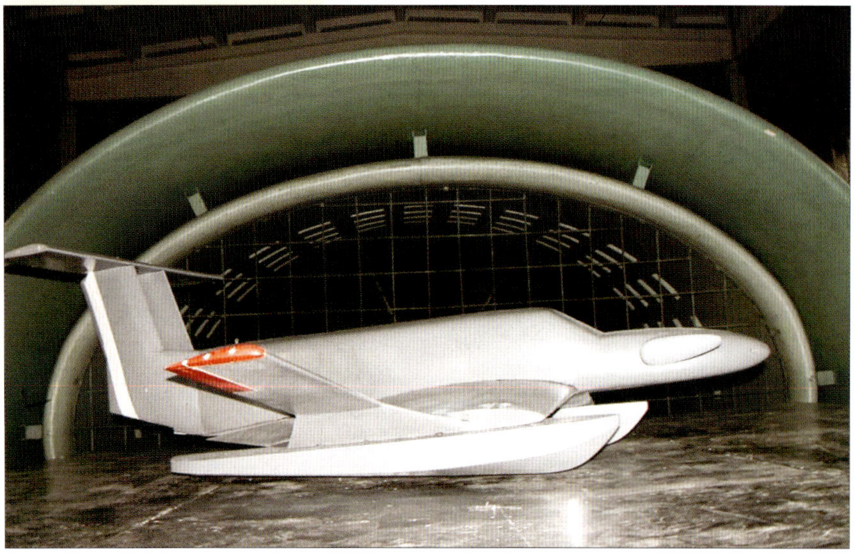

lar versions of this type in having the floats located below the main wings, rather than flanking them; the outer panels are joined to the main wings directly, without the intermediate angled sections.

A picture of another variation was presented in some internet reports with the caption 'Sterkh-10' but this designation appears to be erroneous (more about this below). This configuration also formed the basis for studying versions adapted for different duties.

However, the final layout chosen for prototype construction featured a tail unit comprising two splayed vertical tails mounted on the fuselage and topped by a horizontal tail, resembling the Orion-15 in this respect. Construction of this machine seating 21 passengers and operated by two pilots was started by the Orion Company at the Volga Shipyard in Nizhniy Novgorod in September 2010; from December 2011 the work was transferred to the production facilities of the former Avangard Shipyard in Petrozavodsk, Karelia. Looking like a low-wing monoplane, the prototype had a roomy fuselage with a rear hatch and boarding/loading ramp, compound wings with a well-developed centre section and narrow-chord outer panels. The whole structure rested on large twin floats turning the vehicle into a catamaran. In its original version it was powered by two 750-hp Motorlet M-601E turboprops with three-blade propellers mounted on horizontal pylons attached to the forward fuselage; they performed the double role of take-off boosters and cruise engines. In the course of testing this machine was fitted with a third (cruise) engine, mounted on struts above the rear fuselage right ahead of the tail fins. Some sources identify this third engine as a 1,025-ehp Glushenkov TVD-10B turboprop, but in the pictures this engine has a nacelle identical to those of the two M-601Es.

Basic specifications include a length of 19.128 m (62 ft 9 in), a wing span of 19.778 m (64 ft 10¾ in), an AUW of up to 10 tonnes (22,050 lb), a speed of up to 250 km/h (155 mph) and a range of 1,600 km (994 miles). It can be used in a variety of

roles, such as cargo carrier, medevac and SAR craft, ecological monitoring platform, as well as a VIP transport or mobile command post.

Initial tests were successful, but in the summer of 2015 the prototype came to grief during tests on Lake Onega. While moving at speed the machine suddenly pitched up into a near-vertical position, stalled and fell into the water, suffering serious damage but staying afloat. The crew survived with only minor injuries.

The vehicle was considerably rebuilt in the course of the ensuing repairs; the result was, in effect, a new machine. Equipped with TVD-10B turboprops instead of the M-601Es, it was capable of carrying 30 passengers or 3 tonnes (6,610 lb) of cargo at speeds up to 250 km/h (155 mph). The vehicle was slightly enlarged and refined aerodynamically, and the rear fuselage was lightened to shift the CG forward and thus cure the propensity for nosing-up. In its new guise it is sometimes referred to as the **Orion-20M** (*modifi***tsee***rovannyy* – modified).

Installation of the more powerful TVD-10B engines on the Orion-20 ekranoplan had been planned already at the beginning of design work on this type. The TVD-10 turboprop initially rated at 960 hp for take-off is not a new engine; it made its appearance in 1965 and was manufactured in series between 1969 and the 1980s. In November 2012 the Omsk Engine Design Bureau reportedly resumed the manufacture of this engine specially for the Orion-20 ekranoplan. In any case, by the time when construction of the modified Orion-20 started, two TVD-10 engines were supplied to the Orion Company. Some reports suggest that the engines were not in the best condition (possibly refurbished second-hand engines), and this may have been the reason for a rather lengthy interruption in the tests.

Opposite page, top: The broadly similar Orion-20A project differed in having the floats underneath the wing centre section (rather than at its extremities) and ordinary outer wings attached to the centre section instead of gull wings attached to the floats.

Centre and bottom left: A model of the Orion-20 built for wind tunnel tests shows fuselage-mounted fins disposed vertically and still only two engines.

Bottom right: This model of the Orion-20 is closer to the definitive configuration, showing an aft-mounted third engine and outward-canted fins.

Above: The Orion-20 prototype (in its second configuration with three M-601E turboprops) flies over Lake Onega in company with a smaller Orion-14 during an EMERCOM of Russia exercise.

Left: The rebuilt Orion-20M with a mixed powerplant featuring two TVD-10Bs at the front and one M-601E at the rear.

In March 2017 the testing of the rebuilt Orion-20 resumed. The craft made its first flight in the twin-engined configuration, but later a third engine – an M-601E – was mounted above the rear fuselage. In April 2018 the testing at Lake Onega was still in progress. In that month the governor of the Yamal Region (a territory in Northern Russia playing a prominent role in oil and natural gas extraction) made a trip to Petrozavodsk and visited the testing site, taking much interest in the possibilities of adapting this new means of transport to the needs of his region.

In September 2018 it was reported that flights had been suspended because the main engines failed to deliver the required power and were to be replaced by new ones. The machine was fitted with an auxiliary power unit for low speed movement (taxying) when afloat. Plans were in hand to install a new autopilot system which was expected to ensure a considerable improvement of controllability.

As mentioned above, there are project versions of the Orion-20 which differ from the prototype described above in having a twin-boom configuration of the tail unit. One of these is the **Orion-20MChS** (*Mini**ster**stvo po chrezvy**chay**nym situ**ah**tsiyam* – Ministry of Emergency Situations/ EMERCOM) which has been studied in several configurations: **Orion-20McChS-P** (*pat**rool'**nyy*) for patrol duties, **Orion-20MChS-E** (*ekolo**gich**eskiy*) for ecological monitoring, **Orion-20MChS-AS** (*ava-**reey**no-spa**sa**tel'nyy*) for rescue missions and **Orion-20MChS-P** (again P – this time standing for *po**zhar**nyy*) for fire-fighting duties and oil spill elimination. There was also a medevac version designated **Orion-20MChS-Med.**

Sterkh-10 and Sterkh-PSE

In 2013 the Russian media reported that a WIG vehicle bearing the name Sterkh (the Russian name for the Siberian white crane) was being developed by Orion JSC to meet an order from the Russian Ministry of Industry and Trade which, incidentally, recommended this designation for the project. At an AUW of 10 tonnes (22,050 lb) the machine was to carry 20 passengers. In July 2013 Chairman of the Ekranoplan Association Yuriy G. Varakosov told journalists that design work on the Sterkh-10 had been successfully completed, and the launching of

The Orion-20M is depicted here while being tested by EMERCOM of Russia; a 'stretcher case' is loaded via the rear airstair door.

the vehicle and its first flight were scheduled for the beginning of August 2013. Actually, he had in mind the **Orion-20** which was indeed launched that month. However, knowledgeable observers pointed out that the designation Sterkh-10 had been mistakenly attributed to the vehicle and, in fact, denoted only one of the research programmes associated with it.

In the wake of a report on the Sterkh-10 yet another item of news made its appearance, citing a project designated **Sterkh-PSE**. It was described as a high-speed WIG vehicle in the B category intended for SAR missions (PSE obviously stands for *poisk**o**vo-spa**sa**tel'nyy ekrano**plan*** – search and rescue ekranoplan) in the High North areas. The machine is considerably bigger than the so-called 'Sterkh-10' (Orion-20) – at an AUW of 14 tonnes (30,870 lb) it is capable of transporting 32 passengers or 4 tonnes (8,820 lb) of cargo; it will be provided with a ramp in the rear hatch for loading vehicles or standard air freight containers. The work on this project was undertaken by Orion JSC under the terms of a contract with the Russian Ministry of Industry and Trade signed in December 2014. Information to this effect was published on a web site in March 2015; no further details are available. Should these plans come to fruition, this machine will presumably crop up under the Orion-20 designation with an appropriate suffix.

Orion-27

This is a WIG vehicle with an AUW of 6.7 tonnes (14,730 lb) powered by two Audi Q-10 automobile piston engines rated at 600 hp apiece. The project was revealed by Yuriy Varakosov in October 2010. Presumably, this is the project which was formerly known as EK-27 (see Chapter Six pp. 287-288 of this book). It resembles a scaled-up EK-12.

An artist's impression of the Orion-40 – a scaled-up version of the early twin-boom Orion-20.

Orion-30

This design was briefly mentioned in a news report on the activities of Orion JSC. No details are available.

Orion-40

This project of a WIG vehicle intended to carry 40 passengers and a crew of four was likewise announced by Yuriy Varakosov in October 2010. This is a passenger WIG vehicle intended for summer and winter operation on big rivers, lakes and water reservoirs and in littoral areas. Its layout resembles a scaled-up Orion-20 in its twin-boom configuration. The vehicle with an AUW of 30.0 tonnes (66,150 lb) measures 26.24 m (86 ft 1 in) in length and 16.20 m (53 ft 2 in) in wing span and has a cruising speed of up to 250 km/h (155 mph); the range is 1,800 km (1,119 miles). Its envisaged roles are exactly the same as for the Orion-15: passenger transport, VIP transport, cargo transport, medevac, SAR, ecological survey and mobile command post. It can also be adapted to special tasks of military agencies.

Performance characteristics of some WIG craft developed by the Orion company

	Orion-12P (EK-12P)	Orion-15 project	Orion-20 initial project	Orion-20 prototype	Orion-20 rebuilt
Length overall	n.a.	13.2 m (43 ft 3½ in)	19.128 m (62 ft 9 in)	19.128 m (62 ft 9 in)	n.a.
Width overall	n.a.	12.3 m (40 ft 4¼ in)	19.778 m (64 ft 10¾ in)	19.778 m (64 ft 10¾ in)	n.a.
Width with wings folded	n.a.	4.8 m (15 ft 9 in)	8.0 m (26 ft 3 in)	8.0 m (26 ft 3 in)	n.a.
Height	n.a.	4.4 m (14 ft 5¼ in)	6.0 m (19 ft 8¼ in)	6.0 m (19 ft 8¼ in)	n.a.
All-up weight, kg (lb)	4,200 (9,261)	4,200 (9,21)	up to 10,000 (22,050)	up to 10,000 (22,050)	n.a.
Passengers	12	15	21	21	n.a.
Payload (cargo), kg (lb)	1,200 (2,646)	n.a.	n.a.	n.a.	n.a.
Crew	1-2	1-2	2	2	2
Maximum speed, km/h (mph)	220 (137)	up to 250 (155)	up to 250 (155)	n.a.	n.a.
Cruising speed, km/h (mph)	185 (115)	n.a.	n.a.	n.a.	n.a.
Range, km (miles)	1,500 (932)1,300 (808) *	1,300 (808)	1,600 (994)	n.a.	n.a.
Engine type	Chevrolet LS-3	Chevrolet	2 x M-601E	3 x M-601E**	2 x TVD-10B1 x M-601E
Engine power, hp	2 x 436	2 x 480	2 x 750	3 x 750	2 x 1,025 +1 x 750

*In ground effect and out of ground effect; ** Some materials indicate a TVD-10B as the third engine, but actually it was an M601E

Design performance of some prospective WIG craft developed by the Orion Company

	Sterkh-PSE(Orion-20)	Orion-40	Orion-110	Orion-275	Orion-1100
Length overall	n.a.	26.24 m (86 ft 10⁴³⁄₆₄ in)	n.a.	n.a.	n.a.
Width overall	n.a.	16.20	n.a.	n.a.	n.a.
Width with wings folded	n.a.	n.a.	n.a.	n.a.	n.a.
Height	n.a.	6.01 m (19 ft 8³⁹⁄₆₄ in)	n.a.	n.a.	n.a.
All-up weight, kg (lb)	14,000 (30,870)	30,000 (66,150)	32,000 (70,560)	275,000(606,375)	1,100,000 (2,425,500)
Passengers	32	40	n.a.	n.a.	1,500
Payload (cargo), kg (lb)	4,000 (8,820)				500,000(1,102,500)
Crew	n.a.	4	n.a.	n.a.	n.a.
Maximum speed, km/h (mph)	n.a.	n.a.	n.a.	n.a.	n.a.
Cruising speed, km/h (mph)	n.a.	up to 250 (155)	n.a.	n.a.	n.a.
Range, km (miles)	n.a.	1,800 (1,119)	n.a.	n.a.	n.a.
Engine type	n.a.	2 x VK-2500	2 x TV7-117S	4 x PS-90A	6 x NK-44
Engine power, hpor thrust, kgp (lbst)	n.a.	2 x 2,500	2 x 3,000	4 x 16,000(35,280)	6 x 44,000 (97,020)

Detail design work on this project was to start in 2011, but financial issues had not been solved by that time, and the project obviously failed to make a significant progress.

Incidentally, the advertising image of the Orion-40 closely resembles that of the PE-40 published in Chapter Six of this book (see p. 290), which leads to the assumption that this is the same project under a new name.

Orion-50

According to advertising material, this WIG vehicle with an AUW of 50.5 tonnes (113,350 lb) is designed to carry up to 150 passengers and a crew of four at a speed of up to 300 km/h (186 mph) over a distance of no less than 1,600 km (994 miles). Its powerplant comprises four Klimov VK-2500 turboshaft/turboprop engines of 2,000-2,400 shp apiece. Dimensions include a length of 26,24 m (86 ft 1 in) and a wing span of 26.5 m (87 ft 0 in) reduced to 13.0 m (42 ft 8 in) with the wings folded. The height is 8.5 m (27 ft 10¾ in).

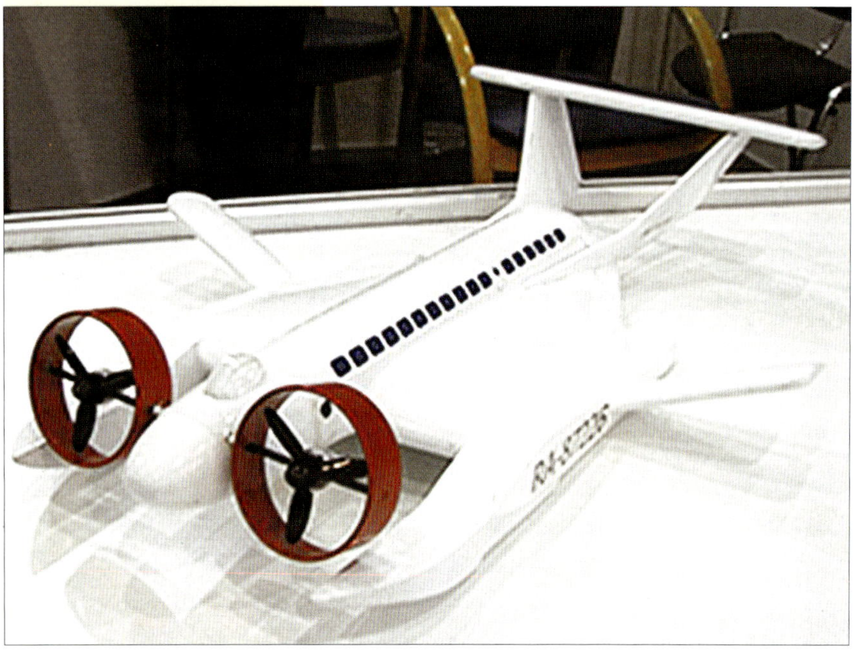

This model shown at the Interpolitech-2010 exhibition in Moscow in October 2010 probably depicts the Orion-110. It looks like a scaled-up EK-75 but with twin fins instead of the T-tail. The registration RA-87225 in the Yak-40 block is spurious.

Orion-110

This is a WIG vehicle with an AUW of up to 32 tonnes (70,560 lb) powered by two Klimov TV7-117S turboprops rated at up to 3,000 hp apiece. The existence of such a project was revealed to a journalist by Director of the Ekranoplan Association Yuriy Varakosov in October 2010. No confirmed illustration is available.

Orion-275

This WIG vehicle with an AUW of 275 tonnes (606,375 lb) is powered by four Solov'yov PS-90A turbofans delivering a thrust of 16 tonnes (35,280 lb) apiece (these engines power the Tu-204/Tu-214 and Ilyushin IL-96 airliners and the current Russian-built versions of the IL-76 transport and IL-78 refuelling tanker). This project was likewise mentioned by Yuriy Varakosov in conversation with a journalist in October 2010.

Orion-1100

This is a project of a gigantic WIG vehicle with an AUW of up to 1,100 tonnes (2,425,500 lb) powered by six Kuznetsov NK-44 turbofans delivering a thrust of 44 tonnes (97,020 lb) apiece (the NK-44, under development since 1992 for large capacity airliners, has not reached the hardware stage to this day). The ekranoplan is intended to transport up to 1,500 passengers and 250 tonnes (551,250 lb) of cargo in combi configuration, or 500 tonnes (1,102,500 lb) in all-cargo configuration. Once again, the project was mentioned by Yuriy Varakosov in a press interview in October 2010. No image is available.

Left and below: An electrically powered model of a Mirel WIG vehicle prepared for towing basin trials.

Mirel JSC

Mirel JSC is a relatively small and little-known enterprise engaged in the development of ekranoplans and closely associated with the Orion Company. A project emanating from this design team was mentioned and illustrated in Chapter Six of this book (see p. 299). According to some reports, in 2010-11 the Mirel company was a subsidiary of the Orion JSC. Like its parent company, it joined the Ekranoplan Association when the latter was formed in 2011. Little is known about Mirel's present activities. In October 2010 it presented a model of a WIG vehicle (reportedly designated **Mirel-4**) at the Interpolitekh police hardware exhibition in Moscow. The machine resembled in its layout some of Kolganov's projects, such as the EK-17 (see above in this chapter). Another project, designated **Mirel-5**, was fleetingly presented in the shape of a small computer-generated image which formed part of the advertising material posted by the Ekranoplan Association on a web site. The layout of this diminutive WIG vehicle also betrays kinship with Kolganov's concepts.

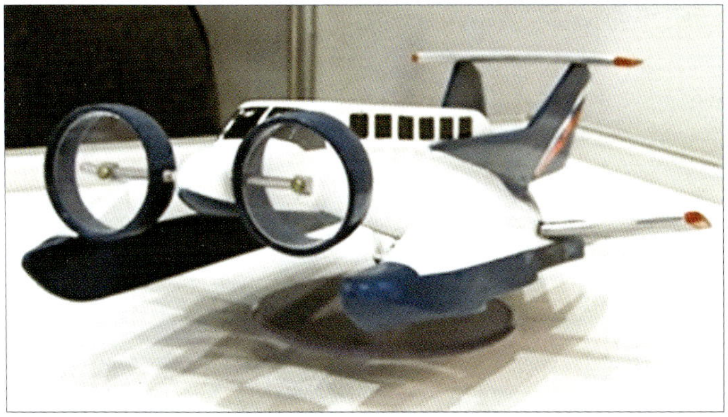

Below left: display model of the Mirel-4 passenger ekranoplan. The similarity to some competing designs is striking.

Below: A computer-generated image of the Mirel-5 passenger ekranoplan, a rather elegant vehicle.

Sky plus Sea Design Bureau Burevesnik-24 and further projects

The activities of the **Sky plus Sea** (in Russian: ***Neb**o plus **Mor'**e*) Design Bureau dating back to the beginning of the 2000s have been described in the main text of this book (see Chapter Six, pages 311-312). It is a private company based in the Mytishchi District of the Moscow Region, with Vladimir Bukovskiy as both Director-General and chief designer. The company's work is financed only by private investors, without any government support. Since 2002 the company has built several prototypes of a 24-seat WIG vehicle called **Burevesnik-24** (the version tested in 2009 was described in the main text of the book). Since then further prototypes have entered the test programme. One of them was the prototype known as **Burevesnik-24M**. It was completed by the summer of 2016 and was to be launched in June of that year. This improved model featured a new control system and a new life support system. Development work on this model was conducted with assistance from the Duks Company (this enterprise is engaged in the development and production of air-to-air guided missiles, but also acts as a sponsor for small companies dealing with light aircraft and ekranoplan construction).

One of the Burevesnik-24 prototypes on the Lena River during trials; the inscription on the nose reads *ispytaniya* (trials).

In September 2017 the machines Nos. 6, 7 and 8 were undergoing tests in Mytishchi and in Yakutia. Incidentally, V. Bukovskiy refers to his designs as 'high-speed amphibians' (VSA – *vy**so**koskoros**na**ya am**fib**iya*) and mentions the designation VSA-7 – presumably with reference to the seventh machine. The local government of Yakutia displayed considerable interest in the machine which, it was believed, could prove very useful in solving the region's transport problems. The Burevesnik-24 was tested on the Lena River, navigating the stretches from Yakutsk to Pokrovsk 78 km (48.5 miles) upstream and Olyokminsk 530 km (329 miles) upstream. Tests were conducted during the summer and winter seasons; the machine acquitted itself very well under all kinds of weather, including severe frost. The vehicle proved very sturdy, not least thanks to the use of a special composite material developed by the design team. According to Bukovskiy, this material is both lighter and stronger than duralumin. Various improvements have been introduced into the design of this highly unusual WIG vehicle, the most obvious being the addition of

Another view of the Burevesnik-24 accentuating the downturned wingtips and the strut-mounted navigation/collision avoidance radar. Note the slightly different floats.

Burevesnik-24 Performance figures	
Maximum AUW	6,100 kg (13,450 lb)
Payload	2,850 kg (6,280 lb)
Maximum speed	280 km/h (174 mph)
Cruising speed	200 km/h (124mph)
Take-off time	20 seconds
Range	1,200 km (746 miles)
Crew	2
Passengers	up to 24

downturned wingtips (a sort of inverted winglets) on the upper wings. Alterations were introduced into the powerplant; notably, several types of propellers have been tested, including three-blade, six-blade and finally four-blade propellers. The fuselage has also been subjected to some changes. The machine undergoing tests in September 2017 had a displacement of 7 tonnes (15,435 lb) and a payload of 3 tonnes (6,615 lb), the empty weight being 4,350 kg (9,590 lb). It had been undergoing tests at the Pirogovskoye Reservoir near Mytishchi for a year by then; the tests revealed some faults which needed to be corrected. In September 2017 Vladimir Bukovskiy said in an interview that, given adequate financing, a year would be required to complete the testing under summer-time and winter-time conditions and to verify all the aerodynamic and hydrodynamic characteristics. The example transferred to Yakutia was delivered to a specially set-up transport company called SKAT-R (*skoros***noy** *amfi***beey***nyy* ***trahns****port, rech***noy** – High-Speed Amphibious River Transport) whose task was to conduct operational testing of the vehicle under Siberian conditions.

According to some reports dating back to 2014, the powerplant of the Burevesnik-24 comprised two AviaSmart B-V12K piston engines, each of them delivering 421 hp at a maximum rating and 350 hp in cruise mode.

The Burevesnik-24 features a modular design; the floats; for example, can be replaced by new ones within an hour. After dismantling the machine can be accommodated in a marine container which can be transported on a ship, by rail or road transport.

Vladimir Bukovskiy revealed to a journalist his plans for constructing a WIG vehicle with an AUW of 10 tonnes (22,050 lb) in cooperation with the abovementioned Duks Company. No details are available, however. Moreover, the Sea plus Sky Company reportedly was studying the possibility of building a 100-seat ekranoplan.

The figures in the table on this page apply to one of the Burevesnik-24's configurations.

Vladimir Bukovskiy, the craft's designer and Director-General of the Sky plus Sea Design Bureau, with one of the Burevesnik-24 prototypes.

The Aerokhod A-18 Tungus in an early test flight (note the uncowled engines).

Project from the Aerokhod shipbuilding company (Nizhniy Novgorod)

The Aerokhod shipbuilding company based at Nizhniy Novgorod has in the last two decades designed and put into production a number of amphibious air cushion vehicles capable of transporting anywhere from six to 50 passengers. They are specially adapted for work in the harsh climatic conditions of the Arctic region. One of the company's designs known as **A18 Tungus** (an old name for the Evenks, one of the indigenous peoples of the Russian North) and described as an air cushion vehicle with aerodynamic offloading is for all practical purposes equivalent to an ekranoplan in the A category. It is intended to be operated in two basic modes, in which it is sustained respectively by a static air cushion or by a dynamic air cushion. The first operational mode is used for movement along minor rivers or stretches of major rivers with difficult navigating conditions; in this mode the vehicle travels at speeds between 50 and 90 km/h (31-56 mph). In the second basic operational mode the vehicle travels at speeds between 160 and 200 km/h (99-124 mph); this mode is used for long-range routes on major rivers and in littoral areas.

The prototypes undergoing test at present feature a layout reminiscent of the Lippisch designs but lacking the upturned wingtips. The wings are fitted with two floats on each side of the hull (an unusual feature), and the rear portion of the hull is topped by a T-tail with strut-braced stabilisers. Two piston engines with tractor propellers are mounted on struts above the wings.

The pictures showing the vehicle under test were revealed in August 2015. They show the vehicle in slightly varying configurations. The current status of the programme is not known.

The same prototype at a later stage of the testing with engine cowlings added.

Arctic Trade and Transport Company (ATTK, Chkalovsk)

After 2010 the ATTK (see Chapter Six, pp. 265-282) continued its activities for a while, turning its attention to promoting the sales of its five-seat Aquaglide 5 WIG vehicles. By the middle of June 2011 seven machines had been completed and a further three were nearing completion. Negotiations were pursued with prospective customers for the sale of this batch; a price of 386,000 Euro was quoted. The ATTK had plans to resume the production of this type on a limited scale and for the modernisation of the machine. The Aqualglide 5 was demonstrated at the Hydroaviation Show in Ghelendzhik in 2012. The company was transformed into ATTK Invest and joined the Ekranoplan Association. There were

A preserved example of the Aquaglide-5 in 'low flight'. The craft, which is on display in Nizhniy Novgorod's Victory Park, has been named 'Viktor Razzhivin'.

plans for a scaled-up 8-seat version of the Aquaglide-5; some hopes were pinned on the development of its 30-seat Aquaglide 30 project described earlier. In 2011 the company's chief Ruben Nagapetyan expressed the hope that the prototype of the Aquaglide 30 would be completed by the end of 2013 and possibly followed by the 60-seat Aquaglide-60 in 2014.

However, the company's expectations failed to materialise; the lack of orders eventually forced it to cease its activities. The ATTK went into liquidation on 16th March 2015.

Amphicon (Nizhniy Novgorod)

Some of the numerous projects in the NVA-series, developed under the guidance of N. N. Nazarov, notably by Amphicon Company, are described in Chapter Six of this book (see pp. 300-305). After 2010 this company, based at Nizhniy Novgorod, continued its design activities for some time. In 2011 it joined the newly formed Ekranoplan Association.

In 2012 one of the projects obviously belonging to the NVA range was demonstrated at the Hydroaviation Show in Ghelendzhik (see pictures here). This particular design (not described in the main text of this book), a large vehicle propelled by two powerful turboprops, shares the basic lifting body layout with Nazarov's other projects but differs from them in having no tail unit. The model was presented as a *high-speed marine passenger vessel with aerodynamic off-loading* under the designation **'Aquaplan';** it was exhibited under the auspices of the United Shipbuilding Corporation (apparently acting a sort of parent company or sponsor to Amphicon). No further information on this project or any other activities of the Amphicon company has come into the public domain in subsequent years.

The Amphicon company went into liquidation on 11th April, 2018.

Two photos of a model of the Aquaplan 'high-speed marine passenger vessel with aerodynamic off-loading' exhibited at the Hydro Aviation Show-2012 in Ghelendzhik. Note the windows in the rear part of the cabin roof and the small canard surfaces at the front of the floats.

A model of the AMS-400 Odissey passenger craft. Note the nose air intake for the booster engine; the splayed tail surfaces are not visible.

A model of the AMS-440 passenger craft.

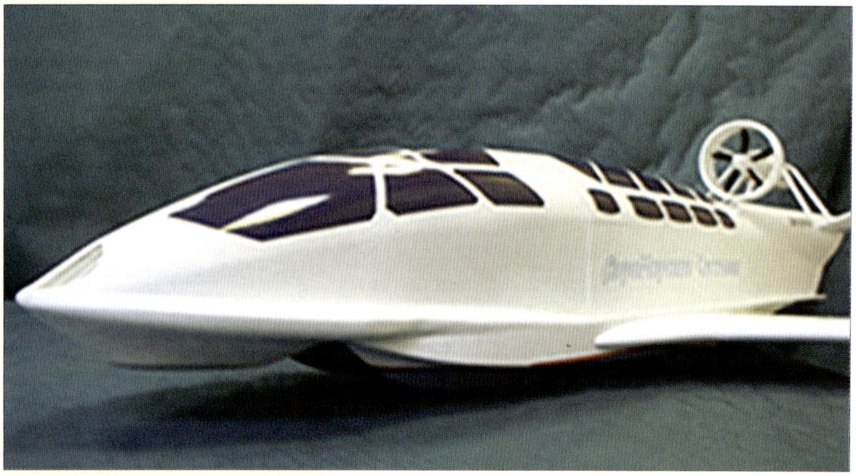

Aviasystems JSC (formerly AeroMarine Systems Company)

Projects of AeroMarine Systems Company were described in the first edition of this book, see Chapter Six, pp. 316-317). In August 2010 the company's General Director Aleksandr Makiyenko publicised ambitious programmes which, in addition to several light aircraft, included two types of WIG vehicles: the AMS-400 *Odissey* (Odysseus) described earlier and the AMS-410 Sea Hunter. The latter was a project of a patrol WIG vehicle with an AUW of 5 tonnes (11,025 lb) powered by two turbojets. Furthermore, design studies were initiated on a Class C WIG vehicle powered by two Fairchild J-44 turbojets and designated AMS-500 Korvet (Corvette). The company contemplated the construction of a factory intended for the manufacture of lightplanes and, eventually, of ekranoplans. A design not previously mentioned cropped up recently; it is a WIG vehicle designated AMS-440. No information on it is available, apart from the picture published here.

In 2011 the company undertook rebranding. On 13th May 2011 it was registered under the name *OOO Aviasistemy* (Aviasystems Limited Liability Company), with Aleksandr Makiyenko as General Director. The new company joined the Ekranoplan Association. In August 2016 it was included into the register of small and medium-sized enterprises. Activities of Aviasystems Limited encompass a wide range of development work and services associated with aircraft systems; during recent years the company has not undertaken any active promotion of its WIG vehicle projects which apparently are not in the centre of its interests.

Projects from the Beriyev TANTK (Taganrog Aviation Scientific and Technical Complex, TANTK)

Be-1000 and Be-2500

The original Be-2500 project, developed at least two decades ago and publicly unveiled for the first time at the Hydro Aviation Show 2000 in Ghelendzhik in September 2000, was described in the first edition (see Chapter Three, pages 194-199 of this book). Apparently, this project has no immediate prospects of implementation at present, but the company keeps reminding the world of its existence. In August 2013 Viktor A. Kobzev who headed TANTK at that time stressed that the development of super-heavy Class C WIG vehicles within the framework of broad international co-operation was 'one of the prospective directions of TANTK's activities'. He expressed the opinion that '*all the advantages of the concept of super-heavy airborne vehicles can be fully implemented in the projects of the Be-2500* ekranolyot (Class C WIG vehicle – *Auth.*) *with an AUW of 2,500 tonnes (5,512,500 lb) and a maximum payload of up to 1,000 tonnes (2,205,000 lb)*', but added: '*At present, as a transitional stage to the Be-2500, studies are being pursued on the concept of the Be-1000 super-heavy* ekranolyot *with an AUW of 1,200 tonnes [2,646,000 lb] and a payload of 400 tonnes [882,000 lb], designed around existing engines*'.

Statements in the same vein were made by Yuriy V. Grudinin, who was the Beriyev TANTK's General Director and General Designer until April 2019. In September 2018 he was quoted as saying that preliminary design work on the Be-2500 was in progress. '*The enterprise is studying the performance and technical features of the machine and is conducting negotiations with prospective customers. Depending on the results of this work, decisions will be taken on further activities*', said Grudinin.

Be-2500-2

A new facet to the subject of super-heavy ekranoplans was added at the Hydro Aviation Show 2010 in Ghelendzhik in September 2010. The Beriyev

TANTK presented to the public a picture of a huge transport vehicle bearing the name Be-2500-2. One would be wrong, however, in surmising that this was a direct development of the original Be-2500 concept. Apparently the similar designation merely indicated this was a vehicle in the same overall weight category of 2,500 tonnes (5,512,500 lb). As for the aerodynamic layout, the new monster looked much rather like a revival, in scaled-up form, of Bartini's VVA-14 VTOL amphibian in its WIG version – the 14M1P (see Chapter One, p. 160 of this book). It must be borne in mind that Bartini's design team developed this vehicle while being a part of the Beriyev design bureau.

Judging by the available illustration, the Be-2500-2 has a large wing centre section possessing a wide chord and small span (that is, a low aspect ratio). The wing centre section is flanked by floats doubling as endplates and creating a chamber for the dynamic air cushion. It is supplemented with unswept outer wing panels with a high aspect ratio and much smaller chord featuring large vertically disposed winglets. The tail unit consists of two surfaces attached to the rear part of the wing centre section and canted outwards at an angle of about 45°. Placed outboard of these tail surfaces are high-thrust turbojets which, surprisingly, have axisymmetrical supersonic air intakes with shock cones. The aircraft (or WIG vehicle) is apparently provided with an air-cushion or VTOL landing device; its exact configuration is not clear but the device may well be based on the use of lift jets. This is suggested by six panels on the upper surface of the wing centre section which may be the covers of the lift engines' air intakes. The flight crew cabin is attached to the leading edge of the wing centre section.

It is surmised that the Be-2500-2 may be used as a carrier vehicle for a prospective aerospace transport system intended for the delivery of large-size rocketry devices to launch sites in equatorial areas (these areas possess distinct advantages for sending loads into orbit). This possibility is suggested by the illustration which depicts the Be-2500-2 as carrying a suborbital space launch system piggy-back, the system comprising a manned booster vehicle with an unconventional tail-first/twin-fin layout and a small space shuttle.

An artist's impression of the giant Be-2500 ekranoplan carrying a two-stage suborbital space launch system with a small space shuttle.

Projects from the RDC Aqualines Company

RDC Aqualines is a relatively recent newcomer to the ekranoplan design and production field. Based at Nizhniy Novgorod, this company started its activities in 2013. It is a subsidiary of the local holding company called RDC Company which finances its activities. In the course of a few years it has developed several projects of WIG craft differing in size and passenger carrying capacity. They were the product of a joint effort of the company's founder and director Pavel F. Tsarapkin and chief designer Eduard Vasil'yev who had worked for several years in Rostislav Alekseyev's famous design bureau. From 2000 he had been working on his own concept for an ekranoplan which came to be embodied in the new company's designs. Sadly, E. Vasil'yev died on18th June 2016.

The company has embarked on a programme of civilian ekranoplans. It envisages the development of several types of cargo/passenger WIG vehicles of different sizes, ranging from an experimental two-seater to a huge craft intended to carry 300 passengers. The main effort is concentrated on medium-sized vehicles carrying 15 to 50 passengers.

All designs developed by RDC Aqualines have the same basic layout. They have a fuselage shaped as a boat hull with planing steps, incorporating a retractable hydroski. The hull is fitted with low-set short wings of low aspect ratio. The wingtips carry floats which, in addition to balancing the craft when afloat, act as endplates and thus create a cavity beneath the wing which serves to build up a dynamic air cushion during the take-off run. In all cases the tail unit is formed by twin splayed fins and rudders mounted on the aft part of the hull and topped by the horizontal tail whose parts outboard of the fins have slight dihedral. The powerplants (turboprop engines) are located behind the cargo/passenger compartment, driving pusher or tractor propellers. All types are provided with retractable beaching gear.

A peculiar feature of all designs is the use of 'boat architecture', notably in shaping the contours

A computer-generated image of the RDC Aqualines EP-2 two-seat leisure ekranoplan.

on the forward part of the hull. The latter incorporates a deck which facilitates the embarkation/disembarkation of passengers; railings are provided to help move about on deck. A peculiarity of the designs is the provision of fillets at the intersection of the wing leading edge and the hull, as well as at

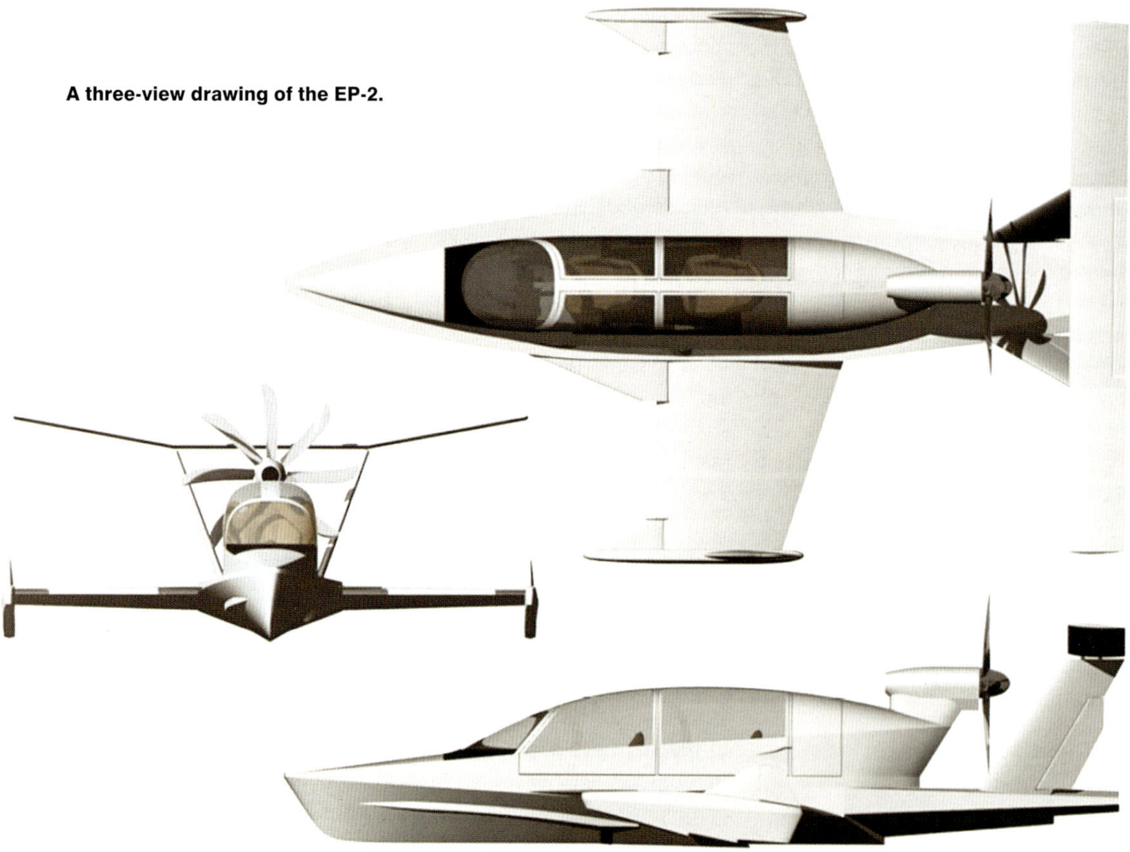

A three-view drawing of the EP-2.

the intersection of the wing leading edge and the float (endplate). The floats are topped by vertical fins at their aft end.

In general, the outward appearance of these vehicles is strongly reminiscent of the designs in the RT and MT series described elsewhere in this chapter, which cannot be a mere coincidence.

The RDC Aqualines was planning to start the assembly of its ekranoplans at the production facilities of another company – the Aerotekhnologii Science and Production Association which is affiliated to the Sokol aircraft factory in Nizhniy Novgorod. In January 2015 RDC Aqualines' Director Pavel Tsarapkin expressed the hope that the Russian Ministry of Industry and Trade would provide some financing for the company's R&D programme, while series production would require participation of private investors.

At present the company is making a stake on the EK-15 civil ekranoplan intended for passenger transportation on short sea routes. This 15-passenger craft is to be followed by EP-50 for 50 passengers, EP-150 for 150 passengers and EP-300 for 300 passengers. A brief description of these designs follows.

EP-2

This small two-seat research WIG craft was built and tested by RDC Aqualines in August 2016. The company had plans to construct an improved version of the EP-2 which would benefit from the experience gained with the initial model. The updated EP-2 was to be tested in France (no further information on that score is available). Should the test results prove encouraging, the company would embark on developing a full-scale passenger model – the EP-15.

The EP-2 is intended for pleasure rides, for official duty travel, for the transportation of small cargoes and for the monitoring of water areas. It has an extensively glazed cabin seating two persons in tandem and is powered by an 80-hp Rotax UL/A/F piston engine placed aft of the cabin and driving a pusher propeller (the computer-generated image shows an engine installation with an eight-blade propeller; the use of such a propeller is expected to reduce noise). The craft is 7.3 m (24 ft) long, 4.88 m (16 ft) wide and 1.97 m (6 ft 5½ in) high. It has an empty weight of 300 kg (661 lb), a maximum take-off weight of 500 kg (11,025 lb), a cruising speed of 143 km/h (89 mph) and a range of 350 km (218 miles). The craft consumes 10-11 kg (22-24 lb) of fuel per hour and can perform cruise flight over waves up to 3 m (10 ft) high.

The EP-2 is fitted with a hydro-ski which is provided with a shock absorber and is extended during take-off.

Small research vehicles of the RDC Aqualines company

In connection with the development of the EP-15 ekranoplan (described separately below) the company built two small vehicles purely for research purposes. One of them, styled as 'a self-propelled model of the EP-15', is a single-seat vehicle with an open cockpit, obviously intended to verify the soundness of the basic layout adopted for the EP-15. Furthermore, a small pilotless craft was built. In January 2017 this pilotless vehicle was used for testing various types of powerplants (engines and propellers) intended to be used later in the EP-15 WIG vehicle.

EP-15

This is a medium-size passenger ekranoplan capable of transporting 15 passengers and two crew. It has been advertised by the RDC Airlines company at least since 2015. Notably, during the MAKS-2015 airshow in Zhukovskiy the organisers of the show announced as one of the events in their business programme the signing of a contract on the delivery of 15 EP-15 sea-going cargo and passenger ekranoplans to a customer in Estonia. The vessels were to be operated on a passenger line on the Baltic Sea. Presumably the contract had actually been signed; reports published in the Estonian press in 2017 and 2018 claimed that the Estonian transport company Sea Wolf Express was planning to launch a passenger service between Tallinn and Helsinki using a Russian-built ground-effect vehicle (evidently the EP-15), with operations starting in 2019 – a promise that turned out to be premature. The Estonian company claimed that the trip with a 12-seater vehicle on the Tallinn-Helsinki route would last approximately 30 minutes. According to these reports, 'the prototype of the ekranoplan was essentially finished", although "hydrodynamic problems occurred during the testing of it' (such were the words used by Ville Hogman, head of Sea Wolf Express, in an interview). It appears that the ride in the vehicle came to be less comfortable than expected – apparently due to the rough sea. (Possibly he was referring to a ride in the EP-2 two-seater.)

As for the testing of the EP-15, it is still a matter for the future. At some time after 2015 General Director of RDC Aqualines Pavel Tsarapkin was quoted as saying that the prototype would be completed *'within two years'*. There are no fresh reports on that score.

Here is a brief description of the EP-15 on the basis of the company's advertising materials.

The EP-15 is to be operated on routes spanning up to 1,000 km (620 miles). It is to be powered by a single 7.4-litre V-8 Chevrolet LSX454 automobile engine of 620 hp. Dimensions are as follows: a length of 16.3 m (46 ft 19 in), a width of 10.1 m

Artist's impressions of the EP-15 passenger ekranoplan.

A three-view drawing of the EP-15.

(33 ft 1⅝ in), a height of 4.6 m (15 ft 11 in). Basic characteristics include an empty weight of 2,600 kg (5,730 lb), a maximum take-off weight of 4,000 kg (8,820 lb), a cruising speed of 185km/h (115 mph) and a maximum speed of 200 km/h (124 mph), fuel consumption 60 kg (132 lb) per hour, range with full payload 600 km (miles) and ferry range with full tanks 2,500 km (1,564 miles); the carrying capacity is 1,400 kg (3,090 lb) of cargo or 15 passengers. The height of cruise flight is up to 5 m (16 ft).

A different source indicates that the EP-15 is intended for passenger transport on routes spanning 50 to 300 km (31 to 186 miles).

The EP-15 provides a sufficiently high degree of comfort for its passengers. In the standard configuration the cabin houses five rows of seats three-abreast with an aisle plus two jump seats. In the VIP version the cabin seats nine passengers in two compartments (4+5) plus two jump seats. In both cases the flight deck accommodates two crew, and a toilet is located aft of the passenger cabin. If needed the passenger cabin can be converted partly or wholly into a cargo hold. Access is ensured through four upward-hinging doors (two on each side, fore and aft). Interestingly, the passenger and crew compartment resembles a superstructure of a ship being surrounded by the deck from all sides (this is also characteristic of the EP-50).

EP-108

This light sea-going ekranoplan, under development for border guard troops, is a military version of the EP-15. It is intended for patrolling and troop transport in littoral areas. The military version will have more powerful engines. The company states that the EP-108 can be adapted to all sorts of naval requirements.

ES-108

Looking like a direct derivative of the EP-108, the ES-108 is a SAR vehicle (ES is deciphered as *ekranoplan-spasatel'* – rescue ekranoplan). It is intended for SAR operations in littoral areas. At an AUW of 4 tonnes (8,820 lb) it can carry 12 persons or a cargo of 1,4 tonne (3,090 lb) over a distance of

A computer-generated image of an ES-108 civil search-and-rescue ekranoplan taking on shipwrecked sailors from a lifeboat.

The ES-108 in flight.

600 km (373 miles) at a cruising speed of 185 km/h (115 mph). The vehicle is powered by a single Chevrolet LSX454 engine of 620 hp; it is supplemented by an auxiliary engine of 40 hp for taxying when afloat. Two upward-hinging doors and two sliding doors facilitate the versatile use of the cabin

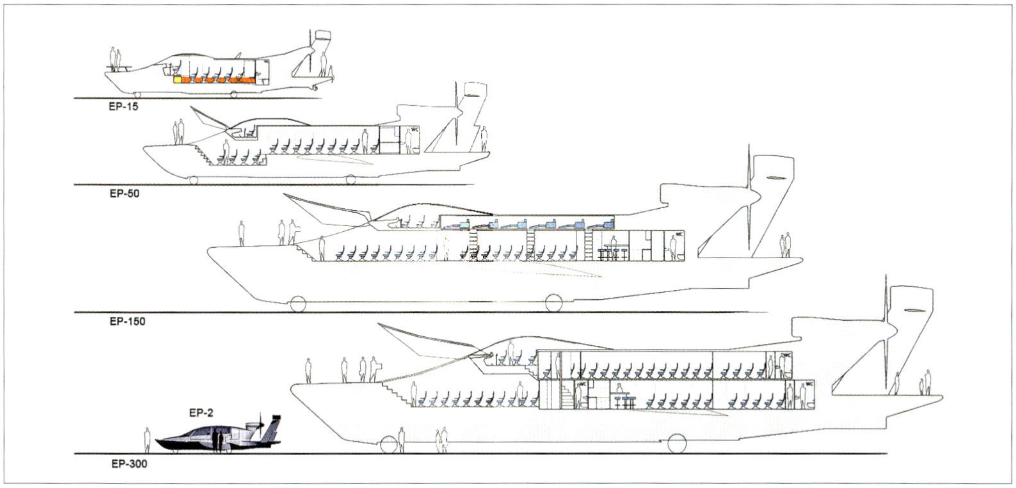

Opposite, top: An artist's impression of the EP-50 passenger ekranoplan operating a river service.

Opposite, bottom: A three-view drawing of the EP-50.

Left: A diagram showing the comparative size of the ekranoplans developed by RDC Aqualines. Note the sleeping berths on the upper deck of the EP-150 – with very little headroom.

space. All-round glazing of the pilot's cockpit enables observers to have 360° visual coverage during search operations. Equipment may include an intensive care unit; the cargo compartment can also be used for the delivery of rescue means.

EP-50

This WIG vehicle nominally intended to transport 50 passengers looks like a scaled-up version of the EP-15. It is powered by a single Klimov VK-2500 turboshaft/turboprop rated at 2,500 ehp. Actually, its passenger carrying capacity may vary from 48 to 60 seats. With a full payload it can cover the distance of 620 km (385 mph) at a cruising speed of 206 km/h (128 mph). Interestingly, the passenger cabin of the vehicle is arranged on two levels, the forward part of the cabin being placed lower, under the flight deck. In addition to the all-passenger configuration (53 seats), two mixed cargo/passenger configurations are envisaged, with 45 seats and one container or 15 seats and three containers. The all-cargo version can accommodate five standard containers. The four side entry doors are supplemented by an upward-hinging hatch in front of the flight deck.

EP-150

This WIG vehicle is intended to transport 150 passengers or a cargo of up to 13.5 tonnes (29,770 lb) over a distance of 1,050 km (622 miles). The powerplant is listed as two Izotov TV3-117 turboshafts rated at 2,200 eshp apiece (actually, a turboprop version of this helicopter engine, namely the TV3-117VMA-SBM1 powering the Antonov An-140 airliner, is rated at 2,500 ehp).

EP-300

The machine bearing this designation is intended to carry 294 passengers on two decks (114 seats on the upper deck and 180 seats on the lower deck. Some further details can be found in the table on this page.

Design performance figures on the RDC Aqualine projects

	EP-2	EP-15	EP-108	ES-108	EP-50	EP-150	EP-300
Length	7.3 m (23 ft 11 13/32 in)	16.3 m (46 ft 10 in)	16.3 m (46 ft 10 in)	16.3 m (46 ft 10 in)	24.5 m (80 ft 4 1/2 in)	31.6 m (103 ft 8 1/8 in)	55.0 m (180 ft 5 23/64 in)
Width	4.88 m (16 ft 0 1/8 in)	10.1 m (33 ft 1 5/8 in)	10.1 m (33 ft 1 5/8 in)	10.1 m (33 ft 1 5/8 in)	15.8 m (51 ft 10 in)	19.5 m (64 ft 0 in)	48.0 m (157 ft 5 49/64 in)
Height	1.97 m (6 ft 5 1/2 in)	4.6 m (15 ft 11 in)	4.6 m (15 ft 11 in)	4.6 m (15 ft 11 in)	5.2 m (17 ft 0 3/4 in)	6.2 m (20 ft 4 in)	11.0 m (36 ft 1 5/64 in)
All-up weight, kg (lb)	500 (11,025)	4,000 (8,820)	n.a.	4,000 (8,820)	13,000 (28,665)	19,300 (42,570)	80,000 (176,400)
Crew	1	2 pilots	n.a.	2	2	2 pilots	2 pilots
Passengers	1	12	n.a.	12	48-60	150	320
Cargo, kg (lb)	100 (220)	1,400 (3,090)	n.a.	1,400 (3,090)	4,500 (9,920)	13,500 (29,770)	32,000 (70,560)
Max speed km/h (mph)	n.a.	200 (124)	n.a.	200 (124)	238 (148)	n.a.	n.a.
Cruising speed, km/h (mph)	143 (89)	185 (115)	n.a.	185 (115)	206 (128)	180-225 (112-140)	184-230()
Height of cruising flight, m (ft)	0-3 (0-10)	1 (3)	n.a.	1 (3)	n.a.	0-5 (0-16)	0-5 (0-16)
Range with max payload, km (miles)	350 (218)	600 (373)	n.a.	600 (373)	620 (385)	1,050 (622)	1,650 (1,025)
Engine type	Rotax UL/A/F	1xChevrolet LSX454	n.a.	1xChevrolet LSX454	1xVK-2500	2xTV3-117	1 M70F
Engine power, hp	80	620	n.a.	620	2,500	2x2,2000	1x14,000
Low speed engine, hp	n.a.	40	n.a.	40	n.a.	n.a.	n.a.

Projects from TsAGI (Central Aero-Hydrodynamics Institute)

TsAGi has always played an important role in studies and investigations concerning the aero- and hydrodynamic properties of ground effect vehicles, providing assistance to design bureaux engaged in developing practical designs in this category. In parallel, TsAGI is responsible for a number of conceptual WIG craft designs of its own, only a fraction of these having come to public knowledge. One of these has received a measure of publicity and can be presented here.

According to some reports, in October 2018 TsAGI started wind tunnel testing of a model of a heavy transport aircraft with a blended wing/body layout known under the Cyrillic acronym TTS-IS (*tya***zho***lyy* **trahns***portnyy samo***lyo***t inte***grahl'***noi* **skhe***my* – heavy transport aircraft featuring a BWB layout). In fact, however, the vehicle does *not* have a BWB layout in the form used on modern fighters and some other aircraft. The TTS-IS was revealed more than a year prior to that – it was presented as a model at the MAKS-2017 airshow in July 2017.

The TTS-IS features a twin-boom layout and incorporates a fuselage/lifting body supplemented by low aspect ratio wings with downturned wingtips. The powerplant consists of four turboprop or propfan engines of a very high power rating installed in pusher configuration on pylons above the rear fuselage between the booms carrying the tail unit. The latter is formed by twin vertical tails topped by a horizontal tail. The fuselage houses cargo compartments with front loading hatches (closed by hinged sections of the wing leading edge), housing six rows of airfreight containers on each side of a central bay occupied by fuel tanks.

Available drawings and reports show that the project envisages the possibility of using cryogenic fuel, namely liquefied natural gas (LNG). A huge

A model of TsAGI's TTS-IS conceptual heavy transport aircraft undergoing wind tunnel tests.

LNG tank will be housed in the lifting body along the centreline, between the cargo compartments.

During the first stage of wind tunnel tests researchers investigated the main aerodynamic characteristics in flight out of ground effect at high altitude above the water. During these tests they checked the efficiency of control surfaces and the influence of the airframe parts such as engine nacelles, wingtip shape and varying forward fuselage contours on the vehicle's performance. The second stage of the tests was devoted to investigating the stability and controllability of the model in ground effect mode. Yet another stage of the testing was intended to visualise the air flow on the model's surface, for which purpose the model was covered with wool tufts.

It is hoped that successful completion of the tests will make it possible to develop an ekranoplan which can deliver a payload of 500 tonnes (1,102,500 lb) at a speed of 500 km/h (311 mph) over a distance of more than 6,000 km (3,730 miles). The flight in ground effect is expected to be performed at a height of 3-12 m (10-40 ft) above the sea or ground surface. The vehicle can perform a take-off from conventional runways.

It is obvious that implementation of such a project involves huge investments and great technical risks; at present it appears to be clearly beyond the practical possibilities of the Russian state and the Russian aeronautical industry. Such visionary projects can so far be only classed as futuristic.

Ekranoplan with air cushion landing gear (a TsAGI project)

In September 2016 TsAGI demonstrated a large radio-controlled model of an aircraft with an air cushion landing gear at the Hydroaviation Show 2016 in Ghelendzhik. Experiments with this model became an object of public interest in March 2019, when the Russian media published reports on the work conducted by TsAGI specialists for the purpose of creating a new means of transport for Siberia, the High North and Far Eastern areas of Russia. The reports included a photo of a model closely similar to the one from 2016. The vehicle in question is described as an ekranoplan with an air cushion landing gear. It looks like a transport aircraft with a bulky square-section fuselage, high-set cantilever wings, a twin-fin tail unit and two turboprop engines mounted on the wings. The lower part of the fuselage is flanked by voluminous inflated sponsons which serve as the landing gear (also on water) and at the same time create a chamber for the air cushion which ensures a smooth take-off and equally smooth landing. This chamber is closed in front by a flexible curtain and at the rear by a hinged flap. According to the reports, the vehicle is capable of performing flight in ground effect mode.

Plans in hand envisage the development of several vessels based on this concept and intended to transport 20, 50 and 100 passengers. The basic 20-seat version will have a length of some 20 m (65 ft), a wing span of 11 m (36 ft $1\frac{5}{64}$ in) and an AUW of 10 tonnes (22,000 lb).

A radio-controlled flying model of an ekranoplan with an air-cushion landing gear developed by TsAGI, shown here during tests in 2019.

The same model three years earlier as an exhibit at the Hydro Aviation Show 2016 in Ghelendzhik.

Top and above: A model of the VSA-500 ekranoplan proposed by MGTU, showing its unconventional wing design.

Below: The homebuilt light WIG craft designed by Ivan Bryukhanov. Here it is seen as originally built, without the upturned 'winglets'; the legend reads *ispytaniya* (tests).

WIG vehicles and projects developed or built by enthusiasts

Bauman Moscow State Technical University (MGTU)

This renowned educational institution is noted for various innovative projects in various branches of air transport developed by its students and teachers. In April 2019 the public was given a chance to get acquainted with one of their projects associated with WIG technology. Presented in model form was a concept of a vehicle which, according to its creators' description, combines the properties of aerosleigh, ekranoplan and amphibious vessel. A 1:25 scale model of the vehicle bearing the designation **VSA-500** was presented in St. Petersburg at a conference entitled 'The Arctic region – Territory with room for dialogue'. The choice of this forum for the presentation was no matter of chance – the authors of the project are convinced that the VSA-500 and similar vehicles of various sizes can provide a tangible contribution to solving the transport problems of the Russian North.

Judging by the pictures of the model, the VSA-500 is configured as a combination of a tail-first aircraft and a catamaran vessel. The layout is reminiscent of some of Bartini's projects, such as PVA-62 and OVA-62 (see above in this chapter). The wide-chord wing centre section of relatively small span resting on two floats is supplemented by narrow-chord outer wing panels. The leading edge has a rather odd S shape – possibly even with negative sweep at the tips; the trailing edge is parabolic. Twin vertical tails and the location of two turbojet engines atop the rear part of the wing center section also are similar to Bartini's designs. Peculiar features of the VSA-500 include the ogival shape of the wing leading edge and the provision of canard surfaces on the forward fuselage. The downturned tips of the outer wing panels obviously are intended to enhance the dynamic air cushion during the vehicle's movement in the ground-effect mode. The vehicle can move in aerosleigh mode on the snow, making hops to a height of some 10-15 m (33-50 ft) to negotiate obstacles; in WIG mode it can fly above the water surface, eventually rising to altitudes of up to 150 m (490 ft) and reaching a speed of 300 km/h (186 mph).

The MGTU team engaged in this work have declared their intention to develop projects for a huge ekranoplan capable of carrying a payload of up to 300 tonnes (661,500 lb), and for passenger ekranoplans seating 60 to 80 persons.

Ivan Bryukhanov

In the summer of 2015 Ivan Bryukhanov, an enthusiast designer from Irkutsk, completed a small WIG vehicle closely resembling a scaled-down ESKA-1 (see Chapter Five, p. 216 of this book). It took him three years to build this vehicle of wooden construction, with fabric-covered plywood skin. Initially it differed from the ESKA-1 in having no upturned winglets outboard of the wingtip floats, but they were added at a later stage. It was shown with an open cockpit and, surprisingly, no windshield. This small craft was powered by a motorcycle engine of 17 hp and was intended to reach a speed of 70 km/h (43 mph). Dur-

Left: The Skat homebuilt light WIG craft in its original configuration (with short upturned 'winglets').

ing initial test runs on the water Brykhanov refrained from exceeding 20 km/h (12 mph) for safety reasons. No information on further testing is available.

Vladimir Sedykh

Skat (continued tests in 2014-15)

This small WIG vehicle built by Vladimir Sedykh, a resident of the city of Bratsk in Siberia, was briefly described and illustrated in Chapter Five (pp. 261-262). In the period after the publication of the 2010 edition Sedykh continued his experiments with this vehicle, introducing some improvements and modifications. New pictures which became available since then show this craft with upturned wingtips in the fashion of the ESKA-1 and Lippisch designs. It appears to be the vehicle's original configuration dating back to 2004; subsequently it was modified and the small wing panels outboard of the floats received a very moderate dihedral.

Vladimir Sedykh went on performing flights on the Skat for several years. In September 2016 local river police authorities placed charges against him for operating his vehicle 'illegally' because he had allegedly failed to obtain the necessary permissions and technical certificates. He faced prosecution but apparently succeeded in extricating himself from this contingency. The chief point in his self-defence was that his vehicle was legally no more than a small boat requiring no special permissions. To avoid legal problems, Sedykh chose forthwith not to class his vehicle as an 'ekranoplan', referring to it instead as '*aeroglisser*' (aquaplaning boat with aerial propulsion) with aerodynamic off-loading. To further stress this point, he went as far as to provide his vehicle with a nose-mounted hydroski. This permitted him to perform runs in the 'dual' mode, with the hydroski touching the water and the rest of the vehicle flying above it on the dynamic air cushion.

Below left: The Skat and its team of designers and testers. For the initial flight tests the craft was fitted with a bicycle landing gear featuring skis.

Below: Another view of the Skat in early form, showing the ski landing gear.

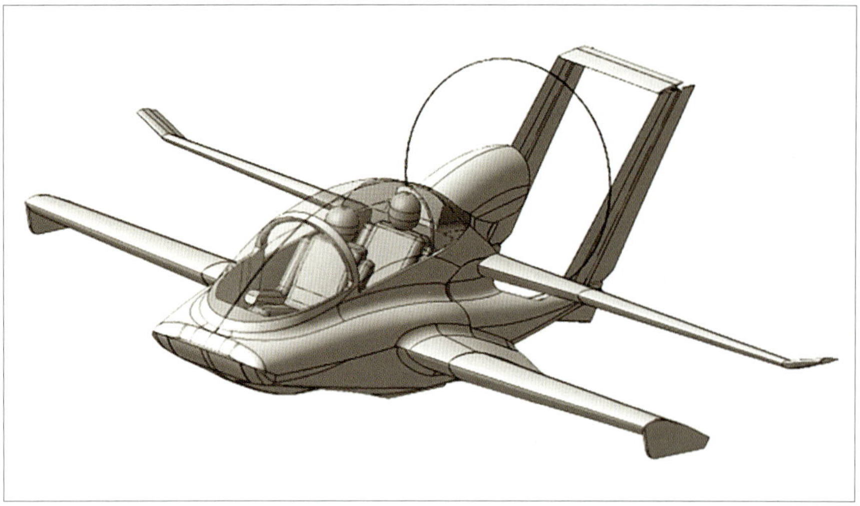

A computer-generated image of the ORCA-1 (with an apparently robotic crew).

Another image of the ORCA-1; the propeller is not shown in this instance.

An artist's impression of the larger ORCA-100. The object in the nose is apparently a booster blower helping to create an air cushion.

Far-Eastern Federal University, Vladivostok

In 2014 specialists from the Far-Eastern Federal University in Vladivostok embarked on an ekranoplan project. A report to this effect published on a web site did not disclose any significant details, apart from mentioning a 16-seat passenger vehicle as the basic version. Obviously, this is in some way connected with the ideas of introducing ekranoplans on local sea routes connecting Vladivostok with Russian cities in the area, as well as with some cities in Japan, South Korea and China. Such plans were discussed on the level of local sea transport companies.

Igor' Biryukov's designs

In 2002 this enthusiast from the city of Tobol'sk on the Irtysh River built a small WIG vehicle named Kasatka-1 (see Chapter Six of this book pages 310-311). Featuring a tandem-wing layout, this little craft made runs in aquaplaning mode, but failed to achieve a true ground effect flight. Plans for the construction of similar vehicles of larger size did not materialise. Nevertheless, Birykov continues to promote his paper creations which, he claims, possess advantages over ekranoplans of other designers. Some of his projects bear the designation ORCA. These are the **ORCA-1** and **ORCA-100** (Roman alphabet is used in the original). Both of them belong to Class C (*ekranolyot*, in Russian parlance) and feature a tandem wing layout (Biryukov puts it as 'semi-tandem'). The two-seat ORCA-1 is powered by a single Hirth 2703 engine of 55 hp driving a pusher propeller, while the 10-seat ORCA-100 is powered by two engines of an unspecified type driving tractor propellers. For other particulars, see the table on this page.

Biryukov seeks investors for the larger type and offers the smaller one to those who might be tempted to build it on their own, using instructions and documentation supplied by the designer (!).

Speficications of the ORCA

	ORCA-1	ORCA-100
Length	5.8 m (19 ft in)	7.2 m (23 ft 7½ in)
Width	5.4 m (17 ft 8½ in)	8.0 m (26 ft 3 in)
Height	1.9 m (6 ft 2¾ in)	2.6 m (8 ft 6½ in)
Empty weight, kg (lb)	330 (898)	800 (1,764)
Maximum AUW, kg (lb)	600 (1,323)	1,800 (3,969)
Optimum height of flight, m (ft)	0.5	1.5
Theoretical ceiling, m (ft)	3,500 (11,480)	3,500 (11,480)
Touch-off speed, km/h (mph)	65 (40)	75 (47)
Max speed, km/h (mph)	180 (112)	280 (174)
Wave height at take-off, m (ft)	0.3 (1.0)	0.5 (1.64)
Crew	1 pilot	1 pilot
Passengers	1	9

INDEX

AIRCRAFT

ENGINES

LOCATIONS (USSR/CIS)

TEST/RESEARCH ESTABLISHMENTS